HOW TO LOSE A REFERENDUM

THE DEFINITIVE STORY OF WHY THE UK VOTED FOR BREXIT

JASON FARRELL AND PAUL GOLDSMITH

Biteback Publishing

First published in Great Britain in 2017 by
Biteback Publishing Ltd
Westminster Tower
3 Albert Embankment
London SE1 7SP
Copyright © Jason Farrell and Paul Goldsmith 2017

ISBN 978-1-78590-195-9

10 9 8 7 6 5 4 3 2 1

A CIP catalogue record for this book is available from the British Library.

Set in Adobe Garamond Pro

Printed and bound in Great Britain by
CPI Group (UK) Ltd, Croydon CR0 4YY

This book is for Kerrie, Charlie, Millie, Emily, Ellie and Josh
Our book widows and orphans
We hope this is worth it.

This book is also for everybody who would like to know, or think they already know
Why Britain voted to leave the EU.

CONTENTS

INTRODUCTION

At 3 a.m. on 24 June 2016, business behind the bar of the ground floor café in Millbank Tower was swell. For the revellers, the night was still young. The drink was still flowing, the chatter decibel level still rising and, on the fake grass lawn outside, cigarettes still needed to be smoked. Indeed, the high proportion of smokers and the density of purple and tweed combined with the odd 1940s trilby hat made the whole event unmistakably UKIP. If you're a non-smoker in UKIP, you're going to miss half the meetings.

For the numerous broadcast journalists at the event, it was the crossover hour; several were coming to the end of a rollercoaster all-night shift reporting for special programmes as the results of the counts dripped in. Other journalists, including co-author Jason, had stolen a few hours' sleep in nearby hotels and were preparing for the six o'clock breakfast shows, getting ready to break the result of the EU referendum to the waking world, and embarking on what would become the most momentous and unforgettable day in modern British politics.

The reason so many journalists had come to the Leave.EU event – a factional Out campaign group closely affiliated to UKIP – was because the official Out campaign, Vote Leave, had cancelled their party. It was widely thought they came to this decision because they assumed they were going to lose. But was it actually because they feared how things would look if they won? How would Conservative voters feel about images of Conservative bigwigs such as Michael Gove and Boris Johnson toasting a victory that would almost certainly lead to their party leader and Prime Minister's resignation? And so, if the UK did decide to leave the EU that night, it would be UKIP purple and tweed that the world would see basking in the glory of victory.

The only person missing from the picture was Nigel Farage. It was not like the party leader to miss a party. Just five hours before he had practically conceded defeat in the EU referendum. But as the pendulum seemed to be swinging back the other way, Farage was having a quiet moment of reflection, having slipped away from the throng to the nearby home of his strategist Chris Bruni-Lowe.

When the polling stations closed at 10 p.m. and the TV channels began their night-long shows, a YouGov survey predicted the result at 52:48 per cent to Remain. Ipsos MORI had the gap slightly wider at 54:46 per cent. According to insiders in Downing Street, the Prime Minister had been certain his side would win with a margin of around eight or nine points. Bookies agreed; earlier in the day they had suggested over a 90 per cent chance of the UK voting to remain in the EU.[1]

The only person who had any figures suggesting anything different was the organiser of the Leave.EU event in Millbank Tower. The UKIP donor Arron Banks had conducted a secret poll of 10,000 people that suggested the opposite to YouGov: that the UK would vote to leave by 52:48. He'd first seen the figures at around lunchtime and shared them with Farage, telling him to 'stop bloody worrying'. His poll had done something the others hadn't. It had actively dug into the cohort of people who didn't usually vote, and discovered that this time they had – and these non-voters were voting to leave.

As the party bustled around him through the long night, Banks's figures started to be confirmed. First, at midnight, Newcastle upon Tyne only narrowly voted to remain. The expectation had been that the city was more strongly in favour of EU membership. Then Sunderland went 61 per cent Leave. A Leave vote had been expected, but not by as wide a margin. Pollsters tapped these new findings into their laptops to reconfigure their predictions and suddenly they were getting the kind of results Banks had seen fourteen hours earlier. Currency traders began to press the sell button on their holdings in sterling. Arron Banks quietly watched everything unfolding as he'd expected.

As the Sunderland result came, Brexit campaigner and soon-to-be Brexit Minister David Davis was on the BBC's election programme. In an off-air aside, the perennial presenter of BBC election shows David Dimbleby leant across and said, 'You could win this.' Davis replied, 'We just have.' He had looked up at the overall count and could see that so far nationwide a million votes had been counted, bigger than any poll – and Leave were in front.

In the offices of Stronger In, the official designated Remain campaign, they were using special demographic-based software developed by Jim Messina, the former White House deputy of staff under President Obama and specialist in highly developed digital techniques for targeting individual voters. Messina had helped the Tories win the general election in May 2015, and reluctantly George Osborne had agreed to allow the cross-party Remain group to use some of his alchemy for their campaign. The Messina software worked out what each location in the UK should score if the result was going to be a 50:50 split. A team based in Downing Street and another in Labour HQ tapped the initial results into the model then conferred with the press team at the Stronger In office, which was headed up by Nick Clegg's former campaign manager James McGrory.

McGrory, who was Stronger In's head of media, would interpret the results into lines that could be spun out by partygoers at their media event in the Royal Festival Hall on the South Bank. The Sunderland and Newcastle results had been disappointing but not disastrous, only 1 or 2 per cent lower than where they should have been on the 50:50 split, so pretty much in the rough margins of what was expected.

The problem for McGrory was that as the night wore on, the 1 or 2 per cent below expectation was becoming a pattern. Consistently, both in areas where they won and in those where they lost, they were just below where they should have been – 59 per cent where it should have been 60 per cent, or 44 per cent instead of 46 per cent.

At 1 a.m. the swing seat of Swindon went nine points for Leave, then more Labour heartlands declared for Brexit: Tyneside, Swansea, Middlesbrough, Hartlepool, Bury, Redcar and Cleveland. By 2.30 a.m., a Remain vote from Glasgow only offered light relief to the Stronger In campaign: it was a low turnout in the city that in 2014 had voted avidly for the break-up of the United Kingdom.

They were falling behind the curve, but McGrory wasn't going to accept defeat yet: he was also hearing that Remain had piled up massive votes in London, and a couple of strong areas had come in way over the expected threshold. He wasn't prepared to write it off, even though the Messina software was now giving his team exactly the same figure Arron Banks had – 52 per cent Out.

Arron Banks stood with a broad smile but with apparent sobriety compared to the ever more red-faced frivolity around him. The question now was whether Scotland, London and other big pro-EU cities such as Liverpool and Manchester could hold out in large enough numbers to sway the outcome.

But as London suburbs such as Watford came out for Leave, it countered the anticipated strong Remain votes coming from inner-city places like Hammersmith and Wandsworth.

At this point Banks began to suggest to the circles around him that his figures had been bang on – the UK was going to leave the EU. Shortly afterwards he was saying the same to journalists.

Word spread that Nigel Farage himself was about to rejoin the party. Excited chatter filled the room, only offset by the serious tone blaring out of the two wall-hung TV sets, which occasionally sucked all the noise out of the room. It happened again at 3.20 a.m., a hush for the announcement from Coventry. The bellwether city voted 67,967 Remain; 85,097 Leave. There was a roar of delight from the sixty or so partygoers. Cameras flashed, reporters prodded microphones into the excited crowd and suddenly the scene in the room was replicated on the two TV sets. 'I can't believe it,' said someone. 'We are going to win!' His words echoed back to him from the wall screens.

By 3.30 a.m. the late night café erupted again as TV straplines showed the chances of Brexit at 80 per cent. Now images on the screens switched to another party – a not-so-happy one. Across the Thames in the Royal Festival Hall, the Stronger In campaign was starting to enter paralysis. There were tears and looks of disbelief. The scales were falling from the eyes of the Westminster bubble and they could see the revolution beyond the metropolis. And what they could see was not just angry frustration against the European Union, but one part of the country taking its revenge on the other. A graph showed the value of the pound plummeting, but no one in Millbank Tower seemed to care. Nigel Farage had finally arrived. He was ploughing through the sweaty Ukippers, photographers and journalists in a scene that later could only be broadcast with a stern warning of flash photography.

'Ladies and gentlemen, dare to dream that the dawn is breaking on an independent United Kingdom...' he yelled to ear-splitting cheers. His voice double-backed from the TV screens. 'This, if the predictions now are right, this will be a victory for real people, a victory for ordinary people, a victory for decent people.' He spat the words out, challenging those who had questioned the values of Leave voters. He told the crowd that this was their referendum. Love him or loathe him, it's hard to argue with that. Then he finished with a flourish. 'Let June the 23rd go down in history as our Independence Day!'

He stayed only another twenty minutes – time to tour the room, speak to supporters and give journalists their moment with the victor. 'What does this mean for David Cameron?' asked co-author Jason Farrell as Farage squeezed towards the doorway. 'It's curtains for Cameron. He'll be gone by lunchtime,' was Farage's reply.

As he made his way to the exit it seemed we were watching the most influential politician of our time at the pinnacle of his career. But Farage's face didn't wear the ecstatic expression of a lottery winner or even the dazed crimson-glowing glee of others in the room. Instead, he looked like a hardened gambler after a long but successful night at the tables. He had walked into the political casino twenty-five years ago with barely a dime; now he was walking out holding everybody's chips.

David Cameron was out of the game. He had maintained an air of calm throughout the evening, absorbing each shock as it came in with a few glasses of Scotch, occasionally offering words of encouragement as he watched the results with his closest aides in the Thatcher Room at 10 Downing Street, his daughter Nancy asleep on his lap. He didn't stick around for Farage's speech but announced at around 3.30 a.m. that he was going to bed. Instead, though, he lingered around the corridors of No. 10 and at 4 a.m. went to his private office, inviting in his long-serving aide Liz Sugg, his Cabinet Office Minister Matt Hancock and director of communications Craig Oliver. The Prime Minister slumped into his desk chair while Sugg and Oliver sat on wooden chairs and Hancock made use of the office sofa.

Two days earlier, Cameron had confirmed to his team, including George Osborne, that if they lost the campaign he would resign. But as the reality dawned, he wondered if he really needed to specify straight away when he was going to go. A heavy pall of depression hung over the room. This was no time to sugar-coat things. 'I may be wrong but I can't see how you can stay.' Oliver told him. Cameron knew he was right. Having campaigned for Remain, he couldn't lead the country through Brexit. He said: 'The trouble with all options other than going immediately is they collapse like a concertina. And the truth is, I wouldn't believe in it.'[2]

Sugg valiantly made the argument that people would expect him to stay on because that's what he had consistently said he would do, but no one else bought it. The mood was one of defeat. After a circular conversation, the team hugged and went their separate ways. Cameron's final decision of his premiership was made. He would resign first thing.

Craig Oliver walked out into the crisp night, through the famous black door his boss would be opening in a few hours' time. Out he went into the quiet of Downing Street, past the police guard at the wrought iron gates and on to the broad empty thoroughfare of Whitehall. He was back in the real world: a changed world. As he approached the memorial opposite the Ministry of Defence, his body went into a spasm and he retched hard, harder than he had ever done before. Nothing came up, but he kept retching all the same.[3]

At around the same time, James McGrory pulled his team into a room to break the news. He'd known for sure when the Sheffield result came in. He knew Sheffield. It was Nick Clegg's constituency and going into the vote they'd expected to win it, but the city backed leave by 51 per cent. They needed big areas like Sheffield; if Sheffield went Leave then so would Birmingham. It did.

It was time to admit defeat, at least to his team. 'You've all worked every hour God has given … We couldn't have tried harder.' The words sounded strangely familiar. McGrory had been a recipient of a similar speech from Nick Clegg thirteen months earlier when the Liberal Democrats were wiped out at the general election. He watched the despair and disbelief on the young faces in his team – he'd been there. What did it mean? Can we un-fuck this? Questions for another day. He briefed some lines for those left in the Royal Festival Hall and announced that it was time to go to the pub. And so they went from despair to Hope: the Hope pub in Smithfield – a rare establishment that opens for its clientele in the early hours and closes at lunchtime. The strange timings cater for fishmongers from the market, who end their shifts at around 5 a.m. In amongst the blood-stained overalls and stench of gutted fish, the defeated defenders of Britain's place in the EU found a place to drink themselves senseless until lunchtime.

Meanwhile, Michael Gove's phone rang. The Justice Secretary and prominent Conservative Leave campaigner had gone to sleep assuming that he would spend the day expressing disappointment. The caller was excited: 'Michael, guess what? We've won.' Gove was in shock. He turned to his journalist wife Sarah Vine, who also struggled with the scale of what had happened while they were asleep. 'You were only supposed to blow the bloody doors off,' was the first thing she could think to say.[4]

Similarly, in his bed in Islington, Jeremy Corbyn awoke, having dozed off at around 2 a.m. He'd spent the evening with his trusted head of media Seumas Milne at Labour's Southside HQ. The Labour Party had an on-the-ground ops team run by Labour's executive head of elections, Patrick Heneghan. Throughout the evening Heneghan had been extrapolating the results and feeding his analysis back to Corbyn. Their initial intelligence had suggested Remain would get around 54 per cent of the vote, but by 1.30 a.m. new analysis had come in warning them that Leave was now odds on to win. It was around this time that Corbyn had headed back to Islington to get some rest, leaving Milne to work overnight on the scripts he could use whichever way the result went.

The Labour leader needed to recharge for the morning round of interviews on College Green. As he woke, about three hours later, he picked up his iPad to check the news. A banner crept across the screen, 'Britain votes to leave'. 'Oh shit,' he said. In a few hours, his adversaries would be out and blaming him. He spoke to his press team to go over some lines for people to use about how he had 'led from the front' during the campaign. But by the time he met up with Milne outside 4 Millbank, a 'traitor' had leaked the script to the media.[5] Soon two MPs would be calling for a vote of no confidence. They were out there almost immediately down on College Green, a small corner of Westminster, Glastonbury-style: MPs going from one broadcasting tent to another churning over the surreal events of last night and churning the grass to mud. As Corbyn arrived, he could see Farage facing a battalion of cameras, giving his second victory speech of the morning.

The Green always has a TV camera on it – but on 24 June there were at least fifty of them. The broadcasters had built huge structures to elevate temporary studios above the lawn. And something happened that never happens – crowds of the general public massed around the triangle of grass just to look. Politics had become a spectator sport. Those who got there early could see Peter Mandelson, the silky-tongued Professor Snape of politics, talking to a rather tired-looking Sky News journalist and choosing his words as if mixing a noxious potion. 'The thing about Jeremy is in every sense he was in the right place at the right time. It's just that voters didn't know where that place was,' he said. 'You've just got to consider sometimes whether you've really found yourself in the right job.'

Across the river in the offices of Vote Leave, the 'operations room' in Westminster Tower was littered with empty beer cans and champagne bottles from the private party the night before. As staff surveyed the mess, Boris Johnson came bursting in, triumphant, hugging and congratulating those in the room for a job well done. He had missed the office booze-up and instead watched the results come in from his home in Islington. Rather than tapping into the sophisticated software of election gurus, he'd obsessively followed the odds on Betfair as his guide to how the UK might vote. Talk in the office was of how MEP Daniel Hannan had, when they knew they had won, stood up on a desk and broken into the rousing soliloquy of Shakespeare's *Henry V*. Everyone had their stories of the night before. The director of Vote Leave Dominic Cummings was already looking to the future. He told Boris that when he became Prime Minister he should announce an extra £100 million per week for the NHS (along the lines of the pledge made by Vote Leave, albeit falling short by £250 million). 'Absolutely. Absolutely. We must do this,' said Johnson.[6] But first they needed to prepare for their press conference. It was victory – but it would have to be rather sombre in tone, because of what was happening at Downing Street.

As David Cameron descended the stairs of No. 10, only the Prime Ministers whose portraits hung on the walls could really understand his feelings. But, like him, they all wore faces of pure stoicism. He was about to deliver a speech he'd never thought he would have to make. He must have been exhausted. It wouldn't just have been the lack of sleep: he is a master of the power nap and it had served him well during his six years as Prime Minister. This time the tiredness was also caused by gravity, pulling him into the centre of the earth. 'The British people have voted to leave the European Union and their will must be respected.'[7] That's what he would say, but the words had been so hard to imagine just a few hours ago. How could it have gone so badly wrong? This was going to be his legacy. People were already saying it – he'd gambled and lost. That he'd only done it to placate his backbenchers in a spectacular, foolhardy act of arrogance.

The black door opened onto Downing Street to the noisy flutter of cameras, as if a plague of insects was amongst people behind the railings. It was so similar and yet so different to thirteen months earlier, when Cameron had been last man standing in a political bloodbath. Now, it was his turn to take a wash.

Watching TV at her home in Maidenhead was Theresa May. Cameron's Home Secretary didn't know for sure how her Prime Minister would react to the result. She hadn't been party to his conversations with Osborne and others, but as the door opened she saw it wasn't just David but also his wife Samantha walking out into the street. Then she knew.

'I love this country, and I feel honoured to have served it,' said Cameron. His wife fixed her gaze on him as she stood five paces to his left. A dapple of light under her feet was her spotlight for this extraordinary moment on stage. He would be gone by autumn, he told them. Actually, it would be much sooner. 'I will do everything I can in future to help this great country succeed. Thank you very much.'[8]

As they walked back through that black door, someone had already dug up a Cameron tweet from 4 May 2015, three days before his most triumphant achievement, a general election majority that no one had predicted. It said: 'Britain faces a simple and inescapable choice – stability and strong Government with me, or chaos with Ed Miliband.'[9] How wrong could he have been?

It wasn't supposed to be this way. Historically, referendums are called to rubber-stamp decisions that have already been made. Governments know and plan for the direction the voters will go. Prime Ministers don't lose referendums. How had this happened to Cameron?

At the point he re-entered 10 Downing Street, the Brexit revolution was already being recorded as a triumph and disaster of a few key players in Westminster; the actions of a small band over the past six months had effectively rewritten the course of UK history. The two factions involved in the Leave campaign were patting their own backs and starting what has since become an interminable argument over whose campaign was responsible for their victory, refusing to acknowledge that they were in fact vital to each other. Indeed, the whole Brexit revolution, which came as such a shock to the establishment, was something far more significant than a reaction to the messaging of Westminster strategists over the previous six months, and far more complex than simply a defeat for the Prime Minister and his team. They say victory has many fathers and defeat is an orphan – but in this case defeat had numerous parents.

One can imagine David Cameron going back up those stairs at No. 10, arriving at the top having passed the portraits of post-war Prime Ministers Attlee, Churchill, Eden, Macmillan, Douglas-Home, Wilson, Heath, Callaghan, Thatcher, Major, Blair and Brown. He feels their accusing eyes. *He* is the one who took this country out of the European Union. But as he reaches the last one, Cameron would have been justified in turning around and snapping at his predecessors: 'Don't look at me like that. This is as much your fault as it is mine.'

Britain's decision to leave the European Union was the result of not one

Prime Minister's blunder, but those of a succession of Prime Ministers, foreign ministers, civil servants and European leaders to boot. Brexit was as much their responsibility as Cameron's.

It wasn't just about politicians; it was about people's lives. It was economic, it was social and there was a heavy dose of events – yes, 'events, dear boy' – that led to Britain's decision to depart the EU. That, and an ingrained attitude of non-cooperation and misunderstanding of the vision and idea behind European unity dating back to its very beginning; the UK's historic approach to Europe played a huge role.

This book argues that there are eighteen main reasons why the UK chose to leave the EU. Some individuals make the list, one being Nigel Farage, who not only pushed the referendum onto the agenda but also identified a section of disgruntled voters and the messages they wanted to hear. David Cameron is on the list for calling the referendum, raising expectations and falling short in his negotiations. The lukewarm campaigning of Labour leader Jeremy Corbyn has also been blamed for the defeat, and we analyse whether he really was a significant cause. The 'Mad Men' of the Vote Leave campaign obviously make the shortlist, and we spend significant time understanding the work put in over many years up to the referendum to achieve the result they did. The political figures who got behind Vote Leave were important. They didn't just get Vote Leave the official designation from the Electoral Commission, but also added huge weight to their campaign. So the actions of Michael Gove and Boris Johnson are resoundingly on this list. We also look closely at the shortcomings of the Stronger In campaign and why 'Project Fear' didn't scare the public into voting for the status quo in the way it had during the general election and the Scottish referendum. Then there was the final month of the campaign, when 'purdah' rules were in place, stopping the Remain campaign from having the full government machinery behind them, while the Leave campaign, who had backloaded their finances and their tactics, were able to come off the ropes like Muhammad Ali in the 'Rumble in the Jungle' and deliver the final knockout blow.

But for the root causes of the UK's decision to leave the EU you have to look beyond the political personalities and the campaign. We have to examine the EU itself – the way it was created and how it evolved. For instance, the UK was nowhere to be seen when the European project started, kept out of it by a Labour government that didn't want anyone interfering with their post-war rebuilding of Britain. We will hear about the civil servant sent to the meetings that set up the full European Community in 1955 with strict instructions not to agree to anything. We will find out about the two applications to join the EC that were rejected, meaning the UK was out of the EC in the 1960s. We will see how this led to a European organisation being created that possessed a higher authority than nation states, able to pass laws and set regulations over and above national parliaments. We assess the political and economic contortions Britain had to go through in order to eventually join the European Community, originally without a referendum, then with one that was seen as having been hugely unbalanced and potentially misleading. We learn how the Labour Party was historically Eurosceptic but how many Conservatives turned against Europe as Margaret Thatcher and then John Major signed away many powers to the European Union. Then, we see the impact of the decision in 2004 to open the UK's borders to immigrants from the new, mostly Eastern European, accession countries. This all built up to a European Union that was incredibly difficult to defend, when the time came to defend it.

We also have to look at other influences, such as the unique circumstances at the time the referendum was held and the impact of the financial crash in 2008. Then there's the role of the media, not just during the campaign but in the decades of cynicism about the EU and what one Remain campaigner described as 'the steady drum beat of just a relentless negativity about European membership'. And why was it that people had 'had enough of experts'? We argue that the rather shocking remarks made by Michael Gove were indeed spot on.

This book began as an argument. The two authors were on a drive, taking their daughters to Peppa Pig Land. The quarrel was over whether David Cameron was doomed from the moment he called the referendum. Was the referendum ever winnable? Was it lost through the course of history, or by more recent events and his own mistakes? Certainly, we've come to an agreement that you can't assess matters by simply recounting the four-month campaign leading up to the referendum. If you want to understand the result, you have to go back much further. And so this book travels back to the creation of the European Union, tracking its evolution and Britain's awkward involvement all the way forward to the UK's decision to press the eject button.

This is how to lose a referendum.

REASON 1

ABSENT AT THE BIRTH

Sir Edwin Plowden had a problem. He needed to get an answer back to the French Foreign Minister Robert Schuman as to whether Britain would take part in the creation of the European Coal and Steel Community, the very first step towards what we now know as the European Union. Schuman had announced his plan at a dramatic press conference in Paris in May 1950, and the past few weeks had been spent trying to persuade the British to accept the main principle of it being a 'supranational' organisation and join the negotiations to create it. Fed up with waiting for an answer, Schuman had issued an ultimatum on 1 June that an answer had to be given on 2 June. As Chief Planning Officer in the Treasury, Plowden was the most senior advisor to Chancellor Stafford Cripps. But Cripps was on holiday in France, as was Prime Minister Clement Attlee. Foreign Secretary Ernest Bevin was ill in hospital. So, someone had to track down the Deputy Prime Minister, Herbert Morrison, who was in charge of the country that evening. Having been dispatched to find Morrison, who was on a night out in theatre land in the West End of London, Plowden finally tracked him down to the Ivy restaurant, near Leicester Square. They found a passage at the back of the restaurant where spare tables and chairs were stored and Plowden asked Morrison what the answer would be. Morrison shook his head gravely and said, 'It's no good. We can't do it. The Durham miners will never wear it.'[1]

Every time a Leave campaigner reminded the voters during the 2016 EU referendum campaign that they could 'take back control' by leaving the European Union, we can trace the loss of that control to the UK's absence from its creation. We can trace that absence directly to the joy of victory in the Second World War in 1945.

Winning the war began a series of misinterpretations and misjudgements that were to cause Britain to refuse to take part in the formation of European unity.

This refusal proved to be at the cost of any decisive British influence in moulding the eventual outcome. Michael Charlton, who provides probably the seminal work on this subject in his series of interviews with almost everyone involved in Britain's relationship with Europe, called his BBC Radio programmes and the associated book *The Price of Victory*. Right at the start, Charlton says: 'In the beginning Britain was asked to lead this movement; at various stages to participate in it; throughout she tried to stop it taking the direction it did; and finally felt compelled to join it.' Charlton concludes the opening to his first chapter by saying that the 'price of victory' was that being absent at the creation of the European project meant Britain couldn't play a role in 'shaping that specific nature and character which the European Community assumed at the start, and which we find painful to live with today'.[2]

This absence meant that the European Community we eventually joined was a political and economic entity that went against British conceptions of sovereignty and would require a huge number of changes in how Britain was governed before we did join. The result was an organisation that was extremely hard for pro-Europeans in the UK to defend from the moment it was created to the day we joined – and up to the minute we voted to leave.

Let's start at the turn of the twentieth century. The UK was sitting in what was termed by late nineteenth-century political leaders as 'splendid isolation'[3] from the continent of Europe. The country had a small agricultural sector, relying on cheap food imports from its colonies, with whom they traded freely with no tariffs. As a maritime power and an island, Britain relied on the navy to defend it. The only need for an army was to defend India from what was thought were covetous Russian eyes, requiring, according to Lord Kitchener, an army of thousands of men and around 3 million camels.[4]

Perhaps no one summed up this outlook better than Sir Eyre Crowe, a diplomat in the Foreign Office, who wrote in 1907:

> The general character of England's foreign policy is determined by the immutable conditions of her geographical situation on the ocean flank of Europe as an island State with vast oversea colonies and dependencies, whose existence and survival as an independent community are inseparably bound up with the possession of a preponderant sea power ... A maritime State is ... the neighbour of every country accessible by sea.[5]

The existence on the other side of the world of a white population of British stock in Australia and New Zealand was seen as a testimony to that sea power and global reach.

By 1945, however, Britain had found it impossible to live in isolation from Europe. The UK had fought two world wars in alliance with France. This was in large part to preserve Britain's own independence, which was seen as not worth much if a hostile power controlled France. So when France had found itself threatened from the East in both 1914 and 1939, Britain had had to get involved.

So involved, in fact, that in 1940, as it looked as if France was sliding towards surrender to Germany, Winston Churchill went as far as to offer France an 'indissoluble union', sharing the costs of the war, even though France's bill would be much greater. The proposal was submitted to the French government led by Prime Minister Paul Reynaud at 4.30 p.m. on 14 June 1940. A constitution would be created to provide for 'joint organs of defence, foreign, financial and economic policies' and 'every citizen of France will enjoy immediate citizenship of Great Britain; every British subject will become a citizen of France'. Although Reynaud was in favour of acceptance, his colleagues weren't. Reynaud resigned and at half past midnight Marshal Pétain initiated the negotiations leading to the French surrender.[6]

Britain withdrew back over the English Channel while remaining in the war. The fact that it never fell under Fascist rule, and eventually won the war, despite an early defeat, showed that it didn't need to stand or fall as a nation in the same way the other nations of the Continent did. Meanwhile, its continued ownership of an empire, and presence at the talks at Yalta and Potsdam on rebuilding the world order, showed it remained a great power with a reach beyond Europe.[7]

Britain may have felt like that, but the original six countries which formed the European Community – France, Germany, Italy, Belgium, the Netherlands and Luxembourg – felt very differently about themselves. Most Continental countries had succumbed to Fascism or Nazism and thus had much to be ashamed of as the Second World War ended. They also had to start over again with their entire political systems, including their constitutions. European unity was driven by the need to get their act together, as decisions were being made for them by the United States and Russia. Seeing that Hitler had exploited divisions amongst the European powers to establish dominance over them, it was also hard to escape the conclusion that it had taken a common, supranational, European struggle to defeat him.

At this point it is important to explain three key political concepts: sovereignty, intergovernmentalism and supranationalism. Without these three notions it is hard to explain the way the European Community and then Union was put together and to explain the issues that many people in Britain have with the result.

Sovereignty is the authority of a state to govern itself. It is composed of three important and distinct factors: First, de jure sovereignty entails *the right* to be the ultimate authority within a defined territorial space. Secondly, de facto sovereignty entails *the ability* to actually control what happens within that defined territory. By leaving the EU, Britain regains some de jure sovereignty, as Parliament regains complete legislative authority over the UK to make its own laws and rules over, for instance, who can cross its borders. But, critically, that doesn't mean it necessarily regains de facto sovereignty, as the forces of globalisation, the power of multinationals and the compromises of any trade deal made with the EU can reduce that ability for Parliament to really control what happens in the UK. The country with the most de facto sovereignty in the world is North Korea, which really does exist in not-so-splendid isolation from the world. The final part of sovereignty is that there needs to be external recognition of a nation state's right and ability to be the ultimate authority within a given space. All three factors are important for a government to be regarded as 'sovereign'.

Intergovernmentalism involves arrangements where nation states cooperate with each other on matters of common interest in situations and conditions they can control. States are free to cooperate or not and have the ability to set the level of cooperation. This is often operated through states having a veto, enabling them to block any proposal presented by other parties. So, for example, although the UK is part of NATO and the United Nations, it retains a veto over actions these organisations can take, and whether or not to approve these actions. Crucially, these circumstances involve no loss of sovereignty.

Supranationalism, however, sees states delegating some responsibility for decision-making to a body or decision-making forum that stands above the nation state. States lose the right to veto and agree to be bound by the majority decisions of cooperating states and thus lose some control. This means that in some circumstances states may have to go along with a policy that contravenes their particular preferences. Essentially, supranationalism takes inter-state relations beyond cooperation towards integration.

These three concepts are so critical to the European story because, firstly, right from the start, the founding members of European unity intended to 'pool' their sovereignty, which means that they decided to collectively make decisions, with each one agreeing that the central authority they created could make decisions in certain policy areas. This means that the central authority could make rules that override the rules and laws and therefore the sovereignty of the parliaments of member states. However, states have to give permission to have their sovereignty become part of this 'pool' via treaties and can in theory withdraw from the EU at any time.

Secondly, that difference between de jure sovereignty (having the *right* to authority) and de facto sovereignty (actually being able to use it to control their territory) was becoming important given the growing influence on Europe of the USA and Russia in 1946 and then the further influence of major international trends associated with globalisation (including trade, climate change and combating terrorism). By giving up some de jure sovereignty and pooling sovereignty at a European level, the idea was for European states to be able to collectively use their weight in a more globalised world to increase their de facto control over what happened in their countries. A large European superstate would have more clout in negotiations with the world's main superpowers.

The main catalyst for European cooperation was Russia's actions in supporting the Communist coup in February 1948 that ousted the government in Prague, Czechoslovakia, the blockade of Berlin that following summer and the revelation of the first Soviet atomic bomb threat. The Americans were looking for a way to help West Germany recover economically as well as perhaps to rearm without creating too many security concerns for France. Under pressure from US Secretary of State Dean Acheson, French Foreign Minister Robert Schuman engaged in frequent discussions with the new West German Chancellor Konrad Adenauer over the two central problems in Franco-German relations: security and the status of the coal-rich Saar region. The Saarland had been economically annexed by France after the war, under the 'Monnet Plan' created by civil servant Jean Monnet. Adenauer said the Saar issue was 'political dynamite' for his people, who demanded the region's return to Germany. Schuman began to realise that there was a need for a change in French post-war policy towards its former enemy, rather than continuing to depend upon West Germany remaining weak and on US support, both of which were fuelling French and German animosity.[8]

It was Jean Monnet himself who came up with the inspiration for the solution to this impasse. He describes his epiphany, which he developed on a meditative walking holiday in the Alps in the early spring of 1950, as the realisation that:

> if only the French could lose their fear of German industrial domination, then the greatest obstacle to a united Europe would be removed. A solution which would put French industry on the same footing as German industry, while freeing the latter from the discrimination born of defeat – that would restore the economic and political preconditions for the natural understanding so vital to Europe as a whole.

Monnet then underlined that 'coal and steel were at once the key to economic power and the raw materials for forging weapons of war ... to pool them across frontiers would reduce their malign prestige and turn them instead into a guarantee of peace'.[9]

Returning to Paris in March 1950, Monnet produced nine drafts of his proposal before sending it to Prime Minister Georges Bidault on 20 April 1950 and, having received no reply, to Foreign Minister Robert Schuman on 28 April. Along with the plan, Monnet worked with his American friend John McCloy, who, usefully, had become US High Commissioner to West Germany, to persuade Secretary of State Acheson that he ought to let Schuman know how important German rehabilitation was to the USA. Key to this was convincing Schuman that the Americans would proceed without France if they had to.

It worked. Robert Schuman adopted Monnet's plan, took charge of it and used secrecy, discretion and speed to bypass most official and industrial opposition. By late afternoon on 9 May, what was to be known as the Schuman Plan had been approved by the French Cabinet and was to be announced at a crowded press conference at the Quai d'Orsay, the French Foreign Ministry, in Paris.

The key paragraphs of the Schuman Declaration are right in the middle of what Robert Schuman read out at the press conference on 9 May 1950. They make clear that the eventual aim of the European Coal and Steel Community was the economic and political union of the countries of Europe:

It proposes that Franco-German production of coal and steel as a whole be placed under a common High Authority, within the framework of an organization open to the participation of the other countries of Europe. The pooling of coal and steel production should immediately provide for the setting up of common foundations for economic development as a first step in the federation of Europe, and will change the destinies of those regions which have long been devoted to the manufacture of munitions of war, of which they have been the most constant victims.

The solidarity in production thus established will make it plain that any war between France and Germany becomes not merely unthinkable, but materially impossible. The setting up of this powerful productive unit, open to all countries willing to take part and bound ultimately to provide all the member countries with the basic elements of industrial production on the same terms, will lay a true foundation for their economic unification.[10]

The ECSC's 'High Authority' was a supranational body that eventually became what we now know as the European Commission. Members of the body were appointed by member states with the mandate to represent the common European interest, rather than the interests of the member states themselves. France and Germany were joined by Italy, Belgium, the Netherlands and Luxembourg. Sixty-seven years on, 9 May is Europe Day on the Continent, and some call it Schuman Day. There have been numerous attempts by the Catholic Church to beatify Schuman, but no evidence of a miracle could be produced.[11] Some would argue that the joining together of France and Germany in industrial cooperation so soon after the war was in itself a miracle.

It is not an overstatement to say that 9 May 1950 was also the most important date in Britain's post-war relationship with Continental Europe. Britain had had nothing at all to do with the Schuman Declaration, as Clement Attlee's Labour government had decided not to take part in the discussions. This choice turned out to be a key factor in Britain's decision to vote Leave in 2016.

At the time, this was perfectly understandable, for reasons about to be explained. But in fact it became apparent very quickly that not being in at the start meant that Britain was unable to stop Europe working together in a manner that Britain would feel highly uncomfortable being part of. Once the UK did join the European Community in 1973, the economic and political adjustments it was forced to make were so great that many quickly began to wonder whether it was ever going to be in the UK's interests to make them.

The key to understanding the problem comes from knowing that Parliament in the UK is completely sovereign. This situation has no parallel on the Continent and has been the case since the parliamentary monarchy was established during the Glorious Revolution of 1688. So continuous and undivided is the sovereignty of Parliament that the UK doesn't have a written constitution (a written-down set of fundamental principles or established precedents according to which a country is governed) because Parliament can do what it likes.[12]

Compare this to the constitutions of the continent of Europe. Italy's was written in 1947, Germany's in 1949 and France's in 1958. For these countries, and especially countries like Spain, Greece and Portugal, who were to join the European Community in later years, European unity was like a show of democratic virility, having escaped the world of dictators. Being able to start again, there was little problem in creating a European constitution at the same time. But the UK had never lost democratic responsibility, so it had no need to regain it.

Worse still, the principles of the European Union undermine this parliamentary sovereignty by enacting laws with a direct effect on UK citizens and which our Parliament cannot amend or alter, making Westminster a subordinate legislature to the European legislature. Other international organisations of which the UK was a part, such as the UN and NATO, were intergovernmental, so member states can choose whether or not to cooperate. The European Union from the start was more supranational: a law-making body making laws directly applicable to Britain and whose laws are superior whether Westminster approves of them or not.

The Labour government of Clement Attlee, which had been voted in straight after the end of the Second World War in 1945 and remained in government until 1951, had not disengaged with Europe during this time. Its focus was on helping the Continent rediscover democracy while recovering economically, as well as receiving defence cover when needed. So Britain signed the Treaty of Brussels (an alliance with France and Benelux) in 1948, and that was expanded in 1949 into NATO – an explicit commitment that an attack on any one member of the alliance was an attack on all, and every member should go to the aid of the attacked country. Furthermore, Britain played a leading part in 1949 in the establishment of the Council of Europe, composed of members of national parliaments and governments, which produced the European Convention on Human Rights (ECHR) – now enshrined in British law as the Human Rights Act.[13]

Importantly, these organisations were intergovernmental. NATO and the Council of Europe didn't involve any form of power-sharing or merging of sovereignty. The Labour government felt they needed to balance their three key relationships – with Europe, being head of the Empire and being part of the special relationship with the USA. Tilting in any particular direction would be to put the other relationships at risk.

Take the British Empire as an example. This was being transformed into a multiracial Commonwealth, with Britain at its head. India had gained independence, and the Labour government had a great attachment to Canada and Australia. Many soldiers from the latter two countries had died in support of Britain in two world wars, and many of their citizens had relatives in Britain. The Commonwealth countries had, in the words of Ernest Bevin, Foreign Secretary in Attlee's government, 'raw materials, food and resources, which can be turned to very great common advantage, both to the people of the territories themselves, to Europe, and to the world as a whole'.[14] The feeling was that joining Europe and merging sovereignty in any way might mean jettisoning the Commonwealth, so it should be resisted. To this should be added Bevin's natural distrust of the European movement in general. On hearing of the creation of the Council of Europe in 1949 and the demands for a European assembly to be created, Bevin was famously reported to have warned that 'if you open that Pandora's Box, you never know what Trojan 'orses will jump out'.[15]

For a while, as initial discussions on British–French economic cooperation progressed in the late 1940s, some European statesmen insisted that the UK being involved with Europe wasn't mutually exclusive with its support of the Commonwealth. In a meeting with Acheson and Schuman in 1949, Schuman told Bevin that 'Europe was inconceivable without Great Britain and the British people must not feel that they had to choose between the Commonwealth and Europe'.[16]

As an aside, it is extremely interesting to note that less than six months after this meeting – not only was 'Europe' going to be without Great Britain, but Great Britain, in the form of Ernest Bevin, had not even been consulted on its creation. Much has been written about Bevin's reaction to this, which includes telling Schuman that relations between the two countries would never be the same again,[17] and berating Acheson, while in a 'towering rage', for keeping the plan from him.[18] But that doesn't mean Whitehall didn't carefully sift through the implications of full participation. In truth, there was a more important concern for Labour when it came to judging whether to participate in the Schuman Plan, and that was how it would conflict with their political and economic plans at home.

Attlee's government had received a massive mandate at the 1945 election to put the UK on the road to socialism. Creating the modern welfare state, the National Health Service free at the point of use, the nationalisation of key state industries and the maintenance of full employment involves a necessary amount of government control of the country, and that requires complete sovereignty, at least until the task is complete. Giving up any of that sovereignty to a European unity project would be untimely, even unworkable.

Labour's programme was, in the eyes of its proponents, nothing less than a new social contract between the government and the people. Government could be a highly effective instrument of social transformation, encouraging a notion of 'social patriotism'. The Labour Party hoped that Britain would draw collective pride from this programme of policies, which would stand as a 'unique statement of how solidarity, fairness and rationality could be combined in a national community'.[19] This was perhaps best put by Deputy Prime Minister Herbert Morrison, who declared: 'Planning as it is now taking shape in this country is something new and constructively revolutionary which will be regarded in times to come as a contribution to civilisation as vital and distinctly British as parliamentary democracy and the rule of law.'[20] This meant that Britain owed it to others, as much as to itself, to ensure that this experiment was allowed to develop without interruption by an excessively close association with the unstable political economies of Western Europe.

Take full employment as an example of Labour's commitments. This requires careful economy management and control of government spending, as well as control over the movement of labour. Labour had nationalised the UK's coal and steel industries, while the ECSC was to be built up on the basis of private ownership. The concept of the European Coal and Steel Community was that a decision could in theory be taken by a supranational higher authority on how much should be produced, or even to close down production at a plant. It was this threat to employment that most exercised politicians.

When the UK government rejected participation in the Schuman negotiations, Chancellor Stafford Cripps suggested that the 'supra-national high authority ... could cause a whole coalfield or steel centre to go out of production without any social or political responsibility for their action'.[21] This, of course, implied that the ECSC would have ever been designed to allow the high authority to close down major parts of industries without the agreement of member governments. The French would certainly not have let that happen, but, as the UK found in 2016, all kinds of fears and hypotheticals tend to be used when Europe is involved.

Even if the ECSC was not as powerful as Cripps feared, the UK had other motives to treat it with suspicion. The British Board of Trade noted that Europe's industrial and agricultural goods were in competition with those of the UK, whereas the Commonwealth economy was complementary. Countries from the wider world generally supplied raw materials not available in the UK. The Commonwealth and UK could thrive together, with Britain at the centre. Revived German industries meant more local competition, so British governments were naturally cautious about irrevocable commitments to Europe.[22]

Key to all this was the realisation that the higher authority meant decisions would be taken by people who were not accountable, and were put into place by a system that was not democratic. So, for the UK, it was the wrong time for a non-democratic, non-accountable body with sovereignty over its member states to be created. Con O'Neill, who at the time was working in the Foreign Office but who would eventually rise to lead the negotiations for Britain's entry to the European Community in 1973, explained that 'the idea that there should be a body with real authority over the decisions of national governments – admittedly in a small and perhaps unimportant field, but *real* authority – was something we felt was grotesque and absurd at the time'.[23]

Future Prime Minister Harold Macmillan, in opposition at the time, spoke to the Council of Europe in 1950, saying that 'fearing the weakness of democracy, men have often sought safety in technocrats', but that he was concerned that 'we have not overthrown the Divine Right of Kings to fall down before the Divine Right of Experts'.[24]

The 'divine right of experts' would be questioned sixty-six years later by Leave campaigner Michael Gove during the referendum campaign. 'People have had enough of experts,' he told Sky News political editor Faisal Islam in a TV interview. The sentiment almost mirrored Macmillan's – railing against the idea that expertise should dare to trump instinct and a simple conviction that it was better to be in control.

This fear of the lack of democratic accountability of the High Authority created by the Schuman Declaration in 1950 was also well expressed many years later by the words of the left-wing Labour stalwart Tony Benn, who argued that democracy allowed the people to ask five questions of those in power: What power have you got? Where did you get it from? In whose interests do you exercise it? To whom are you accountable? How can we get rid of you?[25]

The inability to find satisfactory answers to the final four questions has dogged pro-Europeans ever since: in 2016, the Leave campaign constantly invoked the concept of democracy and how being in the EU compromised it, and those leading Remain struggled to explain the benefits of this compromise.

Probably the biggest fear for those governing Britain at the moment of decision about whether to join the ECSC was where it would lead to. Sir Ivone Kirkpatrick, head of the German section of the Foreign Office, noted two days after the Schuman Declaration that 'if the United Kingdom is required to join, or if economic factors prevent our staying out, British participation is likely to involve us in Europe beyond the point of no return'.[26] This fear was confirmed by the Cabinet's official rejection of the Schuman Plan for Britain, which announced that the UK could not be committed irrevocably to Europe 'unless we could measure the extent and effect of the commitment'.[27]

Therefore, having not been consulted over the Schuman Declaration, Britain chose not to be involved in the eventual creation of the European Coal and Steel Community. Germany and France tried to cajole them, but the final moment was precipitated by that ultimatum set by Robert Schuman on 1 June 1950 that Britain must stop delaying their response and either commit to the talks to create the ECSC or withdraw from them by the end of the next day, 2 June 1950.

Which brings us to the hurried meeting between the Deputy Prime Minister and his Treasury official in a back passage of the Ivy restaurant in London's West End. The answer that Herbert Morrison gave Edwin Plowden that night once he had been tracked down was the result of a Cabinet meeting earlier that day. The minutes from it suggest ministers didn't want to send out mixed messages. 'Nothing would be more likely to exacerbate Anglo-French relations than for us to join in the discussions with mental reservations and withdraw from participation at a later stage.'[28] To this rather pious thought can be added the demand by Jean Monnet that Britain accept the 'principle' of supranationalism before entering any talks.

The principle had been made clear to Plowden and Lord Sherfield (then Roger Makins, in charge of the management of Britain's European policy in the Foreign Office) by Jean Monnet himself. Monnet had come to London on 10 May 1950 and asked to meet with Plowden and Makins at the Hyde Park Hotel. He showed them the rather short piece of paper containing the Schuman Declaration, and in it was a suggestion that a condition for participating in the ECSC project would be accepting the principle of a federal Europe (a supranational authority). This was extremely important to the French because of the protections having a supranational authority would give them against any German backsliding from their obligations. Makins asked, 'Does this mean if we are not prepared to accept the principle of a federal Europe that we're not in, we're not wanted?', and Monnet answered, 'Yes, that is the position.'[29] This was not something the government could do, the cautious nature of British government being uncomfortable with accepting any principle before discussing it.

Yet the Dutch had accepted the invitation to enter the negotiations by saying that they accepted the principle, but made a reservation about their commitment if it didn't turn out to be to their liking – that they could withdraw from the negotiations later. According to the then Secretary of State for Commonwealth Relations, Patrick Gordon Walker, when this was presented back in Cabinet, some people – amongst them, Herbert Morrison – commented that 'in principle' has a different meaning in French than in English: 'In English it means that you have burnt your boats. In France it means you have just opened an argument!'[30]

Gordon Walker went on to point out that when the UK did join the Common Market in 1973, it accepted a variety of principles and was then in a position to 'argue like billy-o', but that in 1950, those in government and supporting the government felt that the British way of doing things was the best way, the British use of words was the best use. So the Cabinet agreed not to join the negotiations.

This decision would, in the words of Kenneth Younger, who was standing in for Ernest Bevin at that fateful Cabinet meeting, have a heavy cost. 'While we might be able to join in the Plan before it reached finality,' Younger wrote, 'we should, by failing to participate at the start, greatly reduce our chance of getting a scheme worked out on lines proposed by ourselves.'[31]

In his attack on Labour's decision not to enter the negotiations for the implementation of the Schuman Plan, opposition leader Winston Churchill made what the President of the Board of Trade and future Prime Minister Harold Wilson said was one of his best-ever speeches. Wilson paraphrases Churchill's words as: 'Let's go and talk, and say why we don't like it, or see if we can improve it to the point where we *can* go in. Don't let's just sulk on the sidelines.'[32]

Oliver Franks, who had been Britain's Ambassador to the USA at the time of the Schuman Plan's emergence, was highly influential in cultivating the atmosphere of non-participation. He reflected later that 'the decision cost us the leadership of Europe which we had enjoyed from the end of the war until May 1950'.[33] It proved Europe could integrate without the UK being involved. France and Germany became the motors of European cooperation and thus the dominant powers in the new Europe. US Secretary of State Dean Acheson was even more damning. He said that Britain's refusal to join in negotiating the Schuman Plan was 'the greatest mistake of the post-war period'.

What happened next was almost farcical. The Labour government decided to set up a small interdepartmental 'working party' to monitor the developments of the Schuman Plan as it began to be negotiated into what would become the Treaty of Paris in March 1951. The working party was placed under the direction of Sir Duncan Wilson at the German Economic Department at the Foreign Office. Wilson reports that, as the draft of the Paris Treaty emerged around the beginning of 1951, he was given a rather strange remit: 'We were told to find out what the text of one or two of the crucial articles meant, but to show no interest in doing so!' Wilson gave an example of this.

> I remember being told in casual conversation with the French, you know, to 'find out what Article 51/2 on exports to the Community really means'! Well, this was not a very easy remit, going cold into the subject, so to speak! Going up to Monnet or any of his officials and saying by the way 'It's a fine day, and what does Article 51/2 really mean?'[34]

This chapter could be accused of insisting that had Britain not been absent at the creation of the European unity project, it *would* have turned out differently. Daniel Hannan, the intellectual godfather of the Eurosceptic movement, argues that 'it is simply false to argue that, had Britain joined at the outset, the

EU would have been a looser arrangement, based on free trade and national democracy'. Hannan goes on to insist that 'it was precisely because the six founding members did not want these things that they went ahead without the United Kingdom'.[35]

There is some truth in this assertion, because the supranational nature of the ECSC had a far-reaching vision that was much more important than simple economic cooperation. In the middle of the Schuman Declaration were these words: 'The solidarity in production thus created would make all war between France and Germany not only unthinkable but materially impossible.' In the event of conflict, it was coal and steel that would need to be mobilised, yet under the ECSC it would not be readily available for any unilateral aggression by one European Community country against another. West German Chancellor Konrad Adenauer himself pointed out that, at the very least, a European Coal and Steel Community would make the aggressive plans of any one country transparent to its neighbours. If one member state started diverting production from what would be an intricate network of transnational trading contracts, it would trigger an early warning system. The ECSC stopped restricting German production and instead internationalised it.

Most importantly, instead of restraining sovereignty, it was sharing sovereignty – so it was a loss of absolute, but not relative sovereignty. In actual fact, the Schuman Plan actually made Germany more, not less sovereign than it had been. This is why the head of the Foreign Office's German Department suggested it was the first French scheme that had a chance of being acceptable to the Germans 'since it places Germany on the same footing as France or any other participating country'.[36] As we will see, Europe is a political vision more than an economic marriage of convenience, which is why simply measuring costs and benefits using economic indicators misses the point.[37] So, in one sense, Daniel Hannan is correct: perhaps there was no chance that the European unity project *would* have turned out differently had Britain been involved at the start.

But most people involved at the time came to admit that at the very least it *could* have turned out differently. Winston Churchill, in his speech to Parliament leading the attack on the Labour government's decision not to take part in the talks, insists that Britain could have entered on the same terms as the Dutch by accepting the 'principle' of supranationality but reserving the right to withdraw. He then runs through all the ways in which the Labour government could have addressed the parts of the Schuman Plan it was worried about, before turning to Chancellor Stafford Cripps and saying:

> If he asked me, 'Would you agree to a supranational authority which has the power to tell Great Britain not to cut any more coal or make any more steel, but to grow tomatoes instead?' I should say, without hesitation, the answer is 'No.' But why not be there to give the answer?[38]

Very soon, Labour was out of government. Having had their majority reduced from 146 to five in the 1950 election, Attlee was put under pressure to call another election, which he did in 1951, resulting in the Conservatives taking over with a majority of seventeen, putting Winston Churchill back in Downing Street. This would surely be, in the words of Harold Macmillan, 'hailed throughout Europe as likely to mark a wholly new approach towards the question of European unity'.[39]

Or was it? In truth, having missed the boat of the ECSC, Britain was now destined to miss the tanker of the European Economic Community.

RIGHT PLACE, WRONG MAN

Russell Bretherton was a well-known economist and rather less well-known amateur entomologist. In his day job he was a civil servant at the Board of Trade, but in the summer of 1955, Bretherton found himself acting as the UK's representative around a table in Brussels with the Foreign Ministers of Germany, France, Italy, Holland, Luxembourg and Belgium. It was one of the biggest moments in EU history and the choice of the United Kingdom's delegate says much of what we need to know about the country's attitude to the creation of the European Economic Community, the forerunner to the EU. The UK's man was not only out of his depth in this high-level gathering, he was under strict instructions not to agree to anything.

In explaining how this happened, we enter the battle between Europhiles and Eurosceptics over the mind and views of Winston Churchill. During the 2016 referendum campaign, some of Churchill's quotes were used to promote the Leave campaign while his grandson Sir Nicholas Soames claimed the wartime leader would have backed Remain, and even the Prime Minister evoked the spirit of Churchill in his fight to stay in the EU.

In 1942, in the middle of the Second World War, while he was Prime Minister, Winston Churchill wrote to his Foreign Secretary, Anthony Eden, that he was looking forward to a 'United States of Europe, in which the barriers between the nations will be greatly minimised and unrestricted travel will be possible'.[1] After the war, it was Churchill, giving a speech in Zurich in 1946, who suggested the formation of a Council of Europe as part of a 'United States of Europe'.[2] It was Churchill who said: 'My counsel to Europe can be given in a single word: "Unite!"'[3] It was Churchill who claimed, in November 1949, that 'Britain is an integral part of Europe, and we mean to play our part in the revival of her prosperity and greatness'.[4] Churchill had even shown during the Schuman Plan debate in 1950 that he understood the limits of national sovereignty in pursuit of a great vision, saying: 'National sovereignty is not inviolable and … it may be resolutely diminished for the sake of all the men in all the lands finding their way home together.'[5]

So it came as a surprise to many when, in 1951, having been returned to government, Winston Churchill decided not to join the European Coal and Steel Community (ECSC). Was this a massive U-turn by someone whose attack on Labour's decision was purely political rhetoric? The most likely reason for this apparent change of heart is that Churchill took a look at how the ECSC had been created (he came to power after the Treaty of Paris had been signed in 1951) and had decided that what had been set up in Britain's absence was harmful to Britain's interests and went against the way his subjects would consent to be governed.

That this could be spotted so early in the EU's development tells us a great deal about why so many in Britain have always been against the UK's membership of the EU. When it came to the 2016 referendum, there were still many fundamental factors about it that made it such a hard sell and such an easy target. In fact, Churchill believed that the ECSC that would have emerged had Britain been involved in the discussions would have been intergovernmental rather than supranational, and so no referendum would ever have been needed to rubber-stamp Britain's involvement in it.

It should be said that Churchill as Prime Minister in 1951 was a waning force. Coming into Downing Street aged seventy-seven, he deferred a great deal to his Foreign Secretary, Anthony Eden. In fact, Churchill's son-in-law, Christopher Soames, also his Principal Private Secretary at the time, suggests Churchill had surrendered authority over foreign affairs to Eden, who was hostile to Britain's role in European unity. According to those who worked most closely with him, Eden had a fundamental distaste for the whole *emotional* approach to Europe, feeling that it would never engage the deepest feelings of the British people.[6] As he told Evelyn Shuckburgh, his private secretary: 'What you've got to remember is that if you looked at the post-bag of any English village and examined the letters coming in from abroad, 90 per cent would come from way beyond Europe.'[7]

To be fair to Eden, nobody in his job could ignore the need for the 'three circles' of the USA, the Commonwealth and Europe to be maintained. Britain was still involved in the Korean War and the imperial sun had not yet completely set.

Eden was a man of European culture, he spoke French and some German, and he would never dream of carrying a supply of cornflakes on the cross-Channel ferry (something that many British people did at the time). He simply did not think that Schuman and Monnet's concept of 'Europe' would ever work. His knowledge of history told him that nationalisms were for ever the raw materials with which foreign secretaries did their work, and could not be abandoned for what was to him an alien construct. Nowhere is Eden's attitude better summed up than in his own words to Columbia University in New York in January 1952:

> If you drive a nation to adopt procedures which run counter to its instincts, you weaken and may destroy the motive force of its action ... You will realise that I am speaking of the frequent suggestion that the United Kingdom should join a federation on the continent of Europe. This is something which we know, in our bones, we cannot do ... For Britain's story and her interests lie far beyond the continent of Europe. Our thoughts move across the seas to the many communities in which our people play their part, in every corner of the world. These are our family ties. That is our life: without it we should be no more than some millions of people living in an island off the coast of Europe, in which nobody wants to take any particular interest.[8]

So began a series of attempts to negotiate a special position within Europe without sacrificing too many of the benefits. The 'Association Agreement' with the ECSC in 1954 was a bit like 'country membership' of London clubs, where a limited subscription reduces your obligations but gives you only some of the benefits. As part of this agreement, Britain established a permanent commission in Luxembourg, headed by Cecil Weir. Weir became a huge enthusiast for the idea of an economically integrated Europe, and often rushed around the corridors of the Foreign Office, Board of Trade and Treasury singing its praises. He was met by a wall of bored indifference, as most in those departments thought the whole organisation to be totally insignificant.[9]

Britain also stayed away from the attempt in the early 1950s to create what would have become a 'European Army'. The European Defence Community (EDC) Treaty was signed in 1952, providing for German rearmament within the framework of European cooperation, with the German Army to be responsible to the EDC, not the German government. This happened under pressure from the USA, who believed Europe would need to strengthen its defences against any attempts by the Soviet Union to expand. The realisation had dawned during the late 1940s and early '50s that the massed forces of NATO were not required any more to guard the borders of France and Benelux against West Germany, but were instead needed on West Germany's Eastern border with the now Russian-controlled East Germany and Poland. For this to happen the West Germans would need to be rearmed, otherwise the only Germans who would be armed if the USSR decided to invade would be East Germans. Should that happen, West German loyalties might be confused, as Ernest Bevin hinted when commenting on his fear of 'being made to appear as fighting Germans to prevent the reunification of the country and its liberation from occupation'. As long as the East could portray NATO as an army of occupation rather than protection, the Soviet propaganda machine would make considerable headway in West Germany. Therefore, US Secretary of State Dean Acheson proposed that German troops should be able to take their place alongside NATO allies.

But for France the prospect and the proximity of a rearmed Germany posed particular fears. In fact, Jules Moch, the French Defence Minister at the time, burst into tears when Acheson first proposed German rearmament in 1950. He reminded the Atlantic Council, the governing body of NATO, that France had been invaded by Germany once a generation for each of the past three generations, so these objections were from the 'recent personal experience of practically every Frenchman'.[10]

There was an answer to these fears, and it came from René Pleven, the French Minister of Defence from 1952 to 1954, who had been Jean Monnet's assistant in wartime London. Monnet had wondered about who would recruit the first German soldiers if not a national war ministry in Germany, and who would give them orders, if not a German general staff? Pleven, inspired by Monnet and Schuman's federalism, suggested a supranational European Army, under a single European defence minister.[11] The first German soldier recruited would be 'a European, in European uniform, under European command'.[12] Having launched the plan when Britain was still governed by the soon to be defeated Labour Party, Pleven was pretty sure the Conservative government would be in favour and the British would be involved. After all, Churchill had proposed a motion for a common 'European Army' at the Council of Europe in Strasbourg in 1950. He had said at the time that such an army would be a message 'from the

House of Europe to the whole world' and that Britain should be included, as 'we should all play a worthy and honourable part'.[13] What happened next was seen as a betrayal of Europe, both by some in Britain and by those abroad.

Anthony Eden was troubled by the idea of Britain's place in a European Army. He knew it might work for the Europeans, and he knew the Americans wanted it, as part of the Marshall Plan of financial aid to help rebuild Western Europe. They wanted Europe to stand on its own two feet militarily as well as economically. But he didn't think Britain should be involved in any supranational organisations. Eden was also one of the first practitioners of 'détente' with the Russians, and didn't want to upset the apple cart. Added to that was a personal rivalry between a small but influential group of Conservatives at the forefront of the European movement, such as Harold Macmillan, Duncan Sandys and David Maxwell Fyfe. It was Maxwell Fyfe who bore the brunt of this rivalry on 28 November 1951.

The Tory Cabinet had discussed the Pleven Plan in detail, and Maxwell Fyfe, the Home Secretary, travelled to the Consultative Assembly of the Council of Europe in Strasbourg armed with a carefully worded statement that was the outcome of protracted and difficult argument. The idea of the statement was to hold out the promise to the Europeans that British attitudes to supranational cooperation would be more forthcoming, starting with the Pleven Plan. 'I cannot promise our full and unconditional participation, but I can assure you of our determination that no genuine method shall fail through lack of thorough examination ... There is no refusal on the part of Britain.' Maxwell Fyfe said later that he believed he was giving the view of a senior Cabinet minister, acting on the authority of the Cabinet, that Britain had 'agreed to the very principle of joining a European Army'.[14]

A few hours after Maxwell Fyfe had delivered this statement, however, Anthony Eden, the Foreign Secretary, who had been a party in the Cabinet to drafting that statement, called a press conference in Rome, where he had been attending a NATO meeting. At the press conference, Eden was categorical: Britain would *not* participate in a European Army on any terms.

Back in Strasbourg, the European delegations were greeting the British with reproachful cries of 'betrayal'. Paul-Henri Spaak, the President of the Council of Europe (which at the time was separate from the ECSC and was really only a 'talking shop'), resigned in desperation at Britain's behaviour (Spaak will reappear in our story very soon). David Maxwell Fyfe called Eden's dismissal of the possibility of British participation 'the single act which above all other destroyed Britain's name on the Continent'.[15] This was a strong rebuke of his own Cabinet colleague, showing how divisive Europe could be amongst the Conservatives even back then. But Eden was fiercely protective of his autonomy on British foreign policy, and didn't believe that Britain was a European nation. That said, he remained extraordinarily sensitive about this particular episode, even instructing lawyers to sue Maxwell Fyfe over the latter's retelling of this episode in his memoirs in 1964.[16]

Winston Churchill also believed that the UK shouldn't be treated like the European states, none of whom had the advantages of the English Channel and who were thus more easily conquerable. At a dinner with Monnet in Paris, he called the idea of a European Army a 'sludgy amalgam', and then held forth at a dinner with US President Dwight Eisenhower on the presidential yacht in Washington in early 1952 with a sustained caricature of how a European Army would or would not function. Dean Acheson reports that:

> He pictured a bewildered French drill sergeant sweating over a platoon made up of a few Greeks, Italians, Germans, Turks and Dutchmen, all in utter confusion over the simplest orders. What he hoped to see were strong national armies marching to the defence of freedom singing their national anthems. No one could get up enthusiasm singing 'March NATO, march on'.[17]

Ultimately, Churchill and Eden believed that, whatever their reservations about it working, if the EDC kept Western Europe stable, it would be in the UK's interests. But the UK's lack of participation in it was one of the most significant reasons why the French Assembly, after a long internal debate, voted down the EDC in 1954. Edouard Herriot, at eighty-two years old still the leader of the radical left and a former Prime Minister, reduced many in the chamber to tears when he recalled the German wars and pleaded for the survival of the French Army. The French Assembly had called a temporary halt to the country's political and intellectual leadership of European unity.[18]

Anthony Eden proposed a more light-touch approach – the Western European Union (WEU), which would keep a check on the armaments and forces of European countries, and allow defence to be discussed at an intergovernmental level. But what did come out of the experience with the European Defence Council was a reinforcement of the British conviction that methods of European collaboration that involved weakening of national sovereignty were not going to work. The Coal and Steel Community would continue to exist but there would be no more expansion. This was combined with a belief that British policy-makers' own pragmatic approach to European cooperation was the wisest way to go. So when the Benelux countries proposed an extension of the ECSC into a general 'common market' at a meeting in Messina, Italy, the British foreign policy establishment was unable to take it seriously.

By 1955, Winston Churchill had passed the leadership of the Conservative Party (and thus the keys to Downing Street) onto Anthony Eden, who had called and won a resounding general election victory. The Western European Union had been ratified and West Germany allowed into NATO. This provided 'a new atmosphere of security in which continental integration efforts could successfully progress'.[19] Unlike in 1950, Britain would be openly invited without conditions to take part in that progression.

The initial driver was the Dutch Foreign Minister, J. W. Beyen. He produced a document which he finessed with the help of the other smaller members of the ECSC (Belgium and Luxembourg) into a proposal which at first disturbed and rather horrified the larger members (France, Italy and Germany). It committed the six members to the belief 'that it is necessary to work for the establishment of a united Europe by the development of common institutions, the gradual fusion of national economies, the creation of a common market and the gradual harmonisation of ... social policies'.[20]

Jean Monnet had stepped down as the head of the ECSC to launch a high-profile pressure group to campaign for further supranational integration in other areas, notably atomic power. He was replaced by the Belgian Foreign Minister, Paul-Henri Spaak (who had resigned from the Council of Europe in protest at Britain's behaviour back in 1951). Spaak and Monnet thought further supranational integration would be achieved by forming further communities like the ECSC – one for air transport, one for nuclear energy and so on.

J. W. Beyen, however, had another idea. He argued that it would be better to form a full 'customs union', yoking the six national markets into one. A customs union would be like a 'common market' and involve free trade between the member states but a common external tariff on products from outside the union.

It would also involve the possible harmonisation of social laws and monetary policy. The most significant part of this was that a customs union has only one, shared trade policy with countries outside it, unlike a free trade area, which still leaves countries to have their own trade deals with external nations. One trade policy for a group of countries means a need for a centralised authority to make those trade deals on behalf of its members. This was a bold agenda, and the Foreign Ministers from the six members agreed to meet in Messina, Sicily, to discuss it.

The Messina conference eventually broke up having made what Jean Monnet called a 'timid step towards the making of Europe'. Spaak's principal aide, Baron Snoy, reported the need to have been extremely cautious on questions of sovereignty after the collapse of the EDC Treaty in France.[21] There was no mention of the word 'supranational', and all that was agreed was to set up some committees of experts to discuss the 'functional possibilities' of working together on roads, railways, canals and energy, and a central committee, headed by Spaak, to discuss the creation of the Common Market. It was also decided, without conditions attached, to invite Britain to participate in these committees as a full and equal partner.

There had been no British 'emissary' at Messina. The British government more or less ignored the conference. The British Ambassador to Rome reported that his Dutch colleague had said that the meeting had never meant to achieve much and that the Foreign Ministers had enjoyed their holidays. The meeting had only been held in Messina because the Italian Foreign Secretary, Gaetano Martino, had an election coming up in Sicily so refused to hold the conference in Rome. What's more, at exactly the same time, British newspapers were reporting the Old Bailey trial of the... wait for it... Messina brothers, who had been charged with pimping and racketeering. So mention of Messina in Britain in May 1955 inspired only thoughts of prostitution and extortion by oily Italians running a corner of London gangland.

J. W. Beyen himself came to London to explain the intentions of the Messina resolutions at a series of meetings presided over by the Chancellor of the Exchequer, Rab Butler. Beyen delivered a formal invitation to Britain to take part. Harold Macmillan, now Foreign Secretary, and in San Francisco at the time at the tenth birthday of the UN, asked that any decision on a response to the invitation be delayed until he got back.

Thus it was not until 30 June 1955 that the Cabinet discussed whether to take part in the Spaak Committees. Rab Butler had conceded that Britain might send an 'observer', who would open proceedings with a statement making it clear the UK fundamentally objected to the supranational basis of the enterprise. Harold Macmillan thought differently. At a meeting of the Foreign Office on 29 June, Macmillan argued that this was a chance to 'relaunch' Europe, and if this was to be a version in which the British should join, they had to be there to shape it.[22] Cabinet minutes from the next day report Macmillan suggesting that the UK might be able to exercise greater influence in the forthcoming discussions if it were to enter them on the same footing as the other countries and not in the capacity of an observer.[23]

Eventually, Macmillan was allowed to reply to the invitation to participate in the work of the Spaak Committees. He sounded a word of warning, saying that 'there are, as you are no doubt aware, special difficulties in any proposal for a European common market', but then moved on to say that Britain would be happy to take part in studying the problems 'in the hope of reaching solutions which are in the best interests of all parties concerned'.

What Macmillan meant by 'problems' was that if there was to be a European customs union, tariffs would have to be imposed on imports from the Commonwealth. Britain would not want to breach the system of imperial preference established in 1932, whereby Britain gave free entry to Commonwealth produce and in return was given preferential rates on tariffs into those countries. It may be hard to imagine being so preoccupied with the Commonwealth when reading this book in the twenty-first century, but at the time the British government was under the impression that the Empire would be going strong for another fifty years, as opposed to the reality, which was that it was over by the '60s.

Macmillan also reported that Britain would appoint a 'representative' to take part in the studies. The word was chosen carefully. A representative didn't have to be committed to the Messina resolution, unlike the 'delegates', as the Foreign Office believed they would be, from the other countries. This meant that the representative could take part in discussion but, in diplomatic terms, a 'representative' suggested 'close association with' but in the end 'detachment from' full involvement in the talks. Anthony Nutting, Minister of State for Europe at the Foreign Office, pressed hard to be at the meetings. Anthony Eden wouldn't allow it. A minister, or any politician, would be expected to have some elected authority to make decisions and commitments. No, this was a purely economic affair, and so it would be natural to send someone from the Board of Trade. The most appropriate person the Board of Trade had to send to Brussels was its representative on the OEEC (Organisation for European Economic Co-operation – set up to administer and distribute the aid money from the Marshall Plan), one Russell Bretherton.

Bretherton had been a fellow of Wadham College, Oxford for seventeen years, teaching economics, before he got into the Board of Trade. One of his students at Oxford had been future Prime Minister Harold Wilson, who was elected to the House of Commons in 1945 and quickly rose at the age of thirty-one to become President of the Board of Trade. Toiling on the lower corridors of that department was the tutor who had taught him much of what he knew about economics.[24]

Russell Bretherton's experience and expertise in the economics of trade, gleaned from his time working on the economic side of the conferences that created the Marshall Plan and NATO, made him perfect for this particular task. London would rather this whole integration process was not going ahead, but if it was, it would pitch its contribution purely on trade.

Bretherton was, according to Roy Denman, who worked under him at the Board of Trade, pipe-smoking, spare and austere. 'His views were clear and firm, carefully enunciated, they brooked no contradiction.' Bretherton would open meetings that he chaired, make a statement of the issues to be discussed, and then outline the rational solution. Denman then reports that 'glaring round like a basilisk he found neither discussion nor dissent. Gratefully I was able to record, "There was general agreement with the Chairman's approach."'[25] Bretherton spoke no foreign language; Continentals, he believed, were unreliable fellows, apt to get up to mischief if not kept under control.

Bretherton was sent to Brussels for the Spaak Committee meetings, which started on 9 July 1955, with clear instructions from Peter Thorneycroft, the then President of the Board of Trade: Britain was a member of the OEEC, which covered the whole of Europe, and any 'common market' should cover all of the countries of the OEEC as a multilateral solution, rather than dividing Europe. He was also told to cooperate but avoid all commitments. Ever the professional, Bretherton went to do his job, intending to follow his instructions to the letter – he was to 'wait and see'.

When Russell Bretherton arrived in Brussels, he was startled to find that every other participant in the process was at Foreign Minister level. He was referred to, for the only time in his life, as 'Your Excellency'. He was even more startled to find that the other countries had arrived with very different attitudes about what could be achieved. Back in the UK, the Cabinet Mutual Aid Committee had advised the Chancellor of the Exchequer that there was very little chance of the Messina process leading anywhere, as the conflicts of national interest were too great. This advice had been well wide of the mark.

Bretherton's first report was clear that the first meeting of the Spaak Committee had shown 'firm determination to implement the Messina proposals'; the project was indeed 'predominantly political'. He also went back to London to tell colleagues that his brief, to 'steer the Spaak Committee Britain's way', was unlikely to be achieved. The customs union was already almost agreed in principle, and he was becoming more of an observer of this process than actually achieving anything. What's more, with no British Ambassador in Brussels, Bretherton felt on his own, unhooked from ministerial or Whitehall control. Telephone communications were awful and the diplomatic bag took four days to reach Brussels, so it was impossible for him to be briefed on his response to every turn in the discussion.[26]

Meanwhile, the other participants in the Spaak Committees were noticing Bretherton. Robert Rothschild, one of Spaak's assistants, remembers Bretherton as 'a very pleasant fellow and very courteous', but that he contributed little. 'He usually had a rather cynical and amused smile on his face, and he looked at us like naughty children, not really mischievous, but enjoying themselves by playing a game which had no relevance and no future.' For his part, Bretherton felt that he did contribute, but mainly to point out the technical difficulties of a customs union because of the UK's links with the Commonwealth, and how a free trade area would be a good deal easier.[27]

As July turned to August, Bretherton found himself being drawn in. No longer able to 'influence' or 'steer' the discussions, he started to fear the implications of his continued presence. 'If we take an active part in trying to guide the final propositions,' he wrote to a colleague, 'it will be difficult to avoid later on the presumption that we are, in some sense, committed to the result.' This meant that Britain could end up insisting on such-and-such a point, get it into the conclusions, but then renege on the whole deal. 'On the other hand, if we sit back and say nothing, it's pretty certain that many more things will get into the report which would be unpleasant from the UK point of view whether we in the end took part in the Common Market or not.'[28]

As luck would have it, it was at this point that Spaak adjourned the discussions until September. Bretherton said that Spaak had intended to work right through the holiday period. 'But when we go into August this was more than could be stood even by the Europeans, and a lot of people found that their daughters were getting married or their grandmothers were getting buried; and eventually he agreed that we should have a break.'[29]

So Russell Bretherton went back to London, and Paul-Henri Spaak followed him, to try to persuade London to change its mind on its approach. He managed to get a meeting with Chancellor of the Exchequer Rab Butler, at which his aide Robert Rothschild was present. Rothschild recounts that:

> It was obvious that Spaak was not convincing Butler. I can still see him, very immobile, looking at Spaak without saying a word, and the colder he became the warmer Spaak became, and the warmer Spaak became the colder Butler obviously became. After a while we realised it was no use going on. We said goodbye and went off ... As we walked back, Spaak turned round to us and said, 'I don't think I could have shocked him more, when I appealed to his imagination, than if I had taken my trousers off.'[30]

Before going back to Brussels, where he knew the talks were getting to the point where decisions were going to be called for and treaties prepared, Bretherton wrote another letter to his political masters. In this letter is a passage that sums up perfectly the missed opportunity that not taking part in the Schuman Plan and not taking a serious part in the Messina process entailed: 'If we are prepared to take a firm line, that we want to come in and will be a part of this, we can make this body into anything we like. But if we don't say that, something will probably happen and we shan't exercise any influence over it.'[31]

Bretherton's advice was ignored. He received no further instructions and no change in the instructions he had. In Brussels, Jean Monnet and Paul-Henri Spaak had engineered a change in procedure which would bring matters to a head. The many functional committees were disbanded and there was to be one committee at which experts would speak and decisions would be made on the Common Market. A rapporteur would be appointed to draft what would become the Treaty of Rome, and Monnet's personal assistant, Pierre Uri, was that man.

This was a step too far for the British government, who had commissioned a report on the benefits and risks of joining the Common Market that had come down on the side of the benefits not being enough to outweigh the risks. More importantly, in terms of the Common Market being created at all, the report stated four objections:

1. It would weaken relations with the Commonwealth;
2. The concept of the common external tariff would be contrary to the British idea of free trade in food;
3. It might lead to further political federation – and public opinion was against that;
4. It would remove protections for British industry against foreign competition.

The committee that produced the report suggested that the establishment of a European Common Market would be bad for the UK, and if possible should be frustrated, which meant it should be made clear through Russell Bretherton that the British were against the idea.[32]

Thus it was that Russell Bretherton was provided with a speech to read out. Uri remembers Bretherton reading out this speech in 'the dullest possible way'. Uri accepts that Bretherton was a faithful civil servant, under instructions, reading a brief that his heart wasn't in and with which he didn't want to be associated. Uri thought it was a very sad situation. 'I must say, later on when he saw what we produced, the so-called Spaak Report, he said, "This is a damned good report. I wish we had been in it."'[33]

What was in the speech that Bretherton read out? The official record, stemming from the report of J. F. Deniau, a member of the French delegation, is that Bretherton said the following to the others involved in the negotiations: 'Gentlemen, you are trying to negotiate something you will never be able to negotiate. If negotiated, it will not be ratified, and if ratified, it will not work. Au revoir and bonne chance.' He then walked out, although Bretherton insists that what in fact happened was that Spaak 'blew up' and asked him to leave.

This line has been repeated over and over again in slightly differing variations ever since, including by European Commission President Jacques Delors in late 1991 to illustrate his view of the attitude of the then British government to Europe, and in numerous BBC and magazine specials on the issue. But there is no official record of Bretherton having spoken the line, and the record of the coded message he received mainly mentions the duplication of the Common Market arrangements with those already in place for the OEEC.

Russell Bretherton was sent to the negotiations on the Common Market with specific orders to carry out the Cabinet's decision, which was not to commit the country to anything. If he did say the words that Deniau had reported, it was only to state the view of the UK government at the time. Therefore, no responsibility for what happened nor its consequences should be put on his shoulders. The consequence of the approach Bretherton was ordered to take was what some have called the greatest missed opportunity of the UK's post-war history, the opportunity to shape the European Union.

The Treaty of Rome was signed on 25 March 1957, coming into force on 1 January 1958 and creating what was officially called the European Economic Community (EEC) as one of three European Communities alongside the ECSC and the European Atomic Energy Community (Euratom), a way of cooperating on nuclear power. The EEC was not just a customs union – with free trade between the states and a common tariff on outside countries' exports into the Common Market – but also a single market for goods, labour, capital and services. It also proposed the creation of common transport and agriculture policies and a European Social Fund and established the European Commission.

So this was where some of the most controversial parts of the European project (as far as the 2016 EU referendum campaign is concerned) came from. In the preamble, the signatory states said they were 'determined to lay the foundations of an ever closer union among the peoples of Europe'.[34] Pierre Uri, one of the drafters of the treaty, said the aim was for the wider European Community to take responsibility for what used to be the role of individual states – in his words, 'to provide welfare, security and full employment and to increase prosperity for all its citizens'. Uri then noted that 'this in the long run implied and was meant to imply fiscal, social, monetary and, ultimately, political union'.[35]

Although the EEC was mainly establishing freedom of movement of goods, the Treaty of Rome also established the concept of aiming for freedom of movement of labour. A Common Agricultural Policy (CAP) was adopted, which to this day absorbs the majority of the EU budget while protecting European farmers from competition. Furthermore, a supranational authority, the European Commission, was created, consisting of 'elected officials' who can propose legislation, implement decisions and uphold the treaty agreements.

From that moment, what was created was a political and economic entity that was anathema to British conceptions of sovereignty and which would require a huge number of changes in how Britain was governed if it ever wanted to join it. As Russell Bretherton said, had Britain played a full and constructive part in the discussions and negotiations involved in creating the European Economic Community, and the European Coal and Steel Community before that, they might have got exactly what they wanted. But they didn't play a full and constructive part.

The result was an organisation that was extremely hard for pro-Europeans in the UK to defend from the moment it was created, to the day we joined, and up to the minute we voted to leave. It was also an organisation as difficult to change from the inside as it was impossible from the outside, something David Cameron would find when he attempted his renegotiation in 2016.

Jean Monnet, the godfather of the European unity movement, expressed many years later his initial bewilderment and eventual explanation for Britain's actions during this time. 'I never understood why the British did not join this, which was so much in their interest. I came to the conclusion that it must have been because it was *the price of victory* – the illusion that you could maintain what you had, without change.' To this can be added an off-the-cuff remark that Monnet was recorded to have made to Labour Chancellor Stafford Cripps way back in the early summer of 1950 when Britain was refusing to participate in the negotiations for the Schuman Plan: 'I hope with all my heart that you will join from the start. But if you don't, then we will go ahead without you; and because you are realists you'll adjust to the facts when you see that we've succeeded.'[36]

It didn't take very long after Britain had walked away from the negotiations for the creation of the European Economic Community for them to see that the other six had succeeded, and that they would need to adjust to the facts.

REASON 3

OUT IN THE COLD

On the afternoon of 14 January 1963, the International Press Corps gathered in the Élysée Palace, Paris, for the twice-yearly press conference of General Charles de Gaulle, President of France. He spoke with no notes, his arms upraised to emphasise his doubts, his expression a parade of grimaces and concerns. Without actually saying 'Non' but by using an avalanche of negatives, de Gaulle had argued that Great Britain was not ready to join the European Communities. 'One might sometimes have believed that our English friends ... were agreeing to transform themselves ... It cannot be said that it is yet resolved... Will it be so one day? Obviously only England can answer ... after a profound change...'[1] This would come to be known as the 'veto' of Britain's first application to join the EU.

It is important to tell the story of how and why it happened because, while some argue it was beyond our control, it was in fact another of Britain's great missed opportunities in Europe. The length of time the government took to decide to apply, the decision to try to reform before joining instead of the other way around, and the time they took to negotiate the terms of entry were enough. But to that should be added the timid way the government managed the press, public opinion, politicians and the Commonwealth. Britain's first, vetoed application was the final of our triumvirate of missed opportunities for Britain to get in at the start of the European unity project in time to shape it to its needs and interests.

We pick up the story in the mid-1950s, with the creation of the European Economic Community by the signing of the Treaty of Rome on 25 March 1957. The EEC was aimed at bringing about economic integration amongst its member states, including a common market (meaning free trade, with no tariffs on imports, and free movement of labour and capital) and a customs union (meaning a common external tariff (CET) on imports from countries outside). There was also mention of 'ever closer union', which would eventually mean an attempt at increased political union.

Between Britain leaving the negotiations and the treaty being written, the French had brought up the need to include Algeria and its colonial and overseas territories in the agreements. This was so that they could involve them in trade, eliminating tariffs for the imports of raw materials and agriculture from them. This request was accommodated into the treaty.

One of the reasons the British had left the negotiations was because of the perceived effect of Common Market membership on trade with the Commonwealth. Yet here were the French overcoming a similar obstacle simply by getting stuck into the negotiations. Pierre Uri, who drafted the treaty, claims of Britain that '*had* they been there, provided they accepted the main and the key idea – that we were all working together for a common project – I think they would have got the same deal as the French did'. This view is backed up by Hervé Alphand of the French Foreign Office, who said:

> I think the invitation to the British was made with the intention of bringing Britain inside the Community and to discuss with Britain the articles of a Treaty, and then, had Britain accepted, the Treaty would have been different probably. I think we would have had to take into consideration probably the special interests of Britain with overseas Commonwealth trade.[2]

But the British were not inside the Community, and were also beginning to be troubled by what that meant. Harold Macmillan, who was then Chancellor of the Exchequer, wrote to his Permanent Secretary at the Treasury in February 1956: 'I do not like the prospect of a world divided into the Russian sphere, the American sphere and a united Europe of which we are not a member.'[3] Macmillan decided to act when the Spaak Committee report was completed, leading to a meeting in Venice in April 1956 at which 'The Six' decided to draw up treaties containing the report's proposals. Now it became clear that 'The Six' meant business, Macmillan instructed the Treasury to draw up a variety of strategies to deal with the new European bloc. Plans A to G were drawn up and it was 'Plan G' that was chosen.

Plan G was based on a free trade area (FTA) in industrial goods only. It would be run by the OEEC (which was, remember, an intergovernmental organisation). This would involve all members of the OEEC and include 'The Six' as a single entity. The mere fact that Plan G named 'The Six' as a single entity was an admission that they would probably succeed in forming their common market. Most historians believe that Plan G was an *alternative* to the EEC, with the aim of binding the EEC to the other members of the OEEC and minimising the ill-effects on Britain of a Continental customs union from which it was excluded.[4]

Plan G demonstrated several aspects of the continuing overconfidence the British government had in dealing with Europe. Effectively, it showed that they still felt Europe needed them more than they needed Europe, particularly after the failure of the European Defence Community (explained in Reason 2). So, the proposed FTA would exclude foodstuffs in the interests of British farmers and the Commonwealth; Britain would reserve the right to reimpose certain trade restrictions if necessary to protect sterling; and there should be 'no discrimination by the Messina Six ... against us'. This overconfidence was without foundation, but the whole FTA plan did persuade Paul-Henri Spaak, the leader of the talks on the EEC, to speed up discussions amongst 'The Six' about their own arrangements, fearing it was an attempt to sabotage the Common Market.

Plan G failed for a variety of reasons, but it is worth focusing on two economic issues and two political issues. The first economic issue was called 'trade deflection'. The aim of the free trade area was to allow free trade between all the countries in the OEEC, including not only 'The Six' of the EEC but also the countries on its periphery. But the EEC was a customs union whose members were agreeing to have free trade amongst themselves and a common external tariff with the outside world – so any imports into the EEC would be subject to a tax. Meanwhile, the peripheral members of the FTA could pursue their own trade policies with the rest of the world – vital to preserve Britain's trade with the Commonwealth. But this could mean that countries around the world could circumvent the EEC's common external tariff by their goods entering, say, Britain with no tariffs and then being traded freely to the EEC. This would be unacceptable to member states such as France and Italy, whose agricultural industry benefitted from the protection that tariffs provided.

The second economic issue was that of 'discrimination'. The EEC were committed to reducing tariffs between themselves as quickly as possible. But if they did that more quickly than they reduced tariffs with the outside FTA members, or reduced tariffs on a wider range of products than did the FTA, this would mean trade discrimination between the two groups. Effectively, consumers within the EEC would find EEC products cheaper than those from outside in the FTA. Britain wanted to avoid this, but the French government saw no point in offering all the commercial benefits of the EEC to the FTA, otherwise, why had 'The Six' accepted all the political obligations of the Treaty of Rome?[5] Here was an early example of Britain not actually being able to both 'have cake' and 'eat cake', either in joining or in leaving the EU.

Like Brexit, Plan G was also influenced by external political problems. The political issues were even more serious and far-reaching. First was that the USA didn't support the plan. The Americans saw Plan G as a step away from the principal aim of their post-war statecraft in Europe – which was the encouragement of a community that would stand on its own feet and outgrow the old nation state antagonisms. Given the choice between supporting the EEC or supporting Plan G, it was a simple choice to go for the former. Worse, the Americans felt that the FTA would be discriminatory against US trade without compensatory political advantages. In fact, George Ball, an advisor on Europe at the State Department, advised President Eisenhower that 'all this was going to do was to complicate Britain's ultimate relationships with the Continent', calling it a 'major tactical error'.[6]

An even bigger, longer-lasting problem was the Suez Crisis. Colonel Nasser of Egypt had precipitated a crisis with the West by nationalising the Suez Canal (which linked Asia and east Africa with Europe). Britain and France were the two countries with major stakes in the Suez Canal Company, and they concluded a secret agreement to regain control of the waterway. They conspired that Israel should invade the Suez region and France and Britain would come in to 'separate' the Egyptian and Israeli forces. The French and British leadership forged some very strong relationships during the planning for the Suez operation, during which French Prime Minister Guy Mollet attempted to convince his co-conspirators to move back into the European Community creation process, but to no avail. Worse, once the fighting broke out, the Americans were horrified, as were the Russians. Both saw the action as destabilising a strategically vital region. Considerable pressure was put on Prime Minister Anthony Eden to withdraw. The pound came under sustained attack, and the US refused to loan the UK the billion dollars they needed to support their currency. Thus, humiliated, the British called a halt to the Suez operation.

It was a wake-up call. Britain, it seemed, no longer carried the clout to take part in unilateral military operations around the world. The answer they came up with was to double-down on trying to maintain their 'special relationship' with the USA. This was to the considerable dismay of the French, who argued, according to the British Ambassador to Paris, Gladwyn Jebb, that 'American policy favouring the Asiatic races will drive the United Kingdom further in the direction of Europe'.[7] German Chancellor Konrad Adenauer summed up what should happen now when he said to his counterpart Guy Mollet that 'for Britain, France and Germany, there was only one way of playing a decisive role in the world: that is to unite Europe. We have no time to waste. Europe will be your revenge.'[8]

France agreed, moving decisively to push her version of the Union to the front of the agenda, in turn bringing the Treaty of Rome process to a constructive climax.

This was before Britain tried two last desperate throws of the dice: David Eccles, the President of the Board of Trade, commented at a Commonwealth Chambers of Commerce meeting that 'although it is not military or hostile in its intent – six countries in Europe have signed a treaty to do exactly what, for hundreds of years we have always said we could not see done with safety to our own country'.[9]

Harold Macmillan, who had become Prime Minister shortly after Suez, went further. Seeing that an old acquaintance from the Second World War, Charles de Gaulle, had been elected President of the French Fifth Republic at the end of 1958, he travelled over to Paris to make a radical proposal. He believed that de Gaulle owed him a debt of gratitude for having been responsible on more than one occasion for saving de Gaulle's political life. (President Roosevelt and Winston Churchill had both tried to terminate it during the Second World War, fearing him to have the makings of a Fascist dictator.) De Gaulle's memoirs recount Macmillan saying the following to him in their first meeting: 'The Common Market is the Continental system all over again. Britain cannot accept it. I beg you to give it up. Otherwise we shall be embarking on a war which will doubtless be economic at first but which runs the risk of gradually spreading into other fields!'[10]

Too late. De Gaulle authorised the rejection of the free trade area at the end of 1958. Britain did try a second plan – to create their own, entirely separate, gang – negotiating an alternative free trade area with six other countries not in the Common Market – Denmark, Norway, Sweden, Austria, Portugal and Switzerland. This became the European Free Trade Area (EFTA), with free trade in industrial but not agricultural goods, no common external tariff and no pretensions. The weaknesses of this plan were quickly spotted. The six members of the EEC were a strong core of major Western European powers, while the seven members of the EFTA were a weak periphery. David Eccles summed up the prospect as 'a climb-down – the engineer's daughter when the general manager's had said no'.[11]

At this point, Harold Macmillan seems to have decided to take stock of Britain's position within Europe. He had already realised that Britain was in a political pickle. In December 1959, he wrote to his Foreign Secretary, Selwyn Lloyd, that 'for the first time since the Napoleonic era, the major Continental powers are united in a positive economic grouping, with considerable political aspects, which though not specifically directed against the United Kingdom, may have the effect of excluding us, both from European markets and from consultation in European policy'.[12]

When he had entered Downing Street to replace Anthony Eden in 1957, Macmillan had pinned some words from a Gilbert and Sullivan opera, *The Gondoliers*, to the green baize door that separated the Cabinet Room from his private office at No. 10. The words, written in his own hand, were 'Quiet, calm deliberation disentangles every knot…'[13] These words became the signature tune of the Macmillan years of government and, according to Michael Charlton:

> He made it a watchword for all at Downing Street as he set out to restore the lost national self-confidence of Britain and keep the country buoyant in the sea of troubles which flooded in upon it in the bitter, divisive aftermath of the Suez failure – and after what was becoming obvious by 1958: the breakdown of the European policy.[14]

The trouble was, time was no longer on Britain's side. Macmillan's quiet, calm deliberation was a part of the next missed opportunity for Britain in Europe.

Armed with a majority of 100 seats from a crushing victory at the 1959 general election, Macmillan's mood was less jovial when reviewing the economic figures. Between 1954 and 1959, for example, unit labour costs (the cost to make a unit of output) in the manufacturing industry had risen by 25 per cent in Britain, which was twice as fast as in other industrial countries. This rise in costs would at some point have to feed through to prices, both at home and in exports to other countries. In 1955, after a few years of expansion, the balance of payments (essentially the value of exports minus the value of imports, an important measure of the competitiveness of British products) went from a surplus to a deficit. In 1958, the West German economy overtook the British economy in terms of output as well as exports. From 1950 to 1960, average annual growth rates were: West Germany 7.8 per cent, Italy 5.8 per cent, France 4.6 per cent and Britain 2.7 per cent.

Now, one could easily dismiss these figures, as the Continentals had started from a lower base. But the economist Peter Oppenheimer noted in 1970 that these figures were a seed-bed of a pattern in which all the other countries of north-west Europe had surpassed Britain in output per head by the time the Conservatives left office in 1964.[15]

Until 1959, the political class had convinced itself that Britain could defeat the economic power of Europe anyway, believing that French and German growth rates were purely due to rising from wartime destruction. In truth, another price of victory of the Second World War for the British was that the *lack* of destruction, combined with the full employment policies followed by the governments from that point, meant that the day of reckoning had never come. Any economic depression wasn't serious enough to force government to give manufacturing a higher priority and address the competitiveness problem. In the case of Germany in particular, the need to rebuild and the pool of unemployed labour led to deep thinking about their education system and methods of production, resulting in an economy that is far more productive to this day. Britain hadn't *needed* to rebuild like that, so they chose not to.

Furthermore, relying on the Commonwealth for trade wasn't working as well as it should, not being as strong or coherent an economic force as it used to be. The colonies were disappearing too, gaining independence. The idea that Britain's growth could be based on the *complementary* economies in the Commonwealth, who could provide raw materials that Britain couldn't, with Britain having the manufacturing expertise that they didn't, was running out of steam too. The fastest growth in world trade was between industrialised countries, almost *because* they were competitive to each other, meaning industries and firms within had to become more efficient to survive and prosper.

Dean Acheson, the former US Secretary of State, summed up the dilemma facing the UK at the start of the 1960s devastatingly in a speech at the naval military academy at West Point. His main point was that 'Britain has lost an empire and not yet found a role'. To this he added:

> The attempt to play a separate role, that is a role apart from Europe, a role based on a Special Relationship with the United States, a role based on being the head of the Commonwealth, which has no political structure or unity or strength, and enjoys a fragile and precarious economic relationship by means of the Sterling area and preferences in the British market, this role is about to be played out.

So, really, Britain decided to join the EEC for lack of an alternative – or *faute de mieux*, as the French would say.[16]

At the end of the 1950s, however, economic realism in the UK was still superseded by political resistance. *Plus ça change*, as the French would also say. But some officials, whose job it was to give straight advice to politicians, were sounding the alarm. One was James Marjoribanks, who was minister (economic) at the British Embassy in Bonn, West Germany. Marjoribanks wrote a dispatch to London which suggested that unless the free trade area could reach a practical understanding with the European Economic Community, Britain faced 'disaster', with exports falling and economic power diminishing. 'Our position would be changed from the biggest market, and the second largest exporter of manufactured goods to Europe, to a member of what would be very much a second eleven scattered round the fringe of an increasingly powerful and rapidly growing United States of Europe.' He advised his political masters to stop waiting for 'The Six' to make concessions allowing Britain entry into their industrial markets and freedom from their agricultural rules. 'I think it is vitally important for us all to rid ourselves of the feeling that the Six cannot do without us ... The consequences for them of the United Kingdom being excluded are far less than the consequences for the United Kingdom of being shut out of Europe.'[17]

Here is an argument that would rumble on for sixty years – the counterpoint to this was made by Vote Leave's Boris Johnson in a BBC televised debate at

Wembley three days before the referendum in June 2016: 'Everybody knows that this country receives about a fifth of Germany's entire car manufacturing output – 820,000 vehicles a year. Do you seriously suppose that they are going to be so insane as to allow tariffs to be imposed between Britain and Germany?' Yet when he became Foreign Secretary, Johnson was swiftly disabused of this notion during a conversation with Carlo Calenda, a former Italian envoy to Brussels. Johnson had suggested to Calenda that Britain would want access to the single market without accepting freedom of movement. Calenda reports what happened when he told Johnson that was not possible: 'He said, "you'll sell less prosecco". I said, "OK, you'll sell less fish and chips, but I'll sell less prosecco to one country and you'll sell less to twenty-seven countries".'[18]

Back in the early 1960s when BMW was still developing its New Class Sedan, a blueprint car that would dominate European markets for years to come, the UK's decision on joining the EEC centred on similar questions to those fought over during the 2016 referendum campaign: trade and sovereignty. It was Frank Lee, Joint Permanent Secretary to the Treasury, who delivered the most emphatic push towards joining the EEC. It started with a memorandum dispatching any number of illusions, read by Macmillan on 27 May 1960. The memorandum made clear that Europe was now divided and Britain was linked to the weaker grouping. It noted that the success of the Commonwealth depended on the economic well-being of Britain, and if Britain was shut out of growing European markets, the Commonwealth was 'not likely to flourish'. Britain should put out of its mind that it could secure its objectives on the cheap, as industrial free trade, without a price recognising the economic strength of Continental farmers, was simply out of the question. Some difficult and unpalatable decisions were now required, including the contemplation of some surrender of sovereignty. Lee was thus asked to form and act as chairman of the Economic Steering (Europe) Committee in the middle of 1960, and they produced a report in the form of the answers to twenty-three questions.[19]

This time, Lee's advice was far less ambiguous than in his memorandum. A flavour of the report, considered at Cabinet on 13 July 1960, comes from the answer to Question 7 – what joining the Common Market means.

We cannot join the Common Market on the cheap. Joining means taking two far-reaching decisions. First, we must accept that there will have to be political content in our action – we must show ourselves prepared to join with the Six in their institutional arrangements and in any development towards closer political integration. Secondly, there must be a real intention to have a 'common market', and this implies that, in so far as the members of the market consider that production inside the market requires protection against outside production, this must also apply in our corner of the market; that is to say, in general we must accept the common tariff.[20]

Essentially, the report of the Economic Steering (Europe) Committee shows how far 'The Six' had come, and how Britain was now probably too late to change the way they operated. Lee (although the report was anonymised, those who know him say the style was unmistakably his) is admitting that joining the EEC involves accepting what is known as the *acquis communautaire* – the full range of decisions, policies, rules and treaties already agreed.

This is where the missed opportunity of the first attempt to enter the EEC lay. Harold Macmillan had persuaded his Cabinet to support the policy of entry and appointed pro-Europeans like Duncan Sandys (Minister for the Commonwealth), Christopher Soames (Minister of Agriculture) and, most importantly, Edward Heath (Lord Privy Seal and the minister responsible for leading negotiations). He then spent a year in exploratory talks with the EEC's members and finally announced Britain's intention to apply to the EEC to the House of Commons on 31 July 1961. There was then a period of one and a half years of negotiations before it all broke down. Had Britain started off by accepting the *acquis communautaire* as they stood, joined the EEC then negotiated from within, they were still in a position of power from which they might have been able to change the organisation from the inside. This was before so many areas that would not be negotiable by the time Britain actually joined (the CAP, the Budget etc.) had been set. Edward Heath called this the 'Monnet line' – as Jean Monnet had urged Britain to say yes to becoming a member then adjusted themselves *inside* the Community, getting the Community to adjust too. Heath believes that strategy wasn't followed as parliamentary and public opinion didn't really understand the nature of the Community.[21]

Instead, it was the 'quiet, calm deliberation' that was Macmillan's mantra. By the time that was done, the EEC had already changed beyond measure, de Gaulle had a majority in the French Assembly, and Britain's application was vetoed.

So what was holding Britain back from early commitment? There were two issues: sovereignty and the Commonwealth.

The sovereignty issue was never solved, and was laid bare to Macmillan first by the Cabinet's leading lawyer – the Lord Chancellor Viscount Kilmuir – and then by the USA's new President – John F. Kennedy.

We have met Viscount Kilmuir before, when as David Maxwell Fyfe he took part in the embarrassing episode in 1951 of announcing, in his role as Home Secretary, that Britain would consider joining the EDC a few hours before Foreign Secretary Anthony Eden announced that they would not.

The Prime Minister had asked Edward Heath to consult Kilmuir on any legal and constitutional issues around joining the European Community. Kilmuir's response to Heath and Macmillan was that the loss of sovereignty would be considerable in three main respects: first, Parliament would surrender some of its functions to a Council of Ministers, which could, by majority vote, make regulations that became the law of the land. Second, the Crown's treaty-making power would in part be transferred to an international organisation. Third, British courts would sacrifice some of their independence by becoming subordinate in some respects to the European Court of Justice. Kilmuir insisted that these were serious matters and argued that 'it will not be easy to persuade Parliament or the public to accept them'. Also, they should be 'brought out into the open now', because otherwise, 'those who are opposed to the whole idea of the Community will certainly seize on them with more damaging effect later on'. It is fair to say Kilmuir's advice on bringing these matters out into the open was ignored, but he was extremely prophetic about the 'damaging effect' that arguments over sovereignty would bring.[22]

The second way in which the effect on sovereignty of joining the EEC would be laid bare to Macmillan was in conversation with John F. Kennedy. Kennedy had appointed George Ball as Under Secretary of State. Ball had been asked to come to a meeting in London with Frank Lee and Edward Heath, in which they had told him that the British government was thinking of applying for membership of the European Community. When Harold Macmillan came to the US to speak to President Kennedy about the idea of applying, the young President told George Ball to give Macmillan the answer, which was this:

If Great Britain were to make application for membership in adherence to the Rome Treaty and do so in the recognition that the Rome Treaty was not a static document but indeed was a process leading toward greater and greater unity, including political unity, and might even ultimately lead to some kind of confederal or federal system for Europe – that I thought this would be a great contribution to the cohesion of the West.

But then Ball sounded a warning: 'We would not favour any British move if the intention of that move was to water down the Treaty of Rome, or try to transform the Community into anything that would be simply a loose consultative arrangement.'[23]

The little backbench Tory opposition there was to entering Europe was based on sovereignty and led by Derek Walker-Smith, who made an exquisitely polite and lawyerly speech in the parliamentary debate on the application in August 1961, the words of which have rung true from the early 1990s until now:

> If we adhere to the Economic Community now and the Six proceed, as they are entitled to proceed, to the next stage of political union, what then is our position? If we do not want to go along with them on the political side, could we stay in on the economic side, or could we get out at that stage even if we wanted to? Or is the real position this, that if the decision is taken now we forfeit the power of political decision? ... If we tried to come out of the Community in those circumstances, would not the Six be justified in saying to us, 'But you knew all along of our enthusiasm for the next political step. If you did not share it, why did you join in the first place?'

Walker-Smith's answer to this was simple: 'Tell the Six that we wish them well and that we want the maximum co-operation with them which is compatible with our own independent sovereignty and duty to the Commonwealth'[24] – in other words, we seek no more than to associate with them, never to belong.

So, the threat to Britain's sovereignty was one issue. Yet many of the arguments about that were carried out privately. A much more public, and thus significant, issue was the Commonwealth. All through the period leading up to the announcement on 31 July 1961 in the Commons that Britain would seek entry into the EEC, reams of papers spewed forth from the Treasury and Board of Trade about the need to consider what would happen to tropical and temperate foodstuffs, woodpulp and aluminium, Rhodesian tobacco and New Zealand butter. It seemed that Whitehall was stuck on the idea that the five countries other than France, at least, might let us have it both ways, allowing Britain to sustain the special treatment for her Commonwealth premises, and the cheap food that went with it.[25]

On the topic of agriculture, the French had been pushing for a while by then to get a Common Agricultural Policy agreed by the other five members of the EEC. This would mean a series of subsidies and minimum pricing policies to guarantee incomes for farmers (who were very politically influential in France). This was a concern for Britain for a variety of reasons. Firstly, it would be paid for by increasing prices for consumers instead of the way Britain funded subsidies for their farmers, through taxation. Secondly, it would involve very little gain for Britain, with only 4 per cent of its labour force being in agriculture in 1961, as against 12.5 per cent of Germany's, 20 per cent of France's and 25 per cent of Italy's, but considerable cost, with Britain having to import 50 per cent of its food due to its climate.

So it was that Harold Macmillan's announcement to the House of Commons came to be rather tepid. He made it clear that there had been no decision that Britain should join the EEC or even apply. The negotiations were to initially be about whether to negotiate.

> We have now reached the state where we cannot make further progress without entering into official negotiations … the Majority of the House and country will feel that they cannot fairly judge whether it is possible for the UK to join the EEC until they have a clearer picture before them of the conditions…[26]

It sounded like while Britain recognised the necessity of making this move, it was far from welcoming it. The *Manchester Guardian* commented that 'his approach is so half-hearted that it must diminish the chances of success in the negotiations'.[27]

Democracy is the art of persuasion and explanation. It seems that Harold Macmillan was so afraid of the implications of Britain joining the EEC that he decided democracy was in fact the art of pretending. His public approach to this movement towards Europe was similar to the approach of every other British political leader up until the 2016 referendum, all of whom did the same. It was to present the move they were making as absolutely essential to the British national interest but at the same time saying that nothing whatsoever would change in the British way of life and government. In the case of Macmillan, he said nothing about sovereignty, despite what Viscount Kilmuir had communicated to him. He seemed to prefer not to think through or pronounce upon the fact that 'Europe' was a political venture that had huge implications in terms of reducing the independence of both Parliament and the courts.[28]

George Ball wrote to President Kennedy that Macmillan's tactic was to 'move crabwise into the Common Market, sideways, and not to face the basic issues as to what the genius of the institutions was, that they were an attempt to move towards political unity'. Macmillan had, according to Ball, given 'simply a kind of tradesman's view of the Community'.[29]

This minimalism in presentation, this pinched, apologetic stance, meant that public opinion was never prepared for, still less won over by, a visionary leap into the Common Market. Over the course of the negotiations to follow, wary approval drifted to an unhelpful scepticism – with Gallup polls showing a fall in support for the policy from 53 per cent in December 1961 to 36 per cent in June 1962. Without the public behind the government, it was never possible to say that Britain was 'ready' to join. Furthermore, it was the first in many missed opportunities to sell the vision of European unity to the public rather than just present it as a pragmatic, economic choice that could be measured in numbers.

That said, Edward Heath started well with the eloquence and vision of his introductory statement in Paris at a ministerial conference of 'The Six' to launch the negotiation:

> The British Government and the British people have been through a searching debate during the last few years on the subject of their relations with Europe. The result of the debate has been our present application. It was a decision arrived at, not on any narrow or short term grounds, but as a result of a thorough assessment over a considerable period of the needs of our own country, of Europe, and of the Free World as a whole. We recognise it as a great decision, a turning point in our history, and we take it in all seriousness. In saying that we wish to join the E.E.C., we mean that we desire to become full, whole hearted and active members of the European Community in its widest sense and to go forward with you in the building of a new Europe.[30]

He then went on to set out the three problems Britain faced: access for the Commonwealth, the fortunes of British agriculture and what would happen to EFTA.

> It would be a tragedy if our entry into the Community forced other members of the Commonwealth to change their whole pattern of trade and consequently perhaps their political orientation. I do not think that such a development would be in your interests any more than in ours ... I now turn to the question of United Kingdom agriculture ... Provided we can see that in future – with the new methods decided upon – we are able to maintain the stability and living standards that we have established for our farmers, I believe that the problems raised by the differences in [our] present methods are in no way insuperable ... I should next like to consider the position of the countries associated with the United Kingdom in the European Free Trade Association. It has long been our view that the present division of Western Europe into two economic groups – a division which in our opinion has political as well as economic dangers – should be brought to an end ... As you will know from the statement issued by the E.F.T.A. Council on the 31st of July, we concluded that each member of E.F.T.A. should examine the possibility of entering into a direct relationship with the Community.

Although the speech was extremely well received in general, as they later read and digested it, 'The Six' began to have doubts. It seemed that the opening nego-tiation position from the British was not much better than the old free trade area plan rejected in 1958. Britain seemed to be expecting Commonwealth producers to have tariff-free access to the EEC. It was also expecting to play a full part in drafting the Common Agricultural Policy and asking for 'transitional arrange-ments for between twelve and fifteen years from joining'. Finally, it was urging the creation of a 'wider trading area' between the Community, the members of EFTA that had not joined, and Greece.

It is no surprise that several commentators argue that the British had started the bidding too high and had come too slowly to more realistic positions. The negotiations were held up for a variety of reasons beyond British control. The French held them up, first to insist that there would be no collective negotiation with 'The Six'. Unlike the Brexit negotiations that started when Article 50 was

invoked in March 2017, in which the European Commission had the authority to negotiate on behalf of the member states, de Gaulle was wary of the in-
fringement on national interests of giving too much power to the Commission.
Therefore, the French wanted Britain to have individual negotiations with each
member country. Secondly, 'The Six' refused to negotiate with EFTA members
en bloc on what would happen to them. This was a thorny issue thanks to the
London Agreement of June 1961. As part of this agreement, Britain had agreed
rather rashly not to enter the EEC until the interests of the other six EFTA
members were assured. It became clear very quickly that to join the EEC, Britain
would have to renege on that pledge.[31] Thirdly, no negotiations could take place
on agriculture until the principles of the CAP were agreed, which happened on
14 January 1962, ready to be fully implemented by 1970.

But the real problem was the whole negotiation approach of the British.
Journalist and author Hugo Young describes it as 'a conditional and tentative
venture, creeping in a state of high suspicion towards this moment of historic
destiny, declining to make a commitment until the Europeans had shown what
ground they were prepared to surrender, and reserving even then the option
of a British veto'. Young goes on to suggest that the British were not, actually,
applying: 'They made it clear that they wanted the Treaty of Rome, which they
had declined to participate in drafting, unpicked in certain parts.' They seemed
to be offering nothing in return for this.[32] Heath came to realise in hindsight that
he should have got the negotiations finished by August 1962, when they could
have then gone to the party conferences and the House of Commons and said,
'This is the agreed broad outline. We can have as long a debate as you like about
it, and if you accept this outline we can move forward very quickly on the details
and settle the agreement for ratification.'[33]

Under Edward Heath, the deputy leader of Britain's delegation was Eric Roll.
He explains how there was also a parallel negotiation going on with public and
party opinion at home. As well as our negotiating partners, we were talking to
the Commonwealth, to the farmers and the consumers, the British public, the
House of Commons and the House of Lords, and each one required a somewhat
different presentation because their interests and concerns were different.

Although some of the press were in favour of the application, they were particularly exercised about the effect on the Commonwealth. The *Daily Telegraph*
stressed that 'membership of the Common Market is a bigger issue for Britain

than for any other major Continental power. That is ... because of the Commonwealth and the vast role that the Commonwealth plays in our trade, our investment and our ways of political, social, legal and cultural thought.'

Meanwhile, Lord Beaverbrook's *Daily Express* acted as the mouthpiece of those sections of British industry with a vested interest in the maintenance of a special trading relationship with the Commonwealth. It came out unequivocally against the application, and accused the Prime Minister of putting 'Europe ahead of the Commonwealth'.[34] At the Commonwealth premiers conference, which began on 10 September 1962, Macmillan tried to focus on how Britain could be stronger, and thus better able to defend Commonwealth trade, from *within* the EEC. But the premiers of Canada, Australia and New Zealand all feared for their future trade with Britain, and the Afro-Asian nations could see little benefit for them from the EEC.[35]

Opposition in the Commons was led by Labour Party leader Hugh Gaitskell, who provided the classic model of criticising entry into Europe on the terms being discussed rather than entry itself. In his 1962 Labour conference speech, Gaitskell became the first major political leader to raise the issue of sovereignty in public. Gaitskell said that the European Commission, which had been set up as a supranational authority in the Treaty of Rome, would mean 'that powers are taken from national governments and handed over to federal parliaments. It means ... that if we go into this, we are no more than a state, as it were, in the United States of Europe, such as Texas or California.'

Gaitskell explained that while he understood the desire of those who created the European Community to have a political federation, he didn't feel this was the right path for Britain. He continued:

It does mean, if this is the idea, the end of Britain as an independent nation state. I make no apology for repeating: it is the end of a thousand years of history. You may say, alright, let it end, but my goodness, it is a decision that needs a little care and thought.[36]

Gaitskell's speech received a rapturous ovation at the conference. He was from the right of the party, and half of those of his political hue were actually supporters of European entry. However, the left, with which he had done battle on Clause Four (nationalisation of the means of production) and nuclear disarmament, rose as one to hail him, leading his wife Dora to remark worriedly that 'all the wrong people are cheering'.[37]

With public opinion turning against the government, Macmillan was faced with considerable problems when negotiations resumed on 8 October. These worsened when de Gaulle and his supporters easily won the French general election, winning a majority in the French Assembly and thus giving him full authority for foreign policy, most pressing of which was the British application.

Events moved rapidly to a climax when Macmillan ran into problems over the issue of nuclear weapons. De Gaulle wanted to have genuine nuclear forces in France and Britain, which American could not control. Britain had tried to build their own but had failed, and the Americans were offering a replacement, which Macmillan, never slow to flaunt his excellent relationship with the President, was going to fly to Nassau in the Bahamas to negotiate over.

During what was to be their final meeting at Rambouillet, de Gaulle organised some pheasant shooting, which he didn't take part in, preferring to stand behind Macmillan and other guests and comment loudly when they missed. After that, the French President expressed as forcefully as he could that if Britain wanted to join Europe, the special ties with American would have to be cut. De Gaulle managed to reduce Macmillan to tears of frustration at his intransigence. De Gaulle's Prime Minister, Georges Pompidou, summed up the difficulties as being not merely technical but, in his words '...*d'un problème de conception même du marché commun et son avenir...*', the problem of the basic viewpoint of the Common Market and its future.[38]

Macmillan then went to Nassau and persuaded Kennedy to let Britain have the Polaris submarine nuclear deterrent. He asked the President to grant to the UK, as a last resort in a moment of supreme national interest, the ability to independently launch the missile. He then negotiated the same deal for France on the same terms. Rather than gratitude, for de Gaulle this was the final straw. Having asked Macmillan to detach from the USA, he finds even further evidence for his fear that if admitted, Britain would act as the US 'Trojan Horse' within the Communities.

So, in January 1963, Charles de Gaulle abruptly called a press conference to announce his veto of the UK's application. He started by saying that the six states who had signed the Treaty of Rome had 'a feeling of solidarity because not one of them is linked on the outside by any special political or military agreement'.

Meanwhile, 'England is, in effect, insular, maritime, linked through its trade, markets and food supply to very diverse and often very different countries. Its activities are essentially industrial and commercial, and only slightly agricultural.'[39]

Let's have a look at those words again, with the hindsight of seeing our relationship fifty years on. De Gaulle was saying that the nature, structure and economic context of the UK differed profoundly from those of the other states of the Continent. Perhaps Charles de Gaulle was right then, and is right now?

It is fair to say that the British reaction to de Gaulle's veto was rather extreme. Princess Margaret's trip to Europe was cancelled, and one tabloid told de Gaulle to 'take your dreams of independent power and stick them up your Eiffel Tower'. Even some of de Gaulle's compatriots weren't sure about his decision. A former French Prime Minister, Paul Reynaud, wrote to de Gaulle asking, 'Does this not show ingratitude in view of Britain's role as an ally of France in two World Wars?' Reynaud received an empty envelope back, with, written on the outside, 'Re-direct to Agincourt, Somme or Waterloo, Belgium'.[40]

However, one British reaction to the veto was telling: that of Edward Heath. Heath had been the chief negotiator in Europe, travelling back and forth to Paris and Brussels nearly 100 times. He said, at the final session of the negotiations, the following:

> There have been times in the history of Europe when it has been only too plain how European we are, and there have been many millions of people who have been grateful for it ... We in Britain are not going to turn our backs on the mainland of Europe or on the countries of the Community. We are a part of Europe; by geography, tradition, history, culture and civilisation. We shall continue to work with all our friends in Europe for the true unity and strength of this Continent.[41]

The veto of Britain's first application to join the European Communities was the end of a traumatic period for the country's self-esteem. The embarrassment of Suez, the realisation that its economic performance was lacking, and the success of the Treaty of Rome in bringing together 'The Six' into a functioning customs union put Britain in a position where they probably had more to gain from joining than 'The Six' would gain from their entry. Although the remnants of old-school politicians and officials still clung to the belief in British superiority, the many times from 1956 to 1963 that Britain ended up with its tail between its legs hit it hard.

Still, Britain ignored advice from the US to agree to join on the basis of the existing arrangements and then try to change from the inside, at a time when many issues were still up in the air. It dragged out the negotiations to the point where the one person who might have the power to veto them suddenly gained that power. It overplayed its hand with its relationship with the USA, who was far more interested in the success of the European Communities than Britain wanted, and whose help in the nuclear field wasn't viewed as positively by its negotiating partners as it might have been. Finally, it didn't honestly and clearly sell the benefits of European unity to the public, the press and its politicians in a way that would show Charles de Gaulle in particular that it was 'ready' to join, that it could indeed be European.

This was the final in a triumvirate of opportunities to shape the political and economic arrangements of the European Communities. It meant that when Britain finally did join, it had to contort itself politically and economically way past the level at which it was comfortable. The 2016 referendum ended up being a vote to leave a set of institutions that were extremely difficult to sell as beneficial to the national interest.

REASON 4

JOINING PAINS

On 1 January 1973, the United Kingdom finally joined the European Communities. It was the most imaginative achievement by a British government for generations and, at last, a chance not missed. Yet it came at a constitutional, economic and political price that was far higher than it would have been had Britain entered earlier. Some of those costs weren't fully apparent to anyone at the time, nor even by the referendum in 1975, and so the 2016 EU referendum was the first occasion when the public had a chance to decide whether they really wanted to continue to pay them.

In 1964, Labour won the general election. A year later, Edward Heath became leader of the defeated Conservatives and by 1970 he was Prime Minister. The man who had been lead negotiator in the UK's first application to join the EEC would be the man who in 1973 led Britain into Europe. Before all that, French President Charles de Gaulle vetoed a second application in 1967. Far more importantly, though, two little-noticed court cases would change how all member states of the EEC were governed forever.

These two cases determined that the laws of the EEC were superior to the laws of the member states and would have direct effect on *all* of the member states, whatever their parliaments did. The cases and their results were ignored in Britain at the time, and even ten years later, when the UK *did* enter the EU, it is fair to say that many public lawyers did not understand the ramifications.[1]

The first case was Van Gend en Loos *vs* the Netherlands Inland Revenue. The Dutch had tried to levy a tariff on goods from Germany. This was ruled by the European Court of Justice (ECJ) to be against the provision of the Treaty of Rome, and the Dutch government was ordered to remove the tariffs. This ruling established the principle that EEC law had 'direct effect' on member states' legislatures and individuals, whether the legislatures approved of it or not. 'Direct effect' meant that legislation from the EEC was like federal legislation in the USA having direct effect on Florida and Connecticut, whether the people of Florida or Connecticut like it or not. The EEC was now a new legal order, the subjects of which were the member states and individuals, and laws it made became part of the legal heritage of the member states.[2]

The second case was Costa *vs* ENEL. Mr Costa objected to the Italian government nationalising the electricity industry (in which he was a shareholder), which he said violated the Treaty of Rome. The ECJ ruled that the principle of Community law was supreme over the law of member states. That meant that if there was a conflict between the law of a member state (Italy) and the law of the EEC, the EEC law prevailed. The wording of the judgment speaks volumes: 'The transfer by the States from their domestic legal system to the Community legal system of the rights and obligations arising under the Treaty carries with it a permanent limitation of their sovereign rights, against which a subsequent unilateral act incompatible with the concept of the Community cannot prevail.'[3]

In clearer English, the law cannot vary from member state to member state or there is no Community. European law is thus not only directly effective but also superior to the law of member states.

But let's focus on seven words of the ECJ judgement in the Costa *vs* ENEL case: 'a permanent limitation of their sovereign rights'. Britain would join an organisation in 1973 which could not only limit her national sovereignty (which can happen any time you join an international organisation like NATO) but also her *parliamentary* sovereignty. Parliamentary sovereignty cannot be shared. You are either sovereign or you are not. Either Parliament can do what it likes or it cannot. Either we vote for our lawmakers or we don't. These two 1964 court cases meant that when the UK joined the EEC in 1973, Westminster became a subordinate Parliament.

In the 1972 European Communities Act (Section 2(1))[4] (the legislation that would allow Britain to join the EEC), it is made clear that Parliament would have to legislate consistently with European law. The terms of the European treaties, as interpreted by the European Court of Justice, would require national parliaments to limit their sovereignty, by Parliament giving direct effect to European law. Furthermore, Acts of Parliament have to be made accordingly with European law. This means Parliament lost the power at that point to legislate in any manner they wished to. The 1972 European Communities Act was a constitutional revolution, as it broke the convention that no parliament can bind future parliaments when it makes law. In this case, future parliaments were bound by the terms of the Act unless they expressly repealed it.[5] In effect, leaving the EU does just that.

More than 90 per cent of the over-65s turned out in 2016, and many of them voted to leave. Many of those said that they had voted Yes in 1975 but had felt 'duped' then, not realising the loss of sovereignty the Common Market entailed. They also felt Europe had moved on from what they signed up to. But given how few people in Britain understood the implications of these two court cases fully at the time of the 1975 referendum (held to decide whether the UK should stay in the EC), it is no surprise that they weren't mentioned during the campaign. So the over-65s had a point, and the 2016 referendum was the only opportunity they ever got to make it.

That said, before the UK's 1970s attempt to join the EEC, a little battle had been won by France's President Charles de Gaulle – he got the national veto. De Gaulle was worried about a challenge to the Common Agricultural Policy. The arrangement favoured France and had been won with great difficulty. But a loosening of the voting threshold on the Council of Ministers posed a risk. A group of member states might be able to wrestle through changes. France needed a way to block any future amendments and, until that could be found, announced its intention to be absent from the Council. This boycott was known as the 'empty chair crisis' and was only ended by the working out of the 'Luxembourg Compromise'. This stipulated that if a member state believes that its vital national interests are at stake and no compromise could be reached, that state could have a right of veto. What counted as 'vital national interests' was not defined – this was left to the judgement of the state in question.[6]

De Gaulle's stand would enable successive British governments to argue that the existence of a national veto meant British sovereignty was always protected. Ironically, it was the mother of Euroscepticism Margaret Thatcher who would get rid of it. More on that later.

The second attempt to join the EEC, in 1967, was led by the Labour Party Prime Minister Harold Wilson, although the application failed before it got off the ground.

It may seem odd that the Labour Party had led this application, given that five years earlier they had attacked the Conservative government's first attempt.

The general view of the Labour Party was that the European Community was a Catholic and capitalist conspiracy which, if Britain were foolish enough to join, would stifle any attempt to create a socialist Britain.[7] But this masked some division amongst the parliamentary party, one third favouring a positive approach, one third opposing membership on any terms, and one third either uninterested or unconvinced.

As far as Harold Wilson's own view was concerned, historians have found it surrounded by contradictions. The truth is that he probably lacked strong views of his own on Europe, and was far more interested in party political issues. Many of his Cabinet wrote diaries during this period, so we know that he tended to say one thing to pro-marketeers and another thing to anti-marketeers. We also know that he became more pro-European once Prime Minister but kept it quiet to maintain Cabinet unity because his party had such a small majority of four seats.[8] After his second election victory in 1966, the majority was ninety-seven, so his approach could change. But, perhaps to appease certain sections of his party, he would mock his opposite number, Edward Heath, over the Conservative leader's affection for Europe. After de Gaulle's veto success, he said in Parliament: 'One encouraging gesture from the French government and the Conservative leader rolls on his back like a spaniel ... Some of my best friends are spaniels, but I would not put them in charge of negotiations into the Common Market.'

Wilson was made aware in early 1966 of the support of businessmen, White-hall officials and public opinion for another application. He could see links with the Commonwealth weakening, both politically, with the furore over the future of Rhodesia (where a white minority led by Ian Smith had illegally declared independence despite Britain's insistence that it would only be granted if the black majority had a share of power), and economically, with the major Commonwealth countries forging trade links elsewhere. He knew that Britain would always be of secondary importance to the USA compared to its own interests. Thus, feeling that the 'three circles' foreign policy of triangulation between the USA, Commonwealth and Europe that had been the focus for the UK since the Second World War was no longer working, Wilson chose to focus on Europe, with conditions. Labour stated in their 1966 election manifesto that Britain was ready to enter the European Communities 'provided essential British and Commonwealth interests are safeguarded'.[9]

In economic terms, things had also moved on. During the first application in the early 1960s, the UK economy was showing warning signs of being in trouble, but by the time Harold Wilson and his Chancellor Jim Callaghan entered 10 Downing Street, those warnings were now reality. On Callaghan's first day in his office, his Tory predecessor, Reggie Maudling, is said to have passed him on the way out, stopped with his coat on his arm and apologised: 'Sorry to leave such a mess, old cock.'[10]

This was a problem for Wilson, whose campaign had been based upon what he called 'purposive' modern planning – a scientific revolution which would require wholesale social change. 'The Britain that is going to be forged in the white heat of this revolution will be no place for restrictive practices or outdated methods … Those charged with the control of our affairs must be ready to think and speak in the language of our scientific age.'[11] That was all very well, but in the first instance it would need some money.

Over-reliance on declining industries, lack of investment and low productivity had caused a massive gap between imports and exports, which meant a balance of payments deficit the government was going to need to close. League tables showed Britain was at the wrong end of figures on strikes, inflation and economic growth, while virtually all other European countries were experiencing a renaissance. There were three short-term solutions: import controls, deflation (reducing the amount of money in circulation), or devaluation (reducing the value of sterling). The government tried imposing import controls in 1965, but this angered their EFTA partners and there was always a threat of retaliation, which Britain couldn't afford as it was unusually dependent on foreign trade. Deflation was a non-starter because it would mean huge public spending cuts and unemployment returning to 1930s levels. Devaluation of sterling, which would make exports cheaper and imports more expensive, would help the economy grow again but Wilson and his fellow leaders saw it as humiliating, cruel to poorer nations who kept their money in sterling (which was still a 'reserve currency') and would remind the country of the fact that Labour had been forced to devalue the pound when they were last in government in 1949. The short-term solution was a $2 billion loan from the US, which simply postponed the day of reckoning. The balance of payments sank further into deficit, unemployment and inflation rose, strikes became more widespread and the economy lurched from one crisis to another.[12]

Eventually a national seamen's strike in 1966 along with another depressing set of economic indicators forced Wilson's hand. The head of the Department of Economic Affairs, George Brown, urged a break with the US, and advised instead that the UK should devalue the pound and join the EEC. A story was doing the rounds in London at the time that Harold Macmillan had left a black box in Downing Street, to be opened by a future Prime Minister in a moment of despair. Inside was a simple message: 'Join the Common Market.'[13]

So it was that on 22 October 1966, after having put pro-European ministers in important places, Harold Wilson called an all-day meeting at Chequers for what would be the first full Cabinet discussion on Europe. Amongst the preparatory papers for the meeting was one by Con O'Neill, the chief civil servant in the Foreign Office. It was an appeal to consider joining the EEC that was above mere accountancy. Rather, it was an appeal to lift their minds to a vision of high politics.

> For the last 20 years, this country has been adrift. On the whole, it has been a period of decline in our international standing and power. This has helped to produce a national mood of frustration and uncertainty. We do not know where we are going and have begun to lose confidence in ourselves. Perhaps a point has now been reached when the acceptance of a new goal and a new commitment could give the country as a whole a focus around which to crystallise its hopes and energies. Entry into Europe might provide the stimulus and the target we require.[14]

Given that no politician could have said this in public, because it essentially admitted that Labour politicians had failed in their past two years in charge, Wilson demanded no leaks of what was said at the meeting. We know from the many published diaries of Cabinet ministers that the economic arguments were well balanced, partly because the entry date was to be 1968, before CAP funding (which Wilson said could be influenced from the inside) was agreed. But the political arguments significantly revolved around there being no alternative for Britain if it wished to be an important power. Wilson managed his Cabinet by promising to examine equally joining the newly created North Atlantic Free Trade Area (NAFTA) and 'going it alone' (GITA). He then explained his plan to embark on a tour with his new Foreign Secretary George Brown to 'probe' the leaders of 'The Six' and to explain the seriousness of the new British bid.

Those who were against the application decided not to fall out with Wilson by opposing the attempt.[15] Minister of Power Richard Marsh complained to other ministers after the meeting that it looked like Wilson was going to apply to join the EEC whatever the results of the 'probe', and Commons leader Richard Crossman replied, 'Of course he does, but the General will save us from his own folly.'[16]

The General, of course, was French President Charles de Gaulle. Wilson visited de Gaulle as his second stop on his tour of European capitals. Knowing how de Gaulle felt about Britain, one would have thought that Wilson would prepare in detail for this meeting. Instead, during the ministerial Economic Steering Committee meetings held before he went, the Prime Minister said he would 'free-wheel' in the discussions with the General, rather than try a particular line of persuasion – an astonishing display of overconfidence.[17] In his meeting with the French President, Wilson made much of the possibility of a new 'technological community' forming – which was supposed to appeal to de Gaulle's wish to challenge American dominance and also suggest a shared objective. De Gaulle was unimpressed, saying that technological cooperation could take place whether or not Britain was in the EEC. He informed Wilson that the conditions Britain would demand for entering the EEC and their close relationship with Washington were still issues, as was the link between sterling and the dollar.

Although Wilson and Brown tried to remain optimistic, and Britain's second application to the EEC was approved by Parliament by a large majority, it had become obvious that for an application to be successful, Britain would have to go *around* de Gaulle. In May 1967, the President called a press conference and announced that entry would only be possible when 'this great people, so magnificently gifted with ability and courage, should be on their own behalf and for themselves achieve a profound economic and political transformation which could allow them to join the Six Continentals'.[18] Wilson thus tried to keep up the pressure. The UK even issued threats. In an off-the-record talk with journalists in October 1967, junior Foreign Office minister Alun Chalfont said the UK would have to review its military commitments in Europe if de Gaulle used his veto.

None of this worked. It didn't help that in November 1967, Wilson was finally forced to devalue the pound, very soon after denying he would have to do it. The Prime Minister also managed to devalue himself during the process, by claiming in a TV appearance that 'it does not mean, of course, that the pound here in Britain, in your pocket or purse or in your bank, has been devalued'.[19] This may have been true at your local shop, but not when buying the many imports Britain needed to buy to sustain itself.

De Gaulle called a press conference on 27 November 1967. He argued that Britain was fundamentally not ready to join the EC. The Common Market was incompatible with everything that mattered: Britain's relationship with the USA, the way she fed herself, the state of sterling and her enormous external debts.[20]

However, rather than withdrawing its application as it had done in 1963, the British government left it 'on the table' to be reactivated whenever 'The Six' saw fit, which was a euphemism for when de Gaulle was either dead or gone. That day came quite quickly. Civil disturbances in May 1968 weakened his grip on power. He called a referendum on some constitutional changes in 1969, framing them as a vote of confidence in him. The referendum was lost and de Gaulle stepped down. He was dead by 1970.

The reason the failed second application for joining the European Community is important in explaining the result of the 2016 referendum is because of what happened between it and the successful application.

That successful application was to be delivered via a formal speech in Luxembourg on 30 June 1970. At that point, the applicants, who included Norway, Denmark and Ireland as well as the United Kingdom, would need to accept the full *acquis communautaire* of agreements, policies, rules, laws and treaties. The trouble was that at the same meeting in December 1969 at The Hague at which 'The Six' had agreed to the formal opening of negotiations with the four countries that had applied, the full pill that Britain would have to swallow had become a lot more bitter.

For one thing, 'The Six' became fully committed to linking their exchange rates as the first step towards full monetary union. The special position of sterling as a 'reserve currency' made this difficult. Being a reserve currency meant that sterling could be used across the world for trading, but also that many countries held sterling as their foreign currency reserves. This in turn meant that Britain could not easily adjust its exchange rate in line with other EC countries as that would affect so many other countries around the world.

More importantly, France's new President, Georges Pompidou, insisted that the financing of the Common Agricultural Policy, the largest part of the

Community Budget, must be agreed before negotiations could open with the applicants.

The CAP involved a system of guaranteeing minimum prices for farmers within the Community by buying up any surpluses they produced (having been incentivised to produce those surpluses by the guarantee of minimum prices!) as well as enforcing the common external tariff on non-EEC agricultural products.

This meant that considerable financing was required, to be collected through 1 per cent of each country's VAT tax receipts and by collecting the import duties (tariffs) on non-EEC agricultural products. With 50 per cent of its agricultural goods having to be imported, Britain would be collecting a large amount in tariffs, but would have to give them to a central pot to be distributed, because the tariffs were and still are regarded as the EC's 'own resources'. With only 4 per cent of their workforce being farmers, compared to 25 per cent of Italians and 20 per cent of the French, this would make the UK a much larger contributor than recipient. Fast-forward to 2016 and the Leave campaign using this EU budget contribution as a stick to beat the Remain campaign with, and you can see how significant this gap would become.

The CAP also had far-reaching consequences for British taxpayers and consumers. The UK always had a system of using taxation to subsidise its farmers. Taxation is generally 'progressive', meaning the rich pay a higher proportion of their income in taxes than the poor. But the CAP meant *all* consumers would need to pay higher prices for their food, which would mean the poor spending a higher proportion of their income on food, making this system of funding regressive. If this wasn't enough, the use of VAT to fund the CAP meant that VAT would have to replace the 'purchase tax' that the UK had been using to tax consumption. The purchase tax was levied far more heavily on luxuries, which again meant that the rich paid more of it as a proportion of their income than the poor. VAT, on the other hand, is levied on a wider range of goods, which meant again that it would have a greater impact on the poor. The establishment of the CAP in the 1960s meant that it had become non-negotiable by the time Britain put in its formal application in 1970. The inequity of this settlement was to remain a running sore in Britain's relationship with Europe.

Harold Young, a now retired accountant who was working for an agricultural food supplier around this time, explains just how inequitable the CAP became in his eyes. In fact, the CAP is what turned him against the EU. Young explains:

The deficiency payments system that held sway in this country subsidised the British farmer to ensure he invested. It reduced the farmers' costs to the world cost – at some expense to the taxpayer. But we had the most efficient and highly capitalised farming industry in Europe. So when that had to be phased out, the cost of basic foods went up 15–30 per cent. I remember heady price increases because instead of lowering the price to the world price we were having to raise the price to the French agricultural price.

Then, Young recalls, the policy changed:

First of all there was this massive surplus of food the French were being paid to produce – a massive waste of money. Barns going up everywhere to store this stuff, but there was no buyer for it at the price they were being paid to produce it. So they discussed this problem and CAP changed from one that improved production to one which helped poorer farmers – so it became a sort of social policy. With our farms being twice the size of everybody else's at the time, our subsidies went down to zero and everybody else's went up. We were robbed blind in the end.

Harold is one of the many who voted Yes to the EC in 1975 and to Leave the EU in 2016 (the next chapter explores this phenomenon in more detail).

A White Paper produced by Wilson's government in February 1970 on the cost of entering the Common Market estimated food prices would go up by 18–26 per cent, the cost of living by 5 per cent and the balance of payments deficit perhaps by up to £1 billion. Although the Prime Minister wanted it to remain on record that he still favoured entry on the right terms, Wilson watchers noted that he was preparing a line of retreat. He was even berating the pro-Europe Tories in the Commons for being willing to sacrifice cheap food from the Commonwealth without any corresponding advantage.[21]

It's not clear what Wilson would have done next because on 18 June 1970, there was a political shock as the Conservatives won a general election. Some bookmakers had given odds of twenty to one on Labour winning. Sir Roy Denman, who had been appointed to the negotiating team that Wilson had set up for the application to join the EC on 30 June, thinks that had Wilson won the election, negotiations for entry would have failed and Britain might never have joined the European Union. Denman argues that Wilson was a tactician rather than a visionary and regarded the countries of the Community with suspi-cion. Denman commented that 'to imagine Wilson manoeuvring with ease and conviction in a polyglot Continental grouping would have been tantamount to imagining General de Gaulle switching happily to a diet of warm beer, pork pie and HP sauce'.[22] Wilson's main concerns were party unity and the security of his own leadership, and the difficult negotiations would not have lasted the splits in his party that would have come. So he would have broken them off, telling the pro-marketeers he had done his best and the anti-marketeers that the country's national interests had not been adequately protected.

Denman's argument gains more force as he tells the tale of Georges Pompidou's visit to London as French Prime Minister in July 1966. Wilson had cancelled a meeting at short notice, then cut out of a dinner given in Pompidou's honour at the French Embassy. Denman's French contacts told him Pompidou returned to Paris convinced that Wilson was not serious about joining the Common Market. The soon-to-be French President had none of those concerns over Wilson's re-placement at 10 Downing Street, Edward Heath.

Heath was by far the most qualified European in Tory politics, with a history of progressive interventions. His maiden speech in Parliament was during the debate over the Schuman Plan, in which he was convinced that the ECSC would work to 'bind in' Germany to Europe in a positive way. He had led the negoti-ating team during the first application, making speeches at the start and the end of the negotiation that showed his almost unique (amongst the British) under-standing of the vision of Europe, and making friends on the Continent with his earnest negotiating style. In 1967, he had made a series of speeches at Harvard University, in which he worried about the fresh arrangements and institutions that were being created in Britain's absence and also showed an understanding of how Europe was about working together to reach accepted goals.[23] These speeches – called the Godkin Lectures – found their way to then French Prime Minister Georges Pompidou through Michel Jobert, his private secretary. Heath had forged a friendship with Jobert during the first negotiations, and when Pom-pidou read the lectures, his comment to Jobert was: 'This shows that Heath is a European.' So when it came down to the third and final application, the French President already knew he was dealing with the right man.[24]

Heath's performance over the next two and a half years was a textbook exercise in most of the arts of government, producing a rare phenomenon: the complete attainment of a political objective. He managed to achieve this without ever really explaining to the British people what being in Europe was for, nor what the implications would be. Although Heath never tired of reminding everyone that he was the father of European Britain, the way he accomplished that goal was to contort his country's constitutional, economic and political arrangements to the point where they spent the next forty-two years ready to burst out from the box they had been put in.

Just think about what had to happen between 18 June 1970 and 1 January 1973 in order for Britain to join. Having not been there at the creation of the European Community, Britain would have to submit to a political system where an unelected organisation can make laws for the UK and overrule its own laws. This was complete anathema to the system of parliamentary sovereignty that had existed in the UK since 1688. Also, Britain needed free trade in industry with some industrial protection, but the EEC had been set up so that there was free trade in industrial products and agricultural protection under the CAP. The CAP plus the Common External Tariff would raise the cost of living in the UK and desperately hurt the economic future of many Commonwealth partners – particularly New Zealand lamb and dairy farmers and Caribbean sugar producers. With tariff income having to be paid directly to a central fund in Europe, Britain would contribute far more than they would benefit from the CAP. Worse, this would not be compensated for by benefits from free access for British industrial goods for the EEC. This was because it wasn't clear whether Britain could cope with the competition from German industry, not helped by the rise in the cost of living feeding through into higher wage demands in the more unionised industrial sector, making Britain's goods even more uncompetitive.[25]

But that wasn't all. At midday on 20 June 1970, the applications to join Europe came in from Norway, Denmark, Ireland and the UK. At 9 a.m. that day, the incumbent six members of the EEC agreed and signed the Common Fisheries Policy (CFP). They had realised that the four applicant countries happened to control the richest fishing grounds in the world (encompassing four fifths of all the fish in Europe). So it seemed a great idea to draw up Council Regulation 2141/7 to give equal access to all members to all fishing waters within the Common Market. Because it was signed before the accession states applied, the CFP became part of the then 13,000 pages of the *acquis communautaire*, so, if they wanted to join the EEC, the four applicants had to accept it.

Today, the *acquis* weighs over a tonne when printed out, and so it can hardly have been ignored by David Cameron when he attempted his renegotiation. As explained in Reason 15, treaty changes have to be ratified by all member states, so Cameron's chance to achieve the reforms he wanted during his renegotiation involved refusing to recommend ratification of a new treaty unless his reforms were included. At the time of the Bloomberg speech, it was thought there would need to be a treaty change to accommodate the reforms needed to deal with the Eurozone crisis, but that never happened. So, in the absence of the treaty change process, for Cameron to achieve the reforms he wanted the *acquis communautaire* would have to be untied. This was never going to happen.

Although there have been numerous histories of these negotiations written, perhaps the most significant is that of Con O'Neill, the chief official negotiator. As a civil servant, his record of the negotiations was kept secret until thirty years later, but when it emerged, it was worth waiting for.[26]

In O'Neill's view, the whole negotiation was 'peripheral, accidental and secondary' because of the imperative that Britain should join the Continent: 'What mattered was to get into the Community,' said O'Neill. He continued with a set of fundamental facts that lay bare the existential reality about 'Europe' as it stood at the time of the negotiation. 'None of its policies were essential to us … Many of them were objectionable.' Yet they all had to be accepted for the larger purpose. If Britain had been there at the creation, O'Neill said, 'we would never … have allowed a situation to develop which made it so difficult, for instance, to ensure fair arrangements for New Zealand dairy products or developing Commonwealth sugar, or to create a situation of equity in respect of our contribution to the Budget'. These, along with fish, proved to be the most contested items in the deal, but it was laid down from the start that they were absolutely non-negotiable.

They all had to be swallowed from the start not because of malice or political enmity, said O'Neill, but because 'almost every conceivable Community policy … is the resultant of a conflict of interests between members, and has embedded in it features representing a compromise between the interests'. If it were to be opened up, just because the British had a strong argument, the whole laborious compromise would fall apart.[27]

We should take a step back and look at what this really meant. The CAP and CFP didn't benefit the UK or any of the new members. They benefited countries with a larger agricultural sector and way of life, and countries who did not have access to large pools of fish. As examples of sheer, naked, unbalanced audacity, the CAP and CFP were strong examples of why Bismarck, the nineteenth-century German Chancellor, once said that 'Europe' was usually heard from 'those politicians who demanded from other powers what they in their own name dare not request'.[28] They were not in Britain's interests, but Britain signed up to them when they joined. Did the British people know what was being signed up to in their name?

Take a step forward to the penultimate week of the 2016 referendum campaign. A group of fishermen decided to take a flotilla of thirty boats down the River Thames, with Nigel Farage on one of them, to highlight the effects of the Common Fisheries Policy on the fishing industry – in particular, the statistic that British fisherman were only allowed to catch 20 per cent by value of the fish that swim in British territorial waters. They were met outside Parliament by a fleet of boats led by the musician and international charity campaigner Bob Geldof, representing the Remain campaign and playing 'The In Crowd' over loudhailers. The picture of multimillionaire Geldof literally sticking two fingers up at Farage and the fishermen and the 'establishment' connotations of the song 'The In Crowd' were not lost on those seeking to highlight how insular liberal metropolitan Londoners had become. Not only did they fail to understand the negative effects of EU membership on some parts of the UK society but they actively mocked people for complaining about them. It did not help the Remain campaign. But it can't all be blamed on Captain Bob. The CFP was a covetous manoeuvre by Europe that snagged in the nets of UK fishermen for more than forty years.

Back to the negotiations, and Con O'Neill reports that within three months, the British team were reduced to debating how to mitigate the unavoidable changes required of membership. They couldn't rewrite the rules so they discussed transitional arrangements. New Zealand butter and Caribbean sugar was allowed lower tariffs to give those countries access to the EC market, but only for a while. This was, nonetheless, vital as meat and dairy constituted 80 per cent of New Zealand's exports and they supplied nearly half of Britain's imports of butter and cheese. Jack Marshall, New Zealand's Deputy Prime Minister, had been sent to watch over the negotiations and if the result had not been to his liking, he would have denounced it as unacceptable, which would have made it impossible to get the final agreement through the House of Commons.[29] So

New Zealand had a virtual right of veto over the negotiations. O'Neill thus believed that the real winners of the negotiation were the New Zealanders.

But that in turn caused a further problem. The British wanted to negotiate bit by bit, without any linkages between what they were negotiating. The French were having none of that. They linked the New Zealand problem with the problem of Britain's budgetary contributions. The more that was won on New Zealand, the more the UK would be expected to put in the pot. In the end, O'Neill thinks getting what he got for New Zealand cost the British taxpayer around £100 million in 1972 money (over £1 billion in today's money) over five years. On the budget, while it was agreed by all that the contribution should start lower and rise over a period of years, the first British offer was to pay only 3 per cent of the EEC budget in the first year, whereas the French said it should be 21.5 per cent. This led President Georges Pompidou to comment that 'one readily recognises that the British have three qualities: humour, tenacity and realism. I sometimes think we are still a little at the humour stage. I do not doubt that tenacity will follow. I hope that realism will come too, and triumph.'[30]

That triumph took a while. Spring was turning into summer in 1971 when the British Ambassador to Paris, Christopher Soames, and Michel Jobert, Secretary-General at the presidential Elysée Palace, set up a bilateral summit between Heath and Pompidou. The two men met on 19 May and talked for two days. There were no officials, just Edward Heath and Georges Pompidou and two interpreters. It wasn't about the details, it was about the vision. Was Heath a genuine European? Did he share the vision of Europe that the six members shared?

The answer was communicated at a joint press conference at 9 p.m. on 20 May, held in the Salon des Fêtes at the Elysée Palace, the very room where de Gaulle had announced his first veto in 1963. Although the negotiations were not over, Pompidou signalled that he saw no reason why they wouldn't be successful. More importantly, recent history could be undone and the ghost of de Gaulle could be laid to rest.

Begun and pursued throughout with the greatest possible frankness, our talks ended in a spirit of trust ... Many people believed that Britain was not and did not want to become European and that it wished to join the Community only to destroy it or to divert it from its goals. Many also thought that France was ready to use any pretext to impose a new veto on Britain's accession. And, this evening, you can see before you two men who are convinced of the contrary.[31]

Pompidou then said that he had put four questions to Heath, to which he had replied yes:

1. Do you accept the very basis of the European Community for agriculture, the principle of Community preference whereby members would feed themselves in the first place within the Community?
2. Do you accept the veto, the rule of unanimity?
3. Do you accept that Sterling should end its role as a reserve currency and Britain should play her part in the development of monetary union?
4. Would Britain become really European? Would Britain, an island, decide to moor herself to the Continent, and come in from the wide seas which had always drawn her?[32]

Edward Heath had convinced Georges Pompidou that his conception of Europe was in fact similar to the French. So that was it, all settled. Britain was in Europe. The remaining problems for British membership, although often technically complex, were now dealt with speedily. Special arrangements were made to protect the markets of New Zealand dairy products during the early years of membership, and a compromise was reached whereby Britain's financial contribution to the EEC would increase annually until 1980. Although the Treasury were concerned about this potential outflow of money, Edward Heath hoped that once inside the EEC the UK would gain money from the proposed European Regional Aid Fund (which was to go to depressed industrial areas). Furthermore, should real problems arise over the British contribution, it would always be possible to reopen the issue with the other members. After all, the minister in charge of the negotiations, Geoffrey Rippon, had reported to the House of Commons on 10 December 1970 that the European Community had assured his negotiating team that 'should unacceptable situations arise ... the very survival of the Community would demand that the institutions find equitable solutions'.[33]

There was, however, a problem. The deep, existential meaning for Britain of getting into 'Europe' was never considered. The way that Britain would have to change once it joined the European Union wasn't in the remit of the techno-crats who were negotiating the deal. There is, for instance, no mention at all of sovereignty in the whole of Con O'Neill's report on the negotiations. Some in Parliament thought that wouldn't be necessary. Anthony Meyer told the Commons in January 1971: 'Frankly, I do not think that it depends on the terms at all. I believe that it would be in the interests of this country to join the E.E.C. whatever the terms.'[34] In the Lords six months later, Lord Crowther said, 'You do not haggle over the subscription when you are invited to climb into a lifeboat. You scramble aboard while there is still a seat for you.'[35]

Let's be clear, though, about what happened on 1 January 1973, when Britain became a member of the European Community. The subscription for entry was pretty high – it was a fundamental change in how the country was governed, involving some eye-watering economic and political contortions that were extremely hard to ever explain as being in Britain's national interests, right up until 23 June 2016. Britain was also no longer an independent country, and sovereignty had been diluted. Had this been done with the consent of the people? That was the context of the battle that was about to be fought.

REASON 5

THE IMMACULATE DECEPTION?

Lifelong Labour voter John Francis* voted Yes to keeping Britain in the European Community in the country's first ever national referendum in 1975 'without reservation or much thought'. He says: 'One listened to one's betters in those days and all the expert advice was in favour, as I recall. Also, I thought we were joining a free trading market without relinquishing very much independence. Britain was in a pretty bad way in the '70s and any change was something to cling on to.' Preoccupied as he was with a new wife, house and children, and having just become a partner in a civil engineering firm, John didn't really have time to read newspapers, and if he had, he would not have been told anything different from what he thought he knew.

On 23 June 2016, John Francis stepped up to the ballot box again and voted for Britain to leave the EU with a similar lack of doubt. He was one of many 1975 Yes voters who made the same conversion. Let's find out why.

In 1975, the electorate were asked to decide through the ballot box whether Britain should remain in the European Community. Conservative Prime Minister Edward Heath had taken the UK into the EEC without consulting the electorate, and Labour leader Harold Wilson had made holding a referendum on EEC membership a manifesto promise in the 1974 general elections. The question was 'Do you think that the United Kingdom should stay in the European Community (the Common Market)?', and the answer was a resounding yes, with 67 per cent of the electorate voting in favour on a 65 per cent turnout. You would have thought that such a massive victory would be the end of the matter. But it was just the beginning, as the true implications of what the public

---

* 'John Francis' is a pseudonym, but we have used this voter's actual words. He contributed to this book on condition of anonymity, due to the sensitivity of his family and friends, most of whom were 'horrified' that he voted Leave.

had voted for became clearer very quickly. To an initially quiet but growing chorus of Eurosceptics, Britain had submitted itself to political and economic contortions that it wasn't ready for. Instead of ending the debate, the 1975 EEC referendum was the beginning of the wave of Euroscepticism that washed ashore with remarkable and unpredicted consequences on 23 June 2016.

The previous chapter explained why the conditions of a seat on that lifeboat were hugely onerous and possibly inappropriate for the UK. Surely, if the British people knew that, why did the UK enter the EEC?

Well, the answer to this question is extremely important. Ninety per cent of people aged sixty-five and over voted in the 2016 referendum – the youngest of them would have been twenty-four years old at the time of the 1975 referendum which kept the UK in. There's a reason many of them had waited forty-one years to reverse their decision.

The 1970 Conservative manifesto included words that would come back to haunt Heath. Announcing a cautious positivity towards joining Europe, it read: 'Obviously, there is a price, we would not be prepared to pay ... Our sole commitment is to negotiate; no more, no less.'[1] But far more memorable was that just before the election, in a speech to the British Chamber of Commerce in May 1970, Heath said that Europe could not be enlarged without 'the full-hearted consent of the peoples and Parliaments of the applicant countries'.[2]

These words were intended to mean that the current members of the EEC couldn't press the applicants' governments too hard, as whatever was agreed would have to pass some democratic tests. In the language of the time, what Heath meant was the consent of Parliament, perhaps filtered through a more than usually thorough appreciation of public opinion. Britain had never had a referendum at that point, with most politicians believing its use was alien to British parliamentary traditions. Furthermore, Heath had always argued that if Europe suspected that whatever was decided would be subject to a veto of the British electorate, it would make the task of negotiators almost impossible. It was thought that a good deal for the UK was more likely if ratification only required parliamentary approval, and would not be subject to the whims of the electorate. So, while many commentators these days choose to look back at Heath's May 1970 speech as the beginning of some sort of fraud on the British people, it was never Heath's intention when making that speech to be seen to be promising a referendum.[3]

But there was a problem, both theoretical and practical, with claiming in 1970 that Parliament had a mandate from the people to take Britain into Europe. All three mainstream political parties (Conservatives, Labour and Liberals) had been in favour of joining Europe in their manifestos for the 1970 election. This means that there had been no method through which a voter who didn't think the UK should enter the European Community could show that through a democratic vote.

Philip Goodhart, a young Tory MP, planned to produce a pamphlet arguing the pros and cons of a referendum on entry into the Community. The Conservative leadership blocked this project, as a referendum was contrary to party policy. Goodhart protested: 'If we are not to be saddled with the charge of dragging the country unwillingly into the Market, then there has to be some visible test of public opinion, somewhere at some time.'[4]

Heath didn't intervene personally at this point, but one can't help wonder if the April 1970 Gallup poll showing 59 per cent of the electorate disapproving of the government even applying for membership, against only 19 per cent in favour, was influencing his views on consulting the public.[5] That said, while this opposition continued into 1971, it was reduced by October 1971, thanks to a perception that the negotiated terms were satisfactory, the government having a clear policy, and a massive information and propaganda campaign.[6]

In July 1971, Heath's government published a White Paper.[7] This paper showcased the tendency that has most animated those who switched their vote from Yes in 1975 to Leave in 2016: the exaggeration of economic benefits offered by entry and the downplaying of the issue of sovereignty.

The White Paper runs through the economic benefits of EEC entry: 'The government are confident that membership of the enlarged Community will lead to much improved efficiency and productivity in British industry, with a higher rate of investment and a faster growth of real wages.' This improvement in efficiency 'should enable the United Kingdom to meet the balance of payments costs of entry over the next decade' and, it is claimed, 'will also result in a higher rate of growth of the economy... [which] will make it possible to provide for a more rapid improvement in our national standard of living as well as to pay for the costs of entry.'

Bearing in mind that by 1976 Britain was going cap in hand to the International Monetary Fund for a loan, even the economic benefits of the decision may have quickly seemed rather overstated.

Then the paper states that 'the Community is primarily concerned with economic policy' and uses the language of 'harmonisation' and 'co-ordination' of
policies that Britain will be able to influence from the inside. It also mentions
economic and monetary union, pointing out that if Britain were not to join, the
Community would move forward to economic and political union regardless.
'Thus the options open to future British Governments would be limited without
their having any say in the matter.' This may be so – but what comes next is
more controversial.

> The Community is no federation of provinces or counties. It constitutes a
> Community of great and established nations, each with its own personality and
> traditions. The practical working of the Community accordingly reflects the re-
> ality that sovereign Governments are represented round the table. On a question
> where a Government considers that vital national interests are involved, it is es-
> tablished that the decision should be unanimous.

This, as we know, is the all-important 'veto' which came as part of the Luxembourg Compromise in 1966 and was given away as part of the Single European
Act in 1986. That veto was used throughout the ensuing campaigns to justify
what came next in the White Paper.

> Like any other treaty, the Treaty of Rome commits its signatories to support
> agreed aims; but the commitment represents the voluntary undertaking of a sov-
> ereign state to observe policies which it has helped to form. There is no question
> of any erosion of essential national sovereignty; what is proposed is a sharing and
> an enlargement of individual national sovereignties in the general interest.

The key term here is 'essential' sovereignty. What is deemed essential to the Eu-
rophobe may be dispensed with by the Europhile. The White Paper did concede
that entry into Europe would change the popular concept of an independent
nation through selective immersions in a larger pool of multinational power,
presided over by a supranational body. But how many of the public realised the
true implication of the supremacy of European law, the special power of the
European Commission as the sole initiator of European policy, and the advent
of majority voting to take some issues out of British control?

It is quite possible that no one in government, nor lawyers, academics, nor anyone who should have noticed it realised the effect of the two key cases at the European Court of Justice from the mid-1960s, mentioned in the previous chapter. These ensured that national sovereignty was *already* eroded. If they didn't know it then the many members of today's over-65 cohort who said in 1975 that they thought they were voting for free trade and the Common Market and no erosion of sovereignty had a point.

Could Heath be blamed for this confusion? Well, on the one hand yes, as the White Paper phrases were a hostage to anyone wanting to later mount a case for there having been a deception pulled on the British people. But on the other hand no, because Heath genuinely believed that sovereignty was not just a theoretical concept but something far more flexible. It could be solitary or pooled, and exercised separately or together depending on its pragmatic usefulness at each moment. Heath once told a meeting in 1994 that 'sovereignty isn't something you put down in the cellar in your gold reserve, and go down with a candle once a week to see if it is still there'.[8] Others argue that a country either has sovereignty or it doesn't.

These were fundamental differences between the Remain and Leave campaigns in 2016. The Leave campaign's arguments on sovereignty boiled down to leaving the EU meaning 'taking back control'. But David Cameron, in an interview on the BBC just after naming the referendum date, argued that sovereignty was more about the best ways to 'get things done'.

He said:

Now, on sovereignty, yes of course if Britain were to leave the EU that might give you a feeling of sovereignty, but you've got to ask yourself is it real? Would you have the power to help businesses and make sure they weren't discriminated against in Europe? No, you wouldn't. Would you have the power to insist that European countries share with us their border information so we know what terrorists and criminals are doing in Europe? No you wouldn't. Would you, if suddenly a ban was put on for some bogus health reasons on one of our industries, would you be able to insist that that ban was unpicked? No you wouldn't. So you have an illusion of sovereignty but you don't have power. You don't have control. You can't get things done.[9]

So, having joined the EEC on 1 January 1973 without a referendum, how did the

UK end up having a referendum on it two years later in 1975? As with the 2016 referendum, it was a unique constellation of political stars aligning in such a way that it couldn't be avoided.

The first issue was that once he had won over French President Georges Pompidou, Edward Heath had to win over Parliament. He had a majority of thirty in the 1970–74 parliament, but more than thirty Conservative MPs would vote against joining Europe under any circumstances. With only six Liberal MPs, Heath had to look to Labour Party MPs for support.

This shouldn't have been a problem. The Labour Party had applied to join the EEC in 1967 when in government, and left its application on the table when initially rejected. This meant that in their 1970 general election manifesto they were committed to the reopening of negotiations to join.[10] George Thomson, who would have been in charge of those negotiations had Labour won in 1970, declared on hearing about the deal Heath had agreed that 'these are terms which I would have recommended a Labour Cabinet to accept'.[11] Had Harold Wilson been Prime Minister, he would almost certainly have pushed through entry on those terms and, having won a third election, could have survived any revolt from anti-Europeans. But Wilson wasn't Prime Minister. He wanted Heath's contribution to be discredited and he was not prepared to risk party unity to secure a vote for entry on what he called 'Tory terms'.

Harold Wilson's political history can be best described as thinking first of party unity and his own leadership. Since the 1970 election, anti-marketeers had been strengthened by Trade Union Congress (TUC) opposition and by an increase in the proportion of left-wingers in the parliamentary party after the 1970 election. This increased the volume of the socialist objection to being in Europe, which labelled it a capitalist cartel, a 'rich man's club' that could take powers of economic management away from the British government and make socialist planning in Britain impossible. This included the 'state aid' rules that prohibited national governments from subsidising struggling industries (because a subsidy had the same effect as a tariff in reducing competition). This meant that regional policies in areas like Wales, which were totally reliant on industries subject to the ups and down of competition, would not be possible. The final issue for those on the left was the loss of cheap food, particularly for those on low incomes, due to the Common Agricultural Policy and its effect on the Commonwealth.[12]

If Wilson had any intentions of endorsing the UK's membership, his shadow

Home Secretary Jim Callaghan did his best to curtail them. A popular politician, Callaghan made a speech in Manchester in May 1971. The press were briefed beforehand to come and hear the next leader of the Labour Party. In response to President Pompidou's comment that French was the language of Europe, while dismissing English as the language of the USA, Callaghan said:

> Millions of people have been surprised to hear that the language of Chaucer, Shakespeare and Milton must in future be regarded as an American import from which we must protect ourselves if we are to build a new Europe. We can agree that the French own the supreme prose literature in Europe, but if we are to prove our Europeanism by accepting that French is the dominant language in the Community, then my answer is quite clear, and I will say it in French to prevent any misunderstanding: Non, merci beaucoup!

The last three words were plainly towards Europe, and Callaghan's actions were plainly a threat to Harold Wilson.[13] The left of the party seemed to be moving against Wilson, pointing out that the Europe issue was a chance to remove Heath and perhaps bring the Tory government down, and if he wasn't prepared to do it, they would find someone who would.[14] This belligerence was exemplified by a newly elected 29-year-old Welsh firebrand called Neil Kinnock, who declared: 'Because I want to see the Tories beaten, and because I am willing to use any weapon to beat them, I am against EEC entry on these terms at this time.'[15]

So, in July 1971, a special Labour Party conference was called at which the Labour Party adopted the specific policy of voting against entering Europe. They nearly voted to withdraw the application altogether. However, deputy leader Roy Jenkins had let it be known that he would vote for membership whatever the official line of the Labour Party was, an unusual position for a deputy leader. Jenkins, who had been a Labour Chancellor and Home Secretary, felt so strongly about Europe that he was prepared to launch a battle that would destroy his reputation in the Labour Party and eventually drive him out of it. He tried to persuade Harold Wilson to do what Edward Heath had done and allow a free vote for his MPs (Heath did so to encourage Labour rebels to come and support him), but Wilson was persuaded to impose a three-line whip by anti-marketeers who reminded him that the party had decided on its view and that must be enforced on MPs. Not allowed to speak in the October 1971 final debate on EEC membership, Jenkins led sixty-eight other Labour MPs through the 'aye' lobby to vote with the Tory government. With thirty-nine Tory rebels voting with the opposition, the parliamentary majority for entry was 356 to 244.

Edward Heath returned to his flat in Downing Street and played the First Prelude from Book 1 of Bach's *Well Tempered Clavier*. Harold Macmillan lit an enormous bonfire on the cliffs of Dover which was answered by another waiting on the shores of France. And Roy Jenkins, proud of having stuck to his principles, was contemplating what he himself called the 'civil war' over Europe that was dividing the Labour Party.[16]

Harold Wilson had found a way to keep his party together, and many political commentators and biographers argue that his greatest success was to maintain his freedom of manoeuvre for the future, should he return to power. In fact, the story that is about to be told was, in Ben Pimlott's view, 'one of Wilson's most remarkable achievements, perhaps the greatest triumph of his career'.[17] The formula that emerged was thanks to Tony Benn, the leader of the Eurosceptic left of the party. Benn's idea was first mooted in 1970, and it was that Europe was so large a question that it should be put to a referendum, because what the party could not agree, the people could settle. Labour would vote in Parliament against what they would call entry to Europe on 'Tory terms'. They would then support a renegotiation if the Labour Party won the next election, and this renegotiation would be put to the British people in either a new general election or a referendum.

Benn's journey to pushing for that referendum is interesting. He was a supporter of Europe when Minister of Technology in Wilson's Labour government of the second half of the 1960s. But after the 1970 general election he wrote a letter to his Bristol constituents saying that:

> If the people are not to participate in this decision, no one will ever take participation seriously again. It would be a very curious thing to try to take Britain into a new political entity, with a huge potential for the future, by a process that implied that the British public were unfit to see its historic importance for themselves.[18]

Politics students may spot the irony of a representative of Bristol arguing for the importance of needing the people's opinions in an exercise of direct democracy. In 1774, Edmund Burke, addressing *his* Bristol constituents, had laid out the doctrine of representative government: 'Your representative owes you, not his industry only, but his judgment; and he betrays, instead of serving you, if he sacrifices it to your opinion.'[19]

To its opponents, the very nature of the Common Market was that it undermined the sovereignty of Parliament, the foundation of Britain's constitution, and diverted control away to institutions overseas over which the British electors would have no control.[20] As Benn himself was to put it in a second letter to his Bristol constituents in the run-up to the 1975 referendum:

In short, the power of the electors of Britain, through their direct representatives in Parliament to make laws, levy taxes, change laws which the courts must uphold, and control the conduct of public affairs has been substantially ceded to the European Community whose Council of Ministers and Commission are neither collectively elected, nor collectively dismissed by the British people nor even by the peoples [of] all the Community countries put together.[21]

So, it was all very well talking about representation, but the powers of the representatives were being removed from them, and that should require the consent of the people they represent.

Wilson opposed the referendum at first, and Benn couldn't find a seconder at his first attempt to put the idea before the party's National Executive. But after the Bristol letter became public, Jim Callaghan commented that Benn's idea was a 'rubber life-raft into which the whole party may one day have to climb'.[22]

Climb aboard they did. By 1971, the three countries other than the UK (Denmark, Ireland and Norway) had decided to have a referendum on entering Europe. Then President Pompidou announced that France was going to have a referendum to find out if the French people approved of the new accession states' entry into Europe. He did this for internal party politics reasons, to weaken his opponents on the left, but it added credibility to Benn's idea. The result in France was a 68.3 to 31.7 per cent vote in favour of accession, on a 60 per cent turnout. A cynic wrote to the newspapers to suggest that when Edward Heath had spoken of the full-hearted consent of Parliament and people, he must have meant the full-hearted consent of the French Parliament and people.

Labour's National Executive began to consider Benn's idea more seriously as a potential manifesto promise. The Heath government then announced that Northern Ireland would have a referendum on whether its people wished to remain in the UK or join the Irish Republic, so now the direct democracy dam was well and truly broken. The Labour shadow Cabinet agreed the party's policy was to vote against joining Europe on 'Tory terms' and commit to a referendum if in government.[23] It was a party-unifying policy. To those who wanted a harder stance on Europe, Harold Wilson warned he would resign if the Labour conference voted to commit Britain to a withdrawal. To Europhiles like Roy Jenkins, they would have to concede that the public should have a say on membership.

In some ways Wilson was like David Cameron, trying to mend his divided party while those around him picked at the seams in the name of principle and conscience. In an early 1973 shadow Cabinet meeting when Jenkins had once again insisted he could not in conscience follow the party line, Wilson exploded: 'I've been wading in shit for three months to allow others to indulge their conscience.'[24] It had been more like three years, but if Labour won the next election, a referendum on Britain's membership was promised.

In January 1972, Edward Heath signed the Treaty of Accession in Brussels. He invited Harold Wilson to attend, but Wilson declined. The UK joined the European Community on 1 January 1973. Heath says in his memoirs: 'I saw this as a wonderful new beginning and a tremendous opportunity for the British people.'[25] Within a year, Edward Heath was out of Downing Street.

Disaster struck almost the moment Britain joined the EEC. There was a rise in food prices and thus the cost of living, making it harder to achieve an incomes policy deal with the unions. Incomes policies were economy-wide wage and price controls used to manage inflation, and were used in Britain after the Second World War up until 1979. During this period, when successive governments tried to maintain full employment, the unions had an unusual amount of market power, so incomes policies made sense to keep wages and prices down. Since wage demands were also based on the cost of living, the rise in food prices made it much harder to justify wage controls. Heath had floated the pound, which had previously been tied to the dollar, to allow it to drift downwards, making exports cheaper. President Pompidou had been angered by this, as he felt that fixed exchange rates were vital for the proper functioning of the Common Market. Exchange rate volatility increases uncertainty for firms and so discourages trade. Therefore, small steps towards aligning the exchange rates, a very early precursor to monetary union, were being pushed by France and Germany. They tied these steps to the establishment of a European Regional Fund, which would give the more rundown industrial areas of Britain the kind of support the Common Agricultural Policy was giving French agriculture. However, when Britain floated its currency it lost the chance to get money for its depressed industries and regions.

Then the Yom Kippur War broke out in the Middle East, with Egypt and Syria attacking Israel to seek the return of Arab territory Israel had captured in the 1967 Six Day War. The Arab oil states, which operated the OPEC (Organization of the Petroleum Exporting Countries) cartel, said they would reduce oil production by 5 per cent each month until Israel withdrew from those occupied territories. This led to a four-fold increase in oil prices – once again wreaking havoc on the British economy and the anti-inflation policy. Then France floated the franc in January 1974, which meant that all possibility of monetary union was ended for the foreseeable future. If all currencies were able to freely float up and down then exchange rate volatility would discourage the Common Market countries from trading with each other, because they would have little idea how much money they would make from selling to each other or how much buying from each other would cost. Although all members knew that some form of monetary union would be important for the success of the project, European solidarity was being undermined by national pressures.

The key point here is that in the 1960s, economic prosperity had strengthened the loyalty of the six founding members to Europe. But just after Britain joined, the long boom ended, and the association in the minds of the British people between Europe and economic prosperity began to wane. Attitudes might have been different had Britain joined in the mid-1960s, but by the beginning of 1974, just 39 per cent of British people thought membership had been helpful to Britain. It was not a good time for the incumbent of Downing Street to be the most pro-European Prime Minister Britain has ever had.

As European solidarity collapsed, Edward Heath lacked the communication skills to persuade the British people of the value of the European adventure. One man within his own party *did* have enormous powers of persuasion, but when it came to Europe, Enoch Powell was an enemy. Powell was probably the most popular politician in the country at the time – so much so that if the UK had had a presidential system, he might have won it. Like Boris Johnson in 2016, support for Powell transcended traditional party lines – but he wasn't a particularly easy colleague to work with, and so he had no chance of becoming Conservative leader. But when someone is as popular as Powell, attracting his ire to the extent that Edward Heath did is not a good idea.

Powell was opposed to entering Europe due to the restrictions it placed on British sovereignty. His argument went like this: Britain's long and uninterrupted history means that Parliament plays a crucial role in Britain that it doesn't play in the other Continental countries. The UK had stood alone against the Continent in numerous wars, being hard to defeat because of the presence of the English Channel. Powell noted that all of the original six countries in the EEC had been either Fascist or occupied by Fascist countries. All had needed to start again with new constitutions, being happy to build new institutions, something the UK doesn't like to do and didn't need to do. The UK is evolutionary, relying on adapting the institutions of the past – such as the House of Commons, House of Lords and the monarchy – not creating new ones. Europe, therefore, was just not appropriate for the UK.

Yet, to Powell's horror, Edward Heath was taking Britain into Europe, and thus sovereignty away from Parliament, without consulting the British people. He saw that the Labour leadership had committed to having a referendum on Europe if they won the next election. So, in June 1973, he made a speech arguing that the principle of self-government was more important than party allegiance.[26] Powell said that he was prepared to face Labour rule for the rest of his life if that preserved the sovereignty of Parliament. Powell had voted with Labour against entry into Europe, but could anyone really believe he was serious about wanting a Labour government?[27]

Days before the February 1974 election, Powell showed just how serious he was. He started his speech by saying: 'A vote for Labour is the only way to ensure that Britain stays out of Europe.' He then went on to talk about himself:

> Here is a man who promised his electors, in 1970, that he would do everything in his power to prevent British membership, who voted against it in every division, major or minor, which took place in the ensuing Parliament, who did so even when success would have precipitated a dissolution, who allied himself openly on the subject with his political opponents, who made no secret of his belief that its importance overrode that of all others, and who warned that was one of the issues on which men will put country before party.[28]

Sure enough, Powell then said he would not stand as a Conservative. There was only one way that people could get rid of Edward Heath and keep out of Europe. The day before the election, Powell announced that he had voted by post for the Labour candidate in his old constituency of Wolverhampton South West. The only modern-day parallel would be Boris Johnson announcing before the 2015 general election that he had voted for Labour, and that he did so because he was putting 'country before party'. You can get a sense of what that looked like from what happened to the 2016 EU referendum campaign when Boris Johnson chose to join Leave.

Labour won a narrow victory in 1974, with a hung parliament, and Heath was unable to form a government with the Liberals. A host of factors were important – but no one doubts that Powell's intervention made a difference, especially considering the resulting swing against the Conservatives in the West Midlands was larger than anywhere else (3.9 per cent against 1 per cent across the country). It was Europe that was the catalyst for this result, and so it was Europe that played a large part in the Conservatives' and Heath's defeat. But if Labour gained from Heath's political death, Enoch Powell was holding the dagger.

So, after a series of unique political events, Harold Wilson was back in Downing Street. Having limped around for a few months as a minority government, he called another election in October 1974 and won an overall majority of just three seats.

Labour's February 1974 general election manifesto insisted that 'a profound political mistake made by the Heath government was to accept the terms of entry to the Common Market, and to take us in without the consent of the British people'. The manifesto demanded various changes in the European Community and claimed that a Labour government would be seeking 'a fundamental renegotiation of Britain's membership'. Labour argued that the 'Tory terms' had involved 'the imposition of food taxes on top of rising world prices, crippling fresh burdens on our balance of payments, and a draconian curtailment of the power of the British Parliament to settle questions affecting vital British interests'.[29] Thus, Labour would seek major changes in the Common Agricultural Policy, particularly the way it limits access to Britain for low-cost Commonwealth producers; 'new and fairer methods of financing the Community budget'; and 'the retention by Parliament of those powers over the British economy needed to pursue effective regional, industrial and fiscal policies'.[30]

Much of what was actually achieved was cosmetic, with the other members of the EEC being as helpful as they could without being seen to capitulate to British pressure. The Lomé Convention of February 1975 was signed, guaranteeing quotas and tariff exemptions for developing countries' exports. The special agreements for sugar from the Commonwealth and New Zealand butter were extended. Then there was the size of Britain's budget contribution. In May 1974, the Treasury forecast that by the end of the transitional arrangements, Britain would be contributing 24 per cent of the budget, even though it had a share of GNP (gross national product – a measure of the output of British firms in Britain and abroad), of only 14 per cent. After much debate, a formula was agreed in the European Commission that awarded a rebate to any net contributor satisfying certain criteria (relating to its balance of payments, growth rate, share of GNP) and limited to around £125 million. In hindsight, this concession actually gained nothing for Britain, and the matter had to be renegotiated again in 1984 by Margaret Thatcher in what became known as the Fontainebleau Agreement.

Reviewing the outcome, it is hard not to recall the criticism of David Cameron's 2016 renegotiation deal by Tory MP Jacob Rees-Mogg: 'The thin gruel has been further watered down.'[31] The sums involved in Harold Wilson's renegotiation achievements added up to very little, and nothing that might not have been achieved through the continuous negotiation month by month which is a fact of European Community life.[32]

Wilson still presented it as a battle in which a vital British national interest was at stake, and he wanted to be presented himself as a St George figure, who knew how to stand up to foreign dragons and would never sell his country short.[33] But his officials weren't fooled. Michael Palliser, a key player in the renegotiation diplomacy, felt 'that the whole object of the exercise was to keep Britain in, and get something that could be presented to the British as politically adequate'.[34] But Roy Denman, also involved in the negotiations from his position at the Board of Trade, argued that what had in fact been achieved in Europe by Harold Wilson was 'the minimum of gain for the maximum of irritation'.[35]

There are further parallels between the 1975 referendum campaign and the 2016 campaign. In 2016, nobody involved in or out of politics seriously thought David Cameron would ever campaign for anything other than to Remain, whatever the result of his renegotiation. In 1975, the Prime Minister in charge of the negotiation, Harold Wilson, had made it quite clear before the negotiations were ended that he would be campaigning to stay in the European Community. This was further proof of how cosmetic the renegotiations really were, with commentators pointing out that the whole exercise was mostly part of the campaign to get the British people to accept membership of the Community rather than an actual attempt to alter the terms.[36]

The second parallel was that, like Cameron, Wilson created an 'agreement to differ' with his Cabinet that abandoned collective responsibility during the referendum campaign. Had this not happened, the anti-Europeans would probably have had to resign their ministerial jobs or even give up the party whip, which could have brought the government, with its tiny majority, down. In 1975, seven Cabinet members chose the path of 'agreement to differ', staying within the Cabinet but campaigning for No. They included future leader Michael Foot as well as Tony Benn and Barbara Castle, along with a leading figure from the right of the party, Peter Shore. Before the renegotiations, a vote in Cabinet had been twelve for remaining in the EEC and eleven against. Now, it was sixteen for and only seven against. This was rather like what happened in 2016, when after David Cameron's renegotiations some well-known Eurosceptic Cabinet ministers such as Theresa May, Philip Hammond and Sajid Javid rather surprisingly came out as Remain supporters.

The third parallel was that each Prime Minister was leading a highly divided party, at odds with its own supporters. While Cabinet supported the 1974–75 renegotiation, Labour MPs in Parliament voted *against* the renegotiated terms, by 145 to 137, with thirty-three abstentions. Then, at a special conference in April, the Labour movement voted two to one against membership. This was to mark the birth of a movement within the Labour Party that would lead to a commitment to leave the European Community in their 1983 election manifesto and result in the actual splitting off of many members into the Social Democratic Party just before that.

Back in March 1975, when the legislation for the first national referendum the UK had ever had was introduced to the Commons, Edward Short, the Labour leader of the House of Commons, was clear on why it was necessary: 'The issue continues to divide the country. The decision to go in has not yet been accepted. That is the essence of the case for having a referendum.'[37]

Edward Heath, whose decision it was to go into Europe without a referendum, was not impressed. Having lost two elections in 1974, Heath had lost the

Conservative leadership to Margaret Thatcher in February 1975. This marked the start of what political commentators would call Heath's 'incredible sulk'. But Europe was important enough for Heath to join together with Thatcher to launch the Conservative Party's pro-Europe campaign. Heath pointed out that 'the party has made its view clear that it is opposed, in any case, to a referendum as a constitutional device. We regard it as abhorrent. We also regard it as unnecessary. We regard it as part of a party political manoeuvre.'

Thatcher then stood up and set out the positive case for Britain staying in the Community:

> First, the Community gives us peace and security in a free society, the peace and security denied to the past two generations. Second, the Community gives us access to secure sources of food supplies, and this is vital to us, a country which has to import half of what we need. Third, the Community does more trade and gives more aid than any other group in the world. Fourth, the Community gives us the opportunity to represent the Commonwealth in Europe, a Commonwealth which wants us to stay in and has said so, and the Community wants us to stay in and has shown it to be so.[38]

So, the Labour government were split and the Conservative opposition MPs were almost completely united in supporting the Yes campaign in 1975. If this was a pretty stark inversion of the party positions in the 2016 referendum, the fact that the Nationalist parties – SNP in Scotland and Plaid Cymru in Wales – were implacably against the EU is a complete inversion of the situation in 2016.

The SNP led the Remain campaign in Scotland in 2016 and were 'rewarded' with what to them was the ultimate prize – a Remain vote in every counting district in Scotland combined with a Leave vote in the rest of the UK – enabling them to push for a second Scottish independence referendum. In 1975, the SNP were looking for the opposite for the same reason – a comprehensive No vote in Scotland but the rest of the UK voting to stay in Europe.

It is fair to say that the 1975 Europe referendum was unbalanced. Britain in Europe, the Yes umbrella campaign, raised more than £1.3 million in addition to the £125,000 received from public funds, helped by almost 100 per cent support from the City. The No umbrella campaign, rather oddly named 'The National Referendum Campaign', raised £6,354.[39] Not a single major newspaper supported the No campaign. The *Daily Mail* and *Daily Express* were the strongest newspapers for remaining in Europe – with the former saying food supplies would be in danger if Britain left. The only newspaper against was the *Morning Star*, a Communist paper, along with the right-wing *Spectator* magazine.

The approach of the press during the campaign has come in for particular scrutiny from historians, many of whom argue that their pro-European sentiments meant that they didn't necessarily tell their readers what to think, but what to think about. While some sections of the press tried to discuss the issue of sovereignty and the federalist nature of the European project, they focused primarily on the familiar bread-and-butter issues of prices, income levels and economic security. It is argued that the issue of sovereignty was complex, and difficult to deal with in a manner deemed appropriate for the readership of the more popular newspapers, and therefore avoided. We know from the 2016 campaign that the message of 'take back control' was simple and effective. The suspicion in 1975 was that the pro-Community press focused on the mundane issues because it allowed the renegotiated terms to be presented more positively.

More importantly, the media came to focus hugely on the personalities involved in the campaigns rather than the issues. With the Liberals, led by Jeremy Thorpe, maintaining their consistent position of supporting Britain's place in Europe, the most startling imbalance was that of political leadership between the two campaigns. People at the time still trusted their political leaders completely, and Wilson, Thatcher and Thorpe were all supporting staying in. Such was the strength of the politicians campaigning for Yes that Harold Wilson, Jim Callaghan and even Margaret Thatcher were able to take a back seat, allowing Roy Jenkins, the Labour Home Secretary, and Willie Whitelaw, the Conservative deputy leader, to lead the Yes campaign. This was vital, because it meant that the 1975 referendum couldn't be seen as a referendum on Harold Wilson's premiership, unlike in 2016, when the lack of an interested Labour leader or popular senior Conservative MP left David Cameron no option but to lead the Remain campaign himself.

Against continued membership was the very right-wing Enoch Powell, very popular with some but extremely unpopular with others. There was the very left-wing Tony Benn and Michael Foot from Labour, joined by the Reverend Ian Paisley, leader of the Democratic Unionist Party in Northern Ireland; the National Front (predecessor of the British National Party); the Communist Party;

and the main trade union leaders, who were, at the time, bitterly unpopular. What the No campaign didn't have were the likes of Michael Gove and Boris Johnson, with the respective credibility and popularity to be presented in the last month of the 2016 campaign as a possible alternative government.

Like the Leave campaign in 2016, Powell and Benn ran with an anti-establishment message. The country was in economic difficulty, and the political establishment had failed to solve these problems. In some ways, it is hard to understand why that approach would fail as miserably as it did in 1975. It must have been particularly bewildering after what had happened in Norway in 1972. Here, all main party leaders had backed the Yes campaign, and the No campaign went down the anti-establishment route. They made it a referendum on their party leaders' ability to govern effectively at a time when the creation of the Common Fisheries Policy put at risk one of the country's main sources of income.

But the reason this approach had worked in Norway was the emergence of new leadership from outside the established politicians, backed by a grassroots movement opposed to Europe. They won, the Norwegian PM resigned and Norway is still not in Europe. The credibility of that 'new leadership' in Norway was key. Equally, in the UK, the 1975 referendum could be placed as not really being about Europe at all, but about who would run the country. Roy Jenkins said, at the final rally of the Britain in Europe campaign: 'For Britain to leave now would be to go into an old people's home for fading nations ... I do not think it would be a very comfortable old people's home. I do not like the look of some of the prospective wardens.'[40]

Reflecting on the referendum after the result came in (a resounding victory for Yes by 67 per cent to 33 per cent), Harold Wilson noted that, as Vernon Bogdanor puts it, 'the main reason for voting yes was that victory for no would empower the wrong kind of people in Britain, the Benn-left and the Powell-right, who were often extreme nationalists, protectionists, xenophobic, and backward-looking'.[41]

Perhaps more significant is Roy Jenkins's comment after the referendum that 'people took the advice of those they were used to following'.[42] As we will see later in Reason 16, that was no longer the case in 2016.

Matthew Elliott, the chief executive of Vote Leave in 2016, recalls a campaign image from 1975. It pictured Tony Benn, Enoch Powell and Ian Paisley and was captioned 'The Professionals'. It clearly played on the fact that the Out campaign was led by people on the extremities of politics. As we'll see in Reason 14, Elliott kept that image in mind as he approached the task of formulating his campaign strategy to take the UK out of the EU.

This takes us back to 2016, and that massive turnout of over-65s who had voted to remain in Europe in the 1975 referendum and would now vote to leave. We know now that 2016 was when they decided to stop taking the advice of people they were 'used to following'. Why? Well, it was partly because the EU had changed, partly because the situation Britain was in was different in 2016 than in 1975 (the 2008 financial crisis and its outcome and the 2009 expenses scandal had reduced trust between the people and their politicians), but also because many voters felt that forty years ago they had been deceived.

The referendum happened at a time of considerable national anxiety. In the winter of 1973/74, Britain had undergone the economic and national trauma of a three-day week brought about by a dispute between the government and the miners. Inflation had reached 25 per cent, combined with widespread and sustained unemployment for the first time since the 1930s. Responsible pundits and politicians began to fear a shortage of raw materials and basic foodstuffs. In this context, the Common Market had become a reassuring fixed point in the status quo. Anything that put jobs at risk or added another element to the turbulence was an adventure not worth undertaking.[43]

David Butler and Uwe Kitzinger, who wrote one of the definitive histories of the 1975 referendum, agree with this assessment:

> The referendum was not a vote cast for new departures or bold initiatives. It was a vote for the *status quo*. Those who had denounced referenda as instruments of conservatism may have been right. The public is usually slow to authorise change; the anti-Marketeers would have had a far better chance of winning a referendum on whether to go in than one on whether to stay in. Before entry, to vote for going in would have been to vote radically. But after entry, it was at least as radical and unsettling to vote for leaving ... The verdict was not even necessarily a vote of confidence that things would be better in than out; it may have been no more than an expression of fear that things would be worse out than in.[44]

Because of this, Butler and Kitzinger argue: 'The verdict of the referendum ... was unequivocal but it was also unenthusiastic. Support for membership was wide but it did not run deep.'[45] This can go some way to explaining some of the movement from Yes to No on Europe forty-one years later.

A far more serious point, and one that motivated many who voted Yes in 1975 to vote Leave in 2016, was the feeling that they were misled into thinking they were voting only for a free trade area and nothing else. They hadn't realised that the European Community would turn into the far more political European Union, that monetary union would emerge to the point where Europe had its own currency, that sovereignty would no longer be absolute and that Britain's Parliament was now subject to a superior legal order. None of this was spelt out in the 1975 campaign.[46]

For instance, look at the question that was asked. It was: 'Do you think the UK should stay in the European Community (Common Market)?'[47] Let's start with the brackets. The 'Common Market' was highlighted. If the vote was just about being in a Common Market, there may never have been a need for another one. Harold Young, the retired accountant we met in the previous chapter who was one of the many who voted Yes in 1975 and Leave in 2016, recalled in an interview for this book that 'Harold Wilson made out that this isn't about marriage, this is about divorce. The emotional way of talking about the question was – do we get divorced when we've hardly been on the honeymoon?' Young went on to say that Wilson 'had already rigged the question in a way'.

Had he? Let's compare the question wording with that of 2016. In the original EU Referendum Bill, the proposed question was: 'Should the United Kingdom remain a member of the European Union?' and the answers were 'Yes' or 'No'. Eurosceptic MPs realised that question would mean the government would own the Yes vote. They wrote to the Electoral Commission, arguing that an ICM poll published in early June 2015 had found that if voters were asked 'Should the UK remain a member of the EU?' then 59 per cent said Yes. But if the question was 'Should the United Kingdom remain a member of the European Union or leave the European Union?', only 55 per cent voted to Remain. So there was a 4 per cent difference between a yes/no question or a remain/leave question. The Electoral Commission agreed, saying that while the original question was 'not significantly leading', it was doubly unbalanced, since only the Remain option was explained in the question, and the Yes response for the status quo.[48] The question was changed to: 'Should the United Kingdom remain a member of the

European Union or leave the European Union?'[49] The 2016 referendum victory margin? 52 per cent to 48 per cent. 4 per cent. So Harold Young has a point when he argues that the 1975 question was 'rigged'. The 2015 Electoral Commission report basically said so.

It wasn't for lack of trying by the No campaign. Their official propaganda document ran through the fundamental dangers, saying that the Common Market:

> sets out by stages to merge Britain with France, Germany and Italy and other countries into a single nation ... As the system tightens – and it will – our right, by our votes, to change policies and laws in Britain will steadily dwindle ... Those who want Britain in the Common Market are defeatists; they see no independent future for our country.

But this was hardly an appeal to the moderate voter, whose support the No campaign needed in order to win.

The Yes campaign, along with the government, dealt with this issue differently. Looking through the campaign documents, historians are struck by the wariness about what to say, and in what context. Throughout, according to the journalist and author Hugo Young, there is a 'golden thread of deceptive reassurance that runs through the history of Britain's relationship with the European Union up to the present day: our entry was essential, our membership is vital, our assistance in the consolidation is imperative – but nothing you really care about will change'.[50]

For instance, on the supremacy of the European Court of Justice, the Yes campaign document says this: '*English Common Law is not affected.* For a few commercial and industrial purposes there is need for Community Law. But our criminal law, trial by jury, presumption of innocence remains unaltered. Scotland, after 250 years of much closer union with England, still keeps its own legal system.' That may have been true at the time, but since then, many British cases have been won using British laws, created by legislators British people can vote for, only to be overturned on the basis of European laws, created by legislators British people cannot vote for.

On sovereignty, the Yes campaign tried to change the way the public thought about the concept. They called the current sovereignty argument a false one, arguing that it was 'not a matter of dry legal theory' but could be tested in the wider context of British interest in the world. Not remaining in the European Community would not stop the EC taking decisions, but the UK would have no say in them: 'We would be clinging to the shadow of British sovereignty while its substance flies out of the window.' It also pointed out that, given the existence of the national veto, 'all decisions of any importance must be agreed by every member',[51] meaning that no important new policy could be decided in Brussels without the consent of a British minister, answerable to a British government and a British Parliament. What constitutes *any importance* was not clear. For instance, the Treaty of Rome provided for majority voting on agriculture.

The key point is that the leaders of the Yes campaign never disclosed what the next steps were, nor the ultimate goal. There was nothing about the single market, tax harmonisation, majority voting, enlargement or the single currency – all of which became reality in the next thirty years.[52]

Those who defend this campaign argue that monetary union, for example, may have been an objective but, with all the major currencies recently having been floated freely, it was so unlikely to happen in the near future that it wasn't worth mentioning. Others argue that both monetary union and political union had been mentioned in Parliament. In the House of Commons in 1971, Edward Heath said that he had told President Pompidou that Britain 'looked forward wholeheartedly to joining in the economic and monetary development of the Community'.[53] Furthermore, when heads of government of the European Community states met in October 1972 – with Britain involved, as their entry had been successfully negotiated – a communiqué was issued stating that their aim was to 'transform, before the end of the present decade, the whole complex of their relations into a European Union',[54] and that this included economic and monetary union. The problem, of course, is that most people in the country don't follow reports from Parliament and European Community meetings – so it may be that most people in the country didn't know that economic and possible monetary union was on the 'ticket' in the 1975 referendum.

The fact is that at the time, there was genuine and almost universal uncertainty about where the Community was going. Nothing much was happening as Europe struggled with economic problems. Furthermore, in poll after poll at the time, over 50 per cent of respondents were concerned about the effect of Europe on the cost of living, but no more than 9 per cent registered alarm about sovereignty or national independence. So the Yes campaign knew that prices rather than independence was where the voters needed reassurance. Contrast this with the 2016 referendum, where Leave voters listed sovereignty as their key motivation, above immigration.

Rather than arguing that they were deceived, it is probably truer to say that the average voter in the 1975 Europe referendum didn't know what they were voting for, because nobody really did. They could legitimately state that having voted for free trade within the Common Market in 1975 they were surprised to find that they had instead committed themselves to an organisation with a superior legal status to their Parliament, to an organisation with a single currency, freedom of movement of workers and the eventual aim of political union. On 23 January 2013, David Cameron announced in a speech at Bloomberg's office in London that he would put a commitment to an In/Out referendum in the Conservatives' next election manifesto. We explore what came to be known as the Bloomberg speech in more detail in Reason 11, but within it Cameron did make a good point when he claimed that 'democratic consent for the EU in Britain is now wafer-thin'.[55] Even Cameron knew the 1975 voters hadn't voted for what they were now getting.

Civil engineer John Francis was one of those voters. He had built up a litany of concerns.

> It was gradual. I began to think that hardly anyone knew how decision-making was done in Europe, or how many of our own laws were initiated there, or even whether it was at all a democratic process. The media hardly reported what was happening, say, in the European Parliament, unless there was a brawl between MEPs or something similar.

Francis was uncomfortable with the effect of the CAP and the CFP on the country. He had a growing feeling that the British government had lost control, particularly in the area of immigration, and that trade agreements were taking a long time to conclude, given that any could be scuppered by any of the twenty-eight members, most of whom had different priorities. The only way, John thought, to make the EU truly 'work' would be to have a central unified government, which is what the originators anticipated. Instead, there is a mishmash of mixed sovereignties with some majority voting and some veto control, and it wasn't working. Ultimately, John saw a sclerotic, inward-looking organisation on the brink of serious turmoil and knew he had one chance to help free Britain, and more specifically his children and grandchildren, from the effects of the mistake he now thought he had made in 1975. So when the 2016 EU referendum came around, millions of people like John were ready to make up for their 'mistake'.

REASON 6

CARELESS THATCHER

As Geoffrey Howe rose to his feet to make his resignation speech on 13 November 1990, he was greeted with the silence that is customary in those circumstances. Margaret Thatcher's former Chancellor, Foreign Secretary and Deputy Prime Minister, Howe was a heavyweight political figure. Heavyweight political speaker, he was not. But on that day, this reasonable and mild man's frustration with his Prime Minister's behaviour over Europe propelled him to heights of oratory so disdainful and lethal that it led almost directly to the unseating of a once all-powerful leader. His speech was an explanation of how Thatcher's abandoning of proper Cabinet government in favour of her own prejudices against the European ideal was hurting the national interest. It ended with the words of a British businessman, trading in Brussels and elsewhere, who had written to Howe the week before.

> People throughout Europe see our Prime Minister's finger-wagging and her passionate 'No, No, No' much more clearly than the content of the carefully worded texts. It is too easy for them to believe that we all share her attitudes; for why else has she been our Prime Minister for so long? This is a desperately serious situation for our country.[1]

It is amazing to think that Geoffrey Howe was speaking about the Prime Minister who took the UK further *into* Europe than anyone except Edward Heath. Under Thatcher, institutions, markets and laws became far more deeply combined within the Continent. With Thatcher's voluble support, the unity project underwent a step-change from unanimous to majority rule. Yet, almost immediately she had signed the Act that catalysed these changes, she began to lead the opposition to her own actions. If the most elementary task of a politician is to secure popular support for their policies, Thatcher's stoking of the fire of those who opposed the integration she herself had encouraged is one of the odder political stories of our time.[2]

The key element of the story of Margaret Thatcher's relationship with Europe is her enthusiastic enacting of the Single European Act (SEA) in 1985–87. It started off as an attempt by Thatcher to support her economic policies of free trade and market liberalisation by removing 'non-tariff' barriers to trade (regulations that reduced competition across Europe in goods and services). It ended as a treaty change, meaning that whatever was agreed in Europe could be enshrined in the domestic law of every member state and thus enforced in the courts. Within the SEA was a significant transfer and sharing of national sovereignty, and a commitment to monetary and political union. Thatcher and other heads of government reduced their right to veto any policy or directive they disliked apart from in a few areas.

The Leave campaign's key slogan, repeated ad infinitum at debates and speeches, was: 'Take back control'. It was their hero Margaret Thatcher who lost a lot of that control. Some say she was deceived and didn't properly understand what she had signed up to. That suggestion about a woman who worked harder than most to master the implications of policies she supported was condescending to say the least. Ultimately, it was most probably an underestimation of what being 'European' meant to the other members of the European Community. Whatever it was, the implication of that one signature on a treaty was to light the fire of mainstream Euroscepticism that would burn all the way to June 2016 and beyond. That the flames were then fanned by Thatcher herself is what led to Geoffrey Howe's resignation speech and her downfall. Not the first and definitely not the last Conservative Prime Minister to be brought down by Europe.

The irony of all of this is that when Margaret Thatcher became Prime Minister in 1979, the other members of the European Community breathed a quiet sigh of relief, thinking that she would bring a more determined and positive attitude towards the EEC.

After the 1975 referendum, Britain's reputation as an awkward partner under the Labour government had gathered steam. In July 1975, the attempt to build a common environmental policy was almost derailed when Britain insisted on exemptions from emissions limits designed to curb river pollution, as its faster-flowing rivers cleared pollution more quickly than Continental ones. Britain then refused to pass the 1976 legislation to reduce the maximum number of hours lorry drivers could spend at the wheel. Meanwhile, Harold Wilson insisted that Britain, as a prospective oil producer (North Sea oil was about to come on stream) should have their own seat at the Conference on International Economic Cooperation on energy, instead of the EC being represented as whole. Wilson eventually backed down, but only after German Chancellor Helmut Schmidt wrote a letter to the other Community heads of government declaring that his country would not go on subsidising Britain indefinitely if they refused to act in a manner which was communautaire (the term for acting in the interests of the Community as a whole).

That may have put an end to that issue, but in the first half of 1977 Britain held the presidency of the EC, meaning British ministers would chair meetings of the Council of Ministers. The UK was therefore responsible for maintaining the Community's impetus and direction. During this time, Britain isolated itself in two disputes, both in the field of agriculture, which was led by John Silkin, the Minister for Agriculture. He was also a highly ambitious Eurosceptic who saw a chance to burnish his leadership credentials by appearing to block Community advances. Hence, Silkin refused to move an inch on fishing quotas following the general declaration of 200-mile fishing limits. He then held up the agricultural price review for a month for the sake of 1½ pence a pound on the butter subsidy. Commentators on this period argue that Labour ministers seemed to believe that the EC presidency simply meant 'a *carte blanche* for Britain to get her own way for six months',[3] and had once again achieved the minimum of gain for the maximum of irritation.[4]

While this was happening, Helmut Schmidt and French President Valéry Giscard d'Estaing decided to press ahead with integration. This came in the form of two significant projects: direct elections to the European Parliament, and a revival of the idea of monetary union.

The idea of holding direct national elections for members to the European Parliament had featured in the Treaty of Rome. Most countries saw this as a way of ensuring national democratic control over European business. But in the UK, Labour's national executive argued that a more democratically legitimate European Parliament would lead to a power struggle with the UK's own Parliament. Jim Callaghan, who had taken over as Prime Minister in 1976, decided not to plunge himself into an early internal party dispute, so instead took a head-in-the-sand approach. His government took no steps to draft any legislation to implement the elections. So once again, because of the priority given to domestic political considerations, Britain appeared to be in breach of the spirit of the European Community.

Meanwhile, the first concrete step that Europe took towards monetary union was promoted by a British politician. In January 1977, Roy Jenkins, feeling he no longer had a place in British politics, accepted a role as the President of the European Commission. While on a picnic outing to the Forêt de Soignes, Jenkins developed his argument for creating monetary union within the bloc. He explained the case for it during a lecture in October 1977,[5] using his considerable skills as an orator combined with a highly developed understanding of how to explain political and economic concepts, as might be expected of a former Chancellor of the Exchequer and Home Secretary.

It is useful here to consider Jenkins's argument, because it explains very well the attraction of monetary union to European politicians at that point. The idea was to take gradual steps from where Europe was, with freely floating exchange rates, to full monetary union. The benefits of this would be economic at first, but eventually political.

The pound-loving Brits have often been perplexed by other European nations' desire to fix their economies together and share a currency. To understand why Europeans wanted to do this, the question you need to ask is: what problem was it trying to fix? The answer was exchange rate volatility. When exchange rates move up and down, it is extremely difficult for customers, businesses and governments to plan their consumption, production and policies. Even if you are only building a free trade area, volatile currencies are a problem, because you cannot know how much you will pay for goods and services from outside your country, nor receive for those you sell. As we know, the European Community wasn't just a free trade area. It was a customs union, with trade within the union encouraged as much as it could be. Trading with confidence is difficult if you cannot forecast prices from one day to the next. Businesses that cannot plan with confidence tend not to take risks and invest, and this can cause unemployment. Stabilising currency fluctuations, according to Jenkins, would promote 'steady and more uniform economic policies favouring investment and expansion'.

It would also help reduce inflation. Price rises were bedevilling Europe at the time. Should a country's exchange rate suddenly fall, the price of imports would go up, meaning costs would be higher for those businesses importing raw materials. The price of exports fall and that may help the job market, but would push up demand without increasing a country's productive capacity. This increase in demand without an increase in supply also pushes prices up and causes inflation. Stabilising and managing demand across the European Community would be advantageous to all, even more so with the prospect of new countries Greece, Portugal and Spain joining the bloc. If European monetary union brought inflation down to a lower and more even rate then this would again help give economies more confidence.

Politically, Jenkins noted that 'spasmodic, local economic difficulties' were being 'magnified by exchange rates and capital movements into general crises of confidence'. So monetary union could 'change radically and for the better the institutional weaknesses that have been hindering our ability to restore high employment in conditions of price stability'.[6]

Those are the economic arguments for monetary union. They were adapted in the 1980s by many members of Margaret Thatcher's Cabinet as arguments for joining the Exchange Rate Mechanism (ERM). As we will find out, Thatcher resisted this until the very last moment. The main reason is the loss of sovereignty over economic decisions that it would involve. Roy Jenkins, in his 1977 speech, does not shy away from this downside. Yet he argues that fluctuating exchange rates are reducing economic sovereignty anyway, once again explaining the difference between de jure sovereignty (the right to control) and de facto sovereignty (whether that control actually exists).

> The relocation of monetary policy to the European level would be as big a political step for the present generation of European leaders as for the last generation in setting up the present Community. But we must face the fundamental question. Do we intend to create a European union or do we not? Do we, confronted with the inevitable and indeed desirable prospect of enlargement, intend to strengthen and deepen the Community, or do we not? There would be little point in asking the peoples and governments of Europe to contemplate union, were it not for the fact that real and efficient sovereignty over monetary issues already eludes them to a high and increasing degree. The prospect of monetary union should be seen as part of the process of recovering the substance of sovereign power. At present we tend to cling to its shadow.[7]

Jenkins's idea was pushed forward by German Chancellor Helmut Schmidt, who once again found that Jim Callaghan was not prepared to play ball. With the British economy still struggling, Callaghan didn't want to have any external influences on his ability to act. He offered instead to join the European Monetary System (EMS), the broad arrangements that attempted to link EEC countries' exchange rates to each other, but *not* the Exchange Rate Mechanism, a more rigid scheme which tied member governments to policies that maintained their currency exchange rate with the German Deutsche Mark within a 2.25 per cent band (6 per cent for Italy and Ireland). Callaghan's compromise was that he would endeavour to maintain the value of sterling as though it *were* in the ERM, without actually being in it. It was yet another example of the UK's refusal to put national interests aside as an 'indicator of a certain European *spirit de corps*'.[8]

Conservative leader Margaret Thatcher commented in Parliament when Callaghan reported back on his decision that it was 'a sad day for Europe, in that the nine member countries have been unable to agree on a major new initiative which will affect us all'.[9] But perhaps a more damning indictment of the Labour government's attitude to Europe came from Roy Denman. He was the senior civil servant who'd worked on the small print of the treaty ahead of the UK's entry into the EU. He'd already become increasingly disillusioned by Wilson's laborious, and in his view bogus, renegotiations. Now he had equal contempt for Callaghan, writing in his memoirs:

> There seemed no understanding in London, among both ministers and many senior officials, of the simple point that the process of European unification could not be stopped. If we wanted to remain part of it, then, short of leaving the Community, the British interest could best be served by our fighting our corner among partners convinced that Britain, in her heart, was at one with them in moving to the 'ever closer union' proclaimed as the European goal by the Treaty of Rome.[10]

If Britain's European partners thought the return of a Conservative government would bring a new dawn of cooperation, they were swiftly proved wrong.

In June 1979, Sir Nicholas Henderson, continuing the tradition of departing ambassadors of writing valedictory dispatches, left his role in Paris with a rather grim update. 'Our decline in relation to our European partners has been so marked that today we are not only no longer a world power, but we are not in the first rank even as a European one.'[11]

Armed with a parliamentary majority of forty-three, the highest majority for any government since 1966, Thatcher had her own answer to these problems. She was influenced by 'monetarist' theorists like Milton Friedman and Friedrich Hayek, to control money supply to lower inflation, which would then lead to sustained economic growth. Believing in the power of the free market, she aimed to reverse the interventionist consensus that had animated British economic policy since 1945. Therefore, she would 'privatise' (sell off) the nationalised industries, diminish trade union power, restrain public expenditure, cut taxes, remove obstacles to free enterprise and try to widen the basis of property and share ownership.

Thatcher had a vision of the European Community as a zone of prosperity and freedom, uniting a substantial part of 'free Europe' against the Soviet menace, encouraging cooperation particularly in foreign policy. She also lauded the benefits of the EEC in economic terms, reminding audiences that membership brought access to an enormous and prosperous market, encouraged inward investment and enabled Britain to negotiate as part of the world's largest trading bloc.[12]

That said, not everything was rosy in her eyes about the European Community. Chief amongst the problems she chose to tackle as soon as she entered 10 Downing Street was what became known as the 'British Budgetary Question' (BBQ). In 1979, Margaret Thatcher saw that because Britain collected more tariffs on goods imported from outside the EEC and had an efficient agriculture sector, it paid more into the EC budget but was rewarded with far lower subsidies. Britain was looking at a net contribution in 1980 of over £1 billion and it was rising fast. At home she was trying to reduce public expenditure. She'd take any savings wherever she could find them. But she was also offended by the very principle of the UK's deficit between contributions and receipts. Furthermore, picking this fight would help burnish her credentials as a slayer of foreign foes.

The importance of the BBQ is not in the result, which was overall seen as a win for Thatcher. It is more about the way in which she achieved that result, which was to show her counterparts across the European Community that she had little understanding of the European ideal. It would stiffen their resolve to integrate deeper, with or without her.

For instance, from the moment she went into battle, she started referring to the budget contributions as 'our money', or even 'my money'. The rest of the club didn't see it like that. The 1957 Treaty of Rome had contained within it a concept of the EC's 'own resources'. These resources came from tariffs and levies on anything imported to the bloc from outside, a proportion of VAT income, and a portion of gross national income.[13] To other nations, this wasn't just some kind of annual joining fee that you could haggle over – the money belonged to the member states – it was Europe's money!

So the BBQ became irreverently referred to as the 'Bloody British Question'. Thatcher raised it as soon as she could, and at the Dublin summit in 1979, Helmut Schmidt feigned sleep during one of her harangues while Valéry Giscard d'Estaing kept his motorcade drawn up at the door, engines revving. The two sides, which is the only way one could describe Britain and Europe, were miles apart. Europe offered a £350 million a year rebate; Thatcher wanted at least £1 billion. The Europeans suggested that a simple way to reduce the UK's contribution was to consume less, and when they did consume to buy inside the Community rather than out, which would reduce both import duties and VAT.

The whole dispute was to last four more years. A temporary settlement was reached in May 1980 when UK Foreign Secretary Lord Carrington managed to get a rebate of two thirds of the British net contribution for the next three years. But Thatcher wanted a permanent solution. On she went, threatening in 1982 to veto the decision on agricultural prices for the next year unless a permanent solution to the BBQ was reached. Given the Luxembourg Compromise only allowed the right of veto to be used on issues of vital national interest to a member state, and agricultural prices were definitely not one of those, this was brushed aside as a foolish threat.

By the time the problem was solved in 1984 by the Fontainebleau Agreement, the leadership of France and Germany had changed. The French were led by the Socialist François Mitterrand, and the Germans by Helmut Kohl, who was a Christian Democrat. This may have meant Kohl was nominally a conservative, but Christian Democrats believe fully in Europe as a federalist project.

Mitterrand decided he had had enough and it was time to get a deal. When he became President of the European Community in 1984, he publicly suggested that it would be better for all concerned if Britain ceased to be a full member of the Community and instead negotiated a 'special status'.[14] The catalyst for this new sense of purpose was the increasing technological and thus economic gap between the USA and Japan on the one hand and the European Community on the other. Europe needed to get its act together. So President Mitterrand instructed his Foreign Minister Roland Dumas to announce that if a budget agreement was not reached, France would call a meeting without the British to discuss political reform.

Margaret Thatcher had put Britain into a position of self-excluding stubbornness, just as Anthony Eden's government had when sending Russell Bretherton to the Spaak Committee in 1955. This meant that instead of leaving an empty chair, obstructing all EC business by refusing to attend (the device used by Charles de Gaulle to help the French get their own way with the Luxembourg Compromise in 1966), the British had exasperated other members almost enough to have an empty chair forced on them.[15]

Finally, Margaret Thatcher came through – helped by an admirable command of her brief, honed not only by her weekly preparation for Prime Minister's Questions but also by her little 'handbag points' lists that she could use to batter her adversaries. (Mrs Thatcher famously kept briefing notes in her handbag that she would bring out when up against it in meetings, leading the Oxford English Dictionary to introduce 'handbagging' as a verb, meaning 'to ruthlessly crush'.) The deal came down to numbers. The British had asked for 70 per cent of the difference between its VAT contribution and its receipts from the budget. The Germans offered 50 per cent, the French 60 per cent. Eventually, the agreement was for 66 per cent, in return for the Community's take from VAT rising from 1 per cent to 1.4 per cent.

For many years, the Fontainebleau Agreement was lauded by those who took part in it. Official Treasury figures for the amount of money cumulatively saved for Britain by 2015 was £78 million. It was claimed by one Foreign Office diplomat to be 'the most valuable financial agreement this country ever negotiated'.[16] The rebate payments would be handed over automatically each year, rather than subject to a vote in the European Parliament. The eventual mechanism meant that the rebate was discounted off the annual budget contribution, so the UK never pays its full contribution.

In the 2016 referendum campaign, Vote Leave (the main designated Leave campaign) would constantly refer to the full gross contribution of £350 million a week having to be paid to the EU, whether on their bus or in debates. We look into this claim in more detail in Reason 14, but given the rebate never left Britain's shores, it was highly controversial. The amount actually paid in 2015 was just under £250 million a week, and that was before the money that Britain gets back from the EU in subsidies and grants – which added up to another £79 million a week, meaning the true figure sent to the EU was around £170 million a week.[17] That said, the subsidies and grants are at the whim of those in the EU who distribute them, and will not always match what the British government might think should be the priorities. Furthermore, the rebate has never been inserted into a treaty, so it isn't a full and final settlement. It is therefore up for discussion every seven years as part of the EU's long-term budget process. But given that the budget has to be approved by all twenty-eight members, the UK has a veto over any process that could scrap or reduce it.

As we are about to find out, however, vetoes don't last forever.

As far as Europe goes, the Single European Act was Margaret Thatcher's greatest triumph, and her greatest mistake. The moves that it made to create a single Common Market opened it up to British financial services in particular in a way that helped them thrive. But her mistake was to think this could be done without any serious threat to the sovereign powers of Westminster.

As Thatcher surveyed the European Community, she saw no internal tariffs on goods – a customs union in practice – but she also saw a collection of 'non-tariff' barriers. Some of these were subtle, such as different national standards on health and safety, regulations discriminating against foreign products, public procurement policies, delays and over-elaborate procedures at customs posts. Britain was more or less excluded from markets in which they would excel, for example from the German insurance and financial services markets. In return for these non-tariff barriers being removed, Thatcher conceded she would have to agree to there being more majority voting in the European Community (a reduction in the number of areas in which the national veto could be exercised). Without this compromise, the single market could never be created because countries would succumb to domestic pressures and prevent the opening up of their markets. But she would make clear that any extra power for the European Commission should only be used to create and maintain a single market rather than to advance other objectives. Finally, she was going to achieve all of this while resisting any attempt to make treaty changes which would allow the Commission to pile extra burdens on British businesses.[18]

Margaret Thatcher's aim, then, was to create a single market without ceding extra powers to the European Commission and without treaty change. It's argued with hindsight that she was being naive. But signs that her plans were overambitious were there at the time, and she appears to have ignored them.

In 1981, the Foreign Ministers of Germany and Italy, Hans-Dietrich Genscher and Emilio Colombo, had written a paper in which they had argued for greater European political integration. The Genscher–Colombo plan laid the ground for a European state and called for a 'European Act' to advance it. National governments were always asked whether they supported these papers, which would one day form the basis of treaties. And at times it seemed good diplomacy to show willing. At the time, Thatcher's Foreign Secretary Lord Carrington suggested that if she wanted a satisfactory outcome on the BBQ, it would be good to 'provide them with evidence of simultaneous progress on the wider, vaguer and more theological issues' such as those laid out in the Genscher–Colombo plan. She received similar advice from Carrington's replacement, Francis Pym, in 1983, when the plan was being developed into a 'Solemn Declaration' on European union by the heads of government at the meeting of the European Council in Stuttgart on 19 June 1983. Pym used the rather ingenious approach of arguing that Thatcher should sign the document in order to deny it any credibility: 'If on the other hand, we were to refuse to sign, we would run the risk of appearing to attach more credibility to the document than it either warrants or deserves.'

Recalling this advice is important, because for years Margaret Thatcher was advised that the 'windy rhetoric' and 'theology' of European declarations like that of 1983 were worth putting up with in order to achieve the concrete advantages she wanted. So the 1983 declaration's references to progressing towards economic and monetary union and the need to decide within five years 'whether the progress achieved should be incorporated in a Treaty on European Union'[19] could safely be ignored, as could the wording of the draft treaty on European union promoted by Italian federalist Altiero Spinelli and adopted by the European Parliament in February 1984.[20] But, as Charles Moore points out,

What was conceived by Genscher-Colombo in 1981 and solemnly declared at Stuttgart in 1983 would be framed as a treaty obligation at Luxembourg in 1985, included in the Single European Act in 1986, set in train at Hanover in 1988, confirmed at Madrid in 1989 and Rome in 1990, and implemented in the Maastricht Treaty in 1991.[21]

Every treaty, declaration, protocol and directive was a building block for the next, and fear of being left out in the cold in a 'two-tier' Europe meant Margaret Thatcher was trapped inside what they were building. She had little understanding of the deep emotions underlying the drive for European Union. On 22 September 1984, on the field that had seen the terrible First World War battle of Verdun, Helmut Kohl and François Mitterrand stood together, hand in hand, to symbolise the reconciliation of France and Germany. Watching on television, Thatcher was asked whether she thought the scene was moving. 'No, it was *not*,' she answered. 'Two grown men holding hands!'[22] Much as she was in favour of EEC developments, she never shared the European religion.

When the British put forward a document for discussion called 'Europe – the Future'[23] at the Fontainebleau meeting in 1984, it met a decidedly unenthusiastic reception from other heads of government. It explained why opening up the internal market would help deal with the growing technological gap with the United States and Japan as well as deal with the high levels of unemployment in the Community, both genuine concerns of the other member states. It suggested cooperation on pollution, foreign policy and defence – all very communautaire. But there were only very weak proposals on institutional reform, which was the central issue for the other member states in giving new impetus to the Community. So, the Community decided to set up a committee to look into the question of institutional reform, under the chairmanship of James Dooge of Ireland.[24]

Meanwhile, Jacques Delors had somehow ended up with Margaret Thatcher's endorsement as President of the European Commission. That the most successful European integrator since Jean Monnet partly owed his position to Thatcher was due to his record for financial discipline. He had guided François Mitterrand away from the journey to what Thatcher saw as a socialist-inspired financial meltdown that the country appeared to be making in the early 1980s. There is no record of any discussion within Thatcher's circle about his attitude to European integration. This was unfortunate, given that he was to mastermind the two treaties that drove Europe towards economic and political union.

Thatcher also drove the appointment of Arthur Cockfield as the new European Commissioner for the internal market and services. Cockfield's appointment was typical of Thatcher's habit of ignoring a candidate's view on European integration and focusing more on whether they were 'one of us' – meaning whether they shared her economic beliefs. Cockfield was a tax expert and a businessman but, it turned out, 'tended to disregard the larger questions of politics – constitutional sovereignty, national sentiment and the promptings of liberty'.[25] He produced a White Paper identifying 297 imperfections in the single European market, with timetabled proposals for eliminating them by 1992. As part of this drive, Cockfield insisted that all fiscal barriers should be removed, including harmonising indirect taxes (making taxes like VAT the same in every country). This for Thatcher was beyond the pale, because the ability to set tax rates was at the heart of parliamentary sovereignty.

Then the Dooge Committee reported back. It argued that institutional reform was essential for the future of the Community, as its goals could only be achieved if there were more rapid procedures for decision-making. So the veto should be abandoned in favour of majority voting, except for specific areas designated in advance as being too sensitive for national interests to be overruled. The Committee then argued there should be an increase in the powers of the European Parliament. There was also mention of 'the achievement of a European social area' (meaning shared social policies) and the promotion of 'common cultural values'. This was all topped off by a rebranding of the European Community as the European Union.[26] The only way these ambitious propositions could be enacted would be through the summoning of an intergovernmental conference (IGC), which the Treaty of Rome had insisted would be needed in order to negotiate any amendments to the European Community.

No treaty can be ratified without unanimity, but an intergovernmental conference can be called with only majority support. Britain was against a new treaty, concerned that anything agreed would have to be implemented in every member state and be backed by law and almost certainly against national interests. Margaret Thatcher and Geoffrey Howe suggested a compromise. There would be a 'Constitutional Convention': a gentlemen's agreement, written but without legal force, to treat the single-market agenda as though the unanimity rule had been set aside. This meant that purely for the purpose of removing the protectionism of non-tariff barriers, qualified majority voting (QMV), a mechanism allocating voting weight to each country roughly according to its size, could be used. Once agreement was achieved, the EC could go back to having national vetoes.

When national leaders converged on Milan for a European Council meeting on 29 June 1985, Thatcher was met by a pincer movement from the French, German and Italian governments that many argue was payback for the way Thatcher had triumphed in the budget negotiations. Kohl and Mitterrand circulated a 'Draft Treaty on European Union' just before the meeting, and at the meeting Italian Prime Minister Bettino Craxi called for a vote – the first ever taken at a European Council – on whether to hold an IGC. The Foreign Office were embarrassed at their lack of foresight; Margaret Thatcher was apoplectic. But she knew that if she was going to get her internal market, she would have to accept treaty changes, and so she sent her officials off to negotiate the kinds of treaty changes that would expedite the internal market decisions.[27]

The result was the Single European Act,[28] which was formally signed by the European member states in February 1986 and came into force on 1 July 1987. It was the first major revision to the 1957 Treaty of Rome, and it established the goal of creating a single European market by the end of 1992, providing for the extension of qualified majority voting to achieve this.

Britain had won some concessions in the process, in addition to the freeing of the internal market. Specifically excluded from the rules on majority voting were the areas of taxation, free movement of persons, health controls and employees' rights. No major increase was proposed in the powers of the European Parliament.[29] But amongst the policies introduced by the Act were economic and social cohesion, monetary union, which was mentioned for the first time in a treaty, and the development of common social and environmental policies.[30] For example, Article 21 of the Act extends QMV over matters concerned with health and safety at work. Thatcher had been concerned this could result in heavy burdens being imposed on small businesses, and in the end she was right: QMV on health and safety was used in the 1990s to impose social legislation that Britain didn't want.[31] The biggest issue was that instead of marking the limits of integration, as Thatcher had hoped it would, the SEA contributed to the momentum for further change, by creating new opportunities for the proponents of union.[32]

This is why Margaret Thatcher developed a love–hate relationship with the SEA. She loved the trade and commercial aspects but was concerned about and came to hate the political and constitutional aspects. She had thought at first she was sufficiently protected from those, but came to realise that she had got it wrong. Some argue that she was unaware of the implications of the SEA, but David Williamson, her senior Europe advisor, remembers her walking down the stairs at No. 10 one morning and saying, 'I've read every single word of this treaty, and I am happy with it.'[33] What she didn't and couldn't predict was the way that her European counterparts, led by Jacques Delors, would use the wording of the treaty to push for further European Union, and in particular monetary union.

Parliament was not much help either. The European Communities (Amendment) Bill came to the Commons in April 1986 and it took only six days to see it through all its stages. The SEA was a major constitutional measure, but there were hundreds of absentees from Parliament on the days of the votes. Littered throughout the debate are contributions from sceptics whose names would become a lot better known in the next few years[34] – but they still voted for the guillotine motion proposed by the government to cut off debate not long after it started.

What happened instead is that the Single European Act became a fact. Significant sovereignty was surrendered. Margaret Thatcher backed it, her Cabinet backed it, her parliamentary party backed it. Once they realised what it meant, the Conservatives couldn't face the consequences of what they had done.

If the signing of the Single European Act was the high-water mark of Thatcher's influence and 'success' in Europe, it didn't take long for her downfall to begin. Jacques Delors, who became the catalyst for her Europhobia, noted how drastically Mrs Thatcher had underestimated the extent to which her acceptance of the SEA brought her along the conveyor belt to closer union.[35] Nowhere was the effect of the Act more vastly underestimated than in the rather opaque and vague commitment to monetary union, giving Delors a base from which he could launch a campaign in favour of a single currency.[36] This campaign would intersect eventually with the campaign within Thatcher's Cabinet for Britain to join the Exchange Rate Mechanism.

We now know that Britain eventually joined the ERM in October 1990 and crashed out of it on 'Black Wednesday' in September 1992. It would be fair to say that that experience has coloured many people's view of what it was trying to achieve. But in 1985, just at the point that the SEA was being created, Nigel Lawson, Thatcher's Chancellor, had joined together with the Foreign Secretary, Geoffrey Howe, and the Governor of the Bank of England, Robin

Leigh-Pemberton, in agreement that the time was 'ripe' for joining the mecha-nism. Had Britain joined then, history might have turned out very differently than it did.

The basis of the ERM was a weighted average of all the currencies involved, known as the ECU (European Currency Unit). However, the German Mark became the currency against which all other currencies involved would be meas-ured. Currencies would enter at a particular rate against the Mark and then could adjust around it (plus or minus 2.25 per cent in some cases, 6 per cent in others). If it was found that the entry rate was not right (too high or too low for the country's economic conditions), there could be a realignment, with the currency pegged at a different level against the Deutsche Mark.

Margaret Thatcher was against joining the ERM because she believed that membership would severely limit the government's freedom of action in eco-nomic policy, leading to high interest rates, enforced reductions in public expenditure, and higher unemployment. Interest rates are linked to exchange rates because, for instance, higher interest rates encourage international financial flows into the country, raising demand for the pound and pushing up the exchange rate. Maintaining Britain's position in the ERM would mean interest rates being used to control exchange rates to react to movements in other nation states in-stead of responding to purely British economic and political needs. Thatcher also argued that sterling was in a different position from any other European currency, as Britain was an oil exporter, and more vulnerable to fluctuations in the dollar, as oil was bought and sold in dollars. She was even less keen on full monetary union, as she believed that it meant 'the end of a country's economic independence and thus the increasing irrelevance of its parliamentary democracy'.[37]

Nigel Lawson's main argument was that joining the ERM would provide the necessary discipline to bring down the inflation rate, which he termed 'the judge and the jury' of economic policy.[38] The Conservative government had for six years used control of the money supply to do this, but Lawson had come to realise that the explosion of economic activity that had come from market liber-alisation had made it difficult to interpret what movements in the money supply meant. Lawson felt that linking sterling to the Deutsche Mark would protect businesses from exchange rate gyrations and foster an anti-inflation climate. Although he had thought highly of this idea since 1981, he wanted to wait until the 'right opportunity' to persuade Margaret Thatcher of its merits. A dramatic

fall of the pound against the dollar at the start of 1985 was that moment, because however much Thatcher spoke about leaving the market to its own devices,
she would have found pound–dollar parity intolerable. So Lawson broached
the subject.

Thatcher's close advisors warned her against joining the ERM. Alan Walters,
her economic advisor, had always argued that it was better to leave everything to
the market. John Redwood, head of her policy unit, advocated instead a more
pragmatic approach that 'keeps our destinies in our own hands and not in those
of the Germans; and still leaves us free to try and track the DM exchange rate if
we wish to do so'. David Willetts, also of the policy unit, linked the economic
and political aspects of the problem:

> If God had intended us to join the Exchange Rate Mechanism, we would be
> as productive and moderate in our wage demands as the Germans ... Will the
> average home-owner happily accept a rise in his mortgage rate once he knows its
> purpose is to maintain the pound's value against the German Mark?[39]

Eventually, a meeting of ministers was set for 13 November 1985. Lawson presented the case he had long prepared the ground for, having circulated to all
present reams of papers and tables laying out the economic advantages ERM
members were gaining over Britain, and exposing the much-lowered risks
of joining at that time. Every single person present at the meeting bar long-
term Eurosceptic John Biffen, way down the pecking order as Leader of the
House, backed him. Even Willie Whitelaw, Thatcher's trusty deputy, simply
said: 'If the Chancellor and Governor say the time is right then that is OK for
my money.'[40] Eyes turned to Thatcher to await her response. When it came,
it flummoxed everyone present. Reports of her decision run from not putting
the interest rate into someone else's hands in the run-up to an election to 'I'm
afraid we're not going to do this. I'm sorry',[41] to 'If you join the ERM, you
will have to do so without me.'[42] It was the implication of that final reported
line that was the most shocking, particularly for what it said about the balance
between Prime Minister and Cabinet. Government policy, which had hitherto
accepted that one day Britain would join the ERM, was reversed by fiat of a
Prime Minister who regarded her word alone as sufficient to kill it for ever.
Geoffrey Howe mused whether to get such high-handedness reversed would

require him and friends 'to go almost off the constitutional map', and Nigel Lawson called it 'the saddest event of my time as Chancellor, and the greatest missed opportunity'.[43]

It was a missed opportunity, because, in the words of Howe, joining the ERM in 1985 would have 'delivered a more restrained monetary policy', which would have stopped for instance Nigel Lawson's policies for economic growth that led to an unsustainable boom, causing uncontrolled inflation and ultimately a recession. More importantly, 'we would have been able, as more mature, streetwise members of the system, to play a much more credible and thus fuller part in shaping the Delors Report [on progress to monetary union]'.[44]

Jacques Delors was on the move, with every step being backed by the words of the Single European Act. In February 1987, the Commission produced a package of reforms that Delors described as a 'European Social Area' in a speech called 'Making a Success of the Single Act'.[45] Delors looked for a substantial increase in the legal limit on the annual income of the Community, linked to a new system of funding based on member states' relative shares of the Community's GDP, reflecting more accurately their relative ability to pay. He also wanted reform of the CAP to lower support prices and replace them with direct subsidies. Finally, he pushed for a large increase in EC funding for research, transport and the environment, and a doubling of regional aid and job training by 1992. When the European Council met to approve this package in June 1987, Margaret Thatcher refused to do so, dividing the community eleven to one and leaving Geoffrey Howe 'shaking with anger'. Thatcher's view was that she would only agree to raising the Community's budget when the limits to CAP expenditure were firmly agreed, while the other countries wanted agreement on all parts of the package together. It took until February 1988 for agreement to be reached, with Thatcher receiving tight and binding controls on the rate of increase of CAP expenditure and a continuation of the Fontainebleau rebate mechanism in return for an increase in the budget.[46] This may have been a step forward, but by the end of 1988, relations between Thatcher and Europe had been almost irretrievably broken.

It started in Hanover in June 1988. The French and the Germans argued at this European Council meeting that a single European currency was an essential component of a single market. A single currency would reduce transaction costs, because there would be no need to exchange one currency for another in order to trade; it would provide certainty on prices, because they wouldn't be subject to currency fluctuations; and it would make price differences more transparent, because they would all be in the same currency. Furthermore, monetary union would be strengthened by the creation of an independent European Central Bank (ECB), in charge of monetary policy. To that end, they set up a committee of national central bank governors under Jacques Delors to look at the steps needed to strengthen the European Monetary System. Delors was excited by the way the SEA could bring about economic, social and political unity in Europe and how monetary union could help by leading to common budgetary policies to stabilise the currency, which in turn would affect each member's economic and social policies.[47] Once again, Thatcher was sidelined, protesting that 'I neither want nor expect to see such a bank in my lifetime, nor, if I'm twanging a harp, for quite a long time afterwards'.[48] We now know that the Delors Committee reported back in April 1989, recommending a three-stage approach from currency alignment to the creation of a single currency.

Meanwhile, Jacques Delors, emboldened by having been re-elected for a second term at the Hanover Council, was to make two speeches that acted like a stick poking at the hornet's nest of Euroscepticism in Margaret Thatcher's mind. She was provoked into making what would become a famous speech in Bruges, facilitating the creation of what is called the 'Bruges Group' – an influential Eurosceptic think tank – and leading ultimately to the attack on Delors in the House of Parliament in November 1990 that persuaded Geoffrey Howe to resign in such devastating fashion.

In July 1988, Delors made a speech to the European Parliament in which he predicted: 'In ten years, 80 per cent of economic legislation – and perhaps tax and social legislation – will be directed from the Community.'[49] He went on to say that 'we are not going to manage to take all the decisions needed between now and 1995 unless we see the beginnings of a European government'.[50] His *chef de cabinet*, Pascal Lamy, who had written the speech without this line but seen Delors add it spontaneously while speaking, said:

> I buried my head in my hands as I heard Delors make this claim. I knew just what a disaster it would be around the national capitals of Europe to be told that the work of their governments and parliaments in passing legislation would disappear to be replaced by European law-making.[51]

Delors's aim in making the speech was to provoke national parliaments into considering the political realities likely to flow from the Single European Act. We know now that national parliaments still decide most of the key laws that affect their population. At the time, to Margaret Thatcher, it seemed he was belittling the importance of the House of Commons as the only source for law in Britain. Suggesting that soon eight out of ten laws would be decided outside its frontiers was to attack the very democratic foundations of the island's history.[52]

Her concern over those remarks turned to anger when Delors addressed the annual conference of the Trades Union Congress on 8 September 1988. This was the moment when the Labour movement, including the parliamentary party, moved from Euroscepticism to support of the European ideal. In 1980, Michael Foot had been elected leader of the party, and the Eurosceptic left had contributed to a change in party policy to a call to quit the European Community without a referendum if elected. This decision was one of the key reasons for a major split, as a group of prominent pro-European MPs formed the Social Democratic Party (SDP). The 1983 election saw Labour's worst electoral performance since 1918. From this low point, a new leader, Neil Kinnock, backed by new entrants into the Commons like Tony Blair and Gordon Brown, turned Labour away from its anti-European course. By 1988, with Thatcher having won a third election in 1987 and with a majority of 100, the unions in particular were concerned about whether there was ever going to be a parliamentary means to achieve social and employment protection in the face of Conservative resistance. So it's fair to say Jacques Delors had an open door to their hearts and minds.

The speech explained the single market project, didn't attack the British government and was actually rather pro-competition, market economics and capitalism. Yet it also suggested that economic benefits should be maximised while minimising the social cost. Delors argued that it was impossible to build Europe on only deregulation, saying: 'The internal market should be designed to benefit each and every citizen of the Community. It is therefore necessary to improve workers' living and working conditions, and to provide better protection for their health and safety at work.' This meant that Europe could have a social dimension which would mean:

- The establishment of a platform of guaranteed social rights, containing general principles, such as every worker's right to be covered by a collective agreement, and more specific measures concerning, for example, the status of temporary work.

- The creation of a Statute for European Companies, which would include the participation of workers or their representatives...
- The extension to all workers of the right to lifelong education.[53]

Delors received a standing ovation. They chanted 'Frère Jacques' and sang the miners' hymn 'Here We Go' to the tune of the French revolutionary song '*Ça Ira*', reducing him to tears.

Margaret Thatcher was appalled. She had requested a paper from officials spelling out in precise detail how the Commission was pushing forward its frontiers into new areas of culture, education, health and social security. Thatcher herself reports that:

> It set up 'advisory committees' whose membership was neither appointed by, nor answerable to, member states ... It carefully built up a library of declaratory language, largely drawn from the sort of vacuous nonsense which found its way into Council conclusions, in order to justify subsequent proposals. It used a special budgetary procedure, known as '*actions ponctuelles*', which enabled it to finance new projects without a legal base for doing so. But, most seriously of all, it consistently misemployed treaty articles requiring only a qualified majority to issue directives which it could not pass under articles which required unanimity.[54]

So Thatcher decided to use a speech to the College of Europe at Bruges to set out her concerns about the direction of the EU and to advocate a Europe built around sovereign states.[55] In the speech, she argued that the Treaty of Rome in 1957 had been intended as a charter for economic liberty. This was being undermined by the development of monetary union, proposals for a common currency and for a social Europe, all of which concentrates powers at the centre. She then made this famous remark: 'We have not successfully rolled back the frontiers of the state in Britain only to see them re-imposed at a European level, with a European super-state exercising a new dominance from Brussels.' That said, she did insist that Britain's destiny is to remain in Europe as a part of the Community. For instance, she called for a stronger European defence and foreign policy. But this was ultimately the first major attack by a head of government involved in the European unity project on the sharing of sovereignty and supranational government. She wanted to push instead for '...willing and active cooperation between independent sovereign states'. This, then, is not an anti-Europe speech, but a repudiation of the direction of European cooperation. Charles de Gaulle would have liked it. Other European heads of government certainly didn't.

Foreign Secretary Geoffrey Howe spotted immediately that Thatcher's solution to the problems she had identified was 'to misunderstand or misrepresent the Community as it already existed and to inhibit its future in defiance of the texts that we had ourselves negotiated'.[56]

She certainly seemed to misunderstand what a 'single market' meant. No marketplace operates without rules, including those to protect consumers from harmful products and employees from mistreatment. The removal of non-tariff barriers, which Thatcher had wanted so much, meant that the Germans had to abandon their centuries-old rule that beer must be brewed in a special way. It meant the French had to accept that British beef was safe after the outbreak of mad cow disease. A single market is not the same as free trade. The single market prevents any favouritism or protectionism, obliging national or regional governments to tender for the cheapest product irrespective of where it comes from. Free trade allows every nation to decide the terms of trade, but a single market obliges every European country to allow their consumers to buy Marmite and English muffins delivered across borders by British lorries. This requires some supranational supervision and an enforcement mechanism.[57]

Margaret Thatcher's acknowledged economics hero is Friedrich Hayek. His book *The Road to Serfdom* is often cited as the founding charter of post-war economic liberalism; an assault on the collectivist, statist, social democratic and socialist ideas emerging as a response to Nazism and Communism. But as he contemplated the organisation of the post-war world, he identified the nation state as the source of problems: 'There is little hope of lasting peace so long as every country is free to employ whatever measures it thinks desirable in its own immediate interest.' Therefore, Hayek suggested, 'What we need is ... a superior political power which can hold the economic interests in check and in the conflict between them can truly hold the scales.' Thatcher was a devoted admirer of Hayek, yet he argued that to make a fully open or liberal economy work in Europe, some federal or political direction was required. She signed the Single European Act, ignoring the bits about increasing integration and closer union even though they were vital for the single market she wanted to operate.[58]

As trailed earlier in this chapter, when the Delors Committee on European Monetary Union reported back in April 1989, it recommended a three-stage process. Stage One was the closer alignment of currency values via the ERM, and Stages Two and Three would involve the gradual loss of monetary independence by member states, the creation of a European Central Bank and a common currency. Having rejected these proposals, Thatcher was told by Chancellor Nigel Lawson and Foreign Secretary Geoffrey Howe that they would resign if she didn't sign up to joining the ERM by 1992 at the European Council in Madrid in June 1989. This led to a particularly constructive performance by Thatcher in Madrid – with her announcing that Britain was ready to make a start on Stage One and join the ERM subject to inflation being under control and progress being made in the Community towards a single market. She insisted she wouldn't be able to get Stages Two and Three past the House of Commons, but she accepted that an intergovernmental conference would need to be convened to consider the changes to be made to the treaties to allow further progress.[59]

Within months, however, Howe had been demoted from Foreign Secretary to Leader of the Commons and Nigel Lawson had resigned anyway, fed up of the undermining influence of Thatcher's economic advisor Alan Walters. Typically of Thatcher, she replaced them with two men she thought were 'one of us' in terms of economic views but who in fact were pro-European integration: Douglas Hurd as Foreign Secretary and John Major as Chancellor.

The years 1989 and 1990 saw the biggest changes in the world for nearly fifty years. Communism collapsed and Germany was reunited. European leaders believed that the new Germany should be anchored in the West by more integration. Mrs Thatcher thought differently. She had grown up with an ingrained distrust of Germans. She writes in her autobiography: 'I do not believe in collective guilt ... But I do believe in national character ... Since the unification of Germany under Bismarck ... Germany has veered unpredictably between aggression and self-doubt.'[60] This would explain why she attempted to stop German reunification, and told a former German ambassador during a banquet to celebrate forty years of Anglo-German friendship: 'You need another forty years before we can forget what you've done.'[61]

In July 1990, her Secretary of State for Trade and Industry, and one of her most loyal allies, Nicholas Ridley, had to be sacked after saying in an interview for *The Spectator* (ironically, to Nigel Lawson's journalist son!) that a move towards monetary union was 'a German racket designed to take over the whole of Europe', and then insisting that 'I'm not against giving up sovereignty in principle, but not to this lot. You might just as well give it to Adolf Hitler, frankly.'[62] Nigel Lawson commented that the reason Ridley felt it had been safe to make those comments was that 'he had many times heard Margaret utter precisely the same sentiments in private – as, indeed, had I'. [63]

Polls had support for German reunification at over 70 per cent, so Thatcher was falling increasingly out of touch with public opinion. This had been shown even more starkly by the failure of the Conservatives in the European Parliament elections in 1989, when Labour achieved a majority in Britain's Strasbourg representation despite the Conservatives insisting that 'if you don't vote Conservative next Thursday you'll live on a diet of Brussels'.[64]

In June 1990, Margaret Thatcher's concerns about sovereignty were given a face (Spanish fishermen) and a name (Factortame – their fishing company). For the very first time, the European Court of Justice ordered British courts to suspend the implementation of an Act of Parliament. Under the Common Fisheries Policy, which was supposed to provide free access to the waters of all member states, quotas had been set to try to manage the amount of fish each member state was catching. To get round that, Spanish fishing boats were registering themselves as British under the 1894 Merchant Shipping Act. After British fishing companies complained, the 1988 Merchant Shipping Act was enacted to make sure a vessel could only be registered as British if it had a 'genuine and substantial connection with the UK'.

Factortame was one of the Spanish fishing companies affected by this law change. They argued that the 1988 Merchant Shipping Act was contrary to their right under EU law not to be discriminated against on the grounds of nationality, the rights of individuals and companies to establish themselves in business anywhere in the EU, and the right to own a company in another member state. The case made its way all the way up to the European Court of Justice, where the judgment was laid down that the British courts should have disapplied British law if it was in conflict with European Community law. Uproar ensued in the House of Commons, where it was pointed out that this was the very first time any court had ever told Parliament to suspend or nullify a law. Teddy Taylor, who would become better known in the 1990s as one of the most implacable Conservative Eurosceptics, even argued that Parliament may as well stop any business as there was no guarantee that any laws they made would prevail.[65]

When the case went to the House of Lords, it was again upheld, with the law lords (there was no Supreme Court at the time) arguing firstly that the Merchant Shipping Act 1988 was not in direct conflict with EC law but instead was incompatible with the treaty obligations that had been signed up to when Parliament passed the European Communities Act in 1972. What followed, though, was more significant. Lord Bridge argued that the European Communities Act 1972 made it 'the duty of a United Kingdom court when delivering final judgment, to override any rule of national law found to be in conflict with any directly enforceable rule of Community law'.[66] This means that the passing of the ECA was one of those rare occasions when Parliament has voted to bind further parliaments, which was until then thought not possible under Britain's constitutional arrangements. Given the law lords' decision on Factortame was delivered around the same time Margaret Thatcher was having to consider a further surrender of sovereignty over monetary policy, it is no wonder her sensitivities were heightened.

The decision taken by Mrs Thatcher to let sterling join the ERM was similar to almost every other British decision on Europe. It was postponed as long as possible, and when it did happen, there was far less advantage than there would have been had it happened earlier. Britain joined at the prevailing exchange rate of DM2.95 to the pound, which was unsustainably high. Thatcher gave in to pressure from Hurd, Major and the Labour Party, but entering simply because the PM's resistance had finally collapsed meant there was no real assessment of the downsides of entering at that exact time. What eventually happened (explained in the following chapter) has meant there has been no sensible debate about the benefits of European monetary union ever since.[67]

Having been driven to an action she was so reluctant to endorse, she was determined to take the very next opportunity to show that this defeat did not mean she had caved in to the Delors Report and the single currency. She headed to the European Council in Rome, only to find that the Italians had pushed for a vote on a target date of 1 January 1994 for Stage Two of the Delors plan for monetary union: the bringing together of economic policies centrally. The outcome was the usual eleven to one, and Margaret Thatcher appeared at a press conference afterwards to insist that the Community was 'on the way to cloud-cuckoo land', that the British Parliament would 'never agree to a single currency' and that 'we shall block things which are not in British interests, of course we shall'.[68] This was lapped up by the British tabloid press, with *The Sun* coming up with their famous headline 'UP YOURS DELORS'.

Returning home, she calmed down a little when she reported back to the House of Commons, even admitting in her prepared statement that there was a remote, undesirable yet nonetheless real possibility of Britain joining a single currency, should the people and governments choose that route. Then came the questions, and with no text to hold her down, she resumed her almost lone battle. 'What is being proposed now – economic and monetary union – is the back door to a federal Europe,' she said, having previously turned her rage on the federaliser in chief, Jacques Delors:

> Yes, the Commission wants to increase its powers. Yes, it is a non-elected body and I do not want the Commission to increase its powers at the expense of the House, so of course we differ. The President of the Commission, Mr Delors, said at a press conference the other day that he wanted the European Parliament to be the democratic body of the Community, he wanted the Commission to be the Executive and he wanted the Council of Ministers to be the Senate. No. No. No.[69]

Geoffrey Howe had had enough. He stood up in the Houses of Parliament only days later and delivered his devastating resignation speech. His ultimate contention was that Thatcher's scaremongering was 'minimising our influence and maximising our chances of being once again shut out'.[70] Then, having explained his reasons for resignation, he suggested that 'the time has come for others to consider their own response to the tragic conflict of loyalties with which I have myself wrestled for perhaps too long.'

The following day, Michael Heseltine announced his decision to challenge Thatcher for the leadership. Heseltine had resigned as Defence Minister in 1986 over Thatcher's support for an American company buying Britain's ailing helicopter manufacturer, Westland, instead of his preferred European buyer, and had spent his time on the backbenches writing books and speaking in an unfailingly pro-Europe manner.

Having failed to secure a clear victory on the first ballot, Thatcher reluctantly accepted the advice of her colleagues and withdrew from the contest.[71]

Europe wasn't the only reason Margaret Thatcher lost the support of her party. The economic miracle was failing; the poll tax was a disaster; her authoritarian style of government was alienating colleagues and the public. Opinion polls were also signalling that she was unlikely to lead her party to a fourth election victory. But for many of Thatcher's colleagues, Europe was the main reason she had to go.

The best conclusion to any description of Margaret Thatcher's relationship with Europe is provided by Hugo Young:

> There is straightforward inconstancy: once routinely favouring Europe, she became its passionate enemy. There is more than a touch of dissimulation: though apparently the upholder of the sovereign nation, she acted to increase the collective powers of the Community. There is the preaching of illusion: as Prime Minister she fully understood the interlocking of Britain with Europe, but when she left she flirted with the dream of Britain Alone. There is contradiction: leading Britain further in, she tried to talk Britain further out. And there is incompetence: she lost four senior ministers to the Europe question, a record of instability that culminated in her own eviction.[72]

Margaret Thatcher's shadow loomed large over the 2016 EU referendum. Her battles on the budget implanted in the minds of many the idea that even a penny leaving these shores to go to Brussels is a penny too much, and that the European project's shared resources are in fact abusing 'our money'. The Single Market Act that she championed was one of the largest concessions of sovereignty ever signed off by a British Prime Minister, leading more than any other treaty to the political and economic integration that fuelled the sense of betrayal in many 1975 Yes voters. Her capitulation over the ERM at a time when the rate was fixed at an unsustainably high level led to the exit in 1992 that meant no sensible discussion of joining monetary union could take place in this country. As we are about to find out, her leadership of the group of implacable Conservative Eurosceptics who almost brought down their own government in the years immediately after she resigned created the team of people who were to drive the push for a referendum and then the case for leaving the EU. Finally, her repeated inability to report back from any European meeting with any indication of care for European interests, always framing their achievements solely in Britain's interests, was replicated by every single future Prime Minister. This meant that the Remain campaign's attempts to explain why the EU project was important, why Europe's interests mattered, and why membership of the EU was in Britain's interests, came almost forty years too late.

REASON 7

THE BASTARDS

It was late on the afternoon of Friday 23 July 1993 and Prime Minister John Major had just finished his interview with ITN's Michael Brunson. He was elated but exhausted after coming through one of the most dramatic parliamentary episodes of the past century. The Maastricht Treaty that created the European Union had been ratified, but only after two unruly votes had taken the government to the brink of collapse. All this for a treaty that Major had negotiated and Parliament had previously agreed with massive majorities. To resolve the situation, caused by a large number of rebellious Tories, he had tabled an emergency motion of confidence in the government, making it clear that defeat would lead to a dissolution of Parliament and an immediate general election – the ultimate gamble for any Prime Minister. The Tory rebels had claimed they were acting out of conviction and principle, so John Major offered them a new principle: support the policy upon which they had been elected, or defend their seats in a new election. He had won by thirty-nine votes; the battle of Maastricht was won, although the European policy war was far from over.

After all, three of Major's Cabinet ministers had threatened to resign over this European policy. So, with the interview over and the technicians clearing away their equipment, Brunson asked whether the Prime Minister had thought of replacing them. What Major said next was caught by a 'feed' cable which had carried an earlier interview he had given to the BBC, and which was still switched on. It has gone down in infamy:

> Just think through it from my perspective. You are the Prime Minister, with a majority of eighteen, a party that is still harking back to the golden age that never was and is now invented ... I could bring in other people. But where do you think most of this poison is coming from? From the dispossessed and the

never-possessed. You and I can think of ex-ministers who are causing all sorts of trouble. Do we want three more of the bastards out there?[1]

When Major's words became public knowledge, they caused uproar, and were worn as a badge of courage by those who argued they were fighting Britain's integration with Europe to defend the principle of parliamentary sovereignty. These same 'bastards' never lost their spirit, or their faith, and, although much older by 2016, formed the bedrock of the political support for the Leave campaign.

Part of that bedrock was a previously barely heard-of MEP named Daniel Hannan. He was one of a small group of true Eurosceptic believers who dreamed and schemed of 23 June 2016 for twenty-five years. They worked for little else, with no reward and no sign they would ever prevail. Hannan, it is suggested, contributed more to the ideas, arguments and tactics of Euroscepticism than any other individual – fomenting, protesting, strategising, undermining, writing books, writing speeches and then delivering them without notes.

It was John Major's approval of an early draft of the Maastricht Treaty that first motivated Hannan to found the Oxford Campaign for an Independent Britain at the age of nineteen while in his first term at Oxford. In the spring of 1993, just before he graduated, he wrote offering himself as a researcher to all twenty-two Conservative MPs who had rebelled against the bill to ratify the Maastricht Treaty the previous May, almost bringing down the government. A dozen agreed to form the European Research Group (ERG), with Hannan as its secretary.

The job of the ERG was to keep the European debate alive as part of a lattice of energetic new anti-EU organisations. This became even more important when Tony Blair became Prime Minister in 1997 and, a year later, praised the single currency. Hannan helped to create a single-issue pressure group called Business for Sterling. This set the template, and included some of the key personnel, for the 2016 Leave campaign – its campaign director was a former investment analyst called Dominic Cummings.

Hannan started to understand the mechanics of campaigning and the best way to craft his message. For instance, talking about keeping the pound rather than opposing the euro was 15 per cent more effective in polls. Business for Sterling found language and symbols – like the Queen's head on a fiver – that could touch the nerves of millions of people. Fifteen years later, Cummings would do the same with 'take back control'. Its campaigning helped keep opinion polls set against the euro and deterred the Labour government from joining, or even holding a referendum on whether to do so.

Theresa Villiers, who has been Northern Ireland Secretary and a Minister for Transport in David Cameron's governments, met Hannan when she was an MEP at the time of the Business for Sterling campaign. She claims that Hannan 'radicalised' her during this period, and when it came to the 2016 EU referendum, not only did Villiers campaign for Leave, she played a central role in persuading David Cameron to allow his Cabinet to campaign freely during the referendum. She recalled that 'on the morning of 24 June, I texted Dan congratulating him on changing the course of European history'. Importantly, Villiers is certain that the twenty-five years that Hannan and the band of Eurosceptic, mainly Conservative MPs had spent campaigning against Europe helped them during the campaign.

> Almost at every point I assumed Remain would win. But it certainly did occur to me the disadvantage they had was they had been thinking about this referendum for possibly a year. Whereas people like Dan, it has been their life's work. The whole of their adult working life had been building to this moment.[2]

This is the crucial point. The Maastricht Treaty was first approved as an early draft two weeks after Margaret Thatcher resigned and John Major took over. Its commitments were fully put in place in the middle of 1997, just after Major was defeated by Tony Blair. Therefore, the arguments about it raged over Major's entire premiership. There was something about this treaty that motivated, even radicalised a group of people to fight their leader then and provide the intellectual and political muscle behind the campaign that would lead to Britain voting to leave.

The story of 1990–97 is one of a decent man starting off trying to put Britain at the heart of Europe but ending up with Britain more isolated than ever. It is the story of a Prime Minister trying to accommodate rather than confront the anti-European elements within his party. It is a story of those anti-European elements deciding that they had truly had enough, and would never go away. Europe had involved an organic shift in the nature of the nation-state, breaking with a history that many revered, seeming to imply a threat to the heart and soul of Britishness. Opposing Europe now became for some politicians and campaigners the central purpose of their life.

John Major was born in St Helier, Surrey, and brought up in Brixton, south London. His father was a circus performer before starting a business selling garden gnomes. The family was short of money and Major was short of ambition, leaving school at sixteen to go into clerical work. Meanwhile, the Young Conservatives had captured him, and he became a political junkie, eventually gaining a seat on Lambeth Council. Entering the House of Commons at the age of thirty-six in 1979, he moved quickly up the ministerial pole, starting as a whip, then becoming Minister of State for Social Security. He was efficient and amenable, and soon Margaret Thatcher anointed him 'One of Us' and made him Chief Secretary to the Treasury in 1987. When Geoffrey Howe was sacked as Foreign Secretary and then Nigel Lawson resigned as Chancellor, Mrs Thatcher didn't have to look hard for a capable and deferential replacement.

As Foreign Secretary, he spoke of the need for a 'stronger, more united Western Europe', and asserted that 'our active membership of the Community is a fixed point in our future'.[3] Not burdened with Thatcher's extreme convictions, he actively sought to dissolve differences and heal wounds over Europe. When he became Prime Minister, he began the same mission – to persuade the Conservative Party that there was a middle way between the anti-Europe passions of the vocal minority and the pro-Europe necessities that had become a part of the task of government.

It was Major, as Chancellor, who had convinced Margaret Thatcher to join the ERM. The senior collective at the Treasury had persuaded him the time was right. Sterling had fallen in value by 17 per cent in 1989, making Britain's exports cheaper and imports more expensive, so causing inflation. Major had economics on his side, but he was also aware of the politics of the move. National leaders had decided at the end of 1989 to call an intergovernmental conference to agree changes to the Treaty of Rome needed for a single currency. Joining the ERM would put Britain in a better position to influence this conference, which was eventually held in the otherwise nondescript Dutch town of Maastricht. If Britain didn't take monetary union (EMU) seriously, he minuted Thatcher, Britain would be exiled to the outside of a 'two-tier' Europe. Thatcher thought that Major should not be so concerned about the two tiers 'if the other tier is going in the wrong direction'.[4]

We now know that the pound had risen steadily from 1989, when the decision was taken to join the ERM, until the moment Britain did join in November 1990. It was put into the ERM at DM2.95, meaning the government would have to intervene if it fell below DM2.778. This exchange rate was much higher than any figure reflecting the real competitive relationship between the German and British economies. As we will find, it would cause by itself the loss of the Conservative Party's reputation for economic competence.

The day John Major became Tory leader, he kept a date 200 miles away in a town called Altrincham near Manchester to make a party speech. He said, amongst other things, that he thought Britain should stop shouting from the terraces and start playing on the field of Europe.[5]

In the early months of his premiership, Major's government went about this task with aplomb. In the fog of the war that followed, this short period of time is often forgotten, but it was certainly appreciated by Major's contemporaries in Europe, who were impressed by the change of tone. The Secretary of State for Employment, Michael Howard, met with Vasso Papandreou, the EC Commissioner for Social Affairs, to point out that Britain would accept almost half of her proposed social directives and that it was the only member state to have implemented all eighteen of the social directives already agreed. Norman Lamont, the new Chancellor, stressed that the British were happy to modify their ideas for routes towards monetary union, including coming up with some convergence criteria (criteria a country is required to meet to enter monetary union, including inflation control, similar interest rates, and exchange rate stability), which seemed to imply that Britain could accept they would join an eventual monetary union. Foreign Secretary Douglas Hurd talked of his hope for more foreign policy cooperation at a lecture in Luxembourg.[6] Then Major himself, in a speech given in Bonn, Germany in March 1991, stated: 'My aim for Britain in the Community can be simply stated. I want us to be where we belong. At the very heart of Europe. Working with our partners in building the future.'[7]

This speech stirred the Eurosceptic hornets' nest. The wounds from Margaret Thatcher's departure were still fresh. Her most devoted supporters had convinced themselves that her policy of resisting European integration was the principal cause of her fall, so any change of direction must be opposed. Thatcher herself, unconstrained by office, willingly became a figurehead for hostility to European integration. The Bruges Group had been set up, in homage to the former PM's Bruges speech, and they produced a pamphlet accusing Major of favouring federalism in Europe. The involvement in all this of her old Cabinet ally Nicholas Ridley convinced many that the Bruges Group had become a vehicle for Thatcher's views. Her behaviour during the next seven years is certainly unique. Former Prime Ministers rarely even comment on government policy, let alone do what Thatcher did, which was to actively encourage Conservative MPs to rebel against their own government.

As John Major approached the pivotal Maastricht summit, a problem arose that was to provide grist to the mill of the Eurosceptic case. Even under Margaret Thatcher, the government had accepted that freeing the internal market of the European Community needed to be accompanied by the setting of minimum EC-wide standards on health and safety at work, or employers could try to achieve a competitive advantage by reducing safety standards. Therefore, they accepted during the creation of the Single European Act that there could be majority voting on health and safety issues rather than them needing a unanimous vote. But when the treaty was created, Thatcher had expressed concern that health and safety wasn't closely defined and could be used as a banner under which all kinds of burdens could be put on small businesses. So when Papandreou produced proposals for directives for maximum working hours and maternity rights under the health and safety banner, it seemed Thatcher's concerns had come true. There was actually a move within the Maastricht Treaty to make social affairs as a whole come under majority voting, but this was flatly rejected by the British.[8]

There had been two drafts of the Maastricht Treaty. One was produced by Luxembourg, and proposed a 'European Union' with three pillars – the EC being one, intergovernmental cooperation on justice and home affairs being the second, and intergovernmental cooperation on common foreign and security policy being the third.[9] But when the Dutch assumed the presidency in July 1991, they produced a second draft, and dropped a bombshell, seeming, according to Major:

> to sweep up the nightmares of every anti-European and put them into their text: new powers to decide foreign policy and home affairs at Community level; more authority for the European Court of Justice; power for the European Parliament to overrule decisions taken by sovereign government; more majority voting to decide issues of social affairs, health and education. In short: a United States of Europe.[10]

This was where Major's improved relationships with European leaders helped. Armed with help from German Chancellor Kohl, the Dutch text was seen off. But the simple fact that it had been floated encouraged suspicion amongst Eurosceptics that there was a hidden agenda on European policy. They saw Maastricht as a trap, a now-or-never last chance to exercise a British veto over what would be an irreversible integration. Mrs Thatcher demanded a referendum on a single currency in a speech in Parliament[11] and six Tory MPs voted against the pre-Maastricht declaration of support. Knowing there were constitutional objections to referendums in his Cabinet, Major said no to Thatcher's suggestion, and then saw his predecessor go on television to accuse him of 'arrogance'.

John Major achieved what he thought were significant concessions at the Maastricht summit. Seeing off the Dutch text meant that justice, home affairs, foreign and security policy remained outside the European Commission, Court and Parliament. Britain got references to the 'federal' goal of the European Union removed from the treaty. There was also a reference in the treaty to 'respecting the principle of subsidiarity', which was defined as extending Community competence 'only if and in so far as the objectives of the proposed action cannot be sufficiently achieved by the Member States'.[12] So, it could be said that some infringements of sovereignty had been held off.

There were two more significant victories. Major had made clear in Maastricht that Britain was not ready to enter a single currency, and spoke of his concerns that the economic circumstances had to be right for monetary union to begin. He argued there must be no suggestion of compelling unwilling countries to enter the new currency.[13] Jacques Delors had proposed a formula earlier in 1990 that would allow Britain an 'opt-out' clause on movement to a single currency, giving any member the right to consult its national parliament before adopting a single currency. In the end, Britain got this 'opt-out' clause written into the new treaty[14] but it referred specifically to Britain, once again isolating it as the awkward partner in the Community, and risking lower investment in Britain in future due to the uncertainty over whether it would join the single currency. Other member states were not prepared to accept a general opt-out provision because they wanted to tie the Germans into future monetary union, without which the whole project would collapse.

The opt-out from the single currency was in the end a smooth victory. The second opt-out that John Major won, from joining the 'Social Chapter', was not. The Social Chapter, extending majority voting to a much fuller range of social affairs, was problematic to the Tory government, who saw it as a chance for Europe to place more burdens on British companies. Major felt that the Social Chapter would reverse the reforms to the labour market that the Conservatives had spent years fighting for (such as making it more flexible in terms of hiring and firing and the ability to respond to changes in demand, as well as reducing trade union power), and would push up unemployment. He knew the Tories would face accusations of being in favour of 'low wages' and 'sweated labour', but he believed British workers were better off in jobs than on the dole. Major was attacked for his position by many on the left, including French Socialist President François Mitterrand, but stuck to his line firmly enough that the Social Chapter was removed altogether from the main text and added as a protocol to the treaty.[15]

That said, Major also made numerous concessions. The French had put in a starting date for the single currency of 1 January 1999, meaning that if Britain ratified the treaty, they were officially recognising not just that it would happen, but when. The existence of any social chapter at all was a concession, meaning that majority voting in the Council of Ministers *was* extended over quite a few more areas than before Maastricht. Eurosceptics felt that monetary union should have been vetoed completely, and knew that an opt-out could be easily ended by a future government (they were correct in terms of the Social Chapter, which Tony Blair signed up to as soon as Labour took power). The European Parliament was also given significant new powers, and the treaty established a new 'citizenship of the European Union', which gave every citizen *the right to move and reside freely within the territory of the Member States*.[16] This enshrined freedom of movement even further into the European constitution, meaning that there could be no discrimination at all in a member state against a citizen of another member state. This applied in particular to the jobs market – a major advance on the freedom of movement principle in the 1957 Treaty of Rome.

Finally, there was an official name change – from the European Community to the European Union. It all seemed, according to the academic and former MEP Andrew Duff, to suggest the 'existence of a common popular sovereignty to complement – or rival – the common sovereignty of the states'.[17] It wasn't going to stop, either, because the treaty committed the EU states to a further IGC in 1996 to examine how well it was working and suggest further institutional reform.[18]

When he returned to London, the pro-Conservative newspapers immediately took up the claim of the Downing Street press office that it was 'game, set and match' to the Prime Minister. In the Commons debate on Maastricht on 18–19 December, Conservative MPs were similarly adulatory, and in a vote only seven MPs opposed the treaty, with three (including Thatcher) abstaining. The Prime Minister's foreign policy advisor, Percy Cradock, felt that, given the government's aims in the Maastricht talks, 'It is difficult to see what more could have been done ... and a certain triumphalism ... could be excused.'[19]

Yet neither Major's pro-European nor his anti-European critics were satisfied. The former observed that the 'two-tier' Europe Major had warned Thatcher about in early 1990 had become a reality. The latter couldn't help noticing that while Major was lauding the intergovermentalism of the three-pillar structure and his 'opt-outs', playing down the supranational elements of the Maastricht Treaty, Jacques Delors had other ideas. He was telling the European Parliament that very same day that the Maastricht Treaty had relaunched the Community, emphasising the significance of the decision to proceed to monetary union. He went on to talk up the federalist aspects of the treaty and repeated this to the European media. Bells started to ring across Europe, particularly loudly, and in tones of warning, in the heads of the British Eurosceptics.

What happened next has to be put into the domestic political context. A recession had begun at the end of 1990 and tightened its grip throughout 1991. Although the stabilising effect of membership of the ERM was beginning to lower inflation, unemployment rose from 1.8 million to 2.6 million and output fell by almost 2 per cent. Somehow, in the midst of all this, and helped by some serious misjudgements by the Labour Party, John Major managed to win the 1992 general election. He gained the highest number of votes any political party leader has ever achieved, despite the economy being mired in recession during the campaign.

However, his parliamentary majority fell from eighty-eight to twenty-one. Throughout the next parliament, the Conservatives lost every by-election that was held, meaning that by the time of the 1997 general election, the government actually held a minority in the Commons. This made it particularly susceptible to pressure from its backbenches. Facing this down required strong leadership, but Major was not a strong leader, and he also presided over a fractious and divided Cabinet. What happened in the next five years was that European policy was conducted against a domestic background of an internally divided government, with an increasingly precarious parliamentary majority, which was unpopular in the country and subject, as time went by, to numerous scandals and misfortunes.[20]

Hostility to the EU was shared by longstanding backbenchers like Bill Cash and Teddy Taylor, the former Prime Minister and many of her colleagues, such as Peter Lilley, but it was also shared by some younger Cabinet ministers such as Michael Portillo and John Redwood, along with the Home Secretary, Michael Howard. It was Portillo, Howard and Lilley whom Major is widely thought to have referred to as the 'bastards'. Lilley is unapologetic, arguing that 'it was only because of "bastards" like me that he secured his greatest triumph which was securing an opt-out from the Euro'.[21]

Peter Lilley has a wider point, which is that little time has been spent investigating and understanding the key arguments of those who chose to rebel against their Prime Minister and risk bringing down their government.

John Biffen was a Cabinet minister for eight years under Margaret Thatcher, but back in 1972 he had voted against the 1972 European Communities Act more times than any other Tory. Biffen's core motivation was his belief in the nation as the only entity capable of commanding popular authority. He carried in his wallet a quotation from Charles de Gaulle's memoirs:

> Now what are the realities of Europe? What are the pillars on which it can be built? The truth is that those pillars are the states of Europe … states each of which, indeed, has its own genius, history and language, its own sorrows, glories and ambitions; but states that are the only entities with the right to give orders and the powers to be obeyed.[22]

By 1992, as a backbench elder statesman, Biffen saw himself as teacher and strategist of the rebels, the 'Fagin of Euroscepticism'.[23]

A fellow elder statesman of the time was Teddy Taylor, who fought the Heath application to the EC on the grounds of what it meant for national independence, leaving the government on account of it, and never got back into government through the Thatcher years due to his anti-Europeanism.

Bill Cash had started his professional life as a lawyer, and prided himself on his Euro-awareness from a legal point of view. In the run-up to Britain joining the

EC, he had been warning his law partners to remember that the Treaty of Rome would become a superior law, with the European Court of Justice handing down superior judgments. He even wrote to the President of the Law Society and the Prime Minister to try to make solicitors realise that course studies in European law for solicitors' exams was an absolute fundamental.[24] Once in Parliament in 1984, he was quickly taken onto the Select Committee for European Legislation. 'It was then that I realised what was really going on. The European Community was in danger of rapidly becoming a political federation.'[25] Although he voted the 1986 Single European Act through, he can be found expressing alarm about what it meant, telling the Commons that: 'It is essential to maintain the democracy of this house and its sovereignty and to ensure that we do know that the legislation done in our name is known to have been done on behalf of the people of this country.'[26]

Ultimately, the Eurosceptics were pretty powerless during the late 1980s and very early 1990s, partly out of wilful submission to their trust in Margaret Thatcher's vigilant leadership, but also because of the size of the Conservative Party's majority. But they were responsible for John Major's election as leader, as the most Eurosceptic of the alternatives. Then, in April 1992, they had a government with a majority of twenty-one (so their opposition mattered numerically as well as rhetorically), and a target, the Maastricht Treaty.

The problem with the Maastricht Treaty for the now growing band of Eurosceptics was that even with the opt-outs negotiated by John Major, Maastricht was a watershed. The opt-outs would not prevent the treaty from existing. The only way to stop the creation of a European Central Bank, the introduction of EU citizenship, the framing of a common defence policy, the single institutional framework for matters of justice and home affairs and other diminutions of borders and nation state powers was not to ratify the treaty. Just in case it needed to be clear what the Maastricht Treaty meant, Helmut Kohl helpfully clarified in April 1992 by saying that:

In Maastricht we laid the foundation-stone for the completion of the European Union. The European Union Treaty introduces a new and decisive stage in the process of European union which within a few years will lead to the creation of what the founding fathers of modern Europe dreamed of after the last war: the United States of Europe.[27]

So, for the Eurosceptics, it was now or never.

For Bill Cash and his band of rebel Eurosceptics, the irrevocability of the scheme was the ultimate reason it had to be stopped. The opt-outs would be of modest consequence, the treaty would affect every European Union member, becoming a baseline against which every country would be obliged to measure its real independence. Britain would have to travel on or risk exclusion from the engine room of the train.[28]

Vote Leave chair Gisela Stuart, in an interview for this book, sums up what motivated the 'bastards', Dan Hannan and so many others to begin their fight to stop the ratification of Maastricht and, once that happened, to leave the European Union. She argues that 'the referendum in 2016 was the logical consequence of the Maastricht Treaty'. The creation of a single currency which Britain was not willing to be part of meant that 'the notion of a two-speed Europe was for the birds, because two-speed implies the same destination – but at that moment you had a two-destination Europe'. As we will find out in a later chapter, Stuart believes that no 'architecture' was created that allowed for a two-destination Europe, so whoever was outside the euro was for all purposes outside the European Union.

So, if the Conservative leadership wouldn't use their power of veto, perhaps Parliament could be made to use it instead. Rejecting the legislation could bring the entire Community venture to a halt.

The Maastricht Treaty (now called the Treaty of the European Union, or TEU for short) was formally signed on 7 February 1992. It was not ratified by Britain until 2 August 1993, as the Eurosceptics in Parliament turned the battle over Europe into all-out war. It had been decided not to attempt a pre-election ratification because two months would not have been enough time. So when 21 May 1992 came around, and the Maastricht ratification bill passed its second reading by 376 votes to 92, it escaped few people's notice that twenty-two Tory MPs voted against it. Labour had officially abstained, so the government won securely. As long as Labour continued to abstain, there would be no problem.

Then, a referendum in Denmark saw the TEU defeated. It was by a narrow margin, but it unleashed Europe-wide doubts over the future of the project. Britain's Eurosceptics argued that since the TEU needed to be ratified by all the governments to enter into force, it was now effectively dead. Margaret Thatcher led calls for a referendum on the TEU, which she described as 'a treaty too far', then said she would vote against ratification in her first speech in the House of Lords.[29] Under pressure, Major suspended the ratification process. But François Mitterrand had other ideas. He decided to risk his political reputation on a referendum in France on the treaty.[30]

The trouble was that the French too had their doubts about the growing powers of the European Community. As evidence grew that the French might vote against Maastricht, the whole EMU project looked in question, and the money markets started to sell several European currencies that were part of the ERM, including sterling.

Suddenly, it looked like sterling would fall out of the bottom of its ERM band. Germany's interest rates were necessarily high as they needed to borrow to finance their reunification. This meant that to keep sterling within the banding, the British government would have to raise interest rates in the teeth of a recession, which could cause further unemployment, or borrow money to buy pounds and keep up sterling's value. There was talk of realigning currencies (another word for devaluation), but that would undermine the whole purpose of ERM, which was to have currency stability. Both Major – politely – and Lamont – far less politely – tried to get the Germans to lower their interest rates or devalue their own currency, but the Germans were not prepared to do either, thinking both inappropriate for their current economic situation. Eventually, this strategy was given up, too, not helped by the Bundesbank President Helmut Schlesinger publicly hinting that sterling should be devalued.[31] Sarah Hogg, head of John Major's policy unit, was on a walking tour of Scotland before the days of mobile phones so had to find a police phone box to call Major. With the two constables listening in, she had to be careful. So she said, 'Prime Minister, I don't think we can rely on the Germans,' at which point the two constables were heard saying, 'Dead right!'[32]

On 16 September 1992, with currency speculators like George Soros frantically short-selling the pound (he made over £1 billion selling pounds he didn't own and buying them back at a lower price), Norman Lamont raised interest rates from 10 per cent to 12 per cent to 15 per cent. £3.3 billion was spent trying to shore up sterling. Eventually, though, Major and Lamont had to give in, the latter announcing Britain had 'suspended' its membership of the ERM. In the background of the TV shot that evening, as Lamont announced this, was one of his advisors, a certain David Cameron.

16 September 1992 became known as 'Black Wednesday', *the* turning point

of the Major premiership. It crippled the Conservatives' claim to be the party of sound economic management, it provoked grave popular dissatisfaction with Major and it gave Eurosceptics wind in their sails. They came to call the day 'White Wednesday'. Margaret Thatcher had been proved right on the ERM, and from that moment on there has rarely been any possibility of sensible discussion about monetary union in Britain. This despite the fact that the single currency could have been an answer to the problems of the ERM, as there would be no currency fluctuation within the EU at all, which was in the end the way the French went on the matter. The whole event soured relationships with Germany, which had been important to the success of EC diplomacy, not helped by Major and Lamont openly blaming them for what had happened. John Major summed it up by saying that leaving the ERM was 'a political and economic calamity. It unleashed havoc in the Conservative Party and it changed the political landscape of Britain. On that day, a fifth Conservative victory, which always looked unlikely unless the opposition were to self-destruct, became remote if not impossible.'[33]

The irony of it all is that with the pound falling to DM2.30, Britain's exports became cheaper. Demand rose and, free from the strictures of the ERM, interest rates could fall, helping growth immensely. Many have argued that being in the ERM had finally squeezed inflation out of the British economic system, and from 1992 to 1997, Britain had on average 3 per cent growth while inflation remained under 3 per cent. The economy improved in reverse correlation to the popularity of the Conservatives until 1997, when Labour took over with a massive majority and a thriving economy to back their plans.

Nobody, least of all the Eurosceptics, would have known that would happen at the Conservative Party conference in 1992. Foreign Secretary Douglas Hurd reached back into history, pointing out that splits in the Conservative Party had kept the Tories out of a majority government for twenty-eight years (following the 1846 Corn Laws) and seventeen years (thanks to 1903 tariff reform), and begged the party to not do the same over Europe. But then former party chairman Norman Tebbit stood up and asked the conference three questions: 'Do you want to be citizens of the European Union? Do you want to see a single currency? Do you want to let other countries decide Britain's immigration policy?' The answer to which from the audience was a resounding 'No'![34]

But John Major was not prepared to undermine the treaty, nor to support its amendment. On 25 June 1992, he had told Parliament that:

The Maastricht Treaty was negotiated in good faith by all member states. I have no intention of breaking the word of the British Government that was given on that occasion; nor do I have any intention of compromising what we agreed on that occasion and wrecking this country's reputation for plain and honest dealing and good faith.[35]

Major decided to revive the ratification of the TEU in November 1992. But thanks to a rebellion of twenty-six MPs, the government could only muster a majority of three, and to get that, Major had to promise that final ratification would not take place until after the second Danish referendum. There were two issues arising. Having abstained in May, the Labour Party now saw a possible opportunity to oust the Conservative government and make their feelings clear about Major having opted out of the Social Chapter. The second issue was that it turned out that Margaret Thatcher had been meeting with backbenchers to encourage them to vote against the treaty the next chance they had, to overturn the policy of her successor that had been a manifesto commitment in a successful election held six months before.

Before the next vote, the committee stage of the bill involved some 210 hours' debate spread over twenty-three days, and the consideration of more than 600 amendments. On 17 May 1993, the second Danish referendum resulted in a clear victory in favour of the TEU. Major had arranged for the Danes to be given some of their own opt-outs at the Edinburgh Council in December 1992. A week after the Danish result, Parliament voted. Forty-one Conservatives rebelled and five abstained, but still Major managed to win. He had got Labour to back him by promising they would have a separate vote on the opt-out of the Social Chapter.

This vote took place on 22 July 1993. Labour were united in voting against the government's policy of having an opt-out, while some Conservative sceptics realised that however much they detested the Chapter itself, voting with Labour to approve their amendment might mean the whole TEU would have to be rejected by the government. Labour's amendment to give notice that they intended to adopt the Social Chapter in future was voted on first, resulting in a tie at 317 to 317. Then the government's motion to have the opt-out was voted on, and the government lost that vote by 316 to 324, meaning in theory that the government could not proceed with its policy of not adopting the Social Chapter.

At this point, John Major felt he needed to reassert his authority over the House. The European Communities Amendment Act, ratifying the Maastricht Treaty, had been given royal assent two days earlier, on 20 July. Furthermore, he had intimated at Prime Minister's Questions that day that he would ratify it even if the government lost the amendment vote on the Social Chapter.[36]

So, he decided to call a vote of confidence on the policy for the following day. He still had a majority in the House, and he knew that the Conservative Eurosceptics would fear electoral annihilation if the vote was lost and Major went to the country, with Labour currently 20 per cent ahead in the opinion polls.[37] It was that evening that the fateful interview with Michael Brunson ended with Major seeming to have called three of his Eurosceptic Cabinet ministers 'bastards'.

The ratification of the Maastricht Treaty signalled only the end of one stage in John Major's difficulties over Europe. His Eurosceptic rebels were given solid support from the jingoistic and frequently xenophobic popular press. Even though they had lost the battle over Maastricht, the key arguments used to back an accusation of betrayal by Major centred on security, prosperity and sovereignty, which the Eurosceptics believed had lain at the heart of Conservative electoral success since 1979. The EU was being taken over by Continental federalists who were using every opportunity to force Britain into unwanted further integration. Therefore, Britain should not just say 'No' to that, but to try to 'repatriate' powers that had already been transferred.[38]

To try to placate them, Major tended to throw them some regular bones, some of them with plenty of red meat on them. Later in 1993, he wrote an article in *The Economist* with a strident insularity little different from the Bruges speech of Mrs Thatcher:

> It is clear now that the Community will remain a union of sovereign national states … We have opposed the centralising idea. We take some convincing on any proposal from Brussels. For us, the nation state is here to stay … The plain fact is that economic and monetary union is not realisable in present circumstances and therefore not relevant to our economic difficulties … I hope my fellow heads of government will resist the temptation to recite the mantra of full economic and monetary union as if nothing had changed. If they do recite it, it will have all the quaintness of a rain dance and about the same potency.[39]

To this burst of chauvinism dictated by domestic pressures can be added two others: the first occurred because Sweden, Finland, Austria and at the time Norway were joining the EU. More member states meant there would have to be new rules over majority voting. At the time, under QMV it required twenty-three out of seventy-six votes to block a proposal; the EU wanted this changed to twenty-seven out of ninety. This was seen as a proportional increase, but the UK saw that they'd need to get more votes if they needed to stop legislation passing through the EU Commission. So they opposed the change in the number of votes needed. Major was warned by the Commission that enlargement was being threatened by his actions. Ministers from the enlargement countries were furious that their membership might be delayed. Some Labour Party MPs used the issue as a stick to stir divisions in the Conservative Party, with Giles Radice asking Major: 'Which is more important to the Prime Minister – a blocking minority of twenty-three on qualified majority votes to the Council of Ministers, or an enlargement of the European Union?' Major retorted by accusing the Labour leader John Smith (who, remember, hadn't even asked him the question) of being 'the man who likes to say yes in Europe – Monsieur Oui, the poodle of Brussels'.[40]

Eventually, at a meeting of Foreign Ministers in Ioannina in Greece, Douglas Hurd was presented with a take-it-or-leave-it deal that would raise the blocking vote to twenty-seven, but allow a delay in any legislation objected to by two large countries and one small country. The UK capitulated. It was, as author and former EC negotiator Roy Denman calls it, 'the most humiliating diplomatic climbdown in post-war British history'.[41]

In July 1994, Major decided to single-handedly veto the choice of the eleven other member states for the next President of the European Commission: Belgian Prime Minister Jean-Luc Dehaene. The Belgian was, Major claimed, too federalist and too centralising. Instead, he wanted Jacques Santer from Luxembourg as Commission President. He won, and Santer showed from his very first day that he in fact was the more committed federalist of the two. After all, this was the man responsible for the successful launch of the euro, who saw through preparations for the largest enlargement the EU has ever had, and even worked, together with the then Luxembourg Prime Minister Jean-Claude Juncker (wonder what happened to him?) to try to involve the European Union in the campaign to create jobs, by using EU money to fund training schemes and employment creation schemes in member states.[42]

In June 1994, there had been elections to the European Parliament. The Conservatives ran on a manifesto entitled 'A Strong Britain in a Strong Europe', adopting a distinctly nationalistic tone. The outcome was the worst vote proportion – 27.8 per cent – they had obtained in a nationwide poll in the twentieth century, and a cut from thirty-two to eighteen seats. In the middle of the campaign, Major had spoken of the advantages of a 'multi-speed and multi-track Europe':

> I have never believed that Europe must invariably act as one on every issue. Trying to make every country conform to every plan is a socialist way of thinking; it's not for us. I don't happen to think that it threatens Europe if member states are free to do some things in their own way and at their own speed.[43]

None of this was working. Whatever John Major said or did, however much he thumped his tub on the European stage, he could do nothing to staunch the flow of bile around and out of the Tory Party. It seemed as if appeasing them just left them wanting more, and not even punishing them was working – Major had withdrawn the whip from eight diehard sceptics in November 1994 after they had voted against an EU finance bill despite being told it was a vote of confidence. Clearly, it had had little effect.

So then he decided he owed the Eurosceptics the opportunity to dispose of him. On 22 June 1995, he walked onto the Downing Street lawn and announced that he had resigned as leader of the Conservative Party and would stand as a candidate in a leadership election, offering his enemies the chance to 'put up or shut up'.[44] Unfortunately for the Eurosceptics, the best they could put up was John Redwood. Despite gaining support from the prominent Eurosceptics (including the group now called the 'whipless' eight), despite having the tacit approval of Margaret Thatcher (who refused to endorse John Major when asked to) and despite the Eurosceptic press coming out in force with headlines such as 'Redwood vs Deadwood', the truth was Redwood was not the right person. He had the appearance of a Vulcan from *Star Trek*, the otherworldly intellectualism of the policy wonk that he had been under Thatcher, and his alternative programme was more eccentric than substantial. So Major won by 218 votes to 89, and the Conservative government entered what was now its terminal phase.[45]

As the 1996 Intergovernmental Conference in Turin to launch the review of the Maastricht Treaty and agree any further institutional changes approached, scientists confirmed a possible link between 'mad cow disease' (bovine spongiform encephalopathy – BSE for short) and its human equivalent – Creutzfeldt-Jakob disease (CJD for short). BSE had caused many countries around the world, including America and even the British colony of Hong Kong, to ban beef imports from Britain. But now the EU quickly decided to protect their consumers by banning beef from Britain too.

When the Turin IGC began, the Europeans promised Major financial help to destroy the cattle involved. Major took a different line. He chose to attack the beef ban as 'collective hysteria' and threatened all sorts of retaliation, including a counter-ban on European meat products and 'empty chairing' the conference. In the end, he announced a policy of 'non-cooperation' with Europe, with British ministers blocking as many as seventy measures, including some against EU fraud which they themselves had promoted. When he gave in to a deal in Florence involving a partial lifting of the ban as long as EU vets could invigilate and approve the accompanying cattle-slaughter programme, the media and his political opponents ridiculed him yet again for his retreat and ineffectualness.[46] Twenty years later, the Eurosceptics who were around back in 1996 had to have a giggle when the Remain campaign's umbrella organisation was christened 'Britain Stronger in Europe' – or BSE for short.

Britain was no longer at the heart of the single currency debate, as it had opted out, although it was still in limbo over the matter. There were increasing demands on the government to either reject membership or hold a referendum. They had to take a position eventually, as Sir James Goldsmith was threatening to spend £20 million on a campaign to run Referendum Party candidates in all constituencies in the next election. Goldsmith wanted a referendum on Britain's place in Europe as a whole; instead, Major promised that, if he won the next election, he would hold a referendum on the euro.

Even that wasn't enough. On 6 December 1996, the government finally lost its Commons majority. At a bitter Cabinet meeting on 19 December, ministers insisted on a discussion on whether British membership of the euro should be definitely ruled out, resulting in the official government policy changing to a 'wait-and-see' approach. This was based upon it being unlikely, in their view, that enough economic convergence would have taken place for the euro to begin on 1 January 1999. Even if it were achieved, Britain would not be part of it. As the election campaign started in early April, government ministers were issuing election material opposing the single currency.[47]

When the polls closed on 1 May 1997, the Conservatives won only 165 seats and Labour had a majority of 179. It was the worst Conservative performance since universal suffrage was introduced.

During John Major's time as Prime Minister, the British had made themselves pretty much detested and certainly ignored by the same leaders he had started his premiership wanting to join 'at the very heart of Europe'.

Meanwhile, the Eurosceptic 'bastards' got to go away to the safety of opposition, in which they no longer had to be involved in the compromises of government, and plan their comeback. The Maastricht Treaty had been ratified, the European Community was now the European Union, the euro was about to become a reality, and the same problems of sovereignty still remained.

What happened in the next thirteen years was that another chemical was added to this already toxic mixture. A decision was to be made, without input from the electorate, that brought 3 million people to the country. It would galvanise the Eurosceptic movement like no other.

REASON 8

POLISH PLUMBERS

Prime Minister Gordon Brown was having a walkabout in the northern Labour heartland of Rochdale in the middle of the 2010 general election campaign. Towards the end of it he was accosted by a 65-year-old widow named Gillian Duffy. A lifelong Labour supporter, she had worked for her local council for thirty years, but her support for the party was wavering. Getting Brown's attention, she launched into a litany of issues she had, beginning with the size of the national debt, running through how difficult it was for the truly vulnerable to get benefits and for her grandchildren to afford university. In amongst all this was a question about immigration: 'All these Eastern Europeans what are coming in, where are they flocking from?' Brown handled the questions calmly, even managing to turn Mrs Duffy around to saying she would vote Labour and was happy with how he had answered her. He then got into his car to be driven to a radio studio for a BBC interview. Brown's Sky News microphone was still on, however, and the conversation was recorded and then broadcast. 'That was a disaster. Should never have put me with that woman ... whose idea was that?' he asked his team. They asked him what she had said that made the conversation, in his words, 'ridiculous', and Brown said: 'Ugh, everything – she's just a sort of bigoted woman, said she used to be Labour. It's just ridiculous.'

To the 2016 EU referendum Leave campaign, no story better exemplified the contempt with which the political class had held anyone who stated concerns about immigration during the thirteen years of New Labour's reign. Also, no story better exemplified the way the political class can be charm personified in public but dismissive and insulting in private. Brown's comments were replayed to him once he was at the radio studio and a fixed camera showed him bury his head in his hands as he heard them. Although he went back to Rochdale to apologise to Gillian Duffy, the damage was done. The BBC's political editor,

Nick Robinson, noted that Brown had 'insulted one of the very type of voter it's so vital for his party to hang on to – older, white and traditional Labour'.[1]

We know now that Labour didn't hang on to older, white, traditional voters. We also know that they lost younger, white, traditional voters, both at general election time and also in the 2016 EU referendum, and particularly outside London. But Brown wasn't to blame by himself. The rot had started a long time before.

Some historians date it to the 1964–70 Harold Wilson-led governments who liberalised the country socially without focusing on the socialist objective to help the working class. Some date it to the 1976–79 Jim Callaghan government who accepted a loan from the International Monetary Fund then instituted crippling tax rises and public spending cuts to meet their conditions, falling out with the trade unions in the process. Some think that Margaret Thatcher attracted many working-class voters by offering them the right to buy their council houses as well as a route to riches if they happened to possess the skills, motivation and wherewithal to take advantage of opportunities. The disappointment traditional voters felt about Tony Blair's Labour government's lost chance to create a socialist utopia left many working-class voters looking for another political home. But the final straw was probably the decision to let in 3 million immigrants, many of them from the new Eastern European accession countries to the EU. Labelling those who complained about it as racists or bigots didn't help.

Tony Blair was born in 1953, and matured when the Second World War was becoming a distant memory. His father, Leo Blair, was chairman of the Durham Conservative Association. The son, harbouring more progressive and social democratic views, gravitated towards Labour. We remember Blair as being pro-Europe, but he entered Parliament at the age of thirty on the back of a Labour manifesto that had said 'withdrawal from the Community is the right policy for Britain',[2] the very same election that brought Jeremy Corbyn to the Commons for the first time. By the time Blair became a shadow Cabinet minister, Labour's position had changed, driven by Neil Kinnock, their leader from 1983 to 1992, and inspired by Jacques Delors's TUC speech in 1988 which had marked the EC out as an alternative route to socialism. From 1992 under John Smith and 1994 under Blair's leadership, Labour stood apart from the European issue that was tearing their political opponents apart. They kept unity on the issue as they saw a way to bring the government down by voting against the Maastricht Treaty on the principle of wanting to sign up to the Social Chapter from the start.

'The Third Way' was the ideological background to what would be known as 'New Labour'. Not expressly socialist (Blair rewrote 'Clause IV' of the Labour Party constitution to remove the commitment to nationalisation of the means of production), the Third Way aimed to harness the best of the Thatcherite freeing of markets with social democratic help for the vulnerable.[3] As it became clearer that Labour would be in government after the next election, Blair started to set out his new programme, which included working with the grain of globalisation rather than against it.[4] That incorporated running with the grain of Europe too.

In a speech in 1995, Blair set out a position that 'the drift towards isolation in Europe must stop and be replaced by a policy of constructive engagement'. Europe could be criticised, but not in an anti-European atmosphere. Britain 'should set about building the alliances within Europe that enable our influence to grow'. He then went to Bonn in Germany and said: 'If we do not now make persuasion the condition for moving forward, then the initiative will pass to those hostile to the whole project of Europe.' This made clear to the Europeans that if Labour won they could expect something better than the impotent posturing of John Major, while making it clear to the British that the national birth right would be safe in his hands.[5] As a summary of what came next over the ten years of Tony Blair's time in power, followed by the three years of Gordon Brown, there is little better.

Before Blair, the normal British approach to Europe had been to say there was no need to interfere with European institutions; instead, the policies (like the CAP) should be improved. This served Britain badly, as the European institutions *did* need reform in order to adjust to enlargement, to reflect the evolution of the union and to adjust to new priorities like crime and terrorism. As we have found throughout this story, in the minds of most of its members the EU is an unfinished project, which always needs developing. If a Prime Minister goes into treaty revisions with a purely defensive agenda, they give an image of Britain as grumpy and negative but they also miss the opportunity to shape Europe. Tony Blair arrived with a majority of 179 and with a modernising agenda putting Europe at the heart of Britain as much as the other way round. As Simon Berlaymont, a pseudonymous writer with extensive professional knowledge of the inner workings of the European Union, pointed out, Blair 'was the first Prime Minister from the post-war generation; his memories were not of defending Britain against evil Germans and assisting the feckless French'. He had built New

Labour on respect for German social policy and French economic success. He spoke French well and had built good relationships on the Continent.[6]

Yet, balancing the good European that Blair was, on the other shoulder was always the shadowy figure of Rupert Murdoch. In 1995, Blair had accepted an invitation to address Murdoch's News Corporation conference on Hayman Island in Australia. Murdoch owned highly influential British newspapers such as *The Sun* and *The Times*. Labour's surprise 1992 general election loss had been attributed by some (most of all Murdoch) to *The Sun*'s vicious campaign against Neil Kinnock. Blair's view was that if the country's most powerful newspaper proprietor, whose publications have hitherto been rancorous in their opposition to the Labour Party, invites you into the lion's den, 'You go, don't you?'[7]

The discussions that went on between the two men in Australia have never been properly examined, and probably never will be. Even though *The Sun*'s support for Labour in the 1997 election was a significant factor in their victory, many Labour MPs call whatever they agreed a 'Faustian pact'. Professor David McKnight, in his book *Murdoch's Politics*, says that 'from the very start of Murdoch's support of Blair, he was explicit that he wanted assurances that a Labour government would not favour further integration into Europe'. Blair wrote an article for *The Sun*'s then 10 million readers, saying: 'Let me make my position on Europe absolutely clear. I will have no truck with a European super state. If there are moves to create that dragon I will slay it.' Professor McKnight believes that Murdoch wanted more than chest-puffing language:

> The key device by which Murdoch blocked any British move into Europe was his insistence on a commitment from Blair that he would call a referendum before joining European monetary union. This would mean fighting out the issue in a public campaign in which Murdoch's popular newspapers would be at their loudest and most influential.[8]

Thus, it is just about impossible to find a single occasion where Blair made or wrote an unashamedly pro-European speech or article promoting and explaining the European ideal to the British public. Instead, European integration continued apace with the British public in blissful ignorance of the idealism behind it. EU membership has always been explained to Britons as a cost–benefit decision, purely pragmatic. Therefore, it is judged purely on pragmatic, cost–benefit terms. In Tony Blair, the country had the most pro-European Prime Minister since Edward Heath, *and* he was a great communicator, unlike Edward Heath. This was a chance to properly sell Europe as an ideal to the British people, and it was lost due to domestic political pressures that inhibited the Prime Minister even through eight years of massive Commons majorities.

This explains some of the policy decisions on Europe that Blair made, and perhaps his constant appointment of Eurosceptics like Robin Cook and Jack Straw to the position of Foreign Secretary. It also explains why his autobiography contains so little about Europe. He boiled it down to this:

> In general terms, for me, Europe was a simple issue. It was to do with the modern world. I supported the European idea, but even if I hadn't, it was utterly straightforward in a world of new emerging powers. Britain needed Europe in order to exert influence and advance its interests. It wasn't complicated. It wasn't a psychiatric issue. It was a question of realpolitik.[9]

What followed over the first five years or so of Blair's premiership were some extremely positive exchanges with his European counterparts where his constructive approach was rewarded with a variety of small but significant concessions. The key issue for Europe at the end of the 1990s was to be perhaps its greatest success, and Tony Blair helped achieve it. Yet how he achieved it influenced the number of people who voted to leave the EU in the 2016 referendum.

Perhaps the most astonishing achievement of the European Union was how it extended its community of law and democracy more widely into Central and Eastern Europe. The transformation of those countries into market economies and stable democracies is without precedent. History, both recent and not-so-recent, suggests that revolutions like the one that overthrew Communist Russia in 1989 normally bring with them violence and authoritarian rulers like Pol Pot, Lenin and Ayatollah Khomeini. What a difference it made for the eight countries that joined the EU in 2004 and the next two that joined in 2007 that they had a community of democracies close at hand and able and willing to help. The prospect of EU membership, backed up by NATO protection, offered sufficient motivation for them to create and sustain the institutions needed and the respect for the rule of law and human rights that was required.[10]

In order for this to happen, the European Union needed to adjust its own institutions. This resulted in the 1999 Treaty of Amsterdam, and the 2003 Treaty of Nice. The process wasn't completed in 1997 because, even after over a year of negotiations, too many issues remained on the table. Not, for once, because of British objections, but because of German ones, fuelled by domestic political concerns.

An organisation that was soon to have twenty-seven members would need to extend majority voting into far more areas – such as employment, social exclusion and data protection. The driving force was an acceptance that unanimous voting was almost unworkable amongst twenty-seven countries unless the issue was of particular national sensitivity. Two further measures were included to improve EU flexibility: first, the concept of 'constructive abstention' was added – where a member state could opt out of certain commitments on security and foreign affairs without stopping other members from continuing. Second, there was the possibility of 'enhanced cooperation', allowing some members to cooperate more closely on areas outside the remit of the EU treaties which other members didn't want to take part in. It was also agreed for there to be a stronger role for the European Parliament, which would have to agree with decisions made by the EU Council of Ministers on far more matters than before – a procedure called 'co-decision'.[11]

Even though the key conference for Amsterdam took place only six weeks after Labour's May 1997 general election victory, Britain was able to play a constructive role in the discussion. Labour had been given access to civil servants for the month before the election under the traditional convention whereby an opposition party has meetings with civil servants to prepare Whitehall and the possible future government for a change of party in office. During those meetings, particular time had been given to the contribution they wanted to make to the Amsterdam process. More importantly, the election manifesto had committed the new Labour government to a number of constitutional changes, including devolution for the Scottish and Welsh Assemblies, changes to the House of Lords and the introduction of proportional representation voting for the European Parliament elections (in line with other countries). Making institutional reforms to the EU was simply part of their general constitutional change programme, and held no fears for them.

Blair also won a few important concessions during the conference. He did this by signing the EU Social Chapter, which extended majority voting to some areas of social policy, such as equal opportunities and working conditions – meaning, in effect, that all member states would be obliged to implement laws passed in Europe in these areas. During the 2016 referendum campaign, socialist campaigners argued that staying in the EU would protect these laws, safeguarding workers' rights. John Major had negotiated an opt-out for Britain during the Maastricht Treaty process (see Reason 7), which had caused the Social Chapter as a whole to be annexed to that treaty in a protocol instead of being included within the treaty proper. Major had asked for an opt-out as he felt the Social Chapter would reverse the Tories' labour market reforms and place more burdens on British companies, potentially making them less competitive. It is one of the policies that Leave campaigners would later bemoan as Brussels 'red tape'. Blair simply saw that the provisions of the Social Chapter were a legal minimum that would stop EU states from undercutting each other, as well as being consistent with the general tenor of the 1997 Labour manifesto.

Blair's signature meant that the Social Chapter could now be included in the Amsterdam Treaty, as no country was now opted out. He showed here that he understood the EU 'system' – member states have red lines and objectives but need to be prepared to show tangible concessions in order to achieve their aims. In the case of the Social Chapter signing, Blair was willing to act in Europe's interests in order to protect Britain's interests. Having shown that willing, Blair was able to block majority voting on any taxation issue. He was also able to arrange an opt-out from the Schengen Agreement, which abolished border controls between the other EU countries, fully implementing freedom of movement between them. Therefore, the Amsterdam Treaty process was seen generally as a success for Britain, although it wasn't so successful from a European point of view. Thus they agreed to meet again for another IGC to solve the institutional problems that had been left on the table.

The conferences in 1999 and 2000 that contributed to the creation of the Treaty of Nice involved rancorous negotiations about what have since been dismissed as 'technocratic' rather than 'democratic' arrangements. Britain again was not part of the problem, playing a constructive role throughout as national interests overtook European solidarity.

The arduous arguments were over how the votes of each country in the enlarged European Union would be re-weighted in the European Council. Qualified majority voting was to become the norm, and the new countries needed to have a vote. Because the issue of how many votes countries would get under QMV was opened up, Germany tried to get more votes than France, and the Netherlands more votes than Belgium, due to the difference in populations that had emerged since the previous allocations were agreed. France refused on the basis that the EU had been based on an equal power balance between France and Germany, and Belgium was not going to concede more power to its northern neighbour.

To reduce the number of members of the European Commission, the bigger countries (Germany, France, United Kingdom, Italy and Spain) tried to get smaller countries to rotate places on the Commission. This was refused, and the bigger countries had to go from two Commissioners each to one. There was an attempt then to abolish any existence of a national veto, but that was fought off by national governments. It was also agreed that there would be three ways to block any Council decision: eighty-eight votes would be needed (one small and three big countries), or a simple majority of member states, and a demographic verification clause would be included for Germany's benefit so that 62 per cent of the EU's population had to vote for a proposal for it to be adopted.[12]

So, other than the Social Chapter, nothing controversial for Britain's interests was involved in the Treaties of Amsterdam and Nice. But, in between, Blair dealt with some other European issues that have had far-reaching implications.

In 1996, Blair had been bounced into committing a Labour government to holding a referendum on Britain joining the single currency, which was to enter operation in 1999. His argument at the time for this policy was that European monetary union was not well-formed enough for any country to decide upon entry by May 1997, so he couldn't put entry into his manifesto. Therefore, a later referendum would be the only way to secure the people's consent.[13] This commitment meant that Europe played a far smaller role in the general election than the Tories would have wanted, and Blair thus had considerable room for manoeuvre on the issue once in government.

Or so people thought. Blair, however, wasn't convinced. Previous Labour governments had collapsed under the weight of economic disasters, and he perhaps wasn't prepared to stake his reputation on something that hadn't proved its worth and was so domestically controversial. He dared not risk a referendum on euro entry given that nearly all the press would campaign for a No vote. However popular he was at the start of his premiership, a referendum on the euro would have brought the Conservative Party back into life, united in opposition, and Labour might have split. Losing that referendum might have hurt Blair's carefully won position in Europe, to the extent that he insisted in the end that 'I am not going down in fucking history as the Prime Minister who took Britain out of Europe'.[14]

It should be noted that as part of the 'deal' that Blair had made with Gordon Brown to let him run for leader, he had given Brown autonomy over economic policy. Brown in turn had granted independence to the Bank of England, which took monetary policy out of political control. Some thought this might be in preparation for the European Central Bank eventually gaining control of British monetary policy, but Brown had other ideas. He asked a Treasury committee to come up with some tests to define whether a clear and unambiguous case could be made to join a successful single currency. On 27 October 1997, Brown stood up in the House of Commons and announced that those tests were: 'First, whether there can be sustainable convergence between Britain and the economies of a single currency; secondly, whether there is sufficient flexibility to cope with economic change; thirdly, the effect on investment; fourthly, the impact on our financial services generally; and fifthly, whether it is good for employment.'[15] In June 2003, Brown reappeared in front of the House to give a promised update on those five tests, and admitted that four of them had been failed.[16] So, even though there were undoubted benefits to joining the euro, and even though it had been shown to work, as by that time the euro was a 'reality' and being used by most of the other member states, Britain was kept out.

We know now that to have been in the Eurozone when the financial crisis came around in 2008 would have drastically reduced the flexibility with which Brown himself as Prime Minister could have acted to stave off the worst impacts. We have seen now how the imposition of monetary policy from Frankfurt meant that interest rates were too low for most of the 2000s, allowing countries like Ireland, Italy, Portugal, Spain and Greece to fund unsustainable growth through borrowing at inappropriately low rates for their economy's position. We know now that the inability to devalue their currencies, as Iceland was able to do by 50 per cent, nor use any other appropriate monetary policy, ended up giving these countries precious little room to manoeuvre once their debt crises hit.

But Britain didn't join the euro. In the late 1990s, Britain and Europe were at different stages in their economic cycles. Britain was growing; many countries in

Europe were in recession. But, ultimately, the most powerful reason was that the wish for interest rate and currency flexibility was too strong. This was particularly so in the case of the housing market. Britain has far higher home ownership than most countries in Europe. Those homes are owned using mortgages with far higher multiples of the buyers' income than most countries in Europe. Far more of those mortgages tend to be on variable interest rates than the rest of Europe. So interest rate changes imposed elsewhere would have had a much greater effect on Britain.

This doesn't mean the euro was removed completely from the EU referendum debate in 2016. The political instability and economic depression within the Eurozone made the EU seem a far less attractive place to be trading with. The Leave campaign insisted that Britain could still be taken into the euro in the future, and might still be asked to participate in bailouts of countries within the Eurozone. Thus, they argued, it was more risky to stay in.

An even more controversial part of the EU referendum debate was the UK's commitment on human rights. In 1998, as promised in their manifesto, Labour enacted the Human Rights Act, based on the articles of the European Convention on Human Rights. This meant that British judges must read and give effect to legislation in a way that is compatible with the ECHR, and made it unlawful for any public authority to act in a way incompatible with the ECHR. Should the courts decide that an Act of Parliament breaches the human rights in the ECHR, they can make a 'declaration of incompatibility'. It is then up to Parliament to decide whether or not to amend the law.

The ECHR was created in 1950 and has been in force since 1953. After the Second World War, the UN had issued a Universal Declaration of Human Rights – the first global expression of rights to which all human beings are inherently entitled. The court that enforces it is responsible for monitoring respect for the human rights of 800 million people in forty-seven member states across Europe.[17]

There are seventeen key articles – with the most contentious one in Britain as far as the referendum was concerned being Article 8: the right to respect for private and family life. Those who want Britain to withdraw from the ECHR argue that these articles reduce the sovereignty of Parliament as well as affecting the ability of the government to keep us safe and informed. Article 8, for instance, was felt by some to have been abused by foreign national prisoners and illegal immigrants to avoid deportation. Home Secretary Theresa May had told the 2011 Conservative Party conference that the meaning of Article 8 had been 'perverted', then said: 'We all know the stories about the Human Rights Act… about the illegal immigrant who cannot be deported because, and I am not making this up, he had a pet cat.' This provoked an immediate response from the Judicial Office at the Royal Courts of Justice, which issues statements on behalf of senior judges, saying the pet had 'had nothing to do with' the judgment allowing the man to stay.[18] It had actually been because the man had an unmarried partner with whom he had been in a relationship for over two years, and the UK Border Agency had failed to follow May's Home Office's own guidance, which was to give more weight to 'partnerships akin to marriage' when making immigration decisions.[19] Senior immigration judge Judith Gleeson had cheekily also mentioned the couple's pet cat in her judgment, allowing the Eurosceptic press to wrongly attribute the reversed deportation to the cat.[20]

Then there is how the right to privacy (Article 8) and the right to freedom of expression (Article 10) can come into conflict in the arena of press reporting. This issue came into particular focus during the debate on the behaviour of the British press arising from the phone-hacking scandal and the reporting into the private lives of celebrities. During this debate, Max Mosley, the former president of the organisation that ran Formula 1 motor-racing (who had been subject to a 'sting' by the *News of the World* in which aspects of his sex life had been reported), had gone to the European Court of Human Rights (ECtHR) to argue that Article 8 required member states to legislate to prevent newspapers printing stories about individuals' private lives without first warning the individuals concerned. The ECtHR argued that given Mosley had been awarded damages in the British courts, UK law had sufficient protections. In the ensuing discussion about the case, it was pointed out that the problem with turning that balance between privacy and freedom of expression into a matter of law is, according to the human rights watchdog Liberty, that 'the principles … won't just be tested when the tabloids splash details of a celebrity's sex life across the front page but will also come into play when journalists want to report on a corporation's unethical activities or even a politician's expenses'.[21]

The key problem with all this is that the European Convention on Human Rights is completely separate from the European Union. Yet often Eurosceptics have cited not having to be bound by the ECHR as a reason to leave the EU.

The European Court of Justice *is* part of the EU, and in fact enforces its laws. So Britain will not leave the ECHR when it leaves the EU – that will have to be a separate process. Leave campaigners have pointed out, though, that to remain a member of the EU, a state has to adhere to the ECHR, so leaving would at least give the country the choice. The states that joined the EU in 2004 all had to sign up to the ECHR as a condition of membership, though there is disagreement amongst lawyers as to whether this applies to existing members.[22] For those who say that leaving the EU means 'taking back control', Britain having a free choice about laws and rights is key. Leaving the EU would give the opportunity for a British Bill of Rights to be created. Whether a British Bill of Rights would be better or not is, in the view of Brexiteers, a moot point compared to the fact that it would be British. This debate was given more force by the Charter of Fundamental Rights, which was created as part of the negotiations for the most controversial treaty that Tony Blair and Labour were involved in: the Lisbon Treaty.

In 2001, the Laeken European Council meeting decided that the current constitutional situation surrounding the European Union was too messy. It was agreed that the enlarged bloc of twenty-seven member countries would work better if all earlier treaties could be rolled into one – with extra bits. A Constitutional Convention was called, including representatives from the governing and opposition parties of each member country, and meetings were held in public. The new Treaty establishing a Constitution for Europe (TCE) formally recognised a flag, anthem and motto for Europe. It also restated key EU principles (including the superiority of EU law over member states' law), aims, values and scope. The TCE stated explicitly for the first time that the EU had a legal personality, meaning, for instance, that it could enter into trade agreements and treaties by itself. It also tried to make the Charter of Fundamental Rights legally binding, something Britain had objected to. Added to this, new positions of President of the European Commission and a Minister for Foreign Affairs were created to represent the Union to the outside world separately from its member states. Finally, for the first time, a process was set out for a member to leave the EU.[23]

The press and political Eurosceptics once again rose up and declared this Constitution for Europe a step too far. With the 2004 European Parliament elections and a possible general election coming up, Blair was persuaded to neutralise the issue by committing the next Labour government to hold a referendum on whether to ratify it. Whatever the protests of European leaders that the Constitution was merely a 'tidying-up' process, many within the member states argued that it was more a betrayal of national interests. France, the Netherlands, Spain and Luxembourg held referendums, and others would have as well, except France and the Netherlands both delivered a No vote, meaning the Constitution could not be ratified. It was at this point that then Luxembourg Prime Minister and holder of the EU presidency Jean-Claude Juncker first came to British notice. He claimed during the French campaign that the EU leadership would need to keep going whatever happens: 'If it's a Yes, we will say "on we go", and if it's a No we will say "we continue"', he said.[24]

Continue they did, creating a treaty instead that amended the Maastricht and Rome Treaties, as opposed to an entirely new Treaty. This meant that political leaders could claim, as Tony Blair and then Gordon Brown did, that a referendum to ratify it was not required. This was despite the obvious similarities between the two documents – described by the House of Commons' European Scrutiny Committee as 'substantially equivalent'[25] and debated fruitlessly for fourteen nights in Parliament.[26]

The truth is that the Lisbon Treaty, which was eventually ratified in 2009 by the last government – that of the Czech Republic – *was* remarkably similar to the Constitution for Europe. In fact, Valéry Giscard d'Estaing, the architect of the abandoned Constitution, admitted in an open letter to *Le Monde* in 2007 that 'the institutional proposals of the constitutional treaty ... are found complete in the Lisbon Treaty, only in a different order and inserted in former treaties'.[27] The most important achievement of the treaty in terms of tidying up European governance was the end of the 'three pillars' of the EU. This was where the European Communities (EEC, ECSC and Euratom) had been one pillar, with supranational powers, and the other pillars – one for foreign and security policy and the other for police and judicial cooperation – had been intergovernmental. This was done in the name of 'simplification' but it did give the opportunity for the formerly intergovernmental pillars to become more integrated and centralised. Also included was Article 50 – setting out the processes and deadlines that would govern a country leaving the EU. It was not a particularly well-worded part of the treaty, as those who drafted it didn't envisage it being used.[28]

During the Lisbon process, Britain had insisted on what it called an 'opt-out' from the Charter of Fundamental Rights, which had been incorporated into the Lisbon Treaty, making it legally binding on all EU institutions and member state governments. The aim was to add all the rights from the case law of the ECJ to the articles of the ECHR, then add other rights and traditions from the common constitutional traditions of the EU member countries and put them into one document. By opting out of this, Tony Blair argued that he was stopping the Charter being used to challenge current UK legislation in the courts or to introduce new rights in UK law.[29]

Blair insisted it was an opt-out, Foreign Secretary David Miliband insisted it was an opt-out in 2008, and even coalition Justice Secretary Kenneth Clarke insisted it was an opt-out in 2011. But over the years running up to the EU referendum, it became increasingly clear that the Charter had actually created new rights within the EU (called 'third generation' fundamental rights) in the areas of data protection, bioethics and transport administration, and also that the Charter of Rights had become part of UK domestic law.

In 2013, NS, an Afghan national who had entered the EU via Greece, claimed asylum in the UK. The UK sought to return him to Greece because the Dublin Convention determined that asylum seekers' applications should be processed by the country through which the applicant had first entered the EU. NS argued that the treatment of asylum seekers in Greece was degrading, and so violated not only Article 3 of the ECHR (the prohibition of torture) but also Articles 1, 4, 8, 19 and 47 of the Charter of Fundamental Rights. The UK High Court ruled that a litigant in the English courts could not rely on Charter rights directly. The case was referred on appeal to the ECJ in Luxembourg, which ruled that Protocol 30 of the Lisbon Treaty (the opt-out) was not intended to exempt the UK from the obligation to comply with the provision of the Charter. In other words, the opt-out wasn't an opt-out.[30]

Later that year, ruling on a separate asylum case, Judge Mostyn of the High Court referred to the case of NS. It is worth recalling what he said in its entirety:

> The constitutional significance of this decision can hardly be overstated. The Human Rights Act 1998 incorporated into our domestic law large parts, but by no means all, of the European Convention on Human Rights. Some parts were deliberately missed out by Parliament. The Charter of Fundamental Rights contains, I believe, all of those missing parts and a great deal more. Notwithstanding

the endeavours of our political representatives at Lisbon it would seem that the much wider Charter of Rights is now part of our domestic law. Moreover, that much wider Charter of Rights would remain part of our domestic law even if the Human Rights Act were repealed.

This time, Leave campaigners were right in insisting that leaving the EU would free the UK, should it choose, from these obligations.[31] As we'll see in Reason 16, Boris Johnson's wife Marina Wheeler was extremely exercised about this issue. Is this what finally tipped one of Britain's most popular politicians into the Leave camp?

Britain's EU presidency term coincided with the Lisbon process. The previous time Britain had the presidency was during the optimistic, friendly times of early 1998. By 2005, an almost irrevocable schism had occurred between Blair and many of his counterparts after the British Prime Minister had joined with the USA in invading Iraq. It was believed at the time that had the EU acted together, the USA may not have taken part in that ill-fated adventure, but that wasn't to happen. The fallout wound back the considerable advances Blair had made in the UK's relationship with EU leaders when he became PM, making it more likely they would harden their stance in any negotiations with him.

A central development under the second British EU presidency was the budget settlement, and many Eurosceptics argue that Blair caved in during this process – giving away a large amount of Margaret Thatcher's painstakingly negotiated rebate in return for the promise of reforms of the way the budget is spent (particularly on the CAP) that never actually happened.[32] That is to ignore the context of the new deal on the rebate. When Margaret Thatcher agreed the rebate in 1984, Britain was in a far worse financial state, compared to the other members, than it was in 2005. Margaret Thatcher's heavily reported insistence during the early 1980s that Britain's contribution was unfair and was 'our money' had created the political idea that any compromise on the rebate would be viewed as automatically wrong. But Blair argued that a Labour government could not ask the far poorer Eastern European countries to contribute to the United Kingdom's coffers just because of UK domestic political pressures. So he agreed that Britain should no longer receive a rebate on non-agricultural spending in member states that joined the EU after 2004.

Yes, this has reduced the rebate quite considerably, and yes, the financial reforms have not really been pushed through, and yes, this has greatly annoyed many Eurosceptic commentators. That said, the size of Britain's budget contribution is around 1 per cent of GDP every year, which is a sizeable chunk of money but in reality a small proportion of total spending, and is given in return for benefits of membership of the EU. While it became a major issue in the 2016 referendum campaign (£350 million on the side of a bus), it could be argued that this is because those who want to leave the EU see even £1 going across the water as too high a price to pay for those membership benefits.

What was happening in the Conservative Party throughout all this? Well, there had been a steady line of anti-European leaders since 1997, each contributing in their own way to the culture of hostility to Europe that helped influence the eventual vote to leave. The first Tory leader to follow Major was William Hague, whose 2001 general election campaign was a chronic failure despite the populist claim that Britain had only the days up to the election to 'save the pound'.[33] One of his speechwriters was Daniel Hannan, whom we met at the start of the chapter on John Major's travails, when he was a student at Oxford railing against the Maastricht Treaty. In 2001, Hannan helped William Hague write what became known as his most notorious speech:

> Just imagine four more years of Labour. Try to picture what our country would look like. Let me take you on a journey to a foreign land – to Britain after a second term of Tony Blair. The Royal Mint melting down pound coins as the euro notes start to circulate. Our currency gone forever. The Chancellor returning from Brussels carrying instructions to raise taxes still further. Control over our own economy given away.[34]

The electorate wasn't convinced. Hague lost his election challenge against Blair that year and was replaced as Tory leader by Iain Duncan Smith, whose only real qualification for the leadership was his determined hatred of Europe (he had been one of the original Maastricht rebels). His performance was so poor that before he had the chance to fight an election he was replaced by Michael Howard, in November 2003. Howard had led the group in Cabinet in opposition to John Major signing the Maastricht Treaty. Pro-European MPs had almost completely disappeared from the party leadership. In 2005, after yet another election loss to Blair, so came the next contest for leader. The runners included Europhile Ken

Clarke, knocked out in round one – and Thatcherite Liam Fox, who fell at the second ballot. That left a face-off between shadow Home Secretary David Davis and shadow Education Secretary David Cameron.

At this point, the Conservative MPs who had supported Fox asked both candidates to withdraw from the European People's Party (EPP) – the centre-right federation of parties in the European Parliament. The EPP was an avowedly federalist grouping, committed to further EU integration, and Eurosceptics wanted out as continued membership would mean the Conservatives had to follow that agenda. Only Cameron agreed, citing his opposition to the EPP's commitment to federalism. It was Eurosceptic Dan Hannan, working from within the European Parliament as an MEP, who led the Tory drive to get out of the EPP grouping, which was actually one of the most powerful political groups within the EU, with parties extremely loyal to each other. Leaving the group meant a loss of influence for anyone who may have important negotiations on the horizon. For Cameron, that would prove problematic in a few years' time; for Hannan, it was another inch gained, another bolt loosened.

Cameron won the leadership contest on 6 December 2005 with 68 per cent of the vote. He now felt compelled to commit himself to a steady stream of anti-European political initiatives. Included in this category was a 'cast-iron guarantee' that if elected Prime Minister, he would offer a referendum on the Lisbon Treaty.[35]

The trouble was that the treaty was ratified and in force while Cameron was still in opposition. Once this happens, you can only reopen a treaty with the consent of a qualified majority of member states. That probably wasn't possible, so holding a referendum, should it result in a No vote, could have committed Cameron to leaving the European Union as the only way to remove Britain from its treaty obligations. Labour could have held a referendum before signing the treaty but chose not to; Cameron felt he couldn't turn back the clock and had no choice but to abandon his 'cast-iron' pledge on entering Downing Street. For Hannan, this just wasn't good enough. Having supported Cameron's leadership, he felt let down, and resigned his post as the Conservatives' legal affairs spokesman in Brussels. He decided from that moment to devote himself full time to lobbying for – and winning – a referendum on EU membership.

We will learn more about Hannan's role later and explore further how Cameron was hamstrung by his U-turn on the Lisbon Treaty, unable to change the fact that the treaty had been fully ratified but also unable to undo the promise he'd made to have a referendum on it. But a bigger issue would emerge from the Blair–Brown era where again their successor as Prime Minister made an unworkable, unachievable promise. By far the most fundamental change to the EU over this period was the enlargement of the bloc by countries to the east and south. The impact this had on immigration to the UK was something Blair failed to predict, Cameron failed to control and much of the UK failed to see in anything but a negative light.

Since the Second World War, there had been two major influxes of immigrants before New Labour came to power in 1997. The first was between 1948 and 1962 and consisted mainly of young men, and eventually their families, from the Caribbean and south Asia. This wave of new arrivals was inspired by the 1948 British Nationality Act, which declared that all subjects of the King had British citizenship, and effectively gave some 800 million people around the world the right to enter the UK. Not many of this 800 million did move – after all, transport costs were expensive at the time. Half a million people did arrive, but it was relatively uncontroversial at the time, particularly because it was accepted that Britain needed manpower to rebuild following the war. The country was growing economically, and thus could easily absorb the new arrivals, many of whom were entrepreneurial, starting numerous businesses. That said, the 1948 British Nationality Act was not in any manifesto: it was a politician's decision, not given any mandate by the people.

Restrictions on immigration started to be put in place with a quota system in the 1962 Commonwealth and Immigrants Act. Just before that, the first influx of immigrants was completed by a large migration of Pakistanis and Indians from the Muslim province around Kashmir, straddling the border between India and Pakistan. These men came to work in the labour-short textile mills of Bradford and surrounding towns, as well as other manufacturing towns like Leicester. This group were far more likely than the Caribbeans to send for their families and far less likely to integrate with their communities. Andrew Marr described this group as:

> more religiously divided from the whites around them and cut off from the main form of male white working-class entertainment, the consumption of alcohol. Muslim women were kept inside the house and ancient habits of brides being

chosen to cement family connections at home meant there was almost no sexual mixing, either. To many whites, the 'Pakis' were no less threatening than the self-confident young Caribbean men, but also more alien.

That wasn't the end of it. In 1963, Kenya had won independence and told its 185,000 Asians to surrender their British passports and take full Kenyan nationality, or become in effect foreigners, dependent on work permits. They started flooding to Britain, by 1968 numbering around 2,000 a month. These Asians were well educated, tending to be civil servants, doctors and business people. But Labour's Home Secretary Jim Callaghan rushed through an amendment to the Commonwealth Immigrants Act to try to impose an annual quota. Alongside this, a Race Relations Bill was brought forward, setting up courts that would try cases of discrimination in employment and housing. It was all stirring up considerable disquiet amongst the British public, who were noting again that the new immigrants were arriving and changes were happening in their communities without the electorate ever having given a mandate.[36]

Into the middle of all this stepped Enoch Powell. A member of the Conservative shadow Cabinet, and someone strictly committed to the sovereignty of Parliament, he had been observing what was happening in his and surrounding West Midlands constituencies. Powell had seen how concerns about immigration had achieved a 7.5 per cent swing for Conservative candidate Peter Griffiths, who won the nearby Smethwick constituency in the 1964 election, at the expense of Labour's proposed Foreign Secretary Patrick Gordon Walker.[37] Griffiths had run an unashamedly racist campaign, including the slogan 'If you want a nigger for a neighbour vote Labour', pointing out how his opponent lived in a wealthy garden suburb and thus had no idea of the impact of Smethwick's then comparatively large immigrant intake on the local population. Although Griffiths lost his seat two years later, with Labour Prime Minister Harold Wilson calling him a 'parliamentary leper', the issue hadn't lost its potency. Malcolm X visited Smethwick in 1965, having heard about the campaign, and Enoch Powell became convinced that the political class were being wilfully blind to the effects of immigration. He eventually spoke up at a speech in a small room in Birmingham's Midland Hotel on 20 April 1968.

Powell started by telling the story of a constituent who wanted to leave the country because 'in fifteen or twenty years' time the black man will have the whip hand over the white man'. Powell then went on to question why he should be reporting this inflammatory rhetoric, but claimed to feel a responsibility to speak up for the 'hundreds of thousands' thinking the same thing, 'not throughout Great Britain, perhaps, but in the areas that are already undergoing the total transformation to which there is no parallel in a thousand years of English history'.[38] 'We must be mad, literally mad, as a nation to be permitting the annual inflow of some 50,000 dependants, who are for the most part the material of the future growth of the immigrant-descended population. It is like watching a nation busily engaged in heaping up its own funeral pyre.' Having told a few more stories of constituent concerns, he ended by saying: 'As I look ahead, I am filled with foreboding; like the Roman, I seem to see "the Tiber foaming with much blood"' – essentially a warning of unrest and rioting if this unmandated immigration didn't stop. The outcry to the speech, thereafter labelled the 'Rivers of Blood speech', was immediate, and his party leader Edward Heath sacked him from the shadow Cabinet, saying he found the speech 'racialist in tone and liable to exacerbate racial tensions'. Asked by the *Daily Mail* if he thought he was a racialist, Powell replied, 'We are all racialists. Do I object to one coloured person in the country? No. To 100? No. To a million? A query. To 5 million? Definitely.'

It is important for the story about to be told to know about Enoch Powell's speech because he provided a bogeyman that could be used as a quick, lazy comparison to cut off as quickly as possible any debate about one of the key background policies of New Labour's time in power. Becoming compared to Enoch Powell was what happened if you questioned the benefits of multiculturalism and immigration.

When New Labour came to power, Britain had already become a multiracial society, with a settled minority population of about 4 million people: 7 per cent. Every decision made from 1997 onwards on this issue could be described as reasonable on its own terms, but put together they have added up to annual gross inflows of around 500,000 people a year, resulting in an overall net quadrupling of migration into the country – with the UK population being boosted by 2010 by more than 2.2 million immigrants – twice the population of Birmingham. It was the largest peacetime migration in Britain's history. Many places in Britain previously almost untouched by immigration, such as rural communities and market towns, became host to significant migrant communities.

Some decisions were published in their manifestos – such as the 1997 commitment to scrapping the 'Primary Purpose rule', which had barred entry into Britain for thousands of people married to British citizens unless they could prove that the primary purpose of their marriage was not to obtain British residency.[39] Most decisions, however, were not.

Looking back at some of these choices, there is a case to be made that the key government players were simply trying to cope with a new world of rapid population movements across porous borders caused by numerous conflicts in Africa and the Balkans, along with the natural forces of globalisation, such as cheaper air fares and mass telecommunications. The rapid internationalisation of higher education meant that Labour could finance their policy of expanding university education in the UK through encouraging foreign students into the country. The booming economy and low unemployment saw some pressure from some business sectors to increase work permits, and when asylum seekers from the Balkans increased in number, there was pressure to move them as quickly as possible to the work permit route, away from the costs and dependency of the asylum system.[40]

But there is also a case that the encouragement of immigration was a deliberate policy by the Labour government to make the UK truly multicultural. A former No. 10 and Home Office advisor, Andrew Neather, wrote much later about how 'the policy was intended – even if this wasn't its main purpose – to rub the Right's nose in diversity and render their arguments out of date'.[41] In other words, immigrants tended to vote Labour. Most commentators who were involved with these decisions rubbish Neather's claim.[42] Barbara Roche, Labour's immigration minister from 1999 to 2001, argues that the previous Conservative government had introduced a failed computer system and then made cutbacks that left only fifty officials able to make asylum decisions on a backlog of 50,000 cases. Blair's 1998 Human Rights Act also gave a higher priority to the protection of the rights of these asylum seekers than before. This, however, was seen to get mixed up with economic migrants using the asylum process to get into Britain. The right-wing press began to highlight these issues, conflating asylum with economic immigration and confronting the government with a number of controversial issues.[43]

The biggest decision of them all was made quietly, using inaccurate and wrongly interpreted data, and was to lead in almost a direct line to Brexit.

On 1 May 2004, the former Communist countries of Central and Eastern

Europe were to join the EU. At that point, every single member of their pop-ulation would, according to the Maastricht Treaty, become an EU citizen. This meant that unless the member states took the opportunity to put in place what were called 'transitional controls', citizens of these much poorer states (per capita GDP was less than half the EU average) could move anywhere, without having a job offer waiting for them, and would be entitled to all the rights and privilege of a national citizen in all member states.

The transitional controls meant that this process would be delayed for seven years. Of all the big European countries, only Britain decided not to take up those transitional controls. This was based, it said, on research commissioned by the Home Office from a team led by Professor Christian Dustmann in 2003, which suggested that only 26,000 immigrants would arrive in the first two years. We know now that Dustmann added in the report that immigration to the UK would be much higher if, as happened, Germany and other countries decided to impose the transitional controls.[44] But that figure, 13,000 a year, led to a deep distrust amongst the public of all official migration statistics, providing yet more fuel for Michael Gove's claim that 'people have had enough of experts'.

The rest, as we know now, is history. Home Secretary David Blunkett stood up in the House of Commons, talked of the 500,000 job vacancies in a growing economy, and announced that Britain would allow workers from the accession states access to the labour market. Blunkett also talked of a worker registration scheme which would help the government find out where migrants had gone in order to organise public services for them, and insisted they would not receive benefits until they had been contributing tax and national insurance within that scheme for two years. 'Whether they are plumbers or paediatricians,' Blunkett said, 'they are welcome if they come here openly to work and contribute.'[45]

By the time of the 2016 EU referendum, almost 2.5 million more migrants from other EU countries were living, and many of them working, in the UK. As Sir Stephen Wall, EU advisor to Tony Blair from 2000 to 2004 said: 'We simply didn't take account properly of the pull factor of England for people with skills who could probably find a bigger market for their skills – you know, the Polish plumber.' Unlike non-EU migration, by simple fact of being a member of the European Union, the UK government were not allowed to control their movement in and out of the country. This was another massive change to Britain with no mandate from the British people. Transitional arrangements were being talked about before the 2001 UK general election because German Chancellor Gerhard Schröder had talked to the German population about them in 2000. It is instructive to read what he said:

> Many of you are concerned about expansion of the EU ... The German government will not abandon you with your concerns ... We still have 3.8 million unemployed, the capacity of the German labour market to accept more people will remain seriously limited for a long time. We need transitional arrangements with flexibility for the benefit of both the old and the new member states.[46]

The British people were not consulted at all. This, said some Labour advisors of the time, is because the research that they had done made them sure that immigration would bring benefits to the UK as a whole. A 73-page report was produced by the Performance and Innovation Unit at No. 10 claiming that the foreign-born population in the UK contributes around 10 per cent more to government revenues than it receives from the state.[47] The Home Office were charged with controlling immigration, but were put under considerable pressure from the Foreign Office (traditionally pro-immigration for diplomatic reasons), the Department for Education (keen on the money from foreign students), the Treasury (keen on extra tax revenue) and the Business Department (keen on willing and able workers to fill vacancies and fuel growth).[48] To the extent that immigrants bring skills that Britain might need, fill jobs that Britons might not do, and are often younger and less needful of public services, this enthusiasm was understandable, for the country as a whole. But the country as a whole isn't a human being. Human beings vote in referendums, and many of them were not happy.

By February 2006, Labour MP for Southampton Itchen John Denham had written a memo to Tony Blair, Gordon Brown and then Home Secretary Charles Clarke to warn them that the number of immigrants was far higher than the government's figures had forecast. Southampton by itself had received about 14,000 Eastern European migrants in the eighteen months since the countries had joined the EU. They were putting immense pressure on public services and leading employers to pay lower wages. Denham noted that many new arrivals weren't using the worker registration scheme, as many were self-employed, offering themselves to construction sites. The daily rate as a builder in the city had thus fallen by 50 per cent in those eighteen months. What's more, hospital accident and emergency services were under strain because migrants tend not to use GPs as the first port of call, as they do not have a similar service in the country they came from. A local further education college had to close its doors after 1,000 migrants attempted to sign up for an English-as-a-second-language course in one day. Denham argued for the government to reassess how it was dealing with the surge in immigration. The response was indifferent. They had based their approach on evidence-based research from a credible academic source and they thought any fuss would all calm down.

It didn't. John Harris is a *Guardian* journalist who has, with cameraman John Domokos, been going around the country for the past few years in search of 'real politics', away from London, for a series called 'Anywhere but Westminster'.[49] In a series of thoroughly absorbing ten-minute films, Harris has toured the country to speak to people about their lives and how they are affected by politics. There are many telling vignettes available, but the most significant include the builder in South Shields in the north-east of England whose pay went down from £14 to £11 an hour from 2004 to 2010,[50] and the employment agencies in Peterborough whose only adverts are at rates and with working conditions only migrants would take.[51] Needless to say, the citizens of Peterborough, South Shields and Southampton Itchen all voted Leave.

In April 2017, *The Economist* published a study of areas in the UK that had seen the sharpest increase of new migrants in the ten years from 2005 to 2015. It found this to consist of market towns that had previously seen little immigration. These areas in the UK that the magazine dubbed 'migrant land' saw real wages fall by a tenth over this ten-year period, faster than the national average, while the government's index of multiple deprivation suggested that health and education had also become relatively poorer in these places. But the study also found that 'migrant land' was disproportionately affected by the decline in the manufacturing sector as well as cuts to public services during the coalition government's drive to rebalance the public finances. It is therefore hard to quantify how much the fall in wages was down to cheap migrant labour as opposed to industrial decline and increased unemployment due to vanishing local authority jobs. No matter, the result was that 'migrant land' voted on average 60:40 in favour of leaving the EU.[52]

Poll after poll and journalist after journalist have found the same thing since

23 June 2016. Most people who voted Leave have nothing against the Polish people they know – after all, devoutly Christian, family-loving, football-mad beer drinkers with a strong work ethic are hardly Britain's toughest ever integration challenge.[53] But the speed and scale of their arrival seemingly caused headaches for the labour market and for public services. Furthermore, there was also the issue, explained by John Denham himself, of 'the fundamental desire most people have to live in a community that provides some sense of cohesion based on some shared experience, shared obligation to one another and shared values'.[54]

Vernon Briggs is a leading labour market economist at Cornell University in the US. He was asked to testify in front of Congress back in March 1999 and there has rarely been a better explanation of the problem of the gap on immigration between the 'political class' and the people whose decisions they affect:

> The 'costs' of immigration need to be taken into account as much as do the 'benefits' when it comes to designing the appropriate policy. The concerns of the 'losers' are as relevant as those of the 'winners.' Such is especially the case when those most adversely impacted are the least advantaged persons in the population and labor market.[55]

Or, as put more crudely by Tim Finch and David Goodhart, 'The further down the social scale you go, the more likely it is that an immigrant will be an unwelcome competitor.'[56]

The argument goes like this: the availability of a large pool of immigrant labour tends to result in lower wages, fewer incentives for firms to train their workers, lower productivity, more housing shortages and increased inequality within a country. It also raises the benefits bill in the UK, because the lower wages are topped up with tax credits, also known as 'in-work benefits', which would be reduced if wages had to improve because that pool of available immigrant labour was reduced. The MD of a large recruitment firm once lamented to the present authors that his firm had 250,000 job vacancies, mainly because British workers felt the wages were too low, the working conditions were not good enough, and the location of the work was inconvenient. However, he admitted that without uncontrolled immigration, the pay might be better, as might the working conditions and probably the location of the jobs.

The same issue could be said to apply to the NHS and state education, which would, apparently, collapse without immigrant labour. This situation, though, might have been caused by a long-term government policy of employing cheap, willing immigrants rather than improving pay and conditions so that Britain can train and retain its own workers. This strategy furthermore deprives poorer developing countries of workers with those skills,[57] meaning there are some African countries who actually give Britain more aid, in terms of the involuntary donation of trained medical staff, than Britain gives them.

There is a counter-argument to all of this. The decision by the Labour government to forgo transitional controls meant that many of the immigrants who came were young, highly skilled and university educated, and many of them contributed tax and national insurance to the economy. Germany still got immigrants from Central and Eastern Europe, despite their transitional controls, because freedom of movement still existed in terms of people being able to move around and travel anywhere as tourists – but many of them stayed as illegal immigrants, finding work on the black market, and tended to be older and less qualified.

Professor Klaus Zimmerman of the Institute for the Study of Labour in Bonn told *The Economist*:

> Legal migration by an estimated 1.5m eastern Europeans since 2004 is often accused of acting as a recruiting sergeant for the far right in Britain. Well just try a boom in criminality and black market illegal labour and see what that does to support for the far right, is my response.[58]

It can thus be concluded that transition controls or not, opening up the EU for the first time to countries a lot poorer than the existing member states was always going to result in a lot of Eastern Europeans moving to Britain, and the only way to even try to control that would have been to leave the EU. David Cameron rather recklessly attempted in the run-up to the 2010 election to say he would try to limit net immigration to the tens of thousands. However, every time the immigration figures came out – particularly the ones a month before the 2016 referendum saying that a net 333,000 had come in – the futility of that commitment was laid bare.

Perhaps the biggest issue is that Tony Blair never tried to explain that he had chosen to increase legal immigration to Britain, and why. In a democracy, voter angst cannot be ignored. In Britain, it wasn't just ignored, it was actively suppressed. Those who complained about the scale of immigration were told they were racist,[59] or the Prime Minister called them a bigot once he was in his car, thinking he was safely out of earshot.

The best explanation for this was that many at the top of New Labour, and many of its activists, were influenced by the metropolitan cultural liberalism which saw immigration as an inherently good thing. The party leadership, trying not to appear soft on immigration for electoral reasons and wanting to create a modern, multicultural Britain with a dynamic open economy, also had a lingering belief that tightly controlling immigration was somehow tinged with racism. The New Labour hierarchy were children of the '60s and '70s, when struggles for racial equality were at their peak. They relished diversity, and were part of a metropolitan-minded class that had reaped huge benefits from immigration. Strong lines on immigration control were taken by hate figures like Enoch Powell, Margaret Thatcher and Norman Tebbit.[60] A micro-example of this was the reaction of Barbara Roche to her new job: 'When I was told, in the July 1999 Cabinet reshuffle, that I was moving from the Treasury to become the Minister of State for Immigration and Asylum at the Home Office, I was appalled.' How could she, as a Jew, and with a political outlook shaped by campaigning against racism and inequality, disentangle these issues from the public perception of immigration, she wondered.[61]

Is it racist to be angry that a government decision has reduced your pay? Are you a bigot if you express frustration that you can't see your GP or get a place in your first-choice school after a local influx of immigrants? There is no doubt that some of these frustrations were overblown or unfairly attributed to immigration rather than cuts to public services implemented by the coalition government of 2010–15, but there was also a growing reluctance in politics to fully consider the social impact of immigration. In the 2005 general election, Conservative leader Michael Howard's slogan – 'It's not racist to impose limits on immigration' – was greeted with outrage by the New Labour establishment.[62] This then cowed David Cameron in opposition from speaking up on the issue as he tried to detoxify the Tory brand. But core Labour voters were beginning to think what Howard was thinking and looked to someone in politics who was prepared to take what at the time was a considerable risk of talking about it. Into this conversational void came first Nick Griffin of the BNP and then Nigel Farage of UKIP.

Britain never became a country of angry nativists and racists. OK, maybe about 7 per cent of the population are, according to latest estimates.[63] But there is a larger group of people who are comfortable with difference at a 'micro-level' at work or in their social life but don't like the 'macro-change' to their city or country and worry that too many newcomers fail to integrate. There is also still a reliance on national social contracts and the belief that national citizens should be first in the queue for school places, hospital beds or social housing. The latest British Social Attitudes survey found that 72 per cent of people think immigration increases pressure on schools and 62 per cent say it increases pressure on the NHS. On the economy, 42 per cent think immigration is good and 35 per cent say it is bad.[64] But within that, 15 per cent of graduates think immigration is bad for the economy, compared to 51 per cent of those with no educational qualifications. These are the people most likely to feel like a replaceable cog in the economic machine.[65]

Is it any wonder that when the first chance came to reset the machine, so many people took it?

REASON 9

THE RISE OF THE DISPOSSESSED

Iain Duncan Smith was on his way to Elstree studio in north-west London to appear on the early part of the BBC's coverage of the referendum results when he received a call from a local Conservative Party activist in his constituency of Chingford in Essex. The activist wanted to tell the former Tory Party leader and Work and Pensions Secretary some interesting news. 'We're getting turnout on these housing estates of 80 per cent, we've got queuing,' Duncan Smith was told. The Leave campaign had feared that a two-day extension to the voter registration implemented by the government after the registration website had crashed had benefited Remain by mostly adding young people to the voter roll. But this news suggested something else might have happened in that window of time. Duncan Smith certainly thought so. He said:

> Housing estates don't vote – well, not much – so if you get turnouts of 30 or 40 per cent, that's quite high. Eighty per cent is unheard of and loads of them are having to be shown what to do because they've never voted before. So it was quite interesting actually, that surge in registration was assumed to be Remainers. I don't think it was. I think a lot of it was Leavers in housing estates, at that moment realising they could vote.

When Duncan Smith got to the studio, he bumped into an old friend, Labour deputy leader Tom Watson, who told him: 'This turnout is happening all over the northern seats.'[1] The 2016 referendum was about to be decided by the rise of the dispossessed.

Over 17 million people voted to leave the European Union. There has never been a single decision backed by more people in the history of the United Kingdom. These 17 million comprised many different types of person with a variety of motivations. But in the course of writing this book we have found that both Remain and Leave campaigners believe that the key group, the one that put Leave 'over the top', was one that hadn't voted before. These were people who had been 'left behind' by the political establishment over the past forty years. This was happening alongside the story we have just told about Britain's relationship with the European Union, and we need to tell their story separately, because it focuses on what was going on outside that relationship. Fed up with their personal circumstances, the 'left behind' voted for change. Given that the normal response of the British public is to veer towards the status quo should they be undecided, the significance of the Leave campaign having persuaded this large bloc of voters to vote, and to vote for change, is huge. Let's find out why they did so.

Our story begins on 8 May 1945, VE Day. Conservative Prime Minister Winston Churchill joins the royal family on the Buckingham Palace balcony in front of teeming hordes of ecstatic citizens, celebrating one of Britain's greatest war victories. On the balcony, they stood in a line, the two Princesses, Elizabeth and Margaret, flanking their parents, King George VI and Queen Elizabeth. As they waved, the crowd cheered appreciatively. In the middle of the family, Winston Churchill waved, and the crowd roared. At the time, Churchill had approval ratings of well over 80 per cent, the highest ever for a serving Prime Minister.

So it came as quite a surprise that less than three months later, when counting had finished in the general election Churchill had called that summer, the Labour Party, under the leadership of Clement Attlee, had won 393 seats and an overall majority of 146 seats in the House of Commons. The swing from the Conservatives to Labour was 12 per cent, which has never been matched since then.

In terms of electoral surprises, this took some beating. Such was Winston Churchill's dominance over British politics that even most of the Labour leadership assumed the Conservatives would win and Churchill would be returned to Downing Street. City experts, trade union bosses, the press and diplomatic observers in Moscow and Washington agreed. On election day, the *Daily Express* said: 'There are reasons for expecting that, by tonight, Mr Churchill and his supporters will be returned to power.'[2]

Now, there was actually one group who *did* predict a Labour victory, and that was the nascent polling industry. On the eve of polling day, which was

5 July, there were polls suggesting Labour had a six-point lead. These polls were assumed to be inaccurate, as the electorate was scattered and disrupted. The electoral roll, for instance, was so inaccurate, with so many clerical errors, that Winston Churchill himself found he had no vote.

So, why did Churchill and the Conservatives lose the 1945 election at a time when his personal popularity couldn't be higher? How did Clement Attlee, a man of so little charisma that Churchill had once allegedly commented that 'an empty taxi drew up outside 10 Downing Street, and Clement Attlee got out of it',[3] achieve such a landslide victory? More importantly, what's all this got to do with the result of the 2016 EU referendum? The answer is that on both occasions a large group of voters took a look at their personal circumstances and voted for change, with little care what that change might bring.

The answer goes back to who voted for Labour in 1945, and what had happened to many of those voters over the previous decade and a half. It goes back to the response of successive governments in Westminster to the economic depression in the 1930s. It includes the added deprivations caused by the war, which were bound to continue for the next few years. Quite simply, many voters decided it was time for a transformation in how the country was run. They felt that a vote for Labour offered that transformation, while a vote for the Conservatives didn't.

The depression began in 1929 with an economic collapse in the United States that led in the UK (reliant for income on exports being sold abroad) to a collapse in demand for British products, with the value of exports falling by 50 per cent and unemployment rising by over 10 per cent. With little or no unemployment benefit, many in Britain's population became impoverished. The response to the resulting pressure on the UK's budget came in the form of tax rises and government spending cuts, causing further unemployment. Unemployment benefits that were paid out only occurred after a humiliating and much resented process of means testing that was never forgotten by the working class.

It wasn't as if there had been no alternative to the UK government's strategy. Eminent economist John Maynard Keynes had been promoting his idea of reducing the impact of the depression by putting money in the population's pockets through government spending on public infrastructure (bridges and roads), which would increase consumer spending, giving firms more funds to create jobs, and so on in a virtuous circle. In the US, Franklin Roosevelt had used these ideas as the basis for his New Deal, centred on massive infrastructure spending. The British government ignored Keynes, making, he believed, the depression much deeper than it needed to be. This was not forgotten by many of the electorate when it came to the 1945 election.

Just when the depression was lifting, the Second World War intervened, and the same people who had been so impoverished by the depression were further impoverished by the deprivations of war. However necessary those sacrifices might have been, by 1945 much of the population had had enough and wanted something different.

The Conservatives' election campaign was based entirely upon the shoulders of Winston Churchill, focusing on his record in office and asking voters to give him the opportunity to 'finish the job'.[4] Labour, meanwhile, had published the first official manifesto, entitled 'Let us Face the Future'.[5]

The key point to all of this is that many of those who voted Labour on 5 July 1945 did so because they just wanted a change in their personal circumstances, and they knew voting for the Conservatives wouldn't bring that change, but voting for Labour would. Crucially, at the time, many reported not knowing what change Labour were actually offering; they just knew a change was coming.

Even a cursory knowledge of British political history will reveal that those working-class (and many middle-class) voters who asked for change got lucky. They got Clement Attlee and possibly the most talented government the country has ever had. They got many of the recommendations of the 1942 Beveridge Report[6] on rebuilding Britain after war, which had called for the end to the 'Five Giant Evils' of want, squalor, disease, idleness and ignorance. They got the National Health Service. They got the modern welfare state. They got the nationalisation of the 'commanding heights of production' to try to ensure essential goods and services were provided by the state and not left to the vicissitudes of the free market. They got a commitment to maintaining full employment (for John Maynard Keynes was now being listened to) and the building of thousands of homes. The policies of the 1945–51 Labour government directly improved the lives of the people who voted for them. This is a thought worth holding when considering what happened on 23 June 2016.

It is worth holding another thought too. Most of what Clement Attlee's government did would not have been possible without the absence of one particular force and one particular institution. Attlee was able to implement his manifesto without it being influenced by uncontrollable factors. It is worth noting when comparing the outcomes of the 1945 election and the 2016 referendum that a government's authority to govern itself (de jure sovereignty) is *not* the same as a government's ability to control what happens in the country (de facto sovereignty).

As Attlee took office in 1945, the forces of globalisation were not yet an influence on UK politics. Countries around the world were barely able to provide for themselves, let alone trade with others, and there was thus little global movement of workers, goods, services or money. There were very few multinational companies around, let alone ones with income greater than most countries' gross domestic product.

Nor did Attlee's government have to worry about the influence of a higher form of sovereignty such as the European Coal and Steel Community, which came along in 1951. Essentially, the implementation of socialism in a country, which was Labour's aim, required the state to have the capability to control wages and employment in a manner that is impossible under outside influence.

The truth is that much of what the Labour government did would be illegal under European Union state aid law.[7] These rules prohibit actions (such as subsidies or tax reliefs) which use state resources to give recipient firms an unfair advantage over competitors from other countries, thus distorting trade between those two countries. To achieve full employment, a government would have to replace revenue a firm might not be using (say, due to a recession) with public funds so that they don't need to make redundancies. This would be illegal state aid under EU law. So would some of the nationalisation that Labour undertook – as some readings of EU competition law suggest that any action that lessens competition would be illegal.

Most importantly, 1945 was a unique opportunity for a major adjustment in how the country operated that could deliver real and tangible results for those who voted for it. It wasn't just short-term either: what followed became known as 'the post-war settlement', which lasted until around 1970, through thirteen years of Conservative government from 1951 to 1964 as well as a further six years of Labour government until the end of the '60s.

This settlement, also known as 'the post-war consensus', featured a general agreement between the two parties of government on how the country would be run. Most importantly, in terms of explaining why so many older people voted to leave the EU on 23 June 2016, the central aim of the consensus was that no one would be 'left behind' by the economic management of the country. This consensus, combined with falling import prices as the countries who provided Britain with its raw materials (agriculture and minerals) came back 'on stream' after the war, and the technological and manufacturing advances made globally, led to the longest uninterrupted economic boom in modern British history. Critically, this was a boom in which the vast majority of the British population shared.

At the end of ten years of Conservative rule, in 1961, unemployment stood at around 1.3 per cent of the population, dropping as low as 300,000. Harold Macmillan's 'One Nation' government had built 500,000 new homes and was embarking on massive infrastructure projects such as building the M1 motorway, in addition to other routes. As Macmillan pointed out in a much-misquoted 1957 speech: 'Let us be frank about it, most of our people have never had it so good.'[8]

As we now know, the next ten years saw a gradual realisation that the British people might never have it so good again, and there were two failed attempts to join the European Community, both vetoed by Charles de Gaulle. These European humiliations weren't seen as too serious for the UK while the economy was still booming and jobs were still being created, which was the case until the onset of the late 1960s. But the 1970s saw the breakdown of the post-war settlement, and nothing would ever be the same in the UK again. Here's what happened.

A government policy of maintaining full employment necessarily reduces spare capacity in the economy, meaning that should a firm (or the government in the case of nationalised industries) want to raise production or increase its scale, it is difficult to find new employees. Basic economics will tell you that when supply of a factor of production is low, the price of that factor of production should rise. In this case, trade unions pushed for wage rises for workers. Firms having to pay higher wages would then mean they had to charge higher prices to be able to pay those wages. From the very start of the full employment policy, various government ministers had attempted to negotiate with unions and businesses to achieve some sort of pay restraint, but pressure had built up beneath the surface of the British economy throughout the '60s.

The Wilson government tried to reach an official accommodation with the trade unions under the guise of Barbara Castle's 'In Place of Strife' industrial relations White Paper.[9] This was legislation that put some controls on the power of unions to strike that would subsequently seem tame by 1980s Thatcher standards, but the agreement was fought off by the unions as an unacceptable restriction of the rights of workers. So wages continued to rise, and when they didn't, strike action quickly ensued.

Related to this was the breakdown of the idea that if you put more money into British workers' pockets they would buy more British firms' products, creating more jobs in a virtuous circle. As wages rose and prices rose, British goods became less price-competitive. In addition, British employers (whether public or private) were finding it difficult to persuade British workers who were not in fear for their jobs to learn new working methods, adopt new technology or increase their productivity. This meant that British goods were also less competitive in terms of quality. All this not only meant that demand for British exports from countries abroad lessened, but that British consumers were increasingly turning to foreign imports for their consumption.

This caused two problems: firstly, the reduction in demand for UK exports and increased expenditure on foreign imports hurt Britain's balance of payments figures (the value of exports minus the value of imports, which was important at a time of fixed exchange rates) – which put more pressure on the government's finances, as it had to make up any shortfall. Second was the impact on job creation, which began to creep downwards as unemployment crept upwards, crossing the 700,000 barrier in 1971.

Meanwhile, as we know, the resignation of Charles de Gaulle and the election of Edward Heath as Prime Minister, the most Europhile leader the UK has ever had, paved the way for Britain to join the European Community. We also know that when the UK joined the European Community, it had to sign up to the full *acquis communautaire* – the treaties and agreements that existed at the time. The most relevant of these were the Common Agricultural Policy and the Common Fisheries Policy. The CAP established the concept of 'European preference', meaning that the members of the EC first looked to each other to buy agricultural products over countries outside the EC. In practice, this involved tariffs (taxes on imports) being put on agricultural products in addition to subsidies being paid to agricultural producers. Significantly, whereas Britain had a policy of subsidising farmers through the tax system (which made it progressive, as higher-income consumers paid a higher proportion of their income in tax than lower-income consumers), the CAP subsidised farmers through higher consumer prices (which made it regressive, because if everyone pays the same price regardless of income then those on low incomes pay a higher proportion of their income for the same goods).

What this means is that almost immediately after the UK joined the EC, food prices went up. Food being a necessity, workers demanded higher wages from their employers, but employers were struggling to meet those demands without large price increases, leading to the start of a 'wage–price spiral', with each forcing the other up.

Another consequence of this change of trading focus was a reduction in trade coming into the west of the UK. Now that anything from the Commonwealth and the Americas were subject to tariffs, there was less reason to import from them. The reduction in ships that came from the west meant that those ports facing that direction – particularly Liverpool and Glasgow – started to see a decline in business going through them from 1973. These cities were thus the first major places in Britain to be left behind by UK politicians' decisions.

They weren't the only ones: the Common Fisheries Policy was worse in terms of its effect on certain members of the UK population. The CFP was signed by the existing members (whose waters contained relatively little fish) on the morning of the day on which the applications of the UK, Ireland, Denmark and Norway (whose waters contained four fifths of all fish in Europe) to join the EC were handed in. Thus the CFP was part of the *acquis communautaire* the applicants had to accept on joining. The Norwegians had a referendum on membership of the EC, which resulted in a resounding 'No'. The UK, which didn't have a referendum, thus opened up its fishing waters to the whole of Europe, and the end of its traditional fishing communities was nigh. It wasn't as if those communities received help from the European Regional Fund, which saw depressed industries and regions receive money from a central pot. Access to the regional fund was linked by France's President Pompidou to Britain joining monetary union, so there was no respite for one of our island's oldest industries. The fishing community was one of the groups who voted Leave en masse on 23 June 2016.

As explained in Reason 5, all this was compounded in autumn 1973, when the Yom Kippur War in the Middle East led to a four-fold increase in oil prices, affecting the whole of Europe. France also floated its currency under national pressures, so ideas of monetary union had to be put on hold. The association of Europe with economic prosperity was ended. This prosperity had strengthened the loyalty of the six founding members to each other, but after Britain joined, luck for pro-Europeans ran out, as economic difficulties ended the long boom.

Britain immediately sank into economic and political chaos. Faced with a massive rise in energy costs, firms had to raise their prices. Added to the additional cost of domestic energy and food prices, workers demanded higher wages and weren't taking 'no' for an answer. Strikes closed coal mines and power stations, and Heath had to propose a three-day week. He called an election in 1974 to decide 'who governs Britain' and it turned out that it wasn't him, as he lost to Harold Wilson's Labour Party.

As we've seen, one of the reasons that Wilson won is that his party had come to an agreement to offer a referendum on Britain's membership of the Common Market. This occurred in 1975 and is described in more detail in Reason 5 of this book. A key point about the 1975 referendum here is how unbalanced it was, with all three major party leaders, the entirety of the mainstream press and most businesses supporting the Yes campaign. An even more key point, for better or worse, was that many people who voted Yes to staying in the Common Market felt deceived as time went on by how the Common Market (presented as a free trade area and little more) gradually changed to involve ever closer monetary and political union. There was no talk of the European Community being a superior legal order, creating legislation that couldn't be repealed or amended by Westminster. As we know, there was a national veto at the time on important policies, but that was more or less given away in 1986 by Margaret Thatcher in return for the voting through of the single market in the Single European Act.

To those who felt betrayed and left behind by the mainstream political establishment, the way the 1975 referendum was conducted was another example of their needs not being taken into account. The youngest of those who voted in 1975 were fifty-nine years old in 2016, and over 90 per cent of over-65s voted in the 2016 referendum. Many of them felt they wanted another chance to vote on a political and economic arrangement that they believed they had never given consent to.

Wilson was forced out in 1976, and when Jim Callaghan and Denis Healey took over, Britain was mired in such deep economic chaos, with unemployment reaching seven figures, combined with inflation of over 25 per cent, that they went cap in hand to the International Monetary Fund (IMF) for a bailout. The rise in taxes and cuts in government spending imposed by IMF policies meant another round of pay policies (caps on pay increases) had to be attempted by Callaghan at the end of 1978. The response was a series of strikes that paralysed the country in what *The Sun* called the 'Winter of Discontent'. Rubbish bags went uncollected, filling up Leicester Square at one point, and bodies went unburied as even gravediggers went on strike. Britain was labelled the 'sick man of Europe', and looked in desperate need of something different.

Into this mess rode a putative white knight, wielding a completely different economic model. No analysis of the effect of Margaret Thatcher's policies on the UK is possible without understanding the condition of the country when she became Prime Minister. It is also important to explain what Thatcher was aiming to do, and separate her motives from the consequences of her actions. That said, by the end of the 1980s, a vast swathe of the United Kingdom had been cut loose from the protection of the government. Critically, this was the moment when people started getting left behind.

Put simply, Margaret Thatcher overturned the post-war economic consensus by arguing that government money should no longer be spent underwriting loss-making industries. Instead, production in the UK should be left to the forces of the free market. State-owned industries were to be sold off and opened up to competition. She argued that this competition would encourage firms to become more efficient, producing what customers wanted at cheaper prices and investing in a wider choice of products and services.

Many who defend Thatcher point out, for instance, that Labour Prime Minister Harold Wilson closed more coal mines. This is true, but Wilson led a more activist employment policy that subsidised alternative employment. Thatcher assumed instead that as her policy of non-intervention hit home, those who lost their jobs through coal mine and industrial plant closures would be incentivised to retrain for other jobs and also move to where those jobs were.

But there were problems with this assumption. Firstly, many of those who worked in coal mines were only skilled at working in coal mines. They had often left school at a young age, and may not have possessed transferable skills (including reading and writing) to enable them to retrain for different jobs, so they were faced with either unemployment or very low-paying alternatives. There was no plan to mitigate this.

Secondly, many of these mining and industrial communities existed because of the mine or factory they worked in. So the idea that people would uproot their families and move away from communities in which their families had lived and worked for sometimes over a century was unrealistic to say the least. Despite Thatcher's Employment Secretary Norman Tebbit regaling the 1981 Conservative Party conference with stories of how his father 'got on his bike and looked for work'[10] when he lost his job, it turned out many lacked both the will and the ability to do so.

Unemployment, which had been just over 1 million when Thatcher took over in May 1979, reached over 3 million by 1982. Thatcher assumed this would be a short-term issue as the economy 'sorted itself out'. But for many people, it never did. The country was left pockmarked by scars of unemployment and poverty. The communities most affected, spread around the country, were essentially left to rot, with many still unemployed to this day, or stuck in low-paid employment.

Concurrently, Thatcher opened the country up fully to the forces of globalisation. Exchange controls (which stopped people taking more than £50 out of the country) were relaxed, and in 1986 the 'Big Bang' allowed foreign banks to relocate to a far less regulated financial services regime in the UK, particularly London. More firms shut, unable to deal with competition from abroad. What's more, the uptick in foreign holidays spelt the death knell for seaside communities such as Great Yarmouth, Blackpool and Skegness.

This book is not about the overall rise in GDP and fall in inflation that were key to analysing the Thatcher years economically. But it is about who benefited from that growth and, more importantly, who did not. The south-east benefited greatly. Many people got extremely rich. When Thatcher was convinced to react to the desperation of communities that had lost their main source of income, investment was concentrated mainly in cities such as Liverpool and Birmingham.

So, in the EU referendum, 79 per cent of voters chose Remain in Hackney, east London, 75 per cent in Camden, north London, and 69 per cent in Kensington and Chelsea in west London. Meanwhile, 73 per cent voted Leave in Castle Point in Essex, 72 per cent in Great Yarmouth in north Norfolk and 66 per cent in Redcar and Cleveland in the north-east of England.[11]

As Britons defined themselves more as consumers than as producers, many people got left behind. These people became the 'losers' from unfettered competition and globalisation. They weren't 'living in the past' and they weren't lazy.

Their now troubled existence was a new phenomenon. As new as globalisation, which by its very nature involves losers.

As time went on and the Conservatives entered their fourth term in government in the early 1990s, a continuous lack of investment in public services such as education and healthcare brought with it literally crumbling schools and hospitals in the very regions where they were most needed. But hope was on the horizon for those left behind by globalisation.

Tony Blair entered Downing Street as Labour Prime Minister on a sunny day in May 1997. At last, here was someone who was going to save the day for those who had been abandoned by the Conservatives. Surely, with a majority of 179, he and his government would be free to bring back socialism, concentrate the focus of government on the most vulnerable and help those who most needed it. At a most basic level, New Labour did just that. There was the institution of the national minimum wage (NMW), the Disability Discrimination Act, and the adoption of the Social Chapter, but, ultimately, the NMW was set too low, and Blair's government were committed to Conservative spending plans for two years and a freeze on income tax while in government (such had been their fear of not getting elected in 1997, they had made a lot of commitments that held them back from really making a difference to those most in need). Even the obvious victory that was going to come in the 2001 election didn't encourage Labour to commit to rescuing those communities left behind by globalisation. In fact, things were about to become much worse.

The second half of Reason 8 in this book details the impact of the eight Eastern European countries having joined the EU, many of whom had a GDP per capita less than half that of the UK. It tells the story of how the fifteen 'incumbent' members of the EU applied transition controls on the freedom of movement of these workers into their countries, which lasted seven years, while the UK government, led by Tony Blair, decided not to apply those transition controls, because it was believed the booming economy required a new supply of skilled workers.

As with Margaret Thatcher's reforms, the importance of this influx of migrants is not about whether or not they benefit the country as a whole. It is not about whether or not they pay more in tax than they take out in benefits. It is their effect, or actually their perceived effect, on the lives of Britons, and in particular Britons already left behind economically. As we also know from Reason 8,

Labour MPs like John Denham were telling Blair and his team about the impact on jobs, wages and public services and asking for help and support to mitigate the impact on parts of the population who tended to need those jobs, wages and public services the most – a group that was supposed to be New Labour's core constituency of voters.

The consequences of this combination of lack of government support, exposure to the full force of globalisation and freedom of movement of workers and money can be best seen from what has come to be known as 'the elephant curve'. This was created by World Bank economist Branko Milanovic and his colleague Christophe Lakner in 2012.

The chart lined up everyone in the world in order of income on the horizontal axis and showed the percentage change in their real income (taking out the effects of inflation) from 1988 to 2008. The key group are those at the 77th to 85th percentile. They are the working-class, lower-skilled people in developed countries such as the UK. Around 80 per cent of the world has an income below them, but over the past thirty years their inflation-adjusted income has fallen. They are the only people in the world this has happened to. The middle class in middle-income countries have done very well (e.g. China's middle class, which accounts by themselves for a camel-like bump in the curve at around 50 per cent). The richest 1 per cent's line is almost vertical. [12]

In real terms, this translates to the working class in developed countries seeing their jobs outsourced to other countries while simultaneously watching immigrants come to their countries. This, they feel, increases the supply of labour without an increase in demand, and so has also been responsible for pushing down their wages.

What did Tony Blair do about this? Well, *Guardian* journalist John Harris, introduced in the previous chapter as probably the pre-eminent chronicler of these changes taking place around the UK, tells a story from 2005 that sums up how little he actually did. Harris starts off in May 2005 with Blair standing on the steps of 10 Downing Street after his third general election victory had reduced his majority massively, and his party had received only 35.2 per cent of the popular vote, a mere 22 per cent of the total electorate's vote. With humility, Blair spoke of how he had listened and learned and would focus on how life is a real struggle for many. He then devoted one section of his speech to rising public angst about immigration.

Five months later, Harris was watching Blair make his twelfth annual conference speech as party leader. The humility had vanished, to be replaced by his mission to toughen up the country in response to the endless challenges of the free market and globalisation. Here are the words that Harris picked out:

> Change is marching on again ... The pace of change can either overwhelm us, or make our lives better and our country stronger. What we can't do is pretend it is not happening. I hear people say we have to stop and debate globalisation. You might as well debate whether autumn should follow summer ... The character of this changing world is indifferent to tradition. Unforgiving of frailty. No respecter of past reputations. It has no custom and practice. It is replete with opportunities, but they only go to those swift to adapt, slow to complain, open, willing and able to change.[13]

Harris remembers what he thought watching the speech and listening to those words: '"Most people are not like that." The words rattled around my head: "Swift to adapt, slow to complain, open, willing and able to change." And I wondered that if these were the qualities now demanded of millions of Britons, what would happen if they failed the test?'

The answer came to Harris eventually:

> If modern capitalism was now a byword for insecurity and inequality, Labour's response increasingly sounded like a Darwinian demand for people to accept that change, and do their best to ensure that they kept up. Worse still, those exacting demands were being made by a new clique of Labour politicians who were culturally distant from their supposed 'core' voters, and fatally unaware of their rising disaffection.[14]

Those left behind by Thatcher's Britain and then by Blair's Britain tried to make their rising disaffection clear, focusing on the effect of immigration on their lives, as that was the most visible manifestation of the changes wrought on them by the free market and globalisation. But when they complained about it, they were called racist and ignored. Reason 8 of this book starts with the story of Rochdale pensioner Gillian Duffy's attempt to talk to Gordon Brown about it, resulting in her being dismissed as a bigot the minute the PM got in the car. The chapter ends with an explanation of how the metropolitan-minded class of New Labour politicians who had grown up during the struggles for racial equality in the '60s and '70s and thus relished diversity had come to equate controls on immigration with racism.

Around 2006, the political point was beginning to be made that mainstream, 'respectable' parties of the centre-left and centre-right, which tend to win general elections, cannot and will not do anything about globalisation's negative effects. The elephant in the room to be added to this was race. Those left behind by globalisation were seen to speak or respond to the language of racial or ethnic backlash, which meant that 'respectable' mainstream political parties stayed away from them. Those left behind by globalisation had nobody to represent their interests. The left spoke to the dispossessed working class economically, but they didn't speak to them culturally (in fact, they actively dismissed them as racists for years). Meanwhile, the right spoke to the dispossessed working class culturally but didn't speak to them economically.

This is not about simple racism. This is why Reason 8 talked of the work of John Harris and video journalist John Domokos as they travel around the country meeting people far away from the London political bubble for a *Guardian* series called 'Anywhere but Westminster'. Listen to the builder in South Shields talk of how his hourly rate had come down by £3 from what was already a small amount due to new arrivals from Eastern Europe. See the former docker in Liverpool stare at a row of empty warehouses, asking: 'Where is the work?' Hear people in Peterborough claim that job agencies would only hire non-UK nationals who would work insane shifts for tiny rates of pay. Watch the mother in Stourbridge in the West Midlands ask for a new school for 'our kids'. It all shows a shortage of homes and public services and an impossibly precarious job market – and little sign of anyone wanting to do anything about it. Economic growth is no use to this demographic if a by-product is a visible worsening of their lives.

At this point, the only political party who seemed to speak up for those who had been completely left behind by political parties was the British National Party. The BNP's rather unpalatable platform on race was leavened by what could best be described as extremely left-wing industrial policies involving subsidies for declining industrial areas. In the period from 2006 to 2010, they enjoyed a political ascendency involving winning two seats in the European Parliament and a seat on the London Assembly. But, ultimately, the nature of their barely concealed racism pushed away the more left-wing of those voters being discussed.

Notably, then, this portion of Britain's population entered the second decade of the new millennium feeling unrepresented by the political system but with very little way to express their frustrations. Thirteen years of Labour government had given way to the Conservative-led coalition with the Liberal Democrats that was imposing austerity policies in response to the build-up of a massive deficit from the 2008 financial crisis. Austerity, featuring in particular a reduction in government spending, would further hit those most vulnerable and most in need of help from government. At the same time, the banking system had been bailed out, suggesting that some people in society would never get left behind.

Then, in 2012, Nigel Farage and UKIP stepped up the intensity of their approach to the left-wing voters who had become totally alienated from the Labour Party. This new demographic could be added to the Conservative voters that UKIP's right-wing libertarian platform had been attracting for a decade.

As we will hear in future chapters, Farage, whose party had gained almost a million votes at the 2010 election but no seats in the Westminster Parliament, was talking to a bunch of Conservative MPs fed up with the influence the Lib Dems had on the ability of their party to implement their manifesto. The threat of these MPs defecting, added to some concerning polling, brought David Cameron to make his fateful promise to hold an In/Out referendum on the EU by the end of 2017.

Mahatma Gandhi, the leader of the Indian independence movement, was once quoted as saying: 'First they ignore you, then they laugh at you, then they fight you, and then you win.'[15]

The fightback of the dispossessed, fed up of their personal circumstances, feeling that the political establishment wasn't interested in them, started in earnest in May 2014, when UKIP became the first political party outside Labour or the Conservatives to win a national election since 1906. They came first in the elections to the European Parliament, becoming Britain's largest party in Brussels. But it was the European Parliament, so the Westminster bubble ignored them.

Then, in 2015, UKIP achieved 4 million votes in the general election. But the electoral system, which requires geographical concentration of votes rather than sheer numbers, gave those 4 million votes one seat. Meanwhile, the Scottish National Party got 1.5 million votes and fifty-six seats. This time, despite the obvious unfairness of the result, the Westminster bubble laughed at them.

But possibly the most unexpected outcome of the 2015 election was that the Conservatives won outright, which meant they were suddenly committed to delivering their entire manifesto. We will look elsewhere at whether the entirety of their manifesto was ever meant to be delivered – or whether the more difficult and controversial aspects were intended to be traded away in coalition negotiations. Suffice to say one of the commitments was to hold the EU referendum that had been so rashly promised by David Cameron.

When Cameron came back from Brussels with the results of his attempted renegotiation in February 2016 and named the date of 23 June 2016 as Referendum Day, the dispossessed suddenly had access to a democratic mechanism that made them extremely powerful. The vote of each of those builders in South Shields who had seen their hourly wages fall was now worth as much as David Cameron's vote. General election campaigns often see massive disparities in funding of the different parties. Rich donors can 'buy' access and influence to the governing parties to persuade them to adopt favourable policies. National campaign limits are quite flexible. But the very strict rules and caps on referendum campaign spending meant that this one couldn't be bought.

In the next section of the book, we will see that the Westminster bubble, with all the leaders of the mainstream political parties supporting the Remain campaign, tried to fight them. On social media they were called racist and lazy and told of the economic Armageddon that would ensue should they vote to leave the EU.

The problem with this approach was that Project Fear, as it was labelled by the Leave campaign, told people who had little to lose that their lives would get worse, when they didn't believe that was possible.

The Leave campaign focused on either getting the voters they needed to the polls or persuading voters to take the risk of voting Leave. They told a large mass of people who were unhappy with their lives and who wanted change that leaving the EU would control immigration, give the government more money to spend on them, and allow them to 'take their country back'. Whether or not any of that was true was not the point. As in 1945, the economically dispossessed wanted a change in their personal circumstances, and voting to leave the EU offered them that change. They were willing to take a risk that unknown change would be better than the status quo offered by Remain's Project Fear.

So, the mainstream respectable centrist politicians of all major British political parties reaped the consequences that occur when you ignore the needs of a significant group of people who are mad as hell at being ignored and aren't going to take it any more.

Those people were ignored, laughed at and fought. Then they won.

THE PIED PIPER OF THE DISAFFECTED

We have established that there was a group within society primed for some kind of revolution. But what is also required is for someone to show the way. Someone who can point at the Bastille and say, 'We need to attack that,' and 'If we do, *this* will happen.' If you are going to lose a referendum, there has to be an outsider, a disrupter of the status quo, someone who pokes at the structures and has the tenacity to keep prodding. In short, a Nigel Farage. So how did he do it? And what motivated him in the first place?

Rebels are generally defined by the politicians and politics they oppose – and we tend to think of Nigel Farage as the adversary of David Cameron's administration and a crusader against immigration. But it didn't begin with immigration and he was created much earlier than David Cameron's political stage entrance. Farage was in fact a product of Margaret Thatcher and John Major, adapted and enhanced by Tony Blair. In 1991, Nigel Farage was a Conservative. Had he remained so, events twenty-five years later might have turned out very differently. But two things changed his mind about his chosen party and planted a seed for what would come.

The first was the Conservatives' decision under Margaret Thatcher to join the European Exchange Rate Mechanism in October 1990 at far too high a rate and at an inappropriate time for the UK's economic cycle. As detailed in Reasons 6 and 7, this meant Thatcher's replacement, John Major, had to raise interest rates during a recession and use the country's reserves to buy sterling just to keep the pound within its band.

As a commodities trader, Farage believed in free market fluctuation, be it the metals he traded or currencies that rose and fell depending on economic factors such as productivity and confidence. He didn't like the idea of the pound in a straitjacket. He describes his as a 'global view' and maintains that fixing the rate of one currency to another or to the gold standard was 'always a catastrophe'. He also believed the ERM was a prelude to something even more undesirable. 'In October 1990 I was absolutely furious that we joined the ERM. I thought it was going to be a bloody disaster and it turned out it was,' he said in his interview for this book.

As we know, Farage was right about the impending 'bloody disaster'. On 16 September 1992, the UK left the ERM, but not until £3 billion was spent trying to keep the pound above the lowest rate set and raising interest rates to an eye-watering 15 per cent. The pound was 4 per cent down on the day – 15 per cent down by the end of the month. The currency wouldn't see a nosedive like it again until the early hours of 24 June 2016. The Conservatives lost their reputation for economic competence for a political generation. They also lost Nigel Farage's trust.

'It was perfectly clear to me that, unchecked, the Tories would have taken us into the euro. It wasn't called the euro, no one quite knew what it was going to be called, but it was pretty clear the British establishment wanted us to join it.'

The second thing Nigel Farage strongly objected to was John Major signing the Maastricht Treaty, which stipulated 'ever closer union' between European member states. Reason 7 tells the story of how twenty-two Tory rebels voted against ratification of the treaty but the rebellion was quelled when Major tied the question into a vote of confidence in his government. The chapter begins with Major's famous recorded 'off-the-record' exchange with ITN political editor Michael Brunson in which he referred specifically to Cabinet members who under other circumstances might have been sacked for going against government policy as 'bastards'. Just after Major used that word, he asked the question 'What's Lyndon Johnson's maxim?' before someone, presumably an ITN technician, pulled the plug on the live microphone he was wearing. Johnson's maxim came from when he decided not to sack FBI director J. Edgar Hoover with the reasoning: 'It's probably better to have him inside the tent pissing out, than outside pissing in.'

Major's problems were no different from those of his successor David Cameron, who would also discover he had 'bastards' in his Cabinet who were plotting to defy him on Europe when they got the chance. But there was one Conservative, during the Major era, who wasn't content to sit quietly and wait. Nigel Farage was disgusted that the Maastricht rebels 'didn't have the guts to vote

THE PIED PIPER OF THE DISAFFECTED

against the confidence motion'. Having once thought he would always be a Conservative, he now felt that the party had betrayed everything it stood for. 'There was no point trying to change the establishment from within. I may as well try to change it from the outside,' he said. In other words he decided to stand outside the tent and piss in.

And so Farage became the real bastard of the Tories: the illegitimate Conservative in self-imposed exile. At this point, he had just two things: 'absolute belief' that he was right, combined with 'a total lack of faith in the government and the political class'. These were two essential requirements to start a revolution – but of course – he needed much more. He would need extensive funding, a message of broad appeal, and a vehicle to harness this self-belief into a saleable package – and so he became one of the founding members of UKIP.

A Eurosceptic party had already been set up in 1991 by the historian Alan Sked, originally called the Anti-Federalist League. Sked initially thought his party would 'convert the Tory Party to Euroscepticism'.[1] But the Tories turned against him and he was thrown out of the Bruges Group for putting up candidates against Conservatives. It was at the public meeting where Sked was ambushed into standing down from the Bruges Group that he first met Nigel Farage.

Farage became an activist under Sked and in 1993 the party was renamed the UK Independence Party. Using a right-wing platform, it gradually increased its support, attracting a few more Tory rebels to the fold, but to start with it hardly left the establishment shaking in its boots. During the European parliamentary election of 1994, it captured only 1 per cent of the vote. Compare that to twenty years later, when UKIP won the European elections of 2014, becoming the first party for 100 years to beat both Labour and the Conservatives in a national election. How did they do it?

Let's start with funding.

The first funding boost for the cause actually came from a rival party. Multimillionaire James Goldsmith's Referendum Party, founded in 1994, had a similar message to the UK Independence Party but a lot more money behind it. Initially, this was a problem. It seemed this wealthy rival might destroy UKIP. Members crossed over to what looked like a much more powerful party machine with Goldsmith as its charismatic leader.

In the 1997 general election, the Referendum Party stood in 547 constituencies and finished fourth in vote share, racking up over 800,000 votes (approximately 2.5 per cent). In comparison, UKIP got only 0.3 per cent of the vote, just over 100,000. Of 194 candidates, Nigel Farage, standing in Salisbury, was the only one who got more than 5 per cent and was thus able to keep his deposit. Where the two parties stood against each other – in 165 seats – UKIP came top in only two.

James Goldsmith himself managed only 1,500 votes. So, like Farage, he never got a seat in the House of Commons. Standing in the swing seat of Putney, he did, however, get the pleasure of taunting a government minister, David Mellor, as he lost his seat to Labour. On the platform after the results were announced, Goldsmith shouted, 'Out, Out, Out.' Mellor mocked him back, saying 1,500 votes was 'a derisory figure'. He told Goldsmith to 'get off back to Mexico knowing that your attempt to buy the political system has failed'.[2]

When Goldsmith died later that year, his party went with him, but he had done something Farage's party could never have afforded to do. In the run-up to the election, he had delivered a videotape to 6 million UK households. The twelve-minute film presented by the *That's Life* presenter Gavin Campbell warned of the emergence of a 'federal European superstate'.[3] Goldsmith was the first person to bankroll the campaign for a referendum – and many of the candidates he attracted to the Referendum Party were left with nowhere to go but UKIP.

At this stage, Farage was yet to become UKIP leader, but he was learning the importance of funding. 'Ultimately, it was very complementary,' he says. 'Jimmy massively raised the profile of the European issue. A direct result of what he did helped us to get three people elected to the European Parliament in 1999.' The 35-year-old Farage was one of them, elected to the European Parliament for the South East region. The same intake included the European Parliament's other most disruptive MEP: 27-year-old Daniel Hannan. Alongside them, the future leader of the Green Party Caroline Lucas also got a seat – all three were elected together at Winchester Town Hall. One man in the room, Gawain Towler, recalls Labour MEP Peter Skinner shouting 'Fascist, fascist,' at Farage. Towler says: 'I thought, well, Lucas is essentially a Communist and you're happy with that, and all he is saying is Britain should be independent.' It is notable too that Farage's campaign at this stage made no mention of immigration.

Towler, who was a Conservative at the time and described himself as 'vaguely Eurosceptic', also ended up in Brussels as a journalist, where he slowly came to the conclusion that 'you couldn't be in Europe and not run by Europe'. A stringer for the *Daily Telegraph*, he also worked for magazines and was *Private Eye*'s Brussels correspondent until one day when Farage approached him in a pub. The conversation went as follows:

'You're a Eurosceptic?'

'Yes.'

'You're a journalist?'

'Yes.'

'You take the piss, don't you?'

'Yes.'

'Do you want a job?'

'Yes.'

Towler became Farage's head of press and together they began to build up Farage's and UKIP's profiles. He recalls:

If *Newsnight* wanted to speak to Nigel in Brussels for a one-minute slot and he happened to be in Kent, he would get on a train to Brussels for that one minute and spend £250 to do it – because you had to. There was no question of turning down any bid. If you are not famous and you get a bid, you do it. It took him a long time to build that reputation.

Slowly, Eurosceptic funders began to respect UKIP as a viable agitator against the system. In 2004, the party got a further publicity boost when TV presenter Robert Kilroy-Silk, a former Labour MP, became a UKIP candidate for the EU parliamentary elections. That year, he helped push the Lib Dems into third place; UKIP went from three seats to twelve in the EU Parliament. But soon afterwards the party fell out with its new star, who, according to Towler 'within minutes thought he should be leader'. The current leader, at this stage former Conservative MP Roger Knapman, refused to stand aside, and so Kilroy-Silk left to form his own political group called Veritas.

It was three steps forward, two steps back. In this manner, it took years for UKIP to build up its profile and financial support base. Small parties have a habit of disintegrating into internal warfare or being wiped out by the challenges of the electoral system or lack of funding, but the European elections helped at least with the latter. The European Parliament gave UKIP's politicians well-paid careers. Furthermore, the EU's grant system, which gave money to parties with MEPs in the Parliament, was also a useful source of funds. UKIP would later face allegations of inappropriately channelling these funds into election campaigns in the UK. Ironically, the party's first leader, Alan Sked, thought the party should have nothing to do with the EU's 'gravy train'.[4] If UKIP had stuck with his opinion, the party probably would not have survived.

In terms of large-scale backing, UKIP's story didn't really transform until the likes of millionaire Conservative donors Stuart Wheeler and Arron Banks came onto the scene – but getting those funds and at the right time proved crucial. Wheeler, who'd made his money with a spread betting business, was so opposed to the Lisbon Treaty that he tried to take legal action to stop the Labour government completing ratification on the grounds that it was a breach of their manifesto agreement. The Conservative donor supported Liam Fox in the Tory leadership race that followed the resignation of Michael Howard, and he was disappointed with Cameron's U-turn on his promise to hold a referendum on Lisbon. It was following this that on 28 March 2009 he donated £100,000 to UKIP, and by 2011 he was party treasurer.

Wheeler was a crucial source of party funds, but UKIP's most famous backer was a latecomer to the party. Insurance tycoon Arron Banks seemed to come out of nowhere. He was announced as a UKIP donor only during the 2014 Conservative Party conference, but in those crucial years leading up to the referendum he became the bank of UKIP, and much more. It was leaked to co-author Jason Farrell at Sky News on the day of the Prime Minister's speech at the Conservative Party conference in October that Banks was offering the party £100,000. Sky ran a report that morning. William Hague, first on the stage that day, quipped to the conference hall that he'd never heard of Banks, who'd previously donated £250,000 to the Tories. He said: 'It's certainly not going to overshadow the Prime Minister's speech today that someone we haven't heard of has gone to UKIP.'[5] Insulted by the joke, Arron Banks decided to increase his donation to a more noticeable £1 million. 'I understand Mr Hague called me a nobody,' said Banks. After that, Banks and Farage never looked back.

Not only did Banks go on to fund the party's election poster campaign in 2015, he also set up the activist group Leave.EU, a vehicle for Nigel Farage, which bid to become the official Out campaign group for the referendum. We'll look in more detail at the significance of this group in later chapters, but when

Leave.EU's bid for the Electoral Commission's designation failed, Banks continued to chart his own course through the referendum – providing essential financial backing to keep UKIP on the road and also investing in a social media campaign. From his office in Bristol, he managed to attract nearly a million supporters online. He created videos watched by 6 million people – essentially, Nigel Farage had found himself another James Goldsmith.

Farage had to wait his turn to become leader of the party. He played his part in the ousting of previous leaders including founder Alan Sked, Sked's successor Michael Holmes and then Holmes's successor Roger Knapman. Throughout this time, UKIP remained a fringe party, bumping along the bottom of the polls below the likes of the BNP. So when Farage was elected leader of UKIP in September 2006, his goal was to broaden UKIP's appeal from being a single-issue protest party. He introduced new policies such as bringing back grammar schools, cutting taxes and the issue that would dominate the rest of his career, controlling immigration. He was mixing some of his conservative values with policies that wouldn't necessarily repel blue-collar voters. His target audience could be encapsulated in a single phrase, 'decent working people', but early on he had another sub-group in mind.

In his maiden speech to the UKIP conference, on 8 October 2006, Farage told delegates that the party was 'at the centre-ground of British public opinion'. He said: 'We've got three social democratic parties in Britain – Labour, Lib Dem and Conservative are virtually indistinguishable from each other on nearly all the main issues,' adding: 'You can't put a cigarette paper between them, and that is why there are 9 million people who don't vote now in general elections that did back in 1992.'[6]

It's interesting to contrast that reference to non-voters in his first speech as leader to that of his last speech on the eve of the referendum vote ten years later. On 22 June 2016, he said:

If you've never voted before, because you think voting won't change anything, then tomorrow is your opportunity to make a difference. Go out and do it. Vote with your heart, vote with your soul, vote with pride in this country and its people, and together we can make tomorrow our Independence Day.[7]

For ten years, Nigel Farage held faith that there was a group out there of disaffected people who simply didn't vote in general elections any more, but might vote if they were asked the right question. On this matter, it seems he was right. The turnout for the 2015 general election was 66.1 per cent. The national turnout for the referendum was 72.2 per cent: a difference of nearly 3 million people.

Significantly, the Remain camp had always feared that lazy young voters could cost them victory, as although overwhelmingly in favour of remaining in the EU, younger voters are less likely to actually take part in any election. Post-analysis of the result suggests that indeed the young were more reluctant to turn out, especially in strong Remain areas including London and Scotland, which also featured below average turnout. Glasgow was the lowest city at 56.2 per cent.

So it wasn't the disengaged young but disengaged older voters, many of them the people Farage was referring to in his maiden speech in 2006, who turned out to vote in the EU referendum.

Unlike the Scottish referendum, the rebels were not loud students with banners. They were people who had grumbled for years to their children and grandchildren about 'the way this country is going'. A generation born into or just after the war, the generation who had endured the '50s, or swung the '60s, or became mods and rockers in the '70s meeting for fights in Clacton – now they had retired to places like Clacton. Their youth was long behind them, but not their ability to rebel. Nigel Farage convinced them that the EU referendum was their chance.

In his interview for this book, Farage admits that 'the latter stage of the campaign was all about trying to get people who didn't normally vote out to vote, and they did. What was the difference between winning and losing? It was the increased turnout between the general election and the referendum – and that is clearly non-voters.'

Many analysts thought that if turnout was high, the Leave campaign would lose; indeed, even the official Vote Leave campaign was of the view that anything above 60 per cent would not bode well because it would mean that young people with a tendency for 'In' had bothered to go to the polling booths, but the UKIP leader says he had always thought differently. 'I always took the view: low turnout, Leave wins; high turnout, Leave wins – if it's in the middle, Remain wins.'

So Farage had identified this elusive group of non-voters, who are in large part made up of the people we identified in Reason 9: the 'dispossessed losers of globalisation'. Part of the way he was able to attract them was by being like them – outside of the traditional political system, shunned by 'the elite political class', using his status as an outsider as a selling point. As he put it, 'People either go into politics to become something, or to change something.' He saw himself as the latter. Of course, he would also 'become something': a thorn in the side of the establishment and pied piper of the disaffected. But if he was going to have electoral success, he also needed the backing of traditional Conservative and Labour voters.

It was in the mid-2000s that Farage says he first noticed that 'something fundamental' had changed. While canvassing in a Westminster by-election in 2006, he realised that despite the party being full of ex-Conservatives, UKIP's anti-EU message was getting traction in Labour heartlands.

It's no coincidence that two years earlier, the European Union had seen its largest single expansion in terms of territory, the number of states and the level of population. The newcomers comprised Cyprus, the Czech Republic, Estonia, Hungary, Latvia, Lithuania, Malta, Poland, Slovakia and Slovenia. However, the economic output of these countries was much lower than that of the existing members. Seven of these countries were part of the former Eastern Bloc, and three years later two more countries would join, Bulgaria and Romania.

As explained in Reason 8, existing EU member states took different approaches on how to handle the movement of people from these new territories. Some, such as Germany and Austria, initially maintained transition controls such as work permits and bilateral quotas on the numbers of immigrants. The UK and Ireland had no restrictions other than access to welfare.

We know now that this decision was partly justified by a government report in 2003 that predicted an additional net migration of between 5,000 and 13,000 from these new EU members. The authors had based the figures on Commonwealth countries from Australia to Swaziland and had stated that these figures would only hold true if all other countries also lifted transition controls. The reality turned out to be quite different. Between 2004 and 2012, the net inflow from the new bloc was 423,000.

Hence, there was a noticeable influx of people from Eastern Europe looking for work in the UK and because salaries were low in their home countries, they were offering cheap labour in the UK. The caricature of the Polish plumber was born.

'By 2005, it was obvious that something quite fundamental was going on,' says Farage. 'People were saying, "We're being seriously undercut here."'

A year later there was a by-election in Bromley and Chislehurst following the death of Eric Forth. Nigel Farage stood as a candidate. It was in this election that UKIP beat the Labour Party for the first time. They were still third behind the Conservatives and the Liberal Democrats, but for the man who was soon to become leader of his party, it became clear to him while knocking on doors that it was the traditional Labour areas where he was getting support. From this moment on, UKIP's time, effort, money and people were 're-tacked and rejigged' to reflect this. And his message was also adapted to focus more on immigration.

Before long, the delegates to party conference were travelling from places other than the Home Counties. At one conference, the party leader told co-author Jason in an interview:

> When I first started out, for the first five years or so, I could tell you exactly what a UKIP delegate looked like, what their background was, what they did in the war – now there is no typical UKIP delegate. We have former Labour councillors, people who have never been in politics in their lives, along with ex-Conservatives of forty years.

The main parties in Westminster may have introduced numerous policies to combat immigration, but they still seemed to underestimate the groundswell of public resentment caused by the influx of European migrants. Foreign builders, waitresses and bar staff were for the most part welcomed as a response to the needs of the economy. But the financial crash of 2008 and the resulting fall in living standards stoked resentments. Amid deprivation and neglect, immigration still thrived from an even more economically damaged EU. So migrants were blamed for shrinking wages and the Labour Party was blamed for immigration. During the course of Tony Blair and Gordon Brown's governments between the years of 1997 and 2010, net migration figures quadrupled. The combination of people fleeing conflict in the Middle East and the expansion of the EU meant the UK's population was boosted by 2.2 million people – more than twice the population of Birmingham. Over time, this gave Nigel Farage lots to talk about and plenty of people willing to listen.

In the run-up to the 2010 general election, David Cameron's pledge to reduce immigration to the tens of thousands was at least a recognition of the issue. And during this election UKIP only gained 3 per cent of the vote – a paltry 1 per cent improvement on the previous general election. That said, it still amounted to nearly a million votes, and could have been the difference between an outright win for Cameron and a hung parliament. But once in power, Cameron's immigration pledge appeared to be little more than wishful thinking. The political vacuum opened even wider for Nigel Farage, and popularity for UKIP began to surge, up to 15 per cent by 2012.

Soon the UKIP leader was a regular feature on BBC's *Question Time*. His years of racing across the Channel for a one-minute hit with *Newsnight* were over. He was a mainstay of British television news. What's more, he now had a newspaper behind him. In November 2010, the *Daily Express* became the first national newspaper to call for the UK to leave the EU. Two months later, its front-page cartoon was a crusader standing on the white cliffs of Dover. 'Get Britain out of Europe', said the headline. The knight says in a speech bubble, 'We demand our country back.'[8] So began the tabloid's six-year campaign to get the UK out of Europe. *Daily Express* political editor Patrick O'Flynn had been instrumental in persuading the newspaper tycoon Richard Desmond to take the stance. O'Flynn would soon leave the paper to become UKIP's director of communications.

By 2012, UKIP noticed something that had never happened before. Journalists began to turn up to their party conferences. Gawain Towler recalls his shock at seeing first Channel 4's Michael Crick, then ITV's Romilly Weeks arrive for the event in Birmingham. Farage was even invited on to the BBC's *Today* programme ahead of his speech. *The Guardian*'s Andrew Sparrow had never been to a UKIP conference before and recalled that previously, 'any half-decent political correspondent volunteering to attend would have been dismissed by colleagues as eccentric'. They were still a minor party with no MPs, but things had changed.

'They came second in the European elections in 2009, they are level-pegging with the Lib Dems in the polls and they exercise a potent influence on Conservative party politics. Anyone interested in the British political scene would be foolish to ignore them,'[9] wrote Sparrow.

The party began to really notice a breakthrough in the council elections of 2013, where they picked up 400 seats. A man called Ian Smith became a UKIP councillor in Dorset, just by putting his name on the paper. He'd entered so late in the day he wasn't included in any UKIP literature. The retired IT consultant didn't deliver any leaflets and he didn't attend the election count. The first time this 'paper candidate' realised he'd become a county councillor was when a local newspaper turned up at his front door. Smith called the UKIP press team for advice and was told, 'Invite them in for a cup of tea.'

The main question surrounding UKIP was how much their popular surge was applying pressure to Cameron to adopt a more Eurosceptic stance. The Conservatives, as a more rabid survivalist party than Labour, began looking for a new bone to throw to voters. If a pledge to bring immigration down to the tens of thousands couldn't actually be delivered, how about the promise of a referendum? We will discuss David Cameron's 2013 decision to hold a referendum in the next chapter – but it was clearly the breakthrough Farage had been working towards for two decades. What is also significant, though, is what it meant for Labour. The party had to choose between the pro-European instincts of its Westminster parliamentarians and addressing the concerns of many voters in its heartlands. Ed Miliband chose the former, opposing the referendum and hence giving Nigel Farage an additional reason to hone his message towards the blue-collar vote.

For the 2014 UKIP autumn conference, he deliberately held the event in Doncaster, the Labour leader Ed Miliband's constituency. Nigel Farage claimed: 'We are parking our tanks on the Labour Party's lawn.'[10] It took an awful long time for Labour to see them coming. Conservatives MPs defecting to UKIP only served to confuse the Labour Party even more. UKIP was a right-wing party, wasn't it?

David Owen, a former Labour Foreign Secretary who had left to form the Social Democratic Party in 1983 but was once again a Labour donor at the time, tried to persuade Miliband he should offer a referendum. But Miliband calculated that if he did so and then won the general election, the Tories would replace Cameron with a Eurosceptic leader and Labour would face the challenge of a strong Tory Leave campaign. The result of the referendum could well have been the same. It also wasn't in Miliband's nature to pander to UKIP.

If populist politics is difficult for the mainstream to understand, it is even harder for them to combat. The first response is usually to ignore, deplore or ridicule. Just look at Donald Trump in the 2016 US presidential elections. He completely outmanoeuvred the Republican Party's attempts to suppress his rise. The Washington bubble saw him as a joke, laughed at his wall to keep out the Mexicans and recoiled at his mix of casual racism, Islamophobia and misogyny.

Yet, one by one, he managed to see off sixteen other contenders to become the party's presidential candidate and then the financial and political might of Hillary Clinton to win the White House. In his convention speech in Cleveland, he said: 'Ignored, neglected and abandoned ... These are the people who ... no longer have a voice. I am your voice.'[11]

Subtle isn't a word you'd use often with Nigel Farage, but he was a more subtle version – a very English version – of Donald Trump. His beer-swilling, ordinary man down the pub image wasn't necessarily put on – but he did play to it. Like Trump, he focused on the fears of what he described as 'ordinary people' and he 'gave them a voice', in particular on immigration.

Mr Farage attended Donald Trump's Cleveland convention in July 2016 and said it was like a UKIP conference – 'the sheer unpredictability of it'. He found the Republican delegates saw Brexit as a 'sign of hope that the establishment can be beaten'. In August 2016, Trump asked him to speak at a rally, sparking the beginning of a relationship that eventually saw Farage not only pictured in Trump Tower with the President-elect the weekend after Trump won but even recommended as British Ambassador to the US by his new friend.

Like Trumpism, the chaotic nature of UKIP disguised the growing potency of its message. For years, journalists and Westminster politicians focused on the headline-grabbing farce: MEP Godfrey Bloom hitting a reporter on the head with a manifesto and calling women 'sluts' at their 2013 party conference; a cranky UKIP councillor in Henley-on-Thames blaming floods on the successful passage through Parliament of gay marriage and a UKIP candidate in Essex who joked about shooting peasants. All this became the stuff of wry newspaper columns: interesting and reportable but, like Donald Trump's hair, it was a distraction.

It was easy and fun to gently mock the haphazard nature of these wacky outsiders – in the same way that the people of Hamelin laughed at the man who danced off with the rats. Conservatives rubbed their hands, assuming it was actually helping detoxify the right wing of their party. UKIP attracted all the 'nut-jobs'. If the party held a conference in Torquay, it was a comedy 'Fawlty Towers' conference and analogies could be made with the mad hotel proprietor: 'Don't mention the war!' Even the Prime Minister felt comfortable enough to dismiss them as 'fruitcakes'.[12] So what did the fruitcakes do? They started to call themselves fruitcakes. They embraced the fruitcake. They served fruitcake at their party conferences.

Like any farce, the bombastic action seemed to build to a crescendo, as did the publicity and the rhetoric and indeed the popularity, in what we now compare to a Trump-like craziness. Nigel Farage invented this craziness. Like Trump, he learned the positive value of an attention-grabbing comment, or indeed a controversial poster.

His first big experiment with this strategy was in February 2014 at the 'Fawlty Towers' conference in Torquay. He was bolstered by figures released that week showing that net migration had risen by 40 per cent over the course of twelve months, from a net figure of 154,000 to 212,000. David Cameron's self-imposed target of reducing this figure to below 100,000 seemed at best wide of the mark, at worst a pipe dream.

That weekend, the tone of Farage's language about immigration was stronger than many journalists in the room could remember hearing from any senior politician in many years. He said:

> The fact [is] that in scores of our cities and market towns, this country in a short space of time has frankly become unrecognisable.
>
> Whether it is the impact in local schools and hospitals, whether it is the fact that in many parts of England you don't hear English spoken any more. This is not the kind of community we want to leave to our children and grandchildren.[13]

Note how well this message is directed to the people who've been wondering all these years 'what this country is coming to'. Then, in a question-and-answer session with journalists, he went even further. He described a train journey out of London, where no one in his carriage spoke any English. 'It was not till we got past Grove Park that I could actually hear English being audibly spoken in the carriage. Does that make me feel slightly awkward? Yes, it does.'

You see? An English Donald Trump. He wasn't suggesting the building of a wall or the banning of all Muslims, but in that stiff upper lip 'what's going on here with Johnny-foreigner' type of a way, Nigel Farage was connecting with what he felt was a large proportion of British people who also felt 'slightly awkward' but were just too polite to say anything about it. He was 'their voice': the guy who complains about the noisy table in the restaurant, saving everybody else the embarrassment of making a fuss.

He said afterwards to co-author Jason in a pub that he'd 'thought long and hard' about making the comment. The next day, in an interview for Sky News, asked why his train journey was so disturbing, he replied: 'I was in England… It made me feel uneasy and I think that sense of unease is actually shared by the vast majority of the population. It's impossible to integrate people if they are coming in in such vast numbers.'

He added: 'Almost by definition, if people are speaking a foreign language and have a very limited or in some cases zero use of English, that divides society.'

Farage's train journey was also an analogy for how separate London was to the rest of the UK. The account of his trip was a message to the wider country that taking public transport out of the metropolis was like slowly emerging from a foreign country, and he was warning people that multiculturalism was creeping out. He said he knew this story of reluctant discomfort would resonate because the year before he had toured the country in the run-up to the local elections, 'from Cornwall up to Hadrian's Wall', where he met people who would tell him, 'I hate the way I'm feeling now, but I really don't like seeing what is happening to my town.'

It is interesting to note, at this point, that research done after the EU referendum found that it was towns with relatively low immigration that voted more strongly for Brexit. Some market towns with more recent sharp rises in migration bucked that trend, but larger cities with high levels of immigration voted Remain. One might conclude that the fear of immigration was a greater motivation than the reality of it. At the very least, the UKIP leader's language was tapping into this fear – many argue he was instrumental in stirring it up.

Around this time, the British National Party, generally acknowledged to be a racist party, was imploding with a bitter civil war in its ranks, its demise already being linked to the rise of UKIP. Farage was certainly happy to mop up its voters – but not its members. Indeed, he changed his party's constitution to ban anyone associated with the BNP from joining UKIP. But it was clear that a calculated, divisive tone had crept into the UKIP leader's idiolect. He even knowingly converted what used to be a BNP slogan, 'Love Britain, Love the BNP', to the slogan for UKIP's February conference: 'Love Britain, Love UKIP'.

Add to this UKIP's 2014 poster campaign. They included an image of an escalator up the white cliffs of Dover, a British worker as a beggar with the slogan 'EU policy at work' and a large finger pointing with the strapline '26 million people in Europe are looking for work. And whose jobs are they after?' It led to a full Easter weekend of debate on whether we lived in a Christian country. Had we really become the xenophobic nation of Europe? Wasn't immigration helping to build Britain rather than destroy it? But amongst all this argument came the question – what are the main parties doing about immigration? Regardless of whether the posters were moral or immoral, UKIP was winning on this issue – and promises by the mainstream parties to 'get tough' and 'have an open debate' were starting to wash over the electorate.

Of course, from time to time, Farage did get savaged by journalists, most memorably by LBC's James O'Brien, who suggested that 'the mask had slipped' when the UKIP leader said he wouldn't want to live next door to Romanians. O'Brien asked, 'What about if a group of German children [moved in]? What's the difference?'

The UKIP leader, who is married to a German and therefore has half-German children himself, declared: 'You know what the difference is … An "open door" to immigration has been an open invitation to the traffickers.'

O'Brien responded: 'I asked you a question about Romanians and you started talking about people traffickers!'[14] The interview got even more bruising over Farage's links with far-right parties through his Europe for Freedom and Democracy group in the European Parliament. In the end, UKIP's director of communications, Patrick O'Flynn, stepped in to close off the verbal punches.

But the media and the political class were starting to do what they do best when they sense the undesirable rise of an underdog – they play the man not the ball. To be fair, Farage's language made him an obvious target and made it easier for his adversaries to suggest he was at the very least xenophobic. Even the UKIP founder Alan Sked claimed that the party had become 'Frankenstein's monster' under Farage's tenure. In an interview with *The Guardian*, the history professor said he had wanted a more liberal Eurosceptic party and that the UKIP leader was 'a racist political failure'.[15]

Personal attacks make good headlines but, justified or not, personal attacks don't always work. Margaret Thatcher once said, 'I always cheer up immensely if [an attack] is particularly wounding because I think, "Well, if they attack one personally, it means they have not a single political argument left."'[16] Farage certainly believed that was what was happening. With no clear indication of how the government or the main opposition could reduce net migration to the tens of thousands, it was easy for UKIP to suggest that any outrage at their message was simply an attempt by the 'liberal metropolitan elite' to shout down the debate on immigration. Much of the British public must have thought the same because in May 2014 they handed UKIP victory in the EU elections.

For the first time in modern history, neither Labour nor the Conservatives won a British national election. Nigel Farage unleashed his long-promised political earthquake across British politics, beating Labour by four seats and pushing the Conservatives into third place. Nick Clegg's Liberal Democrats, the only party that dared to face the UKIP leader in a debate in the run-up to the poll, lost all but one of its eleven MEPs. For all the lambasting of Farage's 'racist' comments, he seemed to be speaking a lot of people's language.

He now knew with certainty that all that mattered was one thing: getting heard. People needed to be talking about him, about his campaign, about immigration. With the Conservatives currently in coalition with the Liberal Democrats, Nigel Farage began to believe that maybe in the next election his party could hold the balance of power.

The result of the 2014 EU elections, one year after David Cameron had committed to a referendum, should have sent alarm bells ringing all across Westminster, but two things might have given the other parties reason to moderate their fears. Firstly, UKIP may have won, but only with 26.6 per cent of the vote – the Conservatives got 24.4 per cent and Labour 23.1 per cent – so if we assume UKIP has in this instance mopped up all the Eurosceptics, just over a quarter of the electorate, that means they would lose a referendum. Secondly, the result could easily be dismissed as a protest vote – a decision to actually leave the EU was a much more serious proposition.

However, if David Cameron had any doubts about calling a referendum to help him win the next general election, these were dispelled by the defection of two of his MPs to UKIP, Douglas Carswell and Mark Reckless. Both stood for their seats in by-elections – and both won. As we shall see in the next chapter (Reason 11), Carswell's motivation was in part to 'detoxify' UKIP, but he also bolstered its perceived risk to the Tory Party. By the end of 2014, UKIP had two MPs in the House of Commons – both former Conservatives, now on the opposite benches to the Prime Minister. Farage was claiming that UKIP might, with ten MPs, be part of the next coalition government. It was starting to look possible.

Of course, we now know it didn't happen. UKIP didn't get close to holding the balance of power. Only Douglas Carswell held on to his seat in Clacton.

Mark Reckless lost Rochester and Strood. The UKIP leader failed to win in South Thanet despite focusing his entire national campaign in one constituency. He briefly resigned and this was welcomed by Carswell, who thought Farage had become off-putting to mainstream voters, but the UKIP leader changed his mind and was immediately reinstated. The fact was, however, that 3.9 million people had voted for UKIP in the Westminster elections. The size of their success was disguised by the first past the post system, which gave the party only one seat for 12.6 per cent of the vote, while the SNP took fifty-six seats with 4.7 per cent of the vote.

Was UKIP really still a protest vote? 'For years and years people conned themselves that it was a protest vote,' said Farage. His polling, however, indicated that 'they were voting UKIP because they believed in the solutions on offer'. In his view, the other parties were in part blinded by the 'tribal' nature of British politics that has been nurtured through the first past the post electoral system. The UK voting process, which favours creating strong parties over coalitions, has encouraged a binary form of politics. 'They are so stuck to their tribes that they think anyone outside isn't someone they can do business with… If you are outside the mainstream you are a maverick,' says Farage.

This aversion to the maverick outsider remained an aspect of the referendum campaign. When Eurosceptic Conservatives outed themselves following David Cameron's renegotiation deal in 2016 (more of this later), they joined the campaign group Vote Leave, which refused to work with Nigel Farage. UKIP donor Arron Banks wanted to see Farage front and centre of the referendum alongside whoever came out for the Conservatives. He initially tried to bring everyone together, but the Tory Eurosceptics forming Vote Leave thought this would be a bad idea.

Eventually, three factions formed. Leave.EU was the Arron Banks and Nigel Farage group. Grassroots Out was made up of some backbench Conservatives and Labour's Kate Hoey. Vote Leave was a mostly Conservative operation, with its cross-party nature depending heavily on one Labour MP, Gisela Stuart, and UKIP's only MP, the Conservative defector Douglas Carswell. Carswell said in an interview for this book: 'Some of us underestimated Nigel's determination to stay on – and continue to campaign with a tone and a style that not only lost in Thanet South but also lost us [UKIP] votes and very nearly cost us the referendum.'

Nigel Farage, who'd clearly fallen out with his only MP, treated Vote Leave with equal suspicion. He and Banks criticised them for failing to put out a full-blooded Leave campaign. Instead, they seemed to be campaigning for EU reform. They were suspicious too that Vote Leave was full of former Conservative special advisors (spads) who might be government insiders looking to scupper the campaign. Farage also condemned their failure to use either John Longworth, who'd resigned as chair of the British Chambers of Commerce to campaign for Brexit, or Mick Cash, the Eurosceptic general secretary of the Rail Maritime and Transport Workers' Union. In the UKIP leader's view, 'They weren't there to win the referendum; they were there to fight internal battles for supremacy of the Tory Party.' In other words, according to Farage, it was all about getting Boris Johnson and Michael Gove into No. 10. The most he will accept is that 'they would rather have won than not won', but he insists that leaving the EU wasn't their key motivation. As we shall see, Vote Leave equally saw Farage as motivated by self-promotion. Both sides were against each other to win the coveted designation to become the official Out campaign group. In order to win the Electoral Commission's approval, these opposing camps acted like presidential candidates in the primaries, aggressively lambasting each other's credibility. At stake was a grant worth up to £600,000, campaign broadcasts and free mailing. The winning camp would also be allowed to spend up to £7 million, instead of £700,000, the limit that applies to other registered campaign groups.

Each side tried to win over the crucial support of MPs which would bolster their cross-party credentials in the eyes of the Electoral Commission, and to this endeavour Banks wrote an open letter to MPs warning that Matthew Elliott, Vote Leave's chief executive, and its campaign director Dominic Cummings were 'two of the nastiest individuals I have ever had the misfortune to meet' and that he 'wouldn't put them in charge of the local sweet shop'.[17]

Leave.EU increased its chances when it joined forces with Grassroots Out. That gave them Conservatives Peter Bone and Tom Pursglove as well as Labour's Kate Hoey, but it wasn't enough. Once a large section of the Cabinet joined Vote Leave, it was always likely that they would win the designation. In the assessment of their campaign director Dominic Cummings, the civil servants who make up the Electoral Commission were not going to 'put themselves in the history books' by giving the official campaign to Arron Banks while telling Boris Johnson and Michael Gove, 'That's just tough.' His view was that if they'd done that and the Leave campaign had gone on to lose, it would have been considered an establishment stitch-up. He adds: 'I always thought for purely self-interested reasons that the Electoral Commission would go with what they always do – the line of least resistance.' On 13 April 2016, Vote Leave was award-ed the designation.

It seemed like a blow to Farage, but standing apart from the Conservative Eurosceptic faction made a huge difference to the way the UKIP leader was able to campaign, and in hindsight he acknowledges this.

To start with, there were two campaign slogans. Vote Leave pumped out the highly disputed '£350 million a week' that they claimed was sent to the EU, while UKIP's key message, 'We want our country back', focused on the themes Nigel Farage had honed over several years. The two factions worked apart and yet in tandem.

'I did try to get people together under a big tent, and that didn't happen,' says Farage. 'But the irony is that it was probably a better campaign as it was with us all doing our own thing, and reaching different target audiences.' It meant that Farage could do all the things he had learned through his years as an anti-EU campaigner: focusing on the disaffected voters, targeting the blue-collar workers while leaving the heavy lifting of getting the Conservative vote out to the Tory populist Boris Johnson and the intellectual strategist Michael Gove. The Vote Leave bus toured Tory strongholds such as the Home Counties and the south-west while Farage spent most of his campaign in Labour areas in the Midlands and the big cities of the north of England.

Over the previous decade, since his revelation that there had been 'a fun-damental change' in attitudes towards EU immigration, he had been building a grid of exactly which areas had been attracted to voting for his party. If they were tempted towards UKIP, they would be tempted towards Brexit. Indeed, the EU referendum would be the ultimate poll for this target vote. It wasn't rigged to assist the main parties like the Westminster FPTP system. 'My vote counts the same as the Prime Minister's vote,' someone in Northumberland told co-author Jason, as if this had never happened before. That's how some saw the referendum. It was a once in a lifetime chance for the wretched and neglected, or just the disgruntled and mildly pissed off, to stick it to Westminster. And nowhere would they like the idea of this more than in the northern English regions that Nigel Farage was touring. These would become the cities that sent the first shockwaves through the markets in the evening the referendum results came in.

Farage was assisted here again by a lack of engagement from the Labour Party itself. It is for another chapter to explore how much this was down to the Labour leader himself, but several Labour MPs in the north took the view that their patch was so Eurosceptic it was better not to campaign at all. One told us: 'It would only antagonise them and I'd rather not remind them to vote.'

Nigel Farage took great delight in this approach:

Frankly, what I saw in the Labour heartlands was virtually no [Labour] campaign at all going on. It was fairly easy territory to dig into with a really voracious local newspaper, radio and TV campaign. People were desperate for something to cover – there wasn't much else going on in [places like] Sheffield in the referendum and we made things happen.

That's a boast the former Deputy Prime Minister and former Sheffield MP Nick Clegg might find hard to swallow.

But, more than this, Nigel Farage believes Bob Geldof handed him his biggest publicity boost. As detailed in Reason 4, the UKIP leader led a flotilla of fishing boats up the Thames to urge Parliament to 'take back control of British waters'. His Brexit armada was intercepted by a rival Remain fleet carrying Mr Geldof. The rock star yelled through a loudspeaker, telling Farage he was 'no fisherman's friend' and he was pictured sticking two fingers up, probably intended for Farage, though the gesture was also directed at the fisherman on the UKIP leader's boat.[18]

Afterwards, Farage noticed a massive backlash against Geldof on social media and it played well into his narrative of 'working-class decent people against the rich elite'. He says: 'I thought that morning, we are going to win this and win this big.'

In the later stage of his campaign, he focused on another strength: engaging people who didn't normally vote. At the time, there was a lot of media focus on what was looking like a 'blue on blue' war, referring to an expectation that at some point David Cameron would need to launch an attack on Michael Gove and Boris Johnson in response to what looked a lot like attacks on him – about which more later. Nigel Farage's ground war and poster campaign could pump out messages without much scrutiny. Apart from the flotilla, he pretty much went unnoticed by the national media – well, almost.

The brutal murder of Jo Cox in the streets of Birstall, Yorkshire happened on Thursday 16 June, one week before the referendum. The Labour MP had been an energetic new force in Westminster, outspoken and committed to changing the world for the better; a humanitarian who'd worked eight years for Oxfam. All who met her – including co-author Jason Farrell – were left with the impression that she was likely to have a significant future in politics. She was also a Remain supporter. Her death shocked the nation. Comments allegedly shouted by her attacker, his apparent far-right links and the fact that in court he called for 'death to traitors, freedom for Britain'[19] led to speculation that her murder was linked in part to anti-immigration sentiment that had been whipped up by the divisive rhetoric during the referendum campaign. Journalists looked for an example and seized on a UKIP poster that had been published in four newspapers that morning.

The image was of a queue of mostly non-white migrants and refugees making their way through Europe. The slogan was 'Breaking Point'. Nigel Farage may be right that the media wouldn't have noticed it but for the murder of Jo Cox. He says not a single journalist had called him up about it that morning. But suddenly Dave Prentis from Unison was writing to the Metropolitan Police complaining that the poster was 'a blatant attempt to incite racial hatred … scaremongering in its most extreme and vile form'.[20] Some likened it to Nazi propaganda. Michael Gove said it made him 'shudder' when he saw it.[21]

Had they not been listening to the UKIP leader's comments for the last decade, to his claims that market towns were 'unrecognisable', that foreign voices on trains made him 'uncomfortable', as did living next to Romanians? Nigel Farage had used these messages constantly though the past ten years of his political career as he'd worked out that they led to political gain. Speaking about the poster in an interview for this book, he admitted having mixed feelings about the events that followed. He describes the Sunday and Monday as a low point in his 25-year career, doing 'interview after interview just having to stand my ground, basically being accused of stirring up the kind of conditions that led this man to kill her [Jo Cox] on the streets of Batley'. He added: 'The Remain side decided they would use that [the poster] as a means of attacking the whole motivation behind the Leave campaign, and they did it to an extraordinary extent on the Sunday and it rolled through into Monday.'

But he added that there was a 'strange twist' to it all. By Tuesday morning, the campaigns were back on and Farage reflects:

> When the campaign proper was really back and up and running, what were we talking about? We were talking about immigration. We had said a year ago, if the last week of the campaign is dominated by the economy, we will lose. So, strangely, their choice to demonise me ultimately may have backfired on them.

This is an extraordinary concept: that this terrible event actually achieved the thing Nigel Farage spent his whole career perfecting – drawing attention to immigration – by whatever means. There is no doubt that the murder of Jo Cox took the momentum out of both campaigns – and it was widely thought that it was the Brexit campaign that would be most damaged by what had happened. Prior to the murder, Leave had begun to lead in the opinion polls – afterwards, that advantage appeared to vanish.

However, one could argue that dampening of the poll lead in itself helped Nigel Farage. Market confidence began to return on the belief that the UK would remain in the EU. The polls, the pundits, the media and business began to assume a Remain victory. The pound rose. Confidence was up. What was there to fear?

But if there had been real fear of Brexit in the week before the vote, if there had been volatility and signs of financial doom, if the pound has started falling in the way it did on referendum night – then surely we would all have been talking about the economy. More than any Treasury report that George Osborne could muster, real indicators of economic panic would have resonated with people as they went to the polls. But this didn't happen.

Instead, as Nigel Farage so rightly observes, everyone was talking about *his* poster.

It's hard to imagine the referendum campaign without Nigel Farage. It certainly never would have happened without the pressure applied by UKIP. At conference in 2014, the party chairman Steve Crowther described the influence of UKIP as 5 per cent members, 5 per cent deputy leader and MEPs, and 90 per cent Nigel Farage.

This was about 10 per cent out. Farage practically created a one-man cult. He was a seductive pied piper who adapted his tune to attract the largest possible following. He had just two objectives: first, lead the political class to a referendum and secondly, when that question was put to the public, ensure they followed his tune all the way out of the EU.

There was only one fail-safe way his plan could have been foiled: for the Prime Minister of the day to resist calling a referendum.

CAMERON'S CROWBAR REFERENDUM

So far we have an angry mob and an agitator, but if you are going to prise the UK out of a mesh of treaties with the EU, you need an unsophisticated tool, a blunt instrument with big leverage. Nigel Farage needed a *crowbar referendum* and the only person who could give him that was the Prime Minister. Coincidentally, by 2013 David Cameron realised he needed the same crowbar to get himself back into No. 10.

Whether David Cameron was right to reach into his toolkit and pull out that bent piece of steel is a big question. In fact, it is the pivotal question of this book.

Some say the nation was willing him to do it; others, such as the then Deputy PM Nick Clegg, say he 'allowed the whole country to be hijacked by an internal party feud'. You might expect the former Liberal Democrat leader to say that, of course – but, more unexpectedly, several prominent Leave campaigners also make the case that David Cameron should *not* have called the referendum. All this we will reveal and explore.

One thing you can be sure of is that David Cameron tried to avoid doing it. When he stood on the stage at Bloomberg's offices in London and promised to hold a referendum if re-elected Prime Minister in 2015, it may have looked like it was his idea, but it wasn't. On 23 January 2013, the PM gave the impression of a man who had arrived at a principled position. He announced he would negotiate a 'new settlement with our European partners', and it was only right that this should be followed by a national decision on whether we 'stay in the EU on these new terms; or come out altogether'.[1] But that speech only belonged to David Cameron in the way that a hostage owns a list of demands that his captor has made him read out to a barrage of blue flashing lights. It was less from No. 10, more from Room R.

Room R in Portcullis House has a large white round table and ground-to-ceiling windows overlooking Parliament Square and Westminster Abbey. The letter of the door just happened to be R because it sat between Rooms Q and S, but it might well have stood for 'rebel', or 'referendum', or 'right-wing' considering the occupants who secretly gathered there every Tuesday at 8.30 a.m. The meetings began almost as soon as the coalition government, comprising the Conservatives and the Liberal Democrats, was formed in May 2010.

The right-wing referendum rebels were a group of eight Conservatives who didn't like the idea of being in power with the Liberal Democrats and thought a minority Conservative government would have been preferable. They might never have gathered and plotted against their own government had their party ruled on its own, but they wanted to ensure that right-wing policies would dominate this hybrid administration. Moderate Conservatives would describe them as the head-bangers, and two of them would later defect to UKIP, but many of the things they discussed did eventually become government policy: scrapping the Department of Energy and Climate Change and rolling it into a wider Business Department, tightening planning controls to travellers, and calling a referendum on the EU.

This club of rebels consisted of fairly obscure backbench MPs: Peter Bone, Christopher Chope, Philip Hollobone, Steve Baker, David Nuttall, Douglas Carswell, Mark Reckless and John Baron – none of them household names but all of them committed to leaving the EU, and all would play their part in making that happen. To start with, they simply promoted right-wing amendments to bills and tried to ensure the backbench Conservatives maintained some author- ity within the parliamentary system, but the EU would very often come up in their conversations. If there was anything they could do to sway a motion in Parliament to do with Europe, each of the eight had their own sub-group of MPs whom they could approach to exert influence. Their message was that, on Europe, the Lib Dems couldn't be trusted and for that matter their own leader, Cameron, had a questionable track record.

No one in government knew about Room R, but they could guess that such a breakfast club might exist and had a plan to deal with it. The plan was a simple proposal agreed by both party leaders and worked on by Foreign Secretary Wil- liam Hague and Lib Dem government whip William Wallace. It became the 2011 European Union Act.

The idea was born out of the Lisbon Treaty – something that had discredited the Prime Minister in the eyes of Room R. Indeed, both David Cameron and Nick Clegg had been politically damaged by the treaty, though it had been signed by the previous government in 2008. As mentioned in Reason 8, the treaty itself was designed to update and streamline Brussels institutions but, as with many EU agreements, in practice it granted further powers to Brussels, with new posts such as a President and Foreign Minister and a reformed voting system to make it harder for individual countries to block legislation that the majority agreed upon. It also established a separate legal personality for the EU, enabling it to negotiate and sign international agreements and treaties on behalf of all the member states. Finally, the treaty for the first time also gave member states the explicit legal right to leave the EU and the procedure to do so – Article 50.

In 2007, Cameron had offered a 'cast-iron guarantee'[2] to have a referendum on Lisbon, but U-turned two years later, once the treaty had been ratified by all twenty-eight member states. He had tried to delay the ratification while he was in opposition, writing to the Czech President Vaclav Klaus in 2009 to urge him not to agree to the treaty until after the UK general election. But in November of that year Klaus became the last leader to sign off on Lisbon. In Cameron's view, this meant that 'our campaign for a referendum on the Lisbon treaty is therefore over. Why? Because it is no longer a treaty: it is being incorporated into the law of the European Union.' He could 'no more hold a referendum on the treaty than … a referendum to stop the sun rising in the morning'.[3]

Even some pro-Europeans regretted this decision, because it would mean any future referendum would have to be an all-or-nothing decision on membership of the EU, rather than on a specific treaty. Alistair Burt, a Remainer Tory MP, argued at the time: 'The first chance the British people were going to get to vote on the EU, they'd vote "No", no matter what the question was.' He felt a constitutional question should be put to the British public rather than a Leave or Remain choice.[4]

Nick Clegg had also been burnt by Lisbon. At the time the treaty was being debated, he'd decided that there should not be a referendum on signature, but instead an In/Out referendum on the EU itself. It's surprising, considering what happened later, to think this was his view, but in February 2008 he announced in the Commons:

The Labour Party is terrified of an open debate, whilst David Cameron's Con-servatives are focusing on the sideshow of a referendum on the technical details of the Lisbon Treaty. It's time for the Westminster establishment to stop being so cowardly over Europe and have an open debate with the country. I will be proud to lead the Liberal Democrats in arguing the case for our membership of the EU.[5]

It's worth remembering Clegg's words when we later hear his arguments *against* Cameron calling for an In/Out referendum in 2013. Indeed, the Liberal Democrats felt so passionately about it in 2008 that when the Speaker refused to put their amendment to the vote, they walked out of the Commons. However, a largish chunk of Lib Dems disagreed with their leader on this issue and thought the walk-out was rather undignified.

'I had got into trouble over Lisbon,' Clegg admitted in an interview for this book. 'We did this great flouncing out of the Commons. We were saying, "You can't ratify treaties any more without a referendum." It was a dramatic show of parliamentary petulance.' Clegg probably remembers the moment with little fondness. The circumstances may have been different and no doubt Clegg thought back then a referendum more winnable, but it's ironic that the Europhile Lib Dem leader was at one point the greatest advocate in Parliament for the referendum that eventually happened in 2016.

Clegg, however, learned from the furore over Lisbon that Europe needed some political containment. It was clear that not just the Conservatives but also the Lib Dems had been split by it. By 2010, both party leaders, embarking on a fragile coalition, agreed on a solution for the EU question. Clegg says: 'There was an explicit understanding between us that we should try and find a way of ensuring the coalition government didn't get upturned by Europe.' The 2011 European Union Act was introduced 'to park the issue'.

The new legislation agreed by Cameron and Clegg during their coalition negotiations meant that a referendum would automatically be triggered by any new Brussels power grab. In the words of the Act, it provided for 'a referendum throughout the United Kingdom on any proposed EU treaty or Treaty change which would transfer powers from the UK to the EU'.[6] This would, the two leaders hoped, stop the Eurosceptics banging on about continued erosion of sovereignty while at the same time put Lisbon, and all the other treaties, to bed by agreeing that the UK *shouldn't* have a referendum *unless* more powers were surrendered to the EU. 'We were joking even before the coalition was signed, "Well at least the one thing this government won't be blighted by is Europe,"' says Clegg. By July 2011, the Act was enshrined in UK law and, as far as the two leaders were concerned, that was that.

But the MPs from Room R had another idea and a novel card up their sleeves to ensure that was not that. Two of their members, Philip Hollobone and Peter Bone, were on the Backbench Business Committee (BBC), giving them the power to authorise debates in Parliament. Three months after the European Union Act became law, a debate authorised by the BBC on 24 October would undermine all of David Cameron's and Nick Clegg's efforts.

It's important to note that the BBC powers to call debates were new to the House of Commons in 2010. The previous party-dominated system for scheduling debates had led to the criticisms of 'predictable debates of little concern to the outside world'.[7] But under this new reform backbenchers had more control of the Commons diary – and on twenty-seven days of the year could push forward proposals from MPs on any motion, whether their respective parties wanted to debate it or not. 'It was impartial. We wouldn't allow anything that was party political, or anything put up by the front benches,' says Peter Bone.

Reflecting on what happened as a result of this reform, the Leader of the Commons, Sir George Young said: 'I think the Backbench Business Committee has gone where angels fear to tread, if I may say so, in choosing subjects that the government and, in some cases, the opposition would not have chosen.'[8] The funny thing is that the government was slow to pick up on this, not realising that a committee with the power to put subjects to a vote in the Commons had filled up with party rebels.

In its first session, 2010–12 for example, BBC members Philip Hollobone, Peter Bone and Philip Davies defied the whip a total of 230 times, but by 2012–13 they had been replaced by Bob Blackman, David Amess and Marcus Jones, who between them defied the whip only five times.[9] So it took two years for Downing Street to assert control of this new institution, but those two years were crucial.

In late 2010, Peter Bone recalls sitting next to the Prime Minister in one of the Westminster Palace tea rooms and saying to a friend, 'Isn't it great we've got the Backbench Business Committee and isn't it great they can call votes now on standing motions?' According to Bone, 'tea spurted from the PM's mouth'. He hadn't realised that the Backbench Business Committee could call substantive motions to be voted on in the House of Commons.

In October 2011, Bone, Hollobone and Davis spotted their chance. Normally there was a regular flow of pitches to the committee from other MPs that they had to sift through and consider, but on one Tuesday afternoon session they noticed a gap in the schedule for the following Thursday. On reporting back to the rebels from Room R, it was decided that David Nuttall should propose a debate on whether the UK should hold a referendum on leaving the EU. 'We weren't ready. We hadn't planned to do it on that day but the opportunity came up and we said, "Blow it, we'll take it,"' says Bone.

Tea must have erupted from the Prime Minister's mouth once more when he was alerted to the schedule for the coming week. He quickly decided to move the debate forward to Monday to ensure all his loyal MPs were in the house. A strong three-line whip was issued to enforce a vote with the government and ensure this rebel motion was snuffed out. Speaking ahead of the debate, the PM gave three reasons why it would be a bad idea to call an In/Out referendum:

> First, it is not right because our national interest is to be in the EU, helping to determine the rules governing the single market, our biggest export market, which consumes more than 50 per cent of our exports and drives so much investment in the UK...
>
> Secondly, it is not the right time, at this moment of economic crisis, to launch legislation that includes an in/out referendum. When your neighbour's house is on fire, your first impulse should be to help put out the flames, not least to stop them reaching your own house...
>
> Thirdly, and crucially, there is a danger that by raising the prospect of a referendum, including an in/out option, we will miss the real opportunity to further our national interest. Fundamental questions are being asked about the future of the eurozone and, therefore, the shape of the EU itself.[10]

Proposing the motion, David Nuttall MP said: 'The motion reflects the wishes of the hundreds of thousands of people who have signed petitions calling for a referendum ... Opinion polls clearly show that millions of others agree with them: in fact, the vast majority of the British people want a vote in a referendum.'[11]

Responding for the government, William Hague said: 'I do not believe that most people in Britain want to say yes to everything in the EU or no to everything in the EU.' But his most prescient remarks came when he pointed to the problems of asking such a broad question – rather than voting for or against particular EU powers. He asked:

> If we voted to leave the European Union, would that mean that, like Norway, we were in the European Free Trade Association and in the European Economic Area but still paying towards the EU budget, or, like Switzerland, not in the European Economic Area? If we voted to renegotiate 'based on trade and cooperation', as the motion says, does that mean that we would be in the single market, or not; still subject to its rules, or not?[12]

With that, Hague became the first man to raise the question of a *hard* or *soft* Brexit. But what's interesting is that here in 2011 we have some of the strongest arguments *against* an In/Out referendum being given by the same government that would call for the referendum fifteen months later. David Cameron was clearly arguing that the time was not right and that Britain's best interests were served by being in the EU, yet he would soon be proposing the mechanism to leave it.

One reason for this turn of events was the result of the October debate itself – it shocked everyone. Eighty-one Tories defied the whip, the biggest rebellion ever against a Conservative Prime Minister over Europe. The rebels were more ready than they realised. This was, in part, thanks to a different group of Eurosceptics called the Democracy Movement (successor to Goldsmith's Referendum Party), which had set up the People's Pledge. The cross-party group had a simple idea: identify Labour and Conservative MPs who were threatened by UKIP in their constituency and ask them to publicly support a referendum on the EU. It launched in March 2011 and by the time of the October vote a number of MPs and 100,000 people had signed the pledge. It was organised by Marc-Henri Glendening, Chris Bruni-Lowe (later to become a UKIP strategist) and Tory MEP Daniel Hannan. The same group also set out to hold ballots in key seats asking the public whether they wanted a referendum. In the end, there were only three of these events, in Thurrock (just east of London), Cheadle and Hazel Grove (just south of Manchester), but they managed to generate a turnout of over 30 per cent, with roughly 90 per cent of people in favour. All of this undoubtedly helped the Room R group and other Eurosceptics to convince a sizeable number of their colleagues to vote against the government. Their logic, which seemed to work on many, was that in this instance it wasn't necessarily a vote against the Conservatives – it was a vote against the coalition, against the Lib Dems and against most of Labour. Look at it like that and it was easier to defy one's own Prime Minister, especially when the message goes down well with grassroots Conservatives.

Peter Bone says:

> What happened was Conservative MPs went back to their constituencies, and the party chair and members would say, 'You've got to vote for this motion.' That's why it was such a shock. We thought if nobody peeled off [had second thoughts after committing to voting], we would get fifty. Eighty-one was amazing. From that day onwards it was inevitable that we were going to have a referendum.

Forty-nine of the rebels were new intake MPs, in the job just over a year, but ensuring that Cameron faced a mutiny greater than even John Major had over Maastricht. A new generation of Eurosceptics had arrived in the Tory Party.

Perhaps it should have been Room B for 'bastards', because once again a group of Conservatives was pissing in the tent. Douglas Carswell observes:

> That was the key, key moment when the leadership of the party stopped trying to fight a referendum. After the Nuttall vote, it was all a question of when, how and in what circumstances. They stopped arguing against it in first principle – it was just a question of applying force. It was clear to us that a referendum was coming.

In March 2012, Boris Johnson signed the People's Pledge. Two months later, on 21 May, Cameron met with his Foreign Secretary William Hague and his trusted chief of staff Ed Llewellyn in a pizza restaurant at Chicago's O'Hare Airport. Here, they began to form the plan that would shape British politics for years to come. If the PM could negotiate some form of new settlement with the other member states that could form part of the next EU treaty, then he could approach the electorate for their consent to the deal. The three agreed that this was starting to look like the way forward.

The rebels from Room R kept up the pressure. In June, over a hundred Conservative MPs signed a letter demanding legislation for a referendum after the next election. This time it was John Baron MP who collected the signatures, with each member of Room R drawing on their inner circle to get the maximum numbers and only Baron holding the full list of names, which was never published. The Prime Minister was at a summit in Brussels, from where he said that it was more important to see powers returned from Brussels, which he would push for, than to hold an In/Out referendum, which 'actually only gives people those two choices: you can either stay in, with all the status quo, or you can get out'.[13]

In October 2012, after the EU Commission proposed a 5 per cent increase in the EU budget, fifty-three Conservative MPs defied the whip in a vote in Parliament, demanding that Cameron secure a cut in the budget instead. Again, many Conservatives felt they were not rebelling against their own party but against a dreadful compromise government. Let's not forget that with the Lib Dems sharing power, Nick Clegg could grant thirty ministerial positions in Whitehall, and that meant thirty positions David Cameron couldn't give to his own MPs to buy influence and loyalty within his party. The momentum against him was building.

Cameron's position had been further weakened by his Chancellor's so-called 'omnishambles' Budget, when George Osborne had about-turned on plans to tax hot food and caravans. The Chancellor was even booed at the London Paralympics during a medal ceremony. So the overall popularity of the government was at a low ebb. Respect amongst Cameron's MPs was falling for a leader who couldn't even beat Gordon Brown without the help of the Liberal Democrats. What's more, he was a bit liberal himself. In December 2012, Cameron disturbed Tory traditionalists by setting out his plans to introduce gay marriage by 2014. It was Eurosceptic MPs such as Peter Bone and Bernard Jenkin who were most outspoken against him on this. Nigel Farage sought to exploit the division by threatening to make it a key issue of his campaign in the 2014 European elections. He predicted it had the potential to 'rip apart the traditional Tory vote'. Farage was by now eating into the support base of both the Tories and Labour, and would take any opportunity to attack a perceived weakness.

Another unanticipated side effect of having the Liberal Democrats in government was that they were no longer the party of protest, no longer the challenger against the big two. They had benefited from growing anti-establishment sentiment during their long period in opposition, but now there was space for a new party to replace them. What was worse for Cameron was that this replacement, in the form of UKIP, was magnetic to a certain breed within his party.

Sometimes the chronology over what happened next gets muddled. In interviews, several high-profile figures thought, for example, that David Cameron's Bloomberg speech came *after* the two Conservative defections to UKIP and *after* UKIP won the European elections in 2014. Are some rewriting history in their heads over exactly how much pressure David Cameron was under to call the referendum? Or is it a credit to the PM's political antennae that, actually, his decision to hold a referendum came before these events? He might argue that the UKIP defections would have been more numerous and subsequent election results more damaging had he not offered the referendum when he did. But you could equally say that his referendum gave credence to this Eurosceptic movement, feeding the fire.

Opinion polls and two by-elections in late 2012 did give worrying indications that UKIP was on the march. In both Rotherham and Middlesbrough, Nigel Farage's party came second. In Rotherham, won by Labour's Sarah Champion, the Conservatives slipped from second place to fifth. Their vote dropped from 6,200 to 1,100, while UKIP's rose from 2,200 to 4,600.[14] Furthermore, polling by Lord Ashcroft in December 2012 showed that 12 per cent of people who voted Conservative in 2010 said they would now vote for UKIP.[15] That would be enough to put Labour in office.

Having achieved 3 per cent of the popular vote in the 2010 general election, UKIP were now regularly scoring into double figures in the polls. Labour were ahead of the Conservatives, and many Tories were wondering whether they could keep their seats next time round.

The defections hadn't happened yet, but rumours were starting that UKIP leader Nigel Farage was talking to some Conservative Eurosceptic MPs. As early as 2011, reports circulated that the new UKIP treasurer Stuart Wheeler had wined and dined eight Tory MPs with the express purpose of kindling a mutiny. The rise of UKIP, combined with internal party insurgence, was setting off alarms in Downing Street.

A No. 10 source says the PM and his Chancellor had differing views on UKIP. 'Osborne thought it would rise and fall. Cameron said no – I think it is a big thing.' When Cameron suggested a referendum as a way of addressing the problem, George Osborne warned against it, saying the campaign would 'split the party down the middle'.[16] According to Tim Shipman's *All Out War*, the Chancellor thought: 'There's a good chance we'll lose and it will destroy the

Tory party.' But Cameron told his colleagues: 'Don't worry, I know what I'm doing.'[17] Nick Clegg describes a 'breezy confidence' in the PM, who 'thought it would undoubtedly be won if the referendum was on the extreme option of leaving altogether'.

Clegg may have wanted a referendum during the Lisbon debate five years earlier, but he saw Cameron's decision in 2013 as having nothing to do with the best interests of the UK. He says:

> It is neither politically nor empirically correct to say there was this irrepressible public clamour [for a referendum]. There was a media clamour, and there was a huge pressure within the Conservative Party which goes back to the slaying of the Boadicea figure of Margaret Thatcher and the profound ideological cleavage within the Conservative Party between the globalists and the localists.

Cameron's camp disagrees. 'It was a slow train coming and it had arrived in the station,' according to the PM's director of communications, Craig Oliver. David Cameron decided the referendum was unavoidable. The plan to ensure Europe remained off the agenda had failed. Once again, on every issue to do with Europe, Conservative MPs were rebelling. Oliver recalls that:

> They were looking for issues that were not to do with Europe and trying to amend them to bring it back to issues to do with Europe again. We were coming up to a general election and the idea that you did not promise a referendum was unsustainable. They would have said, 'If you don't do it, we'll have someone else who will as a leader.'

It seems unlikely that this coup would have happened prior to a general election, but aides close to Cameron argue that he would have struggled to win in 2015 without offering a referendum. This was not because of a growing threat from Labour but out of a fear that UKIP would deplete the Conservatives in key seats, enough to let Labour in. Indeed, many Tories believe Ed Miliband's decision not to back the referendum may have lost Labour the general election. Some polls of voters back this up, suggesting that if Miliband had followed Cameron's promise, he would have become PM.[18]

For the Conservatives, the referendum offer could effectively neuter the argument on the EU. Cameron had promised, early in his leadership, to stop the Tory Party 'banging on about Europe'.[19] The rebellions over the Maastricht Treaty in the mid-1990s had been followed by a 2001 general election campaign dominated by a promise to keep the pound. The subject always sowed division in a party that had been historically well disciplined. One way to end the continuing row was to offer some kind of finality to it. A referendum would give Cameron one word he could use to stop Europe distracting him from his wider mission of winning a majority in 2015.

If this sounds like political expediency rather than responding to the needs of the country, Craig Oliver begs to differ:

> People say, 'Oh, it was just a Conservative Party issue' – well, the Conservative Party was the dominant force in politics of that time. Secondly, it wasn't just a Conservative Party issue. UKIP were on the rise to the extent that they not only did well in the 2014 European election – they won.

Even if Cameron's primary purpose in calling a referendum was to save his political skin, there are other arguments that could be used to justify why he had to do it. There are constitutional questions that can't be settled by general elections – and Britain's relationship with the EU was in that bracket. Referendums were becoming more acceptable to the British public. As explained in Reason 5, up to only fifteen years or so earlier, the country wasn't used to them, because it was extremely rare for a referendum to be called. In fact, up until the 1970s, the referendum as a tool was thought to be unconstitutional in Britain. Parliament was sovereign, and elsewhere in the world, history showed that referendums were often weapons used by dictators, not by democratic governments. In the aftermath of the Second World War, Winston Churchill had proposed a referendum to get a mandate from the people to continue as head of his wartime coalition government, but Clement Attlee, the leader of the Labour Party, dismissed the idea as 'a device so alien to all our traditions ... which has only too often been the instrument of Nazism and Fascism'.[20]

Over time, however, it was argued that the use of referendums did not conflict with the concept of parliamentary sovereignty because if Parliament can do whatever it likes, then it can call a referendum. Furthermore, parliamentary sovereignty means it cannot be legally bound by the result. The UK is a liberal democracy and as such government power is consented to by the agreement of the governed. In most cases, the governed express their views through their elected representatives, which is the reasoning for regular and competitive elections. Sometimes, however, there is a strong constitutional case for direct democracy, by way of a referendum, although this would not be a legal case but a political case. The concept of 'consent' means that the people should consent to *how* they are to be governed, and as the European Union began to intrude deeper into that domain, in particular over who has ultimate authority over our laws, it meant that our ever-changing terms of membership needed to be consented to, politically if not legally.

The Conservatives had effectively conceded to this argument by June 2003 when shadow Foreign Secretary Michael Ancram proposed a referendum on the European constitution (the forerunner to the Lisbon Treaty), which he declared should only be ratified by Parliament 'once it has received consent of the British people, democratically given in a referendum'. In his speech to the Commons, he noted that the Labour government had recently begun to use referendums 'with gusto' and popular involvement in decisions was becoming part of 'national culture'. Ancram cited thirty-four referendums over the previous six years on matters ranging from the Good Friday Agreement and devolution for Scotland and Wales to the London Mayor and Assembly and even the Mayor of Hartlepool (a decision which resulted in the town's football club mascot, H'Angus the Monkey, being elected as Mayor). He asked: 'If the people's consent to set up a Mayor of Hartlepool is so important, why is it to be denied for the setting up of a European President of a European political union?' He went on to argue: 'It is impossible to see how a constitutional treaty providing a constitution can, by definition, be said not to have constitutional implications.'[21]

Eventually, all three main parties pledged a referendum on the EU constitution ahead of the 2005 general election. Even Tony Blair made one of the most dramatic U-turns of his career, conceding that it was time to 'let the people have the final say'.[22] Yet, once he was re-elected, somehow the public didn't get a say over Lisbon. This was because, as explained in Reason 8, the constitution had been a completely new treaty whereas the Lisbon Treaty was an amendment of existing treaties (despite containing almost exactly the same provisions). Blair backtracked, Clegg switched to his fated In/Out call, and Cameron's 'cast-iron guarantee' turned out to be made of sand.

So there was a void left by a broken promise to the British public and a constitutional justification for calling a referendum to go with Cameron's party political justification. In his Bloomberg speech, David Cameron noted that 'democratic consent for the EU is now wafer-thin'.[23] He had begun to buy into the idea that there was a democratic deficit. That people had to have been nearly sixty years old to have had a say on the EU and a lot of those who had voted back in 1975 believed it had dramatically changed from what they had voted for. What's more, a large section of society felt they'd been lied to and betrayed over Europe – not just over Lisbon but over other broken promises, such as the assurance that only 40,000 people would come to the UK when the accession countries joined, which turned out to be a million. David Cameron couldn't survive being labelled as another EU fraud. His cast-iron guarantee U-turn risked putting him in that category.

It was Cameron's political instinct to rail against any suggestion that he was a closet federalist. When he was a prospective Conservative candidate in 2000, he had insisted he should be classified as a Eurosceptic and when Sean Gabb, the proprietor of the Candidlist website that classified Tory hopefuls according to their stance on Europe, described him as a Europhile, Cameron emailed him to object: 'No to the single currency, no to further transfer of powers from Westminster to Brussels and yes to renegotiation of areas like fish where the EU has been a disaster for the UK. If that is being a Europhile, then I'm a banana.'[24] So David Cameron, the prospective parliamentary candidate, was either a Eurosceptic or he knew what needed to be said to get selected.

Now here he was as Prime Minister, once again knowing what his party wanted to hear. He had thought the 2011 European Union Act would be enough, but his own MPs had shown him it wasn't. UKIP polling told him that a big enough section of the country was starting to feel the same way. The media was also gunning for a referendum; the same newspapers the Prime Minister would need in just two years' time to help him get re-elected. The coincidence of all this coming together meant that the referendum's time had come – the idea that you could kick it down the road just didn't work. If he wanted to remain in power, it was time to grab the crowbar.

Craig Oliver sums up: 'There had to be a referendum; we held it, Leave won. And the fact that Leave won tells you something, doesn't it, about why there needed to be a referendum.'

You have to admit that it is a rather blunt point from the man who campaigned to remain, and it is also rather hard to argue with. With hindsight, we now know that people voted to leave, therefore even to suggest that David Cameron shouldn't have called a referendum leads you down a rather undemocratic path. But let's go down it anyway.

To begin with, you could say that the Prime Minister's decision to call the referendum legitimised the Tory rebels, gave added purpose to UKIP and put the EU on the agenda at the worst possible time.

His Bloomberg speech came in the midst of the Eurozone crisis and ahead of the migration crisis. We will discuss these factors in greater detail in the next chapter, but news from Europe in the months leading to Bloomberg had focused particularly on a Greek tragedy: bailouts, forced austerity, suicides, food banks, political turmoil and riots. If it wasn't Greece, it was Spain, where youth unemployment was, at the time of Bloomberg, at its peak of 56 per cent. Across Spain, campaigners were forming human shields against forced evictions and whole towns had been built on credit then left empty because no one could afford the homes. If you didn't watch the news, you could still find Europe's misery featured on the BBC's flagship programme *Top Gear*. Jeremy Clarkson and the gang visited Ciudad Real Central Airport in southern Spain. It had been completed in 2012 but never used because the company went into receivership amid Spain's banking crisis. The deserted terminal and weed-filled runways made the perfect racetrack for Clarkson, James May and Richard Hammond to conduct their budget supercar challenge.

So, Europe's house was on fire, with *Top Gear* leaving skid marks on the driveway, and the UK's response was not to douse the flames but to celebrate its own detached status from the euro and consider further options for separation. It's hard not to see Cameron's move as ultimately driven by the Eurozone troubles. The level of political harassment from UKIP and his own party intensified as Europe's fortunes declined. But if Bloomberg was somehow intended to stem this political pressure, it failed. UKIP's poll shares rose into the mid to high teens after Bloomberg. In May 2013, the party won 23 per cent of the vote in the local elections, just two points behind the Tories, and by 2014 it won the European elections.

As for the Eurosceptics within the Conservative Party, they became even more motivated. In May 2013, they put on their biggest show of defiance. Rejecting pleas to show trust in their Prime Minister, 114 Tories voted to 'express regret' over the lack of a bill legislating for an In/Out referendum in the Queen's Speech.[25] It was another rebellion orchestrated by Room R against their Prime Minister, even though he'd promised them the thing they'd been calling for. Room R was beginning to show cracks. Steve Baker MP stopped attending, for example, because he thought the constant attacks on the government were becoming counter-productive and the meeting time clashed with his Bible group. But other sub-groups were forming, each with their own specific mission.

The most significant one, which first met in 2012, was the trio of Mark Reckless, Douglas Carswell and MEP Dan Hannan, who got together regularly at the Tate Gallery. Their purpose was not only to ensure Cameron stuck to his promise, but also to make sure that when the referendum came, the UK voted to leave. After Bloomberg, these three saw an opening that hadn't been achieved in decades of Euroscepticism. They were emboldened to risk their political careers to do whatever was necessary to ensure their PM's promise was kept. According to Douglas Carswell:

> At the time of the Bloomberg speech he used the tone that allowed him to think he had wriggle room. In his speech, he used the phrase fundamental change. But in an article in *The Times* soon afterwards, it then became clear this was not applying to the UK's relationship with the EU – he was talking about internal EU reform.

In truth, Cameron had also used the phrase 'fundamental change' in his speech in the context of describing what was happening in Europe due to problems with the Eurozone – but it was forever misquoted afterwards by Eurosceptics as something he'd called for in terms of the relationship between the UK and the EU.

Almost immediately, the Tate trio decided Cameron's heart wasn't in it – but he'd given them momentum. The next step was for the two MPs of the group, Carswell and Reckless, to defect to UKIP. This would have the dual purpose of triggering by-elections that would apply pressure on Cameron, while at the same time helping to 'detoxify' UKIP. It's an odd concept that MPs should want to join a party that they think is toxic, in order to change it from within, but while the Tate group agreed with UKIP's drive to leave the EU, they also feared that Nigel Farage's tone was off-putting to many potential Out voters. They had noticed a phenomenon they dubbed 'the Farage Paradox': that when UKIP did well, such as winning the 2014 European elections, polls showed that support for leaving the EU amongst the general population actually dropped.

Their conclusion was that Farage was a Marmite character whom many mainstream voters didn't want to associate themselves with. Young people, women and ethnic minorities did not respond well to many of Farage's messages. Hannan and Carswell in particular concluded that if he were to be figurehead of the referendum campaign, Britain would vote to remain in the EU. It's quite possible that the 'Farage Paradox' was nonsense. For example, UKIP won the EU elections in 2014 but wider support for actually leaving the EU may have also dipped in 2014 as the euro crisis began to recede and the migration crisis was yet to fully emerge. There were certainly factors beyond the success of UKIP that influenced mainstream voters' feelings towards the EU. But there is a strong argument too that UKIP could not carry the campaign all the way to 23 June. Carswell says:

> Just look at the number of people who voted to leave in the referendum on 23 June and compare that to the number of people who voted UKIP in the general election. It's not an anti-anyone point. If the SNP had had the good sense to not make support for Scottish independence synonymous with supporting the SNP, they might have won their referendum.

And so, the two Tory MPs decided that by defecting to UKIP they could help improve the overall brand of Euroscepticism. 'I wanted to make it possible for good people who weren't yet Eurosceptic, but could be led to that position, to go to that position and not be put off by some of the people who were already there,' says Carswell. 'If you make arguments in decent, moderate terms, you can say some fairly radical stuff. And I felt that if I establish in people's minds the idea of UKIP as non-scary – it would help.'

So, rather than quelling the political storm, the Bloomberg speech was potentially the trigger for a chain of events that further weakened Cameron's position. The Tate group would have met, but would they have had the impetus to begin structuring the Vote Leave strategy so early on? Would they now know that Cameron was malleable under pressure? The two by-elections had their desired effect. Carswell won easily in Clacton and, despite a huge Conservative effort against him, Mark Reckless regained his seat for UKIP in Rochester and Strood. Shortly afterwards, David Cameron promised to put forward his referendum legislation within 100 days of forming a majority government. Another crucial concession was won. 'What we were arguing for became his flagship policy in the 2015 general election,' says Carswell.

With the Prime Minister questioning the current direction of the European project, he not only legitimised the argument for his party rebels and UKIP, but also put Europe firmly in the centre of the political agenda. An Ashcroft poll at the time of Bloomberg shows the issue had not been high on the public list of priorities up until that point. Indeed, it found that even amongst those considering a vote for UKIP, only just over a quarter of them put Britain's future relations with the EU amongst the top three issues facing the coun-try; only 7 per cent of them said it was the most important of all. Ashcroft concludes that people's attraction to UKIP owed more to their distrust of mainstream politicians than to any policy. Economic growth, jobs, welfare reform, immigration and the deficit all mattered more to potential UKIP voters than the EU.[26]

Other polls came to similar conclusions. Ipsos MORI's Issues Index contains over forty years of monthly data showing people's answers when asked 'What are the most important issues facing the country?' For much of the 1980s, the percentage even mentioning Europe stayed in the low single figures. In late 1990, this climbed to 18 per cent as Britain entered the European Exchange Rate Mechanism, growing to 33 per cent during the Maastricht Treaty debates and slightly higher when Blair flirted with the euro. The NHS and unemployment always remained top and by the turn of the century, interest in the EU began to fall. By the time David Nuttall was insisting his Referendum Bill was introduced because 'the vast majority of the British people want a vote in a referendum',[27] just four in a hundred people told Ipsos MORI that Europe was one of the issues that mattered most.[28]

Ashcroft is partly right, therefore, in concluding that this meant that in 2013 people didn't necessarily consider the EU as important and that their dissatis-faction was with Westminster itself. Even Eurosceptic Cabinet minister Theresa Villiers admits, 'Europe was not often high on the list of priorities in my constit-uency – the referendum was the first time people started talking about it.' But it is also clear that dissatisfied voters on the left and the right were persuaded that Europe had an effect on other issues, especially immigration. What this meant was that you couldn't assess the significance of the EU to people simply by asking them 'How important is the EU?', because it was becoming merged with everything else. Immigration, welfare, housing, education and health were all beginning to drift into a Venn diagram that had Europe in the middle. David Cameron's referendum ensured that it maintained that central position leading into the general election.

Nick Clegg noticed a change on the doorstep. Somehow, three subjects – Europe, welfare and immigration – had mixed into an 'almost uncontrollable brew'.

'I can't put my finger on it – but something happened. When Cameron and I started out, we were pretty confident those three separate things would remain separate. The moment they became conflated, I totally accept, that put a completely different complexion on it.' However, Clegg adds: 'Just because things become confused with each other doesn't mean the solution to that is to hold a gun to the head of the whole country and say, "Right, are we going to leave the European Union?"'

During the course of our interviews for this book, everyone we've spoken to has expressed a view on whether David Cameron should have called the referendum. Some views won't surprise you. Alan Johnson, head of Labour In, for example, says: 'Of course he didn't have to.' The referendum, Johnson thinks, 'was purely about shoring up himself against Tory Eurosceptics and against UKIP. He put that before the good of the country … It wasn't in the British public's top ten concerns. Yes, they were concerned about immigration, but having a referendum on the European Union didn't appear.'

On the other hand, another Labour Remain campaigner, Will Straw, director of Stronger In, says:

My sense at the time was that the referendum had become inevitable – the British public had been promised referendums on the euro and the Lisbon Treaty and there had been a 'referendum lock'. The way it was delivered and put in the manifesto was more about internal Conservative Party management than the national interest, but it had been brewing. When I was a Labour candidate, it came up on the doorstep. Not all the time, but it came up enough.

The most surprising view we discovered was that of Gisela Stuart, co-chair of Vote Leave. Despite the fact that she was one of the most significant players in the campaign to leave the EU, Stuart believes Cameron should never have called the referendum and in fact thought the whole thing was 'an abuse' of democracy. It's worth noting down a section of this interview in full:

JF: Do you think David Cameron should have called a referendum?

GS: No. The way he called that referendum was an abuse of democratic processes. It really was. I've never gone through a voting process where the losers demand of the winners that they explain themselves. This is what happened with the referendum, because you had a binary question. You had no bodies accountable for an outcome. This notion that you can create these campaigning groups that aren't established political parties. Immediately after the referendum with Vote Leave, we resigned as directors and the whole thing was shut down. And that's not good democracy.

JF: So no one is accountable for the decision?

GS: Yes. It comes back to: what are political structures? They are mediators. They anchor responsibility, and I would have been quite happy to have a referendum on Maastricht, I think there should have been. I campaigned for a referendum on the Lisbon Treaty. At that moment, we would have had clear questions. So it wasn't a question of one side or the other coming at each other with threats. You would have had a clear body. This is the text – this is what happens now – you can have this or you can have that. But Cameron just threw this vacuous question into the air.

JF: So the question in your view should never have been about leaving the EU, it should have been on the treaties. But could that have led us to leaving?

GS: It would have been at the time of the treaties and if we had rejected it then they would have been back to the drawing board as the European Union – because we had decided No.

JF: For someone who campaigned to leave the EU – one would assume you appreciated him giving you the option to get out of something you disagreed with?

GS: I think it was the right decision [to leave]. But given what I was asked [Yes or No to the EU] – there was no way I could endorse this. Was I signing up for my membership form for UKIP? No. But essentially what he did – he kind of forced a question – to which I could not say Yes.

JF: But you'd rather he hadn't asked the question?

GS: Yup.

JF: But to say 'Yes' is to accept the status quo?

GS: But as I famously kept saying, the status quo is not on the ballot paper. If after the most intensive negotiations he got nothing, and the British people had said Remain, he wouldn't get any trade deals for years and years – because people would say, 'Mr Cameron, you are the most Eurosceptic of any of the countries and the people have said they are happy the way it is.' You can see the speech Juncker would have given in the European Parliament, the great triumph: 'The people are ahead of their politicians. They've all just said yes! No more requests for changes. They are happy with everything.'

In other words, even Gisela Stuart, a chief campaigner for Vote Leave, felt backed into a corner by the question and by the subsequent renegotiation. David Cameron had created a set of circumstances that left her with a choice she didn't want to make.

This could perhaps be said of the British public too. We well know from polls that throughout the campaign, one third were for Leave, one third for Remain and one third undecided. Many felt they simply weren't qualified to make the decision, or that the question was too stark. As William Hague predicted in 2011, it has indeed left the UK squabbling over what kind of Brexit we actually want.

Former Conservative advisor Paul Stephenson was travelling back to London from a football game when he heard the Bloomberg speech and remembers 'shouting at the car radio' while being driven home by Nick Timothy, who was to become Theresa May's co-chief of staff.

I thought it was a stupid idea, a terrible solution to a short-term political problem, that would give UKIP a huge amount of oxygen. Cameron could easily lose. Indeed, the landscape meant he'd be facing an uphill battle. By the time of the 2015 general elections, immigration had become synonymous with the EU in the public psyche.

Despite not wanting the referendum, Stephenson would later become a key player in Vote Leave's campaign as a director of comms.

As a footnote to this story of how the UK ended up with an In/Out EU referendum, let's hold open the idea that at the time of his Bloomberg speech, Cameron might have envisaged some way of slipping off the bonds of his promise. Like any hostage reading out his captors' demands, surely his head was whirring with possible escape plans. Some suggest the answer to this was obvious – in the next coalition negotiations with the Lib Dems, he could bargain away his pledge. This never happened because he unexpectedly won a majority. But Nick Clegg believes that even if he had found himself in coalition, Cameron could not have yielded on the pledge without severe consequences, and had 'boxed himself in' with a manifesto promise that was central to the Tory election campaign. Lib Dems Danny Alexander and David Laws were already setting out the things they would demand from the Prime Minister in return.

Interestingly, however, the Lib Dem leader had decided that he personally did have a red line on the referendum. 'Privately, I had decided I could not be part of a government that called a referendum on the EU,' said Clegg in an interview for this book. The man who had been pilloried for U-turning on tuition fees could not once again put in power a government that offered the thing he had most vehemently campaigned against. In other words, there was never any chance of another Conservative–Lib Dem coalition forming without Cameron dropping his pledge for a referendum, at least while Nick Clegg remained leader. It throws up fascinating questions over what would have happened had there been a hung parliament as predicted, but it is irrelevant because the Conservatives won outright.

Having laid out the arguments for and against Cameron's decision to call a referendum, we can only conclude that in 2013 the Prime Minister was in a lose/lose situation: likely to come under ever greater pressure and risk losing his job if he held out against it, but inflaming and encouraging Euroscepticism when he yielded.

This is reflected in the schizophrenic speech he made at Bloomberg, which warned of a 'danger that British people will drift towards the exit' while setting in motion the means for this to happen. He hailed the benefits of the trading bloc, asking for safeguards 'to ensure that our access to the single market is not in any way compromised' but later observed that British people had started to 'wonder what the point of it all is'. As Cameron tried to navigate a course between Europhile and Eurosceptic, he landed on a promise of 'fundamental, far-reaching change'[29] to the EU: an unachievable pledge. He set out five principles for a more competitive, flexible, fair, democratically accountable EU, with power allowed to flow back to member states, not just away from them. He set expectations too high. As we shall see later, this overreach was the greatest error of his Bloomberg speech.

In hindsight, it is hard to see what Cameron really thought he could have achieved. Firstly, as we have already established, the opportunity for the UK to mould the EU to its liking was something that was long lost, almost from the outset of the project. Far-reaching reform, of the type envisaged by Eurosceptics, was a near impossible task – so he was setting himself up for a fall.

Secondly, if he were confident nonetheless that he would ultimately win a campaign to remain in the EU, did he expect his problems would end there? Tory division and resentment may well have continued to simmer. 'Do you really think people like Iain Duncan Smith would've gone silent?' asks Gisela Stuart. 'He just poked the hornet's nest. It would not have united the Tory Party if he had won. The only way to unite the Tories was to lose the referendum.'

Cameron had also overlooked something else. The reason he was under such pressure to hold a referendum was because the EU's image was in decline. If one day he was going to campaign to stay in the European project, he needed to start making people believe in it, and that ambition was incompatible with his message that the institution needed fundamental reform. The rhetoric required to get the EU to wake up to his demands could stir up even more resentment at home, especially with the EU jumping from one crisis to another.

REASON 12

BRAND CRISIS

On the morning of Wednesday 4 April 2012, the 77-year-old Dimitris Christoulas walked into Syntagma Square in Athens – one of the most stunning places in Europe. A grand marble staircase rises out of the tree-lined plaza up to the neoclassical edifice of the Old Royal Palace. This is home to the Hellenic Parliament. Its pale yellow façade is beautifully symmetrical and it is by far the cleanest-looking building in Athens, literally shining when the sun catches it against the cloth of blue Athenian skies. That is, unless clouds of tear gas happen to be rising up to obscure the view. And in 2012 this was often the case. In the depths of Greece's debt crisis, Syntagma Square witnessed ugly scenes of fierce uprisings against government austerity. Students fought riot police: Molotov cocktails versus clouds of acrid smoke. TV reporters stayed in expensive hotels overlooking the plaza and pointed their cameras down from balconies on to the mess below.

On this sunny morning in April, there was no gas and there were no petrol bombs. Mr Christoulas was not a youthful protester. He was old. His actions, however, were more profound and devastating than those of the raging mobs in bandanas. Friends and former colleagues would later describe the retired pharmacist as quiet and dignified, yet he too was angry with the authorities. 'I have debts,' he shouted at the commuters streaming out of the metro at rush hour. 'I can't stand this any more.' Then he put a gun to his head and pulled the trigger.

The suicide note found in his coat pocket written in red ink read:

The occupation government of Tsolakoglou has annihilated any possibility for my survival, which was based on a very dignified pension that I alone paid into for thirty-five years with no help from the state.

And since my advanced age does not allow me a way of dynamically reacting

… I see no other solution than this dignified end to my life, so I don't find myself fishing through garbage cans for my sustenance.[1]

'Tsolakoglou' was a reference to a Greek military officer, Georgios Tsolakoglou, who became the first Prime Minister of the collaborationist Greek government under German and Italian occupation during World War II. The phrase 'Tsolakoglou' has the connotation of 'collaborator' or 'traitor'. There is no doubt this suicidal pensioner was referring to Greek politicians 'collaborating' with lenders of the 'Troika' consisting of the International Monetary Fund, the European Central Bank and the European Commission.

It was not difficult to find Athenians, especially those who had lived through the war, who took this view in 2012, feeling that Greece was again on its knees under the authority of Germany. Pensioners at food banks would frequently compare modern life in Greece to a form of German occupation. The country was in its fifth consecutive year of recession and massive debts had been exposed. Bailouts were offered from the IMF, the ECB and the EU, and the taxpayers most liable for all this were Germans. German Chancellor Angela Merkel and her Finance Minister Wolfgang Schäuble could only offer the money needed on strict terms. They demanded Greece tighten the screws on what was considered an unaffordable system. Greece's creditors were dictating the terms of national tax and spend policy. They demanded drastic cuts to public services, pensions and salaries, along with higher taxes, as a condition of the loan.

Life in Greece became truly appalling: pensions were slashed, unemployment soared, suicides increased, the number of women in prostitution increased, as did the number of families putting their children into care. Medication began to run out in hospitals, high street pharmacies closed because prescription debts owed by the government had not been paid, national depression was palpable across the country but particularly in the graffiti-covered streets of Athens, where many pensioners did indeed survive on food scavenged from bins.

It was widely acknowledged that the Eurozone had helped create these conditions. After it adopted the single currency, Greek public spending increased at a faster rate than other Eurozone countries, creating an unsustainable boom. Its economy remained weaker in comparison to the other nations, but it was locked into the same interest rates and currency value as those with low unemployment and high productivity. So as the government ran up debts paying for things like the 2004 Athens Olympics, it wasn't becoming more competitive, it was mostly just paying public sector workers higher salaries while allowing them to retire earlier.

Greece's budget deficit, the difference between spending and income, spiralled out of control. Under the constraints of the euro, it could no longer improve competitiveness by devaluing its currency. Dr Monique Ebell, from the National Institute of Economic and Social Research, called it the 'Eurozone's trilemma', whereby free movement of capital and fixed exchange rates had become incompatible with financial stability.[2] She was amongst many economists who argued that if Greece had had a floating exchange rate, it would have encouraged investment and the drachma would have appreciated.

Greece was also concealing these problems. Its annual debt levels were underreported to give the impression it was meeting the 3 per cent of GDP cap on borrowing that was required of Eurozone members.[3] When the global financial downturn hit, and Greece's hidden black hole was exposed, the country couldn't repay its loans and was forced to ask for help.

In 2010, amid fears of a massive Greek debt default, the European Union stepped in with a €110 billion rescue package. This was followed by a 50 per cent debt write-off in 2011, then another bailout in 2012 for €130 billion. With each intervention came more stringent conditions on Greek spending.

Over this period, everyone appeared to conform to stereotype. Greece was accused of being lazy, Germany was accused of being authoritarian in its demands for austerity, and the UK twitched the curtains and looked from its bay windows in haughty disdain at the whole affair. In many ways, the UK's reaction to this crisis was the most pessimistic.

As the euro crisis escalated, millions of Brits watched it unfold on the evening news. Greece was in flames, month after month. Youth unemployment hit 60 per cent. If Greece left the euro, Spain's banking crisis would deepen and they might leave the euro too. Then what about Portugal and Italy? 'Contagion' became the word of the hour and it could have huge repercussions on the UK's banking system and therefore the British economy. Even though we'd resisted joining the euro, we were not immune to the crisis the EU appeared to have created. In focus groups, people would say, 'It's so bad even Germany's in trouble now because of the euro,' and 'Not even Germany can afford to sort this out.'[4]

Dr Henning Meyer, editor-in-chief of *Social Europe Journal*, noted the loss of trust in European politics: 'Certainties were destroyed in the course of the crisis.'[5] That certainty up till now was the idea that European integration could only bring financial gain. Professor Nicolas Crafts from Warwick University came to the damning conclusion that while the EU could cope with rising income levels and growth, it was not equipped to handle a depressed economy. The ECB was too cumbersome and slow to move to quantitative easing. Crafts said: 'Survival entails serious reform: a fully federal solution and deep economic integration.'[6] If deeper integration was the only solution, where did that leave Britain? Would it be dragged in or isolated? Was Brussels inexorably moving towards a United States of Europe?

Ipsos MORI examines trends in attitudes towards UK membership of the EU. For roughly a decade, since the Maastricht Treaty, the majority of people supported remaining in the EU, but during the euro crisis in 2011 and 2012, British opinion changed and people mostly supported leaving.[7] When pollsters Survation asked the British public, 'Do you think that the EU as a whole would be better or worse off in the long run if the Eurozone currency were to break up?', 43 per cent of respondents chose 'better off', compared to 33 per cent who selected 'worse off'. Similarly, 39 per cent of respondents said that the UK would be better off in the long term if the Eurozone collapsed and the vast majority (77 per cent) thought Greece would leave the currency by the end of 2012[8] – but that's not how the Greeks felt.

Through all this awfulness, polls in Greece during the height of the crisis showed they overwhelmingly wanted to stay in the Eurozone. If you spoke to people in the streets, they would often condemn Germany, but they would blame their own government for the mess they were in. They knew that money had flowed out of the coffers into the wrong places, that the country's income was hit by widespread corruption and tax evasion. In 2012, Greece held two elections in short succession where the mainstream ruling parties were punished. The ballots were often described as a decision on the euro, but even the far-left party Syriza didn't advocate leaving the Eurozone or the EU, only a tearing up of the austerity plan and calling the EU's bluff. Speak to Syriza politicians and their supporters at the time and they wanted a Greek delegation in Brussels and Berlin challenging the severity of the debt reduction programme; few countenanced a return of the drachma. Even suicidal Dimitris Christoulas pointed his finger at his own politicians more than at the EU.

The difference in reaction between the UK and Greece to the Greek crisis comes down to several things, which you could combine to show that the EU already had a bad brand in the UK, and was now suffering a wider brand crisis. If the EU were a product, a Brit might describe it as having an unclear purpose while being overpriced. Now they had discovered it was also hazardous.

When crisis struck the EU institutions, the basic premise of the EU started from a low base in public opinion. On top of this, it had very few defenders and these would become diminished in the approach to 2016. Indeed, if David Cameron had wanted to pick the worst possible time to hold a referendum on the EU, he could not have done much better than 23 June 2016.

So where did this low opinion come from? To begin with, there were a whole set of feelings in Europe about the EU which are generally not shared in the UK. For Greece, joining the union was bound up with them becoming a democratic country, ending the rule of military colonels. Dictators and then a military junta controlled Greece right up until 1974. With the far-right party Golden Dawn gaining popularity in 2012, there was a sense in mainstream opinion that a break from the Eurozone would reopen the cage of fascism. Indeed, many of those campaigning for the UK's departure from the EU also believe that the Union makes political sense for Greece. Spain, Italy and Portugal had similar power structures of dictators and military juntas in the living memory of their populations. In Eastern Europe, meanwhile, membership is linked to the end of the Soviet Union. In Germany, more than seventy years on, two world wars still hang heavy in the public consciousness. Other nations may have moved on, but like the jagged spire of Kaiser Wilhelm Church in Berlin, which has remained intentionally unrepaired since it was damaged by bombing in WWII, Germany is still scarred. European peace and stability is high on their list of reasons for the Union. Ask people about the benefits of the EU from Hamburg to Munich and eight out of ten will say the word 'peace'. So nearly every other country saw the EU as an escape from darker pasts.

This social perspective didn't apply to Britain. To many, the Union was a trading partnership and nothing more. If anything, the historical consciousness in the UK was the opposite to that on the Continent. The EU appeared problematic relative to the UK's own domestic issues and generally seen as a source of disruption. Director of Vote Leave Dominic Cummings says:

If you look at Britain in 1914, you have a country which economically, culturally, politically – in every way – is much more engaged with the rest of the world and Europe is seen as an irritating source of trouble. We wanted to trade with them, but they're always going mad. Every now and then they try and invade – and this is a deep-rooted idea, even before two world wars.

But did this really translate to current times? Modern-day troubles from the Continent came in the form of 'red tape' to Britain's business and the overturning of UK legal decisions. Greece may have had its austerity martyrs, but the UK was years ahead with its metric martyrs. In 1994, several statutory instruments came into force, bringing the United Kingdom into compliance with an EU directive to harmonise the use of units of measurement within the European Community. Instead of pounds and ounces, food should be weighed in grams and kilograms.

Now, some say Sunderland's EU revolt happened on the night of 23 June 2016, but actually it began in 2001 when greengrocer Steve Thoburn decided to test the law by refusing to adopt the EU weights and measures. He was convicted at Sunderland Magistrates' Court for using weighing apparatus that did not comply with the Weights and Measures Act.[9] He and others, dubbed the Metric Martyrs, took their cases to every court they could and, ironically, even the European Court of Human Rights. They lost every time. Although the UK Parliament had voluntarily accepted these rules, the legal cases spoke volumes about the supremacy of EU law, and of course it was particularly prominent on the local news in Leave-voting Sunderland. According to UKIP spokesman Gawain Towler:

> It was the first time ordinary people thought, 'Hold on, what the blazes are they playing at? If I want to go to a market stall and buy a pound of bananas, and the chap in the shop wants to sell me a pound of bananas, why the devil can't we? He's happy, we are happy. Whose business is it to impose themselves between a perfectly normal contract or arrangement between two individuals that we are all perfectly happy with?'

Newspapers soon learned that stories about EU impositions on the UK, or other negative tales about towering sugar mountains and wine lakes caused by the EU Common Agricultural Policy, were all good tabloid fodder. Indeed any

Brussels correspondent wanting to get themselves noticed anywhere other than a small square on page 35 needed to step up their game and get themselves some grime-tinted spectacles. Someone who certainly wouldn't tolerate being ignored was myth-peddler-in-chief Boris Johnson.

The man who would be Mayor of London, Leave figurehead, then Foreign Secretary was the *Daily Telegraph*'s Brussels correspondent between 1998 and 1994, and his trade was to feed readers with stories of silly EU regulations and a bloated Brussels bureaucracy. He wrote about plans to standardise condom sizes and ban prawn cocktail flavour crisps. In the early 1990s he even suggested that the headquarters of the European Commission 'is to be blown up' because of fears that it contained asbestos. It didn't happen, with the asbestos being removed in a less explosive manner, although it was a hugely expensive and delayed renovation.[10]

Brussels correspondent Jean Quatremer of *Libération* says he observed Johnson's methods first-hand and gives an example of him writing that Commission President Jacques Delors lived 'in an immense chateau on the outskirts of Brussels'. Quatremer challenged him about it after the President's spokesman described it as a large house that had a turret, typical of the period in which it was built. 'You see, it's a castle!' Johnson laughed back.

'It wasn't truthful journalism,' says Quatremer, 'but who cared about that? Johnson managed to invent an entire newspaper genre: the Euromyth, a story that had a tiny element of truth at the outset but which was magnified so far beyond reality that by the time it reached the reader it was false.'[11]

Years later, Johnson told the BBC:

[I] was sort of chucking these rocks over the garden wall and I listened to this amazing crash from the greenhouse next door over in England as everything I wrote from Brussels was having this amazing, explosive effect on the Tory party – and it really gave me this, I suppose, rather weird sense of power.[12]

Other Fleet Street editors began to press their own correspondents to follow suit. Martin Fletcher became Brussels correspondent for *The Times* in 1999 and says he suffered the consequences.

Soon, a Europe of scheming bureaucrats plotting to rob Britain of its ancient liberties, or British prime ministers fighting gallant rearguard actions against an increasingly powerful superstate, or absurd directives on banana shapes, became the only narratives that many papers were interested in.[13]

Indeed, in September 1994, *The Sun*, *Daily Mirror*, *Daily Mail* and *Daily Express* all reported that 'curved bananas have been banned by Brussels bureaucrats'. The grain of truth was a commission regulation dictating that bananas must not have 'abnormal curvature'. The observant shopper will notice that still, to this day, there are no straight bananas in UK supermarkets, yet this exaggerated story has refused to die.

The Johnson wit about EU regulation sold stories and it would later win votes. On the campaign trail in 2016, he continued to talk about hoover suction or the curvature of bananas, knowing how well this message struck the public consciousness. After the referendum result, at the subsequent Conservative conference in Birmingham – a city that voted to leave the EU – Sky News quizzed shoppers on what rules they were looking forward to taking back control of now that the UK was leaving the EU. Out of about a dozen, no one could name a single EU regulation, until someone finally said, 'That one about bendy bananas.'

David Cameron's director of communications Craig Oliver says on reflection, 'What had not happened was any positive PR about the EU for forty years. We had allowed it to become a whipping boy – we allowed people to think this was a weird distant place that was not going to allow you to eat prawn cocktail crisps.'

He adds, 'It became this great bogeyman, a dreadful thing that was impacting on people's lives – not true – it was a complicated pooling of energies and resources to ensure that 500 million people had better well-being and international clout.'

One source in Brussels close to the then European Parliament President Martin Schulz bemoaned the British reporting on EU affairs and how it differed from journalism in other European countries: 'They don't get twisted stories,' he said.

They don't get somebody like Boris Johnson or others who sit down and ask themselves, 'What ridiculous story can I dig up about the EU and even if it is only

5 per cent true that will do for me, my editor and my readers.' You do see critical stuff about how for eight years the EU has not got a grasp on the Eurozone and how it's all set up for elites, but you don't get the parody and the ridicule.

In Brussels, the technocrats and politicians were well aware that they got a bad rap from the British press. Some in Brussels have suggested that one reason for this is that they don't have access to influence editors in the way that Downing Street has, nor indeed the power to punish journalists who write negative stories. No self-respecting political reporter has not at some point made it onto the No. 10 blacklist, meaning that for a period of time their organisation is unofficially snubbed for interviews with the Prime Minister or Cabinet members, or rather childishly ignored in press conferences because they had the audacity to ask an embarrassing question or print an article that put the PM on the spot. A few weeks or months later, it's forgotten, but it is part of the give and take in the Westminster Lobby's strange relationship with the politicians it rubs shoulders with. Brussels doesn't have that. So they can be portrayed as pantomime villains with very little comeback.

The most famous rebuke was 'Up Yours Delors' from *The Sun* on November 1990 after the French socialist President of the European Commission pushed for further integration (mentioned in Reason 6). *The Sun* produced T-shirts with the slogan for its readers. But Delors was only the first in a string of hate figures lambasted in the British press over decades, ending with another Commission President, Jean-Claude Juncker, who apparently drank whisky for breakfast, according to the *Daily Mail*.[14] This despite the tabloid's hero Winston Churchill having been well known for doing the same thing. Already poor relations between Juncker and Cameron were not helped when the same paper alleged that Juncker had a Nazi father-in-law.[15] His other low point was a video that appeared to show he was drunk at an EU event in Latvia.[16] The video came to widespread public attention just a month before the UK's referendum, when it was highlighted by the press, even though the actual event had taken place in May 2015.

If it wasn't politicians and regulations then it was interference in the courts. The largest public frustration was over the European Convention on Human Rights – which, as explained in Reason 8, was not linked with membership of the EU. Most notably, it had caused the extradition of extremist Abu Hamza to be delayed for years and had almost stopped the deportation of Abu Qatada. In

Hamza's case, the process of extraditing him to the United States took eight years and fifteen court cases after he first was charged in the US with developing a terrorist camp in Oregon and aiding Al-Qaeda.[17] The process cost the UK millions and the saga seemed unending when the focus later turned to his daughter-in-law, whom the UK wanted to deport because she was considered dangerous.[18]

The woman's case was repeatedly cited by Boris Johnson and other Brexiteers during the referendum campaign to demonstrate that Britain's security was being put at risk by European courts that were hampering the UK's ability to deport dangerous individuals. The European Court of Justice said freedom of movement laws did not allow the Moroccan-born woman to be automatically deported as a convicted criminal because she was the sole carer for her British son, who was a citizen of the European Union. After the referendum result, however, the ECJ found that British judges did have the right to decide on the grounds of upholding public security.[19]

In focus group conversations that Vote Leave has shared for this book, it is clear that the European Court of Human Rights was seen as undermining not only the control of immigration and asylum but also the UK's ability to deal with criminals and terrorists. People repeatedly raised 'the guy with the hook', a story that emotively wrapped together immigration, crime, extremism, benefits and the EU. Here is a quote from one focus group:

> Look at Hamza – we couldn't get rid of him and his family, they had a massive house, we paid for that … European law is a nightmare … All his family are still on benefits in this country, and we can't send them home cos of the Human Rights Act. We pay these 600 MPs and most of the laws are set by European courts. What's the point of voting for them if they just get overruled in Europe?[20]

It was therefore quite a smart move from Theresa May, in April 2016, when she made a speech suggesting the UK should leave the European Convention on Human Rights without leaving the EU. 'The ECHR can bind the hands of Parliament, adds nothing to our prosperity [and] makes us less secure by preventing the deportation of dangerous foreign nationals,'[21] she said. However, May's position was at odds with the PM, who wanted to reform the ECHR, not pull out of it.

Hamza was a regular feature in the tabloid newspapers, but the story that grew throughout the coalition years was that of European immigration. The Migration Observatory notes that over 70 per cent of stories about migrants had no positive aspect to them[22] and, from 2010 onwards, attention switched dramatically to European migration. It became particularly intense in 2014 when the British government, along with other EU governments, was required to lift the temporary restrictions that had been in place on Romanian and Bulgarian citizens' rights to work in the UK.

From 1 December 2012 to 1 December 2013, an important period leading up to the lifting of these transitional controls, Britain's nineteen main national newspapers published more than 4,000 articles, letters, comment pieces and other items mentioning Romanians or Bulgarians. Language used by tabloid newspapers to describe and discuss Romanians often focused on crime and anti-social behaviour. Common words associated with them were 'gang', 'criminal', 'beggar', 'thief' and 'squatter'.

In September 2016, the *Times* journalist Liz Gerard did a study of front pages since David Cameron became Prime Minister and found that the *Daily Express* splashed on migration on 180 occasions and the *Daily Mail* 122 times, with a marked acceleration in the run-up to January 2014. She found the general tone was 'all foreigners are a problem and everything is Europe's fault'.[23]

Here are three examples of *Express* headlines:

'Britain's 40 per cent surge in ethnic numbers'.[24]

'Migrants rob young Britons of jobs'.[25]

'Workers are fired for being British'.[26]

In March 2014, when Nick Clegg debated Nigel Farage over the EU, Clegg brandished a UKIP leaflet which claimed: '29 million Romanians and Bulgarians may come to this country.' Clegg said: 'There aren't even 29 million Romanians and Bulgarians living in Romania and Bulgaria. It's simply not true.' Farage replied, 'That's because 2 million have already left.' At the time, Romania's population was 21.7 million and Bulgaria's was 6.9 million, so his population figures were accurate enough and they did indeed all have the legal right to travel to Britain.[27] But as the UK braced itself for the influx, the actual number who came in the first year from the two countries was 22,000. This was a 15 per cent increase on the numbers of those nationals already in the UK.[28]

The problem for David Cameron was that he had set himself a goal of reducing net migration to the tens of thousands.[29] This was probably incompatible with his goal of reducing the deficit, as migrants contribute to the economy, but it was also unachievable, and people could see that it was unachievable. By setting an unachievable target, he was proving firstly that he didn't have a grip on migration and secondly, it seemed he thought the public would be too stupid to notice. This mistake was simply repeated as the numbers grew, and therefore became more and more absurd. He couldn't have known that the euro crisis would drive economic migrants to the relative security of the British economy, but his policy ensured that any influx had to be viewed as a 'bad thing'.

Polls throughout recent history show that roughly 70 per cent of the population think the UK is overcrowded and there is too much immigration. This figure was as true in the '60s and '70s as it was in 2016. Even in years when net migration was negative, the majority of people surveyed said that immigration was too high. The difference by 2010–16 was the feeling that the government was powerless to control it.

What's more, even though economic concerns were fading in the UK, with employment rising, worries about immigration became more prominent. Home Secretary Theresa May attempted to crack down on bogus marriages and colleges offering visas for phony courses to students outside of the EU, but there was nothing Cameron's government could do about the numbers from inside the bloc. So, like the rules imposed upon metric martyrs, like the apparently ridiculous regulation of bananas, like the impotent judges trying to expel Hamza, here was another example of European policy having unwanted consequences in the UK – and this time feeding into an issue that had been considered a negative for decades. On top of that, as the UK's EU referendum drew closer, the migration issue was about to take on a whole new dimension.

As we've established in Reason 5, when Britain joined in 1975, the EU was seen as providing much-needed economic stability. It was a transactional relationship and there was little to no emotional, historical tie-in with creating a better form of governance, peace and cooperation. So if motivations for membership were based on free trade and prosperity, everything balanced on the question 'What is the cost–benefit ratio?' This meant that when crisis hit, the UK's reactions to those events were different to the rest of the bloc, because it lacked the additional social and emotional attachment. The euro crisis and the financial crisis were felt far more deeply in many parts of Europe than in the UK, but the effect on the perceived brand of the EU was more profound in the

UK because the cost–benefit ratio appeared to have tipped. The term 'financial contagion' had been bandied about so much that the British public began to fear the country was not immune to the euro disease. The same thing happened with the next set of crises: terrorism and migration. The financial crisis exposed the imbalance of a part-integrated financial system. The Eurozone crisis then created a level of distrust between the larger, wealthier states and the poorer southern states, but the arrival in Europe of more than a million asylum seekers over the course of one year unsettled the UK's relationship with the EU like nothing else.

The migrant crisis began to take hold in 2015. A multifaceted war in Syria, ongoing violence in Afghanistan and Iraq and abuses in Eritrea all fed into the largest mass movement of people since World War II. While neighbouring countries such as Libya and Turkey became gatekeepers to this African crisis, housing millions of refugees, it soon spilled over into Europe. Many headed for Greece, taking the relatively short voyage from Turkey to the islands of Kos, Chios, Lesvos and Samos, often in flimsy rubber dinghies or small wooden boats. The boats' lack of seaworthiness, combined with the greed of people traffickers who packed the crafts with bulging numbers of people, turned this tantalisingly narrow stretch of sea into a death trap. According to the International Organization for Migration, 3,770 migrants were reported to have died trying to cross the Mediterranean in 2015.[30]

For the EU, the test was how to cope with this crisis. How to patrol the coast and save lives without encouraging more to take the risk? What to do with the migrants who made it? Nightly news was now dominated with images of desperate families arriving on islands that were better known from the pages of glossy travel brochures. The real challenge was how to cope once these people began to move across the Continent. Now it was the Schengen Agreement that was being put through an unprecedented stress test – and, like the euro, it came out as a fail.

The Schengen zone includes twenty-six EU states that have abolished passport control. This means that the 1.7 million square mile area with a population of 400 million people mostly functions as a single country for international travel purposes, with a common visa policy. As mentioned in Reason 8, Labour Prime Minister Tony Blair secured an opt-out for the UK from the Schengen zone during the process that led to the signing of the Amsterdam Treaty in 1997, but Britons could still see what was happening on the Continent, only thirty miles away.

If possible, the Schengen failure during the migrant crisis was even more visual than the riots in the streets of Athens. It was seen in the burgeoning refugee camps in Italy, Greece and, of course, closer to home in Calais. It was a 13-foot-high fence erected across the border between Hungary, Serbia and Croatia. It was refugees walking in endless lines across railway tracks or sitting on stationary trains going nowhere, throwing themselves on the tracks in desperation.[31] It was a mother offering her child to a Sky News reporter if he could just take her to Germany.[32] It was the body of a three-year-old boy washed up on a Turkish beach. That one photograph of Alan Kurdi face-down in the sand represented thousands of deaths.[33] For a moment the world stopped and saw the humanitarian crisis for what it was. Hearts bled for this one child and his family. Newspapers and broadcasters broke with convention to show the image of the dead boy to its usually squeamish readers and viewers. Apart, that is, from the *Daily Express*, which on this day decided not to focus on immigration and didn't show the photograph anywhere in the newspaper. But after two or three days of the media asking whether one image could change the world, the answer seemed to be no. Attention soon shifted back to the enormity of the problem – and once again 'people' became a 'swarm'.

What had been created to allow the free movement of goods and European workers was now facilitating the massive uncontrolled flow of refugees into countries that were unused to mass migration. The Schengen Agreement wasn't designed to deal with this issue. The EU's Dublin Agreement, under which refugees must claim asylum in the first EU country they arrived in, was also unsustainable. Greece and Italy had to spread the burden. Internally, the EU was borderless and yet it did not have its own coastguard, nor did it have a common management system for its external borders. As a result, it was very slow in making any collective decisions.

Having been Europe's financial rock, Germany's Angela Merkel tried to show moral leadership, and several days after the image of three-year-old Alan appeared in the papers, she took a stand, offering an open-door policy towards refugees from Syria. In September 2015, she said there were 'no limits on the number of asylum seekers' Germany would take in, adding that 'as a strong, economically healthy country we have the strength to do what is necessary'.[34]

Merkel's pledge provoked greater division in Europe and her own country. As Berlin looked for other countries to make similar gestures, it was accused of adding to the burden it was trying to share. Many, including the UK government, argued that now more people would be attracted to make the perilous journey, knowing they had guaranteed refuge in Germany.

The Hungarian Prime Minister, Viktor Orbán, took the opposite approach to Merkel, closing his borders, erecting a fence and saying of the refugees: 'Most of them are not Christians, but Muslims. This is an important question, because Europe and European identity is rooted in Christianity.'[35] Other countries took unilateral decisions on border control and Europe divided into countries of first arrival, transit nations, and wealthier states of final destination. The UK was firmly in the last category – but, not being part of Schengen, could once again loftily view the situation from its bay windows and insist that this was not our problem.

Stefan Lehne, a visiting scholar at Carnegie Europe in Brussels, is an expert in relationships between the EU and member states. He observes:

> The EU's normal practice of defusing political problems through extended technocratic discussions does not work well with issues of great salience to the citizen. And migration certainly belongs to the hottest and most divisive topics on the political agenda. The main crisis managers – the prime ministers and presidents who derive their legitimacy from national elections – naturally approached the issue from the perspective of domestic politics.[36]

Once again, despite being distant from the coalface, the UK appeared to be the most alarmed by events. The UK government insisted it was dealing with the problem at its source, by doing more than any EU country to fund refugee camps in nearby countries such as Lebanon and Turkey. (Indeed, it was these countries facing the real refugee crisis.)

Keen to justify the UK's desire to stay out of the immediate EU migration problem, government ministers called on Europe to get a grip, especially as greater numbers appeared to be attempting to get to Dover either as stowaways in the back of UK-bound trucks or by hitching a lift on freight trains, or even by walking though the Channel Tunnel. In August 2015, the then Foreign Secretary Philip Hammond suggested the migrants mostly had 'economic motivation to try to get to Europe'. In fact, over 60 per cent of those who had reached Europe by boat in 2015 were from Syria, Eritrea or Afghanistan, according to the UN. These citizens from war-torn countries have a right to refuge in Europe. But Hammond added:

> So long as there are large numbers of pretty desperate migrants marauding around the area, there always will be a threat to the tunnel security. We've got to resolve this problem ultimately by being able to return those who are not entitled to claim asylum back to their countries of origin.

Labour politicians accused him of being 'alarmist' and 'dehumanising' about refugees.[37]

A month later, then Home Secretary Theresa May called for Europe to 'get on with the job' of breaking the link between 'economic migrants' making the dangerous journey across the Mediterranean and settling in Europe.[38] Even the Prime Minister David Cameron, referring to the Calais crisis, spoke of 'a swarm of people coming across the Mediterranean, seeking a better life, wanting to come to Britain'.

Acting leader of the Labour Party Harriet Harman responded that he 'should remember he is talking about people and not insects' and called the use of 'divisive' language a 'worrying turn'.[39]

Ten months later, Cameron, May and Hammond would be trying to defend the EU against this kind of language and this kind of message. In 2015, they weren't doing themselves any favours. Indeed, they were making Nigel Farage's point for him – that these were economic migrants, not refugees. In 2016, Nigel Farage's infamous 'Breaking Point' poster was really not far removed from what the most prominent Remain campaigners had been saying only a few months earlier. This issue had become far more ingrained in the public consciousness when this language was coming from the mouths of elected politicians, in items on the news set to images of overloaded boats and squalid holding facilities, than any poster could achieve in the last weeks of the campaign.

Dominic Cummings, director of the Vote Leave campaign, says of the migrant crisis:

> You got such a striking image. I don't know what kind of a value you put on that

in advertising terms but if you talk about millions, tens of millions of pounds' worth of essentially advertising of people on the news and people watching that and thinking the world is changing fast and in a dangerous way, the EU is contributing to this problem and the guys in charge in London haven't got the faintest clue what to do about it.

Nigel Farage also claimed the crisis was being fuelled by 'economic migrants'. But the UKIP leader went further, warning the European Parliament in September 2015 that: 'In addition, we see, as I warned earlier, evidence that ISIS are now using this route to put their jihadists on European soil. We must be mad to take this risk with the cohesion of our societies.'[40]

Two months later, Paris was rocked by a series of coordinated terrorist attacks. Simultaneous shootings and bomb blasts at a football stadium, a concert hall, restaurants and bars left 130 people dead and hundreds wounded. The group was in fact European-born, based in Brussels, but several had gone to Syria to become members of Islamic State before returning with horrific intentions. They had taken advantage of open borders between France and Belgium and two of them had posed as refugees on boats to sneak back into their home country unnoticed. As authorities closed in on the remnants of this terrorist cell in March 2016, the group detonated a bomb at Brussels Airport, killing thirty-two people.

Nigel Farage viewed the carnage as fair game for political point-scoring. He attacked pro-EU politicians for 'putting lives at risk for the sake of political union'.

David Cameron hit out at the comments, saying it was 'not appropriate at this time to make any of those sorts of remarks'.[41] But bookies shortened their odds on Brexit.

It's notable that in its reporting of this spat, the *Daily Mail* article included only one comment of condemnation from the Prime Minister but made reference to Farage's original tweet, then his retweet branding Brussels the 'jihadist capital of Europe'. It then included his full statement that piled blame on the Schengen Agreement. The article then included a quote from UKIP defence spokesman Mike Hookem MEP saying: 'Cameron says we're safer in the EU. Well, I'm in the centre of the EU and it doesn't feel very safe.' Then, just for balance, because you might feel this is quite a UKIP-dominated article, it turned to Peter Whittle, UKIP's London mayoral candidate, who was quoted from LBC

Radio as saying: 'The way things stand, our membership of the EU means we actually have a problem with our security and that is appalling.' Not satisfied with the UKIP content quota, next the article turned to the Twitter account of Michael Heaver, Nigel Farage's spokesman – even though we'd already heard three times from Farage himself. Heaver said: 'Rampant jihadism combined with open borders is a cocktail for disaster.' Then the article gave three paragraphs to President Obama's calls for unity and calm before swiftly moving on to nine paragraphs on Donald Trump's view – which was a defence of his anti-Muslim policy and an observation that European capitals were 'literally disintegrating'.

During the referendum campaign, there was speculation about which newspapers would support Leave and which would back Remain. Let's not forget that, as we saw in Reason 5, every single mainstream paper had supported the Yes campaign in 1975. In 2016, discussion focused on the motivations of *Daily Mail* editor Paul Dacre and media mogul Rupert Murdoch. But actually the UK's biggest broadsheet (the *Telegraph*), the biggest mid-market newspaper (the *Mail*) and the biggest tabloid (*The Sun*) had, through their own reporting, helped to create a Eurosceptic readership that wanted to consume negative stories about the EU. It would have been entirely hypocritical for these papers to support Remain – and potentially damaging to their already dwindling circulations, in what was and is a difficult time for the newspaper industry. Certainly, that is the view of one senior Stronger In source, who said:

> In the *Telegraph* it was purely demographic. They did a survey and almost 80 per cent of the people who buy their paper wanted to leave the EU. It is a dying industry and it does everything it can to suck up to those people who will give that amount of money each day and not cancel their subscription.

On 20 June 2016, the *Telegraph* printed an opinion piece which said:

> In supporting a vote to leave, we are not harking back to a Britannic golden age lost in the mists of time but looking forward to a new beginning for our country. We are told it is a choice between fear and hope. If that is the case, then we choose hope.[42]

Or was it simply aiming to please the readership that it had, over twenty-five years, starting with Boris Johnson, helped turn into Eurosceptics? Having read the article, Stronger In's Craig Oliver furiously texted the editor, saying, 'What if it's a choice between fantasy and reality – what do you chose then?'

The Sun, with its tendency and preference to be on the winning side, also supported Vote Leave, as did the *Daily Mail* and the *Express*. Leave campaigners had the larger readership compared to the reach of Remain-supporting papers the *FT*, *The Times*, *The Guardian*, the *Mail on Sunday* and the *Mirror*. Research by Loughborough University found that during the referendum campaign 60 per cent of articles were in favour of leaving the EU, but when adjusted for newspaper circulations that figure rose to 80 per cent. They also noted that discussions about issues that became important after the vote, such as the Article 50 process (how Britain would actually leave), were almost invisible in the newspaper copy prior to the vote.

As even the Remain camp chose to focus on the negative aspects of leaving rather than the positives of staying, the EU's achievements seemed to go almost completely unreported. Europeans wondered why the debate appeared to side-step issues like unity, peace, freedom of travel, protection of the environment and workers' rights that had been secured in the world's largest single market, that by good fortune happened to be on Britain's doorstep. Instead, the UK media was obsessed with what could be gained from dealing with China.

It could be argued that the national press was simply maintaining Britain's long-standing tradition of holding the EU to account, that its focus on immigration represented the concerns of its readers; others say the coverage was super-charged and designed to inflame 'Little England's' worst instincts.

From a left-wing perspective, there is an even more sinister assessment of what was happening. Justin Schlosberg, a media lecturer at Birkbeck University, says:

The working-class people have had an acute sense that their interests were not being represented by the banks and Westminster. What the right-wing press seeks to do is – rather than identify the true source of the concerns, which is inequality, concentrated wealth and power and the rise of huge multinational corporations that dominate the state. All of that is an abstract, complex story to tell. The story they told which more suits their interests is: the problem is immigrants. The problem is the person who lives down your street who works in your factory, who looks different and has different customs. It plays on those instinctive fears. Ironically, in [the establishment] trying to distract people from the real cause of the crisis [inequality] – which it suited them not to tackle – it manifests in this bizarre situation which leads the UK to leaving the single market, which doesn't necessarily suit them at all.

The 2008 financial crisis underpinned all of this, undermining confidence in government, politicians, big business and banks. London and the EU may have moved on to other things, but real people had not recovered from the recession, still being told to accept lower wages or face unemployment. Now these same people were being told the EU was something else they had to accept. But they'd seen what the EU was on their TV screens – it was a bunch of foreigners trying to deal with a mess by brushing it under the carpet, and no doubt working people would ultimately pay for the clean-up – as they were in Greece.

What's more, to many people this institution was expensive and seemed to have no direct impact on their lives. It seemed to be a 'free hit' at the establishment to vote Leave – absolutely cost-free. Vote Leave's Dominic Cummings notes:

> All those amazed at why so little attention was paid to 'the experts' did not, and still do not, appreciate that these 'experts' are seen by most people of all political views as having botched financial regulation, made a load of rubbish predictions, then forced everybody else outside London to pay for the mess while they got richer and dodged responsibility. They are right. This is exactly what happened.

Some Brussels officials certainly thought British politicians used Euroscepticism as 'a tool – to put the blame on others' and that, having done everything they could to entrench this attitude, they could hardly reverse it in a few months of campaigning. The EU had been portrayed as an opponent by successive Prime Ministers who would 'go in to battle', 'block measures' and 'win crucial victories' against Brussels. Triumph over Europe was especially part of Thatcherite tradition, reinforced by David Cameron with squabbles over the EU budget and Greek debts. The 2015 Conservative manifesto even stated: 'We took Britain out of Eurozone bailouts, including for Greece – the first ever return of power from Brussels.' The impression given was that the EU was always trying to take – the battlegrounds simply shifted – until finally David Cameron beat his chest and said renegotiation or go. Vote Leave's Matthew Elliott recalls one European ambassador saying to him: 'You can't drip poison into a well and then expect voters to drink from it.'

The UK is naturally more anti-EU than other countries and has always been opposed to immigration, but this Eurosceptic feeling in the UK was ever more influenced by events between 2008 and 2016, and was magnified by the government and media reactions to those events. If Cameron called his referendum hoping that Remain would win it, then, more than anything, he needed events to turn in his favour. They didn't.

He made his Bloomberg speech as the country was still recovering from a banking crisis and Europe was in the middle of the euro crisis. Greece was on fire and economic migration to the UK increased. He conducted his renegotiation in the middle of the migration crisis when fears were raised about an uncontrolled influx of people – and in the twelve months leading up to the EU vote, both Paris and Brussels saw their worst terrorist atrocities of modern times. For all we might consider the impact of certain politicians joining certain camps and clever strategists during the campaign, can anything outweigh these factors on the result? It was catastrophically bad timing.

As Nick Clegg puts it:

> Everything that preceded the campaign: the visuals, the Med crisis, the Bataclan bombing in Paris. It is impossible to exaggerate the visceral impact it has on people's sense of insecurity when they are being invited to remain in a continent, which at its borders, at least, seems to be descending into chaos. I just think that is so powerful. That combined with the ongoing scars of 2008, the powerful vested interests in the press, the shallow roots of British attachment to the EU – it's almost a miracle looking back on it that 48 per cent of people voted to remain.

What PR firm could turn around a brand crisis of that magnitude? If there was a check on this apathy, and a desire to push back against Euroscepticism, it was the forces of progressive liberalism in British politics: the pro-EU Liberal Democrats, the centre-left of the Labour Party and the Scottish National Party. These were the defenders of the European project. Surely they would come to the rescue during the referendum?

But after the 2015 general election the Liberal Democrats returned to Parliament with just eight MPs – punished by the electorate for their perceived failings in government. One can only imagine what Nick Clegg with his pre-coalition popularity might have achieved as a Remain campaign leader.

The SNP, while being fully in favour of remaining in the EU, realised that to support it would be to work openly with David Cameron and the Tory leaders, something with which they were extremely uncomfortable. Furthermore, the SNP seemed to realise quite early on that every region in Scotland might vote Remain. But if the UK voted Leave, David Cameron would have to resign and the Conservatives might be left in chaos. What's more, a UK Leave vote combined with a Scottish Remain vote (leavened by a low Scottish turnout) would give them more ammunition to fulfil their ultimate ambition, Scottish independence, because it would meet their manifesto commitment to call a new referendum 'if there is a significant and material change in the circumstances that prevailed in 2014, such as Scotland being taken out of the EU against our will'.[43] Scotland *were* taken out of the EU against their will, with their will expressed in small enough numbers that it never risked affecting the UK result.

Sure enough, on 24 June 2016, leader Nicola Sturgeon was quickly arguing that this exact result could lead to a second Scottish independence referendum. SNP politicians insist they did run an effective In campaign in Scotland, but admit it was not done with anywhere near the gusto of their own referendum for independence. The key focus was on trying to ensure that every region of Scotland voted Remain, but the drive to get the vote out in strong Remain areas was less robust. This was partly because it didn't need to be. The notable thing about Scotland is that there was a very weak Leave campaign, with every party strongly supporting Remain. 'There was no one to fight,' said one campaigner.

The history of British general elections has shown that turnout is at its highest when the campaign is closely fought, with two definable sides seemingly having similar chances to win. Scotland, with a separate media and political environment, didn't have the public battle over this referendum that England was having, and definitely not like their 2014 independence referendum, which had seen turnout of 84.6 per cent. The result was that Remain got 62 per cent of the vote in Scotland, but on a turnout of only 67.2 per cent, with voter participation especially low in the key Remain city of Glasgow.

Of course, the most significant political defender of the EU was the Labour Party. Of their MPs, 218 declared for Remain and just ten for Leave. Led by a progressive Blair-like figure at the peak of his popularity, the party would have been a formidable force for Remain, but circumstances were different. Labour's problems were just beginning.

REASON 13

AGENT CORBYN

A few days after he was elected leader of the Labour Party, Jeremy Corbyn met with Alan Johnson, head of Labour's Remain campaign. Johnson wasn't sure what to expect. He knew that Corbyn had, for most of his career, been part of a group of backbenchers whose mindset on the EU hadn't changed since they had opposed membership in 1975. Given this, the new leader might even try to engineer a shift in the party's position from Remain to Leave. Johnson had been in charge of Labour's pro-EU campaign for four months, but it was possible he was going to be sacked. The best Johnson could hope for was to discuss strategy, give an overview and hope that 'unless he said something to the contrary, he was floating towards having a Labour campaign to stay in the EU'. But the conversation never got on to that. Jeremy Corbyn wanted to talk about something else.

'Jeremy mostly told me about his writing,' recounts Johnson. 'He had partially written five or six books on issues that he was interested in. He'd started books, as lots of people do, and never properly got on with them.' None of these books were relevant to the issue they had met to discuss. None of them were published. Nor, it seemed, had Corbyn began the process of getting a publisher interested in the manuscripts he'd written during his thirty-three years as MP for Islington North. It became clear to Johnson that his leader was angling for some advice on how to get into print.

The former Home Secretary, who had had two volumes of his own memoirs published, told him: 'Now you are party leader, there will be a market, you'll find an agent and a publisher. You should just get on with it.' But, according to Johnson, the conversation about Corbyn's writing aspirations dominated the meeting, and his disinterest in the EU referendum was all too apparent. Johnson left the room deciding that, for now at least, Labour was still a party for Remain and he was still running the campaign. 'He agreed that I stayed in the role. Or rather, the fact that I left the meeting without him telling me I wasn't meant that I was,' says Johnson.

If that all sounds a bit vague, things didn't get much clearer over the next nine months. What follows is a story of frustration, confusion and mixed messages as the Labour Party tried to cope with a leader who didn't seem to have the EU referendum high on his list of priorities. Some even argue he had an underlying plan to disrupt the Remain camp and unseat David Cameron – but there's also evidence to suggest that he simply wasn't that interested in the Europe question, and while everyone else in the Labour boat screamed at the approaching rapids, their leader appeared to be wearing state-of-the-art noise-cancelling headphones that insulated him from the increasing panic.

However, there is more at play here. Labour was at war with itself. There was an ideological tear at the seams at which both sides were, and the EU campaign became a part of that battle. Corbyn was in splendid isolation from Labour's thrust to keep the UK in the EU at all costs, because he came from a different tradition within the party. For a number of reasons, he didn't agree with the way his party wanted to campaign. What's more, Labour's MPs found their enthusiasm for the EU was not shared on the doorstep in their heartlands, adding another layer of complication to the party's approach. The upshot was that Corbyn's leadership became a headache for the Remain camp, and his role is worthy of its own chapter.

The extraordinary rise of Jeremy Corbyn is for another book to tell, but its impact on the Brexit vote should not be overlooked. Nor should certain aspects of his rise to lead the Labour Party, nor where he came from. Vote Leave chief executive Matthew Elliott described Corbyn's election as Labour Party leader on 12 September 2015 as 'a massively good day for Vote Leave'. Politically, Corbyn was never a team player. He'd voted against Labour more than 500 times – 'more times than David Cameron', claimed the *Daily Mail* the day after he was elected Labour leader.[1] Being on the far left of the party, he'd opposed Tony Blair's efforts to relocate Labour in the centre of British politics. He opposed Blair's commitment not to raise taxes and to flirt with big business. He opposed Blair's war in Iraq.

To many activists, Blair was Labour's bad conscience, and Corbyn the wizened sage-like figure who emerged from a black period in the party's history with the moral loftiness of one who had exiled himself from all the nastiness. The controversy over the war in Iraq became the single most trust-eroding political event of recent decades, and by backing Corbyn – the chair of the Stop the War Coalition – Labour members could dump the baggage of the past. This and his firm opposition to austerity made him the champion of the left.

In May 2015, following electoral defeat and the resignation of Ed Miliband, Labour's left-wingers got together to discuss the thing they always discussed when the leadership question arose: Which of them should put themselves forward? It was a tradition that one of them would stand and that that person would come last. Corbyn's shadow Chancellor John McDonnell tells the story: 'We went round the table. I said "I've done it twice and couldn't even get on the ballot paper," Diane Abbott did it last time and so she'd done her duty, and so we looked at Jeremy and said, "Your turn." He said: "OK, I'll do it."'[2]

And so a political movement was born – along with a really good betting opportunity. A week after Corbyn announced he was standing, a poll of nearly 2,000 LabourList readers put him ahead of all the other candidates – and not just slightly ahead but on 47 per cent, compared to his nearest rival Andy Burnham on 13 per cent. These were Labour members – the people who would decide the outcome – and they were backing the rank outsider from the beginning, even though at this early stage Corbyn hadn't made the ballot paper, which required the backing of thirty-five MPs. Those of us who had spotted the poll found ourselves checking the bookies' odds. William Hill had him at 80/1.

Corbyn managed to secure enough MPs required to get himself on the ballot, convincing them that the left needed a token representative to 'open up the debate', or it would seem like a Parliamentary Labour Party stitch-up. Several who gave him their nomination later came to regret it, and one former Blair advisor described them as 'morons'.[3] Those thirty-five MPs might not just have determined a tumultuous future for the Labour Party, but also put in place a significant factor towards Britain's departure from the EU.

What they had all overlooked is that by changing the leadership voting method to one member, one vote, which Ed Miliband had done in an effort to reduce the influence of the unions, Labour activists were suddenly handed more power. Activists tended to be more left-wing than the MPs, who under the previous system had controlled one third of the final vote. On top of this, anyone could vote in the leadership election by becoming a registered supporter for just £3. So people who had abandoned Labour during the Blair years for the

Greens or the Socialist Workers, and even those Trotskyites who'd been banished from the party in the 1980s, could now grab the wheel of the Labour Party and yank it back in their political direction.

Meanwhile, as the leadership contest got underway, a group of MPs considered a different question. How could Labour help keep the UK in the EU? Three things were clear: 1) Labour had lost the general election; 2) the Conservatives had won a majority, so there would be no horse-trading with coalition partners over their manifesto; and 3) the Tory manifesto had promised a referendum. There was no time to lose. Labour MPs decided they needed to put the campaign together immediately. In early June, Hilary Benn and acting leader of the Labour Party Harriet Harman cornered Alan Johnson in the voting lobby of the House of Commons.

Johnson's long experience in office made him the obvious choice. He'd been Home Secretary, Secretary for Health, Education, Trade and Work and Pensions. He was also briefly shadow Chancellor. He says, 'I thought, this is going to be the most important political decision in my lifetime and I'd better get involved in it.'

All concerned decided it was crucial that Labour had a distinctive campaign, separate from the Stronger In umbrella that was likely to be the designated main group that would win the public money via the Electoral Commission. They had learned from the 2014 Scottish referendum that they do not benefit from campaigning alongside the Tories. But Johnson had picked up rumours that, even before Corbyn was elected leader, some of the shadow Cabinet was split on whether the party should be for In or for Out. His one stipulation was that if he was to lead the campaign, the Labour Party had to be 'unequivocally Remain'. With this purpose in mind, he and a small team set about shaping the Labour argument, mostly based on positive aspects of the EU on jobs and working conditions.

When Corbyn was elected in September, everyone took a deep breath and hoped nothing would change. During the leadership debates, he was the only contender who'd refused to reassure voters that he wouldn't vote Out in the referendum. At a hustings in Warrington in July 2015, he said: 'No, I wouldn't rule it out ... Because Cameron quite clearly follows an agenda which is about trading away workers' rights, is about trading away environmental protection, is about trading away much of what is in the social chapter.'[4]

Once leader, it was rumoured he was considering taking a neutral stance on the EU or even campaigning to leave. That was a worry for many MPs. In particular, it was a worry for Corbyn's new shadow Foreign Secretary Hilary Benn and shadow Minister for Europe Pat McFadden. They wanted to ensure the party was seen as pro-Europe. They opposed suggestions made by John McDonnell that Labour wait until after David Cameron's negotiations before declaring a position. Both had asked for certainty about Corbyn's stance when they accepted roles in the shadow Cabinet. The reassurance was vague and, at a hustings with MPs, Corbyn had warned against giving David Cameron 'a blank cheque'.[5] It was possible he was contemplating a reversal of the party's stance, so Benn and McFadden set themselves the task of binding him in.

According to Labour sources, the key thing was to get him away from Eurosceptics in his close circle such as shadow Chancellor John McDonnell and head of communications Seumas Milne. McFadden took Corbyn aside and threatened to resign unless he committed to the campaign to keep the party in the EU. 'I was the shadow Europe spokesman,' says McFadden, 'I wanted to be clear that if I stayed it was on the basis that we would campaign to remain in.'

In the meantime, Benn drafted a Parliamentary Labour Party briefing note. The top line stated: 'Labour will be campaigning in the referendum for the UK to stay within the European Union.'[6] Corbyn, who perhaps thought he had bigger battles to wage over other matters, agreed to sign it. This, according to one former shadow Cabinet member, was the moment they 'pinned him down'.

'That was absolutely exhilarating,' admits Johnson.

Jeremy is not very tough; they had to get him on his own and when McDonnell and Milne found out about this briefing, they were furious. But it was gone. It couldn't be retracted, from the offices of Jeremy Corbyn and Hilary Benn. So that was a real game-changer for us.

Much to the relief of his MPs, Corbyn then wrote an opinion piece in the *FT* that committed his party to opposing Brexit. He said: 'Our shadow cabinet is clear that the answer to any damaging changes that [prime minister David] Cameron brings back from his renegotiation is not to leave the EU but to pledge to reverse those changes with a Labour government elected in 2020.'[7] Within this article, however, there was also the foundation of Corbyn's argument that the EU was far from perfect and needed reforming, but at this stage MPs were just glad he wasn't joining the Leave camp.

When it came to Jeremy Corbyn's first Labour Party conference, the members backed the established stance on the EU. Furthermore, work had already been done to get the unions onside – this mostly involved ensuring that David Cameron wasn't going to negotiate away workers' rights. Johnson had been to Brussels to meet the UK negotiators, who at this stage were 'bored with nothing to do' because Cameron hadn't yet set out his plans. But when it came to opt-outs on EU employment legislation, the negotiators did tell Johnson: 'We've been very clear to him – don't go there, it is not a good idea. How are you going win a referendum if you tell people they're going to lose their right to four weeks' paid holidays?'

Only the GMB union wanted to wait to see what David Cameron came back with from his negotiation. But others argued that even if the Prime Minister came back with an opt-out from the Working Time Directive (which limits working hours to forty-eight per week) or the Social Chapter (designed to improve, or at least provide a basic 'floor' for working conditions), the trade union response shouldn't be to leave the EU, but to campaign to stay in and get rid of David Cameron. Pat McFadden argued this using the example of John Major's government refusing to sign up to the Social Chapter: 'Once Labour was in power, the first thing Blair's government had done was sign the Social Chapter,' he told union leaders. 'So the best thing is to remain in Europe, because if you left, what protection would that give you?' Eventually, this argument won out.

Having the unions onside and a piece of paper with Corbyn's consent for a Remain campaign was one thing – mobilising the leader as an effective campaigner for the EU was another. So here is a challenge: watch any speech that Jeremy Corbyn made during the 2017 general election campaign and compare it to any speech he made about staying in the EU. In the latter, there is a palpable drop in both quality and delivery – he has the demeanour of someone switching from the words he's been saying all his life to a script that's been shoved in his hands five minutes before.

His first big intervention came on 14 April 2016. In a keynote speech at the Senate House, he said Labour was 'overwhelmingly' in favour of staying in. He added, during the questions afterwards, 'That's the party I lead and that's the position I am putting forward.'[8] In the speech he had criticised the EU's 'democratic accountability', arguing that it needed reform. 'Europe needs to change,' he said, but it could be reformed from within if we remained members of the EU 'warts and all'.[9]

The first thing to say about this is it undermines the Stronger In argument that David Cameron had just come back with the reforms Britain needed. Had Cameron asked for the wrong things? Would Europe really accept the next round of reforms that Corbyn was asking for? Was the government really going to ask for them? If not, should we vote to leave? These were the questions left hanging from Jeremy Corbyn's first significant intervention.

But he had no issue with offering this level of confusion. His primary goal was to distance himself from Cameron, making it clear that even if, on this rare occasion, he did want the same outcome as the Conservative leader, it was for totally different reasons. He even made a point of supporting unlimited immigration: 'There is nothing wrong with people wanting to migrate to work around the continent,'[10] he said. Indeed, to be doubly clear he wasn't in Cameron's camp, he also criticised the government for sending out a pro-EU leaflet to 9.3 million homes using taxpayers' money. His spokesman told the press: 'Jeremy is of the view that there should have been an even approach to the information to allow everyone to make an informed decision.'[11] In other words, it wasn't fair to Vote Leave.

Apart from undermining the main campaign, the other problem was that Jeremy Corbyn failed to make a convincing socialist case for remaining in. His next big chance to do this was in May 2016, when Labour launched its referendum battle bus. The weather didn't help. Journalists stood under a makeshift canopy as rain added to the grim feel of a car park on London's South Bank. A group of activists were huddled under a two-metre-square red canopy that one of the journalists present joked was 'Labour's broad tent'. Behind them was a red bus. Not the famous Vote Leave red bus, with the famous message on the side. Few would remember the message on this red bus. It said 'Vote Remain 23 June' (we had to look that up).[12]

After quite a bit of waiting, four figures filed out of the coach into the damp day. Alan Johnson led the way, then came deputy party leader Tom Watson, Gloria De Piero MP and finally Jeremy Corbyn, who spoke last, using the time during the other speeches to check his notes. When he was handed the microphone, he focused on the EU's contribution to human rights, workers' rights and the environment. As he shuffled his increasingly soggy pages, he sometimes moved the microphone away from his mouth, which meant certain phrases disappeared into the drizzle. 'These things [muffle, muffle, muffle] are crucial.'

Even with his notes, the speech was repetitive, constantly returning to his key points: 'human rights, justice, the environment'. That was, until he finished off – and here he didn't need notes as he vowed to ensure the EU didn't press on with its Transatlantic Trade and Investment Partnership (TTIP), which 'we oppose'. That was his final point in a very weak and poorly delivered speech. On the day Labour launched its battle bus to remain in the EU, Jeremy Corbyn rounded off the whole event with another negative.

'You could tell Jeremy's heart wasn't in it,' says Alan Johnson. 'We kept putting into speeches "that's why *I'm* campaigning to remain in the European Union" – and Seumas kept changing it to "that's why *Labour* is campaigning". There's a bit of a clue there.'

After the speeches, Corbyn did a TV interview with co-author Jason Farrell where he was challenged on the point Johnson raises. Here's a brief extract:

JF: You say Labour is overwhelmingly in favour of remaining in – are you overwhelmingly in favour of remaining in?

JC: Overwhelmingly in favour of remaining in – for the opportunities it gives – in particular environmental protection we can get as well as the human rights agenda across Europe. [Notice he still doesn't use the word 'I'.]

JF: You have been a critic of Europe and voted against further integration but you know your party supports the EU. Is this a rare occasion where you are prepared to put politics ahead of your own convictions?

JC: I've made many, many criticisms of the EU. I still make them. I still make criticisms of excessive levels of lobbying by big business and global corporations in Brussels and I'm very critical of the Transatlantic Trade and Investment Partnership, just as I am of CETA [Comprehensive Economic and Trade Agreement, made with Canada].

JF: So how can you persuade voters of something you are so critical of?

JC: On the basis of the jobs that depend on exports to Europe are still going to be defended. I don't want to see jobs especially in the north-east and the Midlands end as a result of an end of trade agreements with Europe.

Bang – there is the key Labour argument for staying in the EU: jobs. This extract is right at the end of the interview in which Corbyn has mentioned workers' rights and the environment on several occasions, but when asked how to persuade voters of the merits of the EU, he knows the answer: one word – jobs. Why did it have to be prised out of him? Why was it preceded by a list of other stuff that was less important and sprinkled with negativity?

It emerged later that ahead of this press conference Corbyn refused to sign off on a quote for the newspapers that mentioned jobs. A press officer asked approval for a quote from Corbyn which was written for him saying: 'Labour is for staying in because we believe the EU has brought investment, jobs and protection for workers and the environment.' Corbyn's spokesman Kevin Slocombe responded that they were unhappy with it, because that wasn't what he planned to say. Nor could they provide an alternative quote. The newspapers would have to do without one.

In an interview for this book, Corbyn's director of communications Seumas Milne said that it was unreasonable for the Labour In camp to provide quotes for the Labour leader to give in speeches or to newspapers and just expect his sign-off. 'They would give us lines to deliver and then complain that he would not deliver them – that's not how being a leader works.' He also says that Corbyn had a general aversion to using the word 'I' in his speeches – which was something they were trying to train out of him. He admits that his boss was at odds with Labour In's message, but argues that Corbyn's approach was more effective. He said:

> They worked closely with the cross-party campaign, they were closely integrated, their line was undiluted and uncritically pro-EU. Jeremy didn't want it – didn't believe it and didn't think it was the most effective message to take to traditional Labour areas – and there's quite a lot of evidence that we were right about that. Polling shows his voice was the most effective towards winning Labour voters towards the Remain vote.

But Pat McFadden disagrees with this explanation.

> It wasn't about being in touch with Labour voters, it was born out of a history of mistrust in the European Union; of seeing it as this 'corporatist body' which, beyond the employment rights directive, he couldn't really think of anything good to say about. So its role in preserving peace in Europe, its post-Cold War role, none of that particularly appealed to him. He would have been unconvinced

about the single market, which had been the centrepiece of Britain's inward investment and trade stance of recent decades.

This issue would arise again and again. In mid-June 2016, Tom Watson asked for approval to make a statement based on analysis by the Centre for Economics and Business Research. The think tank found that EU membership would provide 1.3 million jobs by 2030. Corbyn and his Chancellor John McDonnell looked at the figures and found some of those jobs were based on the EU signing off on its TTIP deal with the US. They told Watson they couldn't support the figures 'because we are not backing TTIP'. Watson gave the speech anyway.

Why is Corbyn's failure to talk about jobs a problem? A YouGov poll for *The Times* Red Box after the Brexit vote asked Leave voters what factors would have changed their minds. A significant increase in unemployment was the most crucial, with more than a fifth saying that would sway them. It was more important than concerns about tariffs on goods, Scotland leaving the UK, needing a visa to travel to Europe or even seeing the price of groceries go up by 10 per cent.[13]

During the 2017 snap election campaign, Corbyn argued that jobs would be at the heart of his negotiation strategy. His message on Brexit was: 'Primarily, it's about getting and retaining tariff-free access to the European market.' Yet, in the referendum campaign, Corbyn didn't just fail to focus on this message about jobs; he made it clear he was lukewarm at best about the European Union. This was exemplified in early June when he appeared on Channel 4's comedy show *The Last Leg*. He told Australian comedian Adam Hills: 'I'm not a huge fan of the European Union.' Asked to give the EU marks out of ten, he probably thought a 7 out of 10 was quite generous. It goes to show how out of touch he was with his party's thinking.[14]

Watching the programme was Labour's Will Straw, campaign director for Stronger In. 'Him saying he was only seven out of ten in favour for staying in, in what was a binary referendum. I mean you can't be seven out of ten. You can be ten or zero – you don't have the option to be seven out of ten!' says Straw.

Corbyn supporters argue it would have been disingenuous for him to give the EU full marks and that pointing to its blemishes made him a more authentic and convincing advocate for remaining in. Seumas Milne says: 'I think that's fine. If you say ten out of ten, it's just stupendous – when you are trying to convince people who are wavering – that's not a very good message.'

Straw disagrees:

He is a politician – you have to give a political answer: 'I accept the EU isn't perfect – but in this referendum there is a choice between remaining or leaving and I am 100 per cent for remain'. That was the only answer that he needed to give in that situation and it shows incompetence that he wasn't able to give a more political answer.

Unlike Alan Johnson, Will Straw was unable to get a single meeting with Corbyn in six months of trying. As executive director of the Electoral Commission's designated campaign to remain in the EU, and someone with long connections to the party (his father Jack Straw is a former Foreign Secretary), this is quite extraordinary. Straw says, 'There were two big problems with Jeremy Corbyn. One was his ambivalence but the second was his competence. He and his team couldn't run a bath.'

Straw complains that Corbyn consistently failed to make interventions cut through and get on the evening news with a clear message, which Straw describes as 'the basics of political communication'. He adds:

Corbyn seemed to take the notion that the way to win a campaign was to speak to crowded church halls in the evenings as a way of getting through. I'm sure they got through to thousands of Labour members that way, but we needed to get across to millions of Labour voters – and they failed to do that.

Corbyn's camp deny the notion that his campaigning was low-key – but argue that the 'air war' was dominated by Straw's Stronger In group, who would only create space for him when it suited them. The agreement amongst the broadcasters was that Stronger In and Vote Leave should be the leading voices on either side, because they were the official campaigns. But equally Corbyn didn't want to campaign alongside the official campaign. 'Photoshoots with David Cameron were the last thing we wanted to do,' says Milne.

He added: 'When they wanted to give us the space, they gave it to us but, by the way, they didn't coordinate it. No one told us that this was the day that Stronger In would shut down so we would get the airtime – it just happened.'

Clearly, there was tension between the two camps. But Corbyn's disengagement with the EU question was also noted within the Labour Party. He didn't turn up, or send a delegation, to the weekly Labour EU meeting. There would be a seat there for LOTO (Leader of the Opposition) and it was always empty. Some of his staff were said to complain that the 8.30 a.m. event was 'too early'. At a Cabinet meeting where Alan Johnson was invited to make a presentation on the EU campaign, Corbyn insisted on devoting most of the meeting to John McDonnell's response to the Budget. When it came to talking about the EU, the Labour leader seemed to forget he'd invited Johnson and asked his new shadow Europe Minister to speak. Pat Glass was forced to remind him, 'Alan is here.' Johnson finally prepared to speak, but he was told to keep it brief. 'Let's hurry this up,' said Corbyn, 'because John McDonnell's got an important statement to make about finance.' Questions off the back were also cut short to give more time to McDonnell. 'It was so obvious that he didn't want to talk about the EU,' says Johnson.

This, in part, was simply a factor of Corbyn's style of leadership and the internal warfare within the party. In January 2016, he had sacked his Europe minister Pat McFadden, sparking resignations of three others from the front bench. In his phone call to McFadden, Corbyn had explained that he thought McFadden had been trying to mock him in the Commons. The Europe minister appeared to have been cutting about his leader's stance on terrorism in the wake of the Paris attacks. McFadden said in the House of Commons: 'Can I ask the Prime Minister to reject the view that sees terrorist acts as always being a response or a reaction to what we in the West do?'

McFadden was a significant player within the Europhile campaign and some within Labour saw his dismissal as McDonnell's revenge for his role in getting Corbyn to sign the party leader up to the Remain campaign. However, McFadden says Europe didn't come up in the phone call when he was sacked.

This internal turmoil was itself destructive. We would see in the days after Brexit how disunited the Labour Party was and how much MPs blamed Corbyn for failing to engage with the campaign. After the referendum, 80 per cent of them voted no confidence in their leader and attempted to oust him. But even during the campaign this disunity was simmering below the surface.

Pro-EU MPs were hamstrung not just by Corbyn's lack of passion but also by the fact that Leave campaigners could point to his history and the fact he had previously been a Eurosceptic. Some even suggested that 'Agent Corbyn' was working for the other side. The handful of Labour Leave campaigners interviewed for this book, such as Kate Hoey and Graham Stringer, consistently said that historically he was always in their lobby when it came to voting on EU matters.

However, this isn't entirely true. In fact, Corbyn's relationship with the EU was much more in line with the indifference he showed during the campaign. It's true that he was against joining the EU in 1975 and he'd campaigned against the Maastricht Treaty. But as the years went on, he was quite often absent from EU votes and he was rarely vocal in debates. Take the referendum vote itself. In a debate in October 2011, Corbyn voted for having a referendum on the UK's membership of the EU. This was against his party's stance. However, in a long debate in the Commons, he didn't contribute. Furthermore, when it came to the actual European Referendum Bill following David Cameron's Bloomberg speech, he was absent from the debate and didn't vote in any of the readings. Not in July 2013, nor in October 2014, nor during the three readings from June to September 2015. Be sure of this: all the key Eurosceptics showed up. Quizzed on this recently by co-author Jason, Corbyn says in those summer months of 2015 he may have been out campaigning for the leadership – but confirms he would have voted to have the referendum.

Corbyn *was* someone who tended to vote against further integration. For example, he voted against the Maastricht Treaty and the Lisbon Treaty, but again he was absent for most of the debates leading up to the Lisbon vote and he didn't contribute to the debate on the day of the final vote. So trying to understand Jeremy Corbyn's stance on Europe was never straightforward.

Most people we have interviewed for this book were unable to say for certain whether he favoured staying in the EU or not. Plenty believe he voted Leave, which he strongly denies. The most common response was that of Angela Eagle: 'You'd have to ask him.' Craig Oliver, David Cameron's then director of communications, says simply, 'I don't think he understood the EU.'

Several within the cross-party Stronger In group began to consider the prospect of the Labour leadership changing its mind and turning hostile towards the Remain campaign. But as the campaign progressed, it became more and more obvious to people like Craig Oliver that they desperately needed Jeremy Corbyn. 'Blue on blue' disagreements between high-profile Conservatives were dominating the media. It was no good just rolling out the Prime Minister. They needed high-profile advocates of the EU who weren't Tories. People who could cut through to non-Conservative voters who were undecided on Remain or Leave. They needed a spokesperson from one of the progressive parties – the largest one being the Labour Party.

In late February 2016, Craig Oliver noted in his diary that:

The Labour party is vital. We can't win it without them. But will the voters turn out for a leader who seems barely competent and seems indifferent on the EU? Perhaps even more worrying, Corbyn was put there by people who think the system is failing them. Will they vote for the status quo option, led by a Conservative?[15]

Liberal Democrats also acknowledged this problem. Nick Clegg's former advisor James McGrory was director of Stronger In's media strategy. He says that in the last fortnight, an effort was made to refocus their entire strategy around the Labour Party: 'Ten days out, we tore up our grid and briefed the fact that we were doing a "Labour fightback".'

The Prime Minister stood aside from a speech he'd been earmarked to do in Leicester to allow Jeremy Corbyn to take the stage – but the Labour leader refused to do it. Indeed, his press team made it clear that Stronger In would have no access to the frontbench team – they would only do Labour-organised events. At the last minute, the former Labour Prime Minister Gordon Brown stepped in to do the Leicester event.

Labour people dominated the Stronger In team. The trouble was they were from the Blairite and Brownite wings of the party and therefore had little influence on the current leadership. They had just fought a bitter campaign against Corbyn only a few months before, with the moderate side of the party warning he would be a disaster as leader. Corbyn had equal disrespect for them. So while Stronger In could consistently deliver Labour's big beasts from yesteryear – Alistair Darling, David Blunkett and Neil Kinnock – or people committed from the backbenches – such as Emma Reynolds, Stephen Kinnock and Chuka Umunna, all strong performers – what they couldn't get at any point during the campaign was the current Labour front bench. And, like it or not, this made Stronger In look very much like the Prime Minister's campaign. In McGrory's view, 'The impact was huge.'

He says: 'Jeremy Corbyn's office and John McDonnell's office were lamentably disengaged. They couldn't be relied upon to do anything. They couldn't be relied upon to campaign, to do speeches, to do media appearances – any of the bread-and-butter things you need doing during a campaign.'

In Craig Oliver's view, Corbyn certainly didn't want to actively help the Prime Minister. He says:

> It was a golden opportunity for a Leader of the Opposition to take this campaign by the scruff of the neck and say 'We believe in the EU' and lead from the front. But what happened was two things: Corbyn was pretty equivocal about the EU and secondly he was surrounded by people who thought, 'Why are we helping David Cameron?' And as a result there was lukewarm, tepid, useless, hopeless campaigning. I think they thought we would get under the wire and do it – but why help David Cameron more than you needed to?

This translated to not helping Stronger In even when key Labour figures were involved. One of the most telling examples came when shadow Business Secretary Angela Eagle was put up by Labour to be one of a team of three in the ITV referendum debate on 9 June. At the time, the former head of media for Tony Blair, Alastair Campbell, emailed her to say: 'This is the biggest thing you have ever done. You need to take it seriously.'[16]

So how much input did the Labour leadership have in this key moment? 'None,' says Angela Eagle. Despite being Jeremy Corbyn's shadow Business Secretary, she was coached for the interview by the Stronger In campaign team, including David Cameron's director of communications Craig Oliver. There were no internal messages from the Labour leader's office on what they wanted her to say. She says:

> I had absolutely no contact whatsoever. I went to be briefed by Stronger In and they were using mainly Conservative messages. There was no interest from the leader's office. There was no good luck message. There was no wrap-up afterwards whether they thought I'd done well or badly, absolutely nothing. I had to go and do it myself. It is unbelievable, but true.

As the division between the leader's office and the rest of the party became more obvious, there were efforts made to counter this perception – but these too ended up having the reverse effect. It happened with three weeks to go until the vote. Immigration figures had come out a week earlier which showed the UK had a net inward migration of 333,000. Alan Johnson recalls:

You could feel it slipping away. It was a gift – not least because Cameron had promised to get net migration down to the tens of thousands. When I was Home Secretary it was 160,000. No credit to me – we'd had Lehman's and the crash. No one wanted to come and work here. Anyway, 333,000 was a record number! It was slipping. You could feel it slipping.

He decided to call the Labour leader:

My message to Jeremy was: 'Look, you've got three weeks. You've got to press on the shadow Cabinet to do their bit.' Some did more than others. Some did nothing at all in terms of getting out there. 'You've got to make the positive case. You seem to be pushing this Remain and reform. You've got to forget about the reform and concentrate on the Remain.'

The conversation then turned to a new plan to combat the impression that Labour was disunited. Phil Wilson, chair of the Backbench European Parliamentary Group, had got 212 MPs to sign a letter to go into the papers that weekend. Johnson had been having some 'to and fro' with Corbyn's office about the wording, but they had eventually cleared it and the letter was sent to a newspaper. It would send a unified message that the Labour leadership and nearly all of his MPs supported remaining in the EU.

However, Seumas Milne, Corbyn's head of communications, had been on holiday and, according to Johnson, he didn't see the letter until it had already been signed off and sent to the *Sunday Mirror*. He apparently wanted to take the word 'united' out of a sentence about the party agreeing that Britain should remain in the EU. He also wanted a more positive message on immigration.

Johnson says:

Milne then intervenes on the Friday after it has gone to the newspaper and says he wants it changed. To which the Labour Party people said, 'Don't be stupid, you can't change it now they've got the original version. If you change it, they will compare it and what is a story about Labour unity becomes a story about Labour disunity.' Pretty simple stuff!

So in this conversation with Jeremy, I said, 'Really, we can't do this.' And he said, 'Oh, I'll have a word with Seamus… Leave it with me.' I leave that with him.

I got up the next morning [and] Seumas had insisted at twelve midnight that the original letter is changed. So we had to drag two people in on a Saturday morning to contact all 212 MPs to say, 'Look, there is this slight change.' Now they were then saying, 'Why is this changed?'

Nigel Nelson, political editor at the *Sunday People*, was then tipped off by someone at the *Mirror* about the changes and wrote a story about Jeremy Corbyn 'at odds with his own MPs', having disrupted his party's appeal for unity.[17] The actual letter was never published.

Milne insists he was right to change the letter. The party wasn't fully 'united'; there were Labour figures in Vote Leave and Grassroots Out camps such as Gisela Stuart and Kate Hoey. He says the changes were minimal, changing the word 'united' to 'overwhelmingly supportive'. 'It's not a big change, just more accurate,' he says. There had also been rumours of a Cabinet defection by John Trickett to Leave. If that had happened around the time of the letter, the leader would have had egg on his face. It would emerge after the referendum that Trickett, who was Labour's election campaign boss, had written an email to Corbyn saying:

> I would like permission to amplify the critical, pro-reform part of the agenda on the basis that I accept that I can't follow my instinct to vote and campaign for No. There will be loads of Labour Euro-fanatics pressing an uncritical case; so at least one of us needs to speak to the hundreds of thousands of Labour voters who are (correctly) sceptical of the EU.[18]

Trickett didn't campaign for Leave, and insists he voted Remain. Milne's explanation for changing the letter seems credible, but on balance, the evidence thus far does suggest that Corbyn was leading a campaign he didn't much care about. He didn't have any skin in the game and he is not the kind of politician who can make himself interested in something that doesn't go to the very core of his own beliefs. And so he became a negative. Indeed, some argue it might even have been better if he had just come clean and campaigned for Leave – or stuck with his initial neutral stance – so that a strong advocate for the EU could have led Labour's campaign.

Often, Alan Johnson or others gave way to Jeremy Corbyn on major interviews that would set the tone for the evening news bulletins. This happened on the last Sunday before the vote. During an interview on the BBC's *Andrew Marr Show*, Jeremy Corbyn took the place of Johnson and said: 'There is no uncontrolled immigration. There is free movement of people across the EU that goes both ways.'[19] He then refused to back his deputy Tom Watson, who had said there needed to be reform of free movement. Once again, it showed disunity even within Labour's Cabinet over the EU, one week before the vote. It suggested that Corbyn was out of touch with voters in northern heartlands who believed there *was* 'uncontrolled immigration'. It prompted Peter Mandelson to warn Stronger In: 'Corbyn and Watson want us to lose this referendum. Everyone needs to wake up.'[20]

But it should be remembered that Labour figures such as Peter Mandelson were desperate for Corbyn to fail. Not to lose the referendum – but to be seen as a failing leader. Is this what was really going on? There is no doubt that many in Labour were looking for an opportunity to oust their leader. So at this stage it is worth exploring some of the key counter-arguments against the theory that Jeremy Corbyn messed up.

Point One: he didn't call the referendum, it wasn't his battle to fight. Let's not outright dismiss this argument. The Conservatives called it and if they wanted to win the referendum, should they have been so reliant on their rivals to get them across the line? Probably not – but it was the role of the Leader of the Opposition to give a clear direction to Labour supporters about where the party stood.

Here, Jeremy Corbyn scored a fail. Three weeks before the vote, a memo leaked to *The Guardian* showed analysis of focus groups which found that around 50 per cent of Labour voters were 'uniformly uncertain' about whether the party was for or against staying in the EU. A closer look at the figures published in Craig Oliver's book *Unleashing Demons*: 'Only 47% of voters believe that Labour party politicians are "mostly in favour" of Remain. Only 11% of voters say they have noticed Jeremy Corbyn making a "persuasive argument" about the referendum over the past week.' Asked whether they thought Corbyn supported the EU, the majority said either that they didn't know or that 'his heart isn't in it.'[21]

Point Two: nearly two thirds of Labour voters backed Remain in the eventual ballot. Some argue that is a good achievement and therefore Corbyn's 'remain and reform' message was effective. But could Labour have done better and, like the Lib Dems and the Greens, got nearer 70–75 per cent? Internal polling seen by Stronger In two weeks before the vote suggested that during the campaign period, Labour supporters slipped from being 70 per cent Remain to 60 per cent Remain, and that was enough to shift the overall result from Remain to Leave.

According to Lord Ashcroft's post-referendum polls, 63 per cent of people who backed Labour in the 2015 general election voted Remain – whereas only 42 per cent of Tory voters did the same.[22] Based on this, you could argue that the Conservative leader had much less influence over the people who voted for him than Jeremy Corbyn did over the people who voted for Ed Miliband. But then, the Conservatives started out more divided on the issue – evidenced by the number of Tory MPs and Cabinet ministers who campaigned for Leave.

But the Ashcroft poll doesn't necessarily give the full picture. Look at the areas where the big shock results came back – Sunderland, Newcastle, Birmingham – all traditionally Labour heartlands. Many of these areas had lost votes to UKIP in 2015 and Labour wasn't winning them back. What's more, many Labour MPs in these areas admit it was people from their stronghold districts within the constituencies who were putting their X in the Leave box, more than local supporters of other parties. Leave campaigner John Mann MP for Bassetlaw said:

> The 2 million people who live closest to where we are now [Worksop], it was 70 per cent to leave, and I know because we've sampled the ballot boxes to see what the approximate results are by area. The Tory areas here were the most pro-EU and in the Labour areas some of the Labour wards were 90 per cent plus to leave, and they didn't see it coming. That's a big problem for the Labour Party.

There is a related factor here that pro-EU MPs don't like to talk about. Just ahead of the referendum, 5 May 2016 saw the local elections, and on the doorstep canvassing many had noted hostility to Labour's pro-EU stance. So when the Labour In campaign wanted to trigger its EU ground war, a number of MPs were reluctant to be seen promoting the cause – especially those in the north of England and in Wales. Look back at the Stronger In data on Labour: it wasn't just that people didn't know where the leader stood – they didn't know where the party stood.

Some MPs saw events in Scotland as a lesson learned. Labour had been decimated by the SNP in the general election and many believed reputations had been tarnished during the 2014 Scottish referendum, when Labour MPs had campaigned alongside Conservatives. They had heard the chants of 'Tartan Tory!' and watched their leader Ed Miliband running the gauntlet past angry Nationalists to make a speech in Edinburgh. The lesson, according to one back-bench Labour MP: 'Don't share a platform with the Tories, because they will toxify you.' Some MPs privately admitted it could be damaging to be seen actively campaigning to remain in the EU. Another says: 'People are so Eurosceptic in my area I don't door-knock because I don't want to remind them of the date to go out and vote.'

Alan Johnson says: 'In Wales … there was a real antipathy to do anything about Europe because they said, "UKIP are our biggest opponents. It will be a gift to them if we make Europe an issue." To which we were saying, "Europe is bound to be an issue."'

Let's look at Wales. Here, 52.5 per cent voted to leave, but even more strongly in Labour areas. Merthyr Tydfil was 56 per cent, Neath Port Talbot was 57 per cent, Torfaen 60 per cent, and Bridgend, the seat of the Labour leader on the Welsh Assembly, Carwyn Jones, 55 per cent.[23] These are all areas where Labour got around 50 per cent of the vote in the general election and where two decades ago the party was getting nearer 70–80 per cent.

On 5 May 2016, the former Conservative MP Neil Hamilton won a seat on the Welsh assembly for UKIP, as did six other UKIP candidates. According to Hamilton, the Labour Party in Wales had 'completely lost touch with its traditional voting base – the white working class'.

For UKIP, the key issue in Wales was immigration. The Oxford University Migration Observatory conducted a 2011 census for Wales comparing data to 2001. It found an 82 per cent increase in the non-UK-born population over those ten years. Note that, even after this, only 5.5 per cent of the total population was born outside of Wales. The most numerous group were from Poland, accounting for 18,023 residents, the majority of them men aged between twenty and thirty-nine, many attracted to factory jobs in the country – so, working-age, working-class men.[24]

Hamilton describes a 'ripple effect'. A fear of what people read in the papers about annual net migration to the UK. Often described as 'a population the size of Cardiff every year', or in nine years, 'a population the size of Wales'.

'People knew this was going to continue unless we can restore control,' says Hamilton.

It's not just actual immigration but the fear of future immigration and what it is going to do to communities, and particularly in low-wage areas, and this is the key to it really. If you look at where the biggest Brexit votes occurred, they tended to be in areas where wages were rather low and places left behind by the twenty-first century and feel a sense of hopelessness and helplessness where they're not represented by the political class.

But weren't these the same people who had backed Jeremy Corbyn to become leader of the Labour Party: The left-behind, disaffected with the political class? Why was Corbyn not their champion, rather than a C-list celebrity and disgraced former Conservative MP? Put this to Neil Hamilton and he will tell you, firstly, that his name has been cleared over the 1980s cash-for-questions scandal; secondly, that a bit of celebrity recognition helps break the ice with voters; and, thirdly, that 'People from the Labour Party were giving them an unpalatable message. I was telling them what they wanted to hear. That's the difference. This is a case of the people leading the politicians rather than the other way round.'

The threatened closure of Tata Steel was another issue that UKIP highlighted as a demonstration of what happens when you give away control – in this case, the levers of economic control. Forty thousand jobs, many of them in Wales, were put at risk in March 2016 when Tata announced it was pulling out of the UK.

While Remainers, and also Tata Steel management, argued that EU membership would help protect jobs at Tata because the EU was by far the largest export market for UK steel, UKIP countered that Britain needed the power to unilaterally take anti-dumping action against cheap Chinese steel imports that were way below the cost of production in the UK. Facing the same problem, the United States had slapped a 522 per cent duty on certain kinds of Chinese steel, whereas the maximum the EU was prepared to impose was 25 per cent. The fact that the UK had wanted the tariffs lower to help the UK car industry, amongst others, was played down.

Furthermore UKIP was also saying that if we left the EU we could have tariff-free trade with countries like China. These inconsistences in their argument didn't matter. It goes back to what Alan Johnson said: Labour politicians in Wales were nervous about taking on UKIP, so a lot of their claims went relatively unchallenged. And Corbyn, as a leader who was ideologically isolated from most of his MPs, had neither the political fortitude nor the inclination to rally his team and take the fight head on in Wales or indeed in central and northern England.

In cities like Birmingham and Bradford, where there was a large Labour-voting Asian population, Euroscepticism was ingrained for a number of other reasons. These were communities descended from immigrants who came to the UK from Commonwealth Asian countries such as India, Pakistan, Bangladesh and Caribbean countries including Jamaica or Barbados. Many of these nations had provided soldiers from what was then the British Empire to fight in the Second World War. More than 87,000 Indians, including from modern-day Pakistan, Nepal and Bangladesh, gave their lives. But as the Home Office tried to reduce net migration figures by clamping down on non-EU migration from countries such as India and Pakistan, so British nationals in places like Birmingham saw the free movement rules within the EU unfairly disadvantaging their families abroad.

Birmingham Perry Barr MP Khalid Mahmood said:

> We can have a far stronger trading relationship, with our Commonwealth history, with people who actually want to work with us if we are outside the EU. Outside the EU we can get people in from the Commonwealth countries based on the contributions they can make, such as the qualifications they have and what they can do, without having the people coming in from Eastern Europe who are undercutting our workers and increasing our benefits bill because of the benefits they are entitled to.[25]

This was a compelling argument in Mahmood's constituency. What's more, a number of British Asians ran small businesses that felt hindered by EU regulations. Birmingham's metal industry was subject to a number of directives over the use of chemicals and by-products that had become increasingly stringent about environmental protection and health and safety. Mahmood himself came from this background: 'I am an engineer by profession and engineering has been decimated by European legislation, particularly in metal finishing industries, where European regulation has clamped down so much,' he said.

Despite all the polls suggesting a third of the population were undecided for much of the referendum campaign, there was a sense amongst many in the Labour Party that people had made up their minds long ago. John Mann, one of the few Labour MPs who campaigned to leave the UK, says there was virtually no traditional campaigning from either side in the north of England.

> What happened round here, people made their own decisions in workplaces, in families, in clubs, a long time in advance of the vote, a long time in advance, and they weren't swayed by any of the arguments. It wasn't Boris Johnson, it wasn't Farage, it wasn't me who affected people's votes. It was their conclusion and they made a decision that they thought was right from their own life experience and they voted in communities and families and workplaces very similarly.

In the Worksop Miners' Welfare Social Club, where co-author Jason spoke to John Mann, around 300 people were playing bingo, pretty much all of them Labour supporters. In a straw poll of the room, Jason found that about 90 per cent had voted Out. 'We're only an island,' said one player, 'and if you can't control how many are coming, how can you cater for them?'

The room was full of working-class patriotism, which many felt Jeremy Corbyn lacked. In general, they disagreed with him on two things: his stance on defence – anti-Trident and anti-NATO, which they considered 'weak' – and the fact that he appeared to have no ambition to cut immigration.

This, according to John Mann, was the fatal flaw in Corbyn's argument. Labour voters wanted some form of acknowledgement that immigration had affected their lives. Migrants had helped create a more flexible marketplace and given companies such as Mike Ashley's Sports Direct greater power over the native workforce. According to John Mann, the government was 'using the health service and tax credits and schools' to help attract immigrants. 'That is the British state subsidising Mike Ashley's employment, and that's a big cost and the fault lies with two people: they're not the Poles who come, the fault lies with Ashley for doing it in that way [and] the fault lies with Parliament for allowing that to happen.'

Mann added:

> What people say to me is, 'John, I've got lovely Polish neighbours, they're far better than the people who lived next door before. I like them, they're good people. I like their children. But it's my job.' That's how it's said to me, and I fully understand what people mean and if you go into more detail, actually often what

they really mean is 'It's my son, my grandson, my daughter, my granddaughter's job, their pay, their prospects, that's what really frightens me. When's it all going to end?' So when they say 'How many more?', this isn't some xenophobia. This is about their family's possibilities, prospects, working, standards of living, ability to buy a car, a house, raise a family in the immediate future. It's about the real world. These are real fears.

Perhaps, then, Agent Corbyn wasn't entirely to blame for Labour's woes – perhaps many voters had made up their minds long ago. As we will explain in Reason 18, research by Vote Leave found Labour voters' views on immigration to be 'indistinguishable' from people who voted for UKIP. The majority of MPs may have been pro-Remain, but many were equally lacking in commitment when it came to campaigning, because they were conscious of their voters' fears, as identified by John Mann.

However, if Corbyn truly wanted to stay in the EU, he needed to try to answer those fears. He needed a strategy to address them. He needed to be talking every day of the campaign about the flipside: the economic dangers that could hit working-class families. He might even have convinced voters that leaving the EU did not mean that £350 million a week would be earmarked for the NHS – which many people in the bingo hall in Worksop believed. He was the one man in politics who was in a sense outside of the political class – without being Nigel Farage. As the 2017 general election campaign showed, he actually had enormous power at his fingertips, but he chose not to use it. The main problem was that even if you followed his socialist 'remain and reform' solution, it wasn't on the ballot paper. These were not the reforms Cameron had negotiated.

In the Remain camp's fantasy world, they would have had a centrist, progressive, passionate Labour leader who was genuinely in favour of the European Union; a David Miliband, an Yvette Cooper or even an Ed Miliband. There would be no negative focus on transatlantic trade deals and the need to reform – Labour voters would have been warned about jobs dependent on the EU, rising prices and what could happen to the value of the pound in their pocket. Yes, you could argue that the broader Remain campaign did warn voters about these things, and the warnings were dismissed as scaremongering, but it may have been seen differently coming from a left-wing Labour leader rather than a former Bullingdon boy.

'Instead, what you got was a reluctant half-arsed effort,' says James McGrory, 'and voters aren't idiots. It came across. It came across that Jeremy Corbyn wasn't that bothered.'

Angela Eagle, who, after the Brexit vote, was first to challenge Jeremy Corbyn for the leadership, says he failed in his duty as leader.

> I think we had a duty to try and maximise the number of Labour voters who would vote to stay in because the effects of coming out actually do hit far more Labour areas in a far harder way. Now, Jeremy, in what was a black-or-white, 'Are you in or out?' question in a referendum, was so ambiguous about it that it gave a lot of people who were worried in Labour heartlands about immigration and other issues permission to vote Leave – and I think that did make a difference.

Post-Brexit, Welsh MP Owen Smith became the eventual challenger for the leadership after 172 MPs voted no confidence in Jeremy Corbyn. In one debate, he accused Corbyn of voting to leave. Corbyn vigorously denied it. But after beating Smith in September 2016 with an even larger mandate from the membership, Corbyn suggested that Brexit was an opportunity to ditch certain aspects of the single market, and he rejected his rival's idea that the final Brexit negotiations should be put to a second referendum. Later, having been re-elected as leader, he called a three-line whip to ensure his party backed the government's triggering of Article 50.

It seems safe to conclude that Jeremy Corbyn wasn't a passionate defender of the EU. In fact, we are still left wondering whether, on balance, he was Remain or Leave – and exactly how much he really cared.

A few weeks after the Brexit vote, Jeremy Corbyn boarded a train to Brussels en route to a meeting with other European socialist leaders, unaware that in the seat behind him were some journalists. This is the dream scenario for any reporter en route to a story – one of the subjects of the story sitting within earshot. You are expecting now to hear about the scoop that they got: a snippet of unguarded conversation about the EU between the Labour leader and his advisors. Perhaps hear a clue as to what the Labour leader really thought about the biggest question facing the UK as he prepared to discuss it with his European counterparts. Unfortunately for the journalists, their delight soon turned to frustration and then boredom. The Labour leader's conversation, which could be heard with absolute clarity, was simply idle chitchat, mostly about making jam.

MAD MEN

Douglas Carswell, the Conservative MP who defected to UKIP, was in Portcullis House when a co-author of this book asked him who he thought mattered most in the referendum campaign. Was it Nigel Farage, Boris Johnson or Michael Gove? He stood, as he always does, like an RAF pilot who's lost his Spitfire, his aristocratic chin jutting on a rakish angle and said: 'What you need to understand is that only three people matter. They are Daniel Hannan, Dominic Cummings and Matthew Elliott. If any of them had got run over by a bus, we would still be in the EU.'

Brexit is universally acknowledged as a rebellion against the ruling elite, and it is ironic that so many people in Westminster are obsessed with attributing this uprising to the actions of a few individuals who lived within the bubble. Nonetheless, these three people Carswell refers to, and others, were the message makers. They built the Leave campaign from scratch in minimal time but on a wealth of knowledge built up over years. That knowledge and experience turned into sound bites and slogans which dominated the campaign. In more ways than one, they were the 'Mad Men' of Brexit; the strategy and marketing gurus – and they warrant some analysis.

There were Mad Men on both sides, of course, – but the Leave camp's were more radical, meaner and hungrier, and they'd studied their subject for longer. There were different factions of Mad Men within the Leave ranks, and they pushed each other on in the maddest of fashions. Yes, the Leave camp was madder, but that was the secret to its success.

In the early years of David Cameron's coalition government, the Mad Men were scattered. Of the three mentioned by Carswell, Dan Hannan was an MEP, Dominic Cummings was working for Michael Gove at the Department for Education, and Matthew Elliott was chief executive of the pressure group the

Taxpayers' Alliance. Their coming together formed the nucleus of a team that would persuade the country that it was OK to tick the box marked Leave.

Matthew Elliott was interviewed for this book in the remnants of Vote Leave's headquarters, several months after the campaign was over. Situated in a tall block on the southern bank of the Thames with space for about forty desks, the vista from the ceiling-to-floor windows takes in the Palace of Westminster, meaning they always had their enemy in their sights. Vote Leave placards were still propped up against the walls of what was otherwise just an empty shell of an open-plan office, with one fishbowl office where Elliott and Cummings honed their strategy and orchestrated the movements of Boris Johnson, Michael Gove and Gisela Stuart.

As he sat at the last remaining desk in what were once buzzing headquarters, Elliott recalled some research he had been doing long before the referendum, in 2012, for a speech he was due to give. He had come across a cartoon that had been published on 24 March 1975 in the *Evening Standard*. It depicted the No campaign against EU membership from that time. People were on a march and at the front, Enoch Powell, Tony Benn and Michael Foot were under a banner reading 'Get Britain Out', while in the crowd of people there were placards saying National Front, Communist Party, Scottish Nationalists, Trotskyists, Anarchists, IRA, Orange Order. The tagline underneath was 'Join the Professionals'.[1] Although it was published before the referendum, it is one of the best illustrations of why the 1975 campaign lost.

Elliott saw the obvious message: 'It was basically saying … they were a rag-tag bunch of people, dominated by extremists.' He knew that if a referendum was coming, the Out campaign would need mainstream players on board. For that, it needed an organisation that could cater for them. In his view, the worst-case scenario would be a UKIP-led purple revolution.

Now why, in 2012, before the 2016 referendum had even been called, was Elliott studying a cartoon from 1975? It's because he was an EU obsessive, and the fact that he and others had a passion for this issue would give them an advantage over their eventual opponents – many of whom were hired to defend the UK's place in the EU less than eighteen months ahead of the vote. Anti-EU strategists were one step ahead simply because they had been thinking about it for longer.

A master lobbyist, Elliott had studied at the London School of Economics and worked for Tory MEP Timothy Kirkhope. That is where he first met Dan

Hannan, who became a close friend. 'He is one of very few people who attended both my weddings,' says Elliott. In his mid-twenties, Elliott had set up the Taxpayers' Alliance, a low-tax pressure group. Later, in 2009, he founded Big Brother Watch, which campaigned against a surveillance state. Then, in 2011, he got involved in the first UK-wide referendum since 1975. The subject was whether Britain should change its electoral system.

No one realised it at the time, but this experience would become a highly significant factor in the EU referendum five years later. Elliott decided to run the campaign to keep the current voting system, in what would become a test run for ideas he would later use in the EU campaign. It brought together strategists, politicians and donors who, a few years later, would form the backbone of Vote Leave. Stephen Parkinson was one such strategist, who five years later left the Home Office to join the Out campaign, running the ground war. Elliott also campaigned alongside Labour MP Gisela Stuart and Lord David Owen for the first time; from different political spheres, they would become invaluable partners in his Out movement.

The question put to the British public in 2011 was whether they wanted to change from the first past the post electoral system, to what is called Alternative Vote (AV). Under AV, voters list their candidates in preference – if the first-choice candidate doesn't get 50 per cent of the votes in round one, then second preferences are taken into account. This means that voters can use their first-preference vote for whomever they wish, knowing that if the candidate (however small their party) is eliminated then their second-preference vote will count and so on. After each round, the candidate with the lowest number of votes is eliminated and those who voted for them have their next available preferences redistributed. The Conservatives opposed it. Labour was split. But it was popular with smaller parties and its biggest advocates were the Liberal Democrats. At the beginning of the campaign, two thirds of voters favoured the new system, but in the end they voted against it.

The NOtoAV campaign didn't bother to focus much on the democratic advantages or disadvantages of the two systems. Instead, Matthew Elliott commissioned a series of controversial posters that aggressively focused on cost. The figure they came up with for the cost of changing Britain's voting system was £250 million: a combination of holding the referendum, which was money already being spent so could never be recouped, and the cost of changing the way ballot papers were counted. The figure was nonsense. Next, they took the nonsense figure and applied it to random but important things the money could otherwise be spent on. A picture of a solider: 'He needs bulletproof vests NOT an alternative voting system.' A newborn baby in an incubator: 'She needs a new cardiac facility NOT an alternative voting system.' Another poster pictured a doctor and the £250 million figure. A caption said: 'Instead our money could provide 2,503 doctors.'

You know where this is going, don't you? The message was clear. At a time of austerity, £250 million could be better spent on things like the NHS rather than on a new electoral system. Political commentators described the posters as crass and infantile. The *New Statesman* said the campaign was 'beyond parody'. Steven Baxter concluded: 'If this is the quality of campaigning we're going to have in the coming days and weeks, it's no wonder that the issue could fail to grasp the public imagination.'[2]

But the NOtoAV campaign was on to something. The polls started to change and on 5 May 2011, nearly 70 per cent of the electorate voted No to AV. Matthew Elliott had discovered a compelling message formula. Find a big figure – it doesn't have to be true – and look for emotive areas where the money could be better spent. Elliott says: 'That proved that you could concentrate an issue on cost and also the potency of health care. The most controversial poster was the baby in the incubator. It was proof of concept. That was the germ of the idea for the referendum bus.'

During the referendum, Vote Leave would claim that £350 million a week sent to the EU could be better spent on the NHS. It was the most controversial claim of the referendum, roundly debunked as a gross figure for Britain's EU contribution which did not account for money that came back in a rebate (£100 million a week) plus roughly another £100 million a week that was spent by the EU in the UK. So the figure should more accurately have been £150 million. Sir Andrew Dilnot, chair of the UK Statistics Authority, wrote to Vote Leave, saying the £350 million figure 'appears to be a gross figure which does not take into account the rebate or other flows from the EU to the UK public sector (or flows to non-public sector bodies)'. He added: 'Without further explanation I consider these statements to be potentially misleading and it is disappointing that this figure has been used without such explanation.'[3]

All the same, '£350 million a week' was probably one of the most effective and important slogans of the 2016 referendum campaign. While Elliott says he would 'defend the figure to my dying day' and makes equivalence to the fact that people talk about gross salaries rather than net salaries, he also knew well that it was at the very least mischievous to suggest that all this money would reach the health service, when a big chunk of it never left the UK, and large swathes of it were already spent elsewhere in Britain – used to support the UK's farming industry for example. Furthermore, nobody making the claim was in a position to promise any such thing.

What Elliott also noticed during his AV campaign in 2011 was that the other side couldn't decide whether to keep quiet about his figure, implicitly accepting it, or to attack it and thereby draw attention to it. Even when Nick Clegg accused them of 'lies, misinformation and deceit',[4] it was still somehow drummed into people's minds that AV was going to be a very expensive system. The same thing would happen during the EU referendum campaign with the £350 million. So the AV victory gave Elliott the confidence in his formula, even when it came under attack – sometimes from his own side.

A year after the AV vote came George Osborne's so-called Omnishambles Budget of 2012. The Chancellor was forced to retract planned taxes on pasties due to public outcry that workers might pay an extra 50p for a hot meal. 'Let Them Eat Cold Pasty' decried the *Sun* newspaper,[5] while George Osborne's face was photoshopped onto the body of Marie Antoinette. David Cameron's political strategist Steve Hilton suggested Downing Street bring someone in to help the PM smooth relationships with the public and business. Elliott, a friend of Hilton's, had good contacts from his role running the Taxpayers' Alliance, and he clearly understood public attitudes towards tax. He had also proved himself an effective campaign operator during the AV referendum, but that was also a problem. During AV, his team had made personal attacks against Nick Clegg. The Lib Dem leader was of course the Deputy Prime Minister of the coalition. 'Clegg won't wear it,' Elliott was told in a phone call. His cheerleader Hilton went off to become a scholar at Stanford University in California. So in 2012 Elliott was left considering his options.

Also considering his options was Dan Hannan, whom we have met in both Reason 7 and Reason 8. By 2012, the Conservative MEP had been a Eurosceptic for twenty years. Aged nineteen, he had despaired at the Maastricht Treaty and decided that recovering self-government was 'the most important issue in politics'. At the time, he was at Oxford University, where he set up the Oxford Campaign for an Independent Britain with two other students. One of them was Mark Reckless, the Conservative MP who would later become a member of Room R (see Reason 11), before dramatically defecting to UKIP. Hannan was never tempted to become a member of the UK's Parliament; a journalist first, then speechwriter for Michael Howard, he decided he was best placed to achieve his goal inside the European Parliament. He was elected in 1999 and waited coiled in anticipation for the revolution. It didn't come as quickly as he'd hoped. His blood got pumping over Blair's promise to hold a referendum on the euro – but it didn't happen. For a decade, opportunities came and went. Hannan became increasingly frustrated that while Euroscepticism was bubbling under the surface in British politics, it wasn't breaking through. 'We were winning the battle of ideas; but we were losing the battle of implementation ... I sometimes felt, like Tolkien's Galadriel, that I was fighting the long defeat.'[6] He was doing it with great eloquence. Hannan's harmonious voice and perfect diction, best suited for Shakespearean soliloquies, was put to use in the European Parliament. When Gordon Brown visited the chamber in 2009, Hannan's attack on him as a 'devalued Prime Minister of a devalued government' became a YouTube sensation.[7]

However, his hopes of a breakthrough continued to be dashed. The Lisbon Treaty came and went without a referendum. 'Had I known it would take so long, I probably would have done something else in those fifteen years,' he says. When, in 2009, David Cameron welched on his cast-iron guarantee for a referendum on Lisbon, it was the last straw. Even if a Conservative Prime Minister gained power in 2010, there would be no challenge to Europe. Hannan decided to resign from his front-bench position in the European Parliament in protest at his leader's U-turn. What happened next has been referred to in Reason 8, but it is worth recalling it in Dan Hannan's own words. He called Cameron's office and spoke to an aide.

> I wanted him to understand that he had just lost his last opportunity to hold a referendum on something other than membership of the EU. After such a climb-down, I told him nothing less than an In/Out poll would do and I thought it only polite to let him know that I intended now to campaign full time to get such a poll. The aide chuckled indulgently and said, 'Well, good luck with that.'[8]

So it was that, three years after Hannan's resignation call and just a few months after Matthew Elliott failed to get a job in Downing Street, the two men sat together in a garden in Norfolk. The pair had been invited on a weekend away at the country home of Rodney Leach and Jessica Douglas-Home. Leach had set up Business for Sterling in 1998 to campaign against the euro. He'd become a Eurosceptic after his wife persuaded him to read the Maastricht Treaty.[9] He would remain a committed opponent of European integration until his death just before the referendum in 2016. That weekend, he'd also invited Max Pearson, director of Open Europe, as well as Andrea Leadsom MP, who would eventually make her mark for the Leave campaign in the television debates. She also ran for leader of the Conservatives in the wake of Brexit, making it to the final ballot before stepping down to make way for Theresa May.

But the most significant conversation of the weekend was that between Hannan and Elliott. 'Over lunch, Dan and I talked about what my next big thing would be,' says Elliott, 'and it seemed obvious from that conversation it had to be something to do with the EU.' By the summer of 2012, Hannan could sense that the mirage he'd been chasing for twenty years was once again forming before his eyes, but this time it looked real. Having spotted the looming oasis, he'd looked around and realised that no one else in the long caravan of Eurosceptics appeared to be acting on it.

Who was considering the campaign that would be required when the referendum came? What was the point of pushing for a referendum only to lose it? Hannan, like Elliott, dreaded the idea of Nigel Farage becoming the face of the Leave campaign. Their fears were not just based on the 1970s cartoon. They were backed up by polling which found that while the UKIP leader was magnetic to his core voters, he was a turn-off to those wavering on the issue of whether the UK should be in or out of the EU. (As we found in Reason 10, those closest to Farage deny this.) Hannan wanted to create a Conservative-led strategy, and who better to do this than his good friend and the man who'd successfully run the NOtoAV campaign?

Hannan had a reputation for 'radicalising' people against the EU. As we have seen in Reason 7, Leave campaigner Theresa Villiers admits he did it to her. As the MEP continued his conversation with Elliott after lunch in the garden, he could sense him coming round: 'I could see he was thinking not as a strategist, but as a patriot ... Matthew was looking at the offer not as an opportunity, but as a duty,' says Hannan. Certainly, both men recognised that any Leave campaign was expected to be unsuccessful, and most likely against the government, and therefore anyone running it could risk damaging their reputation. They would also be up against the rest of the political establishment, most multinational corporations and nearly every foreign leader. But while Elliott admits he was driven in part by a sense of patriotism, he also accepts that Hannan radicalised him too:

> I was always more of a renegotiate man. But he is a very clear thinker and he's also very appealing to people who are more liberally minded. He doesn't put it across like a knuckle-dragging populist, 'kick out the migrants' approach of Euroscepticism that you get from UKIP. He puts it across as an internationalist, forward-looking, free trading approach to the world.
>
> He was basically convincing me that we needed to get going on this. The next big campaign was going to be the EU. An organisation needed to be set up that was battle ready, ready for the referendum, having the right foundation, the right backers having the right tone, coming up with the right intellectual arguments to be ready for that referendum when it happened.

Elliott agreed to take it on. In the spring of 2013, he set up Business for Britain (BfB), with William Norton (who'd worked on NOtoAV) and Eurosceptic financier Daniel Hodson. It operated out of the same address as Elliott's Taxpayers' Alliance. Launched with a double-page spread in *City AM*, its purpose was to attract Eurosceptic business leaders, to get funding for the cause and to find advocates who would give any Leave campaign credibility in the argument over the economy that surely lay ahead. Five hundred business leaders signed up in a matter of weeks and by the eve of the CBI's annual conference in the autumn of that year they had 1,000 signatories for another advert, this time in the *Telegraph*.

Elliott was bolstering his weakest flank. He knew the Remain camp would major on the economy. But, at this stage, his message was not 'Leave the EU', it was 'Change or Go'. To all appearances it was supportive of Cameron's approach in the Bloomberg speech, that the EU needed radical reform. Indeed, a headline in the *Sun* newspaper read: 'PM's EU bid Gets Business Backing'. In that way, it could attract those who wanted to reform the EU, as well as those ready to get out. Elliott says: 'Did most of them want to leave? No. Neither did I – had the PM come back with a decent deal, I would have been fine staying in the EU as well.' But Elliott had high demands of what Cameron should achieve in the negotiations and BfB was in some ways based on an assumption that he wasn't going to meet them. It was all about amassing people into the departure lounge – before directing them to the gate. It would soon become Vote Leave.

Elliott's BfB was inspired by the similarly named campaign group Business for Sterling (BfS), which he believed was the most effective anti-euro lobby against Tony Blair's potential plans to join the single currency, at a time when the Conservatives under William Hague had been weak. Just as Elliott liked the BfS model, he also wanted to tap into their experience, their contacts and their analysis on the EU. The BfS campaign director between 1999 and 2002 was a man named Dominic Cummings.

When it comes to Mad Men, Cummings fits the bill. 'Intelligent and divisive', says his Wikipedia page.[10] David Cameron once described him as a 'career psychopath'.[11] Like Don Draper of the eponymous TV series about 1950s advertising gurus, Cummings spent months refusing to sign a contract for Vote Leave, even after he had been appointed campaign director. His former colleagues use a mix of descriptions: 'mad but very bad', says one, who goes on to suggest Cummings is prone to 'ferocious temper tantrums, and looks like he's been sleeping in a hedge'.[12] But while Cummings put the backs up many a politician, he would generally inspire fierce loyalty from his staff – and this, as we shall see, would save his skin when there was an attempt by MPs to oust him from his job during the EU campaign.

He was born in Durham and his father was a project manager for the construction of oil rigs and other large structures. He describes his father as 'a classic example' of someone left frustrated by the way the EU was sold to the public in 1975. Cummings says:

He was then in his early thirties, and basically believed that this was all about trade, but he became increasingly irritated. This whole set of people of that age thought the EU was based on trade and in fact many were small-business people and they didn't see any free trade benefits; instead, they saw a whole bunch of stupid regulations about what size containers to sell things in – and that's not what they'd been told [in 1975].

Cummings stayed out of politics while studying at Exeter College, Oxford, where in 1994 he took a First in Ancient and Modern History. Then, after a period in Russia, he joined Business for Sterling in 1998. He had no real background in party politics and rapidly lost respect for politicians. Asked for this book what he'd learned from Business for Sterling, he said his main lesson 'was that 99 per cent of MPs are dreadful characters and if you want anything professionally organised you've got to exclude them, which causes a lot of trouble'.

He went on: 'You're faced with a very hard choice. You either give them the platform they want, in which case you will have a fucked organisation, or you exclude them and try and butter them up in various ways.' He believes the selection processes and the incentive structures within parties mean that the wrong kind of people are attracted to becoming MPs, who 'to a large extent are not particularly bright, are egomaniacs and they want to be on TV'.

He also found over his years as part of the Eurosceptic movement that the EU issue attracted 'a particularly unbalanced set of people'. He said:

> The Eurosceptic world is a very old world populated by very odd people. Generally, not always but generally, the longer they have been involved in it, the higher the probability that they will be odd.
>
> There's a sort of self-perpetuating cycle – the kind of people who are likely to take opinions against a long-running establishment tend to be quite contrary characters. By definition, it is quite hard to coordinate their actions, and the cumulative effect psychologically of being called 'nutters' and excluded from things means they become more eccentric over time – that's my experience.

This is the man who would become campaign director for Vote Leave – and you see perhaps why at times the appointment was problematic. But you also see that Cummings approached the campaign through the same lens as Elliott and Hannan: he believed that a mainstream movement needed to be created to counter-balance old-school, eccentric Euroscepticism.

Having done a great deal of market research while running Business for Sterling, in 2004 Cummings had tried to set up an organisation called New Frontier that attempted to 'figure out the whole roadmap for getting out of the EU'. He found he couldn't persuade people to get involved and 'in classic Eurosceptic fashion, we all fell out'.

One thing that his group did do in 2014 was get involved in a referendum campaign in the north-east against John Prescott's plans to create a regional assembly. Like Elliott during the AV referendum, Cummings learned some vital lessons and built up invaluable contacts. He admits it was 'a kind of training exercise' to learn how the referendum process worked, what happened with broadcasters and how the Electoral Commission operated. His campaign depicted the assembly as an expensive talking shop without any real powers. In Cummings's view, it was 'a whole new bullshit level of things that will make things worse rather than better'. His campaign won with 78 per cent of the vote, beating an establishment campaign that had a larger budget and more resources. It was the first time that he sensed the growing void between the northern heartlands and Westminster. He says: 'We exploited this feeling. "Politicians talk, we pay" was our slogan. SW1 ignored the result. It did not appreciate the scale of this growing force even after the financial crash and expenses scandal.'

After the Conservatives formed their coalition with the Lib Dems in 2010, Cummings became a special advisor to Michael Gove at the Department for Education and the friendship they formed became vital to the Leave campaign. To begin with, the PM's advisor Andy Coulson banished Cummings from government, convinced that he was briefing against them. But after Coulson was forced to resign over his role in phone-hacking during his time as editor of the *News of the World*, Gove brought Cummings back in, and he was seen as the driving force behind the Education Secretary's school reforms. He remained an abrasive character within the department. What's more, when he left in 2014, he sniped from the sidelines at the coalition, claiming that education reforms were being held back by the lack of support and sense of purpose from the Prime Minister. He was also scathing about Cameron's chief of staff Ed Llewellyn, describing him as a 'classic third-rate suck-up-kick-down sycophant presiding over a shambolic court'.[13]

But during this time Cummings never left the EU project completely alone. For example, when examining attitudes to school reforms, he would often throw in a question about the EU to his focus groups. 'I think it was just generally useful because it meant I had a feel for what people are thinking and, most importantly, I discovered the vast majority of people knew nothing more about the EU now than they did fifteen years ago.'

This 'feel for how people were thinking' was what made Cummings invaluable. If you want to understand why he would later survive the MPs' attempted coup to get rid of him, you need only to study a report he was commissioned to produce for Business for Britain in 2014.

For this report, Cummings conducted six focus groups in May 2014 in War-wickshire, Thurrock and Hendon. Arguments about the EU were fresh in the participants' minds because it was carried out just after the EU elections. From these conversations and his own experience of attitudes towards the EU, he made an assessment of what might happen in a referendum and how an Out campaign might best navigate towards its goal. It became an extremely significant docu-ment – a blueprint for how the campaign should be conducted – and we've been given exclusive access to it for this book. Here are the first three conclusions that Cummings makes:

1. For decades, the public largely ignored the often esoteric debates on the EU as they seemed disconnected from everyday concerns about jobs and living stand-ards. I was Campaign Director of the campaign to stop Britain joining the euro 1999–2002 (Business for Sterling / the No campaign) and spent a great deal of time researching public attitudes to the euro. There was concern about immigra-tion but it was rarely linked to the debate on EU membership. Now, the EU is seen as important because immigration is such an important issue and it, plus associated human rights issues (like difficulties deporting Abu Hamza), are in-timately connected to the powers of the EU. Regaining control of immigration and human rights 'so we can have an Australian points system' is the strongest argument for changing our relationship with the EU among crucial parts of the electorate. This is the biggest change in people's attitudes towards the EU between my research 1999–2002 and now. This is very bad for the EU's supporters.

2. Given that immigration will likely continue at a much higher rate than people want and all three parties have to admit that none of it from the EU can be controlled except at the margins, it is reasonable to predict that a) hostility to immigration will continue to grow, b) hostility to the three main parties will continue to grow, and c) hostility to the EU will continue to grow.

3. Cameron and the Conservative Party will have a big problem if they stay in government in 2015. If they do have a renegotiation of some sort but either do not try, or try and fail, to take back control of immigration policy from the EU, and Britain keeps anything like the *status quo*, then these swing voters will regard the renegotiation as a big failure. In these groups, people become more

hostile to the EU if it is suggested that Cameron embarks on getting 'a new deal' then fails to change the *status quo* on immigration. It seems unlikely that any remotely plausible political force could persuade them to be positive about this *status quo* given that the public already rejects the combined view about immigration of the three main parties, the CBI, the unions, and most of those who run large media organisations. It is unlikely that the pro-EU forces could change people's minds about immigration even if they spent tens of millions on brilliant adverts.[14]

So the top three points all focus on immigration. Vote Leave set out to create an alternative message to UKIP, and yet in 2014 they identify Nigel Farage's message as the most persuasive case to leave the EU. As we will see, Vote Leave was later criticised for switching its campaign focus to a 'populist' message on immigration rather than an intellectual one on sovereignty and global outlook. But it's clear that even back in 2014, the soon-to-be director of the campaign had already established migration as the number one issue.

This didn't mean he needed to campaign on it. With UKIP focused on immigration, and images of migrants on the news every night doing the job for them, the strategists decided they didn't need to address the subject at all in the early stages.

If they were going to create a movement that would attract mainstream Tory MPs and Cabinet ministers, they would also have to create a more outward-thinking Eurosceptic message, based around Thatcherite concerns on sovereignty and the ability to trade with the world. If the likes of Boris Johnson and Michael Gove were to join the team, its focus would have to be on reclaiming powers from the EU.

Cummings said:

From that report we decided immigration was such a big deal we don't have to make a big deal of it. That was one of the arguments we had all the way through really from the summer '15 onwards, was me saying to people there's nothing we can do that has remotely the force of what people can see on the TV of these guys getting on their boats and sinking. What we have to do is construct our campaign in a certain way and get across other messages until the final crunch point comes. And really the core of that is money in the NHS.

Cummings noted in his 2014 report that people's second priority was to reduce 'all the silly laws' and 'bring down the UK's contribution to the EU budget'. Collating the comments from focus groups, he says the general argument was that by leaving the EU 'we will save a fortune and we can spend that on the NHS or tax cuts or whatever we want to make Britain stronger'.[15] The slogans were being handed to them on a plate.

Cummings and Elliott therefore had a meeting of minds about the £350 million a week message. Reflecting on their use of it during the campaign, Cummings wrote:

> Pundits and MPs kept saying 'why isn't Leave arguing about the economy and living standards'. They did not realise that for millions of people, £350m/NHS was about the economy and living standards – that's why it was so effective. It was clearly the most effective argument not only with the crucial swing fifth but with almost every demographic. Even with UKIP voters it was level-pegging with immigration. Would we have won without immigration? No. Would we have won without £350m/NHS? All our research and the close result strongly suggests No. Would we have won by spending our time talking about trade and the Single Market? No way.

There is another striking theme developed in this report. It recognises the power of harnessing a general feeling amongst the public that they have lost control over various aspects of their lives. In what is a nineteen-page report, the word 'control' is mentioned thirty-seven times. Amongst the quotes from focus groups, a man in Thurrock says simply: 'We have lost control because of Europe.'[16] The expression 'take back control' is used five times. Another conclusion is as follows:

> There is a general argument that applies to almost any specific area: we will be better off if we take back control because then we can control what happens by voting, but 'now we vote and nothing changes because Europe controls so much'. In a referendum, it would be important for the OUT campaign to avoid taking specific positions on many issues as this would only split the campaign. Instead, the OUT campaign should simply say 'whether you think X or Y about Z, the most important thing is we take back control of Z so that *you* can control what happens by voting people out'.[17]

The Leave campaign would eventually adopt the line 'Vote Leave: Take Back Control' as its central, all-encompassing slogan. Take back control of borders, law-making, millions of pounds a week, whatever it is you feel is out of control. It was included in their name and web URL. It was applied to every aspect of the campaign and repeated endlessly in interviews. Not just tested on focus groups, but derived from them, 'take back control' was a combination of the active and the nostalgic, even more so when set against the alternative call to Remain. The whole word is suggestive of complacency: remain = do nothing.

Gisela Stuart reflects: 'The genius of Dom was that on the one hand you had this… The "take back control" phrase – there was no answer to it. "Oh, you don't want to take back control?"' Cummings takes no credit for this phrase. 'All I did was listen,' he says, but he'd done a lot of listening. The complaints he had heard from the public would soon be coming out of the mouths of his Vote Leave politicians.

The idea of control could be used to counter the perceived benefits of the EU. By leaving the single market and customs union, the UK could control its own trade deals with the rest of the world and not be tied into the whims of twenty-seven other nations. The UK could control its own economy and its own rules and regulations. Of course, the biggest aspect of control, as seen by voters, was border control, and focus groups showed that the public also had a solution.

There was a natural inclination in large sections of the British public to suggest that the answer was to introduce an 'Australian-style points system'. So when, later in the campaign, Vote Leave was to propose a post-EU immigration system, the answer was again given to them by the public. It is not clear how it became so ingrained in UK consciousness that Australia had the holy grail of immigration systems. Certainly, Nigel Farage used the expression often – but it is thought that public approval of this idea predated even UKIP's adoption of the concept. Either way, it would soon be Michael Gove and Boris Johnson extolling the virtues of a system they knew the public already believed was the answer.

The Out strategists also recognised the areas where loss of control could be used against them on economic issues – the fear of jobs lost, prices going up, businesses leaving and living standards slipping. 'They think that we put in more than we get out but we might get clobbered financially if we leave,' notes Cummings. However, as we've established, the 2008 financial crisis and the subsequent euro crisis meant Europe was losing its status as an economic stabiliser and it was no longer viewed as it was in the 1970s, when the European project was seen as a life-support to a failing Britain.

People were also more suspicious of big business. Cummings's report found that distrust of business ran deep; corporate interests were perceived as trumping the nation's interests. The general view was: 'They're off on their yachts thinking about themselves, us mugs on PAYE pay the costs…' The report's author predicted: 'Given the extremely low opinions of the City and bankers, it is far from obvious that having Goldman Sachs on the side of IN is an advantage.'

One of Cummings's final points was this:

> When probed, most of these voters have the attitude: *if leaving the EU would have net zero (or a minor negative) effect, then let's get out now.* This is mainly because the prize of an Australian points system for immigration is so great that they are prepared to roll the dice unless something convinces them of economic meltdown.[18]

From all of this, Elliott, Hannan and Cummings came up with a strategy, which they refined over time. But their most interesting conclusion from the report was that an Out campaign would *not* have to focus its campaign on immigration – at least not in the early stages. It was already a massive factor that 'needs no reinforcement'. Instead, their campaign would need to neutralise the fear of leaving and focus on what could be done with the money saved by leaving, both as a positive message and as an answer to the fear of lost trade. Without financial fears, there was nothing holding the UK back from leaving the EU.

The attempt to defuse the economic argument was made through Matthew Elliott's pressure group Business for Britain. In the run-up to the 2015 general election, BfB published research papers and polls to demonstrate that many in the business community wanted either radical reform or to leave the EU. Its central objective was to demonstrate that the business community was divided on the issue and that while the CBI appeared to support membership, others saw opportunities in leaving. The month after David Cameron won a majority in the election, it produced a 1,000-page paper on what his negotiations should look like and how Britain could thrive outside the EU if he didn't achieve these aims. It was an attempt to raise the bar to unreachable levels.

The report, 'Change or Go',[19] called for the UK to secure a veto for the UK over European laws, win back control of employment rules and protect the City from Eurozone regulations. The UK could 'go back to a purely free-trading rela-tionship with the EU', argued Elliott. In retrospect, he admits this would have been difficult to 'go back' to, because there wasn't a period of time in the UK's relationship with the EU when it did have a purely free trade relationship. As we've seen in previous chapters, efforts to do this had failed since the war. But within Elliott's BfB community, the argument was developing that while the Eurozone needed to integrate further to survive, with greater fiscal transfers and debt sharing, the UK had set its own course by not joining the euro.

Equally, there was a group of countries like Norway, Switzerland and Turkey who had varying forms of trading relationships with the EU. 'Why not just have a trading relationship common to lots of different countries outside the EU which is basically based purely on free trade?' argued Elliott. 'Not being members of the single market, not being under the thumb of the ECJ, not being part of the free movement of people but being open to the free movement of workers, a pre-Maastricht, peripheral relationship.'

Of course, David Cameron was never going to negotiate for this level of detachment from the EU. His aides were at that time drawing up their plans. One of their first ports of call was the City of London. During the summer of 2015, Downing Street held a series of meetings with financial experts and their public affairs teams. In one such meeting was Paul Stephenson, a former special advisor at the Department of Health, who had become spokesman for the Brit-ish Bankers' Association.

When he saw the government plans laid out, his first thought was that there were some good suggestions to protect the banks. But as the No. 10 aide got up to leave, his second thought was: 'This is thin – this isn't what I would define as real reform. It's window dressing – just enough to come back and declare victory.'

Stephenson had been head of research for the Eurosceptic think tank Open Europe, he'd campaigned for a referendum on Lisbon, he'd worked with Dom-inic Cummings on the campaign against the north-east assembly, and a few months after seeing the government's renegotiation plans he joined Vote Leave as director of media. 'I had been involved in the EU debate for the last seven years. It felt like going back and finishing off the job. The referendum was taken away from us, in many ways, by Blair. This felt like coming back to finish the job.'

A few weeks later, at a drinks party at Westminster Abbey, Stephenson's former colleagues mocked his decision:

> That was when they were at their arrogant best. They'd just won an election that no one thought they were going to win. Corbyn looked like he was going to lead the Labour Party. They were joking. They said we're going to do the same campaign as in Scotland and we're going to crush you. So they didn't really take it seriously.

But consider this. While Elliott and Cummings had already formulated Vote Leave's strategy and laid the foundations for their campaign, Stronger In was still in its infancy. In the weeks after the general election, Conservative MP Damian Green, Labour grandee Peter Mandelson and Liberal Democrat former Treasury spokesman Danny Alexander got together with Lord David Sainsbury and put out a job advertisement for a director to lead the Remain campaign. In July 2015, they selected Will Straw, the former Labour candidate for Rossendale and Darwen and son of former Foreign Secretary Jack Straw.

By most accounts, he was a respected manager and an excellent debater, but Will Straw didn't have the experience of his opponents on the issue of the EU. The only campaign he had previously run was his bid to become an MP, which he'd lost to Conservative incumbent Jake Berry. At Stronger In, he would work alongside the Conservative (Lord) Andrew Cooper, the lead pollster for the No campaign in the Scottish referendum, who was widely credited with finding the key messages and groups that needed to be swung to prevent the Scots voting for independence.

Nick Clegg's former campaign strategist Ryan Coetzee also joined the team, along with Lucy Thomas, the campaign director for Business for New Europe, which supported the UK staying in a reformed EU. Greg Nugent, the director of marketing for the London Olympics, came on board to look at branding and marketing. It was an impressive enough line-up – but it lacked the deep-rooted experience on the EU issue that Vote Leave had, and it was coming from behind. Research needed to be done. Messages needed to be developed and tested, and quickly. When, in October 2015, the two campaigns were launched, Will Straw had been preparing for four months; Dominic Cummings had been preparing for seventeen years.

At its launch on 8 October, Vote Leave had 'Take Back Control' as its central theme. Its website was voteleavetakecontrol.org. It announced the backing of more than twenty prominent business people, including Joe Foster, founder of Reebok, Christopher Foyle, chairman of the Foyles bookshops, and John Caudwell, founder of Phones 4u. Things were shaping up into the kind of outfit that Elliott and Cummings hoped could lure major politicians such as Boris Johnson and Michael Gove. Elliott had built up a donor base which included billionaire JCB boss Anthony Bamford, a huge contributor to the Conservatives, former Conservative Party treasurer Michael Spencer, Next boss Simon Wolfson and city financier Peter Cruddas, who would prove the most essential amongst them. Cruddas's donation of £1 million to Vote Leave kept it afloat and he even offered to give more cash if other donors didn't come forward.

Business for Britain had also recruited chairmen for eight of the English regions. In the north-east, they signed up John Elliott, chairman of major employer Ebac, whom Cummings had worked with during the north-east assembly referendum. Paul Stephenson had also embarked on organising regional media launches in places like Newcastle, Leeds and Nottingham. Spokespeople were being trained up across the country to do local radio and TV. Cruddas, the former Tory Party co-treasurer and founder of the online trading company CMC Markets, was one of its three treasurers from across the political spectrum. The others were Stuart Wheeler, the UKIP donor who set up IG Index, and Labour donor John Mills, founder of JML. The quote from John Mills given to the newspapers on the day of the launch was: 'If we vote to leave, then the £350m we send to Brussels every week can be spent on our priorities like the NHS.'[20]

Meanwhile, in limited time Stronger In had created a sophisticated video with an upbeat message about the benefits of the EU, backed by impressive celebrity and business endorsements.[21] Some might argue that the patriotic launch video was the zenith of the campaign, as Stronger In would soon descend into a more negative mood. Indeed, watching it back, these were advocates who should have been used more: Richard Reed, founder of Innocent Drinks; Karren Brady, vice-chairman of West Ham; Carolyn McCall, CEO of EasyJet; Sir Hugh Orde, the former president of the Association of Chief Police Officers; Professor Dame Julia Goodfellow, president of Universities UK; and Virgin's Sir Richard Branson. But amongst the numerous advantages of the EU extolled by those in the film, the campaign group had yet to figure out what would resonate with the public. As we shall see later, they had been rather shocked by their initial research.

Vote Leave, though, had already done the groundwork and developed its brand and in doing so created something potent that offered voters a sense of empowerment. 'It is hard to overstate the relative importance in campaigns of message over resources. Our success is an extreme example, given the huge imbalance in forces on either side,' says Cummings.

There is a tendency in writing history to suggest the losers got everything wrong and the winners had God-like foresight. This is not the case. The Remain camp got a lot of things right and the Leave camp would mess up badly. Indeed, a few months later, Vote Leave nearly imploded as it fought against the biggest Mad Man of all: Arron Banks and his rival No campaign group, Leave.EU.

The Vote Leave board, made up of Eurosceptic MPs and donors, had already started to be concerned when, in November 2015, Elliott and Cummings had sent two students posing as businessmen to the CBI conference to unfurl a banner and disrupt the Prime Minister's speech. At this stage, Robert Oxley had joined the group as head of media, and he tipped off Sky News to keep its camera trained on the audience. But no one outside a small handful of Vote Leave people had been told about the stunt, and of those left in the dark about it, most thought it unprofessional that their campaign had childishly disrupted the PM's speech. Elliott and Cummings seemed to be acting too independently, to the detriment of the campaign. The people who'd been the backbone of the Eurosceptic movement for twenty years, such as Bill Cash, John Redwood and Bernard Jenkin, felt they were being side-lined and in January, just as Cummings was close to lining up Michael Gove to join Vote Leave, those MPs launched a coup to get rid of him.

Depending on who you speak to, this was either because of the erratic and irrational behaviour of Cummings or because of the sheer vanity of the MPs. Cummings says:

> The heart of the problem I had was really about the control of policy, the control of messaging, and credit. People like Bernard Jenkin kept saying to me over and over again, 'Bill Cash has sacrificed many things since the 1980s and it's just not fair if this campaign comes along and a whole bunch of people who have not really been involved in the issue, suddenly they get involved and they get the credit, they are in history books.'

Some of them were completely deranged: Bernard, for example, hated the idea of Boris coming on board and said repeatedly in Vote Leave board meetings, 'Dominic is wrong to be going off on secret meetings to meet Boris Johnson, he will be nothing but a negative to the campaign.' That's the degree of craziness we were having to deal with. I'd say: 'Who should be on? John Redwood, right? So you really think we're going to win this campaign by excluding the most popular politician in Britain, and putting John Redwood on TV more? Sorry, we're going to do things differently.'

But others argued that Cummings was a liability. In November 2015, Richard Murphy, who had been hired to run Vote Leave's ground campaign, had resigned, citing that fact that Cummings seemed uninterested in the ground campaign. Others complained that he was either aggressive or in an ivory tower, isolating everyone but Elliott from the workings of campaign – and this was the guy who wouldn't even sign a contract.

Then, there was the lure of the alternative campaign group. As mentioned in Reason 10, billionaire Arron Banks set up Leave.EU to ensure that Nigel Farage was centre stage during the campaign. In the summer of 2015, Leave.EU (originally called In the Know) had got going very quickly. By the winter, they were all-singing, all-dancing. Plus, with their affiliation to UKIP, they had a campaigning structure in place. What's more, websites were rapidly created and people were signing up. They set up a social media campaign group and used Banks's company to create a call centre. Indeed, had BfB not had its platform in place, it would have been virtually impossible to catch them up.

Banks had originally tried to pull the two campaigns together, but was shunned by Cummings and Elliott, who both wanted to keep Farage at arm's length. Soon, Banks was spreading rumours that Cummings and Elliott were agents for No. 10, their job being to deliberately lose the campaign. This wasn't necessarily malicious, but more a genuinely held view by people in UKIP, who couldn't understand, for example, why Business for Britain persisted with its mantra of 'Change or Go' during the negotiations. If it was linked to Vote Leave, why not just say Leave?

Businessman Richard Tice, who had been involved in the campaign to keep the pound, was also now involved in Leave.EU. Tice had several meetings with Elliott and his recurring question was: 'Why aren't you campaigning for Leave?' Elliott tried to explain his strategy:

We need to take people on that journey where you sign them up for Change or Go, and saying the EU should reform – and when it becomes apparent that the EU isn't going to reform then they think, 'Well, we tried. We were serious about it and now we are going to hand on heart say we are for Leave.'

Elliott remained certain that many of his backers 'were not ready for that jump' – partly because they were loyal to Cameron. He was, at this stage, sticking within the centre of gravity of where he thought his business supporters were. He knew that 95 per cent of them were Conservatives, such as JCB's Anthony Bamford and Next boss Simon Wolfson. Under Cameron, they had just unexpectedly won a majority and were therefore willing to at least give Cameron the benefit of the doubt to bring something home from his negotiations. But in Tice's view, Elliott and, by association, Cummings were both giving Cameron too much of a free ride.

As it happened, Cummings had no particular fondness for the PM. His attitude was 'I'll happily chop David Cameron's head off every day in order to win.' So while he had Banks on one side saying he was a saboteur sent by No. 10, others in the Conservative Party viewed him as too anti-PM. Peter Bone MP, for example, was still clinging to the hope that Cameron might join the Out camp. Bone says, 'When the PM said he might campaign to leave, that led to an argument between myself and Cummings. He said: "I don't want the PM near the campaign." That's when I decided to leave.'

Bone had also point-blank refused to hand out messages about giving £350 million a week to the NHS, which he thought was misleading and suggestive that his party wasn't doing enough for the health service. He and fellow Tory MP Tom Pursglove had campaigned during the general election in their neighbouring Northamptonshire constituencies, and in Pursglove's case overturned an almost 8,000 majority from Labour by focusing on an anti-EU message. The pair decided they knew best what worked with voters and set up a brand-new organisation called Grassroots Out, which also lured prominent Eurosceptic Labour MP Kate Hoey away from Vote Leave. Hoey had close ties with Richard Tice and it wasn't long before Grassroots Out joined forces with Farage and Leave.EU. Suddenly this cross-party group began to look like the more serious team, representative of more parties, and more devoted to leaving the EU. With Vote Leave dragging its heels, it seemed Farage and Banks could win the

Electoral Commission's designation as the official campaign group after all. Vote Leave was falling apart.

As mentioned previously, each side in a referendum campaign has one campaign group that is officially recognised by the Electoral Commission. The process of gaining this status is called 'designation'. It is highly coveted because while other groups can still operate, the lead group is awarded state funding to the tune of £600,000, as well as TV advertising and a leaflet campaign sent to every home in the country. They are also allowed to amass large campaign war chests from donors while other groups are restricted. In addition, the media is likely to go to this group first for comments on stories and hence they set the tone and agenda for the entire campaign. If Farage and Banks had won the designation, the campaign would have been very different.

To begin with, Vote Leave's attitude to Banks was: 'He doesn't really understand politics, he'll fade away.' In some respects, he was useful to those, like Cummings, who wanted to kick-start the operation more quickly than Elliott, and needed a bogeyman to frighten him into action. All sides accept this was one of Banks's achievements.

Over the course of the winter, the Vote Leave camp was highly motivated to get the designation. But they also felt that Leave.EU had changed its tack. In a meeting with Nigel Farage before the general election, Cummings was left with the impression that the UKIP leader didn't want to be the figurehead of the actual referendum race. But in a subsequent get-together late in 2015, Cummings found him in a different frame of mind; now he had Banks behind him, Farage wanted to be the front man.

This put the politicians behind Vote Leave in a difficult position, wondering if they would have to choose between Cummings and Farage. Certain Conservative MPs, like Chris Grayling and Bill Cash and David Davis, began to wonder whether following the maverick spad was really a better option than joining forces with UKIP. A campaign that at least included Farage might give the Out camp a broader appeal. They suggested Cummings consider it, but he told the board, 'If you have one campaign, you are responsible for Farage, Arron Banks and Andy Wigmore and what any of these clowns says or does. That enables the media rightly to portray the official campaign as in the grip of a bunch of loonies with sometimes dreadful opinions.'

It has since been suggested that if a UKIP-heavy Leave.EU-style organisation had looked strongly placed to get the designation then the likes of Boris Johnson would never have joined the campaign. Gisela Stuart says: 'If Arron Banks and UKIP got the designation – people like me and Boris would have gone silent and we would have lost the referendum.'

This actually looks at things the wrong way around: Johnson and Gove coming on board provided a massive boost that helped Vote Leave ensure its designation status. They may have disagreed with his message, his approach to UKIP and his management style, but as Gove's former advisor, Cummings was crucial to bringing the Justice Secretary on board – and, as we shall soon see, the Justice Secretary was the bridge to Boris Johnson. But the man bringing them on board was now close to being booted out of the camp.

On 25 January 2016, members of the board decided he had to go. Cummings was called in to meet Daniel Hodson, the chair of City for Britain, at the Business for Britain offices in Tufton Street. When the Vote Leave director arrived at the meeting, Hodson said, 'I am afraid this meeting is not what you thought it was going be. You are no longer going to be campaign director. You're going to resign and that you can say it is for personal reasons.' They had even thought of his cover story: 'Your wife's been pregnant, you could say there's been some problems with the pregnancy. That would be a perfect explanation to everyone about what's happening.'

A document was produced for Cummings to sign, and outside he could see the shadows of lawyers pacing around. Then, in came other members of the board to show support for the decision, including MP Bernard Jenkin. Cummings told them: 'You guys haven't thought this through,' and suggested they go and check with the other staff while he went to Pret a Manger and read through the document. Jenkin tried to stop Cummings from leaving the room while they did this, but was overruled, which gave Cummings time to tip off the staff. By the time the delegation arrived in Westminster, three quarters of the team were primed to walk out if Cummings was forced to leave. Paul Stephenson, director of media, Victoria Woodcock, director of operations, and Stephen Parkinson, director of the ground campaign, all threatened to resign if Cummings was removed. Suddenly, Vote Leave was faced with losing its media team, the entire research team and the ground team. 'They were told, "You won't have an organisation. You'll just have a smouldering room,"' says Cummings.

Cummings was off the hook. The black sheep from the Department of

Education maintained his job alongside Elliott, the man snubbed for a job at No. 10; Stephenson, who had been 'laughed at' at a drinks party for joining Vote Leave; and Hannan, who had been told 'good luck with that' by a senior Cameron aide: all of them were battle-hardened malcontents, the Mad Men of Brexit. And Cummings knew that if he could survive one or two more weeks then he might have some equally colourful politicians on his team too. He'd been meeting secretly with Michael Gove and Boris Johnson for weeks. Even during the attempted coup he didn't tell the other MPs or donors how close these two big hitters were to joining Vote Leave, in case one of them leaked it, but Cummings knew it was close and much hinged on David Cameron's negotiations.

The Remain camp was also sitting tight and waiting – waiting still for many of its key players to join the team. Many from the Conservatives could not be seconded from the government until Cameron had declared he was campaigning for Leave. So it wouldn't be until after the negotiation settlement in February 2016 that they would have a full complement of staff – four months before the vote. Nor would they know until then exactly what benefits they could promote from whatever EU deal the PM could strike. After that, they would have the weight of government and every major political party and much of the corporate world behind them. Until then, their strategy was up in the air, and much depended on what David Cameron would bring home from Brussels.

REASON 15

TAKING NO FOR AN ANSWER

Two hours from Stockholm, driving directly into the heart of Sweden, there is a manor house called Harpsund. The roads seem to narrow as you approach through a countryside of meadows, farmland and sapphire lakes. There are no signposts to Harpsund. If you are lucky enough to find the final turning, a long, thin lane leads you into a forest where, about a mile in, the felled trunk of a giant silver birch blocks three quarters of the road. This form of road traffic management comes with armed guards. Once past the roadblock, there are no other properties for a mile or so, apart from outbuildings containing farm machinery. Inside one barn, several eight-foot tractor tyres have been rolled to the side of the hangar so it can be kitted out with desks and plug points for a media centre. The private estate of 4,000 acres includes a stunning manor house with white painted walls and a terracotta roof, tucked within forests and open meadows and bordered by a massive lake. It used to be owned by an industrialist, but in the 1950s it was given to the Swedish Prime Minister as a country residence. In the summer of 2014, Swedish PM Fredrik Reinfeldt invited David Cameron, German Chancellor Angela Merkel and Dutch Prime Minister Mark Rutte for boating followed by dinner.

For Cameron, it was a chance to exert some influence on his most important allies in the potential EU renegotiations ahead. A key test would be whether he could stop pro-federalist Jean-Claude Juncker becoming the next President of the European Commission. A week earlier, he had warned a Brussels gathering that electing the former Luxembourg Prime Minister could lead to the UK leaving the EU.

It is traditional for the Swedish PM to paddle the visiting dignitaries around the lake, and luckily Reinfeldt was in good shape. He expertly steered his four-man craft across the still waters, and this of course provided great pictures for the media and nautical metaphors for journalists covering the story. That said, the lake's serene stillness didn't necessarily match the mood. At a press conference afterwards, Cameron was given warning of rapids ahead. The Swedish and Dutch leaders were non-committal on the issue of Juncker, but the German Chancellor was furious at Cameron's threat that the UK would most likely leave the EU if he didn't get his way. In a rare public rebuke, she expressed her support for Juncker and added: 'We cannot just consign to the back-burner the question of the European spirit. Threats are not part and parcel of that spirit, that's not how we usually proceed.'[1]

By 2014, Cameron's whole approach to the EU was based on a threat. The British PM needed the EU to reform, or his country would most likely vote to leave. But here was Angela Merkel warning him: don't think you can use this referendum to insist everyone dances to your tune – that's not going to wash. In fact, Merkel wasn't fond of Juncker, but after the British PM's intervention she made sure he got elected. Later that month, the vote was 26–2 in favour, with just Britain and Hungary opposing his nomination. It was just one illustration of how isolated the UK was in the run-up to the negotiations – but many within Brussels felt that Cameron had spent his first four years in power making ene-mies. Now, he was about to ask the EU for a great deal of goodwill.

Earlier in the year, Cameron had begun to set out some of the compromises he hoped the EU would agree to should he win the next general election and start the negotiation process. In January, interviewed on Andrew Marr's Sunday programme, his message was that he wanted to stop the export of benefits across the EU. While he respected that people from Poland might want to come to the UK, he said: 'I don't think ... we should be paying child benefit to their family back at home in Poland.' He added: 'To change that, you've either got to change it with other European countries at the moment or potentially change it through the treaty change that I'll be putting in place before the referendum.'[2] So David Cameron expected Britain's demands to be wrapped up in a brand-new treaty signed and delivered by the EU. This was never going to happen.

At the time, many considered Europe might need a new treaty to deal with the Eurozone crisis and this meant Cameron would have a natural opportunity to tie in his set of changes as part of the agreement. This was important for two reasons. The first was that the changes in the treaty would be binding on all EU countries, giving legal force to whatever agreement Cameron had negotiated.

And, secondly, a new treaty would need ratification by all parliaments, and Cameron would have the opportunity to recommend that Parliament withhold ratification unless he had got what he wanted in return for giving the Eurozone countries something they wanted. It might even have given Cameron the opportunity to hold a referendum on something connected with Europe that didn't involve a simple In or Out choice.

The reason, it was thought, that a new treaty was needed was that the Eurozone bailouts had come with all sorts of regulatory implications that were currently outside of existing treaties. Wealthier governments had set up the European Stability Mechanism (ESM), to provide financial assistance to struggling countries. The ESM came with a set of tax and budget agreements, along with potential penalties for those failing to comply. In 2011, member states had tried to get these added as amendments to the Lisbon Treaty. But in December that year David Cameron had vetoed the idea of 'a treaty within a treaty', on the grounds that Eurozone members could have used the institutions of the EU to undermine Britain's interests and the principles of the single market.[3] In particular, Cameron was concerned about new powers being given to the European Commission to scrutinise national budgets and request revisions, as well as powers to bring in new regulation on financial services, including a Europe-wide tax on financial transactions.[4]

This was the most outstanding example of Cameron frustrating the plans of others to obtain what he hoped would be written up back home as a great victory. Ten hours of talks collapsed in the early hours, with the PM claiming he had to protect key British interests, including its financial markets. One source within the Council at Brussels describes this as 'incredibly unhelpful' and a sign of 'absolutely no solidarity'. The European Stability Mechanism was crucial to the survival of the Eurozone and here was the UK Prime Minister destroying the deal 'for petty British interests'.

Like Margaret Thatcher in the 1980s, Cameron had lacked any sign of showing he understood the meaning of being 'communautaire'. In press briefings and conferences afterwards, he talked only of British interests, without any sign he understood the need to consider the EU's interests. Cameron said that 'membership is in our interests. I've always said, if that's the case, I'll support our membership.'[5] But sometimes, membership involves compromise given as well as compromise taken.

'After that he became toxic,' says one Brussels source. 'The ESM was cost-free for him. Nobody ever understood his arguments; it would never have cost the UK anything, as it was a Eurozone instrument. Everyone was really upset.' Eventually, the deal was done between the other twenty-six nations through agreements outside the framework of the EU. But the ESM still used two EU institutions, namely the Commission and the European Central Bank, in order to carry out its functions. The loans came with strict conditions, agreed by the recipient nations. But these conditions of course affected citizens of those countries, who could in theory challenge their validity under the EU Charter of Fundamental Rights.[6] In short, by 2013 there was a view that, in part because of Cameron's veto, Europe might need to come back to the idea of a new treaty to legislate for the bailouts. And for Cameron, that meant he could tag on the UK's demands into this upcoming legislation.

You can already see how this might be viewed in the rest of Europe. What's more, they had decided to get by without a treaty. The problem with treaties was they often came with disruptive national referendums – and after getting its fingers burnt over the constitution in 2005 when the French and Dutch voted No, the EU sought to avoid new treaties wherever possible. By the time of the renegotiation process, the Eurozone crisis was settling down and other issues such as the migration crisis were now dominating the agenda. One source close to the negotiations in Brussels says:

> This is what happens when you don't listen to the briefings that your permanent representation in Brussels is giving you rather than listening to the four or five people in your private office. Honestly, there were some dim flickers of a chance that a new treaty was on the cards – with the euro and migration crisis – but they were fleeting. It's not only the Brits – people don't listen to the foot soldiers in Brussels who want to explain things without the varnish … We don't get ear-time.

So, by the end of 2014, the President of the EU Council, Donald Tusk, the President of the European Parliament, Martin Schulz, the German Chancellor, Angela Merkel, and the French President, François Hollande, all reiterated that no treaty change was on the table. Without a treaty, how would the UK's renegotiation agreement have any authority? This was a question David Cameron was never able to fully answer.

In discussions with the Council and the Commission, the best they could offer the UK was a settlement signed by the member states, with an agreement that certain elements would be incorporated the next time a treaty came along.

The problem was that in his Bloomberg speech, Cameron had offered fundamental reform, and that required new legislation. Reform can of course mean different things to different people. To Boris Johnson, it meant the return of the sovereign powers of Parliament. To Nigel Farage, it meant complete control of the UK's borders and over the number of migrants entering the UK from the EU. And in 2014, Farage was the greater concern. In the run-up to the Conservative Party conference, two Conservative MPs had defected to UKIP, triggering by-elections. Cameron needed red meat for the Eurosceptics to avoid further defections and bolster Conservative prospects in seats threatened by UKIP. In his conference speech, he pledged to go in to the negotiations and 'get our powers back' from the EU. He would replace the Human Rights Act and reduce the meddling of European judges – all music to the ears of Boris Johnson. On the issue of immigration, he looked directly into camera and down the barrel of the gun as he said: 'Britain, I know you want this sorted so I will go to Brussels, I will not take no for an answer and when it comes to free movement: I will get what Britain needs.'[7]

It was the kind of speech that could help win an election but leave you with problems further down the line. From this moment onwards, Cameron would slowly backtrack on his demands – a subtle erosion that would leave him with a renegotiation that was not meaningless but certainly fell short of others' expectations and was probably more of a negative than a positive in the all-important question of whether it could help him to win the referendum.

Reflecting on this, Craig Oliver, Cameron's former director of communications, says: 'Did we set expectation too high? Yes. When we said, "We will not take no for an answer," we meant one thing, what other people took that to mean was another, and it then became open to parody and caricature.'

That said, Oliver added that:

There is nothing short of a complete end to freedom of movement that would have satisfied the main proponents of Leave. The *Sun* newspaper was not going to accept anything other than an end to freedom of movement. If you have a newspaper that sells 2 million a day and is read by three or four times that amount and is also allowed by other institutions to set the agenda then you've got an issue. I'm not complaining about it, but you've got an issue.

Later that month, the defecting Tory Douglas Carswell won his by-election for UKIP in Clacton. Just weeks before the second by-election in Rochester and Strood, triggered by Mark Reckless, reports emerged that Cameron was considering either a 'quota' or an 'emergency brake' on EU migrants to the UK.

Michael Gove and Oliver Letwin started arguing for Cameron to demand a cap, perhaps set at 100,000, on the number of EU migrants allowed to enter Britain every year. Cameron aides believe it was Michael Gove who leaked the plan to the *Sunday Times*.[8] Downing Street described the reports as 'speculation'. The theory was that the emergency brake in particular could be achieved without treaty change. Under EU rules, a genuine emergency, such as a natural disaster, allowed countries to suspend certain freedoms – for example, on free movement of capital.[9] Capital restrictions were imposed on Cyprus after its banking crisis[10] under Article 66 of the Treaty for the Functioning of the European Union (TFEU), but the treaty does not appear to make the same provision for freedom of movement of workers.[11] With net migration now well above 200,000, could Cameron convince the EU that this measure should be applied to the UK? Alternatively, could there be quota levels on high influx nations such as Poland, or a basic cap on overall migration? The answer to all these questions from Angela Merkel was a resounding no.

Merkel's upbringing in East Germany, where the Berlin Wall restricted movement, is one explanation for her attachment to the travel and work freedoms EU membership gave to its people. When the iron curtain came down, Merkel wanted to ensure there would never again be second-class citizens in Europe. Meeting in the British delegation room in Brussels in October 2014, the German Chancellor told Cameron: 'You will not get support,' adding that such a cap flagrantly breached the EU's rules on freedom of movement.

In an interview for this book, Craig Oliver admits that it was at around this time, a year before his renegotiation even began, that David Cameron realised he was not going to be able to obtain any direct control over the UK's borders against EU migration. He would have to take 'no' for an answer. Oliver says:

The realisation was that we just weren't going to get it. I think it was October 2014 that Merkel was very clear on it. It was well before the end of 2015 we knew we weren't going to get it. Merkel was clear before, during and after [negotiations] that it wasn't going to happen.

In November 2014, Cameron developed a new plan. It was actually stolen from the right-leaning think tank Open Europe, who published a pamphlet on controlling benefits for migrant workers.[12] If he couldn't put a limit on numbers, surely he could change the circumstances that attracted migration to the EU? On 28 November 2014, in a long-anticipated speech, the PM proposed that migrants would have to work for four years in the UK before they could claim benefits. This would include their ability to claim tax credits paid out by the government to people on low wages. By eliminating this automatic wage boost, Cameron would reduce the disparities between the take-home pay earned by EU migrants in Britain and that earned in their home country. It was aimed squarely at the low-skilled end of the labour market. Housing benefits and social housing would also be unavailable for four years, thus reducing dramatically the 'pull factors' that encourage foreigners to come to the UK.[13]

This offer to cut in-work benefits and child benefit to migrants became a key element of the Conservative manifesto. The PM was also clear that if he didn't achieve his goals, he 'wouldn't rule anything out', including campaigning to leave the EU. After he won the general election in May 2015, Cameron had to face the reality of trying to achieve his demands. Free movement, without discrimination, was a fundamental principle laid out in the European treaties, which, as we've established, would be impossible for Cameron to change. Given this fact, he actually did better than anyone in Brussels expected.

At EU Council meetings, pressure was growing on Cameron to spell out exactly what it was he wanted. By late 2015, his answer to that appeared to be that, above anything else, he needed a victory. He needed to come home holding a piece of paper that looked as much as possible like he had got what the UK needed. That meant he had to be careful what he asked for.

A group of 100 MPs led by George Eustice, Chris Heaton-Harris and Andrea Leadsom had drawn up a set of proposals under a project called Fresh Start. They wanted a reduction of the EU budget, an overhaul of the Common Agricultural Policy and repatriation of certain powers, including all social and employment legislation.[14] Business for Britain had also come forward with its 1,000-page document suggesting the UK effectively abandon political union and revert to a pure trading position (see Reason 14).[15] None of this was winnable in the eyes of Cameron and his Chancellor, George Osborne.

In the meantime, the EU published its Five Presidents' report, signed by Jean-Claude Juncker, President of the Commission; Martin Schulz, President of the EU Parliament; Donald Tusk, President of the Council; Mario Draghi, President of the European Central Bank; and Jeroen Dijsselbloem, President of the Eurogroup, which is the financial think tank of the EU. Together, they mapped a route to full political integration for the Eurozone countries.[16] This route was in the opposite direction to the Conservative pressures on Cameron to unpick the treaties.

There are five Presidents, but European government in Brussels is divided into three main centres of power. The European Parliament contains elected MEPs based in a circular drum of concrete and glass. Inside, they assess legislation and in part control the EU budget, and they appoint members of the EU Commission. Martin Schulz was at the time their President.

The Commission, whose President was the controversial Juncker, is the second powerbase. It is an independent arm of the EU, consisting of civil servants and politicians (or, to use the collective term, technocrats) who draw up and implement legislation. Its building is star-shaped, with exterior shutters against the walls to protect workers from the sun's glare and act as sound barrier against noise from the Rue de la Loi. Some might say the giant wall screens are appropriate to the level of transparency from a body that is not democratically elected but wields enormous power.

Across the road from the Commission is the third centre of power, the European Council, where heads of state meet to discuss and define the general direction of the EU. Donald Tusk is their President. Tusk would become Cameron's main point man in the negotiations. Until recently, the Council was based in the Justus Lipsius building, but for a number of years they had been creating something next door that looks like a giant balloon in a cage, also known as 'The Egg'. This building began full use in January 2017.

True to form, David Cameron expressed his 'immense frustration' about the cost of this new development when he was first handed a brochure about it in 2011. The brochure was given to the UK press, with Cameron commenting that the current building was adequate for the Council meetings.[17] It was the kind of thing that five years later UK voters probably didn't recall but which had nonetheless dripped into their subconscious when the time came for Cameron to defend the cost of these Brussels institutions.

It was in a breakfast meeting on 24 September 2015 in the old 'perfectly good' Justus Lipsius building that David Cameron first explained to the President of the Council, Donald Tusk, what he wanted to achieve in the renegotiations. 'It is important we are seen as winning these negotiations if we want to win the referendum,' he told the President. Tusk responded that the EU had 'a mutual interest' in achieving this. His advice was that Cameron should not push his demands too far, but at the same time he had to get something because everybody shared in his desire to show to the British people that he had gained something. If the UK openly demanded too much, it could be thrown out and would be deemed a failure in the eyes of the public; at the same time, he shouldn't ask for too little. 'It was a tricky situation,' observes one person who was present at the meeting.

Cameron then set out four key areas where he felt reforms were needed: competitiveness, the relationship of non-euro countries with the Eurozone, the issue of ever closer union, and migration. The question of migration was 'the most important thing', he said. Some of his staff hoped these four areas could be discussed at the October European council and possibly agreed in December. Tusk told him: 'We need a paper setting out the UK's objectives.' This way, he could start to engage the other nations.

Cameron resisted the idea. He didn't want to make all his demands public in writing because Eurosceptics could begin to complain that he wasn't asking for enough, while some EU nations would insist he had gone too far. If all that played out in the media, it wouldn't read well. His plan was to stick to the key areas and first see what could be achieved behind the scenes. 'I am not going to spring any surprises. I'll keep to my four demands,' Cameron told them, according to our source. But Tusk said the other nations would be sceptical without a document: 'Maybe you'll say one thing today and tomorrow you'll raise another thing. You need to have it in writing with your letterhead, exactly what you want and then we can start talking, but we need to know the parameters.'

Over time, Tusk's team was able to persuade No. 10 to compose a letter. Indeed, although Brussels was not involved in drafting the document, there was 'intense consultation' between No. 10 and the Council about what should be in it. So by the time Tusk was sent the 'Dear Donald' letter dated 10 November 2015, he knew exactly what it would say.[18]

When the letter became public, the Prime Minister also made a speech setting out his 'four baskets' of demands. As expected, Conservative Eurosceptics lined up to savage its lack of substance, while EU officials expressed doubts about the legality of his demands. In the Commons, backbencher Bernard Jenkin said: 'After all the statements made by the Prime Minister … is that it? Is that the sum total of the government's position?' Jacob Rees-Mogg called the plans 'vacuous' and 'pretty thin gruel'. Bill Cash said the renegotiation plans were a 'pig in a poke'.[19]

As we explore what each of these demands were, for the sake of simplicity let's also compare them to what Cameron would eventually achieve three months later in February 2016.

The key areas for negotiation were as follows:

Economic governance: Cameron wanted 'legally binding principles' to ensure that there was no discrimination against any business on the basis of the currency of their country. Non-Eurozone taxpayers should not be liable for operations to support the euro. This included recognition that the euro used by nineteen countries was not the European Union's only currency (the treaty stated that it was, but with an exemption for the UK). Indeed, at the time, nine other EU nations were outside of it, but Cameron's original intentions went further. He wanted to adjust the voting powers of countries in this area so the larger Eurozone bloc could not impose regulations and directives on the single market that might have a negative impact on the City of London. Chancellor George Osborne always considered this the most important element of the negotiations and thrashed out ideas with his German counterpart, Wolfgang Schäuble. There was talk of resurrecting an obscure EU legal instrument that would allow the UK to veto proposed legislation deemed to favour the Eurozone over the others.

But this was interpreted in Brussels as the UK looking for special status to protect its financial institutions. If the UK could halt or skip certain regulations, that would give it a competitive advantage over financial institutions in other European countries. It could also mean that a non-Eurozone country, with no direct link to a particular issue, could hold up or block a matter of extreme urgency within the Eurozone. Sources in Brussels say that this, more than the demands on immigration, raised the most alarm bells in the EU, especially for the French and Belgians. 'If we weren't careful it would have really put a spoke in the wheel of Eurozone integration and banking union,' says one Commission source.

> For example, if the UK has a full say in decision-making on Eurozone banking legislation but was also exempt from certain things, that was a problem in itself. But then, further, why shouldn't other countries have exemptions? There would just be an unravelling of an economic union that is already not integrated enough.

This was an area that ended with intense negotiations between the UK and France on 18 and 19 February 2016, when the final deal was thrashed out. The disagreements were not so much between François Hollande and David Cameron, but when their so-called 'sherpas' got into the nitty-gritty of wording, it became very complicated.

The final draft exempted non-Eurozone countries from paying for bailouts – although this exemption was effectively already in place. Wording was also introduced to allow any single non-Eurozone country to force a debate amongst EU leaders about 'problem' laws – though they could not have a veto. On protections to the City, it was stated: 'The single rule book is to be applied by all credit institutions and other financial institutions in order to ensure the level playing field within the internal market.'[20] So the UK couldn't use the euro as an excuse to opt out of legislation.

Vote Leave chair Gisela Stuart says in an interview for this book that she would not have campaigned to leave had Cameron managed to come back with a particular form of wording in the agreement on this basket. Stuart, who had learned a great deal from being part of the Constitutional Convention that had created the EU Constitution, wanted recognition that 'for ever and ever there would be two kinds of member states'. One kind would be those in the single currency. For the single currency to truly work, its member countries would require deeper political integration, including harmonisation of taxes and a governing central bank. The other kind of country would be those who would never join the single currency, *but* they would be just as much members of the European Union.

Importantly, an architecture would need to be created allowing for both of those kinds of countries to exist. This would then allow for anyone who peeled off from the euro to leave the single currency but still be a part of the European Union. This is what Stuart meant in our Reason 7 when she said that the Maastricht Treaty led directly to the 2016 referendum. That treaty created a two-speed Europe, but it was still moving towards the same destination. She believes that Cameron could have come back with recognition that member states in the European Union could have two destinations. 'If he had come back with that recognition, I would have said, "OK, let's give it a go."' Instead, said Stuart, all Cameron got were 'protections', and in her experience, 'the moment you introduce protection, you will for ever have to fight for it'. Therefore: 'That to me was the moment I knew I could not accept the deal, because the deal amounted to nothing.'

Cameron's second basket was competitiveness: he wanted to cut red tape to businesses to boost productivity and 'drive growth and jobs for all', and set up a single digital market, which was estimated could add 3 per cent to the EU's GDP (and was already happening). He wanted a 'Capital Markets Union', which would help get finance to entrepreneurs and growing businesses. He also wanted Europe to get on with completing massive trade deals with America, China and Japan.

The request to reduce regulation was a badly timed demand, as the EU had just introduced a great tranche of legislation in this area and the demand for even greater cuts left civil servants rubbing their brows. Regulations exist to protect things like workers' rights and the environment, so there were limits to what measures could be pared back. Nonetheless, competitiveness was seen as the easy part: economic recovery was a priority for all the EU nations, and most were in favour of trade liberalisation, single market extension and reasonable deregulation.

The effort to boost jobs and growth was dealt with in a few lines of the agreement that included the EU's commitment to 'increase efforts towards enhancing competitiveness'. It was fairly meaningless stuff. But actually, with more time, if Cameron had made progress in this area, he might have been able to sell the idea that the EU was on the cusp of a great period of growth and prosperity; that a vote to leave now would be to sever the UK from a defining era within the EU. This ability to create a positive narrative about the future seemed to be overlooked. Perhaps it just wasn't in Cameron's psyche. All of his other demands were about rowing back on the EU's tentacles into British life. Here was the one chance of an optimistic, forward-looking outcome, but with only a few months of negotiation, mostly focused on the more complex baskets, very little was likely to be achieved – and it wasn't.

Cameron's third request was for greater national sovereignty. He stated in his letter to Tusk that this issue 'had been central to the debate about the European Union in Britain for many years'. He wanted to end Britain's obligation to work towards 'ever closer union' as set out in the initial 1957 treaty and repeated in others. None of the treaties ever used the phrase 'political union' – it was actually 'ever closer union of peoples' – but it appeared to align every country to a federalist mission. The UK argued that the phrase had influence because it was used as guidance in European courts and could justify pro-federalist judgments. Others contended that it was meaningless while at the same time difficult to preclude because it would mean reopening EU treaties. According to a source in the Commission, the British delegation was told by EU negotiators: 'The way you are interpreting ever closer union is wrong. You're creating a problem that never existed and you're asking us to come up with a solution to a problem that never existed.'

But the final deal included this concession: 'It is recognised that the United Kingdom, in the light of the specific situation it has under the treaties, is not committed to further political integration into the European Union. The substance of this will be incorporated into the treaties at the time of their next revision.'

To many, the UK's immunity from ever closer union sounded symbolic and if anything could be interpreted as setting Britain on an even more divergent path from its partners. But Cameron's team felt this was a great achievement. Craig Oliver says: 'Getting out of ever closer union was the number one thing they [the Tory Eurosceptics] wanted before the renegotiation. When we got it, they said, "Oh, it's nothing, it doesn't really matter."'

When Donald Tusk revealed the EU's willingness to compromise on ever closer union, Boris Johnson was sceptical in his column for the *Telegraph*. He wrote:

> How bankable is this? Will it be engraved in the treaties? Will the court be obliged to take account of this change, or will it be blown away – like Tony Blair's evanescent opt-out from the EU Charter of Fundamental Rights? How can we restore

the force of that Lisbon opt-out, and stop the court making rulings on human rights?[21]

One of the big criticisms made by Tory Eurosceptics is that the PM didn't make reference to specific powers that should be returned to the UK. Key areas were quietly dropped, such as EU social and employment laws. There was, for instance, no attempt to change the working hours directive. Osborne was the key figure in ensuring that Cameron did not make these unachievable demands. He realised that not only would the French oppose them, but setting out this ambition might lose crucial support from the Labour Party.

Cameron's 2010 manifesto had promised:

A Conservative government will negotiate for three special guarantees – on the Charter of Fundamental Rights, on criminal justice, and on social and employment legislation – with our European partners to return powers that we believe should reside with the UK, not the EU. We seek a mandate to negotiate the return of these powers from the EU to the UK.[22]

But this demand vanished from the 2015 manifesto, to be replaced with a greater emphasis on cutting immigration.

Cameron did, however, set out to enhance the role of national parliaments, giving them more powers to act together to stop unwanted legislative proposals. He quoted the Dutch ambition in his letter to Tusk that the EU agreement should be 'Europe where necessary, national where possible'. In the final settlement, he achieved the inclusion of a 'red card' system whereby if 55 per cent of national parliaments agreed, they could block a Commission proposal.

As far as the European Parliament was concerned, this was a big concession because it involved a 'complete change in the theory' of EU government. Normally, national governments controlled the EU through the European Council. Now they would have a 'double entry' through the government first at Council level and then again through their parliaments. This created the prospect of national governments agreeing on something, then sending it through the European Parliament, only to overturn it using parliaments representing the same governments who had initially approved it. Crazy?

On consideration, however, the EU civil servants worked out that 'the

threshold was so high that everybody knew it wouldn't be applied'. The principle might be problematic but in practice could numerous national parliaments,
many of which had two chambers, really club together to block something their
governments had already approved? It wasn't going to happen.

In Dan Hannan's book *Why Vote Leave*, he lambasts Cameron's attempts to
strengthen the powers of national parliaments for different reasons, saying the
'red card' proposal was 'arguably worse than the status quo'.[23] It replaced an
existing 'yellow card' mechanism that required only 35 per cent of parliaments to
be triggered. This was used only twice in six years, although that may have been
because the yellow card didn't have much bite.

Hannan doubted that half the national parliaments could be corralled against
specific legislation. He argued that: 'For the first time in its 750-year history, Parliament is formally recognised as a sub-unit within a larger polity… Parliament
implicitly accepts subordinate status. And all in exchange for a blocking power
that will never in fact be exercised.'[24]

The idea that the UK Parliament is ruled by Europe is a consistent theme of
Euroscepticism but is dismissed by Craig Oliver:

> Where is health policy set? Where is welfare policy set? Where is education policy
> set? What about defence and security? What about national tax? When you get
> past those five things, you are really struggling to say what is of massive signifi-
> cance in this country. This idea that somehow Brussels and Strasbourg define our
> laws for us is utter nonsense.

Cameron and Oliver might well have won that argument had it not been for
immigration. Indeed, many argue that polls after the vote suggest sovereignty was the key issue for voters, above immigration. However, if you ask those
people what laws they wanted to return to the UK, the first thing most will tell
you is for the UK to have powers to control its borders: the sovereignty to stop
ever-increasing net migration. This is the issue missing from Craig Oliver's list.

Basket number four was immigration. 'The issue is one of scale and speed,'
Cameron told Tusk in his November letter. The UK population was set to reach
70 million in the next decades, meaning it would become the most populous
country in the EU by 2050. Net migration was running at over 300,000 a year
and rising. 'That is not sustainable,' said Cameron. The language used in his

letter and his speeches leading into his negotiations would preclude the PM from ever being able to counter the Eurosceptic trump card in the run-up to the referendum vote. Indeed, Cameron told Tusk that because of free movement, 'the pressures are too great' on schools, hospitals and public services. He repeated his plan devised a year earlier, after Merkel told him the emergency brake on numbers was out of the question. 'People coming to Britain from the EU must live here and contribute for four years before they qualify for in-work benefits or social housing,' he demanded. He also wanted to 'end the practice of sending child benefit overseas'.

But there was an element of capitulation in this aspect of his demands. His letter declared his understanding of 'how difficult some of these issues are for other Member States' and he hoped a solution could be found. In an unusual admission in his speech that day, Cameron affirmed that free movement of labour in the EU was 'fundamental'. His lawyers had warned him that his proposals restricting benefits on the basis of race were discriminatory and highly unlikely to pass.

Cameron's efforts to change views on this were herculean in terms of his shuttle diplomacy. The UK effectively lost its Prime Minister for three months in a whirl of bilateral meetings across Europe. Cameron's critics in the EU say he needed years, not weeks, to build up these relationships and build alliances. By taking the Conservatives out of the EPP group when he became leader, he had burnt bridges – and set fire to more with his behaviour in Council meetings over the years. Now he came bearing gifts. He had a present for everybody, ranging from a Beatrix Potter collection for new parent Belgium PM Charles Michel to more consequential promises to countries in the East for defence cooperation.

Those most affected by the proposal were the Eastern European nations that have a political alliance called the Visegrád Four (V4). They include the Czech Republic, Hungary, Poland and Slovakia, who all had sizeable migrant populations in the UK. Cameron embarked on a series of visits to these countries and others, such as Bulgaria, Slovenia, Romania and Austria – the first visit by a British leader to Vienna for thirty-four years. Slowly, there was a softening towards him. In early February 2016, Hungary's Foreign Minister Péter Szijjártó said the EU would be 'permanently damaged' by a British exit and Hungary would 'respect that any member state has the right to cut the possibility of abusing their welfare system'.[25]

Poland mounted the most vocal opposition to the proposals. The country's

Europe minister, Konrad Szymański, said Warsaw had a problem because of discrimination against its people. That said, the ambition of the ruling party in Poland was to stem outward migration and stop the 'brain drain' from the country. If opposition parties would let them get away with it, they were willing to give ground.[26]

Martin Schulz was another problem. The European Parliament President said he had 'strong doubts about the legality of the four-year ban on access to welfare benefit for EU citizens'.[27] He too was schmoozed and invited to Downing Street and St Paul's Cathedral for the 200th anniversary commemoration of the Battle of Waterloo. This charm offensive was less successful. Cameron wanted Schulz to put in writing that any agreement by the member states on benefits would get a free pass through the European Parliament.

On 29 January 2016, Cameron visited Schulz in Brussels asking for a promise that the deal would be upheld by MEPs. 'I cannot do that,' said Schulz. 'I cannot defy or pre-judge a legislative process.' While it might be possible for the Council to reach agreement on the benefits question and for the Commission to promise to propose legislation, what couldn't be promised was that the European Parliament would vote to adopt it. And no vote would take place before the referendum. As one aide to Schulz puts it: 'People were saying, "Oh, Martin Schultz is being a prima donna" – well, you try pre-arranging British legislation. Try that in the House of Commons and see what reaction you get!'

So despite a move towards conciliation by the 'Visegrád Four' nations, the feeling back in Brussels was that Cameron had once again overestimated how much he could bypass the process. While there was goodwill to keep the UK in the EU, they had not forgotten the difficulties he'd caused them in 2011 when they were trying to secure the euro.

One EU official says:

Having come home from EU councils in the past claiming how much he'd won and slagging off the EU constantly and finding it convenient that the tabloids were slagging off the EU to his benefit, then he thought that he would come and, in a matter of months, say 'Let bygones be bygones and actually can I have a super-duper deal?'

That said, it was the European Commission that came up with the eventual compromise. The idea was to 'graduate' benefits so that EU migrants would receive increased payments the longer they remained in the UK over the course of four years. The finer detail of this system became one of the main sticking points on the last day of negotiations on 19 February.

The eventual deal was far removed from Michael Gove's mooted cap on numbers. It was described as an 'emergency brake' not on numbers but on benefits. The UK's ability to implement these restrictions was only authorised by the EU if the conditions were considered 'justified'. Cameron accepted this on the basis that the UK currently qualified for this brake and that it would apply for at least seven years. The whole thing was complex and not easy to sell in a sound bite. For many, Cameron had caved too early on this crucial issue. Boris Johnson wrote in the *Telegraph*: 'Why didn't we try harder to recapture control of our borders, rather than stick at this minor (if worthwhile) change to the law on benefits?'[28]

The 2015 manifesto promise to stop paying child benefit to children outside the UK was also abandoned, replaced by an agreement to pay it at a rate more closely reflecting the local cost of living. This issue alone extended the 19 February negotiations by several hours as Tusk ping-ponged between the delegation rooms of the UK and the V4 representative, Czech Republic leader Bohuslav Sobotka, described by one negotiator as 'flexible, but heavily leant on by the Polish'.

Cameron arrived in Brussels on Thursday afternoon and negotiated into the small hours. It had been hoped that the deal would have been signed over an 'English breakfast' on Friday morning. As it was, the British PM got three hours' sleep in the small hours of Friday before returning for another full day of talks, with 'English breakfast' postponed to 'English lunch' postponed to 'English dinner'.

The leaders got takeouts to keep them going. For Cameron, it was pepperoni pizza; for Merkel, chips and mayo. The delegation team mostly feasted on wine gums, Haribo and Diet Coke. While some negotiators described the last twelve hours as tense, another EU representative insists there was an agreement on Friday morning but things had to drag on 'to show to the outside world that the fight was long'. From this individual's account, all the EU leaders were sitting around waiting, all very unhappy, but thinking, 'Well, if this is what it costs to keep the UK in the EU then we'll do it.'

Others say that while the British Prime Minister had gained 'collegial credit' from his earlier shuttle diplomacy, he hadn't nailed down the detail of how his deals would work and the presence of all the leaders in one building created the required political pressure to sort that out. It seems the final issue was over whether current foreign residents in the UK could continue to claim child benefit at the existing rate. It was settled with agreement that existing claimants could continue at the normal rate until 1 January 2020.

Over dinner, the UK settlement was distributed to the leaders. At this point, the Greek PM, Alexis Tsipras, chose to express his fury that so much time had been given to the British when his country was dealing with the far greater issue of the migration crisis. Why were they spending hours 'discussing the meaning of ever closer union' when the EU was falling down around their ears? The Swedish PM, Stefan Löfven, picked up the settlement and said he needed to consult his coalition partners. Meanwhile, the Portuguese leader António Costa insisted on reading the entire document for twenty minutes while everyone waited. 'Everyone was gloomy and tired,' says one observer. 'Some people call it theatre or posturing. I have no recollection of anything like this ever happening before. It was the crunch meeting that was meant to ratify something that had been cooking for twenty hours and still there were gripes.' Any one of the twenty-seven other leaders could have vetoed the deal, but by the end of dinner they had an agreement.

At 11.10 p.m., a weary David Cameron walked out into the stark white press room packed with around 200 journalists. Mustering what energy he had left, he vowed to campaign 'with all my heart and soul to persuade the British people to remain in the reformed European Union that we have secured today'.[29]

Martin Schulz was still unable to give assurances that these proposals would pass through Parliament and, even if they did, the issues over child benefit could be tested in the European Court of Justice. It could easily be argued that they were in violation of the right to freedom from discrimination by nationality, guaranteed by EU citizenship. One EU official says:

It would've been a matter of controversy in the European Parliament; for sure it was really not the end of the story. The nature of the document, and wanting to amend treaties but without going through the proper procedure to amend them, was in itself problematic. The whole process was shaky.

The perception in Brussels was that Cameron got the maximum he could have got. 'He achieved a lot on the social aspect,' says one of the EU Parliament negotiators. 'He got guarantees to breach the treaty. That is huge.' Another source within the Council said on the issue of benefit restrictions:

> We didn't think the Commission would go that far, but that was an example of how far member states and institutions were willing to go to compromise on something most people thought was going to be impossible – to interfere with free movement. When it happened, it was seen as a huge breakthrough.

Some member states came on board on certain issues because they saw it as an opportunity to make changes. Germany and Austria, for example, welcomed movement on benefits.

But the fact is that once again Cameron had proved that the UK was different from the other nations of the EU, with its own issues and objectives. And even in Brussels, despite giving everything they felt they could give, officials knew expectations in the UK were higher. 'What Cameron thought he could get wasn't something he could deliver. This special status – it doesn't exist inside the EU,' said one EU official. 'And I wasn't surprised people in the UK said no, because that was the real controversy, and you couldn't hide it with a piece of paper.'

By setting certain objectives and slowly pulling back, Cameron revealed to the British public his impotence in Europe. What's more, he spent crucial months in the build-up to the campaign highlighting UK concerns on sovereignty and immigration – without making a substantial sellable breakthrough. He told the nation that he would be prepared to campaign to leave if he didn't get these substantial reforms, but he wasn't. He came back with something that was significant in the technocrat world of Brussels and broke with convention – but it had no meaning to voters. To Eurosceptics, it was feeding time.

Dan Hannan tweeted: 'Britain banged the table and aggressively demanded the status quo. The EU, after some mandatory faux-agonising, agreed.'[30]

He wrote in his book *Why Vote Leave*: 'If this is how unwilling EU leaders are to make meaningful concessions now, when their second-largest member is about to vote on leaving, how much more intransigent would they become should that country vote to stay?'[31]

Richard Tice, the co-chairman of Leave.EU, said: 'The Prime Minister promised half a loaf, begged for a crust and came home with crumbs.'[32]

The Eurosceptic UK press was equally unsympathetic and had been since
Donald Tusk produced the draft deal in early February, when *The Sun*'s headline
read: 'Who do EU think you are kidding Mr Cameron?' The sub-heading was:
'No control of our borders'.[33]

But perhaps the most damning indictment of the whole affair was that the renegotiation deal was dropped as a message by Stronger In almost immediately. It
had achieved not one thing that they could highlight in their campaign, and for
that reason alone must be deemed a failure. Stronger In's executive director Will
Straw believes that there were real achievements in Cameron's package of reforms
but admits the Remain campaign didn't find a way of promoting them. He says:

> The renegotiation became the dog that didn't bark in the referendum. Nobody
> talked about it. It barely came up. Actually, I think there was an argument that
> could have been made quite forcefully on immigration that there had been some
> quite meaningful reforms to who could get what benefits. Cameron talked about
> it a bit in the TV debates, but actually what he got was quite significant.

Straw's complaint, though, is that the negotiations stopped Cameron from
making a positive case sooner. 'I think you cause yourself huge problems if you
say, "We are going to have a referendum; I want to get these reforms but only if I
get them am I going to campaign for Remain."' In Straw's view, this led to Cameron making an impossible switch from calling the EU 'bossy and bureaucratic'
to suddenly saying 'Oh, we are doomed if we leave.'

'It wasn't that our arguments weren't credible. I think people thought that
Cameron and Osborne lost that credibility because they had been so much more
nuanced before 22 February – and if you are going to set some tests, make sure
you get expectations right.'

Straw adds:

> The mistake with the renegotiation strategy was it promised too much; it set
> expectations too high; and it made the points of contention immigration and sov-
> ereignty. So, when we got the campaign going, particularly in the three months'
> run-up to the February council, every day the EU story was about immigration

and sovereignty. But we wanted to be talking about the economy and our place in the world.

It also closed off the Remain camp's option to use a strategy that had been highly effective for the No campaign during the 2014 Scottish independence referendum: to make a 'vow' of further reforms after the vote. The UK's political leaders could offer further devolution to the Scottish people after a No vote because they had the power to offer further devolution to the Scottish people, but with the EU, Cameron had already played his cards. He went in looking for clear wins and came back restating the existing position, one that he himself had so recently denounced as unsatisfactory.

As polling day approached, there was some discussion amongst the Remain campaign, and particularly between David Cameron and Craig Oliver, over whether it would be possible to offer a similar 'vow' on achieving controls on immigration. An idea arose that Cameron could say that freedom of movement would be on the agenda at the first European Council meeting after the referendum, and there was even an initial discussion with Angela Merkel about it. But in the end, the campaign knew that it was powerless to offer any changes on this front with any credibility.[34]

Some have argued that Cameron could have achieved more in his negotiation if he hadn't given the impression to others that he would easily win the referendum. 'He once told Juncker he would win 70/30,' says one Commission source. 'Juncker said, "I wouldn't win in Luxembourg 70/30."' This is denied by No. 10 sources, who say it was other leaders who were complacent about how the UK voters would react. For instance, Dutch leader Mark Rutte had approached Cameron at the financial gathering in Davos in February 2016 and said: 'My understanding is the British people are too conservative. They won't vote to leave.'

As for the Eastern European countries, they wanted the UK to stay in but their part of the deal in the EU was freedom of movement – a fair deal because the big countries get to make themselves better off with a cheaper labour force. Craig Oliver says:

You've got the complacent Rutte view. Then the Eastern Europeans' view: 'That's what you signed up to.' Then you've got the Charles Michel view that everybody should be waking up in the morning and singing 'Ode to Joy' [the EU national anthem]. Then there were the people who were kind of 'Are you serious?' They thought, 'Hold on, you are not in Schengen. You are not in the euro. You are asking for all these other exceptions – you are not really one of us.'

But Oliver insists: 'We didn't feel we overpromised – we allowed expectation to get too high. The deal was a major achievement – and Europe gave more than it wanted to give – but the expectation was being set by people that unless you have complete control of your borders, that's a problem.'

The 2014 report produced by Dominic Cummings for Business for Britain assessed what they expected from the PM's renegotiations and concluded that he would 'raise expectations and then increase disappointment'.[35] They felt that David Cameron was embarking on a reform process that would make people 'more likely' to vote to leave the EU because it would demonstrate the powerlessness of the Prime Minister and undermine his credibility.

Without a major concession on immigration, Cameron lost the natural advantage of being on the side of the status quo, because in many people's eyes the status quo was becoming more and more risky and more undesirable with each quarterly announcement of the ever rising net migration figures. The Leave camp could flip the argument and say that if the UK agreed to stay, there would be huge uncertainties on the horizon. How much more would be demanded for the EU budget? Which other nations might join the EU and add to the influx of migrants?

'My feeling is that Cameron could not have gone further,' says one EU official. 'I'm not judging his talents as a negotiator. The limit was reached, but I also think he set expectations too high in his own country. To win his party, he was playing with the fate of the EU, and he lost both.'

Up until 19 February 2016, David Cameron had complained about and criticised the EU during his entire time in office. Now he was trying to emerge as its defender. How had this change of heart come about? Apparently, it was because of the negotiations. As one EU Council source put it: 'He needed something where he could credibly say, "I've changed my mind" – and only that settlement could give him that platform. He sacrificed the UK's interests for his own personal interests of staying in power.'

Cameron returned to the UK and summoned his Cabinet to a meeting on Saturday morning – the first time a Cabinet had met on a Saturday since the Falklands War. It was time to find out: who would support his deal and who would oppose it? The answer was devastating.

REASON 16

'ET TU, BOJO?'

At 9 a.m. on 11 May 2016, people formed a semi-circle around a large red bus at Truro's Lemon Quay in Cornwall, a county at the south-west tip of the UK. On the side of the bus it said: 'We send the EU £350 million a week, let's fund our NHS instead. Vote Leave. Let's take back control.' The slogan was already infamous, but the gatherers hadn't come for the bus. The star of the show was late. Boris Johnson had been behind schedule all morning as local newspapers and radio shows allowed their interviews to overrun, rarely getting such a high-profile politician into their studios. In the battle for airtime, there was no greater asset than Johnson. The former London Mayor's erudite charm and eccentric unpredictability had always made him a box office guest to have on your show. His job that day was to apply those powers to persuading the south-western counties of Cornwall, Devon and Somerset to leave the European Union. As a net beneficiary from EU funding, many considered it an own goal to sever ties from an important money pot. But Johnson started the day explaining to BBC Cornwall listeners that actually they would benefit. 'We believe passionately in supporting Cornish agriculture, rural development and all the projects that have benefits from ERDF [European Regional Development Fund] funding,' he said, 'but you can do it better at a national level with national priorities.'[1]

The small crowd next to the bus slowly grew. Green-and-white canopies also began to fill the square for market day. Then there was a sudden kerfuffle. Reporters and crews picked up their bags and cameras and ran. In seconds, they had enveloped one of the vegetable stalls. In the middle of the mayhem, the blond-thatched head was unmistakable. Johnson was buying asparagus. Notepads out. Cameras rolling. Earpiece in. Microphones shoved into the throng. 'Are they on us?' 'Are we live?' 'Let's find out, why he is buying asparagus?' Almost immediately, news channels cut out of whatever report happened to be on. 'We can cross over to Truro, where Boris Johnson is launching the Vote Leave campaign bus.' Perhaps in Downing Street the Prime Minister stopped to look. He'd often referred to Boris Johnson as his 'star player' during the general election; now he was playing for the other side – and in a key Tory marginal seat, no less.

With the cameras rolling and the photographers in place, the microphones and Dictaphones recording, Johnson held the asparagus aloft. 'Farming budgets will be unaffected by us leaving the EU, asparagus will be just as delicious – in fact, even better,' he said. Johnson has Dumbo's feather syndrome: he often needs a prop to perform. By the time he'd reached the bus, he'd found another one, a Cornish pasty, which he again raised like a trophy, calling it the 'independence pasty'. In actual fact, in 2011 the European Commission gave the Cornish pasty protected status to prevent cheap knock-offs being produced elsewhere, so pasty makers may not have wanted independence. It also emerged that the bus Vote Leave was using to travel was from Poland. Remain campaigners immediately dubbed it 'Boris's blunder bus'. But these things bounce off Johnson. He said, 'Isn't it wonderful to see our battle bus, which is not funded by the taxpayer? Unlike the £9 million they spent on that government propaganda, that Remain propaganda.' (The reference was to a government-funded leaflet sent to all homes.)[2]

He then told the small gathering and the much larger TV audience that they had a once in a lifetime 'unrepeatable opportunity' to 'take back control'. He followed it up with a warning to his colleagues on the Remain side:

> They think they've got all the big battalions, they've got all the taxpayers' money; we've got the passion, we've got the commitment and we've got right on our side. Fight for our democracy, folks, on June 23rd and let's make sure June 24th is Independence Day.[3]

He was rewarded with a small cheer – nothing like the applause he would get six weeks later, when he used the same line to finish the BBC debates at Wembley Arena.

Throughout the day, Johnson, travelling with Labour MP Gisela Stuart, found more props: beer at the brewery in St Austell, and then to Charlestown for ice cream, which after a few licks he handed to a bystander to finish off. Even in a quiet fishing village more used to celebrity visits for the filming of BBC series *Poldark*, Johnson could pull out a crowd. After a morning of leafleting and hand-shaking, he got on the bus with confidence lifted. 'I must have shaken hands with 100 people. Only two of them actively said they were voting Remain; everybody else said, "I'm with you,'" he told co-author Jason Farrell.

At the back of the bus, past the kitchen food supplies and microwave, there was a sectioned-off semi-circular sofa, where Johnson sat with the ever smiling Gisela Stuart, who correctly described herself as the mother figure of the campaign. Next to her was Johnson's advisor, the affable Will Walden. Here, Jason reminded Johnson of a speech he'd made at the 2014 Conservative conference (in this instance, his prop was a brick), in which he'd expressed confidence that David Cameron would deliver the reforms needed because of his 'natural authority' at the negotiating table.[4] What had gone wrong?

'After the Bloomberg speech, everyone was very confident that there was going to be far-reaching treaty change and fundamental reform – that didn't happen,' said Johnson wearily. 'There's no point crying over spilt milk; a big opportunity was missed.'

'But you were confident he could get what you wanted?'

He just didn't have enough time – the other countries didn't give us what we needed... I really did want to support our Prime Minister and support the government. I think he's a superb Prime Minister and he's done a very good job. But the fundamental question everyone has to face is: do you want to stay in an unreformed EU when it is evolving really quite rapidly now towards a federal state, which is nothing like what we signed up to in 1972? It is a very difficult decision – there are two sides to it. I said in an article two weeks before my decision that I think we would flourish outside – that is my view.

Later, when the bus reached its last destination of the day in Exeter, Johnson was pressed on whether he had another motive. He was holding court amongst his entourage of journalists, who represented just about every national newspaper and broadcaster in the country – perhaps twenty or so. He had just toured half a dozen Tory marginal seats with the entire national media in tow, espousing a message that goes down well with grassroots Conservatives. For Johnson, surely the referendum campaign was his opportunity to display his credentials for the job of Prime Minister? 'It all looks a bit like the battle bus tour of a leadership contender,' suggested Jason.

'Well, I can see how it might look like that, but this isn't for my political advancement. It won't have helped my chances of getting a Cabinet position, and anyway, this isn't just my bus…' said Johnson.

'Well, no one is calling it the Gisela Stuart bus,' responded Rob Hutton, political correspondent for Bloomberg.

The assumption in Johnson's answer was that he expected David Cameron to still be Prime Minister at the end of all this, and therefore Remain was likely to win. No one pressed too hard on that, because all the journalists thought the same. But what one long day in the West Country had shown was the pure gold dust of Johnson in his ability to make the news. The coverage had been wall to wall (and prop to prop). It illustrated exactly why David Cameron should have done everything in his power to keep Johnson on his side. It is not clear that he did.

Really, the key to it all was Justice Secretary Michael Gove. His decision to join the Leave camp provided the final bridge for Johnson to cross. But we should start with Northern Ireland Secretary Theresa Villiers and House of Commons leader Chris Grayling. They were the first Cabinet ministers to open up to David Cameron about their intentions to campaign to leave. The concessions he gave them helped open the door for Gove and Johnson.

It was in late 2015 that Villiers first approached Cameron. She had been concerned about discussions in Cabinet, which in her view suggested that very little was being asked for in the renegotiations. In November, Cameron had first made the broad areas of his demands clear and on 7 December the European Council President Donald Tusk wrote back, setting out what progress had been made on the 'four baskets' the British government was asking for. This and another dispatch from Tusk in early February were done to 'manage expectations', according to his aides. But they gave strong indications to Eurosceptics that the government was watering down its ambitions. Villiers told Cameron she had been 'quite surprised' by the letter. 'I assumed you would ask for more,' she told him. She added that it was 'highly likely' she would campaign to leave.

In an interview for this book, she explained:

> I went to see the PM to ask if there was more I don't know about – is there some rabbit to come out of the hat? I was exploring with him whether the deal he was asking for in public was really as far as they were prepared to go. It didn't seem significant so I wanted to know if they were pressing for more privately.

Villiers wanted a deal that would end the supremacy of EU law and stem the powers of the ECJ.

> I always knew that was going to be hard to achieve inside the EU, but I did think there was a chance the PM might ask for some kind of associate membership. That possibly he could come back with something more radical and take the UK out of some of the treaties.

She also pressed him about the emergency brake on numbers. 'For me, it's a democratic constitutional question,' she told the PM, but she also warned that 'for many people, it's the key issue. That's how the credibility of your deal will be judged. Will it deliver significant change on immigration and free movement?' Tusk's letter had made clear that the negotiations in this area were based solely on restricting benefits. Not enough in Villiers's view.

With the PM telling her he was doing his best, Villiers used Christmas to wrestle with her dilemma. She'd worked hard for two decades in politics to get her Cabinet position and expected she would have to give it up if she wanted to campaign to leave. She hadn't started out on the Eurosceptic wing of the party but, after being elected as an MEP in the European Parliament, seeing the EU in operation had pushed her in that direction.

> I was one of these rare people who was less Eurosceptic in selection than she became in office. It's very rare in the Conservative Party. The normal pattern is for people to bang the table when they are selected as a candidate, to proclaim their Eurosceptic credentials, and then backtrack in office.

Some say this is exactly what David Cameron had done.

Villiers was first elected as an MEP in 1999 and became deputy leader of the Conservatives in the European Parliament from 2001 to 2002. It was here that she met Dan Hannan, who was 'very influential' in her thinking about the EU. She also became frustrated at the system and at the power 'given to people we don't elect and can't remove'.

She'd worked constructively to make changes and mitigate problems, but has plenty of examples of EU legislation that she thought was not in the UK's interests: 'The vitamin supplements directive was immensely frustrating for people in the UK who are perfectly capable of deciding what vitamin supplements they want to take but the EU doesn't let them.' The European Union's ban on lower insurance premiums to women car drivers was another. 'Stats demonstrate that women are less likely to have car accidents than men but under EU law that can't be acknowledged in their premiums because that would be to give them a more favourable rate based on their gender.' She concluded that if the UK were making these laws, it would come up with different answers. She also opposed Britain's entry into the euro, and most other attempts to expand the powers of the EU.

Villiers was elected to Parliament in 2005. She found that Europe was not a big issue on the doorstep in her constituency of Chipping Barnet (Barnet voted 62 per cent Remain). So, as she sweated it out over Christmas, she knew her torment was purely self-inflicted. She used the holidays to get together with Chris Grayling, who was 'never in doubt' that he would campaign to leave. Grayling had already met with Dan Hannan in Brussels to discuss his plans and had been in touch with the key players at Vote Leave. He told Villiers he would approach Cameron as soon as possible and she agreed to do it on the same day. 'I knew even if we got every word we asked for in the negotiations I would have to campaign to leave and I assumed that I would have to resign from the government,' says Villiers. The Villiers–Grayling partnership was never as significant as Gove–Johnson, but they were the pioneer rebels within the Cabinet, and at the time thought there was a good chance they might be the only ones to jump.

On 4 January 2016, at around 9 a.m., Grayling met with the Prime Minister and made clear that he wanted to campaign to leave and that he wanted to get going on it straight away. He offered to resign but also said he would prefer to remain in the Cabinet. Cameron was clear that the latter wasn't an option. It would spread disunity and anyone contemplating joining the Brexit camp could do the same. A Cabinet is supposed, where possible, to operate under 'collective responsibility', meaning they stand together on the government's policy. At that time, the policy on the EU was to remain neutral and positive while negotiations were in progress. 'What's the point of doing it now?' the PM asked Grayling. 'The renegotiation is supposed to be sorted in six or seven weeks.'[5] Grayling told him that the Leave camp was in disarray and he needed to take up the helm.

Vote Leave was indeed under strain at this point. As we saw in Reason 14, there was dissent amongst the ranks, and Grayling was a key player in the attempt to oust campaign director Dominic Cummings. But at this stage he and

Villiers didn't know how close Cummings was to securing other key Cabinet figures to the campaign.

By the time Theresa Villiers met the Prime Minister, Cameron had come up with a compromise. Concerned that Grayling and Villiers would set the year off with a 'referendum crisis', the PM's team decided to 'cauterise the situation'.[6] He offered to suspend collective responsibility, but only after returning from Brussels with his deal in February. Then if Cabinet ministers wanted to go their own way they could, without consequence, but only once the deal was done.

Villiers explained how she also wanted to get going immediately. 'I have a campaign to lead; if that means I have to go, it probably makes sense for me to do it now,' she told him. Cameron acknowledged that Villiers was doing something she believed in and wasn't in it for political positioning. 'He was very graceful and sensible, there was no row.'

Villiers decided the PM's offer was 'generous'. After all, he had appointed her to the Cabinet and shown confidence in her abilities over a number of years. It wasn't unreasonable for him to say you have got to wait until the deal is done. By waiting, Villiers could keep her job and still campaign to leave when the time came. Grayling was given the same offer. Both went away happy.

So once again the PM had given the Eurosceptics what they wanted, with a delay, but with no other conditions attached. His decision to suspend collective responsibility was announced publicly and raised the prospect of any number of Cabinet members and dozens of junior ministers campaigning for Britain to leave the EU. Michael Gove's wife Sarah Vine recalls thinking that day: 'Everything I'd feared was beginning to unfold.'[7] She knew her Eurosceptic husband now had less of an excuse to remain in the background during the campaign. A statement from Downing Street that day suggested the decision had not been taken in response to any pressure, but it is clear from accounts of those close to the PM that it was a reactive move to an immediate problem. He may well have come to this decision anyway, but with more time to consider, he could have imposed conditions on senior Conservatives wanting to campaign for Out, and perhaps insisted on reassurances from senior members such as Gove that they would not take an active role.

At this stage, the other Eurosceptics on the Cabinet were fearful of expressing their intentions, even to each other. 'Everyone was paranoid about ending up in the Sunday papers,' said one. Villiers and Grayling thought they might well be the only senior ministers to defy the PM. Culture Secretary John Whittingdale and Employment Minister Priti Patel were obvious possibilities. Iain Duncan Smith hadn't been clear, even in private. This was partly because, with the PM's negotiations focusing on welfare and migration, the Work and Pensions Secretary didn't want to undermine the discussions. Business Secretary Sajid Javid had also made Eurosceptic noises. Theresa May was a possible but far too difficult to read. Michael Gove was an outside possibility but very loyal to the Prime Minister. They certainly didn't expect to be joined by Boris Johnson.

That afternoon, Cameron and his advisors also speculated about who else might join Leave. Michael Gove was the biggest concern, but Cameron told Craig Oliver that the Gove family had been to stay for New Year at the PM's country residence of Chequers. Gove's wife Sarah had apparently reassured Cameron and his wife Samantha that Michael would support him. Vine was godmother to the Camerons' youngest daughter, Florence. Their children had gone to the same primary schools and Nancy Cameron and Beatrice Gove went to the same secondary school. The friendship ran deep, but later Vine admitted she had 'not been entirely transparent'[8] in her conversations with the Camerons, not knowing for certain which way her husband would jump.

Cameron, Johnson and Gove had a long history. Johnson and Cameron were at Eton and they were all at Oxford University together. The photograph that Cameron hated most in the world showed him and Johnson as fresh-faced students in bowties and tails as members of Oxford's Bullingdon Club. Cameron poses like Hornblower spotting land in the distance; Johnson gives the lens his most raffish glare. About them was an air of entitlement that comes with having enjoyed the very best education that money can buy and gained membership of Oxford's most decadent club. The 200 year-old, all-male Bullingdon Club was not recognised by the university, but was maintained unofficially by wealthy students intent on banqueting, debauchery and setting themselves apart from the others. In 2013, it was reported that members were required to burn a £50 note in front of a beggar as part of an 'initiation ceremony'.[9]

George Osborne would later become a member. Michael Gove, with his middle-class upbringing in Aberdeen, was never a contender. But the innately awkward Gove admits he was intoxicated by Johnson's effortless charisma and became one of his many followers. He told Johnson's biographer: 'I was Boris's stooge. I became a votary of the Boris cult.'[10] Gove helped campaign for Johnson's election to become president of the Oxford Union in 1986 and he would later become president himself.

After university, Cameron worked as an advisor to the Conservatives before going into PR. Gove and Johnson became journalists. Then, in 2001, both Cameron and Johnson were elected as Members of Parliament. At this stage, Johnson was the more recognised figure. He'd graduated from his notorious period in Brussels at the *Telegraph* to become editor for *The Spectator*, and during this time had been invited onto the BBC's satirical news quiz *Have I Got News For You* in 1998. His bumbling language mixed with sharp wit made him perfect for the format and he became a regular on the show.

David Cameron's rise within the party, however, was even more meteoric than Johnson's and he became vice-chair of the party in 2003, having only been an MP for two years. A year later, he was shadow Education Secretary and a year after that he was elected leader following the resignation of Michael Howard in October 2005. Cameron beat David Davis and Liam Fox to get the job. Johnson had supported his campaign, and in return Cameron backed Johnson to become London Mayor in 2008.

But deep down Johnson, who once stated his ambition to be 'World King', thought he was the smarter, more creative, more popular politician who deserved the top job in Downing Street. Another Johnson biographer, Sonia Purnell, observed: 'The fact that Cameron was two years below him at Eton – a terrifically hierarchical school – rankles deeply. As does the fact that it was Boris who shone there, not Cameron. Masters recall Johnson as a remarkable teenager. They do not recall Cameron at all.'[11]

Amid this alpha male rivalry was Michael Gove. It seems unkind to say it, but if you programmed 'geek' into a 3-D printer, it might produce something a bit like the bespectacled Gove. Awkwardness is fused into his DNA. However, it is mixed with politeness, ingrained in that classic English way, meaning he will apologise and thank you profusely for no reason. A TV reporter harassing him on his doorstep after breakfast might not get a question answered, but he will be showered with gratitude for turning up at Gove's house uninvited. 'Are you going to resign, Mr Gove?' would be met by 'How good of you to come, and thank you for your question!' Elected to Parliament five years after Cameron and Johnson, he became a valued friend to both men, who were never themselves socially close with each other beyond the odd highly charged game of tennis. Soon promoted to Education Secretary under Cameron, Gove's high intellect was deployed to reform schools, to studiously examine policy and write good jokes for the Prime Minister to use against his rivals at Prime

Minister's Questions, but he lacked the natural flair for presentation required of a front man, and so he wasn't considered essential to the project.

In 2014, Cameron made clear that Gove was expendable by sacking him from his role as Education Secretary. Gove's controversial school reforms were unpopular with teachers. Election strategist Lynton Crosby decided that he had become a millstone to the Conservatives' re-election strategy. Therefore, Gove was demoted to the lower role of Chief Whip, with a substantial salary reduction. Rather than being immersed in his passion for transforming education, his job was now to rally the team behind the leader. Geeky Gove was back to playing the role of stooge: ballboy to the toffs with rackets.

What also hurt was that No. 10 leaked private polling by Crosby, showing Gove had become 'a toxic liability among teachers'.[12] Did they need to tell the world he was toxic? He was sidelined during the 2015 general election; reduced to organising photobombs at Labour events with an army of young Tories wearing Alex Salmond and Nicola Sturgeon masks. At the time, Gove decided Cameron was doing, rather ruthlessly, what was necessary to win, but 'it soured relationships', says one friend.

In October 2014, a few months after being demoted, Gove was a guest on a bizarre and rather revealing video blog with journalist James Delingpole. After wandering in to the back of shot in Delingpole's garden, Gove, in a supposedly impromptu but clearly staged interview, explains his admiration for the dwarf prince character in HBO's *Game of Thrones*. Tyrion Lannister is a cunning courtier in the series, but his more perfectly formed sister and father overlook his talents and seem to barely tolerate his existence. Gove says:

> The moment I loved the most is when he [Tyrion] leads what's apparently a hopeless charge of his troops in defence of King's Landing against the forces of Stannis Baratheon. And you see there this misshapen dwarf, reviled through his life, thought in the eyes of some to be a toxic figure, can at last rally a small band of followers.

Gove goes on to say the scene reminded him of the words of Winston Churchill: 'Never, never, never surrender.'[13]

Gove did bounce back into a more senior position after the election as Justice Secretary, and those close to him insist his decision to back the Leave campaign was not revenge for his treatment by Cameron, but there's little doubt that when the PM asked for loyalty in 2016, Gove would be forgiven for thinking, 'Where was yours in 2014?'

That moment came on 9 February 2016. A few days earlier, the Prime Minister had read an article in *The Times* with the headline 'Gove "torn" between Cameron and Brexit'.[14] A friend of Gove believes Chris Grayling leaked the story to journalist Sam Coates after the Justice Secretary had an 'injudicious conversation' with the Leader of the Commons about his feelings. In response to the article, David Cameron's chief of staff, Ed Llewellyn, called up Gove and in a rather presumptuous manner said: 'You know the story on the front pages of *The Times*, David wants to put out a line from you just confirming that obviously you'll be supporting the Prime Minister.' Gove responded: 'I can't do that because I haven't made my mind up about what I'm going to do.'

When this was relayed to the Prime Minister, he called Gove in to a meeting with himself and George Osborne at his flat above 11 Downing Street. Here, the Chancellor, who was also close friends with Gove, argued the intellectual case for remaining in the EU and rationalised that, while he understood its imperfections, membership was better than the alternative. The PM made a more personal case, albeit in a calm and measured tone, telling him, 'You know if I lose, then it will destroy me.'[15] But Gove explained that while his views on the EU had been mostly suppressed over the years, it would feel hypocritical to campaign for Remain. He told them, 'I'd put my feelings in a box, and now the box has been opened. My feelings on this have been unleashed. And it's just incredibly difficult for me. If I take a particular view to row in behind you, then everyone will know it's insincere.'[16]

Senior conservatives were dispatched to try to win Gove over and he wrestled with the decision over half-term between playing Monopoly and doing activities with his eleven- and twelve-year-old children. In another meeting with Cameron and Osborne, Gove told them that he wasn't overjoyed at the prospect of campaigning to leave. 'I don't have any relish for it,'[17] he said, and this appeared to convince them he would not play an active role. Later, in her *Daily Mail* column, his wife Sarah Vine recalled:

> Michael has been like a cat on a hot tin roof, locked in an internal struggle of agonising proportions. He has sought counsel from friends, colleagues, relatives. But at the end of the day, only he could make the final decision: to make the choice between loyalty to his old friend, the Prime Minister, and his own heartfelt beliefs.[18]

On the one side was his dislike of 'the unstoppable march of European feder-alism' and the 'erosion of British sovereignty'. But set against that was a valued friendship. The couple went through their old photographs of their wedding in the south of France. Sixty or so friends attended and there was 'Samantha Cameron, radiant and pregnant with her first child; she and David laughing on the coach back from the church'.[19]

In mid-February, Boris Johnson was also staring at the same fork in the road. His memories of Cameron stretched back further but his loyalties were shal-lower than Gove's. Rivals as much as friends, the London Mayor's challenging relationship with the Prime Minister was obsessively followed in Westminster. Johnson regularly defied his leader, who, let's not forget, was his junior at Eton. In 2009, Johnson called for a referendum on the Lisbon Treaty after Cameron had abandoned the idea.[20] He described his PM's reference to a broken socie-ty as 'piffle'. They disagreed on the solution to the UK's air capacity problem, with Johnson wanting to build an airport island in the Thames Estuary while Cameron appeared to be adopting his long-grass strategy of kicking the problem down the road. Boris's signature on Dan Hannan's 'People's Pledge' (demanding an In/Out EU referendum) in 2012 added pressure on Cameron to make his referendum promise.[21] Indeed, they met in September at Chequers, where it's reported Cameron reassured Johnson that the announcement was being readied. Even after Johnson became an MP in the new all-Conservative administration in 2015, he was a loose cannon. At party conference in Manchester, he appeared to criticise his government's plans to cut tax credits, saying everything possible must be done to 'mitigate and palliate' the loss of up to £1,300 a year for millions of families. He later revealed that he had asked City Hall staff to present the government with a study on the impact of the cuts on Londoners. A month later George Osborne was forced to backtrack on the unpopular proposals after they were blocked in the Lords. It was a victory to Johnson against his main rival to succeed Cameron.[22]

As it stood, though, Osborne was better positioned to take over as party leader once Cameron stood down, as long as he could keep the economy on track. In a BBC interview in the run-up to the election, David Cameron had indicated he would leave the job by the end of the parliament – that meant 2019. The race was on. Privately, everyone knew Cameron favoured his Chancellor to succeed him. If the PM had lost in 2015, things might have been different – the party would be looking for a fresh start and Johnson could have campaigned as a new MP while still in his high-profile role as London Mayor.

But in May 2016 he was due to pass on the mayoralty. Thus far, his place in government had been on what's called 'the political cabinet', a periphery to the actual Cabinet. Standing down as Mayor would leave him outside of most government decisions until Cameron gave him a proper job. It was arguably Cameron's biggest political mistake not to address this issue with more immediacy – bringing him closer to the inner circle and guaranteeing him a substantial role in the next parliament. Osborne was already established and getting to know all the new intake of MPs, inviting them to No. 11. In comparison, Johnson's networking was below par while his focus remained at City Hall.

MPs' support was crucial, as they would decide who the last two candidates in the next leadership contest would be, before the final choice was put to the party membership. It's notable that after the referendum, Johnson pulled out of his bid to become leader the moment he lost support from Gove. Despite having a swell of patronage from party members, Johnson felt he simply didn't have the MPs required to make the final ballot without Gove's followers onside. The stooge would become king-slayer, just like his favourite character from *Game of Thrones*.

The situation for Johnson pre-referendum looked just as dire. It wasn't just the lack of support network. With the Conservatives in power and the opposition looking weak, it would be much harder for Johnson to persuade his party not to choose Osborne as the obvious continuity candidate. As one minister put it at the time: 'Boris hasn't got a chance as long as Corbyn is Labour leader. He's the one you pick if we need a bit extra, something special – and, at the moment, we don't.'[23]

James Forsyth wrote in *The Spectator* in October 2015:

At present, it seems like only a political tidal wave could halt Osborne – and one may arrive, in the form of the EU referendum. The Chancellor will almost certainly vote to stay in. Should the Mayor campaign to leave, he would instantly separate himself from Cameron and Osborne and align himself with the instincts of a large swath of both Tory MPs and the grass roots membership. One well-connected Tory peer who will support and raise money for Osborne says, 'If it wasn't for the European issue, George's network would make him unstoppable.'

Johnson must have been very conscious of this and perhaps that is why he delicately made life difficult for his leader over the renegotiations. His approach was subtler than that of Eurosceptics such as Liam Fox or Bernard Jenkin. Johnson would express his confidence in Cameron's ability to renegotiate the reforms, while also raising expectations over what could be achieved. In his view, Cameron needed to obtain wide-scale changes on issues such as the Common Agricultural Policy as well as a repatriation of social and employment laws.

As a newly elected MP for Uxbridge and South Ruislip, Johnson used his first speech in Parliament for seven years to publicly advise the Prime Minister that he should be prepared to walk away if the talks failed. Furthermore, he suggested that Britain could be just as prosperous if it negotiated a free trade agreement with the EU. 'If you are going to go into a difficult international negotiation, you have to be prepared to walk away if you do not get the result you want,'[24] he said.

He later privately asked Cameron to allow him to take on the role of chief negotiator with the EU – which, while it might have been tempting to tie him into agreeing the tabled measures, equally, it could have been disastrous if Johnson had deliberately aimed too high and scuttled the deal. Cameron wanted to be at the helm of his own destiny.

So did Johnson. It's worth considering all of his comments and actions at the time against the recognition that a referendum was perhaps the only way he could disrupt Osborne's route to power. The question is: how much did Cameron appreciate this – and could he have neutralised Johnson by pandering to these aspirations? This is politics, after all. A source close to Cameron says the PM was well aware of Johnson's ambitions and had assured him he would get a top role in a Cabinet reshuffle after the referendum – probably as Foreign or Defence Secretary. The source added: 'Do you seriously think that Boris, Theresa May and Gove did not see this as a career opportunity? How do you stop people seeing it as a career opportunity?'

But Alan Johnson, chair of the Labour In campaign, says he was surprised Cameron didn't have his ducks in a row. He said:

> The big thing I can't understand is, we know Cameron wanted to win – everyone knew if he didn't win he'd have to go. But he didn't seem to do the work that you need to do. So in trade unions in the Labour Party, where we are much more of a membership organisation, you have to do deals to get them onside – we are used to this world and of course he's not used to that world. But I would never

have believed that he'd fail to get Gove and Boris Johnson onside. So here's his problem – he can't even convince his friends!

Alan Johnson says he met George Osborne in February 2016 in Hull and spent forty-five minutes talking about Europe. The Chancellor then told Alan: 'Chris Grayling will be out, but Michael will be fine and Boris will be fine.'

Osborne had read the reports in Westminster that when Johnson had been approached by the Leave camp, he'd told them: 'The trouble is, I am not an "outer".'[25] Furthermore, in an article in the *Daily Telegraph* on 7 February, he'd written:

> It is … true that the single market is of considerable value to many UK companies and consumers, and that leaving would cause at least some business uncertainty, while embroiling the government for several years in a fiddly process of negotiating new arrangements, so diverting energy from the real problems of this country – low skills, low social mobility, low investment etc. – that have nothing to do with Europe.[26]

However, he also described the argument for Brexit as 'balanced on a knife-point'.

He went on: 'Against these points we must enter the woeful defects of the EU. It is manifestly undemocratic and in some ways getting worse. It is wasteful, expensive and occasionally corrupt. The Common Agricultural Policy is iniquitous towards developing countries.'[27] On 15 February, Johnson promised in a TV interview that he would soon 'come off the fence with deafening éclat'. He added: 'Whatever happens, you will hear a lot from me. You don't have long to wait.'[28] Then, on 16 February 2016, came the moment when history became locked onto a certain track. Boris Johnson invited Michael Gove and his wife for dinner at his house in Islington.

Arguably, this dinner was the most significant event of the referendum; the confluence of two men who had been separately wrestling with the biggest question of their careers. Soon their fates would become entwined and equally their decisions would rock the future of their Prime Minister.

In an odd twist, the Russian owner of the *Evening Standard*, Evgeny Lebedev, was also at the dinner, along with Johnson's and Gove's wives. Sarah Vine described Johnson as 'agitated, genuinely tortured as to which way to go'[29] and as the slow-roasted shoulder of lamb was served, a call came in from Cabinet minister Oliver Letwin.

Letwin had been charged by David Cameron with devising a sovereignty law that would allow the UK Parliament to overturn certain EU directives. The legislation was something that had been suggested by Johnson and was being explored in an effort to secure his support for the government. He had floated the idea in November that, as the Germans could use judges in Karlsruhe to overturn EU measures at odds with its constitution, the UK could introduce a similar procedure to ensure authority over the European Court of Justice. One problem is that Britain doesn't have a written constitution for UK judges to use as a guide, and legal minds including that of Justice Secretary Michael Gove had examined the proposal and come up blank.

Ever the optimist, Letwin attempted to convince Johnson that his idea might fly – a unilateral sovereignty plan was still possible. If he could dangle the possibility, Johnson might fall on to the Remain side of the fence. However, when Johnson answered the phone, Letwin's flow was interrupted by him saying: 'Oliver, how good to hear from you. Do you mind if I put you on speakerphone? I've got the Lord Chancellor here.'[30]

Letwin apparently did a good job of swallowing his surprise. It was exactly a week since Gove had revealed to the PM his inability to support Remain, and apart from Letwin, Gove was the only other Cabinet minister with as much understanding of the flaws in his 'sovereignty lock' argument. Cameron was in Brussels beginning the last leg of his negotiations, and now Boris Johnson was entertaining the man they'd only just begun to realise was likely to lead the Out campaign.

Nonetheless, Letwin soldiered on. A lawyer was patched through from Barbados, and as the dinner proceeded, they thrashed though the complexities of EU law. Johnson and Gove listened hard, but the call ended with everyone clear that the sovereignty lock couldn't work. Gove and Johnson talked long into the night – in less than a week they would both out themselves as Outers.

Gove clearly influenced Johnson's eventual decision to support Leave. In many ways, Cameron's best chance would have been to stop the domino effect by convincing his Justice Secretary to back off. To begin with, he was simply blindsided by the belief that his loyal friend would never betray him, and therefore he didn't consider how Gove's decision might influence Johnson.

The London Mayor was not close to other Outers Chris Grayling or Theresa Villiers. His relationship with Iain Duncan Smith was fractious – he'd been a critic of IDS's leadership of the Conservatives when writing for *The Spectator*.

It seemed unlikely he would line up with the usual suspects unless he had a stronger partner in crime.

But director of Vote Leave Dominic Cummings believes Gove might have been persuaded by the PM to take a lower-profile role. He says:

They should have spoken to him properly earlier and got a clearer view. If I had been them, what I would have done, even after the *Times* article cock-up [Gove's indecision being leaked to *The Times*], I'd have said, 'OK, you want to support Leave. When the deal is done and we announce it, you can issue a statement saying you're voting Leave and you can even say why you're voting Leave, but you cannot criticise the deal. You just ignore the deal and you also say that you won't participate in the campaign, because you will be concentrating your entire time on the Ministry of Justice, and that's a fair deal, Michael.

'You are there because of us. We've given you this job. If your conscience tells you you can't support us then OK, but my god, Michael, you can't run around the country campaigning against us for the next two months – it is not on. This deal is fair for both sides.' That's what I would have done if I was them. It was worth a gamble. If they'd gagged him, it would've been all to their game.

Cummings was playing his own game – the director of Vote Leave had had talks with his friend and former colleague over the summer of 2015, and says that by November he was 95 per cent confident Gove would join the Leave camp. Then in January they had another long conversation which included Gove's wife. 'I'm going to be on your side,' Gove told him.

Failing to keep a close watch on Gove was clearly a mistake, and you can see how it happened in the context of the subordinate relationship we've established that Gove had with Cameron. But the bigger error was the lack of investment in persuading Boris Johnson, who was always far more wavering in his views. One government insider says, 'They didn't spend enough time talking to Boris,' adding that at one point George Osborne 'foolishly threatened Boris'. Johnson told a friend just before Christmas that Osborne had walked up to him and said, 'If you support the Leave campaign, I will destroy you.' This did nothing to discourage Johnson's competitive nature.

The day after his dinner with Gove, there was a last-ditch effort from No. 10 to win him over. Johnson was invited to Downing Street, where Cameron tried to get assurances of the Mayor's support. The forty-minute conversation was said to be heated and Cameron handed him a typed response to the points Johnson had made in his latest article in the *Telegraph*. Afterwards, Johnson told an ally: 'He looked down his nose at me. He handed me an essay reply to my article. It was rubbish, utter bunkum. We ended up having a row. He got all pinch-cheeked.' Cameron first made it clear that he didn't consider Johnson a rival, saying, 'I'm not competing with you. We're not competing together. I'm the Prime Minister,' before adding: 'What you're saying is that you can negotiate better than me, and I don't think you can.'[31] Johnson left No. 10 cryptically telling the press pack outside, 'No deal, I'll be back.'

Another unexpected factor in all of this was the role of Johnson's wife, human rights lawyer Marina Wheeler. In November, Dominic Cummings went to Johnson's for a drink and he got talking to Wheeler and discovered she was worried about the ECJ and human rights law. Cummings, whose uncle was a Court of Appeal judge, had a long conversation with Wheeler for a while and Boris sat listening to it all. At the end of it, Cummings was extremely encouraged about the potential influence Johnson's wife might have on him. 'I thought, that's a bit of a wild card.'

On 13 February, Marina Wheeler wrote an article in *The Spectator* magazine expressing concerns that the EU's Court of Justice had extended its reach 'to a point where the status quo is untenable'. She argued that national sovereignty was being eroded and good governance undermined because of new rights being given to the court. Europe, she said, had reneged on an assurance in the Lisbon Treaty. An opt-out called 'Protocol 30' suggested the charter would not affect Britain. But Wheeler cited the case of an Afghan asylum seeker who sought to use a human rights defence when the UK attempted to return him to Greece under the Dublin Convention. The hearing was referred to the Court of Justice in Luxembourg. It ruled that the British opt-out was not intended to exempt the UK from its human rights obligations under the Charter of Fundamental Rights. Thus, the opt-out had no legal force and the Charter of Fundamental Rights applied in the UK. Wheeler expressed frustration at this decision and disappointment that Cameron was not using the renegotiation 'to reassert any form of Charter opt-out or control over its scope'.[32]

Boris Johnson admits his wife did have an influence on him. Friends believe she told him: 'I think you should go for it.' But by the time Cameron entered the final stages of his negotiation, Johnson famously told friends. 'I'm veering all over the place like a shopping trolley.'[33]

As David Cameron was setting off for his final round of renegotiations, Gove became steadfast that he would join Leave; word of this reached Cameron while he was still in Brussels. The other rebel Cabinet ministers had already met in the office of Iain Duncan Smith to stage-manage their announcement. In total, six would rebel, including Gove.

On Cameron's return to London, the PM held his Saturday cabinet at 10 a.m. and one by one each member declared their position, with Gove first to give his reasons for supporting Leave. Immediately afterwards, the Justice Secretary made his way to the headquarters of Vote Leave with his fellow rebels. He was joined by Iain Duncan Smith, the Work and Pensions secretary; John Whittingdale, the Culture Secretary and former Thatcher aide; Chris Grayling, the Leader of the Commons; Theresa Villiers, the Northern Ireland Secretary; and Priti Patel, the Employment Minister who attended Cabinet. The 'Gang of Six' posed next to a signed banner saying 'Let's take back control.' Images were captured that would be used time and again by broadcasters throughout the campaign.

Johnson would wobble for another day. Speculation over which way he would fall grew to fever pitch. On Saturday, he informed the Prime Minister by email before the Cabinet meeting that he would probably be backing Leave, but then later sent a text to say he was 'dithering'.[34] The next morning on BBC's *Marr* programme, the Prime Minister was asked if he had a message for his old university friend. He said:

> I would say to Boris what I say to everybody else, which is that we will be safer, we'll be stronger, we'll be better off inside the EU. I think the prospect of … linking arms with Nigel Farage and George Galloway and taking a leap into the dark is the wrong step for our country.[35]

Johnson's EU-supporting sister Rachel, whom he was staying with in Thame that weekend, told him what the PM had said and asked him how he felt about teaming up with the likes of Farage and Galloway. Everybody knew that this was probably the factor that was troubling Johnson more than anything – but Cummings had promised him Farage would be kept at arm's length from Vote Leave. He spent much of the weekend writing two articles for his morning column, where he had decided he would formally announce his stance. Only one of them would be published on Monday (although the second letter appeared after the referendum in the *Sunday Times*).

First he wrote a Leave-supporting article: 'There is only one way to get the change we need, and that is to vote to go.'[36] Having finished this, he imagined himself in the Remain camp and wrote: 'Britain is a great nation, a global force for good. It is surely a boon for the world and for Europe that she should be intimately engaged in the EU.'[37] The journalist was using trial-by-article to make his decision – and it was here that the natural Eurosceptic came out of him. By any account, even a Remainer would say his first article was more coherent.

On Sunday 21 February, newsrooms had been told to expect the decision in Johnson's Monday *Telegraph* column. As is often the protocol, the article would appear online at around 10 p.m. the night before, in time for the Sunday night programmes – and TV editors could expect some forewarning of the content, which would perhaps be released a few hours early, 'under embargo' until 10 p.m. You can imagine, therefore, that journalists were constantly checking their mailboxes and making numerous phone calls to sources.

At around midday, Sir Nicholas Soames, the former Defence Minister and Cameron loyalist, tweeted: 'Whatever my great friend Boris decides to do, I know that he is NOT an outer.'[38]

Slowly, speculation mounted during Sunday afternoon that Johnson might not stay silent much longer. Naturally, there were reporters outside his home the entire weekend. But at around 4.15 p.m., Faisal Islam, Sky's political editor, was given a tip to get to Islington immediately. He arrived alongside the BBC's political editor Laura Kuenssberg and Robert Peston from ITV, who'd obviously had the same message. They had all had more notice than David Cameron, who received a text nine minutes before Johnson finally emerged to face the pack of journalists who had amassed outside his home.

Standing in a swirl of cameras and microphones, Johnson told reporters that after a 'huge amount of heartache' he had made his 'agonisingly difficult' decision. He said: 'I will be advocating Vote Leave, or whatever it is called – I understand there are many of them.' He then suggested a No vote might not necessarily result in the UK pulling out of the EU altogether, but instead creating a new relationship based upon trade and cooperation, something he would restate in his *Telegraph* article the next day. It sparked speculation that he expected a second referendum, with the UK able to get better terms in Europe once it had voted Leave. It was an idea he would backtrack on a week later.

Johnson tried to temper his choice by telling the press: 'What I won't do is take part in loads of blooming TV debates against other members of my party.' A promise he didn't keep. Then addressing the comments made by the Prime Minister, and indeed his own sister, Johnson was clear that he would not be standing on a podium with 'George Galloway and other individuals – I won't do that either'. These were small consolations for a decision that everyone knew could be devastating to his Prime Minister.[39]

Later, Cameron remarked to a colleague: 'I can't understand why Boris, as leader of the great financial capital, won't support the City.' When he spoke on the phone to Craig Oliver, he described the Mayor as 'a confused Inner', but the pair accepted that they were now entering a new reality. 'It will be a proper fight now,' remarked Craig Oliver in his diary. 'The two biggest Conservatives locked in mortal combat.'[40]

Looking back, there was a certain naivety about Johnson's apparent belief that he would be a back-seat leaver – not taking platforms against Conservatives. As one Leave campaigner put it, 'Maybe he took the plunge not realising that this huge oxygen would rush in behind him and things would only get magnified from here in.'

No one, however, could deny that this moment in Islington was a game-changer. Remain were facing a formidable force – and let's not forget that Johnson could have been a leading player on the other side. Senior figures at Stronger In say if he'd been with them, he would have played a significant or even figure-head role. It is impossible to isolate a single factor behind the crucial 600,000 votes that created a margin of victory. But having the most popular politician in the country on the Leave side, not the Remain side, could easily be the difference between winning and losing.

In the view of executive director of Stronger In, Will Straw, Johnson's decision was the pivotal moment of the campaign.

In a campaign as complicated as this, it is very hard to point to a single decision or moment that was the critical thing for the campaign – but if you had to choose I think that that was the moment. If he had campaigned for Remain or stayed out of it, it is very hard to see how Leave could have won. Because who would they have had as their leader? It's a pretty unpleasant group. And that gave them both a brain in Michael Gove – which particularly helped the right-wing press to carve out an intellectual argument for leaving – and the heart in Johnson who gave them a lot of shy Tories. Let's not forget only 40 per cent of Tories voted for Remain. Corbyn has been rightly criticised and Cameron honourably resigned, but that is pretty extraordinary that only 40 per cent of his own supporters would go with him.

Some of Vote Leave's allure to Conservatives had to be down to Johnson. His decision (as we discussed in Reason 10) would also free up Farage to run his own style of campaign, with Johnson becoming the mainstream face of Leave. Johnson could tour the Conservative heartlands, mostly in the south, leaving Farage free to continue his project as pied piper to disaffected Labour voters, mostly in the north. The former UKIP leader says he was 'overjoyed' when Johnson made his move. However, at the moment he made his announcement in Islington, the question remained as to how much of an active role Johnson would take. It was almost decided for him the next day in Parliament.

On Monday 22 February, the Prime Minister could not contain his anger in the Commons chamber. He described Johnson's idea for a second vote as undemocratic and one 'for the birds'. The London Mayor shook his head and shouted, 'Rubbish.' The gloves were coming off: the old rivalry revealing itself. Cameron then made a remark that was probably not intended as a jibe at Johnson's marriage but was interpreted as such in the papers: 'I have known a number of couples who have begun divorce proceedings, but I do not know any who have begun divorce proceedings in order to renew their marriage vows.' The double meaning of the reference to Brexit was apparently lost on Johnson, but the PM's general line of attack wasn't. Cameron then appeared to question his motivations for backing Leave, telling the House: 'I am not standing for re-election. I have no other agenda than what is best for our country. I am standing here today telling you what I think. My responsibility as Prime Minister is to speak plainly about what I believe is right for our country.'[41]

In the meantime, it was being briefed to the papers that Johnson had only a week earlier assured the Remain side that he would be with them. It was becoming clear that they were ready to smear, discredit and create a narrative around his decision. Unless he started to get full-bloodedly stuck into the campaign, fighting for the cause he said he believed in, the country would simply see him as an opportunist.

Vote Leave's Paul Stephenson says this moment in the Commons pushed Johnson further over the edge. The 'thinly veiled reference to affairs and the second referendum basically humiliated him in front of his peers'. Johnson got on the phone to Stephenson straight after the encounter and said, 'We need a council of war.'

There is a difficult dichotomy here, because it can be argued that later in the campaign the Conservatives backed off from attacking Gove and Johnson – too eager to ensure there would be party unity afterwards. Labour peer Peter Mandelson, who helped orchestrate Stronger In, said:

> All the time we were being held back because the Prime Minister just simply didn't want – and I completely understand why – to deepen the chasm that had broken out in his own party. He thought that at the end of the day after he'd won the referendum he would have to bring everyone together and he didn't want to … poison the atmosphere any more. I said to George Osborne, we feel like sometimes we were taking a spoon to a knife fight.[42]

As we mentioned in Reason 13, there was a natural instinct at No. 10 to reduce 'blue on blue' contact and this was in part for the purposes of party management, but it was also about not provoking Johnson too much. It was difficult. For example, in April, George Osborne accused Vote Leave of being dishonest and 'economically illiterate'.[43] The comments were interpreted as a swipe at Johnson and Gove, and the more they poked, the greater the backlash. Johnson came back at the Chancellor, saying he was using economic warnings to frighten the public with 'an avalanche of scaremongering, a sort of Himalayan snow job of statistics'.[44] These political goliaths may have avoided a face-to-face fight, but it didn't stop the war of words through other means, and it became incredibly damaging for Cameron.

Not least because Johnson, the man who'd said he believed in Cameron's ability to get a deal in Europe, clearly didn't think he'd achieved it. And when the PM suggested that Johnson was just out for political gain and secretly supported Remain, Johnson responded by asking why the Prime Minister wasn't campaigning to Leave, based on the fact that he hadn't achieved the reforms set out in his Bloomberg speech. He also accused the government of 'systematic subterfuge'[45] in the way it portrayed its relationship with Europe. Here was a senior government figure attacking the government. The Mayor of London saying the City will be OK if the UK leaves. A former editor of *The Spectator* who was skilled in writing down his argument, but also one of the great orators in the party, who would fill the Tory Party conference hall whenever he made a speech.

Johnson's other strength was his acknowledged intellect. A self-proclaimed 'liberal cosmopolitan', he could break into German and sing the EU's national anthem. He had closely studied the EU, as he had the ancient languages of Greek and Latin. No one could accuse him of being small-minded: 'I can read novels in French and I can sing the Ode to Joy in German – and if they keep accusing me of being a Little Englander, I will,'[46] he said in a speech in May.

As the punches were thrown back and forth, the strategists at Vote Leave rubbed their hands in glee. When Johnson made reference to a federalist Europe being a realisation of Adolf Hitler's plans,[47] Deputy Prime Minister Michael Heseltine called the comments 'obscene'[48] and suggested that the strain was getting to Johnson. Dominic Cummings says every time someone criticised Johnson, it helped him to persuade his frontman to 'up the ante'.

In early May, Johnson and Gove made their most pointed attack, in a letter calling for the PM to ditch his ambition to limit net migration to the tens of thousands. They described the pledge as 'corrosive of public trust',[49] because, despite constant repetition, it had failed. The numbers were still rising at that time to over 300,000. This really marked the beginning of a gear change in Vote Leave's use of their star players to undermine the credibility of David Cameron. Two Cabinet ministers were openly damning about a promise that had been in their leader's manifestos in both 2010 and 2015 but never achieved. After this, it was open season. On the day of the Vote Leave bus launch in early May, Johnson accused the Prime Minister of 'demented scaremongering'[50] over comments that leaving the EU could threaten peace and security.

On the coach that day, co-author Jason Farrell asked him why he was making such personal attacks on the PM: 'None of those things I said about the Prime Minister personally,' responded Johnson. 'What I said is I think politicians saying that they can control immigration and then failing to do so by hundreds of thousands, a city the size of Newcastle every year, that is corrosive.' But this, of course, was a personal attack. Promising to control immigration, then not managing to do so, is what the Prime Minister had been doing since he entered No. 10, and everybody knew it.

Johnson's assaults were more wounding than any punch Nigel Farage could throw, not just because he was a Conservative but also because he was seen as a potential future leader of the party. This meant he could put forward policy ideas and people might envisage them being implemented. As we shall see later, Vote Leave exploited Johnson's ability to present what many saw as an alternative government with populist policies that had failed to have the same gravitas when previously suggested by the leader of UKIP.

In such a high-stakes game, Cameron did eventually endorse negative posters depicting Johnson rolling the dice, Gove drinking whisky and Farage smoking cigars in a casino together with the slogan 'Don't let them gamble on your future',[51] although he turned down one with Johnson in Nigel Farage's pocket, similar to the poster that had previously been used against Ed Miliband with the SNP during the general election. Former Prime Minister John Major was also unleashed to warn that if Boris Johnson, Michael Gove and Iain Duncan Smith rose to power following Brexit, the NHS would be 'about as safe with them as a pet hamster would be with a hungry python'. It was an extraordinary attack on his fellow Conservatives. He called their campaign deceitful and 'verging on the squalid'.[52]

We can see, then, that Johnson turned the campaign into a 'blue on blue' political death match and that became the best story in town. It meant that many days' coverage was lost on the question of who would be left standing as Prime Minister by the end of the year. It can be argued that this focus helped gloss over some of the essential details in the actual EU debate, but what is indisputable is that it helped Vote Leave set the agenda.

For days, Johnson could hijack the airwaves with stories about the Australian points system, Turkey joining the EU and £350 million being spent on the NHS. 'Broadcasters lapped it up,' says Vote Leave's Dominic Cummings.

> The media is obsessed with process and the snakes and ladders of careers. Many hacks said to me words to the effect: 'I don't care about the issues, I care about whether Cameron will still be PM at the end of the year.' We could not match No. 10 in the golden currency of 'names'. But we could give the media an even more valuable currency – a leadership story.

Within that story was of course a message about taking back control.

'The punch that he gave the campaign – and the ability to get the headlines – was amazing,' says Vote Leave chief executive Matthew Elliott.

We knew that Boris would be the most influential politician in the UK when it came to the decision. Because he had such a stellar Eurosceptic track record with his *Telegraph* articles – and because of his popularity within the Conservative grassroots and because he was seen as being odds on favourite to be the next leader of the Conservative Party. He would have had massive, massive sway if he went to the other side.

Elliott says initially he didn't think Johnson would be leader of the Leave campaign, having spoken to him about it a number of times in the run-up to his decision, but did know he was Eurosceptic. 'Not necessarily a Leaver', but on the Eurosceptic side of things.

But in Johnson, Elliott found his man who could demonstrate to people that Vote Leave 'wasn't just the loons' on the fringe of politics. That cartoon image from 1975 we mentioned at the start of Reason 14 couldn't now be applied to his 'front-bench' team. Johnson was a mainstream, popular, liberal politician and precisely the sort of person who would attract those swing voters he was looking to attract. The Leave side couldn't be portrayed as backwards-looking, as harking back to the 1950s. Here was someone whom the electorate saw as a future Prime Minister, saying to them: 'Yes, you can vote to leave and yes, it will be a great future.' It was hugely powerful compared to the alternative of rather unknown, less charismatic Cabinet ministers such as Chris Grayling, or former Cabinet ministers or politicians last seen in the 1980s, even though they might have been saying the same thing. 'We won by 2 per cent,' says Elliott. 'Boris Johnson brought us much more than 2 per cent. We wouldn't have won without him.'

On the day Johnson declared he would be campaigning for Leave, bookies had their first big influx of people betting on Leave. The pound also fell 1.72 per cent against the dollar, its worst daily performance in nearly six years. Moody's suggested that the UK may have to downgrade the UK's credit rating. It all seemed like a bit of an overreaction to one person's decision, but it wasn't – if anything, it was understated.

FEAR FATIGUE AND THE DEATH OF EXPERTS

On 2 and 3 June 2016, Prime Minister David Cameron and chair of Vote Leave Michael Gove were interviewed on successive nights by Sky News political editor Faisal Islam. It was the first big televised event of the referendum and it would provide the defining quote of the campaign.

Vote Leave chose Michael Gove to do the Sky News debate because their focus groups showed people trusted him. This was quite a turnaround from two years previously, when David Cameron axed him from his role as Education Secretary and sidelined him during the 2015 general election for being 'toxic'. But by 2016, he was reborn as a man of principle. In his move to become a Leave campaigner, he walked through the looking glass and suddenly people liked him, they respected what he said and they applauded his heroic defiance against his old friend David Cameron.

Unlike Boris Johnson, there was no suggestion he was motivated by ambitions for No. 10. If anything, Gove had damaged his career by campaigning to leave and this had bolstered his credibility. A senior Vote Leave source says that the general view of focus groups was: 'They saw a man who had gone against his own self-interest. Essentially, he betrayed his best friend to campaign for Leave and therefore he must be principled and telling the truth. He deserved to be listened to.' That this betrayal was seen as 'principled' already tells us that something was going on in the British consciousness during the referendum campaign.

The Leave camp had a much more obvious choice for the Sky News interview in our protagonist from the previous chapter, Boris Johnson. He had the best opinion ratings of any British politician. This said, however, during the campaign his trust ratings slipped the more he was exposed to scrutiny. It was decided that he wasn't right for the format of a twenty-minute interview followed by a grilling from the studio audience. In early March, he had struggled in his first main appearance as a leading campaigner for Vote Leave on Andrew Marr's Sunday programme. He came unstuck when Marr pointed out that he'd previously said on the show: 'I want to campaign for the single market,'[1] and while Johnson insisted he only wanted free trade with the EU, Marr was able to clearly demonstrate that he'd changed his view. A Leave source admits he'd been badly prepped, partly because at that stage the campaign hadn't decided its stance on the single market.

> We were still a little bit iffy on membership of the single market versus access to the single market and really nailing our phrases… Yes, we wanted to have a free trade option and yes, we wanted a British option that was unique, not the Swiss one not the Norwegian one. But we hadn't really nailed lines to take on that.

It was after Johnson's interview that they decided to sort that out. But the source goes on:

> Boris could make a brilliant speech, but he wasn't a details man like Michael. As Mayor of London, his media appearances were always much more controlled. There were hundreds of pictures of him opening something or holding a cricket bat or a tennis racket, but he actually hadn't had much experience of either the cut and thrust of parliamentary debate or media debate one-to-one.

The Leave team brought in Republican political strategist Brett O'Donnell to coach Gove for the performance. O'Donnell had previously guided Senate candidates in the US and Mitt Romney during his presidential campaign. Now he set out to discipline Gove's messaging during the interview, to focus him on key lines such as 'take back control'. He also wanted to work on his geeky image and make him seem more human. Gove's father's fish processing business had apparently suffered the consequences of EU fisheries policy when he was a teenager, according to Gove (later denied by his father). O'Donnell insisted he should bring this up. Gove later told the authors: 'My views on Europe and the EU were formed over many years by a number of factors. One of them, undeniably, was my father's experience seeing the Common Fisheries Policy cause such damage to Scotland's fishing industry.'

The Justice Secretary was an Oxford Union debater, and was good at writing one-liners for David Cameron to use in Prime Minister's Questions, but had never been a front man on such a big stage. How would he stack up against the Prime Minister? The night before his own Sky News showdown, Gove watched his old friend go through the process. The PM faced a tough line of questioning. Islam asked: 'What comes first? World War III, or the global Brexit recession?' – a reference to the negative campaigning by Stronger In. The audience loved it. The Prime Minister had the humiliation of waiting for the laughter to subside before he could answer. One thing was obvious – there was a visceral public reaction against the use of scare tactics over the EU. Could Gove tap into that disdain?[2]

Islam had also prepped hard for the interviews. The Sky News political editor was getting a rare moment in his career: the chance to interview the Prime Minister in a twenty-minute one-on-one session followed the next night by the same format with the chosen figurehead of the Leave camp. Twenty-four hours would separate them, but it was the closest the PM would allow to a senior Conservative from his Cabinet effectively facing off against him.

Islam spent time going through Cameron and Gove's core messages and attempting to map the interview. His team, led by Sky's head of politics Esme Wren, didn't just prep the questions – they tried to work out the answers and the follow-ups; what buttons could they use to push the interviewees into uncharted territory, to squeeze out something they hadn't expected to say. For Gove, his weak spot had to be the dire warnings from economic experts about the dangers of Brexit.

Not long into the interview, Islam ran off the list of significant people and respected institutions that had signalled the dangers of Brexit: 'The leaders of the US, India, China, Australia, every single one of our allies, the Bank of England...' Gove seemed to know it would be a long list and reached under the desk to douse his drying throat with a glass of water. '...the IFS, the IMF, the CBI, five former NATO secretary-generals,' continued Islam in rapid fire, 'the chief exec of the NHS and most of the leaders of the trades unions.' All of them supported Remain – who did Gove have?

Out came the prepared lines. The public should 'trust themselves' and 'take back control'. A sizeable chunk of the audience applauded. Gove went on: those backing the Remain campaign had done 'very well thank you out of the

European Union'. They had 'vested financial interests' and didn't represent working people because they were 'distant' and 'elitist'. Islam jumped in. How could an Oxford University-educated, Lord High Chancellor attack others for being elitist? Gove pushed back, already calculating that soon would be the moment to mention his father's fishing business. It was time for a 'fair deal' for working people, he said. Islam was trying to cut in again when out came Gove's famous line: 'People in this country have had enough of experts.'

Before Gove could qualify that he meant people with lots of letters after their name who have frequently said they know what is best but have actually been consistently wrong, Islam repeated the line twice in disbelief – 'People have had enough of experts? What do you mean...? This is Oxbridge Trump!' he exclaimed.[3]

Gove believes that his quote was later distorted and used against him. He says:

> I was very specific – I said in terms that the experts people had had enough of were those from organisations with acronyms which had got things consistently wrong in the past. The IMF, OECD and others called the euro wrong, as they called the referendum wrong. But the words have subsequently been consistently misrepresented in an effort to discredit the Leave case.

But Gove had landed on a massive truth. People had had enough of experts, and particularly their deployment in what had been dubbed 'Project Fear'. The British public had lost faith in politicians, economists, FTSE 100 directors, statisticians, pollsters, Bank of England Governors and world leaders. This was a real issue for the Remain camp, and the problem boiled down to two things. Firstly, that what Michael Gove said was true, and secondly that Project Fear – backed up by experts – was all the Stronger In campaign had.

It turns out that even this line about experts was a calculated sound bite put there by Vote Leave coordinator Dan Hannan. 'I may have implanted the idea with Michael,' admits Hannan, 'but I can't claim authorship. I was channelling the great American Conservative Bill Buckley.' Buckley's great dictum was: 'I would rather entrust the government of the United States to the first 400 people listed in the Boston telephone directory than to the faculty of Harvard University.'[4]

Hannan believes this applies well beyond the EU. 'There is a fascinating academic discipline in why clever people make mistakes and it has a lot to do with the "group-think" that comes with self-reinforcing assumptions, especially in careers like economics. Yet we keep trusting them because they have a string of letters after their names.' That trust was fading. In many ways, it had been ground down by overuse.

The first indication of the Prime Minister's expert-led, fear-based strategy came from an account of a private meeting between Cameron and fellow EU leaders, which was leaked to *The Guardian* in July 2015. It stated: 'He believes that people will ultimately vote for the status quo if the alternatives can be made to appear risky.'[5] The leak was embarrassing to the PM because it showed ahead of his negotiations that he was already preparing to campaign for Remain. But it was no surprise Cameron was considering a risk-focused approach, as it was how he had run previous campaigns.

He first deployed the tactics during the Scottish independence referendum in 2014. The phrase 'Project Fear' was actually coined as a joke by Rob Shorthouse, director of communications for Better Together, the cross-party umbrella organisation that opposed Scottish independence.[6]

Pro-independence campaigners seized on the expression in an effort to undermine the series of negative stories pumped out by their opponents. Then First Minister Alex Salmond taunted Better Together chairman Alistair Darling in their first televised debate, asking Darling: 'Why does the No campaign call itself Project Fear?'[7] Darling denied it.

However, the warnings about possible financial consequences of breaking up the Union proved effective, creating uncertainty in the minds of voters over the economics of leaving. Businesses could leave Scotland. Scotland could lose the pound. Experts, economists, business leaders and the Governor of the Bank of England all backed up the warnings. In the battle for hearts over heads, heads won. Scotland voted No to independence by a margin of 55 to 45.

During the general election in 2015, Tory strategist Lynton Crosby once again analysed the British psyche and deduced that they would be susceptible to fear again. Forget positive visions and optimistic promises – pure negativity would claim victory.

On paper, Labour ran a better campaign in 2015, with agenda-setting policy announcements rolled out at least once a week, steering coverage onto popular left-wing issues such as ending zero-hours contracts, closing non-dom tax loopholes, tackling the cost of living and increasing staff numbers in the NHS. By comparison, the Conservatives seemed devoid of any eye-catching new ideas. The £8 billion promise on NHS funding was late in the day and unfunded. A new right-to-buy policy was a throwback to Margaret Thatcher, suggesting a lack of original thought.

When Labour had a good day, like when they attacked non-doms (people taking advantage of a loophole not to pay tax on their overseas income), Crosby would indulge his classic tactic of 'throwing a dead cat on the table'. This meant saying something that would get people and journalists talking about something else besides their opponents' agenda ('Oh look, it's a dead cat'). In this April 2015 case, it was a personal attack by Conservative Defence Secretary Michael Fallon on Ed Miliband. Referring to Miliband beating his brother in the 2010 Labour leadership election and concerns about a future Labour coalition deal with the SNP, Fallon said: 'Miliband stabbed his own brother in the back to become Labour leader. Now he is willing to stab the United Kingdom in the back to become Prime Minister.'[8]

Over the six weeks, Crosby mostly hammered and refined one key message: that a Labour–SNP coalition would leave people worse off. Don't vote for a Labour government 'propped up by the SNP'. The Tories successfully persuaded the British public that this coalition could happen and that it would damage personal finances and endanger jobs. It was the perfect fear tactic because there was nothing people in England could do about the SNP other than watch. The Nationalists, who wanted to break up the UK, were predicted to win a massive landslide against Labour in Scotland and they did. In one Sky News interview, Theresa May used the phrase 'propped up by the SNP' five times in five minutes.[9] It was tiresome, it told us nothing about what the Conservatives would do in power, but it worked. It shattered Ed Miliband's hopes of becoming Prime Minister. England voted Conservative in enough numbers to carry the UK into a majority Tory government.

So the lesson of 2015 was the same lesson of 2014. Australian strategist Lynton Crosby, dubbed the Wizard of Oz, was right: a narrow, relentless focus on the economy was enough. The majority of people in Britain simply wanted to keep their heads down and maintain the status quo. The average man and woman had seen no real salary rise in the past eight years and were mortgaged up to their necks. They clung to the hope that their one asset, if they were lucky enough to own the roof over their head, would continue to increase in value as long as interest rates remained low and the 'long-term economic plan' stayed on track. No one could risk another shock on the scale of what they'd seen in 2008. Surely that same fear would prevail over the EU question?

It seems no one considered that the British public might get fear fatigue; that similar tactics during two referendums and a general election in the space of three years might get wearisome; that expert predictions might lose their hypnotic powers; that other fears might trump economic fear.

The problem, though, from the very start, was that economic fear had to work because Stronger In had no alternative message.

In July 2015, Andrew Cooper, the Conservative peer and chair of the opinion polling company Populus, was recruited to research public sentiment, with a view to developing a line of attack for Stronger In. Cooper had advised Cameron in the coalition period and had been instrumental in the Better Together campaign in Scotland. He put together focus groups using people who were undecided over how they would vote in a referendum on Europe. His team would then just ask them to give positives and negatives about the EU. What the study discovered was disturbing. People with no affiliation to either camp struggled to think of the benefits of remaining in the EU. These were voters that were up for grabs in the referendum and 'they couldn't tell you a single tangible thing that was good about the EU for them and their family', observed Will Straw, the executive director for Stronger In. But they could immediately muster up all of the core arguments for leaving. Unprompted, they would say things like, 'We spend loads of money, don't we, on the EU?' or, 'They make loads of laws in Europe that we have to abide by,' and, as you might expect, 'There's loads of European immigrants.' Without much thought or prompting, people from any walk of life could rattle off the three key messages of the Leave campaign – before the Leave campaign had even begun. Those were: cost, sovereignty and immigration.

When asked for arguments about the positive benefits of the European Union, people in the focus groups had only a very a vague understanding that it was good for the economy but without being able to explain how or why, or in what areas, or what it meant to them. 'For three decades – or longer – since Maastricht there was a steady drumbeat in large parts of the British press, in large parts of the Conservative Party and in large parts of the country of just a relentless negativity about European membership,' says James McGrory, Stronger In's head of media. 'We knew the challenge. You are not going to overturn thirty years of rabid Euroscepticism in Britain and in four months turn it into a nation of Europhiles. This was not going to happen.'

They might, however, be able to pick at that nagging public concern about economics. So, while Stronger In started out with positive messaging about the benefits of the EU, they soon adapted. They decided not to run a pro-European educational campaign, but instead focus on the economy. The slogan was developed: 'Stronger, safer, better off.' It sounds upbeat, but in reality whatever negatives the Leave camp could throw at them, their comeback was an even greater negativity at the prospect of leaving. The early focus groups convinced the Stronger In campaign that there simply wasn't time to change entrenched downbeat perceptions about the EU. So began Project Fear Mark III.

The Leave camp could be thankful that the Scottish referendum had produced a catchy negative name for Stronger In's strategy, and that the public would instantly know it when they saw it. And while the pound in Scotland was something treasured, with consequences of its loss people could understand, EU membership – as we've established – came with built-in public cynicism. So that was problem number one, fear fatigue.

Problem two was overconfidence. Firstly, had anyone questioned how well Project Fear had *really* worked in Scotland? Yes, the Scots voted No. But No had started the campaign with a twenty-point lead and ended it with a ten-point lead. Indeed, had they not had Gordon Brown's last-minute passionate intervention and an eleventh-hour pledge to offer Scotland more powers (not something available to Stronger In when the going got particularly tough in the last month of the campaign) – the lead may have dropped even further. Then look what happened afterwards. The SNP surged and changed the face of British politics. Was fear overrated? Had the Conservatives really pulled off a miracle campaign in 2015, or could people just never really see Ed Miliband as Prime Minister? Was too much credit given to strategic masterminding? As Nick Clegg puts it, 'It had gone to their heads. They believed electorally they could walk on water.'

A Tory sense of invincibility came with Cameron's unexpected victory in 2015, and after the EU renegotiations, David Cameron's team joined the Remain campaign. The PM's head of communications Craig Oliver moved from No. 10 into the Stronger In headquarters in Cannon Street, working alongside former Conservative deputy chair Stephen Gilbert and director of strategy at Downing Street Ameet Gill. Old party rivalries were banished from the war room.

Researchers and press officers who had been at each other's throats six months ago during the general election now all found themselves on the same barricade. Former Labour staffers would have to suck up the bluster of the Downing Street contingent. 'They arrived like an occupying force,' recalls one former Labour staffer.[10] James McGrory and Ryan Coetzee, both former advisors to Nick Clegg, were used to dealing with the Tory team from their coalition days and suspected the decree from the Tory election-winning machine would be to double-down on the economy.

'They said, "That was what won the day in Scotland two years ago, messages about what's best for the economy,"' says McGrory.

> It's what won the Tories the election in 2015 and our polling told us that economic risk for those people in the middle was the most salient factor in their vote, more than immigration. It was a persuasive case – it worked in 2014, it worked in 2015 and our polling says this one can be won on the economy as well. Hindsight might say it was wrong – but that is quite a compelling argument on which to base a campaign.

It was decided, as with 2015, that people would only be persuaded to Remain if they could be convinced Brexit would have a financial impact on them. Craig Oliver says:

> They do not believe in the European project; that Berlin, Paris, Budapest and London are all the same. They do not believe it and if you try and tell them that they say, 'I've had forty years of crap telling me about bendy bananas.' The only thing that persuades them is their pocket.

Any potential weakness in this strategy was masked to begin with by the natural advantages of being on the side of government. In the early stages of campaigning, Stronger In had the Whitehall machine at its disposal. This meant work could be done, reports could be commissioned and leaflets could be distributed using government money and resources. For example, on 6 April, a pro-EU information booklet was sent out to every home.[11] Leave campaigners could argue that this was an abuse of taxpayers' money, but they couldn't stop it and they didn't have the funds to match it. On 27 May 2016, four weeks before the poll, the government would be prohibited from using public resources to publish any material to support their campaign, a period known as 'purdah' (more about this in Reason 18). So they came out of the blocks early.

On 18 April, the Treasury published a report on the long-term impact of Brexit. The Chancellor said that leaving the EU 'would be the most extraordinary self-inflicted wound'.[12] He warned that as a result every UK household would be £4,300 worse off. It's understandable that George Osborne tried to find a figure with which to frame his report. It would help grab the headlines – in the way that Vote Leave had with the £350 million a week banner on their bus. And £4,300 was a stunning figure, a frightening figure – but no one could believe it. Even the Conservative-supporting *Spectator* described his announcement as 'breathtaking dishonesty'. Fraser Nelson wrote: 'I'm a Europhile, but these are the kinds of tactics that make me want to vote "out" – the appalling level of dishonesty with which the government is making the case.'[13]

Osborne had picked 2030 as the date by which this £4,300 figure would become a reality for families, a long way off for any forecast to claim accuracy. How could this prediction be deemed credible? What's more, people wouldn't actually be worse off even by the Treasury's own analysis. It showed the economy would still grow outside the EU, just not as fast. On top of this, Osborne had translated the reduced growth in GDP to loss of household income when in reality the two things are not directly related and don't move in tandem. Finally, he had not allowed for the fact that there would be more households in 2030; he divided the reduced amount by the present-day number. Even if Osborne was right that the decision to leave the EU would leave the UK 'permanently poorer', there were holes in his calculations. It was sloppy.

There was another, more fundamental, reason why this figure didn't have its desired impact. It was making an argument that many people just didn't instinctively believe.

'The majority of people believed that being in the EU was a cost to the UK, and therefore coming out of it would be a saving,' says Stronger In executive director Will Straw. 'So when we said no – it will cost you to leave – they didn't believe that, because that wasn't what thirty years of propaganda had told them. That was where the credibility issue came in – not the number itself – but that we were claiming it was a minus side rather than a plus side to leave.'

Remain campaigners had to explain something that voters didn't immediately understand. Leaving the EU could mean less trade, and less trade might mean less investment and fewer jobs. They also had to try to explain that the pound would fall in value and that could lead to higher prices in the shops. There were a lot of dots to join up, and it couldn't be done with one wrongly calculated figure. Unlike Leave's controversial £350 million a week claim, it wasn't intuitive to the British public. 'They knew successive Prime Ministers had fought to reduce the EU's budget but it kept going up,' says Paul Stephenson, Vote Leave director of communications. 'They knew we put in more than we got back. They knew the EU did not spend their money wisely.'

Will Straw agrees: 'We tested it [the £4,300 figure] in focus groups and we found that people really pushed back on it. You've got to remember that this is in the context of the Leave campaign using a completely discredited figure, £350 million a week.'

An Ipsos MORI poll in the week before the referendum found that 47 per cent of people believed the claim that the UK pays £350 million a week to the EU – but only 17 per cent believed the Treasury's projection that Brexit would make every household £4,300 worse off per year and permanently poorer.[14]

Straw added:

They were putting out some absolutely bogus numbers, and similarly because of that the arms race of rhetoric meant that if you wanted to get on the news then you needed something really eye-catching to splash the papers or to get on top of the bulletins. Bringing out a report that said, 'It's really complicated to put a hard number on this – but we think the range is somewhere between x and y' – it doesn't work – you have to put a figure on it.

This is a hugely significant point Will Straw makes, because it's notable that the £4,300 figure stopped being used. It wasn't used in the BBC debate days before the vote and it didn't feature when David Cameron did TV interviews. There's quite a strong argument that this was a mistake. As Straw points out, the £350 million figure was discredited, but Leave continued to use it. Travelling on the campaign trails, it was noticeable that members of the public knew the £350 million figure and would quote it back. That's the definition of a successful message – people start using it. People become 'the message carriers'. The same was true during the general election of George Osborne's 'long-term economic plan', and 'propped up by the SNP'. These phrases were quoted back to reporters on high streets, in pubs and in workplaces. This never happened with the £4,300 figure.

Perhaps it could have been simplified to the average family losing £80 a week. Could anyone afford that kind of hit? Wouldn't the poorest families be hit hardest? But that message wasn't pushed. The figure was rarely used. What would Lynton have done?

Stronger In did expand its financial argument, but without a consistent, tangible, relatable figure on how it would affect real people. Instead, in some ways, they played into the narrative of representing an out-of-touch elite. The Bank of England Governor Mark Carney was next up, warning of 'material effects' and a 'technical recession', defined as two consecutive quarters of falling economic output.[15] To most people, that didn't have much meaning.

Then came the International Monetary Fund's assessment, which was equally detached from everyday reality. Christine Lagarde's 'tough love' message focused on maintaining London's status as a financial centre and the impact on global markets. It had self-interest written all over it. The IMF predicted losses of between 1 and 9 per cent of GDP. They tackled Leave's £350 million a week claim by warning of 'net fiscal losses' for the UK, because reduced revenue due to lower output would 'more than offset any gains from eliminating the UK's net EU budget contribution of 0.3 per cent of GDP'.[16] Is that a slogan you can put on the side of a bus? Does anyone understand GDP? Did that equate to money for a local hospital?

Robert Kennedy once said of GDP:

> Our gross national product … counts air pollution and cigarette advertising and ambulances … Yet [it] does not allow for the health of our children, the quality of their education … or the strength of our marriages. It measures neither our wit nor our courage, neither our wisdom nor our learning, neither our compassion nor our devotion to our country. It measures everything, in short, except that which makes life worthwhile.[17]

An audience member in a town hall gathering in Newcastle put it even more eloquently during the referendum campaign. When the invited panel of experts began to discuss the potential impact of EU departure on the UK's GDP, he shouted: 'That's your bloody GDP, not ours.'

Voters were not making a personal connection that their own standard of living would be affected by Brexit. Anand Menon, professor of European politics and foreign affairs at King's College, who recounted the moment in Newcastle, says:

> Where jobs are insecure, wages are depressed, housing is scarce, and education levels are far below those in London, there is a profound unease with the kind of aggregate statistics bandied about by experts. Membership [of] the single market may have increased the GDP of the whole country, but it didn't make a difference everywhere.[18]

There's often a lot of focus on why disaffected Labour voters had lost trust in experts, but it was also true of many Conservatives. Retired accountant Harold Young, whom we met in Reasons 4 and 5 and who voted Yes in 1975 and Leave in 2016, had also had enough of Project Fear. 'First of all I didn't believe it, and secondly I didn't care,' he says.

> We needed to make up for the fact that we'd been asset-stripped for the last few decades. The EU economists got it wrong. Look at what happened in Greece – the Germans seemed to think you could get away with selling stuff to people who couldn't afford it. They couldn't work out that if you do that you end up having to give them the money. Economists only work on principles – but they often don't understand how finance works. If you owe the bank £10,000, you've got a problem. If you owe the bank £1 million, the bank has a problem.

So, there was a declining trust in experts in many quarters of society. This was particularly true of matters concerning the EU because some of these institutions had, as Harold Young infers, already blotted their copybooks over the euro. One of the great 'what ifs' of recent history is what would have happened if the UK had joined the euro. It may have helped stabilise Europe in difficult times, but the received wisdom was that the UK had a lucky escape. British interest rates would have been lower during the good times and fuelled an even bigger credit boom, meaning the 2008 banking bust would have ploughed through the UK economy with even more destructive force. Without a Bank of England, the UK would not have been able to use the quantitative easing (QE) programme initiated in 2009, which helped stop money stocks collapsing by 'printing money' and using it to buy bonds from investors, making more money available. Countries unable to deploy QE experienced much worse price deflation and their banking sectors crumpled. The man in the street looked at Greece and Spain on the news and thought, thank God we're not them, and thank God we are not bailing them out. David Cameron reinforced this view by reassuring the country that the UK was exempt from responsibility because it wasn't part of the failing Eurozone.[19]

The problem was that a number of pro-EU politicians, business leaders and the Confederation of British Industry had all wanted to join the euro. This gave Leave the easy hit: 'They were wrong then and they are wrong now.'[20] It helped box in some powerful campaigners. Richard Branson, for example, was unapologetic, saying that if we had been part of the euro, 'our currency would be cheaper'. His track record on supporting the euro damaged his message that 'it would be madness to leave the EU'.[21]

It seemed big pro-EU business leaders could only see things from the perspective of their business ventures. When former M&S boss Stuart Rose became chairman of Britain in Europe, he didn't get off to the best of starts. First, he told *The Times* that 'nothing is going to happen if we come out of Europe in the first five years, probably. There will be absolutely no change,'[22] a quote that was seized upon by the Out campaign. But then he made an even bigger gaffe. Appearing before the Treasury Select Committee, Rose was asked by the Labour MP Wes Streeting: 'If free movement were to end following Brexit, is it not reasonable to suppose that we could see increases in wages for low-skilled workers in the UK?' To which Rose replied: 'If you're short of labour, the price of labour would go up. So yes. But that's not necessarily a good thing.'[23]

The head of the Remain campaign appeared to have let slip that by voting to leave the EU, people might get paid more money.

Rose was of course making the point that it wasn't necessarily good because conversely people might lose their jobs. This is because basic economics suggests that if wages and thus costs go up, and firms can't pass those costs onto the consumer by raising their prices, then they might respond by hiring fewer workers. But good economics doesn't always make good politics, and by saying this Rose reminded us that he isn't a politician. Politicians did, however, seem to fail to convey this key message about job security. During the coalition government, in June 2014, the Liberal Democrats disclosed a Treasury report. It showed that 3 million jobs were directly linked to the EU. The Stronger In campaign was in fact very disciplined about using this fact – always being clear that the jobs were 'linked' to the EU, not dependent on it. They hardly got any criticism for the figure, partly because they were actually too timid in its use.

There is no doubt that Remain had to place emphasis on the economy, but Will Straw, like many others, thinks more should have been done to establish the benefits of being in the EU. His analysis was that if people could see the advantages of being in, as well as the risks to them personally of leaving, then they would almost certainly become Remain voters. If sovereignty and immigration were Leave's trumps, Remain's were the economy and the UK's place in the world. The view Straw's team took was that if the debate ended up being about immigration then they would lose. They had to make it about the economy, and that meant getting the economy in the news. This meant, wherever possible, creating a new story every day. As it would be almost impossible to get a newspaper to lead with a story about something beneficial the EU had done, the easiest way to achieve publicity was to create negative headlines about the risks. As Craig Oliver puts it: 'You can't expect tomorrow's headlines to be more than one thing, and journalism chooses the negative one 999 times out of 1,000. It is a factory setting. Anyone dealing with it has to approach it that way.' So Cameron, Osborne and Oliver continued to prepare their missiles of economic doom. A Treasury report on the short-term risks was in the pipeline. A report found that house prices would fall. Again, something of more concern to London's wealthy than people struggling to get on the property ladder.

Calls went out to the great and the good in order to capture and harness the most powerful endorsers of the Remain argument. They had already rinsed Britain's top business leaders. Back in February 2016, thirty-six FTSE 100 companies had signed their letter to *The Times*, including Burberry, BAE Systems, drinks giant Diageo, and Prudential. It stated that 'leaving the EU would deter investment, threaten jobs and put the economy at risk'.[24] It replicated the business leaders' letter to the *Scotsman* newspaper during the 2014 campaign. Cameron had also learned in Scotland that the method of delivery was as important as the size of the payload. It was Gordon Brown's impassioned speech that helped save the day. Which politician carried that kind of weight on a UK-wide scale? With President Obama making a well-timed farewell visit to the UK as the country celebrated the Queen's ninetieth birthday, it looked like they had a perfect opportunity to drop the mother of all campaign bombshells.

On 22 April 2016, the US President was given the full treatment, including lunch with the Queen in Windsor, becoming the twelfth US President she has entertained, out of a total of forty-five. He also played golf with the Prime Minister over the weekend, and held a press conference under the gilded ceiling of the Locarno Suite at the Foreign Office. It was clear that Obama was coming to lend support to the Stronger In campaign. The ground had been prepared. Two days before his arrival, seven US Treasury Secretaries wrote a letter to *The Times* warning that Brexit would be a 'risky bet'.[25]

Sensing trouble, Boris Johnson decided to fire off his own pre-emptive attack on Barack Obama. In an article for *The Sun*, he recounted a story about a bust of Winston Churchill purportedly being removed by Obama from the Oval Office. 'Some said it was a snub to Britain. Some said it was a symbol of the part-Kenyan President's ancestral dislike of the British empire – of which Churchill had been such a fervent defender,' he wrote.[26] Critics called him racist; even friends and aides warned him it was ill-conceived.

Obama had a good read of the article after his lunch with the Queen, and it did nothing to temper his choice of words to the British press. It was always thought he would hint at a preference for the UK remaining in and perhaps he might talk about unity and joined-up security, but he went much further. At the podium, David Cameron at his wing, a murmur of expectation expelled from the press pack as it became clear he was going to make a direct attack on Vote Leave's claims that the UK would strike a post-Brexit trade deal with the US. He said: 'They're voicing an opinion about what the United States is going to do. I figured you might want to hear it from the President of the United States what I think the United States is going to do.'[27] His answer was that the European bloc would be his priority. The Transatlantic Trade and Investment Partnership (TTIP) negotiation was in progress to create a US–EU free trade zone. If the UK left the bloc it would be 'at the back of the queue'.

Never was a British Prime Minister so chuffed to be patronised. Cameron glowed with pride that without Europe he was a nobody. Indeed, with the use of the British word 'queue' rather than the more American 'line', the speculation was that the White House had conferred with No. 10 over what to say. For good measure, the President rounded on Boris Johnson, explaining that the bust of Churchill was prominently displayed outside his private office in the White House residence, known as the Treaty Room, where he sees it 'every day, including on weekends'. Then, in his lyrical tone, he delivered a put-down that would leave a less bombastic character incapable of ever leaving their house again. He explained that he thought it appropriate to move Churchill so that the first African American President could have a bust of Martin Luther King in the Oval Office to remind him 'of all the hard work of a lot of people who would somehow allow me to have the privilege of holding this office'.

So the leader of the free world trashed the Leave campaign's message and its key messenger, just in time for the six o'clock news. It was confirmation that Vote Leave was exaggerating the chances of possible deals with America once outside the EU. Who was going to listen to Vote Leave on this one, when they were hearing the opposite from the US President? At Vote Leave headquarters on Albert Embankment, the atmosphere was sucked out of the room as they absorbed this sucker punch.

'I'm happy to admit it was one of those rare moments when the office went silent. Nobody was calling up because everybody's watching Obama,' says Paul Stephenson. 'It's powerful and he's such a brilliant performer, like Tony Blair. Hats off to them, it was a good event done well and as a professional you have to admire other people's handiwork.' The mood was gloomy, says another source. 'At that moment I was almost certain we would lose.'

But Leave strategist Dominic Cummings was less awed by it. He walked out of his office and made a speech: 'This will have no effect,' he told the room. Their voters outside of London didn't care what the President had to say.

This only matters to the Westminster bubble. What people in the media are saying and what you are seeing on TV is not the same as what the country will think, so don't get psyched out. We will go off and do focus groups and will find out next week what the true picture is, but don't worry about it.

Internal polling the next day showed he appeared to be right. Obama might motivate the core Remain voters but was having no impact on Leave voters. Many were angered. Indeed, some have since speculated that the Boris provocation had the unintentional result of hardening Obama's response to a level that was unacceptable to the British public. Cummings concludes that Obama had gone in too hard.

If Obama had said, 'Look, this is not going to be good for you guys' in a much gentler way, people would have heard him and thought, 'Oh, that's not good,' but the 'back of the queue'… People's reaction then wasn't 'We're going to suffer', it was 'Who is this guy coming over here and what deal have they done behind the scenes to help Cameron?'

The reason Stronger In kept Angela Merkel and Jean-Claude Juncker at bay during the campaign was to avoid a patronising tone from abroad. They thought they could risk it with Obama – but even he wasn't infallible. Paul Stephenson says: 'They thought it was a winning message to tell the country that "Look, everyone in the world agrees with us and people in power agree with us", and actually that's a fundamental misreading of the British public.'

On Twitter, those who supported Remain swooned, those who supported Leave were disgusted and those in the middle just didn't like being patted on the head and told what to think by an outsider, especially with the undisguised threat that if we made the wrong choice America would put us in our place – much as it might have been presented as friendly advice. The UK got its back up. Hadn't we been by their side in Iraq and Afghanistan? The opinion polls in the week afterwards suggested Obama's intervention either had zero impact or may have even slightly backfired. The most popular global figure after Pope Francis had certainly not made a dent. In a week that began with George Osborne's Treasury warning of economic gloom and ended with endorsement from the US President, Remain appeared to have maxed out, yet they were still neck and neck with their opponents, with two months to go.

This became a recurring theme for Stronger In. They would make an economic argument, line up the expert to enforce their message, and the electorate gave a collective shrug. 'More than anything else, people would say – we just want the facts,' says James McGrory.

So you'd give them some facts, but I think people expected some sort of mythical arbiter on facts to descend from the skies and just decree what the facts were in the EU debate. You'd ask them who they wanted to hear from and they did say experts, they said academics, but then they turned out not to be so enamoured with them.

This seemed to bear out a poll done by YouGov ahead of the referendum that showed Leave voters didn't trust any group of experts. Business leaders were most trusted, but even then only by 27 per cent of people voting Leave. Academics, economists, charities, think tanks, actors, UK politicians and world leaders were all mistrusted. The thing trusted most by Leave voters was 'common sense'.[28]

Two weeks ahead of the vote, Nick Clegg wrote to David Cameron asking him to adopt a message with more emotional punch. 'Why don't you get everybody to say in the last week or so, "Vote remain to keep us safe", from recession, crime, climate change. That resonates with people: keep your kids safe.' He got a prompt reply that Stronger In was going to stick with the economic risk message. Who knows if it would have made any difference?

The final twist of Project Fear came on 15 June. George Osborne warned that he would have to fill the £30 billion black hole in public finances triggered by Brexit with an Emergency Budget. This would mean hiking income tax, alcohol and petrol duties and making massive cuts to the NHS, schools and defence. His message: 'Far from freeing up money to spend on public services as the Leave campaign would like you to believe, quitting the EU would mean less money.'[29] It was interpreted, however, as an aggressive threat to the British public. Osborne described it as an Emergency Budget; Vote Leave got forewarning from a friendly source in the media and renamed it a 'Punishment Budget' and called it 'economic vandalism'.[30] The advance warning also gave them time to compile and release a letter from sixty Conservative MPs vowing to vote against the 'Punishment Budget' just as George Osborne was announcing it.

Even pro-Remainers hated it. 'I immediately thought, sod you,' says Clegg. 'Don't tell me you are going to slash my public services or put up my taxes. It was so gratuitous. It was like *The Sopranos* – "Do what I tell you or I'm going to blow your hands off."'

Cummings believes that, as with Obama, a 'softer approach' would have been more effective. He says, 'By being so aggressive, they undermined their own message. What they ended up doing was "Spinal Tapping" and turning everything up to eleven all the time and by the end of it in the focus groups people were just laughing at them.' This is a reference to the spoof rock band Spinal Tap, who had an extra notch on their amplifiers to make the music louder. 'They're pushing it up to eleven every day. You can't do that. It is more important to get the message right than it is to lead the news.'

Cummings continues:

One strategic error all the way along was Craig [Oliver]'s obsession with leading the news and 'What's the story?' And that sometimes suckers people into making mistakes. If in the end you lead the news with more and more bloodcurdling stories, the actual effect on voters is they're tuning out and saying, 'Bollocks.' You're not making progress; you are just fucking your own strategy – neutralising your own message. Because people stopped buying it.

As far as Stronger In was concerned, they were doing everything right. They had followed not just the Lynton Crosby model but what any guide to political campaigning ever tells you: get in early, frame the parameters of the debate, win it and then just hammer it until it's finished. They played to what seemed their strength: that leading economists, nearly every world leader and the vast majority of politicians in the UK considered Brexit an act of self-harm. None of it worked. According to campaigners, one other very strange thing happened as a result.

'It created an issue which, I'll level with you, we hadn't anticipated,' says McGrory. The Remain campaign began to feel that fear fatigue had even started to take hold in newsrooms. The following story sums up what a number of Remain campaigners have said. One evening, McGrory was doing the late shift, which involved calling newspapers and broadcasters to ensure certain stories were being picked up.

I was here till eleven and I was talking to the broadcast desks about the next day and it was incredible. We had four different massive pieces of economic news. One was from the chair from the Federal Reserve, one from the main guy at Hitachi, one was Aviva and one was something else and they were all proper hard economic arguments about why it would be bad to leave. I was pitching this furiously into the morning programmes and the attitude was like – 'Well, it's just another economic warning.' I'd say, 'Well, no, this is from all corners of the fucking globe! This is the chair of the Federal Reserve here. This is the boss of one of Japan's biggest investors in the UK. It isn't just any old 'this is going to be bad for the economy'. But the feeling was that the media was frankly just a bit bored of us winning the economic argument.

It did leave us with a big problem in the short campaign, which was that our stories on the economy were falling on news desks and people were going, 'Oh well, it's just another bloody sound economic argument from a credible person from the Remain camp. Let me find Boris Johnson to say something ridiculous.'

According to this team of experienced political fighters, the EU campaign took them into new territory. They were being told they'd won a certain aspect of the argument, and therefore another report confirming this was not particularly newsworthy. In many respects, this had to be a good thing. They had nailed the debate to such an extent that it was no longer news. In the Leave camp they couldn't even say what trade model the UK would adopt. They were floundering over the question of access to the single market versus immigration. How could they promise any form of trade arrangement with the EU, when it was bound to come with the proviso of accepting terms on free movement of people? The early victories of the Remain camp over the question of economic uncertainty meant that Vote Leave was pushed into making some choices.

On 19 April, Michael Gove used a speech in London to set out his vision of what the country would look like in the event of a vote to leave the EU on 23 June. He indicated that the UK would leave the single market but still have 'access' to it. In looking for an example of places outside the EU who trade freely with the block, he selected countries 'from Turkey to Iceland'. He argued: 'After we vote to leave, we will stay in this zone. The suggestion that Bosnia, Serbia, Albania and Ukraine would stay part of this free trade area – and Britain would be on the outside with just Belarus – is as credible as Jean-Claude Juncker joining UKIP.'[31]

Critics seized on Mr Gove's 'Albanian model', pointing out that the Balkan country has limited access to the single market, it has no financial services 'passports' and its exports to the EU are subject to customs checks. Even the Albanian Prime Minister, Edi Rama, said: 'When I saw the story of Michael Gove's suggestion that Britain could abandon its partnership with Germany, France and other EU countries and instead enter into a non-EU partnership with Albania, Kosovo, Serbia and Bosnia, my immediate reaction was: "Isn't that a bit weird?"'[32] But who's going to listen to the Prime Minister of Albania on this one?

Remain campaigners say that this is when Vote Leave abandoned the economic argument. Their decision to place the UK outside the single market signalled a huge change in their tactics. That weekend, Michael Gove was unequivocal, saying on the BBC's *Andrew Marr Show* that Britain 'should be outside the single market'.[33] This clarity would allow the Leave camp to focus their message on controlling immigration. 'At the time we thought, "This is extraordinary,"' says Will Straw.

Our strategy had been to chase them round the block on what the alternative looked like – was it Norway, was it Switzerland, was it WTO, was it Canada, was it Albania? To point out that they didn't know what they were arguing for and that every single one of those models was inferior to what we had. And it seemed like a complete capitulation of the economic argument to say, 'Actually, we don't want access to the single market after all.' It was like throwing in the towel and saying, 'We are going to be worse off as a country.'

It opened up Leave's ability to go very hard on free movement. They could now argue that leaving the EU would give the UK complete control over its borders. Stronger In had been wrongly reassured by the glimpses they'd seen of strategy documents that Dominic Cummings had been writing about in his blog, suggesting the focus of his campaign would be economics. Allister Heath at the *Telegraph*, who had good insight into the Leave camp, had written that they would not lead on immigration. Stronger In was also certain that Michael Gove and Boris Johnson, as liberal cosmopolitan social conservatives, would never front a UKIP-style campaign.

'That's ultimately what they did,' says Will Straw. 'At great cost to both of them politically, they marched to Nigel Farage's tune.' One could argue that there was actually no eventual cost to Johnson's political fortunes from this issue, as he would become Foreign Secretary, but Straw was right to think that Gove and Johnson didn't intend to campaign on immigration. They had set out to put forward an internationalist, intellectual argument about the global opportunities outside of the EU, against Cameron's message of economic security within. But what had begun as a rolling up of the sleeves, Queensberry Rules, gentleman's spar between the Prime Minister and his former Oxbridge colleagues rapidly descended into a fight to the death.

What's more, Vote Leave calculated that even if the Remain camp was winning the argument on the economy, there were more compelling ways to appeal to voters. Indeed, while all indicators suggested that in the end the decision would hinge on the economy, in the final two weeks of the campaigns, Ipsos MORI's Political Monitor found the economy had for the first time slipped from being the top ranked issue which would impact how people would vote. It had been replaced by immigration.

REASON 18

LOSING CONTROL

Net migration figures come out quarterly from the Office for National Statistics, and each time, regular as clockwork, political newsrooms at 4 Millbank would get a call from the Home Office to say that James Brokenshire was coming. This sober, unassuming man with oval spectacles and neatly cropped hair looked like he had come to do the company accounts, but he was in fact the Immigration Minister dispatched each quarter to do an equally mundane task. As the net migration figures continued to rise, contrary to government promises to reduce them to 'the tens of thousands', Brokenshire's task was to deflect all the crap.

No one enjoys this process – least of all Brokenshire. Every three months, he would face the same mechanical questions from journalists about broken promises and, as if reading lines off a spreadsheet, he would blandly deliver the same answers. The government had 'cut abuse in student visas' and made it 'harder than ever for illegal migrants to stay under the radar'.[1] All this was true, but only served to demonstrate that the government could do absolutely nothing to stem the rise of EU migration to the UK. And while this seeped into the public consciousness, suddenly these figures became highly charged in the context of the referendum campaign.

Harold Wilson always believed he lost the general election in 1970 because of a bad set of economic figures released in the final week of his campaign. The public mood turned against him when inflation and unemployment rose and the trade deficit went up to £31 million. For the Remain campaign, the bad figures related to the quarterly ONS immigration report on 26 May 2016 – less than a month before the vote. It showed that net migration had risen to its second highest ever peak of 333,000 people. This one figure had a timely impact, further exposing the gaping hole in Stronger In's campaign.

In the course of the year, the number of EU migrants working in the UK had risen 11 per cent to a record 2.1 million. The majority of this increase came from the 'original' fifteen EU countries, in particular those in southern Europe still suffering from the Eurozone crisis. But 58,000 of the new arrivals in 2015 were from Romania and Bulgaria, whose citizens were now making the most of the lifting of labour market restrictions which had occurred in January 2014. It's another reason why the referendum was so badly timed for Cameron.

On this day in May 2016, Brokenshire did his blandest best to boring the story away, insisting that there were 'no quick fixes or simple solutions'. But unlike other months, when the government would collectively leave it to Brokenshire's dry assessment, this time they had a problem. Now some Conservative figures were happy to give a different view. That day, Boris Johnson told the BBC's Laura Kuenssberg in rather less bland terms:

> I think that they [the figures] show the scandal of the promise made by politicians repeatedly that they could cut immigration to the tens of thousands and then to throw their hands up in the air and say there's nothing we can do because Brussels has taken away our control of immigration.[2]

Johnson was clearly hypocritical to criticise the tens of thousands policy that he had campaigned on in the 2015 general election, but the Remain camp really had no answer to it. This was exemplified by the Downing Street spokesman's response to the figures: the PM would 'continue to look at what more might be done'.[3] The particular problem for Cameron was that prior to his renegotiations he had been using the same language as the Vote Leave camp about immigration. Take his speech in November 2014 at JCB. Expressing his desire for EU treaty change, he said: 'It is not wrong to express concern about the scale of people coming into the country. People have understandably become frustrated. It boils down to one word: control.'[4] That one word would lose him the referendum.

It was in late May 2016 that Stronger In lost control of the campaign. The centre of gravity of the argument shifted from the economy to immigration, and the polls shifted with it. A Guardian/ICM phone poll conducted directly after the immigration figures came out showed a four-point lead for Leave. For the first time, the split indicated the eventual result: 52 per cent Leave, 48 per cent Remain.[5] A week earlier, ICM's poll had had Remain leading by ten points.

This shift was not just a result of the immigration figures: the day after they came out, on 27 May, the 'purdah' period began. During this time, usually the twenty-eight days before the vote, the government is prevented from using public money or publishing reports that might assist one side of the campaign.[6] Cameron had attempted to scrap these rules, with a clause in the referendum bill in the summer of 2015, and had he achieved his goal, the result of the referendum might have been different. To understand the success of the Leave campaign in June 2016, we have to go back one year, to events in Parliament in the summer of 2015.

As the EU Referendum Bill was put to Parliament at the end of May 2015, a clause was tucked away in the explanatory notes. It stated: 'Section 125 of the 2000 Act (restriction on publication etc of promotional material by central and local government etc) does not apply in relation to the referendum.'[7] The 2000 Act in this case was the Political Parties, Elections and Referendums Act (PPERA), created to regulate the conduct of elections and referendums to make them more fair and balanced. Despite the clause's remote location, keen-eyed Eurosceptics spotted it and realised what it could mean. 'They hoped to slip it through as a sort of housekeeping necessity – but it would have been a very substantial change in the law,' says Tory MP Bernard Jenkin. Without purdah, the government could continue to use White Papers and government reports to keep their argument on the economy central to the campaign.

Tory MP Owen Paterson wrote in the *Daily Mail*: 'Just imagine. There will be Government White Papers warning of the calamitous effect a "No" vote would have on the economy and how it would imperil the country.'[8] He was right about these plans, and without purdah, George Osborne's Treasury reports could have been produced much nearer the date of the vote, with potentially greater impact on the decision. With purdah in place, the timing of the government's 'Project Fear' strategy would be dictated by the rules – the Treasury reports would have to be released at least twenty-eight days before the ballots opened.

So the revolt in the summer of 2015, led by Bill Cash, Bernard Jenkin and Steve Baker, was an important victory for the Leave campaign – even though most commentators gave it little credit at the time. However, it looked like a hopeless rebellion to begin with. In June 2015, the first rebel attempt to foil the government's plans failed, because although twenty-seven Tories defied Cameron on an amendment tabled by Bill Cash, Labour didn't support them, abstaining from the vote. They had the support of the SNP, who naturally didn't want a precedent set for any future referendums on Scotland's independence, but it wasn't enough.

After the failed rebellion, some Conservatives suggested the government should be wary of surrendering moral authority in the referendum. James Forsyth wrote in *The Spectator*:

> The lesson that David Cameron should learn from this is to be very careful with the details of this EU referendum bill. He should remember that winning the actual referendum is the easy bit compared to preventing a Tory split over the issue... He should not push anything that would allow Tory Brexiters to cry foul after an In vote.[9]

Cameron didn't see it like that, and he was right not to. The government continued to defend its position. In July 2015, the Public Administration and Constitutional Affairs Committee (PACAC) decided to investigate the issue. They called in the most senior civil servant, Jeremy Heywood. He argued that purdah could 'hobble' ministers seeking to represent Britain in EU discussions ahead of the vote. The Cabinet Secretary told the committee: 'The main concern the civil service would have is in relation to the normal activity in Brussels. Maybe not all aspects of that normal activity, but in a typical month you have ten or eleven ministerial councils in Brussels.' He added: 'We need to make sure, in the normal course of business, that our ministers use whichever are the most potent arguments they can use to win points for Britain in those negotiations, in those minute statements and so on.'[10]

However, Speaker's Counsel, Michael Carpenter scotched these arguments. In written evidence to the committee, Parliament's top lawyer said that the purdah restrictions were 'being read more restrictively of the ability to report EU business than is really justified'.[11] In a timely leak ahead of the final debate in Parliament, Carpenter wrote in an email that the government's arguments were 'unsound'.[12] Eurosceptic MP Bernard Jenkin, who was chair of the committee, concluded that the government was simply trying to skew the battlefield. 'The argument the Cabinet Secretary was making turned out to be rubbish – the whole reason for the changes in purdah [was] being presented on a false pretext,' he said in an interview for this book.

His committee members supported this view. Downing Street was starting to look shifty. Over recess, Jenkin had numerous conversations with Labour fixers and MPs to persuade them of the moral argument. Chief amongst them was Hilary Benn, who, though supportive of staying in the EU, could understand that the referendum needed to be seen as fair. What's more, Jenkin could argue, as he did in the Commons, that the 2000 PPERA was a Labour Party Act of Parliament. Did they really want to abandon their principles and allow Cameron to water it down? No doubt a section of the Labour Party simply saw an opportunity to defeat and embarrass the Conservatives, but whatever their motives, they were persuaded to side with the Tory rebels. It was an amendment tabled by the Labour Party that eventually overturned the PM's plans to scrap purdah. The move was blocked by 312 votes to 285.

On reflection, Jenkin says:

You can only conclude that the Prime Minister and George Osborne were trying to get rid of the restrictions for the last twenty-eight days of the campaign. In the run-up to that 28-day period, the government made announcement after announcement, publishing so-called 'White Papers' about Article 50 and leaving the EU, and these were just all propaganda. When that stopped and the purdah period kicked in, there was a transformation in the ability of the Leave campaign to get our stories heard. Before that, everything was smothered by government announcements. Given the result was so close, this was one of the most defining moments of the whole campaign. The government losing that debate was a turning point.

Indeed, there was something in the onset of purdah on 27 May that was reminiscent of the most famous boxing bout in history. In the 'Rumble in the Jungle' in Kinshasa, Zaire in 1974, the 3–1 underdog Muhammad Ali upset the experts who said that, at thirty-two, he was too old to beat the well-stacked 25-year-old George Foreman. Foreman had won all forty of his previous fights, thirty-seven of them by knockout. Ali won the fight by hanging back against the loosened ropes and absorbing the heavy punches until the eighth round, when Foreman had nothing left – then Ali unleashed everything he had. The lifting of purdah was the bell ringing at the end of round seven. With four weeks to go, Vote Leave changed their tack and began to switch focus, knowing their opponent's strength had been sapped.

On 1 June, Boris Johnson, flanked by Michael Gove and Priti Patel, announced support for an Australian-style points system, the very thing Dominic Cummings had noted in his Business for Britain report in 2014 that people cited as the silver bullet solution to their concerns about immigration.[13] It was an adoption of a UKIP policy from the 2015 general election, but this was Johnson, the man who could be Prime Minister, talking of immigration policies that would be enacted by 'the government of the day'. The liberal justification was that the current system discriminated against people outside of the EU; that this was actually fairer while stopping those who didn't have a job coming from the EU. This policy alone would help win the vote of thousands of British Asian nationals who felt their relatives abroad were discriminated against by the EU laws. But, as we've already established, the points system was also widely accepted by many people as a desirable way of reducing immigration.

Opponents warned that actually migration numbers could increase under this system, and what about UK citizens living in Europe – wouldn't they lose their rights in retaliation? But Vote Leave knew the automatic association most people made about the Australian system was that it reduced numbers. By proposing the points system, as well as cuts to VAT on energy bills, the campaign faced allegations of putting forward 'an alternative government'.[14] Gove and Johnson denied it, but here was the blueprint for an alternative strategy on immigration – one that Cameron could not implement without leaving the EU. On top of this, as mentioned earlier, came a letter from Gove and Johnson saying that the government's pledge to reduce immigration to the tens of thousands was 'corroding public trust'.[15] Having suspended the collective responsibility of his Cabinet, Cameron was suddenly facing more than just a handful of ministers choosing to vote differently – it looked like a coup.

To bolster their argument, the next move was to create an immigration bogeyman and weaken the Prime Minister's authority further. On the eve of England's European Championship warm-up football match against Turkey, Vote Leave put out its first salvo on Turkey's potential membership of the EU. It said:

> Since the birthrate in Turkey is so high, we can expect to see an additional million people added to the UK population from Turkey alone within eight years.
>
> This will not only increase the strain on Britain's public services, but it will also create a number of threats to UK security. Crime is far higher in Turkey than the

UK. Gun ownership is also more widespread. Because of the EU's free movement laws, the government will not be able to exclude Turkish criminals from entering the UK.[16]

They further argued that an agreement earlier in the year between the EU and Turkey on tackling the migrant flow across the Mediterranean had injected new impetus into Turkey's membership bid. Brexit supporter and Armed Forces Minister Penny Mordaunt told the BBC's Andrew Marr that it was just a matter of time before Turkey joined. Marr challenged her, saying that the UK had a veto to stop Turkey joining. 'No, it doesn't,'[17] responded Penny Mordaunt. This wasn't true. The UK, and all other member states, did indeed have a veto against expansion of the bloc. Craig Oliver was watching the programme from the green room of another TV studio. He texted the editor of the programme, Rob Burley, to say that Mordaunt was 'plain wrong'.[18] This appeared to reach the earpiece of Andrew Marr at the end of the interview; he again challenged Mordaunt over her claim. Mordaunt looked uncomfortable but couldn't backtrack. 'I don't think that the UK will be able to stop Turkey joining,' she muttered.

According to Oliver, the problem then ensued over how this claim was reported. Broadcasters, keen to be impartial on the argument, spent the day putting forward a seemingly balanced debate on Mordaunt's view that Turkey could join the EU without a UK veto. 'Now, any serious broadcast journalist should have said, "I'm going to stop this at source and point out that there is not a serious credible person in the world, no one, who supports this view,"' says Oliver. 'Why not make some ballsy decisions and actually say this is spurious bullshit, by a minister who clearly doesn't know what they are talking about and has embarrassed herself on national television?' Instead, Oliver watched the six o'clock news with George Osborne outside the Prime Minister's office, 'tearing our hair out because at no point has anybody said, "Turkey isn't going to join the EU, it is nonsense."'

The problem for Oliver was that David Cameron could easily be portrayed as a supporter of Turkey joining the EU. As early as 2005 he had expressed frustration at the accession process being 'desperately slow'.[19] When the Prime Minister visited Turkey in 2010, he gave a speech in which he said: 'This is something I feel very strongly and very passionately about … I want us to pave the road from Ankara to Brussels.' He even drew a parallel between Turkey and Britain, initially prevented by France's veto from joining the Common Market in 1963: 'We know what it is like to be shut out of the club. But we also know that these things can change.'[20]

We live in a world where politics and international relations are nuanced and multifaceted, and Turkey sits almost as a buffer between conflicting ideologies. The British Foreign Office knows Turkey is in a situation where it could move towards the East and extremism, or it could be a Western-leaning liberal democracy. It's clear that the UK wanted to influence the latter direction of travel because, ultimately, for Turkey to be in a position to join the EU, it would have had to have become a Western-leaning liberal democracy. Oliver asks:

> What are the levers that you can pull or the carrots that you can present to them? One of the carrots is getting the Prime Minister to say he would like Ankara to be linked to Brussels, but can you meet a single member of British government who thinks Turkey is going to join the EU? The answer is no. I'd be amazed if Turkey joined the EU in our lifetime – certainly not in the next ten years.

Vote Leave used Cameron's diplomatic language against him, even suggesting that Turkey could join the EU by 2020. On 8 June, Michael Gove made a speech about EU security in which he said that 'official British government policy' was for Turkey to become a member of the bloc. He added:

> With the terrorism threat that we face only growing, it is hard to see how it could possibly be in our security interests to open visa-free travel to 77 million Turkish citizens and create a border-free zone from Iraq, Iran and Syria to the English Channel. It is even harder to see how such a course is wise when extremists everywhere will see that the West is opening its borders to appease an Islamist government.[21]

Given that for Turkey to join the EU it would have to prove it was a 'modern European democracy', it would have to meet dozens of conditions over its governance, human rights and economic well-being. Since its first application to join the EU in 1987, it had made very few steps towards reaching these goals. At a Labour In event in London, Yvette Cooper described Gove's claims as 'shameful' lies. 'It's Oxford Union-style debating, thinking they can just pull anything out, or like a columnist just saying things for the sake of headlines,'[22] she added.

The idea of Turkish membership was high-level scaremongering from Vote Leave, with a grain of truth. Turkey *could* one day join the EU – but that day was probably decades away. However, the Turkey furore reminded voters that during his negotiations Cameron had raised expectations of immigration controls and then failed to secure a significant deal – other than reducing pull factors. On the issue of new accession countries, Cameron had initially promised free movement would not apply until their economies converged much more closely with those of existing member states. This aspect of the negotiation had fallen away.

Vote Leave did everything it could to keep Turkey on the agenda. In mid-June, diplomatic cables were leaked to the *Sunday Times* suggesting officials at the British Embassy in Ankara had discussed granting Turks visa-free travel to the UK. This was all part of a deal the EU was negotiating with Turkey to ensure the country took back migrants crossing the Channel. The EU was offering visa-free travel to the Schengen area in return for Turkish cooperation, and the UK appeared to be at least discussing offering some form of special passport deal. All this would have been well short of free movement, but Leave campaigner Iain Duncan Smith said: 'These documents show that the government and the European Commission are perpetrating an enormous deceit on the British public – saying one thing in public, but quite another in private.'[23]

The Leave campaign had come a long way from its initial Conservative-based message of sovereignty, cutting red tape for business and promoting free trade that was used to attract Gove and Johnson to the campaign. Now they seemed to be wholeheartedly adopting the Farage/Banks mantra on immigration and EU expansion.

Matthew Elliott says it was always a question of timing. 'Let's say our first leaflet in October had been "Vote leave to stop Turkey joining". That's hardly reaching out to the centre-mainstream.' He cites the example of the campaign that Peter Mandelson ran in 1997 to get Tony Blair elected.

They started off saying, 'Of course we will match Ken Clarke's budget; Tory spending plans; tough on crime, tough on the causes of crime.' Very Tory. Then it comes to the short campaign itself, repeating those things but also saying, 'Fifty days left to save the NHS, we are the only party to save the NHS' – their core vote strategy. Having set the parameters of the debate and drawn in new voters, you make sure you have something for your base, to get them out.

But this wasn't just about appealing to the core base, according to Elliott's Vote Leave partner Dominic Cummings. He says: 'About 80 per cent of the country, including almost all swing voters, agreed with UKIP that immigration was out of control and something like an Australian points system was a good idea. This was true across party lines.'

The director of Vote Leave tells the story of a time he took a focus group of what he thought were Conservative voters, in which they talked about immigration and then moved on to the economy. While they held the traditional Conservative/UKIP view about border control, they seemed to sway towards Labour's economic policies.

> I was puzzled and said, 'Who did you vote for?' 'Labour,' they all said. An admin error by the company meant that I had been talking to core Labour voters, not core Tory voters. On the subject of immigration, these working-class/lower-middle-class people were practically indistinguishable from all the Tories and the UKIP people.

Cummings concludes that there was a delusion in Westminster that the third of people who were undecided in the referendum, the 'swing voters', must have a 'moderate' and 'centre-ground' view somewhere between Farage and Corbyn. He was convinced that when it came to immigration, most of them supported UKIP.

How could Stronger In have countered this problem? As we've established in previous chapters, both the Conservatives and Labour were hamstrung by their past on the issue of immigration. Ideally, there would be a single message that everybody could use. Indeed, a script was produced about the benefits of migration for the economy and public services – but it was mostly ignored.

Stronger In's James McGrory recounts:

> If you've got a message on immigration, you want all of your people using it all the time – that's the point of having a script. But obviously the Conservatives had their own issues around the tens of thousands pledge, which made it difficult for them to make the immigration argument in the way that we wanted it made. Meanwhile, the Labour Party were having their own internal debate during the campaign about free movement and about their decision in 2004 [not to impose transition controls on migrants coming from the Eastern European accession countries] and all of that. So in that sense it was difficult. Even if we'd decided to

collectively take on immigration as a campaign, it still would have been difficult, but we didn't even make that decision.

'We did have a strategy around immigration,' says executive director of Stronger In Will Straw, 'it just wasn't implemented.' In July 2015, the Remain camp had set out its war book. In it, they established the positive benefits of the EU and the risks of leaving and they set out what the risks and negatives were for their campaign: immigration was chief amongst them. Straw spent a lot of time with pollster Andrew Cooper testing different groups with different messages to counter this concern. They found that the simple argument that if you leave the EU you get control of your borders was compelling to people. But they also found that public opinion could be swayed by a formula of 'acceptance', 'positives' and 'attack': According to Straw it goes as follows:

1. Acceptance: People have legitimate concerns – 'It is not racist, there has been pressure on public services.'
2. There are positives that most people accept: 'If people come to the UK to work hard and pay their taxes and contribute to society they should be welcome.' Some 85 per cent of people thought that this statement was correct. 'There are a quarter of a million migrants who work in the UK's public services. Many EU migrants set up businesses and employ Brits. Having free movement means Brits can work, study and retire abroad. Being in the EU means there is a border at Calais rather than Dover.'
3. Then the attack messages: 'They are trying to sell you a lemon. They are trying to throw the baby out with the bathwater. An Australian points-based system would increase levels of migration. There's no way we could end free movement without losing access to the single market – pressuring the economy.'

'That's what we wanted politicians to say,' says Straw.

This is the exact script produced by Stronger In that was hardly ever used:

We want fairness in our immigration system, not a free-for-all. People from other European countries should not be allowed to access benefits until they have paid into the system. But those who come here to work hard, pay their taxes, contribute to our economy and support public services should be welcomed.

One hundred thousand EU citizens work in our health and social care system. One and a half million people are employed in businesses owned by EU citizens. And EU citizens have contributed £20 billion more in taxes than they have taken out in benefits. The facts are clear: the overwhelming majority of EU citizens in Britain are contributors, not freeloaders.

The last section of the script touches on the fundamental question that remains as the UK enters negotiations with the EU. It states:

Those who want to pull us out of the EU and end free movement should be careful what they wish for. We lose our access to the world's largest trading area, the single market, costing jobs and pushing up prices. We would compromise opportunities for Brits to work, study, travel and retire freely in Europe. And we would see our border checks moving from Calais to Dover, as the Prime Minister has warned.

Would this argument have persuaded people? It cuts to one of the most interesting questions in politics. How much time do you spend talking about your opponent's core area? If you talk about it too much, you draw attention to it; the Leave campaign are convinced that attacking the £350 million figure was one of the Remain campaign's biggest mistakes – many people only found out about that figure from the Remain campaign complaining about it, when they might have neutralised it by saying, 'OK, we send money to the EU, but it's a membership fee, and here's what we get back for that fee'.[24] It's the same thing if you give a speech about the positive effects of immigration – for all the advantages expressed in the above script, they probably wouldn't change the fact that most people felt immigration was out of control. If you accept this, then a day talking about immigration is a day not talking about the economy. However, the Leave campaign had spent months strengthening its weak spot on the economy by creating a business network (Business for Britain, which brought together Eurosceptic business leaders) and developing messages about the UK standing on its own two feet, cutting red tape and enjoying the free trade advantages outside the EU.

The Remain camp was still floundering over how to address immigration three weeks out from the vote. Matthew Elliott says: 'Long-term on the Leave side, we recognised the economy was our weakest flank and we tried to protect ourselves against it. They never did any long-term planning on their weakest flank of migration – they had nothing to say on that whatsoever.'

Will Straw believes their strategy on immigration was sound, if only politicians had been able to deliver it. He says:

> The Conservatives were always tripped up on the migration cap – they couldn't get through an interview without having to spend 90 per cent of it explaining why they had not hit their migration cap. And Labour politicians fell into one of two camps. Either they had to defend Labour's 'open-door policy' in 2004, or they took a Corbyn line and said, 'There's no problem here', then implying the racist line for dragging it up. So in practice we couldn't find politicians who would use the script.

Instead, Labour's divisions were played out on the airways, with Jeremy Corbyn praising the role of immigration and warning public services would suffer if it was reduced, while his deputy Tom Watson said politicians needed to 'listen to what voters tell them', adding, 'A future Europe will have to look at things like the free movement of labour rules.'[25] It was a debate the party needed to have, but the timing was poor. Arguably, they should have had it over a decade earlier.

There was a genuine cross-party division in the Remain camp around what to do. Some, especially from No. 10, felt the only solution was to try to regain focus on the economy, continuing to come up with eye-catching ways of talking about the dangers of leaving, and pivot back to that. The problem was they had used their biggest guns in that area pre-purdah.

After the migration figures came out, Straw and Peter Mandelson argued the case that they had to take immigration 'head on'. They used as an example the 'Dover speech' that Tony Blair had given in 2005 when he was facing the same pressure on the subject. Blair had said: 'We deal with it, but with care, responsibly and recognising that, in our nation today, our diversity is a source of strength, not weakness, a reflection of a modern country striving to be at ease with the modern world.'[26]

Labour figures within the campaign group tried to persuade Cameron to make a speech where he would set out this positive argument in greater detail and 'rip apart' what Vote Leave was trying to do. This was also supported by some

Conservatives, including Cameron's speech writer Max Chambers. It would be a day's agenda not talking about the economy and some might consider it a day wasted – but it would 'set a really hard marker down', reflects Straw. It would be Stronger In's answer to their main weakness, in the same way that Vote Leave had an answer on the economy. Straw goes on:

> Politicians and other thought leaders and public figures like to echo something that they've heard – that they feel comfortable with – and that would have given people confidence. It would allow Labour people to say, 'Well, I don't agree with David Cameron on much but I heard his speech on immigration and I think there is an awful lot of sense in what he says.' People would have heard an alternative – rather than what we did, which was not engage.

While Cummings's research suggested 80 per cent agreed with UKIP on immigration, there was also an argument that voters didn't want to be associated with some of the more extreme comments made by Farage. While Gove and Johnson had the gravitas to be taken seriously, they also risked reputational damage by shifting to an anti-immigration message. Some strategists within Stronger In wanted to exploit this, with explicit attacks on these rebel Conservatives. As we previously discussed, David Cameron was reluctant, hoping he would be able to reunite his party at the end of it all. McGrory says: 'One thing you have to do in a campaign is characterise your opposition negatively – and we didn't spend a lot of time doing that.'

In Craig Oliver's diary for 29 May, he laments the Gove/Boris letter attacking the government's pledge to reduce immigration to the tens of thousands, which coincided with comments from Employment Minister Priti Patel saying rich people don't understand immigration. 'She might as well have said, "I'm talking about you, Cameron and Osborne,"' says Oliver. And yet Cameron feels his fellow Tories are 'trying to bait us into a blue on blue spat, which makes everyone think it's about the Conservative party – and that depresses turnout'. Cameron reminds Oliver of the expression 'Don't wrestle a pig. The pig likes it and you get covered in shit.' They decide not to unleash a negative poster campaign against Johnson. 'We should stop going on about posters attacking Boris. It's a trap,' Cameron tells his team.[27]

The treasurer of Stronger In, Roland Rudd, later criticised No. 10 for making a huge error. He said the approach of Cameron and his aides meant decisions were 'made in the interest of a party rather than in the interests of what is really needed in terms of the referendum'. In his view, it was a mistake to allow 'the dead hand of Downing Street' to manage the campaign. He blamed them for a lack of strategy on immigration and for refusing to endorse 'blue on blue' attacks. He wrote:

> One of the Stronger In team comes up with a good attack on Boris Johnson's hypocrisy but Cameron vetoes it. Peter Mandelson asks why the campaign doesn't nail Johnson and Gove in a meeting with George Osborne but Oliver parries it away. Even when Gove makes the grotesque claim that millions of Turks are about to arrive in the UK via future EU membership, No. 10 still refuses to criticise him directly.[28]

Vote Leave's Matthew Elliott agrees:

> On a campaigning point of view, they never went for the jugular on Boris and Michael – that was a huge mistake. You would have done everything possible to lash Boris to Farage and the BNP. They would have bought into the idea that all those Leave guys are a bit crazy; Boris is a bit more extreme. It would have been worth more than 2 per cent of the vote.

As discussed earlier, there was a counter-argument that Johnson shouldn't be provoked because it would only increase his dedication to Vote Leave and his attacks on David Cameron – but by the time the campaign reached the purdah period, it seemed the former London Mayor was fully committed to the campaign and comfortable criticising his Prime Minister. However, Elliott says that if No. 10 had retaliated strongly, 'he most likely would have backed off a bit'.

On reflection, Oliver stands by his decision: 'I think it was the right thing to do at the time. Having lost – would I have liked to have had a real go at some of these people? Yes. George Osborne felt strongly we should have been having more of a go at Boris.'

As the last two weeks of the campaign approached, Vote Leave built in another advantage. They had held back most of their budget for the final month, in which they were only competing financially with a rival campaign and not the government as well, and they had spent time and resources calculating exactly where to target their funds.

We've established that at the beginning of the campaign, the country was split roughly into three voting categories. One third were pro-EU: these people were richer, younger and better educated and thought that the EU was a positive thing. Another third were committed to leaving the EU at whatever cost, while the final third, the swing voters, didn't much like the EU either but were worried about the economy and the risks of leaving.

According to Vote Leave's analysis, over the course of the campaign, the core Remain third stayed the same but the core Leave third began to grow to about 44 per cent, as their concerns about the economy were neutralised with alternative messages on free trade and money back from the budget to pay for the NHS. But in the last few weeks they needed to continue to chip away at the 'worried' undecided voters.

Cummings had hired a group of physicists from a data science company who collated different information such as public polling, private polling, door knocking and Census data, and who did what's called 'scraping data' off the internet (extracting data from websites so it can be analysed). They would apply 'some very sophisticated maths' to these data sets and then come back with conclusions such as: 'We think people in the following streets are more likely to vote Leave.' They used automated systems that Cummings describes as 'robots trawling through vast data sets coming up with correlations – and if you haven't got a maths or physics PhD, you're not going to understand it'. Ground teams would be sent to the chosen streets to knock on doors and record data, which would then be fed back into the machine to refine the process. According to Leave strategists, it became more and more accurate as the campaign went on. Early on, experimental adverts were used, mainly on Facebook, to see what messages worked, but the spending on these was very small until the right target groups were established.

Then, ten days out, having spent very little money on advertising, Vote Leave splashed several million pounds targeting 9 million people. Fully 98 per cent of the communications budget went into the digital campaign. There was no newspaper advertising of any kind, and posters were only used tactically to promote an on-the-day news story, not plastered around the country. So roughly £200,000 out of £3.5 million was spent on posters; the remainder largely went on Facebook, directed in the closing days of the campaign to where the physicists told them to spend it: at the 9 million people they thought were the wavering voters, who would sway the outcome.

It is impossible to fully and accurately assess the impact of this strategy. The Remain camp of course did its own door knocking and targeted social media campaigning, using a modelling system developed by President Obama's campaign guru Jim Messina, but they hadn't backloaded their budget to the same extent as the Leave camp.

The key difficulty for Stronger In during the final two weeks was how to wrestle the debate back onto the economy. We discussed in a previous chapter how the impact of Jo Cox's murder may have changed the course of economic indicators that might otherwise have begun to raise alarm bells of impending financial doom. Market jitters in the last week before a referendum could have shifted the conversation back towards the economy – but, as it was, Nigel Farage's poster took centre stage for all the wrong reasons in the last week of the campaign.

Dominic Cummings recalls that the morning before he heard about Jo Cox's murder was the very moment he began to think he'd won. Focus groups and polls were all indicating it was within their grasp. He had locked himself away in a room, sat down and thought, 'We could win this – it is in my hands to win.' He began to consider what needed to be done in the last ten days. 'How do we control this?' At this point, there was a knock on the door. Victoria Woodcock explained what had just happened.

'After that my confidence was gone. A lot of people thought that we were completely doomed. I was genuinely 50/50,' says Cummings. The murder of a pro-EU MP by an apparent right-wing fanatic was perceived as highly damaging and could impinge on members of the public wanting to be associated with the Leave campaign. Certainly, that was the feeling in London, but research conducted elsewhere by Vote Leave found a different view. Henry de Zoete, who conducted this analysis for Vote Leave, reported back from focus groups that 'the rest of the country is totally indifferent and are saying, "What's that got to do with it? Some guy might kill someone, how is that going to affect our vote in the referendum?"'

As with the Obama moment, Cummings gave a talk to his team and he discussed the impact with his analysts. They were ahead in the polls and assumed that if they were still averaging 50/50 on the day, they would win. Cummings also believed that the pollsters' London-centric opinions would make them 'cheat their own methodology – thinking they were making them more accurate, but they were actually making it less accurate'.

Indeed, the weekend before the vote, it was reported that 'pollsters are finding it harder to reach Remain supporters than those backing Leave',[29] according to research by BMG. Michael Turner, BMG research director, said this could mean that opinion polls were understating the level of support for Remain. It's been suggested that some polls were tweaked to reflect this opinion that they had simply 'not reached' the right proportion of Remain voters. Because the polls were skewed to reflect the Remain vote pollsters expected, the markets didn't have a chance to react to what was really coming, and this in turn could have suppressed a panic bounce for the Remain camp, as was seen in the Scottish independence referendum. Henry de Zoete told Cummings: 'The best thing for us will be if the polls stay 51/49 for Remain, as that means that the markets won't panic [which might have led to a knock-on panic upswing in the Remain vote]. They will think that they're gonna be OK.' This is exactly what happened.

Because of the murder, Stronger In cancelled their last big set-piece event with Governor of the Bank of England, Mark Carney, which had been due the Monday before the vote. Carney was actually considered one of the more credible spokesmen by the British public. The general mood of the campaign also switched to a 'choose love, not hate' vibe. While many agreed with the sentiment, this wasn't supposed to be Remain's core argument, which was where they needed to be focusing in the last week as the final TV debates approached.

The last chance to bring the Leave camp down a peg was during the televised debates. The wrangling over how these key TV events would play out was the source of much controversy within the Leave and Remain camps and the broadcasters. There was much discussion about format and who would appear alongside whom, with Cameron keen to avoid high-profile Conservatives attacking each other. A crucial moment came on the evening of Johnson's West Country tour. The journalist pack had gone for pizza with Vote Leave's media spokesman Robert Oxley. Just as the bill was being settled, it was announced that ITV's debate programme would feature the Prime Minister for Remain and Nigel Farage for Leave. Oxley took a call from head office and returned to the table. 'I've got a story for you,' he told the journalists. With Farage considered 'toxic' by Vote Leave, the campaign group had released a furious email: 'ITV has effectively joined the official IN campaign,' said the statement sent to our inboxes. 'There will be consequences for its future – the people in No. 10 won't be there for long.'[30]

It was a highly charged statement and, journalists speculated, one possibly sent under the influence of alcohol. But the next morning, Vote Leave stuck by its comments. 'The reason why we really kicked off that night was not ITV but the BBC,' says Matthew Elliott. 'We knew they were having this crucial meeting to decide what their format would be. There was a feeling [in the BBC] that Cameron should be debating Farage because that would be box office.' Vote Leave thought a robust response to ITV would warn them off. Indeed, the BBC eventually used an all-Vote Leave line-up rather than approaching Farage and Leave.EU.

ITV's referendum debate between Cameron and Nigel Farage on 7 June drew over 4 million viewers, and was the most popular current affairs show so far that year. If Downing Street was hoping Farage would spark negative headlines, it didn't happen. His most controversial moment was to tell an audience member to 'calm down' after she quizzed him on comments he had made previously about immigrants allegedly involved in sexual attacks on women in Cologne in Germany. Farage responded that while some disagreed with his views, his Australian style points system seemed to have been adopted by mainstream politicians. A poll afterwards suggested that the UKIP leader had done more than the PM to persuade undecided voters.[31]

ITV hosted a second debate on 9 June which saw Scotland's First Minister Nicola Sturgeon representing the Remain camp along with Energy Secretary Amber Rudd and shadow Business Secretary Angela Eagle. For Leave, Boris Johnson lined up with Labour MP Gisela Stuart and Andrea Leadsom, the pro-Brexit Energy Minister.

Rudd was finally authorised by Cameron's aides to attack her colleague Johnson for being motivated by personal ambition. She remarked, 'I fear the only number Boris is interested in is the one that says No. 10.' She later added, 'He is the life and soul of the party but he's not the man you want driving you home at the end of evening.'[32] It all seemed to wash over Johnson and he didn't retaliate.

Like Sky News, the BBC held a Question Time format with the PM followed by Michael Gove on two separate nights, but their set piece, called 'The Great Debate', was more ambitious. Like ITV, each side could put up three people for the debate, but this would be in front of an audience of 6,000 in Wembley Arena (an even bigger audience in the stadium was originally considered). As soon as the idea was conceived, every politician, certainly on the Leave side, could suddenly imagine themselves passionately winning over the massive crowd. 'It didn't just derange Farage, it deranged almost everybody. Everybody was obsessed with it – all the way through,' says Cummings.

The debate took place on 21 June – the night before the last day of campaigning. As the crowds gathered outside the Wembley Arena, Remain campaigners pulled in a choir to sing 'All You Need Is Love' by the Beatles. Faces painted in UK and EU flags, their banners read 'Choose love, vote remain.'[33]

In the shadow of the football stadium came the rare sight of both campaign coaches pulling up alongside each other. Leave's notorious red bus arrived first, its infamous slogan still emblazoned across the side, even though they had been forcefully told in the last TV debate to 'get that lie off your bus' by Angela Eagle.[34] Out stepped Vote Leave's team, unchanged from the ITV debate, of Boris Johnson, Gisela Stuart and Andrea Leadsom. Then came Stronger In's bus, adorned in patriotic colours of the Union flag, with its slogan, 'More jobs, lower prices'.

Remain had a fresh line-up: the new London Mayor Sadiq Khan was joined by leader of the Scottish Conservatives Ruth Davidson and Frances O'Grady, General Secretary of the Trades Union Congress. The Remain camp might have been showing its depth, but the consistency of the same three players also showed a confidence in the Leave camp. 'What came across was that we were a team,' says Gisela Stuart. Their message would also remain consistent. 'We knew this was a short, brutal campaign with the brutality of staying on message. When we did the TV debates, if the write-up next morning was, "Oh my God, what a boring bunch of three people, all they could say was 'take back control'" – that's good.'

In effect, this is what happened. Khan and Davidson both put in strong performances, Khan denouncing Vote Leave's immigration tactic as 'Project Hate'. Davidson's fiery delivery matched her bright red suit as she attacked both Johnson and Gove over limp assurances on the economy and jobs. She quoted Johnson saying there 'might or might not' be job losses after Brexit. 'That is not good enough,'[35] she told him. Many assessments had the Remain camp coming out on top, but Leave's message discipline was tight. 'Take back control' and Turkey featured in as many answers as possible. At one point, Sadiq

Khan held up a Vote Leave leaflet on Turkey to attack it, which arguably gave the message more visibility. If there was a memorable moment, it was Johnson's final speech. Suddenly, he was in his element – the master speechmaker in a rousing finale. He said that if people voted leave, 'I believe that this Thursday can be our country's Independence Day!'[36] The atmosphere in the room shifted and, for the first time in the evening, a section of the audience spontaneously stood up to applaud their hero.

There was one other memorable moment of that night which happened behind the scenes in the spin room. An intense argument broke out between Michael Gove and Will Straw, in which a few heated exchanges summed up the campaign. Straw accused Gove of lying about everything from his £350 million claim on money for the NHS to the prospect of Turkey joining the EU.

Gove fired back:

You haven't had an optimistic and positive case about why we should be in the European Union. You haven't argued during the course of the campaign for a single transfer of power from Britain to the European Union. You haven't put the case forward for Europe. You haven't said that the EU is a good thing and that its institutions are powerful and worthwhile.

Straw defended himself, saying that the UK chose to work with the European Union on climate change and on air pollution and this had been mentioned during the campaign 'time and again'. He said, 'We should have confidence in the achievements we have made in Europe.' But, he added: 'You've had decades to prepare and two days to the end of this campaign you do not have a plan for the economy [if we leave the EU].'

Talking over each other, Gove said: 'Well, we have two days to go and we've had no optimistic or upbeat message from the Remain campaign.'

'We have said we are "stronger, safer and better off in Europe",' said Straw.

'That's a slogan, not a plan,' replied Gove.

Straw came back: 'We boxed you in on the economy because you don't have a plan, and you ended up in the gutter on immigration.'

The two men had the measure of each other's campaigns. Neither was perfect, but only one could win and it happened to be the one ruthless enough to climb into 'the gutter', as Straw put it.

The next day, 22 June, the campaign to remain in the EU was nearly lost. Or, perhaps a better way of putting it: at least 51 per cent of voters had decided to vote Leave and there was very little chance of changing that fact. The pollsters didn't know it. David Cameron didn't know it. Boris Johnson didn't know it. But Britain was set to vote Leave – and it just needed one last push.

Often the last day of campaigning becomes a contest to see who can travel the furthest, in a final act of self-punishment to produce a whirl of images and sound bites in the hope that they will stick in voters' minds as their pencil hovers over empty square boxes. Does it achieve anything? Possibly; possibly not. But today one person would give voters an extra nudge.

Boris Johnson's last foray would take him on a 450-mile round trip from posing with salmon at 5 a.m. in London's Billingsgate fish market to aimless high-street rambling in Ashby de la Zouch, before heading north, ending with a pint in Darlington. That morning, 1,280 business leaders, including the bosses of fifty-one FTSE 100 companies, had written a letter warning of the risks of leaving, but the markets remained stable. When co-author Jason interviewed Boris Johnson in Ashby about what might happen to the value of pound if the UK voted to leave, it was easily batted away as there was no evidence of panic. Johnson gave the example of what had happened when the UK left the ERM in 1992, when the pound did fall but then 'rose steadily for fifteen years'. He added: 'If we come out of the EU, we will be on a course to set our own economic destiny.'

After Ashby, he made a speech in Selby. It was nothing we haven't seen before, no new message; the whole day was about mileage. That was, until Johnson got in his helicopter in Selby for the last leg of the trip. The problem for journalists who don't have access to a chopper is that they can't keep up. Travelling by car, some of the Sky News team had to skip the Selby event and head direct from Ashby High Street to the George pub in Piercebridge near Darlington in order to film his final event. Here, Sky News presenter Kay Burley was waiting to give Boris a grilling – if he could be persuaded to do one last live interview. This was far from set in stone. Johnson had been up since 3.30 a.m., he'd been speaking all day and he was tired. His right-hand man Will Walden indicated he might just want to meet supporters and make a short speech before heading home. Burley, having travelled 250 miles to put a microphone under Johnson's nose, probably would have done it anyway without prior permission, but all the better if he would agree to it in advance. For a full hour, several phone calls were made, pressing and getting little more than polite vagueness from Walden. He would discuss it with Boris in the helicopter.

Frustration about the non-committal Johnson was taken out on a plough-man's lunch and washed down with wine. Then, about fifteen minutes before his arrival, a call came from Walden. Johnson was happy to be interviewed by Kay. Not only would he chat on the way into the pub, he would address supporters and do a live interview in the beer garden afterwards. 'Boris wants to talk about Juncker. He's got lots to say,' said Walden.

Around the time that Johnson was leaving Selby, the EU President Jean-Claude Juncker was in Brussels holding talks with the new Austrian Chancellor, Christian Kern. The meeting had nothing to do with Brexit, but when Juncker stepped out to meet the press corps afterwards, he was asked for his thoughts on the UK's big decision. 'Out is out,' said Juncker, sternly (fair enough). 'I have to add … (Did you, Mr Juncker, did you HAVE to add this?) … that the British policymakers and the British voters have to know there will be no kind of any renegotiation.' And, just to be clear, he added, 'We have concluded a deal with the Prime Minister, he got the maximum he could receive, we gave the maximum we could give.'[37]

Bang goes Jeremy Corbyn's message of staying in a 'more reformed EU'. Bang goes David Cameron's suggestion a day earlier that he might negotiate further on free movement should Britain find the current reforms ineffective. No. With a gun to its head, Europe had given everything it could. The flimflammery of February's renegotiations was the 'maximum' anyone could achieve in the EU. Juncker, perhaps knowingly in revenge to David Cameron, who had opposed his presidency, pushed voters towards Brexit. Several Out voters have said those remarks sealed it. It was later claimed that he wasn't referring to potential reforms available if the UK remained in the UK, only if they left. But if he wanted to say that, he should have said it.

So, as Boris Johnson arrived for his pint of bitter in the George pub in Darlington, he had a gift from Brussels waiting for him – something new to say. 'If we stay in, there is no prospect of any further change,' Johnson said. 'This is it, folks. We have been told from the horse's mouth that any hope of further change is absolute illusion.' The news bulletins that night would quote Juncker's words from the EU and Johnson's reaction. It played well for the Leave camp. Britain's bargaining over border control and sovereignty was over. If you don't like what you've got – leave. Sleep on that before you vote tomorrow.

There are some things you can't control, but the Remain campaign lost its grip in the short campaign – in part, at least – because they lost the influence of using the government machine outside of the purdah period. This was thanks to a Commons defeat months earlier which in retrospect, may have had a huge impact. To counter this problem, Remain used up its biggest blows before the short campaign and, as we've described in the previous chapter, sometimes they didn't hit the mark. But, furthermore, they were unable to adopt a coherent message to counter the Leave camp's line of attack on immigration. It was right for Remain to major on the economy, but because their campaign was frontloaded, the Leavers could bounce against the ropes and absorb the punches until purdah kicked in. Then when they attacked on immigration, they found their opponent didn't have his guard up. In the end, it did come down to that one word David Cameron identified in his 2014 speech: 'control'.

The next day, from 7 a.m. until 10 p.m., 52 per cent of the electorate changed the course of history.

CONCLUSION

HOW TO LOSE A REFERENDUM

During Faisal Islam's interview with David Cameron in the first 'debate' of the referendum on 2 June 2016, the Sky News political editor asked a question that sparked guffaws of laughter and not a small amount of scorn for the person who was supposed to answer it. 'What comes first, World War III or the global Brexit recession?'[1] This was a reference to a speech Cameron had made a month earlier, in which he talked about Britain's contributions to the First and Second World Wars and 'the price that this country has paid to help restore peace and order in Europe'. Cameron went on to ask: 'Can we be so sure that peace and stability on our continent are assured beyond any shadow of doubt? Is that a risk worth taking?' Amongst a list of conflicts pre-EU, and including the Balkan conflicts of twenty years earlier, he noted that 'the European Union has helped reconcile countries which were once at each other's throats for decades. Britain has a fundamental national interest in maintaining common purpose in Europe to avoid future conflict between European countries.'[2] The Prime Minister pointed out that military opinion was that 'Britain's departure would weaken solidarity and the unity of the West as a whole' and that those who wish the EU to unravel would 'risk the clock being turned back to an age of competing nationalisms in Europe'.

The press, actively encouraged and cheered on by Leave campaigners, decided to report this as Cameron suggesting that Britain leaving the EU would result in World War III.[3] Cameron's point, which was related to the security benefits of the closest possible cooperation by all countries in the world, was twisted and then lost as this speech was piled on top of all the other 'Project Fear' warnings that could be safely ignored as mere campaigning tools.

Yet anyone with a keen sense of history would find it very hard to deny that the European unity project had indeed achieved what Robert Schuman had suggested it might exactly sixty-six years before at his press conference to launch the Schuman Plan. His declaration predicted that 'the solidarity in production thus established will make it plain that any war between France and Germany becomes not merely unthinkable, but materially impossible'.[4] The pooling of sovereignty was supposed to result in national interests being combined with the interests of the member states as a whole. At a time when Germany had invaded France once in a generation for as long as living memory, Jean Monnet was able to secure a political argument for the European Union as a compact to prevent Germany and France from ever destroying the peace of Europe again. Then you can add the relatively seamless integration of not just the formerly dictator-led southern states of Greece, Portugal and Spain, but so many Eastern European countries, released from Soviet occupation and able to rebuild and democratise in the willing embrace of the countries to their west. It would take a cold heart and an incurious mind to reject the notion that European unity had achieved a peace in Europe nobody had thought possible in.1945.

But this peace was less persuasive as a political argument in Britain than it was in Europe. The United Kingdom alone of the major countries on the Continent had had no need to redraw its constitution and parliamentary arrangements or to completely rethink and rebuild its economic model. Continental Europe rebuilt together, pooling sovereignty for what they hoped would be mutual benefit. Britain's integration into that pool, as we have seen, was painful and difficult.

An example of what this integration led to can be seen in the different treatments by British and French media of the end of John Major's first EU summit as Prime Minister in December 1990. It was a big moment on the road to European monetary union, and thus received blanket treatment on all British TV channels and extensive debate about its implications all through the evening. In France, meanwhile, there was no mention of what had just been agreed on economic integration on the main 8 p.m. news, and the communiqué (the official, mutually agreed announcement released to the media) scraped into the midnight bulletin as the tenth item. This is just one example of the difference in the passion of the debate in the two countries. Contrast the intensity of the UK's democratic challenge to any actions the EU has taken with the way those actions have been almost dozily nodded through in France.

The difference in approach should be celebrated. The UK has a press that scrutinises those in power like no other. But at times the level of the debate in the UK has bordered on the hysterical, and contains some imagined nightmares which are simply not so. Often we have heard in the United Kingdom from anti-EU politicians and campaigners about their fears that continued member-ship of the EU would turn Britons into Europeans, instead of retaining their distinctive cultural identity. Yet after sixty years of being in the Union, creating a single market, subjecting themselves to common laws, taking seats in a Euro-pean Parliament and sinking their economic sovereignty into the institutions of Brussels, the French have remained distinctly French, the Italians are still Italian, the Germans German, and so on.[5]

The British have also remained British. One of the more peculiar consequences of this 'Britishness' has been a determination to observe Community rules while many other members made every effort to evade those rules. The truth is that law-making – and law-abiding – works very differently in Britain than it does on the Continent.

Dan Hannan explains the discomfort the British feel about the way laws are made in Europe and applied in the UK. The legal system of England, Northern Ireland and Wales is based on common law, while the EU's legal system is based on civil law. What this means in practice is that in Britain, a citizen can do whatever they want unless it is expressly forbidden, but in Europe, a citizen can only do something if the law expressly permits it.

How does this apply to the EU rule makers? Hannan goes on to explain the difference in political attitudes he saw every week in the European Parliament.

> Faced with a proposal for some new regulatory power, or some new EU directive, the first instinct of a British MEP is to ask: 'What problem would this solve? Why do we need it?' To which the usual answer is: 'But the existing system is unregulated.' The idea that lack of regulation might be a natural condition, that you shouldn't need a licence from the government before embarking on a new venture, is regarded as an Anglo-Saxon eccentricity. In the mind of a Eurocrat, 'unregulated' and 'illegal' are almost synonymous concepts.[6]

Accountant Harold Young, whom we've referred to sometimes in this book for our grassroots Conservative Eurosceptic voice, puts it like this:

> The European Court of Justice is a prescriptive law – not based on the common

law – and that's why I guess even the British legal experts realise this isn't good. The fundamental rights in this country are assumed unless the law states you can't – whereas EU law seems to imply in the way it is written that you are a slave of the state unless there is a paragraph in here that says you aren't.

What's more, once a law or regulation is in place, whether it is ECJ law or British law, the British obey it, but on the Continent there is almost an entire industry set up to evade laws. As historian and Tory peer Max Beloff told *The Times* in 1994, the Continentals were natural law-breakers, 'prepared to vote for anything at Brussels in the confident knowledge that they will only enforce what suits them'.[7]

What this disparity has led to overall is a feeling amongst British Eurosceptics that Europe restricts the UK in its daily life, while amongst our Continental counterparts Europe may often bring nothing much more than a shrug of the shoulders as they carry on doing what they wish. As we saw in Reason 12, this wasn't an option for the 'metric martyrs'.

Given the British tendency to abide by laws they are supposed to abide by, you would have thought that Britain would send the best people they could to the European institutions to get involved with the drafting and influencing of those laws. But Roy Denman, who spent many years working in Europe as a negotiator and a civil servant, found that Britain fundamentally misunderstood the sheer power of what had been created.

Because the Commission is the supranational executive branch (holding power and governing authority) of the European Union, it is more powerful than a national civil service. Under the treaties, the Commission has a virtual monopoly on the power to make proposals to the law-making body, the Council of Ministers. It also watches over implementation of Community legislation and has the power to take a member state to the European Court if it isn't fulfilling its obligations or if it's flouting Community rules. The Commission negotiates trade and aid on behalf of the member states and acts as a broker between member states in the formulation of common positions and policies. So it is of consider-able importance that the nationals appointed to the European Commission are of sufficient quality. It takes true intellectual clout to present a view that is in a national interest in a way that is in the entire European Union's interest. If that can be done, it can make a sizeable difference to the Commission's conclusion.

This is why France has almost always sent to Brussels Commissioners of high intellectual quality, but Denman noticed that Britain, despite having a first-class civil service, mostly chose not to do likewise. A tradition was established that 'middle-level officials, who would never qualify for the top jobs in Whitehall, are sent to the Commission'. This is because British politicians have tended to regard the Commission as nothing more than an interfering, puffed-up bureaucracy and a rather sinister rival, instead of being an institution in which British interests could be well served by enthusiastic and skilful input and influence.

Denman saw the same problem in the Council of Ministers. He argues that British ministers at a Community meeting are not the figures they are in London, and are not treated in Brussels with the deference they are used to. They tend not to really understand the purpose of the Commission and the Council Secretariat (whose role is to assist, advise and coordinate the work of the Council). They tend to read out their introductory statement then find themselves utterly out of their depth in debate. Their French counterpart, usually a graduate of the formidable École Nationale d'Administration, will know their brief backwards, drawing on it for a few points and asking two or three sharp questions of detail. Outfoxed, British ministers try to go straight to the objective in their brief, essentially stating Britain's needs. The French, and others, get a lot further by putting forward a proposal, seemingly of benefit to all, but in practice largely of benefit to the member's country. British ministers are essentially turning up in Brussels for a rugby match intending to play lacrosse. They return to London complaining bitterly about Brussels bureaucracy.

Small wonder, then, that France has always seemed to the UK to be the main beneficiaries of the European Union while Britain feeds off scraps. The British press have, of course, noticed this and in Denman's view 'lost no opportunity, and invented many, to deride and vilify the jacks in office of Brussels'.[8]

But let us not forget that the British press enthusiastically supported the Yes campaign at the 1975 EC referendum. Is it fair to blame them for causing the British view of the iniquity of Brussels, or was it the entire tenor of British engagement with the European institutions from the moment the UK joined that caused the press's and thus the British view?

This book starts from the beginning of British engagement with the European institutions, and tells the story of how, for the first fifteen years after the Second World War, there was in fact very little engagement with those institutions.

Britain was absent at the creation of the European unity project – the European Coal and Steel Community – because Jean Monnet had insisted that they subscribe to the principle of the supranational nature of the institution created before they even enter negotiations. Yet the Dutch joined on the pretext of saying that they accepted the principle, but reserving the right to withdraw from the negotiations if they didn't turn out to their liking. As Patrick Gordon Walker, Kenneth Younger and Winston Churchill commented, this meant that there was no chance of influencing the scheme in a direction more amenable to British interests. Oliver Franks and Dean Acheson go further, the former arguing that the 1950 decision not to engage cost Britain its leadership role in Europe for ever, and the latter asserting that it was the greatest mistake any country made in the post-war period.

But that was nothing compared to the British attitude to the Spaak Committee talks that led to the creation of the European Communities (EEC, Euratom and ECSC combined). To be invited to send a minister with no pre-conditions set on participation and instead to send a civil servant with strict instructions not to agree to anything can be ascribed to many misperceptions in the British psyche. It was a combination of arrogance and negligence, perhaps, but those terms are best used with hindsight.

It is easier to explain this decision if one understands that British European policy from 1945 to 1955 was based on international intergovernmental cooperation, with an outward-looking, global trading perspective, via bodies such as the OEEC that still allowed them to fit in with the US alliance and the development of the Commonwealth. It contained within it a misunderstanding of the relationship that should exist between the European institutions being built and the nation states that built them. A degree of pooled sovereignty, with governments handing powers in limited areas to common institutions, could actually be in the national interest of member states. But without the same overwhelming national need to pool its sovereignty, and with no leading political figure ready to merge Britain's future with Europe while abandoning the Commonwealth, the massive opportunity to shape the Treaty of Rome was missed.[9] The civil servant sent with instructions not to agree to anything, Russell Bretherton, was himself writing home to his political masters of the time to say exactly that: 'If we are prepared to take a firm line, that we want to come in and will be a part of this, we can make this body into anything we like. But if we don't say that, something will probably happen and we shan't exercise any influence over it.'[10] The fact that the French did take part, did join and got special treatment for their colonies while the British stayed out and thus never achieved the same deal for the Commonwealth shows what might have happened had Britain been in a position to influence the setting up of the European Community.

What was thus created in 1957 was an organisation anathema to British conceptions of sovereignty and one that would require Britain to make enormous political and economic changes to be able to eventually join it.

Yet still there was one more opportunity to influence the European Communities in a substantial way. As Harold Macmillan came to the realisation in 1960 that Britain's exclusion from the customs union was hurting its economy and Britain's exclusion from the top table in Brussels was hurting it politically, there was still much about the European unity project that was up in the air. The method of financing the EC's budget wasn't agreed until 1969, which was also when the Common Agricultural Policy was signed. The Common Fisheries Policy wasn't signed, as we know, until the morning of 30 June 1970. Charles de Gaulle was yet to 'empty chair' the EC in his attempt to secure a national veto.

President John F. Kennedy and his Under Secretary of State George Ball told Macmillan in no uncertain terms that Britain would be best served by joining the European Communities and then negotiating from the inside. Had Britain done so, the EC would still have grown (even de Gaulle couldn't stop that) and vital national interests could have been protected from the inside. Instead, two years were spent dragging out negotiations in a manner that made clear to de Gaulle that Britain was in no sense 'European'. When he was put in a position by French elections in 1962 to have full power to veto their application, he did so.

Roy Denman notes that Britain had remained in 'defiant ignorance and self-assertive insularity' during this time, not recognising changes in the nearby world and suffering from delusions of grandeur. Those delusions had drawn strength firstly from the idea that Britain was the centre of a huge Commonwealth (which in fact was at that time fragmenting) and secondly from the notion that Britain enjoyed a special relationship with the United States (which has never abandoned the tough and unsentimental pursuit of its own interests in the outside world that it has practised since it was created).

But the other source of delusion was, paradoxically, an inner lack of confidence. Denman reports that:

> A Continental observer was struck in the first negotiations for entry to the Community by the anxious desire of the British to have safeguards spelt out in the most detailed form ten years in advance, when robust use of elbow power alone would have been bound to protect our interests.[11]

The first three chapters of our history of Britain and Europe make it clear that the three missed opportunities to join the EC at the start produced an organisation and a set of institutions that by their very nature were hard to explain and defend if you were on the Remain side during the 2016 EU referendum. The basic concepts of freedom of movement of labour, capital and goods and services meant that those on the Leave side who believed in the importance of 'borders' had an easy job to explain to the populace that as long as Britain was a member of the EC, we would no longer be an independent country – as best exemplified by Boris Johnson's last words of the final debate, when he claimed that 23 June would be Britain's 'Independence Day'. Even the Remain camp's Craig Oliver, reflecting on the campaign, said: 'When you sit down and explain to any reasonable person that in order to be part of this international organisation you have to accept immigration into your country which is unlimited no matter what the circumstances, most people would say, "That is crazy."'

The two court cases that took place in the mid-1960s interpreting the provisions of the Treaty of Rome that Britain had played no part in creating were particularly significant. They established the principles that EC law applied to every EU state and that the EC law was supreme over the law of member states. This was really where the strength of 'take back control' as a winning Leave slogan came from. If you believe that you should be able to vote to install and remove those who make your laws, then the concept that you cannot do that with European institutions is a compelling argument against membership. Even if, as many do, you believe that the laws made by European institutions are generally in agreement with your principles (e.g. environmental and social legislation), it takes a very negative view of the British electorate to assume those laws would not exist if presented to the UK voter. One might say it also takes a reasonably negative view of successive Tory governments as well.

Then you have the effect of the Common Agricultural Policy and the financing of the EU budget on the 2016 referendum campaign. This was personified by the red bus, with the claim that £350 million a week is sent to the EU, and that it's money that could be better spent on the UK's priorities, such as the NHS. Britain was not at the table in 1969 to negotiate those budget arrangements, and thus has always been a net contributor to the EU. Britain gets significant membership benefits back from that contribution, but that argument was barely used, being drowned out by 'Project Fear'.

Now add in the Common Fisheries Policy and the effect that its operation has had on the British fishing community. Again, this was something the British had to accept as part of the *acquis communautaire* at midday on 30 June 1970, making the negotiations that followed 'peripheral, accidental and secondary',[12] according to lead negotiator Con O'Neill. When the fishermen came down the Thames to protest this state of affairs (admittedly with Nigel Farage to amplify their protests), they were met by the two fingers of Bob Geldof and a group of leering Remainers dancing to 'The In Crowd'. Geldof used the same arguments politicians have often used about immigration, claiming the CFP has benefited the country as a whole, while completely ignoring the effect it can have on individual fishermen.

The truth is that EU membership has its benefits *and* costs, and did so right from 1 January 1973, when Britain joined. These benefits and costs are political as well as economic.

The task for the British political elite – who were, after all, the people who took the UK into the European Union – has been to use their skill and wisdom to repeatedly repel the forces of nationalism that have always remained in British society, for better or for worse. They needed to create the political context in which the benefits of European integration to both Britain and the EU could be nurtured and supported, explained and clarified. The British political elite have a lot to answer for here.

Take Edward Heath, who was the Prime Minister who finally took the opportunity to take Britain into Europe. Heath barely attempted to explain to the British people the virtues of diluting national sovereignty while pooling it in the European institutions. Instead, he talked merely of extending Britain's influence in the world. This was a triumphalist philosophy that meant a succession of British leaders right up to David Cameron fed the British people a narrative of 'winning' a constant series of zero-sum games against 'opponents' whom they should have considered partners. Not a single Prime Minister, for instance, has ever returned from an EU summit and reported that he or she supported or opposed a decision solely because it was best for the future of Europe.[13]

This is because the British political class has possibly never experienced, and definitely never conveyed, the sense of idealism about the European project shared by many of their European counterparts. Heath until 1974 and then Harold Wilson and the Yes campaign in the 1975 referendum presented European membership as a series of pragmatic benefits – such as a lowering of the cost of food or the number of jobs that might be created. Because Britain was sold EEC membership as a pragmatic step, the British public have always judged the results of membership in pragmatic terms. It has thus been impossible for Britain to become a leading player in the European Union, because it simply does not share the idealism about the project it should have.[14]

The lack of information available at the time of the 1975 referendum on the wider implications of the European unity project is the basis for the sense of betrayal reported by many older Leave voters during and after the 2016 EU referendum campaign. Our chapter on this starts and ends with John Francis thinking he was voting Yes in 1975 for a free trade area and nothing more. It ends with him describing the realisation that he had in fact signed up to political and economic union, with laws made elsewhere and the British government unable to exert control on vital areas such as immigration and trade. Francis genuinely believed on 23 June 2016 that his vote would free his children and grandchildren, providing them with opportunities they could not have as part of the EU. He is one of many people who voted Yes in 1975 and Leave in 2016 whose motivations have, at the time of writing, yet to be understood by the younger generation. Hopefully, if you have come this far in this book, you will understand them better.

What followed the 1975 referendum was complacency. Pro-European UK politicians thought they had won the argument as well as the decision. The other side had lost and should now just shut up. Where the European elite should have continued to try to proselytise the unbelievers, they instead remained inert and baffled by the continued belligerence of those who never gave up. This refusal to engage in discussion and debate meant that there were many missed opportunities to improve the EU's 'brand' in the UK.

For example, in the 1980s there was a huge inward investment into the UK by the Asian car and electronics industries. This was a direct result of Britain being the main access point for Asian companies into the European Union market.

The government, though, was too discomfited by that link to trumpet it to the British press and public. During the 2016 referendum campaign, this link *was* raised, but suddenly bringing it up then when it had barely been mentioned before was again dismissed as just more 'Project Fear' scaremongering.

Complacency also reigned in the British Parliament. Throughout the 1980s and early 1990s, as economic and political integration began to creep further and further forward, Parliament was not persuaded by Commons sub-committees to take what they were reporting seriously. Words that would soon become Community law, such as the 1986 Single European Act, were waved through with astonishing alacrity by a Parliament who were happy to say they were concerned about Brussels dictatorship but did very little to scrutinise or challenge it.

Under this negligence, European union crept up on the citizens of Britain, with repeated encroachments on parliamentary sovereignty going almost unchallenged. These were encompassed in the 1986 Single European Act, the second reading of the 1991 Maastricht Treaty (it was the third reading that attracted the main rebellion), the 1999 Amsterdam Treaty, the 2003 Nice Treaty and the 2009 Lisbon Treaty. Each of these treaties involved a significant transferral of power to the European Union, as the areas in which the national veto could be used were ceded to the majority voting system that would allow the EU to 'get things done', especially as it expanded to the twenty-eight member states it had at the time of the 2016 vote.

Looking back, the Eurosceptics, small band that they were, were correct about the impact of the EU citizenship being created in 1992, and of the Lisbon Treaty making the European Union a separate legal entity. These should have been debated and discussed at length in Parliament, not just at committee stage. In fact, going back to what we said earlier in this chapter, these moves could have been more effectively challenged at Commission level before they were even proposals if Britain had focused more on filling European roles with its best people.

The gradual loss of control and sovereignty that all this entailed was hard to present positively when it came to the 2016 referendum campaign, and so the likes of Michael Gove and Boris Johnson found it easy to present it negatively.

However, as we have said, the 'sovereignty' group of Leave voters probably only account for just over 40 per cent of the Leave voters (so 22 per cent of all voters). Most of the rest were probably motivated to the ballot box by the effect of mass immigration into the UK after the 2004 accession of eight Eastern

European countries into the EU, and many who claim sovereignty as their number one concern can only cite border control as the power they would like to retain.

We have been clear in Reason 8 that whether or not Britain applied transition controls on those new arrivals in terms of their ability to get work permits, they would have come anyway. The lure of countries with more than double your GDP in which you have the same citizenship rights as any other, where you can get free healthcare and education, receive a boost to your income through tax credits and have your human rights protected more than almost anywhere else would have been too tempting to ignore. So once the 'A8' accession countries (the collective name given to the eight Eastern European countries who joined in 2004, excluding Malta and Cyprus, who weren't as poor) were allowed into the EU, the challenge of mass migration and their integration into the UK was always going to exist.

This is why it was so important to have planned properly for those people. In Reason 8, we tell the story of how the government presented data that suggested only 13,000 people a year would arrive, when in fact it has been well over six figures each year. We detail how requiring new arrivals to register in order to be employed should have given the government some knowledge of where they were, thus helping to accommodate them, but the arrival of so many self-employed workers meant this didn't work. The effect of that failure was localised overcrowding of NHS facilities and state schools all over the country. Moreover, skilled workers from abroad were prepared to work for far less than the British public and this affected pay and working conditions. Labour MPs' desire for measures to contain the impact was met with indifference.

All these sins of omission and commission mean that there was a ready mass of people prepared to listen to Nigel Farage, who was also prepared to listen to them. What's more, the people affected by and concerned about immigration were ready to follow Farage all the way to the ballot box.

'Take back control' could be used in many ways. It wasn't just about law-making, or economic policy, or immigration policy; it could be used to say to people who felt left behind that they had this *one* chance to take a bit of control over their lives. This *one* time when their vote wouldn't be subsumed into irrelevance by an inequitable general election voting system. This *one* opportunity to cast a vote that would definitely, really count.

Reason 9 details the side-story of a group of people in the UK who felt abandoned by the political class, for whom politics had nothing to offer. A group of people whose real incomes had fallen while everyone else's had risen, who had seen their communities decimated by decisions taken in Westminster. Although these people thought Tony Blair may improve matters, many found after thirteen years of a Labour government that their position and opportunities had actually worsened. When these people complained about their situation, they were told they were lazy and racist.

might

Almost 3 million people voted in the 2016 EU referendum who didn't vote in the 2015 general election. Most of them voted Leave.

Then we have David Cameron's decision to call the referendum. At the very end of his campaign diary, Craig Oliver, Cameron's director of communications, watches his boss leave Downing Street at the end of his reign as Prime Minister. As Cameron and family wave and get into their car to take them away, Oliver thinks, 'I hope history will be kind to you.'[15]

At the time of writing of this book, David Cameron hasn't produced his autobiography. When he does, we are sure he will explain why he called a referendum many didn't feel he needed to call. Perhaps, as Tony Blair did in his autobiography about his decision to go to Iraq, he will paint it as a principled decision based on what was best for the country. Cameron will be keenly aware that his explanation will help define how history will remember him.

We wonder if he will come clean on whether his constant expressions of Euroscepticism – starting with his attempt to get selected to his seat in Witney, running through his commitment to leave the EPP in the 2005 leadership election, through to his railing against the Lisbon Treaty – were real or emphasised for political gain. We wonder if he will acknowledge the negative consequences of his behaviour in 2011 in not signing the extension to the Lisbon Treaty. That agreement that might have helped the Eurozone, and his consequent trumpeting of the 'national interest' to the press back in the UK meant he lost the pool of goodwill he needed to draw from during the negotiations in 2015–16. Did he really believe his 2013 Bloomberg speech that 'democratic consent for the EU in Britain is now wafer-thin',[16] or was committing to the referendum simply about doing what he thought could keep him in No. 10 for longer? Did he think he might end up in coalition negotiations in which he could give that commitment away? Does he regret raising expectations too high, be it by a promise to reduce immigration to the tens of thousands or by suggesting that he could actually make a difference in his negotiations before the referendum? Does he regret not authorising the 'blue on blue' attacks that might have neutralised the relentless advance of Boris Johnson and Michael Gove during the campaign, even though they were attacking manifesto commitments they themselves had signed up to, and even though they were making some, well, 'audacious' promises?

This book makes clear that David Cameron did not lose the EU referendum alone. It was lost by the succession of Prime Ministers, Foreign Secretaries, civil servants and European leaders who have led this country and Europe since 1945. As we said at the beginning, victory has many fathers and defeat is an orphan, but this particular defeat has numerous parents. You might notice that the pages in this book are almost evenly balanced between what happened before and what happened after the calling of what we've termed the 'crowbar' referendum. So when it comes to the question with which we started this book – was it lost before or after Bloomberg? – it seems we have fallen down the middle. But on balance it seems history was more important than the campaign – and its significance was massively underestimated at the time.

Certainly, when Cameron called it, it didn't look like he would lose. Not many experts or politicians or pundits saw his defeat coming, even on the final day. The polls were obviously wrong, and this in itself was a factor. In Remain's case, their internal poll on 23 June was out by 5 per cent. Their final poll had them winning 53:47; instead, they lost 48:52. That particular Populus poll was in line with many others. Perhaps, then, the polls were five points wrong the whole way along. That would mean Remain was barely ever in front, with the possible exception of mid-May, before purdah kicked in, when Leave was on the rack over the economy.

This perception of being in the lead not only affected political strategic decisions; it also left most members of the public assuming the UK would remain – and that assumption in itself may have affected the vote. It also tells us that, while Cameron may not have been doomed from the moment he called the referendum, he was facing a much bigger struggle than he realised. His confidence was misplaced from the very start. His position was made worse by the very factors that influenced his decision to call the referendum.

So, finally to the wider question of *How to Lose a Referendum*? First, it helps to have history against you. The forefathers of Brexit played a large part. Missing those opportunities to shape the creation of the European Community from 1950 to 1963 was important. So was the decision to join the EC in 1973, first without a referendum but then holding a referendum that lacked a proper discussion of what the country was really voting for. The succession of encroachments on the UK's sovereignty waved through by successive parliaments from 1985 to 2009 didn't help. Nor did the timidity with which the benefits of EU membership have been communicated for the forty-three years between joining and voting to leave.

Secondly, to lose, it helps if you start the campaign with a failure. Once David Cameron decided the only political option he had was to call an In/Out referendum, the lack of goodwill he had built up with other European leaders was not helpful in his negotiations. Although, there is always the question of whether he asked for enough. Clearly, he soon watered down his requests in the face of intractable opposition from Angela Merkel. There is really no question that he set expectations too high for what he could achieve and it would have been useful if he had read the first nine chapters of this book before he laid out his ambitions. It all led to a negotiation so weak that, while it may have been significant in the halls of Brussels, it couldn't be used by Cameron during the campaign and was easy to portray negatively in the Eurosceptic press.

Thirdly, to lose, it is important to have an opposition more passionate and prepared than you are. There was the series of early parliamentary victories by the Leave-supporting MPs. They set the question as Remain/Leave instead of the Yes/No that would have resulted in their campaign being too easy to categorise as negative. There was swiftly organised opposition to the scrapping of purdah, leading to a parliamentary victory that was important in dictating the terms of the campaign. They brutally exploited the weaknesses of Cameron's EU deal and, crucially, unlike 1975, the campaign to leave the EU transformed into something mainstream and credible – indeed, led by one of the most popular politicians in Britain, in addition to one of the cleverest. If you are going to lose a referendum, have your star player on the opposing team.

The resultant awarding of the designation to Vote Leave freed up the agitator and 'Pied Piper of Brexit' Nigel Farage to hoover up those disaffected voters who don't always go to the polls – a freedom he admits was helpful. In some ways, the Eurosceptic movement was a forty-year relay race: the oddballs and extremists of '75 handed the baton to Major's bastards, who ploughed a lonely furrow before Farage ran the third leg. Once the referendum was called, UKIP couldn't have carried the baton to the finish line alone – they needed the figures of Boris Johnson and Michael Gove to run the home straight, with the path smoothed by their 'Mad Men' strategists. Cameron's team was running at a different pace, they didn't anticipate the passing on of the baton and they hadn't been training for nearly as long. Despite the factions within it, the Leave camp had the advantage of refining its message over the course of a much longer race and knowing exactly how to deploy it.

Then there was the flawed Stronger In campaign. Up against the two Leave groups, the rapidly assembled Remainers had to be led by a Prime Minister who had always claimed to have a foot in the other camp. Cameron was hemmed in by his own history. He had spent a decade riding the wave of Euroscepticism, but suddenly he was the EU's last defence, condemned to deliver a shrivelled, negative campaign about the dangers of leaving, because anything else would have been disingenuous.

He also wasn't as popular as narrowly winning the 2015 general election had made him feel. He couldn't even demand loyalty from some of his closest friends, and in part it became a referendum on him as well. And so came the Project Fear strategy that was starting to wear thin on the electorate from overuse in other campaigns, reliant on a past performance that was no longer effective. People were incredulous of experts, tired of Project Fear, dubious of the ruling class and frankly fed up with the EU. Too many of their problems had been blamed on the EU for too long – and those problems didn't seem to be shifting. Add to this a disinterested Labour Party leader and no powerful progressive voice to appeal to the large section of people who don't vote Conservative. There were just too many political headwinds.

Finally, we have the wider backdrop. The 2008 financial crisis had cast a long shadow over the UK; it undermined confidence in government, politicians, big business, banks and all their spokespeople. Outside London, people who'd barely recovered from the recession began to think the same people who'd caused it were once again taking them for fools. Added to this was the euro crisis, the migrant crisis and the terror attacks in Europe. The brand of the EU was in tatters.

The public was rightly furious at the way things had panned out. How can you argue with someone who hasn't had a pay rise for eight years? How can you argue with someone who feels all the money is spent on one end of the country? People felt they and their families were still suffering from mistakes made by bankers, politicians and regulators. Across Europe and beyond, there had been a growth in a more populist and intolerant style of politics. Why? Because for ten years people had seen no improvement in their income or assets. In a Chatham House speech in February 2017, John Major noted:

> In every decade since the 1920s, per decade incomes rose 20 per cent, but between 2007 and 2016 they rose 1.6 per cent … It is unsurprising they are dissatisfied with what has happened and they have shown that dissatisfaction and there is a list of attendant things you can hang to it such as migration across Europe.[17]

Therefore, a final reason the political establishment lost this referendum is that without hope and aspiration, people lose faith in political systems. And in that political climate, people were invited to either 'Remain' or tick the box to 'Leave'. One box says 'Everything is fine'; the other says 'Let's get out of this matrix'. The EU was remote. No one was ever told that there might be any benefit from it, so why would you feel any harm from leaving it? It was a free hit – a chance to kick the system. So some people took this free hit and voted to leave the European Union.

It might sound like we've given you a lot of reasons. But this is how it was. In aviation, they call it the 'Swiss Cheese Model' when an accident is found to have been caused by a number of parallel factors, both immediate and historical – the holes of the cheese line up. You have the missed opportunities, miscommunications and non-cooperation that characterise seventy years of Britain's relationship with the European unity project. You have millions of people who voted Yes to Britain in Europe in 1975 and felt betrayed by the ultimate destination in terms of the political and economic integration of that project. You have the years in which British sovereignty was pooled far further than the leaders involved could have imagined. You have committed politicians and thinkers able to express so well why this is a problem to a people who still possess an 'island' mentality unique on the European continent. You have a population who were never properly sold the benefits of European integration, but many of whom saw the costs personally. You have a particular politician able to explain why those costs were directly caused by the UK government's immigration policies combined with freedom of movement being so integral to the whole European unity project. You have a Prime Minister calling a referendum that could have been avoided, promising a negotiation that to all intents and purposes failed. You have a pro-European campaign riven by a lack of cohesion and the disinterest of one of its potential leaders, making the poll a referendum on the current Prime Minister rather than just on Europe. You have an anti-European campaign able to take advantage of all this, buoyed by the decision of one of Britain's most popular politicians to join it.

Brexit was ultimately the culmination of a constellation of circumstances that had not happened before and might never happen again. Whether the referendum was lost the moment David Cameron called it or whether a stronger campaign might have been enough to change the face of history will remain an open question, but what is certain is that you cannot understand the result simply by looking at the four months leading up to the referendum.

If anyone tells you there is a simple explanation, tell them to read this book.

ACKNOWLEDGEMENTS

This book would not have been possible without the help, support and expertise of a wide variety of people. We start and end with the four most important people. Olivia Beattie and Iain Dale at Biteback Publishing 'got' what we were trying to do with the book, and their encouragement and advice was extremely helpful all the way through. We were often agog at Olivia's editing prowess, which was so skilled and rigorous and made a massive difference to our journey from manuscript to book.

Books like this rely on a number of sources, some of them primary and some of them secondary. A lot of people gave up their time to give us their recollections and views of the campaign, as well as 'colouring in' our history of Britain in Europe. Jason's Dictaphone is full of invaluable contributions from Lee Cain, Douglas Carswell, Nick Clegg, Dominic Cummings, Matthew Elliott, Nigel Farage, Jonathan Faull, Liam Fox, Neil Hamilton, Daniel Hannan, Alan Johnson, John Mann, James McGrory, Seumas Milne, Sir Craig Oliver, (Lord) David Owen, Justin Schlosberg, Will Straw, Gisela Stuart, Gawain Towler and Theresa Villiers. He's also drawn on conversations and interviews with Jeremy Corbyn, Angela Eagle, Boris Johnson, Neil Kinnock, Khalid Mahmood, Theresa May, John McDonnell and correspondence with Michael Gove. We are also grateful to those who gave their time in phone conversations and visits at the European Parliament, Commission and Council.

Both of us are eternally grateful to the many authors who came before us and chronicled the history of Britain in Europe as well as the referendum campaign. Andrew Marr and Vernon Bogdanor inspired Paul with their ability to weave stories around people, deftly turning contemporary historical figures mired in the minutiae of politics into *dramatis personae*. Michael Charlton and Hugo Young managed to get many of those people, whether civil servants or politicians, to speak frankly about the decisions and controversies of their time. Edmund Dell, Sir Roy Denman, Stephen George, Sean Greenwood, Christopher Lord, Alex May and John Young provided invaluable context around which the story could be told.

Colour was added by biographers of those involved, including Alan Bullock, John Campbell, Alistair Horne, Roy Jenkins, Charles Moore, Kenneth O. Morgan, Ben Pimlott, Robert Rhodes James, Anthony Seldon, Martin Westlake and Philip Ziegler.

Meanwhile, the autobiographies, memoirs and diaries of Tony Benn, Tony Blair, James Callaghan, Denis Healey, Edward Heath, Roy Jenkins, Harold Macmillan, John Major, Jean Monnet and Margaret Thatcher provided additional helpful thoughts in explaining the motivations behind the decisions made (and not made) over time.

Just before and immediately after the referendum, books were published that we found extremely helpful in telling the story of this most memorable campaign. For these, we are grateful to Arron Banks, Owen Bennett, Daniel Hannan, Denis MacShane, Sir Craig Oliver and Tim Shipman.

To all this, we add the work of many journalists who reported on the twenty years that led up to the 2016 referendum, the invaluable Hansard (the report of everything said in Parliament) and the CVCE website (a one-stop shop for digital research on European integration).

Wherever possible, we have endeavoured to give proper attribution to all of our sources. If we have not succeeded in doing so, please contact our publisher c/o Olivia Beattie, Biteback Publishing, 3 Albert Embankment, London SE1 7SP and we will do what we can to put it right.

Jason and I want to thank Sky News and Latymer Upper School for their support and encouragement of the work we were doing.

Finally, we couldn't have written this book without the support of our wives, Kerrie and Emily, who also 'got' what we were trying to do, and gave us the time, patience and love we needed to do our topic justice.

ABOUT THE AUTHORS

JASON FARRELL is a senior political correspondent for Sky News. He has been a broadcast journalist for fifteen years and twice shortlisted for the Royal Television Society's Specialist Journalist of the Year Award. He started out at News Direct radio, followed by ITV News, where he covered the 2005 general election. He moved to 5 News in May 2005 and finally Sky News in 2010, where he was head of investigations and a senior correspondent before being promoted to senior political correspondent. He has been at the forefront of the major developments in the run-up to the Scottish referendum, the 2015 general election and the EU referendum. He travelled with David Cameron to European summits during his pre-referendum renegotiations, followed Boris Johnson on his campaign trail through the UK and was at the Leave.EU event with Nigel Farage on the night of the referendum. He covered the momentous political fallout from this dramatic moment in British politics, including the departure of the Prime Minister from No. 10, Theresa May's appointment as PM and the 2017 snap election. As well as news reports and analysis for Sky News, Farrell has also made numerous documentaries for the channel. In 2016, he produced and presented *The Raqqa Resistance* about citizen journalists risking their lives in the ISIS-held city. He also made *Brussels: Terror Central*, which explored the unique aspects of the city that has made it a hotbed for Islamic State converts. In 2017, he made *Primodos: The Secret Drug Scandal* – about a controversial pregnancy test pill. Previously, he's reported on the social impact of the euro crisis in Greece and Spain and carried out numerous exclusive reports and investigations for Sky News. Jason is married with two children and lives in west London.

PAUL GOLDSMITH is a politics and economics teacher at Latymer Upper School in west London as well as a blogger on the same subjects. Having spent ten years in the business world as a management consultant, he qualified as a teacher in 2006. He spent four years at a north-west London comprehensive school, where he led the teaching of economics and politics and was also head of careers education, before moving into the independent sector in 2010 to teach politics and economics and be a head of year. In 2014, Paul started an economics and politics blog which posted analysis every day for a year running up to the 2015 general election. (www.pjgoldsmith.com). With no publicity, the blog was read by over 100,000 people including leading journalists from the BBC, ITN and Sky News who were covering the campaign. Goldsmith has also written online study notes that are used by thousands of A-level politics students. He has an MBA from Cass Business School, City University, part of which involved extensive research, speaking around the world and working with multinational and government clients on the creation, maintenance and destruction of reputation. He is a Fellow of the Royal Society of Arts. Paul is married with two children and lives in west London.

ENDNOTES

INTRODUCTION

1 Hughes, Laura and McCann, Kate (2016), 'Polling day as it happened – June 23rd', *Daily Telegraph*, 23 June 2016: http://www.telegraph.co.uk/news/2016/06/23/polling-day-as-it-happened---june-23rd/

2 Oliver, Craig (2016), *Unleashing Demons*, Hodder and Stoughton, loc. 156

3 Oliver, Craig (2016), ibid., loc. 169–70

4 Vine, Sarah (2016), '"Gosh, I suppose I better get up!" Sarah Vine (aka Mrs Gove) reveals what her husband said when he learned Leave had won the referendum... and how PM's resignation was "absolutely" not intended', *Daily Mail*, 29 June 2016, http://www.dailymail.co.uk/news/article-3665146/SARAH-VINE-Victory-vitriol-craziest-days-life.html

5 Simons, Ned (2016), 'EU Referendum result: Leaked Labour script tells MPs to argue Jeremy Corbyn "led from the front" in campaign', Huffington Post, 24 June 2016, http://www.huffingtonpost.co.uk/entry/eu-referendum-result-leaked-labour-script-tells-partys-mps-to-argue-jeremy-corbyn-led-from-the-front-in-campaign_uk_576cc89ae4b08d2c5638dd7b

6 Cummings, Dominic (2017), 'On the referendum #21: Branching histories of the 2016 referendum and "the frogs before the storm"', blog published 9 January 2017, https://dominiccummings.wordpress.com/2017/01/09/on-the-referendum-21-branching-histories-of-the-2016-referendum-and-the-frogs-before-the-storm-2/

7 Cameron, David (June 2016), 'EU Referendum outcome: PM statement, 24 June 2016', https://www.gov.uk/government/speeches/eu-referendum-outcome-pm-statement-24-june-2016

8 Cameron, David (June 2016), ibid.

9 https://twitter.com/david_cameron/status/595112367358406656?lang=en

REASON 1

1 Donoughue, Bernard and Jones, George W. (1973), *Herbert Morrison: Portrait of a Politician*, Weidenfeld & Nicolson, p. 981

2 Charlton, Michael (1983), *The Price of Victory*, British Broadcasting Corporation, p. 11

3 Phrase used by George Eulas Foster in a speech to the Canadian Parliament, 16 January 1896, praising Britain's foreign policy of isolation from European Affairs – full quote in Partington, Angela (1992), *The Oxford Dictionary of Quotations*, Fourth Edition, Oxford University Press

4 Hyam, Ronald (2002), *Britain's Imperial Century, 1815–1914: A Study of Empire and Expansion*, Palgrave

5 Eyre Crowe, 'Memorandum on the Present State of British Relations with France and Germany' (1 January 1907), quoted in Charlton, op. cit., p. 29

6 May, Alex (2000), *Britain and Europe since 1945*, Addison Wesley Longman Ltd, p. 97

7 For a much fuller description of how Britain had to remove itself from isolation from Europe, see the transcript of the lecture 'Britain and the Continent' by Professor Vernon Bogdanor, delivered 17 September 2013 at Gresham College, London: http://www.gresham.ac.uk/lectures-and-events/britain-and-the-continent

8 Brown Wells, Sherrill (2011), *Jean Monnet: Unconventional Statesman*, Lynne Rienner Publishers, pp. 127–8

9 Monnet, Jean (1978), *Memoires*, Doubleday, p. 274

10 The full text of the Schuman Declaration can be found in many places, but the official website of the European Union seems the most appropriate source: https://europa.eu/european-union/about-eu/symbols/europe-day/schuman-declaration_en

11 For a useful record of these attempts, see https://euobserver.com/political/32291

12 Bogdanor, Vernon (September 2013), op. cit.
13 Bogdanor, Vernon (November 2013), 'From the European Coal and Steel Community to the Common Market', delivered 12 November 2013 at Gresham College, London: http://www.gresham.ac.uk/lectures-and-events/from-the-european-coal-and-steel-community-to-the-common-market
14 HC Deb, 22 January 1948, cols 398–9
15 Quoted in Young, Hugo (1998), *This Blessed Plot: Britain and Europe from Churchill to Blair*, Macmillan, p. 42
16 Dell, Edmund (1995), *The Schuman Plan and the British Abdication of Leadership in Europe*, Oxford University Press, p. 81
17 Lord, Christopher (1996), *Absent at the Creation: Britain and the Formation of the European Community, 1950–52*, Dartmouth Publishing Company, p. 6
18 Acheson, Dean (1970), *Present at the Creation: My Years at the State Department*, Hamilton, p. 385
19 Lord, Christopher (1996), op. cit., p. 41
20 Lord, Christopher (1996), ibid., p. 41
21 HC Deb, 26 June 1950, col. 1940
22 Dell, Edmund (1995), op. cit., p. 85
23 Charlton, Michael (1983), op. cit., p. 106
24 Macmillan, Harold (August 1950), Speech to the European Council, Strasbourg France, quoted in Bogdanor, Vernon (November 2013), op. cit.
25 HC Deb, 16 November 1998, col. 685
26 Memorandum by Sir Ivone Kirkpatrick, 11 May 1950, quoted in May, Alex (1999), *Britain and Europe since 1945*, Longman, p. 101
27 DBPO 77, quoted in Dell, Edmund (1995), op. cit. p. 77
28 Conclusions of a meeting of the Cabinet on the refusal to participate in the negotiations on the Schuman Plan (2 June 1950): http://www.cvce.eu/content/publication/2009/7/6/8737a230-6924-4905-8004-dee4385ad38e/publishable_en.pdf
29 Charlton, Michael (1983), op. cit., p. 99
30 Charlton, Michael (1983), ibid., p. 115
31 Young, Hugo (1998), op. cit., p. 65
32 Charlton Michael (1983), op. cit., p. 110; Churchill's speech: HC Deb, 27 June 1950, cols 2140–56
33 Young, Hugo (1998), op. cit., p. 68
34 Charlton, Michael (1983), op. cit., p. 119
35 Hannan, Daniel (2016a), *Why Vote Leave*, Head of Zeus, p. 89
36 Kirkpatrick, Ivone (1950), 'Memorandum by Sir I. Kirkpatrick on the political implications of the Schuman Plan (11 May 1950)': http://www.cvce.eu/content/publication/1999/1/1/41496a26-f320-4f6a-8d5e-e46f89d7af14/publishable_en.pdf
37 Lord, Christopher (1996), op. cit., p. 114
38 HC Deb, 27 June 1950, cols 2134–40
39 Charlton, Michael (1983), op. cit., p. 123

REASON 2

1   Letter from Winston Churchill to Anthony Eden, 21 October 1942, quoted in Churchill, Winston (2002), *The Second World War*, Random House, p. 622
2   Address given by Winston Churchill, Zurich, 19 September 1946: accessed on CVCE website: http://www.cvce.eu/en/recherche/unit-content/-/unit/02bb76df-d066-4c08-a58a-d4686a3e68ff/e8f94da5-5911-4571-9010-cdcb50654d43/Resources#7dc5a4cc-4453-4c2a-b130-b534b7d76ebd_en&overlay
3   Article in first edition of *United Europe*, the newsletter of the United Europe group; quoted in Joyce, Christopher (2002), *Questions of Identity: Exploring the Character of Europe*, I. B. Tauris, p. 91
4   Rhodes James, Robert (1974), *Winston S. Churchill: His complete speeches 1897–1963*, Chelsea House Publishers, p. 7900
5   HC Deb, 27 June 1950, cols 2170–72
6   Charlton, Michael (1983), op. cit., pp. 135–6, 139
7   Young, Hugo (1998), op. cit., p. 73
8   Eden, Anthony (1960), *The Memoirs of the Rt Hon. Anthony Eden: Full Circle*, Cassell, pp. 36–7
9   Charlton, Michael (1983), op. cit., p. 138
10 Lord, Christopher (1996), op. cit., pp. 109, 111

11 Young, John (2000), *Britain and European Unity 1945–99*, Macmillan, p. 33
12 Charlton, Michael (1983), op. cit., p. 145
13 Young, Hugo (1998), op. cit., p. 74
14 Charlton, Michael (1983), op. cit., p. 146
15 George, Stephen (1998), *An Awkward Partner: Britain in the European Community*, Oxford University Press, p. 25
16 Rhodes James, Robert (1986), *Anthony Eden*, pp. 350, 614
17 Jenkins, Roy (2001), *Churchill*, Macmillan, p. 855
18 Denman, Roy (1996), *Missed Chances: Britain and Europe in the Twentieth Century*, Cassell, p. 194
19 Deighton, Anne (1998), 'The Last Piece of the Jigsaw: Britain and the Creation of the Western European Union, 1954', *Contemporary European History*, Vol. 7, Issue 2, p. 182
20 Young, Hugo (1998), op. cit., p. 80
21 Charlton, Michael (1983), op. cit., p. 175
22 FO 317/116042 – European economic integration: record of FO meeting, 29 June 1955
23 CAB 128/29, 30 June 1955
24 Young, Hugo (1998), op. cit., p. 87
25 Denman, Roy (1996), op. cit., p. 198
26 Young, Hugo (1998), op. cit., pp. 88–9
27 Charlton, Michael (1983), op. cit., p. 181
28 Young, Hugo (1998), op. cit., p. 89
29 Charlton, Michael (1983), op. cit., p. 180
30 Denman, Roy (1996), op. cit., p. 199
31 Charlton, Michael (1983), op. cit., p. 186
32 Bogdanor, Vernon (November 2013), op. cit.
33 Charlton, Michael (1983), op. cit., p. 187
34 http://eur-lex.europa.eu/legal-content/EN/TXT/?uri=uriserv%3Axy0023
35 Denman, Roy (1996), op. cit., p. 200
36 Charlton, Michael (1983), op. cit., pp.307, 166

REASON 3
1 Charlton, Michael (1983), ibid., pp. 299–300
2 Charlton, Michael (1983), ibid., p. 203
3 Young, Hugo (1998), op. cit., p. 116
4 Young, John (2000), op. cit., p. 46
5 Young, John (2000), ibid., p. 59
6 Charlton, Michael (1983), op. cit., p. 215
7 Young, Hugo (1998), ibid., p. 110
8 Quoted in Bogdanor, Vernon (November 2013), op. cit.
9 Denman, Roy (1995), op. cit., p. 203
10 De Gaulle, Charles (1971), *Memoirs of Hope*, Weidenfeld & Nicolson, p. 188
11 Tratt, Jacqueline (1996), *The Macmillan Government and Europe: A study in the process of policy development*, Palgrave, p. 23
12 Quoted in MacShane, Denis (2016), *Brexit: How Britain left Europe*, I. B. Tauris, p. 59
13 Horne, Alistair (1989), *Harold Macmillan 1957–1986*, Viking, p. 13
14 Charlton, Michael (1983), op. cit., p. 228
15 Oppenheimer, Peter, 'Muddling Through: The Economy, 1951–1964', in Skidelsky, Robert and Bogdanor, Vernon (eds) (1970), *The Age of Affluence*, Macmillan, p. 146
16 Quoted in Bogdanor, Vernon (January 2014), 'The Decision to Seek Entry into the European Community', delivered 14 January 2014 at Gresham College, London: http://www.gresham.ac.uk/lectures-and-events/the-decision-to-seek-entry-into-the-european-community
17 Young, Hugo (1998), op. cit., p. 119
18 Wilkinson, Michael (2016), 'Boris Johnson accused of "insulting" Italians over Brexit and prosecco', *Daily Telegraph*, 16 November 2016: http://www.telegraph.co.uk/news/2016/11/16/boris-johnson-accused-of-insulting-italians-over-brexit-and-pros/
19 Young, Hugo (1998), op. cit., pp. 119–24
20 Quoted in Denman, Roy (1995), op. cit., p. 200

21 Charlton, Michael (1983), op. cit., p. 268
22 FO 371/150369, quoted in Young, Hugo (1998), op. cit., p. 126; Booker, Christopher and North, Richard (2005), *The Great Deception: A secret history of the European Union*, Continuum, p. 97
23 Charlton, Michael (1983), op. cit., p. 247
24 HC Deb, 2 August 1961, cols 1507–15
25 Young, Hugo (1998), op. cit., p. 125
26 Denman, Roy (1995), op. cit., p. 215
27 Quoted in Barker, Elisabeth (1976), *The Common Market*, Harvester, p. 76
28 Young, Hugo (1998), op. cit., pp. 129–30
29 Charlton, Michael (1983), op. cit., p. 265
30 Statement by Edward Heath (Paris, 10 October 1961): http://www.cvce.eu/en/obj/statement_by_edward_heath_paris_10_october_1961-en-d990219a-8ad0-4758-946f-cb2ddd05b3c0.html
31 May, Alex (1999), op. cit., p. 34
32 Young, Hugo (1998), op. cit., p. 137
33 Charlton, Michael (1983), op. cit., p. 269
34 Barker, Elisabeth (1976), op. cit., pp. 76–8
35 Young, John (2000), op. cit., p. 75
36 Bogdanor, Vernon (January 2014), op. cit.
37 Young, Hugo (1998), op. cit., p. 164
38 Bogdanor, Vernon (January 2014), op. cit.
39 Press conference held by General de Gaulle (14 January 1963): http://www.cvce.eu/en/obj/press_conference_held_by_general_de_gaulle_14_january_1963-en-5b5d0d35-4266-49bc-b770-b24826858e1f.html
40 Bogdanor, Vernon (January 2014), op. cit.
41 Address given by Edward Heath (Brussels, 29 January 1963): http://www.cvce.eu/content/publication/1997/10/13/d6b554fe-bb82-4499-85fa-02b2407adc65/publishable_en.pdf

REASON 4

1 Description of these cases in Bogdanor, Vernon (January 2014), op. cit., p. 10
2 Judgment of the Court, Van Gend & Loos Case 26–62 (5 February 1963): http://www.cvce.eu/en/obj/judgment_of_the_court_van_gend_loos_case_26_62_5_february_1963-en-4b81dcab-c67e-44fa-b0c9-18c48848faf3.html
3 Judgment of the Court of Justice, Costa v ENEL, Case 6/64 (15 July 1964): http://www.cvce.eu/en/obj/judgment_of_the_court_of_justice_costa_v_enel_case_6_64_15_july_1964-en-cb4154a0-23c6-4eb5-8b7e-7518e8a2a995.html
4 http://www.legislation.gov.uk/ukpga/1972/68
5 Evidence submitted to the European Scrutiny Committee considering the EU Bill and issues of Parliamentary sovereignty in 2011 by Professor Adam Tomkins from the University of Glasgow: https://www.publications.parliament.uk/pa/cm201011/cmselect/cmeuleg/633ii/633we02.htm – section 14
6 The Luxembourg Compromise (January 1966): http://www.cvce.eu/en/education/unit-content/-/unit/d1cfaf4d-8b5c-4334-ac1d-0438f4a0d617/a9aaa0cd-4401-45ba-867f-50e4e04cf272
7 Denman, Roy (1995), op. cit., p. 227
8 Young, John (2000), op. cit., p. 84
9 1966 Labour Election Manifesto: http://labourmanifesto.com/1966/1966-labour-manifesto.shtml, Part 6, Section 4: Better Relations with Europe
10 Marr, Andrew (2007), *A History of Modern Britain*, Macmillan, p. 241
11 Marr, Andrew (2007), ibid., p. 238
12 May, Alex (1999), op. cit., p. 42
13 Frey, C. W. (1968), 'Meaning Business: The British Application to Join the Common Market, November 1966–October 1967', *Journal of Common Market Studies*, Vol. 6 No. 3
14 FO 371/188347 quoted in Young, Hugo (1998), op. cit., p. 190
15 Healey, Denis (1989), *The Time of My Life*, Penguin, pp. 329–30
16 Marsh, Richard (1978), *Off the Rails*, Weidenfeld & Nicolson, p. 96
17 Young, John (2000), op. cit., p. 91
18 Denman, Roy (1995), op. cit., p. 229
19 http://news.bbc.co.uk/onthisday/hi/dates/stories/november/19/newsid_3208000/3208396.stm
20 Press conference held by Charles de Gaulle: the second veto (Paris, 27 November 1967): http://www.cvce.

eu/en/obj/press_conference_held_by_charles_de_gaulle_the_second_veto_paris_27_november_1967-en-d47637f7-b66c-44a7-8cff-2b6b45c53424.html

21   Ziegler, Philip (1993), *Wilson: The Authorised Life*, Weidenfeld & Nicolson, pp. 337–8

22   Denman, Roy (1995), op. cit., pp. 230–31

23   Heath, Edward (1970), *Old World, New Horizons: Britain, Europe, and the Atlantic Alliance*, Godkin Lectures, delivered in March 1967, Oxford University Press

24   Young, Hugo (1998), op. cit., p. 236

25   Bogdanor, Vernon (January 2014), op. cit., p. 4

26   O'Neill, Con (1972), 'Report on the Negotiations for Entry into the European Community, June 1970–July 1972', Foreign Office, unpublished

27   Hugo Young had got hold of the O'Neill report before the thirty years it had to remain secret was up; his description of the contents can be found on pp. 226–33 of his book, op. cit.

28   Quoted in http://www.newstatesman.com/books/2011/03/bismarck-germany-europe-hitler

29   Denman, Roy (1995), op. cit., p. 234

30   Spanier, David (1972), *Europe, Our Europe*, Secker & Warburg, p. 86

31   'The final round' from 30 jours d'Europe (June 1971): http://www.cvce.eu/content/publication/2001/9/13/25b0b206-68d5-44c3-9c28-526f52d86cae/publishable_en.pdf, p. 2

32   Bogdanor, Vernon (March 2014), 'Entry into the European Community, 1971–1973', delivered 11 March 2014 at Gresham College, London: http://www.gresham.ac.uk/lectures-and-events/entry-into-the-european-community-1971-73, p. 7

33   Statement by Geoffrey Rippon (London, 10 December 1970): http://www.cvce.eu/content/publication/1999/1/1/3f0f64d0-43d9-44b0-a730-cfef51f78eea/publishable_en.pdf

34   HC Deb, 20 January 1971, col. 1201

35   HC Deb, 27 July 1971, col. 278

REASON 5

1   1970 Conservative Party General Election Manifesto: http://www.conservativemanifesto.com/1970/1970-conservative-manifesto.shtml

2   Quoted in Wall, Stephen (2012), *The Official History of Britain and the European Community, Volume II: From Rejection to Referendum, 1963–1975*, Routledge, p. 360

3   Young, Hugo (1998), op. cit., p. 239; Ziegler, Philip (2010), *Edward Heath: The Authorised Biography*, HarperPress, p. 286

4   Ziegler, Philip (2010), op. cit., p. 286

5   Young, Simon Z. (1973), *Terms of Entry: Britain's Negotiations with the European Community, 1970–1972*, Heinemann), p. 19

6   Ashford, Nigel (1983), *The Conservative Party and European Integration, 1945–1975*, PhD thesis, University of Warwick, pp. 304–5

7   White Paper presented by the UK Government to the UK Parliament (July 1971): http://www.cvce.eu/en/obj/white_paper_presented_by_the_uk_government_to_the_uk_parliament_july_1971-en-8cf072cb-5a31-46f6-b04f-cb866be92f72.html

8   Quoted in Young, Hugo (1998), op. cit., p. 246

9   Interview with Andrew Marr, BBC1, 21 February 2016 – transcript at: http://news.bbc.co.uk/1/shared/bsp/hi/pdfs/21021603.pdf

10   http://www.politicsresources.net/area/uk/man/lab70.htm#world

11   Ziegler, Philip (1993), op. cit., p. 380

12   Morgan, Kenneth O. (2007), *Michael Foot: A Life*, HarperPress, p. 274

13   Bogdanor, Vernon (March 2014), op. cit., p. 8

14   May, Alex (1999), op. cit., p. 52

15   Broad, Roger (2001), *Labour's European Dilemmas: From Bevin to Blair*, Palgrave, p. 80

16   Jenkins, Roy (1991), *A Life at the Centre*, Macmillan

17   Pimlott, Ben (1992), *Harold Wilson*, HarperCollins, p. 654

18   Bogdanor, Vernon (April 2014), 'The Referendum on Europe, 1975', delivered 15 April 2014 at Gresham College, London: http://www.gresham.ac.uk/lectures-and-events/the-referendum-on-europe-1975

19   Burke, Edmund (1774), Speech to the Electors of Bristol, 3 November 1774: http://press-pubs.uchicago.edu/founders/documents/v1ch13s7.html

20   Morgan, Kenneth O. (2007), op. cit., p. 274

21 http://archive.spectator.co.uk/article/18th-january-1975/5/anthony-wedgwood-benn-on-the-common-market

22 Young, Hugo (1998), op. cit., p. 275

23 Bogdanor, Vernon (April 2014), op. cit., p. 3

24 Ziegler, Philip (1993), op. cit., p. 387

25 Wall, Stephen (2012), op. cit., Routledge, p. 456

26 The Speeches of John Enoch Powell: http://www.enochpowell.info/Resources/May-Aug%201973.pdf, pp. 56–60

27 Bogdanor, Vernon (March 2013), 'Enoch Powell and the Sovereignty of Parliament', delivered 12 March 2013 at Gresham College, London: http://www.gresham.ac.uk/lectures-and-events/enoch-powell-and-the-sovereignty-of-parliament, p. 10

28 This set of speeches can be found here: http://www.enochpowell.info/Resources/Nov%201973-Feb%201974.pdf, with particular focus on Europe in the run-up to the February 1974 election on pp. 3–20

29 Denman Roy (1996), op. cit., p. 247

30 http://www.politicsresources.net/area/uk/man/lab74feb.htm

31 Stone, Jon (2016), 'Tory MPs brand Cameron's EU deal "thin gruel", "watered down" and full of broken promises', The Independent, 3 February 2016: http://www.independent.co.uk/news/uk/politics/david-cameron-insists-eu-deal-is-the-strongest-package-ever-but-his-own-mps-arent-impressed-a6850941.html

32 Denman, Roy (1996), op. cit., p. 249

33 George, Stephen (1998), op. cit., p. 86

34 Young, Hugo (1998), op. cit., p. 281

35 Denman, Roy (1996), op. cit., pp. 249–50

36 George, Stephen (1998), op. cit., p. 92

37 HC Deb, 11 March 1975, col. 292

38 Bogdanor, Vernon (April 2014), op. cit.

39 May, Alex (1999), op. cit., p. 62

40 Butler, David, and Kitzinger, Uwe (1996), The 1975 Referendum, Palgrave Macmillan, p. 183

41 Bogdanor, Vernon (May 2016), 'Learning from History? The 1975 Referendum on Europe', delivered 23 May 2016 at the Museum of London: https://www.gresham.ac.uk/lectures-and-events/learning-from-history-the-1975-referendum-on-europe, p. 9

42 Bogdanor, Vernon (April 2014), op. cit., p. 9

43 Young, Hugo (1998), op. cit., p. 289

44 Butler, David and Kitzinger, Uwe (1996), op. cit., p. 280

45 Butler, David and Kitzinger, Uwe (1996), ibid., p. 280

46 The official campaign leaflets sent out to all constituents – which included one from the Yes campaign, a supporting one from the government, and one from the No campaign – are reproduced here: http://hitchensblog.mailonsunday.co.uk/2015/08/the-1975-common-market-referendum-campaign-documents.html

47 BBC News (1975), 'UK embraces Europe in referendum', 6 June 1975: http://news.bbc.co.uk/onthisday/hi/dates/stories/june/6/newsid_2499000/2499297.stm

48 Shipman, Tim (2016), All Out War, HarperCollins, loc. 1709–13

49 Electoral Commission (2015), 'Referendum on membership of the European Union: Assessment of the Electoral Commission on the proposed referendum question', 1 September 2015: http://www.electoralcommission.org.uk/__data/assets/pdf_file/0006/192075/EU-referendum-question-assessment-report.pdf

50 Young, Hugo (1998), op. cit., p. 293

51 1975 referendum campaign leaflet from the Yes campaign: 'Britain in Europe: Why you should vote Yes, 1975': http://mrc-catalogue.warwick.ac.uk/records/MSX/381/8, p. 4

52 Campbell, John (2014), Roy Jenkins: A Well-Rounded Life, Jonathan Cape, p. 446

53 HC Deb, 24 May 1971, col. 33

54 Statement from the Paris summit (19 to 21 October 1972): http://www.cvce.eu/content/publication/1999/1/1/b1dd3d57-5f31-4796-85c3-cfd2210d6901/publishable_en.pdf

55 Cameron, David (2013), EU Speech at Bloomberg, delivered 23 January 2013: https://www.gov.uk/government/speeches/eu-speech-at-bloomberg

REASON 6

1 HC Deb, 13 November 1990, cols 461–5

2   Young, Hugo (1998), op. cit., pp. 306–307

3   George, Stephen (1998), op. cit., p. 124

4   Denman, Roy (1996), op. cit., p. 254

5   Jenkins, Roy (1977), Address given by Roy Jenkins on the creation of a European monetary union (Florence, 27 October 1977): http://www.cvce.eu/content/publication/2010/11/15/98bef841-9d8a-4f84-b3a8-719abb63fd62/publishable_en.pdf

6   Jenkins, Roy (1977), ibid., p. 11

7   Jenkins, Roy (1977), ibid., p. 17

8   May, Alex (2000), op. cit., p. 65

9   HC Deb, 6 December 1978, col. 1424

10 Denman, Roy (1996), op. cit., p. 259

11 Henderson, Nicholas (1987), *Channels and Tunnels*, Weidenfeld & Nicolson, p. 143

12 May, Alex (2000), op. cit., p. 66–8

13 http://ec.europa.eu/budget/mff/resources/index_en.cfm

14 George, Stephen (1998), op. cit., p. 150

15 Young, Hugo (1998), op. cit., p. 322

16 Moore, Charles (2015), *Margaret Thatcher: The Authorized Biography, Volume Two: Everything She Wants*, Allen Lane, p. 380

17 https://fullfact.org/europe/our-eu-membership-fee-55-million/

18 Thatcher, Margaret (1993), *Margaret Thatcher: The Downing Street Years*, HarperPress, pp. 553–4

19 http://aei.pitt.edu/1788/1/stuttgart_declaration_1983.pdf, p. 7

20 Draft Treaty establishing the European Union (14 February 1984): http://www.cvce.eu/en/obj/draft_treaty_establishing_the_european_union_14_february_1984-en-0c1f92e8-db44-4408-b569-c464cc1e73c9.html

21 Moore, Charles (2015), op. cit., p. 390

22 Moore, Charles (2015), ibid., pp. 389–90

23 https://www.whatdotheyknow.com/request/112377/response/279008/attach/html/4/FOI%20Request%200398%2012%20Europe%20Future%201984.pdf.html

24 George, Stephen (1998), op. cit., p. 176

25 Thatcher, Margaret (1993), op. cit., p. 547

26 http://aei.pitt.edu/997/1/Dooge_final_report.pdf

27 Young, Hugo (1998), op. cit., p. 332

28 http://www.consilium.europa.eu/uedocs/cmsUpload/SingleEuropeanAct_Crest.pdf

29 George, Stephen (1998), op. cit., p. 184

30 Greenwood, Sean (1992), *Britain and European Cooperation since 1945*, Blackwell, p. 114

31 Moore, Charles (2015), op. cit., p. 406

32 Pinder, John (1995), *European Community: The Building of a Union*, Second Edition, Oxford University Press, p. 78

33 Moore, Charles (2015), op. cit., p. 407

34 HC Deb, 23 April 1986

35 Denman, Roy (1996), op. cit., p. 263

36 Young, John (2000), op. cit., p. 141

37 Thatcher, Margaret (1993), op. cit., p. 691

38 Lawson, Nigel (17 October 1985), Speech to Mansion House: https://www.gov.uk/government/uploads/system/uploads/attachment_data/file/308260/document2014-05-01-113932.pdf, p. 17

39 Moore, Charles (2015), op. cit., pp. 416–17

40 Moore, Charles (2015), ibid., p. 420

41 First two quotes from Terry Burns and Robin Leigh-Permberton in Moore, Charles (2015), ibid., p. 420

42 Lawson, Nigel (1992), *The View from No. 11*, Bantam Press, p. 499

43 Young, Hugo (1998), op. cit., p. 343

44 Howe, Geoffrey (1994), *Conflict of Loyalty*, Macmillan, p. 451

45 Address given by Jacques Delors to the European Parliament (18 February 1987): http://www.cvce.eu/content/publication/2003/4/1/5a7c0454-fa33-49c4-a62e-0c2fc3b1a4af/publishable_en.pdf

46 George, Stephen (1998), op. cit., pp. 189–90

47 Young, John (2000), op. cit., pp. 142–3

48 George, Stephen (1998), op. cit., p. 192

49 George, Stephen (1998), ibid., p. 193

50 Young, Hugo (1998), op. cit., p. 345
51 MacShane, Denis (2016), op. cit., p. 70
52 MacShane, Denis (2016), ibid., p. 71
53 http://www.pro-europa.eu/index.php/en/library/the-struggle-for-the-union-of-europe/107-delors,-jacques-it-is-necessary-to-work-together
54 Thatcher, Margaret (1993), op. cit., p. 743
55 http://www.margaretthatcher.org/document/107332
56 Howe, Geoffrey (1994), op. cit., p. 537
57 MacShane, Denis (2016), op. cit., pp. 73–5
58 MacShane, Denis (2016), ibid., pp. 130–33
59 Denman, Roy (1996), op. cit., pp. 266–7
60 Thatcher, Margaret (1993), op. cit., p. 791
61 Denman, Roy (1996), op. cit., p. 259
62 http://www.margaretthatcher.org/document/111535
63 Lawson, Nigel (1992), op. cit., p. 900
64 Denman, Roy (1996), op. cit., p. 266
65 HC Deb, 20 June 1990, cols 923–4
66 Quoted in Craig, Paul P. and de Búrca, Gráinne (2008). *EU Law: Text, Cases, and Materials*, Fourth Edition, Oxford University Press, p. 367f
67 Young, Hugo. (1998), op. cit., p. 366
68 Howe, Geoffrey (1994), op. cit., p. 643
69 HC Deb, 30 October 1990, cols 873–77
70 HC Deb, 13 November 1990, col 465
71 May, Alex (2000), op. cit., p. 77
72 Young, Hugo (1998), op. cit., p. 311

REASON 7

1   Major, John (1999), *John Major: The Autobiography*, HarperCollins, pp. 342–3
2   Knight, Sam (2016), 'The Man Who Brought you Brexit', *The Guardian*, 29 September 2016: https://www.theguardian.com/politics/2016/sep/29/daniel-hannan-the-man-who-brought-you-brexit
3   Young, Hugo (1998), op. cit., p. 417
4   Thatcher, Margaret (1993), op. cit., p. 724
5   Young, Hugo (1998), op. cit., p. 423
6   George, Stephen (1998), op. cit., pp. 238–9
7   Major, John (1999), op. cit., p. 269
8   George, Stephen (1998), op. cit., p. 241
9   May, Alex (2000), op. cit., p. 81
10 Major, John (1999), op. cit., p. 270
11 HC Deb, 20 November 1990, cols 297–8
12 Definition of subsidiarity in Article 3b of The Maastricht Treaty: https://europa.eu/european-union/sites/europaeu/files/docs/body/treaty_on_european_union_en.pdf
13 Major, John (1999), op. cit., p. 278
14 The Maastricht Treaty, p. 193
15 Ibid., p. 196
16 The Maastricht Treaty, op. cit., p. 15
17 Duff, Andrew, Pinder, John and Pryce, Roy (2002), *Maastricht and Beyond: Building a European Union*, Routledge, p. 29
18 May, Alex (2000), op. cit., p. 82
19 Young, John (2000), op. cit., p. 157
20 George, Stephen (1998), op. cit., pp. 235–8
21 Graham, Georgia (2013), 'Peter Lilley: "It's 'bastards' like me who kept us out of the Euro, Mr Major"', *Daily Telegraph*, 23 October 2013: http://www.telegraph.co.uk/active/10397855/Peter-Lilley-Its-bastards-like-me-who-kept-us-out-of-the-Euro-Mr-Major.html
22 De Gaulle, Charles (1971), op. cit., p. 194
23 Young, Hugo (1998), op. cit., p. 377
24 Young, Hugo (1998), ibid., p. 381

25 Cash, William (1991), *Against a Federal Europe: The Battle for Britain*, Duckworth, p. 3

26 HC Deb, 10 July 1986, col. 566

27 Kohl, Helmut (1992), Speech at the Bertlesman Forum, Petersburg Hotel, April 1992, cited in Young, Hugo (1998), op. cit., p. 389

28 Young, Hugo (1998), op. cit., p. 391

29 Bogdanor, Vernon (May 2014), 'The Growth of Euroscepticism', delivered 20 May 2014 at Gresham College, London: http://www.gresham.ac.uk/lectures-and-events/the-growth-of-euroscepticism, p. 8

30 Young, John (2000), op. cit., pp. 159–60

31 Young, John (2000), ibid., p. 161

32 Bogdanor, Vernon (April 2016), *Leaving the European Monetary System in 1992*, lecture to Gresham College, 19 April 2016 – http://www.gresham.ac.uk/lectures-and-events/leaving-the-erm-1992

33 Major, John (1999), op. cit., p. 312

34 Bogdanor, Vernon (April 2016), op. cit., p. 13

35 HC Deb, 25 June 1992, cols 381–2

36 HC Deb, 20 July 1993, col. 191

37 Courtald, Charlie (2001), 'Rupert Allason: A reputation in tatters', *The Independent*, 20 October 2001: http://www.independent.co.uk/news/people/profiles/rupert-allason-a-reputation-in-tatters-9242603.html

38 May, Alex (2000), op. cit., p. 85

39 *The Economist*, 23 September 1993, quoted in Denman, Roy (1996), op. cit., p. 273

40 HC Deb, 22 March 1994, col. 134

41 Denman, Roy (1996), op. cit., p. 274

42 Gerbet, Pierre (2016), 'The Crisis of the Santer Commission': http://www.cvce.eu/content/publication/2004/6/17/7380f95b-1fb2-484d-a262-d870a0d5d74d/publishable_en.pdf

43 George, Stephen (1998), op. cit., p. 260

44 Macintyre, Donald (1995), 'Time to Put Up or Shut Up', *The Independent*, 22 June 1995: http://www.independent.co.uk/news/time-to-put-up-or-shut-up-1587775.html

45 Young, Hugo (1998), op. cit., p. 459

46 Young, Hugo (1998), ibid., pp. 460–63

47 Young, John (2000), op. cit., p. 174

REASON 8

1   http://www.bbc.co.uk/blogs/nickrobinson/2010/04/that_was_a_disa.html

2   http://www.politicsresources.net/area/uk/man/lab83.htm

3   http://www.newstatesman.com/uk-politics/2010/05/labour-policy-policies-blair

4   Bulmer, Simon (2008), 'Constructive Abroad but Not yet Constructed at Home: The Blair Government's European Policy', University of Manchester: archives.cerium.ca/IMG/doc/SimonBulmer-2.doc, p. 16

5   Young, Hugo (1998), op. cit., pp. 485–6

6   Berlaymont, Simon (2007), 'Tony Blair and Europe', https://www.opendemocracy.net/tony_blair_and_europe.jsp

7   Blair, Tony (2010), *A Journey*, Hutchison, p. 96

8   Quoted in MacShane, Denis (2016), op. cit., p. 91

9   Blair, Tony (2010), op. cit., p. 533

10 Berlaymont, Simon (2005), 'What the European Union is', https://www.opendemocracy.net/democracy-europe_constitution/union_2623.jsp

11 Summaries of the Amsterdam Treaty can be found in Piris, Jean-Claude and Maganza, Giorgio (1998), 'The Amsterdam Treaty: Overview and Institutional Aspects', *Fordham International Law Journal*, Volume 22, Issue 6, Article 3, and at: http://www.eu-facts.org.uk/what-is-the-eu/eu-treaties/treaty-of-amsterdam/

12 http://www.historiasiglo20.org/europe/niza.htm

13 Young, Hugo (1998), op. cit., p. 487

14 MacShane, Denis (2016), op. cit., p. 95

15 HC Deb, 27 October 1997, col. 584

16 HC Deb, 9 June 2003, cols 407–15

17 Gani, Aisha (2014), 'What is the European convention on human rights?', *The Guardian*, 3 October 2014: https://www.theguardian.com/law/2014/oct/03/what-is-european-convention-on-human-rights-echr

18 BBC Online (2011), 'Theresa May under fire over deportation cat claim', 4 October 2011: http://www.bbc.co.uk/news/uk-politics-15160326

19 Wagner, Adam (2011), 'Catgate: another myth used to trash human rights', *The Guardian*, 4 October 2011: https://www.theguardian.com/law/2011/oct/04/theresa-may-wrong-cat-deportation

20 Tabloid Watch (2009), 'Mail and Sunday Telegraph: cat-alysts for more anti-immigration feeling', 19 October 2009: http://tabloid-watch.blogspot.co.uk/2009/10/mail-and-sunday-telegraph-cat-alysts.html

21 Liberty (2011), 'Striking the balance between personal privacy and media freedom', 10 May 2011: https://www.liberty-human-rights.org.uk/news/blog/striking-balance-between-personal-privacy-and-media-freedom

22 Commons Briefing Paper SN06577: http://researchbriefings.parliament.uk/ResearchBriefing/Summary/SN06577

23 http://news.bbc.co.uk/1/hi/world/europe/2950276.stm

24 Rennie, David (2005), 'Keep Up the Pressure for a No Vote, Left Warned', *Daily Telegraph*: http://www.telegraph.co.uk/news/worldnews/europe/1490810/Keep-up-the-pressure-for-a-No-vote-Left-warned.html

25 European Scrutiny Committee Report on Lisbon Treaty: http://www.publications.parliament.uk/pa/cm200708/cmselect/cmeuleg/179/179.pdf

26 Francois, Mark (2016), 'The appalling handling of the Lisbon Treaty sowed the seeds of Brexit', 20 September 2016: http://brexitcentral.com/mark-francois-mp-appalling-handling-lisbon-treaty-sowed-seeds-brexit/

27 Helm, Toby (2007), 'Giscard: EU Treaty is the constitution rewritten', *Daily Telegraph*, 29 October 2007: http://www.telegraph.co.uk/news/uknews/1567804/Giscard-EU-Treaty-is-the-constitution-rewritten.html

28 Consolidated Treaty of Lisbon: http://eur-lex.europa.eu/legal-content/EN/TXT/PDF/?uri=OJ:C:2016:202:FULL&from=EN, p. 45

29 Hall, Mark (2007), 'Mixed reaction to "opt-out" from EU Charter of Fundamental Rights', EurWORK, 20 August 2007: https://www.eurofound.europa.eu/observatories/eurwork/articles/mixed-reaction-to-opt-out-from-eu-charter-of-fundamental-rights

30 Case C-411/10, R (NS (Afghanistan)) *v.* Secretary of State for the Home Department [2013] QB 102: http://eur-lex.europa.eu/legal-content/EN/TXT/?uri=CELEX%3A62010CJ0411 – the key phrase is in point 4 of the summary

31 Wheeler, Marina (9 February 2016), 'Cavalier with our Constitution: a Charter too far', UK Human Rights blog: https://ukhumanrightsblog.com/2016/02/09/cavalier-with-our-constitution-a-charter-too-far/   (it should be noted that the author is the wife of Boris Johnson, was to become a prominent member of the Leave campaign)

32 Little, Alison (2014), 'Every household is poorer: Tony Blair's EU renegotiation deal has cost Britain £10billion', *Sunday Express*, 19 May 2014: http://www.express.co.uk/news/uk/476734/Tony-Blair-s-EU-renegotiation-deal-that-cost-Britain-10billion

33 http://news.bbc.co.uk/1/hi/uk_politics/1146210.stm

34 https://www.theguardian.com/politics/2001/mar/04/conservatives.speeches

35 MacShane, Denis (2016), op. cit., pp. 108–15

36 Marr, Andrew (2007), op. cit., pp. 40–42, 192–8, 300–305

37 Jeffries, Stuart (2014), 'Britain's most racist election: the story of Smethwick, 50 Years On', *The Guardian*, 15 October 2014: https://www.theguardian.com/world/2014/oct/15/britains-most-racist-election-smethwick-50-years-on

38 http://www.telegraph.co.uk/comment/3643823/Enoch-Powells-Rivers-of-Blood-speech.html

39 http://www.bbc.co.uk/news/special/politics97/news/06/0605/straw.shtml

40 Goodhart, David (2016), 'A vote against the mass immigration society', *Prospect* magazine, 14 July 2016: http://www.prospectmagazine.co.uk/magazine/a-vote-against-the-mass-immigration-society

41 Neather, Andrew (2009), 'Don't listen to the whingers – London needs immigrants', *Evening Standard*, 23 October 2009: http://www.standard.co.uk/news/dont-listen-to-the-whingers-london-needs-immigrants-6786170.html

42 Finch, Tim and Goodhart, David (2010), 'Immigration under Labour', IPPR and Prospect: http://www.ippr.org/files/images/media/files/publication/2011/05/Immigration%20under%20Labour%20Nov2010_1812.pdf?noredirect=1

43 Roche, Barbara (2010), 'Making the best of immense challenges' in Finch, Tim and Goodhart, David (2010), ibid., pp. 17–18

44 Lowther, Ed (2013), 'Prof says his "13,000 EU Migrants" report "misinterpreted"', BBC News, 7 March 2013: http://www.bbc.co.uk/news/uk-politics-21682810

45 HC Deb, 23 February 2004, cols 23–4

46 Currie, Samantha (2016), *Migration, Work and Citizenship in the Enlarged European Union*, Routledge, p. 22

47 Watt, Nicholas and Wintour, Patrick (2015), 'How immigration came to haunt Labour: the inside story',

The Guardian, 24 March 2015: https://www.theguardian.com/news/2015/mar/24/how-immigration-came-to-haunt-labour-inside-story

48 Cavanagh, Matt (2010), 'Numbers matter', in Finch, Tim and Goodhart, David (2010), op. cit., pp. 30–33

49 https://www.theguardian.com/commentisfree/series/anywhere-but-westminster

50 https://www.youtube.com/watch?v=xGiDuxTROmI

51 https://www.youtube.com/watch?v=TNE_apzz7gY

52 *The Economist* (April 2017), 'Explaining Britain's immigration paradox', 15 April 2017: http://www.economist.com/news/britain/21720576-migration-good-economy-so-why-are-places-biggest-influxes-doing-so

53 Bagehot's Notebook (2011), 'Why Britain should be proud of opening its Labour market to eastern Europe', The Economist, 5 May 2011: http://www.economist.com/blogs/bagehot/2011/05/immigration_britain

54 Denham, John (2010), 'Fairness, entitlement and common obligation', in Finch, Tim and Goodhart, David (2010), op. cit., p. 25

55 Quoted in Browne, Anthony (2004), 'Response to Tony Blair's First Speech on Immigration', Civitas Background Briefing: http://www.civitas.org.uk/pdf/BrowneEconomicsImmigration.pdf, p. 8

56 Finch, Tim and Goodhart, David (2010), op. cit., p. 6

57 Browne, Anthony (2004), op. cit., p. 10

58 Bagehot's Notebook (2011), op. cit.

59 Randall, Jeff (2007), 'It's not racist to worry about immigration', *Daily Telegraph*, 1 June 2007: http://www.telegraph.co.uk/comment/personal-view/3640286/Its-not-racist-to-worry-about-immigration.html

60 Finch, Tim and Goodhart, David (2010), op. cit., p. 7

61 Roche, Barbara (2010), in Finch, Tim and Goodhart, David (2010), op. cit., p. 17

62 Finch, Tim and Goodhart, David (2010), op. cit., p. 6

63 Goodhart, David (2016), op. cit.

64 http://www.natcen.ac.uk/media/1216033/immigration-data-tables-for-web-final.pdf, p. 4

65 Goodhart, David (2016), op. cit.

REASON 9

1 Bennett, Owen (2016), *The Brexit Club: The Inside Story of the Leave Campaign's Shock Victory*, Biteback Publishing, loc. 4143

2 Bogdanor, Vernon (September 2014), 'The General Election, 1945', delivered 23 September 2014 at Gresham College, London: https://www.gresham.ac.uk/lectures-and-events/the-general-election-1945, p. 1

3 Marr, Andrew (2007), op. cit., p. 17

4 BBC Online (1997), 'The 1945 Election': http://www.bbc.co.uk/news/special/politics97/background/pastelec/ge45.shtml .

5 Labour Party (1945), 'Let us face the future: A declaration of Labour policy for the consideration of the nation', 1945 general election Labour Party manifesto: http://www.politicsresources.net/area/uk/man/lab45.htm

6 Beveridge, William (1942), 'Social Insurance and Allied Services', 20 November 1942: http://news.bbc.co.uk/1/shared/bsp/hi/pdfs/19_07_05_beveridge.pdf

7 State aid rules within the Treaty on the Functioniong of the EU (TFEU – the Lisbon Treaty): http://eur-lex.europa.eu/legal-content/EN/ALL/?uri=CELEX:12008E107

8 Macmillan, Harold (1957), quoted in 'More production "the only answer" to inflation', *The Times*, 22 July 1957, p. 4

9 Marr, Andrew (2007), op. cit., pp. 308–11

10 Tebbit, Norman (1981), Speech to the Conservative Party Conference, 15 October 1981: http://www.telegraph.co.uk/news/newsvideo/7858570/Norman-Tebbit-my-father-got-on-his-bike-to-look-for-a-job.html

11 Harris, John (June 2016), 'If you've got money, you vote in … if you haven't got money, you vote out', *The Guardian*, 24 June 2016: https://www.theguardian.com/politics/commentisfree/2016/jun/24/divided-britain-brexit-money-class-inequality-westminster

12 Milanovic, Branko (2012), 'Global Income Inequality by the Numbers: in History and Now – An Overview', World Bank Policy Research Working Paper 6259, November 2012: http://documents.worldbank.org/curated/en/959251468176687085/pdf/wps6259.pdf, p. 13

13 Blair, Tony (September 2005), 2005 Labour Party Conference speech, delivered 27 September 2005: http://news.bbc.co.uk/1/hi/uk_politics/4287370.stm

14 Harris, John (September 2016), 'Does the Left have a future?', *The Guardian*, 6 September 2016: https://www.theguardian.com/politics/2016/sep/06/does-the-left-have-a-future

15 The quote is actually misattributed to Gandhi; there is no actual source in which he says it. It could be paraphrased from a book of his speeches called *Freedom's Battle* (http://www.gutenberg.org/files/10366/10366-h/10366-h.htm), but a closer version can be found in a speech by union leader Nicholas Klein in 1914: https://books.google.co.uk/books?id=QrcpAAAAYAAJ&pg=PA53&dq=%22First+they+ignore+you%22&redir_esc=y#v=onepage&q=%22First%20they%20ignore%20you%22&f=false

REASON 10

1   Mosbacher, Michael and Wiseman, Oliver (2016), *Brexit Revolt: How the UK Voted to Leave the EU*, Social Affairs Unit, p. 13
2   *Daily Telegraph* (1997), 'Sir James Goldsmith – Obituary', 21 July 1997: http://www.telegraph.co.uk/news/obituaries/7720479/Sir-James-Goldsmith.html
3   Referendum Party: 1997 election video: https://www.youtube.com/watch?v=SSXdE8M-9Y4
4   BBC News (2005), 'Profile: UK Independence Party', 5 April 2005: http://news.bbc.co.uk/1/hi/uk_politics/vote_2005/basics/4351871.stm
5   Morris, Nigel and Culzac, Natasha (2014), 'Former Tory donor Arron Banks ups his Ukip donation to £1million following William Hague "nobody" comment', *The Independent*, 1 October 2014: http://www.independent.co.uk/news/uk/politics/former-tory-donor-arron-banks-ups-UKIP-donation-to-1million-following-william-hague-nobody-comment-9768087.html
6   BBC News (October 2006), 'UKIP "voice of British minority"', 7 October 2006: http://news.bbc.co.uk/1/hi/uk_politics/5415252.stm
7   Ashton, Emily (2016), 'Nigel Farage Refuses To Apologise For UKIP's "Breaking Point" Poster', BuzzFeed News, 22 June 2016: https://www.buzzfeed.com/emilyashton/nigel-farage-refuses-to-apologise-for-UKIPs-breaking-point-p?utm_term=.deAPn8YxRR#.bfEyBY67bb
8   *Daily Express* (2010), 'Get Britain out of Europe', 25 November 2010: http://www.express.co.uk/news/uk/213573/Get-Britain-out-of-Europe
9   Sparrow, Andrew (2012), 'UKIP conference and Nigel Farage's speech: Politics Live Blog', *The Guardian*, 21 September 2012: https://www.theguardian.com/politics/blog/2012/sep/21/ukip-conference-farage-speech-live-blog2, 9.15 a.m.
10 Assinder, Nick (2014), 'UKIP conference: Farage Sets Sights on Labour Voters and Balance of Power in Westminster', *International Business Times*, 26 September 2014: http://www.ibtimes.co.uk/UKIP-conference-farage-sets-sights-labour-voters-balance-power-westminster-1429315
11 Mansour, Rebecca (2016), 'Trump champions globalism's "ignored, neglected and abandoned": "I am your voice"', Breitbart News, 21 July 2016: http://www.breitbart.com/2016-presidential-race/2016/07/21/trump-champions-globalisms-neglected-ignored-abandoned-voice/
12 BBC News (April 2006), 'UKIP demands apology from Cameron', 4 April 2006: http://news.bbc.co.uk/1/hi/4875026.stm
13 Hope, Christopher (2014), 'Mass immigration has left Britain "unrecognisable", says Nigel Farage', *Daily Telegraph*, 28 February 2014: http://www.telegraph.co.uk/news/politics/UKIP/10668996/Mass-immigration-has-left-Britain-unrecognisable-says-Nigel-Farage.html
14 Phipps, Claire (2014), 'Nigel Farage's LBC interview – the key moments', *The Guardian*, 16 May 2014: https://www.theguardian.com/politics/2014/may/16/nigel-farage-lbc-interview-key-moments
15 Jeffries, Stuart (2016), 'UKIP founder Alan Sked: "The party has become a Frankenstein's monster"', *The Guardian*, 26 May 2014: https://www.theguardian.com/politics/2014/may/26/ukip-founder-alan-sked-party-become-frankensteins-monster
16 Thatcher, Margaret (1986), transcript from TV interview for Italian television (RAI), 10 March 1986: http://www.margaretthatcher.org/document/106223
17 Sparrow, Andrew (2016), 'EU campaign feuds may lead to no official Brexit group', *The Guardian*, 5 February 2016: https://www.theguardian.com/politics/2016/feb/05/eu-campaign-feuds-may-lead-to-no-official-brexit-group
18 BBC News (15 June 2016), 'Thames: Nigel Farage and Bob Geldof fishing flotilla clash': http://www.bbc.co.uk/news/uk-politics-eu-referendum-36537180
19 BBC News (18 June 2016), 'Jo Cox MP death: Thomas Mair in court on murder charge': http://www.bbc.co.uk/news/uk-36567005
20 Stewart, Heather and Mason, Rowena (2016), 'Nigel Farage's anti-migrant poster reported to police', *The Guardian*, 16 June 2016: https://www.theguardian.com/politics/2016/jun/16/nigel-farage-defends-ukip-breaking-point-poster-queue-of-migrants

21 BBC News (19 June 2016), 'Michael Gove "shuddered" at UKIP migrants poster': http://www.bbc.co.uk/news/uk-politics-eu-referendum-36570759

REASON 11

1 Cameron, David (2013), op. cit.
2 Cameron's 'cast-iron guarantee' was given in an article in *The Sun*, which appeared in the paper on 26 September 2007 but has now been removed from the newspaper's website. See Fawkes, Guido (2009), 'Cameron Flashback: "I will give this cast-iron guarantee"', 1 November 2009: https://order-order.com/2009/11/01/cameron-flashback-i-will-give-this-cast-iron-guarantee/
3 Summers, Deborah (2009), 'David Cameron admits Lisbon treaty referendum campaign is over', *The Guardian*, 4 November 2009: https://www.theguardian.com/politics/2009/nov/04/david-cameron-referendum-campaign-over
4 Author interview
5 Politics.co.uk (2008), 'Lib Dems walk out of Commons in EU row', 26 February 2008: http://www.politics.co.uk/news/2008/02/26/lib-dems-walk-out-of-commons-in-eu-row
6 A summary of the Act can be found here: http://services.parliament.uk/bills/2010-11/europeanunion.html
7 Foster, David (2013), 'Going "Where Angels Fear to Tread": How Effective was the Backbench Business Committee in the 2010–2012 Parliamentary Session?', Centre for the Study of British Politics and Public Life, 13 June 2013: http://www.csbppl.com/tag/debate/
8 House of Commons Procedure Committee Review of the Backbench Business Committee: https://www.publications.parliament.uk/pa/cm201213/cmselect/cmproced/168/168.pdf; George Young quote to be found at p. 63, Q144
9 Foster, David (2013), op. cit.
10 HC Deb, 24 October 2011, col. 27
11 HC Deb, 24 October 2011, ibid., col. 46
12 HC Deb, 24 October 2011, ibid., col. 57
13 Cameron, David (2012), Prime Minister's speech in Brussels, 29 June 2012: https://www.gov.uk/government/speeches/prime-ministers-speech-in-brussels
14 Rotherham 2010 general election result: http://news.bbc.co.uk/1/shared/election2010/results/constituency/d78.stm. Rotherham 2012 by-election result: http://www.bbc.co.uk/news/uk-politics-20541136
15 Ashcroft, Michael (2012), 'The UKIP threat is not about Europe', 18 December 2012: http://lordashcroftpolls.com/2012/12/the-UKIP-threat-is-not-about-europe/
16 Shipman, Tim (2016), op. cit., loc. 358
17 Shipman, Tim (2016), ibid., loc. 487
18 McTague, Tom (2015), 'Ed Miliband would have deprived Tories of majority in election "had he promised EU referendum"', *The Independent*, 19 December 2015: http://www.independent.co.uk/news/world/europe/ed-miliband-would-have-deprived-tories-of-majority-in-election-had-he-promised-eu-referendum-a6780241.html
19 BBC Online (2006), 'Cameron places focus on optimism', 1 October 2006: http://news.bbc.co.uk/1/hi/uk_politics/5396358.stm
20 Toye, Richard (2013), *The Roar of the Lion: The Untold Story of Churchill's World War II Speeches*, Oxford University Press, p. 210
21 HC Deb, 11 June 2003, cols 708, 705
22 HC Deb, 20 April 2004, col. 161
23 Cameron, David (2013), op. cit.
24 Ashcroft, Michael (2016), *Well, You Did Ask: Why the UK Voted to Leave the EU*, Biteback Publishing, p. xvi
25 BBC Online (2013), 'In full: MPs backing the EU amendment to the Queen's Speech', 15 May 2013: http://www.bbc.co.uk/news/uk-politics-22547912
26 Ashcroft, Michael (2016), op. cit. p. xiv
27 Hansard, 24 October 2011, ibid., col. 46
28 Ashcroft, Michael (2016), ibid., p. xviii
29 Cameron, David (2013), op. cit.

REASON 12

1 Papasimakopoulos, Makis (2012), 'Note found on Syntagma suicide victim', *Athens News*, 4 April 2012: http://archive.li/e5JSE

2   Ukandeu.ac.uk (2015), 'Britain and Europe: The Political and Economic Repercussions of the Crisis', Report on Cambridge Network conference on the UK's changing relationship with the EU: http://ukandeu.ac.uk/explainers/britain-and-europe-the-political-and-economic-repercussions-of-the-crisis/

3   Parker, George and Hope, Kerin (2004), 'EU warns Greece for under-reporting deficit', FT.com, 23 September 2004:   http://www.ft.com/cms/s/0/7832d10a-0d87-11d9-a3e1-00000e2511c8.html?ft_site=falcon&desktop=true

4   Cummings, Dominic (2017), 'On the referendum #21: Branching histories of the 2016 referendum and "the frogs before the storm"', 9 January 2017: https://dominiccummings.wordpress.com/2017/01/09/on-the-referendum-21-branching-histories-of-the-2016-referendum-and-the-frogs-before-the-storm-2/

5   UKandeu.ac.uk (2015), op. cit.

6   UKandeu.ac.uk (2015), ibid.

7   Ipsos MORI (2016), 'European Union Membership – Trends': https://www.ipsos-mori.com/researchpublications/researcharchive/2435/European-Union-membership-trends.aspx

8   Jee, Charlotte (2014), 'The Eurozone Crisis – What Do UK Voters Think? Survation For The Mail On Sunday': http://survation.com/the-eurozone-crisis-dark-clouds-gather-but-what-do-uk-voters-think-survation-for-the-mail-on-sunday/

9   BBC Online (2001), 'Trader guilty of metric law breach', 9 April 2001: http://news.bbc.co.uk/1/hi/uk/1269043.stm

10 Dallison, Paul (2016), 'Boris Johnson's 11 best Europe moments', Politico.eu, 23 February 2016: http://www.politico.eu/article/the-eu-is-a-lobster-boris-johnson-best-moments-europe-reporting/

11 Quatremer, Jean (2016), 'The road to Brexit was paved with Boris Johnson's Euromyths', *The Guardian*, 15 July 2016: https://www.theguardian.com/commentisfree/2016/jul/15/brexit-boris-johnson-euromyths-telegraph-brussels

12 Fletcher, Martin (2016), 'Boris Johnson peddled absurd EU myths -- and our disgraceful press followed his lead', *New Statesman*, 1 July 2016: http://www.newstatesman.com/politics/uk/2016/07/boris-johnson-peddled-absurd-eu-myths-and-our-disgraceful-press-followed-his

13 Fletcher, Martin (2016), ibid.

14 Levy, Geoffrey (2016), 'Still sneering at Britain: Jean-Claude Juncker the boozy bully who sums up all that's rotten about the EU', *Daily Mail*, 30 June 2016: http://www.dailymail.co.uk/debate/article-3667054/Still-sneering-Britain-boozy-bully-sums-s-rotten-EU.html

15 Jones, David (2014), 'Cognac for breakfast? Dave's EU nemesis has FAR worse skeletons in his closet, including his nasty habit of blowing taxpayers' millions on white elephants', *Daily Mail*, 5 July 2014: http://www.dailymail.co.uk/news/article-2681298/Cognac-breakfast-Daves-EU-nemesis-FAR-worse-skeletons-closet-including-Nazi-father-law-rumours-love-child.html

16 https://www.youtube.com/watch?v=XPgiI46FCDU

17 Hughes, Chris (2012), 'Hook gets the boot: Abu Hamza has finally left the UK after 8 years, 15 court cases and a £225m bill for taxpayers', *Daily Mirror*, 6 October 2012: http://www.mirror.co.uk/news/uk-news/abu-hamza-deported-from-uk-after-1363430

18 Peck, Tom (2016), 'Moroccan woman in deportation battle is Abu Hamza's daughter-in-law, Tory MP reveals', *The Independent*, 5 February 2016: http://www.independent.co.uk/news/uk/home-news/moroccan-woman-in-deportation-battle-is-abu-hamzas-daughter-in-law-tory-mp-reveals-a6856966.html

19 Cole, Brendan (2016), 'UK judges to decide whether to deport daughter-in-law of Islamist preacher Abu Hamza', International Business Times, 14 September 2016: http://www.ibtimes.co.uk/uk-judges-decide-whether-deport-daughter-law-islamist-preacher-abu-hamza-1581192

20 Cummings, Dominic (2014), 'Report by North Wood for Business for Britain on research into attitudes towards the possible renegotiation of our EU membership and a possible IN/OUT referendum', internal strategy document seen by the authors

21 May, Theresa (2016), 'Home Secretary's speech on the UK, EU and our place in the world', 25 April 2016: https://www.gov.uk/government/speeches/home-secretarys-speech-on-the-uk-eu-and-our-place-in-the-world

22 The Migration Observatory (2016), 'A Decade of Immigration in the British Press', Oxford University: http://www.migrationobservatory.ox.ac.uk/resources/reports/decade-immigration-british-press/

23 Gerard, Liz (2016), 'Liz Gerard on how the Press conspire to brainwash Britain on immigration', *New European*, 30 September 2016: http://www.theneweuropean.co.uk/culture/liz_gerard_on_how_the_press_conspire_to_brainwash_britain_on_immigration_1_4718203

24 http://www.express.co.uk/news/uk/247578/Britain-s-40-percent-surge-in-ethnic-numbers

25 http://www.express.co.uk/news/uk/265665/Migrants-rob-young-Britons-of-jobs

26 http://www.express.co.uk/news/uk/277363/Workers-are-fired-for-being-British

27 Holehouse, Matthew (2014), 'Clegg v Farage: Crunching the numbers', *Daily Telegraph*, 27 March 2014: http://www.telegraph.co.uk/news/politics/UKIP/10727810/Clegg-v-Farage-Crunching-the-numbers.html

28 BBC News (2015), 'Romanian and Bulgarian migration: Rise in workers in UK', 18 February 2015: http://www.bbc.co.uk/news/uk-31519319

29 Prince, Rosa (2010), David Cameron: net immigration will be capped at tens of thousands, *Daily Telegraph*, 10 January 2010: http://www.telegraph.co.uk/news/politics/6961675/David-Cameron-net-immigration-will-be-capped-at-tens-of-thousands.html, repeated in the 2010 Conservative general election manifesto: http://conservativehome.blogs.com/files/conservative-manifesto-2010.pdf, p. 21

30 https://www.iom.int/news/over-3770-migrants-have-died-trying-cross-mediterranean-europe-2015

31 Boland, Stephanie (2015), 'Why are refugees throwing themselves on train tracks in Hungary?', *New Statesman*, 3 September 2015: http://www.newstatesman.com/world/2015/09/why-are-refugees-throwing-themselves-train-tracks-hungary

32 Sky News (2015), 'Refugee Mother's Plea: "Take My Kid to Germany"', 16 September 2015: http://news.sky.com/story/refugee-mothers-plea-take-my-kid-to-germany-10346170

33 https://www.nytimes.com/2016/09/03/world/middleeast/alan-kurdi-aylan-anniversary-turkey-syria-refugees-death.html?_r=0

34 Sky News (2015), 'Germany: "No Limit" To Refugees We'll Take In', 5 September 2015: http://news.sky.com/story/germany-no-limit-to-refugees-well-take-in-10347281

35 Traynor, Ian (2015), 'Migration crisis: Hungarian PM says Europe in grip of madness', *The Guardian*, 3 September 2015: https://www.theguardian.com/world/2015/sep/03/migration-crisis-hungary-pm-victor-orban-europe-response-madness

36 Lehne, Stefan (2016), 'How the Refugee Crisis will Reshape the EU', Carnegie Europe, 4 February 2016: http://carnegieeurope.eu/2016/02/04/how-refugee-crisis-will-reshape-eu-pub-62650

37 Perraudin, Frances (2015), '"Marauding" migrants threaten standard of living, says foreign secretary', *The Guardian*, 10 August 2015: https://www.theguardian.com/uk-news/2015/aug/09/african-migrants-threaten-eu-standard-living-philip-hammond

38 Travis, Alan (2015), 'Theresa May maintains tough stance on "economic migrants"', *The Guardian*, 22 September 2015: https://www.theguardian.com/world/2015/sep/22/theresa-may-tough-stance-economic-migrants-europe

39 Elgot, Jessica and Taylor, Matthew (2015), 'Calais crisis: Cameron condemned for "dehumanising" description of migrants', *The Guardian*, 30 July 2015: https://www.theguardian.com/uk-news/2015/jul/30/david-cameron-migrant-swarm-language-condemned

40 Farage, Nigel (2015), 2015 Speech at the State of the Union, 9 September 2015: http://www.ukpol.co.uk/nigel-farage-2015-speech-at-the-state-of-the-union/

41 Dathan, Matt (2016), 'David Cameron condemns Nigel Farage for suggesting Brussels bombings prove Britain is safer outside the EU … but bookmakers shorten the odds for Brexit', *Daily Mail*, 22 March 2016: http://www.dailymail.co.uk/news/article-3504779/David-Cameron-condemns-Nigel-Farage-suggesting-Brussels-bombings-prove-Britain-safer-outside-EU-bookmakers-shorten-odds-Brexit.html

42 *Daily Telegraph* (2016), 'Vote leave to benefit from a world of opportunity', 20 June 2016: http://www.telegraph.co.uk/opinion/2016/06/20/vote-leave-to-benefit-from-a-world-of-opportunity/

43 SNP Manifesto for the 2016 Scottish Assembly Elections: https://d3n8a8pro7vhmx.cloudfront.net/thesnp/pages/5540/attachments/original/1485880018/SNP_Manifesto2016-web_(1).pdf?1485880018, p. 54

REASON 13

1 McTague, Tom and Chorley, Matt (2015), 'Teetotal vegetarian nicknamed "Jelly": Meet Jeremy Bernard Corbyn, the socialist hardliner raised in a manor voted against Labour more times than David Cameron', *Daily Mail*, 12 September 2015: http://www.dailymail.co.uk/news/article-3230999/Tee-total-vegetarian-nicknamed-Jelly-child-voted-against-Labour-David-Cameron.html

2 Interviewed by Jason Farrell for 'The Battle for Labour', Sky News documentary, 14 September 2016: https://corporate.sky.com/media-centre/media-packs/2016/the-battle-for-labour-8pm-140916

3 Dathan, Matt (2015), 'So, who are the "moronic MPs" who nominated Jeremy Corbyn for the Labour leadership contest?', *The Independent*, 22 July 2015: http://www.independent.co.uk/news/uk/politics/who-are-the-morons-who-nominated-jeremy-corbyn-for-the-labour-leadership-contest-10406527.html

4 Helm, Toby and Doward, Jamie (2015), 'Jeremy Corbyn draws fire for position on Britain's EU future', *The Guardian*, 25 July 2015: https://www.theguardian.com/politics/2015/jul/25/jeremy-corbyn-draws-fire-position-future-britain-eu-membership

5   MacLellan, Kylie and Young, Sarah (2015), 'Corbyn says "no blank cheque" for Cameron on Britain's EU membership', Reuters, 14 September 2015: http://uk.reuters.com/article/uk-britain-politics-labour-eu-idUKKCN0RE0N820150914

6   Wintour, Patrick (2015), 'Jeremy Corbyn: Labour will campaign for UK to stay in the EU', *The Guardian*, 17 September 2015: https://www.theguardian.com/politics/2015/sep/17/jeremy-corbyn-labour-campaign-for-uk-stay-in-eu

7   https://www.ft.com/content/d3ccd904-5d42-11e5-a28b-50226830d644

8   BBC News (April 2016), 'Jeremy Corbyn warns of workers' rights "bonfire" if UK leaves', 14 April 2016: http://www.bbc.co.uk/news/uk-politics-eu-referendum-36039925

9   http://www.labour.org.uk/blog/entry/jeremy-corbyn-europe-speech

10   Stone, Jon (2016), 'Jeremy Corbyn suggests EU-wide minimum wage to give British workers a "level playing field"', *The Independent*, 14 April 2016: http://www.independent.co.uk/news/uk/politics/jeremy-corbyn-suggests-eu-wide-minimum-wage-to-give-british-workers-a-level-playing-field-a6983991.html

11   Waugh, Paul (2016), 'Jeremy Corbyn Slams Cameron's £9m Pro-EU Leaflet As He Calls For "More Even Approach" To Referendum Information', Huffington Post, 13 April 2016: http://www.huffingtonpost.co.uk/entry/jeremy-corbyn-slams-9m-pro-eu-leaflet_uk_570e3f13e4b0b84e2e71a848

12   May, Josh and Whale, Sebastian (2016), 'Alan Johnson under fire over Brexit "extremists" label', Politics Home, 10 May 2016: https://www.politicshome.com/news/europe/eu-policy-agenda/brexit/news/74825/alan-johnson-under-fire-over-brexit-extremists-label

13   Smith, Matthew (2016), 'What would make Leave voters change their mind about Brexit?', YouGov, 27 October 2016: https://yougov.co.uk/news/2016/10/27/what-would-make-leave-voters-change-their-mind-abo/

14   *Daily Express* (2016), 'Flip-flopping Remain campaigner Corbyn admits on The Last Leg he is "not a fan" of EU', 11 June 2016: http://www.express.co.uk/news/uk/678897/Remain-campaigner-Corbyn-admits-he-is-not-an-EU-fan-last-leg-adam-hills-channel-4

15   Oliver, Craig (2016), op. cit., loc. 1478

16   Oliver, Craig (2016), ibid., loc. 4172

17   Nelson, Nigel (2016), 'Jeremy Corbyn angers Labour MPs AGAIN by "hijacking" appeal for unity over EU referendum', *Daily Mirror*, 4 June 2016: http://www.mirror.co.uk/news/uk-news/jeremy-corbyn-angers-labour-mps-8115544

18   Watts, Joe (2016), 'Pro-EU Labour MP claims leaked emails show "in technicolour" confusion of party's EU referendum campaign', *The Independent*, 16 August 2016: http://www.independent.co.uk/news/uk/politics/chuka-umunna-john-trickett-labour-eu-referendum-campaign-leaked-emails-confusion-a7194566.html

19   Schofield, Kevin, Whale, Sebastian and Chambre, Agnes (2016), 'Jeremy Corbyn: There can be no limit on immigration inside the EU', Politics Home, 19 June 2016: https://www.politicshome.com/news/europe/eu-policy-agenda/brexit/news/76327/jeremy-corbyn-there-can-be-no-limit-immigration

20   Oliver, Craig (2016), op. cit., loc. 4761

21   Oliver, Craig (2016), ibid., loc. 3571

22   Ashcroft, Michael (2016), op. cit., p. 109

23   http://www.walesonline.co.uk/news/politics/full-eu-referendum-results-map-11510374

24   Krausova, Anna and Vargas-Silva, Carlos (2014), 'Wales: Census Profile', The Migration Observatory, 4 March 2014: http://www.migrationobservatory.ox.ac.uk/resources/briefings/wales-census-profile/

25   Walker, Jonathan (2015), 'Birmingham Labour MP to urge ethnic minorities to vote "no" to Europe', *Birmingham Post*, 8 November 2015: http://www.birminghampost.co.uk/news/regional-affairs/birmingham-labour-mp-urge-ethnic-10399231

REASON 14

1   The cartoon can be seen here: https://www.adamsmith.org/the-liberal-case-for-leave/

2   Baxter, Steven (2011), 'No to AV's new campaign is beyond parody', *New Statesman*, 22 February 2011: http://www.newstatesman.com/blogs/steven-baxter/2011/02/voting-system-baby-gets

3   Dilnot, Andrew (May 2016), 'UK Contributions to the European Union (EU)'; letter to Dominic Cummings, 10 May 2016: https://www.statisticsauthority.gov.uk/wp-content/uploads/2016/05/Letter-from-Sir-Andrew-Dilnot-to-Mr-Cummings-10-May-2016-.pdf

4   Chorley, Matt and Merrick, Jane (2016), 'Clegg lashes out against Tory "lies" over AV campaign', *The Independent*, 23 April 2011: http://www.independent.co.uk/news/uk/politics/av/clegg-lashes-out-against-tory-lies-over-av-campaign-2274228.html

5   Newton Dunn, Tom (2012), 'Let them eat cold pasty', *The Sun*, 27 March 2012: https://www.thesun.co.uk/archives/politics/486276/let-them-eat-cold-pasty/

6   Hannan, Daniel (2016b), *What Next: How to get the best from Brexit*, Head of Zeus, loc. 366

7   Walker, Kirsty (2009), 'An internet sensation, the Tory who told Brown to his face that he's a disaster', *Daily Mail*, 27 March 2009: http://www.dailymail.co.uk/news/article-1165027/An-internet-sensation-Tory-told-Brown-face-hes-disaster.html

8   Hannan, Daniel (2016b), op. cit., loc. 437

9   Mosbacher, Michael and Wiseman, Oliver (2016), op. cit., p. 19

10   https://en.wikipedia.org/wiki/Dominic_Cummings

11   Oliver, Craig (2016), op. cit., loc. 254

12   Gimson, Andrew (2014), 'A Profile of Dominic Cummings, friend of Gove and enemy of Clegg', Conservative Home, 15 May 2014: http://www.conservativehome.com/thetorydiary/2014/05/a-profile-of-dominic-cummings-friend-of-gove-and-enemy-of-clegg.html

13   Quinn, Ben (2014), 'Michael Gove ally Dominic Cummings in personal attack on David Cameron', *The Guardian*, 16 June 2014: https://www.theguardian.com/politics/2014/jun/16/gove-cummings-david-cameron

14   Cummings, Dominic (2014), op. cit.

15   Cummings, Dominic (2014), ibid.

16   Cummings, Dominic (2014), ibid.

17   Cummings, Dominic (2014), ibid.

18   Cummings, Dominic (2014), ibid.

19   The whole report can be found here: http://2mbg6fgb1kl380gtk22pbxgw.wpengine.netdna-cdn.com/wp-content/uploads/2016/11/ChangeorGo.pdf

20   Pickard, Jim and Cookson, Robert (2015), 'Vote Leave group launches in push for UK exit from EU', *FinancialTimes*, 8 October 2015: https://www.ft.com/content/e926b86a-6dd2-11e5-aca9-d87542bf8673

21   The Stronger In launch video can be seen here: https://www.youtube.com/watch?v=AkSf7XSr2CI

REASON 15

1   Swinford, Steven (2014), 'Don't threaten me over Juncker appointment, Angela Merkel warns David Cameron', *Daily Telegraph*, 10 June 2004: http://www.telegraph.co.uk/news/politics/david-cameron/10888727/Dont-threaten-me-over-Juncker-appointment-Anglea-Merkel-warns-David-Cameron.html

2   http://news.bbc.co.uk/1/shared/bsp/hi/pdfs/05011401.pdf

3   Traynor, Ian, Watt, Nicholas, Gow, David and Wintour, Patrick (2011), 'David Cameron blocks EU treaty with veto, casting Britain adrift in Europe', *The Guardian*, 9 December 2011: https://www.theguardian.com/world/2011/dec/09/david-cameron-blocks-eu-treaty

4   BBC News (2011), 'David Cameron blocks EU-wide deal to tackle euro crisis', 9 December 2011: http://www.bbc.co.uk/news/uk-16104275

5   Traynor, Ian, Watt, Nicholas, Gow, David and Wintour, Patrick (2011), op. cit.

6   Hinarejos, Alicia (2016), 'Bailouts, Borrowed Institutions, and Judicial Review: Ledra Advertising,' EU Law Analysis, 25 September 2016: http://eulawanalysis.blogspot.co.uk/2016/09/bailouts-borrowed-institutions-and.html

7   Cameron, David (October 2014), Speech to Conservative Party Conference 2014, 1 October 2014: http://press.conservatives.com/post/98882674910/david-cameron-speech-to-conservative-party

8   Shipman, Tim (2014), 'PM threatens quotas for EU workers', *Sunday Times*, 19 October 2014: http://www.thesundaytimes.co.uk/sto/news/Politics/article1473074.ece

9   Article 66 of the TFEU: https://europadatenbank.iaaeu.de/user/view_legalact.php?id=772

10   Reuters (2013), 'Cyprus imposes capital controls – the measures', *Daily Telegraph*, 28 March 2013: http://www.telegraph.co.uk/finance/financialcrisis/9958595/Cyprus-imposes-capital-controls-the-measures.html

11   Full text of the TFEU: http://eur-lex.europa.eu/resource.html?uri=cellar:2bf140bf-a3f8-4ab2-b506-fd71826e6da6.0023.02/DOC_2&format=PDF

12   Chalmers, Damian and Booth, Stephen (2014), 'A European labour market with national welfare systems: a proposal for a new Citizenship and Integration Directive', Open Europe, November 2014: http://archive.openeurope.org.uk/Content/Documents/European_labour_market_with_national_welfare_systems__Chalmers_and_Booth__November_2014.pdf

13   Cameron, David (November 2014), JCB Staffordshire: Prime Minister's Speech, 28 November 2014: https://www.gov.uk/government/speeches/jcb-staffordshire-prime-ministers-speech

14 https://www.gov.uk/government/uploads/system/uploads/attachment_data/file/278507/Fresh_Start__full_.pdf

15 http://2mbg6fgb1kl380gtk22pbxgw.wpengine.netdna-cdn.com/wp-content/uploads/2016/11/ChangeorGo.pdf

16 Juncker, Jean-Claude, Tusk, Donald, Dijsselbloem, Jeroen, Draghi, Mario and Schulz, Martin (2015), 'Completing Europe's Economic and Monetary Union', 22 June 2015: https://ec.europa.eu/priorities/sites/beta-political/files/5-presidents-report_en.pdf

17 Traynor, Ian (2011), 'David Cameron enraged by brochure showcasing £270m EU building', *The Guardian*, 24 June 2011: https://www.theguardian.com/world/2011/jun/24/david-cameron-brochure-eu-bulding

18 Cameron, David (2015), 'A new settlement for the United Kingdom in a reformed European Union', letter from David Cameron to Donald Tusk, 10 November 2015: https://www.gov.uk/government/uploads/system/uploads/attachment_data/file/475679/Donald_Tusk_letter.pdf

19 Slack, James (2015), 'Is that it, Mr Cameron? Tories mock his EU wishlist as "thin gruel" while Brussels will fight migrant benefit curbs', *Daily Mail*, 11 November 2015: http://www.dailymail.co.uk/news/article-3312978/Is-Mr-Cameron-Tories-mock-EU-wishlist-gruel-Brussels-fight-migrant-benefit-curbs.html

20 Eur-Lex (2016), 'A new settlement for the United Kingdom within the European Union', 19 February 2016: http://eur-lex.europa.eu/legal-content/EN/TXT/?uri=uriserv%3AOJ.CI.2016.069.01.0001.01.ENG

21 Johnson, Boris (February 2016), 'Voters have to ask Donald Tusk some hard questions before they accept his EU "deal"', *Daily Telegraph*, 7 February 2016: http://www.telegraph.co.uk/news/newstopics/eureferendum/12145593/Voters-have-to-ask-Donald-Tusk-some-hard-questions-before-they-accept-his-EU-deal.html

22 Conservative Party (2010), 'An Invitation to Join the Government of Britain': https://www.conservatives.com/-/media/Files/Manifesto2010, p. 114

23 Hannan, Daniel (2016a), op. cit., p. 138

24 Hannan, Daniel (2016a), ibid., p. 139

25 Khan, Mehreen (2016), 'UK has the right to stop welfare abuse, admits Hungarian foreign minister', *Daily Telegraph*, 5 February 2016: http://www.telegraph.co.uk/news/newstopics/eureferendum/12141935/UK-has-the-right-to-stop-welfare-abuse-admits-Hungarian-foreign-minister.html

26 Foster, Peter and Day, Matthew (2016), 'Poland ready to back David Cameron's flagship EU deal as PM faces down critics', *Daily Telegraph*, 3 February 2016: http://www.telegraph.co.uk/news/newstopics/eureferendum/12138362/Poland-ready-to-back-David-Camerons-flagship-EU-deal-as-PM-faces-down-critics.html

27 Foster, Peter (2016), 'David Cameron's welfare demands split Europe from East to West', *Daily Telegraph*, 10 November 2015: http://www.telegraph.co.uk/news/newstopics/eureferendum/11987099/David-Camerons-welfare-demands-split-Europe-from-East-to-West.html

28 Johnson, Boris (February 2016), op. cit.

29 Cameron, David (February 2016), PM statement following European Council meeting, 19 February 2016: https://www.gov.uk/government/speeches/pms-statement-following-european-council-meeting-19-february-2016

30 https://twitter.com/danieljhannan/status/700802718986797060

31 Hannan, Daniel (2016a), op. cit., p. 142

32 Davies, Mark (2016), '"Cameron promised half a loaf and came home with crumbs": Eurosceptics pour scorn on PM's EU deal after he is forced into climbdown over welfare demands', *Daily Mail*, 19 February 2016: http://www.dailymail.co.uk/news/article-3455418/Cameron-promised-half-loaf-came-home-crumbs-Eurosceptics-pour-scorn-PM-s-EU-deal-forced-climbdown-welfare-demands.html

33 Newton Dunn, Tom (2016), 'Who do you think you are kidding Mr Cameron?', *The Sun*, 3 February 2016: https://www.thesun.co.uk/archives/politics/275289/who-do-eu-think-you-are-kidding-mr-cameron/

34 Oliver, Craig (2016), op. cit., loc. 4449–96

35 Cummings, Dominic (2014), op. cit.

REASON 16

1 *The West Briton* (2016), 'Listen as Boris Johnson guarantees Cornwall won't lose any money if Britain votes to leave the EU', 11 May 2016: http://www.cornwalllive.com/boris-johnson-guaranteed-cornwall-won-t-lose/story-29258605-detail/story.html

2 Molloy, Mark (2016), 'Boris Johnson's bizarre day in Cornwall – the best tweets', *Daily Telegraph*, 11 May 2016: http://www.telegraph.co.uk/news/2016/05/11/boris-johnsons-bizarre-day-in-cornwall--the-best-tweets/

3 Chambre, Agnes (2016), 'Boris Johnson calls for politicians to "man up" over immigration', Politics

Home, 11 May 2016: https://www.politicshome.com/news/europe/eu-policy-agenda/brexit/news/74872/boris-johnson-calls-politicians-man-over-immigration

4 Johnson, Boris (2014), Speech to Conservative Party Conference 2014, 30 September 2014:, http://press.conservatives.com/post/98800242450/boris-johnson-speech-to-conservative-party

5 Oliver, Craig (2016), op. cit., loc. 251

6 Oliver, Craig (2016), ibid., loc. 273

7 Vine, Sarah (2016), 'The torture of watching my husband choose between his beliefs and his old friend the PM: Daily Mail columnist Sarah Vine's intensely personal account of a momentous decision', *Daily Mail*, 24 February 2016: http://www.dailymail.co.uk/news/article-3461103/The-torture-watching-husband-choose-beliefs-old-friend-PM-Daily-Mail-columnist-SARAH-VINE-s-intensely-personal-account-momentous-decision.html

8 Vine, Sarah (2016), ibid.

9 McTague, Tom (2016), 'Bullingdon Club initiation ceremony claim: New members of David Cameron's old club "burn £50 note in front of beggar"', *Daily Mirror*, 23 February 2013: http://www.mirror.co.uk/news/uk-news/bullingdon-club-initiation-ceremony-claim-1725912

10 Gimson, Andrew (2012), *Boris: The Adventures of Boris Johnson*, Simon & Schuster, p. 70

11 Purnell, Sonia (2016), 'Boris Johnson and David Cameron: How a rivalry that began at Eton spilled out on to the main stage of British politics', *The Independent*, 23 February 2016: http://www.independent.co.uk/news/uk/politics/boris-johnson-and-david-cameron-how-a-rivalry-that-began-at-eton-spilled-out-on-to-the-main-stage-of-a6891856.html

12 Watt, Nicholas and Wintour, Patrick (2014), 'David Cameron axes Michael Gove in reshuffle after toxic poll warning', *The Guardian*, 15 July 2014: https://www.theguardian.com/politics/2014/jul/15/cameron-sacks-toxic-gove-promotes-women-reshuffle

13 https://www.youtube.com/watch?v=mnXoQeGnT4Q

14 Coates, Sam (2016), 'Gove "torn" between Cameron and Brexit', *The Times*, 4 February 2016: http://www.thetimes.co.uk/tto/news/politics/article4682358.ece

15 Shipman, Tim (2016), op. cit., loc. 2884

16 Shipman, Tim (2016), ibid., loc. 2885

17 Shipman, Tim (2016), ibid., loc. 2948

18 Vine, Sarah (2016), op. cit.

19 Vine, Sarah (2016), ibid.

20 *Daily Telegraph* (2009), 'Voters could still get say on EU Lisbon Treaty under the Conservatives, Boris Johnson says', 5 October 2009: http://www.telegraph.co.uk/news/politics/london-mayor-election/mayor-of-london/6261277/Voters-could-still-get-say-on-EU-Lisbon-Treaty-under-the-Conservatives-Boris-Johnson-says.html

21 Barrett, Matthew (2012), 'Boris signs the People's Pledge for an In/Out EU referendum', Conservative Home, 25 March 2012: http://www.conservativehome.com/thetorydiary/2012/03/boris-johnson-signs-the-peoplespledgeeu-for-a-european-referendum.html

22 Mason, Rowena (2015), 'Tax credit cuts: Boris Johnson urges moves to "mitigate and palliate" impact', *The Guardian*, 7 October 2015: https://www.theguardian.com/politics/2015/oct/07/tax-credit-cuts-boris-johnson-urges-moves-to-mitigate-and-palliate-impact

23 Forsyth, James (2015), 'Boris in the wilderness', *The Spectator*, 3 October 2015: http://www.spectator.co.uk/2015/10/when-will-boris-take-the-plunge/

24 HC Deb, 1 June 2015, col. 386

25 Maddox, David (2016), 'I won't front the fight to quit the EU, says Boris Johnson', *Daily Express*, 13 January 2016: http://www.express.co.uk/news/politics/634050/Boris-Johnson-EU-Brexit-David-Cameron-Eurosceptic

26 Johnson, Boris (February 2016), op. cit.

27 Johnson, Boris (February 2016), ibid.

28 Staufenberg, Jess (2016), 'Boris Johnson says "don't be afraid" of Brexit ahead of EU membership deal', *The Independent*, 15 February 2016: http://www.independent.co.uk/news/uk/politics/boris-johnson-brexit-dont-be-afraid-eu-membership-deal-a6874916.html

29 Vine, Sarah (2016), op. cit.

30 Shipman, Tim (2016), op. cit., loc. 2758

31 Shipman, Tim (2016), ibid., loc. 3150

32 Wheeler, Marina (2016), 'The crucial missing part of Cameron's EU deal', *The Spectator*, 13 February 2016: http://www.spectator.co.uk/2016/02/the-crucial-missing-part-of-camerons-eu-deal/

33 Shipman, Tim (2016), op. cit., loc. 3246

34 Shipman, Tim (2016), ibid., loc. 3314

35 http://news.bbc.co.uk/1/shared/bsp/hi/pdfs/21021603.pdf

36 Johnson, Boris (March 2016), 'There is only one way to get the change we want – vote to leave the EU', *Daily Telegraph*, 16 March 2016: http://www.telegraph.co.uk/opinion/2016/03/16/boris-johnson-exclusive-there-is-only-one-way-to-get-the-change/

37 Johnson, Boris (October 2016), 'Cripes! I jolly nearly backed Dave on Europe', *Sunday Times*, 16 October 2016: http://www.thetimes.co.uk/article/cripes-i-jolly-nearly-backed-dave-on-europe-wbcqd6b6c

38 https://twitter.com/nsoamesmp/status/701375515219902465

39 A transcript of this impromptu press conference can be found at: http://blogs.spectator.co.uk/2016/02/boris-johnson-i-will-be-advocating-vote-leave-or-whatever-the-team-is-called/

40 Oliver, Craig (2016), op. cit., loc. 1434

41 HC Deb, 22 February 2016, cols 24–5

42 Boffey, Daniel (2016), 'Jeremy Corbyn rules out second referendum on Brexit', *The Guardian*, 7 August 2016: https://www.theguardian.com/politics/2016/aug/07/jeremy-corbyn-rules-out-second-referendum-brexit

43 Watt, Nicholas (2016), 'George Osborne: Brexit campaigners' case is "economically illiterate"', *The Guardian*, 18 April 2016: https://www.theguardian.com/politics/2016/apr/18/george-osborne-brexit-campaigners-case-is-economically-illiterate

44 Dominiczak, Peter (2016), 'Boris and Gove pledge tough new immigration system after Brexit', *Daily Telegraph*, 1 June 2016: http://www.telegraph.co.uk/news/2016/05/31/eu-referendum-boris-and-gove-pledge-tough-new-immigration-system/

45 Wright, Oliver (2016), 'Boris Johnson launches most personal attack on David Cameron yet', *The Independent*, 9 May 2016: http://www.independent.co.uk/news/uk/politics/eu-referendum-boris-johnson-launches-personal-attack-on-david-cameorn-a7020156.html

46 Bennett, Owen (2016), 'Boris Johnson Sings In German To Prove He's Not A "Little Englander"', Huffington Post, 9 May 2016: http://www.huffingtonpost.co.uk/entry/boris-johnson-german-singing-eu-referendum_uk_573076bee4b0e6da49a692bb

47 Ross, Tim (2016), 'Boris Johnson: The EU wants a superstate, just as Hitler did', *Sunday Telegraph*, 15 May 2016: http://www.telegraph.co.uk/news/2016/05/14/boris-johnson-the-eu-wants-a-superstate-just-as-hitler-did/

48 Addley, Eesther. and Mason, Rowena (2016), 'Johnson's "obscene remarks" may have ruined his chances as PM, says Heseltine', *The Guardian*, 17 May 2016: https://www.theguardian.com/politics/2016/may/17/johnsons-obscene-remarks-may-have-ruined-his-chances-as-pm-says-heseltine

49 Shipman, Tim and Harper, Tom (2016), 'Boris and Gove lash Cameron on immigration', *Sunday Times*, 29 May 2016: http://www.thetimes.co.uk/article/boris-and-gove-lash-cameron-on-immigration-5kjl329mx

50 Lowe, Josh (2016), 'Boris Johnson accuses David Cameron of "demented scaremongering"', *Newsweek*, 11 May 2016: http://europe.newsweek.com/brexit-david-cameron-boris-johnson-demented-scaremongering-458531?rm=eu

51 Shipman, Tim (2016), op. cit., loc. 6077

52 http://news.bbc.co.uk/1/shared/bsp/hi/pdfs/05061601.pdf

REASON 17

1 Transcript of Andrew Marr interview with Boris Johnson, 6 March 2016: http://news.bbc.co.uk/1/shared/bsp/hi/pdfs/06031603.pdf

2 Transcript of Faisal Islam interview with David Cameron – https://corporate.sky.com/media-centre/media-packs/2016/the-eu-in-or-out---interview-with-david-cameron-8pm,-20616

3 Transcript of Faisal Islam interview with Michael Gove: https://corporate.sky.com/media-centre/media-packs/2016/eu-in-or-out-faisal-islam-interview-with-michael-gove,-30616-8pm

4 Hartman, Andrew (2015), *A War for the Soul of America: A History of the Culture Wars*, University of Chicago Press, p. 52

5 Nardelli, Alberto and Watt, Nicholas (2015), 'David Cameron plans EU campaign focusing on "risky" impact of EU exit', *The Guardian*, 26 June 2015: https://www.theguardian.com/politics/2015/jun/26/david-cameron-eu-campaign-risky-impact-uk-exit

6 Gordon, Tom (2014), 'I admit it: the man who coined Project Fear label', *The Herald*, 21 December 2014, http://www.heraldscotland.com/news/13194407.I_admit_it__the_man_who_coined_Project_Fear_label/

7 Carrell, Severin and Brooks, Libby (2014), 'Scottish debate: Salmond and Darling in angry clash over

independence', *The Guardian*, 6 August 2014: https://www.theguardian.com/politics/2014/aug/05/alex-salmond-alistair-darling-scotland-debate-independence

8   Delaney, Sam (2016), 'How Lynton Crosby (and a dead cat) won the election: "Labour were intellectually lazy"', *The Guardian*, 20 January 2016: https://www.theguardian.com/politics/2016/jan/20/lynton-crosby-and-dead-cat-won-election-conservatives-labour-intellectually-lazy

9   Farrell, Jason (2015), 'The Worst Campaign May Yet Be The Winner', 5 May 2015: http://news.sky.com/story/the-worst-campaign-may-yet-be-the-winner-10360810

10 Behr, Rafael (2016), 'How remain failed: the inside story of a doomed campaign', *The Guardian*, 5 July 2016: https://www.theguardian.com/politics/2016/jul/05/how-remain-failed-inside-story-doomed-campaign

11 Cabinet Office (2016), 'Why the government believes that voting to remain in the EU is the best decision for the UK', government leaflet sent to all UK households, 6 April 2016: https://www.gov.uk/government/publications/why-the-government-believes-that-voting-to-remain-in-the-european-union-is-the-best-decision-for-the-uk/why-the-government-believes-that-voting-to-remain-in-the-european-union-is-the-best-decision-for-the-uk

12 HM Treasury (2016), 'HM Treasury analysis shows leaving EU would cost British households £4,300 per year': https://www.gov.uk/government/news/hm-treasury-analysis-shows-leaving-eu-would-cost-british-households-4300-per-year

13 Nelson, Fraser (2016), 'The deceptions behind George Osborne's Brexit report', *The Spectator*, 18 April 2016: http://blogs.spectator.co.uk/2016/04/the-deceptions-behind-george-osbornes-brexit-report/

14 Ipsos MORI (2016), 'Ipsos MORI June 2016 Political Monitor – Topline Results', 16 June 2016: https://www.ipsos.com/sites/default/files/migrations/en-uk/files/Assets/Docs/Polls/pm-16-june-2016-topline.pdf, p. 6

15 Robertson, Jamie (2016), 'Brexit vote may spark recession, Mark Carney warns', BBC Online, 12 May 2016: http://www.bbc.co.uk/news/business-36273448

16 Chan, Szu Ping (2016), 'House prices and stock market will tumble if UK votes for Brexit, IMF warns', *Daily Telegraph*, 13 May 2016: http://www.telegraph.co.uk/business/2016/05/13/house-prices-and-stock-market-will-tumble-if-uk-votes-for-brexit/

17 Rogers, Simon (2012), 'Bobby Kennedy on GDP: "measures everything except that which is worthwhile"', *The Guardian*, 24 May 2012: https://www.theguardian.com/news/datablog/2012/may/24/robert-kennedy-gdp

18 Menon, Anand (2016), 'Uniting the United Kingdom: What Comes After Brexit', Foreign Affairs, 6 July 2016: https://www.foreignaffairs.com/articles/united-kingdom/2016-07-06/uniting-united-kingdom

19 Kirkup, James and Waterfield, Bruno (2011), 'David Cameron wins battle to keep Britain out of second EU bail-out for Greece', *Daily Telegraph*, 24 June 2011: http://www.telegraph.co.uk/news/politics/david-cameron/8595806/David-Cameron-wins-battle-to-keep-Britain-out-of-second-EU-bail-out-for-Greece.html

20 *Daily Express* (2016), '"They were wrong then and are wrong now": Farage dismisses Brexit economy fears', 16 May 2016: http://www.express.co.uk/news/politics/670776/nigel-farage-peston-on-sunday-itv

21 Transcript of Andrew Marr interview with Richard Branson, *The Andrew Marr Show*, 28 June 2015: http://news.bbc.co.uk/1/shared/bsp/hi/pdfs/28061502.pdf

22 Thomson, Alice and Sylvester, Rachel (2015), 'If we leave the EU, it will be 20 years before we realise Britain has no clout', *The Times*, 17 October 2015: http://www.thetimes.co.uk/tto/news/politics/article4588253.ece

23 Forsyth, James (2016), 'Head of the IN campaign says wages will go up if we leave the EU', *The Spectator*, 2 March 2016: http://blogs.spectator.co.uk/2016/03/head-of-the-in-campaign-says-wages-will-go-up-if-we-leave-the-eu/

24 *The Times* (2016), 'Business leaders set out their European stall', 23 February 2016: https://www.thetimes.co.uk/article/business-leaders-set-out-their-european-stall-3ll2kjzcg

25 Press Association (2016), 'Brexit would be risky bet for Britain, ex-US finance chiefs warn', *Daily Telegraph*, 20 April 2016: http://www.telegraph.co.uk/news/2016/04/20/brexit-would-be-risky-bet-for-britain-ex-us-finance-chiefs-warn/

26 Johnson, Boris (April 2016), 'UK and America can be better friends than ever Mr Obama… if we leave the EU', *The Sun*, 22 April 2016: https://www.thesun.co.uk/archives/politics/1139354/boris-johnson-uk-and-america-can-be-better-friends-than-ever-mr-obama-if-we-leave-the-eu/

27 Obama, Barack (2016), The President's News conference with Prime Minister David Cameron of the United Kingdom in London, England, 22 April 2016: http://www.presidency.ucsb.edu/ws/?pid=117098

28 Kirk, Ashley and Dunford, Daniel (2016), 'Leave supporters trust ordinary "common sense" more than academics and experts', *Daily Telegraph*, 22 June 2016: http://www.telegraph.co.uk/news/2016/06/16/eu-referendum-leave-supporters-trust-ordinary-common-sense-than/

29 Asthana, Anushka, Mason, Rowena and Inman, Phillip (2016), 'George Osborne; vote for Brexit and face

£30bn of taxes and spending cuts', *The Guardian*, 15 June 2016: https://www.theguardian.com/politics/2016/jun/14/osborne-predicts-30bn-hole-in-public-finance-if-uk-votes-to-leave-eu

30 Evans-Pritchard, Ambrose (2016), 'Osborne's "punishment budget" is economic vandalism', *Daily Telegraph*, 15 June 2016: http://www.telegraph.co.uk/business/2016/06/15/osbornes-punishment-budget-is-economic-vandalism/

31 Goodman, Paul (2016), 'Gove's EU speech: key extracts', Conservative Home, 19 April 2016: http://www.conservativehome.com/parliament/2016/04/goves-eu-speech-key-extracts.html

32 Rama, Edi (2016), 'It's absurd to drag Albania into the battle for Brexit', *The Times*, 26 April 2016: http://www.thetimes.co.uk/article/its-absurd-to-drag-albania-into-the-battle-for-brexit-lknqnm86g

33 Transcript of Andrew Marr interview with Michael Gove, *The Andrew Marr Show*, 8 May 2016: http://news.bbc.co.uk/1/shared/bsp/hi/pdfs/08051604.pdf

REASON 18

1 Settle, Michael (2016), 'UK net migration increases to second highest level on record', *The Herald*, 26 May 2016: http://www.heraldscotland.com/news/homenews/14518189.UK_net_migration_increases_to_second_highest_level_on_record/

2 BBC Online (2016), 'Net migration to UK rises to 333,000 – second highest on record', 26 May 2016: http://www.bbc.co.uk/news/uk-politics-eu-referendum-36382199

3 BBC Online (2016), ibid.

4 Chorley, Matt, Chapman, James and Doyle, Jack (2014), 'I'll veto new members joining EU, warns Cameron as he unveils benefits crackdown… but Germans accuse PM of blackmailing the continent', *Daily Mail*, 27 November 2014: http://www.dailymail.co.uk/news/article-2852457/At-Cameron-acts-migrants-Crackdown-range-benefits-EU-allow-it.html

5 Stewart, Heather (2016), 'UK voters leaning towards Brexit, Guardian poll reveals', *The Guardian*, 31 May 2016: https://www.theguardian.com/politics/2016/may/31/uk-voters-leaning-towards-brexit-guardian-poll-reveals

6 'Purdah' is covered by Section 125 of the Political Parties, Elections and Referendums Act 2000: http://www.legislation.gov.uk/ukpga/2000/41/section/125

7 Parliament Publications (2015), European Union Referendum Bill: Explanatory notes, 28 May 2015: https://www.publications.parliament.uk/pa/bills/cbill/2015-2016/0002/16002.pdf, p. 17

8 Paterson, Owen (2015), 'Why we MUSTN'T let No10 fix this vital vote', *Daily Mail*, 7 June 2015: http://www.dailymail.co.uk/debate/article-3113976/OWEN-PATERSON-MUSTN-T-let-No10-fix-vital-vote.html

9 Forsyth, James (2015), '"Purdah" amendment to EU referendum bill defeated – but only thanks to Labour', *The Spectator*, 16 June 2015: http://blogs.spectator.co.uk/2015/06/purdah-amendment-to-eu-referendum-bill-defeated-but-only-thanks-to-labour/

10 Holehouse, Matthew (2015), 'EU referendum purdah "would hobble negotiations in Brussels"', *Daily Telegraph*, 21 July 2015: http://www.telegraph.co.uk/news/worldnews/europe/eu/11753425/EU-referendum-purdah-would-hobble-negotiations-in-Brussels.html

11 Carpenter, Michael (2015), Supplementary evidence from Michael Carpenter, Speaker's Counsel (EUR16) – written evidence to PACAC Purdah and Impartiality Inquiry, 21 July 2015: http://data.parliament.uk/writtenevidence/committeeevidence.svc/evidencedocument/public-administration-and-constitutional-affairs-committee/eu-referendum-bill-part-one-purdah-and-impartiality/written/22843.html

12 Fawkes, Guido (2015), 'Parliament's lawyer: government's purdah position "unsound"', 7 September 2015: https://order-order.com/people/michael-carpenter/

13 Cummings, Dominic (2015), op. cit.

14 Mason, Rowena, Stewart, Heather and Asthana, Anushka (2016), 'Boris Johnson insists immigration pledge is not bid to oust Cameron', *The Guardian*, 1 June 2016: https://www.theguardian.com/politics/2016/jun/01/boris-johnson-insists-not-presenting-post-cameron-government-vote-leave

15 Shipman, Tim and Harper, Tom (2016), op. cit.

16 Whale, Sebastian (2016), 'Vote Leave accused of "stoking the fires of prejudice" over Turkey security threat claims', Politics Home, 22 May 2016: https://www.politicshome.com/news/europe/eu-policy-agenda/brexit/news/75235/vote-leave-accused-%E2%80%98stoking-fires-prejudice%E2%80%99-over

17 Transcript of Andrew Marr interview with Penny Mordaunt, *The Andrew Marr Show*, 22 May 2016: http://news.bbc.co.uk/1/shared/bsp/hi/pdfs/22051601.pdf

18 Oliver, Craig (2016), op. cit., loc. 3335

19 HC Deb, 19 December 2005, col. 1566

20 Cameron, David (July 2016), PM's speech in Turkey, 27 July 2010: https://www.gov.uk/government/speeches/pms-speech-in-turkey

21 http://www.voteleavetakecontrol.org/gove_and_raab_eu_membership_makes_us_less_safe.html

22 Cooper, Charlie (2016), 'Boris Johnson and Michael Gove "deliberately lying to voters over Turkish migration", Yvette Cooper says', *The Independent*, 9 June 2016: http://www.independent.co.uk/news/uk/politics/eu-referendum-boris-johnson-michael-gove-turkey-migration-deliberately-lying-to-voters-yvette-cooper-a7072661.html

23 Nickerson, James (2016), 'Iain Duncan Smith says government is "perpetrating an enormous deceit on the British public" on visa-free travel to UK from Turkey', *City AM*, 12 June 2016: http://www.cityam.com/243101/eu-referendum-iain-duncan-smith-says-government-is-perpetrating-an-enormous-deceit-on-the-british-public-on-visa-free-travel-to-uk-from-turkey

24 Bennett, Owen (2016), op. cit., loc. 3495

25 McCann, Kate (2016), 'Labour rift over migration deepens as Tom Watson calls for freedom of movement rules to be reformed', *Daily Telegraph*, 14 June 2016: http://www.telegraph.co.uk/news/2016/06/14/labour-rift-over-migration-deepens-as-tom-watson-calls-for-freed/

26 Blair, Tony (April 2005), 'Full text: Tony Blair's speech on asylum and immigration', *The Guardian*, 22 April 2005: https://www.theguardian.com/politics/2005/apr/22/election2005.immigrationandpublicservices

27 Oliver, Craig (2016), op. cit., loc. 3634

28 Rudd, Roland (2016), 'Brexit bound: Roland Rudd on Craig Oliver's "Unleashing Demons"', *Financial Times*, 12 October 2016: https://www.ft.com/content/ed6bf5a0-8fb6-11e6-a72e-b428cb934b78

29 Allen, K. (2016), 'New polling methodology puts Remain on 53%', *Financial Times*, 21 June 2016: https://www.ft.com/content/a56cf4bc-36f5-11e6-9a05-82a9b15a8ee7

30 Bienkov, Adam (2016), 'Vote Leave's undemocratic threat to ITV shows they are losing the argument', Politics.co.uk, 12 May 2016: http://www.politics.co.uk/comment-analysis/2016/05/12/vote-leave-s-undemocratic-threat-to-itv-shows-they-are-losin

31 O'Brien, Zoie (2016), 'Brexit boost: Nigel Farage proved more convincing than Cameron in EU debate, poll reveals', *Daily Express*, 9 June 2016: http://www.express.co.uk/news/uk/678032/Brexit-boost-Nigel-Farage-Cameron-EU-Europe-Referendum

32 Glaze, Ben, Nevett, Joshua and Bloom, Dan (2016), 'David Cameron's "star" Tory minister unleashes whopping personal slur on Boris Johnson', *Daily Mirror*, 9 June 2016: http://www.mirror.co.uk/news/uk-news/david-camerons-star-tory-minister-8153298

33 https://twitter.com/avaaz/status/745299642347290625

34 Nevett, Joshua and Bloom, Dan (2016), 'Trio of politicians turn on Boris Johnson's Brexit claims saying "get that lie off your bus!"', *Daily Mirror*, 9 June 2016: http://www.mirror.co.uk/news/uk-news/trio-politicians-turn-boris-johnsons-8152634

35 Bennett, Owen (June 2016), 'Boris Johnson Accused Of Leading "Project Hate" During Fiery BBC EU Referendum Debate', Huffington Post, 21 June 2016: http://www.huffingtonpost.co.uk/entry/boris-johnson-accused-of-leading-project-hate-during-fiery-bbc-eu-referendum-debate_uk_5769a807e4b0b1f1704f9501

36 Bartholomew, James (2016), 'Boris Johnson's closing speech was the defining moment of the campaign', *The Spectator*, 21 June 2016: http://blogs.spectator.co.uk/2016/06/boris-johnsons-closing-speech-defining-moment-campaign/

37 BBC News (22 June 2016), 'Juncker in "out is out" warning to UK': http://www.bbc.co.uk/news/uk-politics-eu-referendum-36599300

CONCLUSION

1 Transcript of Faisal Islam interview with David Cameron: https://corporate.sky.com/media-centre/media-packs/2016/the-eu-in-or-out---interview-with-david-cameron-8pm,-20616

2 Cameron, David (May 2016), 'PM speech on the UK's strength and security in the EU', 9 May 2016: https://www.gov.uk/government/speeches/pm-speech-on-the-uks-strength-and-security-in-the-eu-9-may-2016

3 Glaze, Ben and Bloom, Dan (2016), '"Brexit" could trigger World War Three, warns David Cameron', *Daily Mirror*, 9 May 2016: http://www.mirror.co.uk/news/uk-news/brexit-could-trigger-world-war-7928607

4 The full text of the Schuman Declaration: https://europa.eu/european-union/about-eu/symbols/europe-day/schuman-declaration_en

5 Young, Hugo (1998), op. cit., p. 501

6 Hannan, Daniel (2016a), op. cit., pp. 111–12

7 Quoted in Young, Hugo (1998), op. cit., p. 403

8   Denman, Roy (1996), op. cit., pp. 279–83, 295
9   May, Alex (2000), op. cit., p. 190
10   Charlton, Michael (1983), op. cit., p. 186
11   Denman, Roy (1996), op. cit., pp. 293–4
12   O'Neill, Con (1972), 'Report on the Negotiations for Entry into the European Community, June 1970–July 1972', Foreign Office, unpublished
13   Young, Hugo (1998), op. cit., pp. 509–11
14   May, Alex (2000), op. cit., p. 198
15   Oliver, Craig (2016), op. cit., loc. 5639
16   Cameron, David (2013), op. cit.
17   Major, John (2017), 'The Referendum on Europe: Opportunity or Threat?', delivered 27 February 2017 at Chatham House, London

INDEX